HUMAN–COMPUTER INTERACTION AND MANAGEMENT INFORMATION SYSTEMS: FOUNDATIONS

HUMAN–COMPUTER INTERACTION AND MANAGEMENT INFORMATION SYSTEMS: FOUNDATIONS

PING ZHANG
DENNIS GALLETTA
EDITORS

FOREWORD BY BEN SHNEIDERMAN

ADVANCES IN MANAGEMENT
INFORMATION SYSTEMS
VLADIMIR ZWASS SERIES EDITOR

LONDON AND NEW YORK

To Gerry DeSanctis for her encouragement and inspiration   *PZ and DG*

First published 2006 by M.E. Sharpe

Published 2015 by Routledge
2 Park Square, Milton Park, Abingdon, Oxon OX14 4RN
711 Third Avenue, New York, NY 10017, USA

Routledge is an imprint of the Taylor & Francis Group, an informa business

References to the AMIS papers should be as follows:
Kasper, G.M., and Andoh-Baidoo, F.K. Advancing the theory of DSS design for user calibration. P. Zhang and D. Galletta, eds., *Human-Computer Interaction and Management Information Systems: Foundations. Advances in Management Information Systems*, Volume 5 (Armonk, NY: M.E. Sharpe, 2006), 61–89.

ISBN-13 978-0-7656-1486-5
ISBN-10 0-7656-1486-3
ISSN 1554-6152

ADVANCES IN MANAGEMENT INFORMATION SYSTEMS

AMIS Vol. 1: Richard Y. Wang, Elizabeth M. Pierce, Stuart E. Madnick, and Craig W. Fisher
Information Quality
ISBN-13 978-0-7656-1133-8
ISBN-10 0-7656-1133-3

AMIS Vol. 2: Sergio deCesare, Mark Lycett, Robert D. Macredie
Development of Component-Based Information System
ISBN-13 978-0-7656-1248-9
ISBN-10 0-7656-1248-8

AMIS Vol. 3: Jerry Fjermestad and Nicholas C. Romano, Jr.
Electronic Customer Relationship Management
ISBN-13 978-0-7656-1327-1
ISBN-10 0-7656-1248-1

AMIS Vol. 4: Michael J. Shaw
E-Commerce and the Digital Economy
ISBN-13 978-0-7656-1150-5
ISBN-10 0-7656-1150-3

AMIS Vol. 5: Ping Zhang and Dennis Galletta
Human-Computer Interaction and Management Information Systems: Foundations
ISBN-13 978-0-7656-1486-5
ISBN-10 0-7656-1486-3

AMIS Vol. 6: Dennis Galletta and Ping Zhang
Human-Computer Interaction and Management Information Systems: Applications
ISBN-13 978-0-7656-1487-2
ISBN-10 0-7656-1487-1

Forthcoming volumes of this series can be found on the series homepage. www.mesharpe.com/amis.htm

Editor-in-Chief
Vladimir Zwass
zwass@fdu.edu

ISBN 13: 9780765614865 (hbk)

CONTENTS

SERIES EDITOR'S INTRODUCTION

Vladimir Zwass, Editor-in-Chief

It is the objective of the *AMIS* monographs to codify research in the field of management information systems (MIS). To fulfill this mission, the volumes in the series need to go beyond presenting the current state of our knowledge. We have to equip researchers with tools for generating new knowledge, by comparatively dissecting the theories, by presenting exemplars of research, and by discussing the streams and methods of knowledge generation within the subfields of the discipline.

The domain of MIS centers on the development, use, and impacts of organizational information systems. The present volume is devoted to human-computer interaction (HCI) research in MIS. The broad area of HCI focuses on human interaction with information technologies. It is vital to appreciate the fact that MIS studies and implements information *systems*. These systems include information technologies—but also, crucially, they include people. In a nutshell, this is why HCI is germane to MIS. The field of HCI has been the subject of study in computer science, the discipline centering on computer technologies; notably, the design of user interfaces has been studied there. Cognitive science has focused, among other issues, on studying how cognitive tasks are apportioned between people and machines. Other scholarly disciplines, including psychology and anthropology, have supplied methods of HCI research.

An obviously vital aspect of study in the domain of MIS is how organizations use information systems to attain their objectives. In any direct sense, organizations do not develop or use systems: people do. It is humans who are system developers, and who find themselves well—or not so well—supported by the development environments in their varied tasks. It is people who implement the system and bring it into good currency in organizations; it is also people who may play the role of counter-implementers, subverting the potential implementation. People are also the maintainers and evolvers of the system—and the malevolent hackers who may find social engineering easy in the given human-computer information system. It is the humans who may become the committed users of the information system—or its avoiders. System users are very often Alvin Toffler's prosumers, as they both develop and use information systems. System usability is intricately interconnected with system functionality: it is for us to know the distinctions that make a difference. Systems that are not perceived by their intended users as supportive, empowering, indeed a joy to work with, are not likely to lead to the envisaged positive organizational outcomes. Users may appropriate the system and have it flourish, they may use it at a minimal level of compliance, or they may utterly reject it. Many system developers recognize that they have an ethical mandate, beyond immediate organizational objectives, to develop systems that are built on human values. Such a system may tap into users' deeply held beliefs, causing organizational benefits to follow. All of this tells us that it is crucial to recognize HCI issues during system development, implementation, and evolution.

It follows that HCI is an organic component of the MIS field, as it addresses the complex set of issues centering on human interaction with information technologies in an organizational context, or for an organization's benefit. The latter aspect has become a broadly researched area with the spread of e-commerce, as the discretionary use of a Web site is in many cases the only locus of interaction between an organization and its customers. For many customers, the Web site's capability to interact is the firm's capability to transact. Thus, the increasing weight of HCI in MIS is no surprise.

The editors of this work, Ping Zhang and Dennis Galletta, have done here a great service for our field. The present work, especially when taken together with their companion volume in the AMIS series, *Human-Computer Interaction and Management Information Systems: Applications*, is a highly ambitious project that aims to establish HCI in its proper place as a vital and vibrant research stream in MIS. As you read the contributions assembled here, you will realize that HCI research has always been a part of MIS work. Yet the conceptualization, the articulation of the goals within the MIS, and the exemplification with leading work, all make these volumes a watershed event in our field.

The two volumes admirably fulfill the objectives of *AMIS*. The papers are authored by the top authorities in the field. A number of them provide a deep perspective on the development of HCI in MIS. Extensive literature citations will help orient a researcher. The volume editors offer a thorough research introduction. The HCI authority *par excellence*, Ben Shneiderman, thoughtfully and graciously introduces the work in his foreword, stressing its milestone importance in further progress. The series editor should know when to get out of the way.

FOREWORD

This remarkable volume needs trumpets to accompany the opening of its pages. But I think many readers will hear those trumpets in their mind, signaling the arrival of something new and important. It is with great pride and enthusiasm that I write this introduction to help tell the story of how human-computer interaction (HCI) has become a key component of the discipline of management information systems (MIS).

The thoughtful introduction and eighteen compelling chapters in this volume are well worth reading carefully with time for reflection. They competently survey the topic, collectively providing readers with an understandable portrait of this emerging interdisciplinary topic.

In addition to the valuable contents of this volume and the follow-up second volume, Ping Zhang and Dennis Galletta's leadership has created a lively community of contributors. This gathering of colorful personalities, leaders of the field, and wise commentators can lay claim to being an authoritative panel that is able to define this topic. The benefits of having this volume and community are enormous as we each promote HCI in MIS with our close colleagues and superiors. This volume will smooth the way for new academic courses, curricula, and degree programs. It will enable industrial researchers to advance their agendas and organizational usability professionals to accelerate their activities.

The authors of the chapters appropriately use calm academic writing styles to thoughtfully convey their contents, so I will use my license as author of the foreword to be more passionate and visionary.

Amidst the taxonomies and historical reviews, I see a shared commitment to making human values a key factor in designing future management information systems. Beyond the authoritative frameworks and extensive references, I recognize a devotion to societal concerns for how information and communications technologies are applied in the workplace. These authors want to be more than respected academics; they aspire to creating a better world.

Their strongly user-centered vision of the world manifests itself in the use of terms and concepts that go beyond technology to focus on people. The gigabytes, megapixels, and megahertz are assumed, and now these authors discuss user acceptance, aesthetics, and affect. They talk about coordination, collaboration, and community. They also have a broad scope of analysis that encompasses cross-cultural design, universal usability, internationalization of products, and the globalization of work. While much of the writing has an optimistic spin, there is enough sober consideration of dystopian scenarios that anticipate dangers and present ethical dilemmas.

The underlying message is that business decision makers, usability professionals, and engaged academics can shape what happens, at least in the world of management information systems.

The implicit challenge is to accept responsibility for the future that we create for employees, managers, customers, and citizens. This is a frightening but invigorating challenge.

To succeed we'll need to put aside our differences, and concentrate on our shared interests in a unified community that promotes HCI in MIS at universities, corporations, government agencies, and non-governmental organizations. Then we'll be able to convince colleagues and superiors that HCI in MIS is worthy of increased support, even at the expense of other topics. Our unified community will gain respect when we reach out to elected officials, industry policy makers, and research agenda setters. Our clear vision will engage journalists who can tell the story to the general public.

Change is often difficult, but with a shared commitment from a vigorous community, much good can be accomplished. We have an opportunity to shape the future of our discipline, shape the way in which technology is deployed, and constructively influence the lives of many people.

THINKING ABOUT THEORIES

In reading the chapters I was impressed with the devotion to theoretical frameworks. Zhang and Galletta refer to the many "strong theories" as they catalog the human issues (demographics, physical/motor, cognition, emotion, and motivation) and the context (global, social, organizational, group). They lay out an overview of the discipline that integrates these human issues and the context with technology, task/job, and interaction design. Since I agree that devotion to theories is important for disciplinary growth, it seems appropriate for a foreword to offer a set of categories for thinking about theories. I see at least five kinds of theories:

Descriptive: describe objects and actions in a consistent and clear manner to enable cooperation. Many of the chapters lay out a descriptive framework, such as the five issues covered by Zhang and Galletta or the three kinds of fit described by Te'eni (Chapter 10): physical, cognitive, and affective.

Explanatory: explain processes that have temporal sequencing or show influence or dependency of one factor on another. Many MIS theories are of this type, such as the coordination theories (Chapter 7) that tie restaurant worker coordination to job satisfaction, or the security theories (Chapter 12) that tie higher employee income levels to better password management.

Predictive: predict performance of individuals, organizations, or economies. These include the traditional human factors results such as Fitts' Law that predicts pointing times based on distance and size of targets. MIS theories seem less concerned with such precise predictive theories, maybe because organizational performance is more vulnerable to high variability and many human values issues are so difficult to measure.

Prescriptive: guidelines that prescribe behavior, recommendations based on best practices, and cautions based on failures. An example is the discussion of Value Sensitive Design (Chapter 16) that offers ten "practical suggestions" such as "identify direct and indirect stakeholders" and "identify potential value conflicts."

Generative: ways to see what is missing and what needs to be done. These are difficult to construct, but are potentially the most valuable for innovators. Some of the research agendas get close to being a generative theory. It seems to me that this is a valuable goal that could accelerate work on HCI in MIS, just as Mendeleyev's periodical table of atomic elements led to discoveries of unknown elements. I've tried to lay out a generative theory based on activities and relationships (*Leonardo's Laptop: Human Needs and the New Computing Technologies*, MIT Press, 2002). The activities (collect, relate, create, donate) form the columns of a matrix and the rows are relationships (self, family and friends, colleagues and neighbors, citizens and markets). The activities are often combined to form compound activities such as shopping which happens by collecting infor-mation about the car you want to buy, forming a relationship between buyer and seller, and then creating the deal. The relationships are organized in order of increasing numbers of relationships, but decreasing shared knowledge, trust, and expectation of future encounters.

These five kinds of theories may not be complete, and some theories fit into more than one cat-egory, but this classification has proven useful to me in thinking about theories. This list helps me understand proposed theories and see opportunities for new theories.

I close with a restatement of my enthusiasm for this collection of papers and for the commu-nity that created them. I see a shared vision of a human-centered approach to HCI in MIS. I'm filled with excitement and enthusiasm and believe that readers will get the message about the importance of human values in HCI in MIS. I believe this volume will motivate colleagues and inspire students to carry out constructive user-centered research. Each of those projects will contribute to the larger goals. There is much work to be done … let's get on with it!

Ben Shneiderman
University of Maryland

HUMAN–COMPUTER INTERACTION AND MANAGEMENT INFORMATION SYSTEMS: FOUNDATIONS

Chapter 1

FOUNDATIONS OF HUMAN-COMPUTER INTERACTION IN MANAGEMENT INFORMATION SYSTEMS

An Introduction

Ping Zhang and Dennis Galletta

Abstract: We begin this introduction to this first of two complementary volumes by providing a general context for both volumes and by giving a brief historical view of management information systems (MIS) scholars' interest in human-computer interaction (HCI) research. We then integrate various HCI issues into an overarching framework that can encompass broad HCI concerns from multiple disciplines. After presenting the classification of HCI topics that guides our organization of the collection, we preview the papers collected in this volume, together with a variety of additional ideas, evidence, and insights. Topics in this volume include different disciplines' perspectives on HCI; our evolving understanding of who users are; theoretical understanding of how to design systems to support humans; theories and models of the cognitive and behavioral aspects of information technology (IT) use; and fundamental understanding of the affective, aesthetic, value sensitive, and social aspects of HCI. Overall, this introduction brings together many literatures and highlights key points in the research's evolution; it thus augments the collected papers to provide readers with a rich picture of HCI research's foundations.

Keywords: Human-Computer Interaction, MIS, Disciplinary Perspective, Computer Users, Design Theory, Fit, Belief and Behavior, Affect, Aesthetics, Socialization, Technology Acceptance Model (TAM), Computer-Human Interaction (CHI), Human Factors, Ergonomics, MIS History

INTRODUCTION

This book is the first of two complementary volumes that present scholarly works from a variety of leading thinkers in HCI, including those who have ties to the field of management information systems (MIS). Volume 1 covers concepts, theories, and models, and general issues of human-computer interaction studies relevant to MIS. Topics in this volume include interdisciplinary perspectives on HCI; our evolving understanding of who users are; theoretical understanding of how to design systems to support humans; theories and models of the cognitive and behavioral aspects of information technology (IT) use; and fundamental understanding of the affective, aesthetic, value sensitive, and social aspects of HCI. Volume 2 covers applications, special case studies, and HCI studies in specific contexts. Topics in the second volume include HCI studies in the areas of electronic commerce and the Web; HCI studies for collaboration support; issues relating to culture and globalization; specific HCI issues in IT learning and training; theoretical understandings of the system development processes; HCI issues in health care and health informatics; and, finally, methodological cal concerns in HCI research. Each volume concludes with thoughtful reflections by well-known authors. In Volume 1, Fred Davis discusses the connection between the technology acceptance model (TAM) and HCI, and Jonathan Grudin reflects on the historical development of three closely related disciplines. In Volume 2, an early, influential, and visible debate on soft versus hard science in HCI studies is revisited and updated from the perspective of one of the original debaters, John Carroll.

We begin this introduction by providing a general context for both volumes, along with a brief historical view of MIS scholars' interest in HCI research. Then we integrate various HCI issues into an overarching framework introduced by Zhang and Li (2005) that can encompass broad HCI concerns from multiple disciplines. We present the classification of HCI topics that guides the organization of this volume; we then preview the papers collected in this volume. We integrate this preview with a variety of additional ideas, evidence, and insights. Overall, we intend this introduction to augment the collected papers in this volume, thus providing readers with a rich picture of the foundations of HCI research.

A HISTORICAL VIEW OF HCI IN MIS RESEARCH

The MIS community includes scholars who focus on the development, use, and impact of information technology and systems in broadly defined social and organizational settings. MIS has seen a steady shift from what could have been labeled techno-centrism to a broader and more balanced focus on technological, organizational, managerial, and societal problems (Baskerville and Myers, 2002). MIS-oriented HCI issues have been addressed since the earliest studies in the MIS discipline. For example, users' attitudes, perceptions, acceptance, and use of IT have been long-standing themes of MIS research since the early days of computing (Lucas, 1975; Swanson, 1974), as have studies on programmer cognition and end user involvement in systems development. MIS scholars have identified information systems failures as the potential result of a lack of emphasis on the human/social aspects of system use (Bostrom and Heinen, 1977), have pointed out the need to attend to user behavior in information technology research (Gerlach and Kuo, 1991), and have attempted to tie human factors, usability, and HCI to the systems development life cycle (Hefley et al., 1995; Mantei and Teorey, 1989; Zhang et al., 2005). Also extensively studied are IS development theories and methodologies (Baskerville and Pries-Heje, 2004; Hirschheim and Klein, 1989), collaborative work and computer-mediated communication (Poole et al., 1991; Reinig et al., 1996; Yoo and Alavi, 2001; Zigurs et al., 1999), representations of information for supporting managerial tasks (Jarvenpaa, 1989; Vessey, 1994; Zhang, 1998), and computer training (Bostrom, 1990; Sein and Bostrom, 1989; Webster and Martocchio, 1995).

Culnan (1986) identified nine factors or subfields in early MIS publications (1972–82). Of these nine, three relate to issues in humans interacting with computers. In a second study of a later period of MIS publications (1980–85), Culnan (1987) found the field to be composed of five areas of study, of which the second, individual (micro) approach to MIS design and use is closely related to human-computer interaction. Vessey and colleagues also considered HCI as a research area when studying the diversity of the MIS discipline, although they considered HCI to be more at the user interface level, and thus placed it within the systems/software concepts category (Vessey et al., 2002). After surveying fifty years of MIS publications in the *Management Science* journal, Banker and Kauffman identified HCI as one of five main research streams in MIS and predicted that interest in HCI research will resurge (Banker and Kauffman, 2004).

These longtime interests in the MIS field have touched upon the fundamental issues of human interaction with technologies, or, even more generally, the broad area of human factors. From the

MIS perspective, HCI studies examine how humans interact with information, technologies, and tasks, especially in business, managerial, organizational, and cultural contexts (Zhang et al., 2002). This differs notably from HCI studies in disciplines such as computer science, psychology, and ergonomics. MIS researchers emphasize managerial and organizational contexts by analyzing tasks and outcomes at a level relevant to organizational effectiveness. The features that distinguish MIS from other "homes" of HCI are its *business application* and *management* orientation (Zhang et al., 2004).

As MIS scholars' interest in HCI has increased in recent years, HCI has gained great importance in the MIS discipline. There is evidence to support these assertions. For example, a large number of MIS scholars report their interest in researching HCI-related issues and in teaching HCI-related topics (Zhang et al., 2002). HCI courses are offered in many MIS programs (Carey et al., 2004; Chan et al., 2003; Kutzschan and Webster, 2005). HCI is considered an important topic in the most recent model curriculum for masters in information systems majors (Gorgone et al., 2005). Both the total number and the percentage of HCI studies published in primary MIS journals have increased over the recent years (Zhang and Li, 2005). Major MIS conferences—such as the International Conference on Information Systems (ICIS), the Hawaii International Conference on System Science (HICSS), the Americas Conferences on Information Systems (AMCIS), the Pacific Asia Conference on Information Systems (PACIS), and the European Conference on Information Systems (ECIS)—have been publishing HCI studies. Most of them have recently included specific HCI tracks (ICIS started in 2004, AMCIS in 2002, and PACIS in 2005; ECIS in 2006, and HICSS in 2007). A workshop devoted to HCI research in the MIS discipline, the pre-ICIS Annual Workshop on HCI Research in MIS, started in 2002. Several special issues on HCI research in MIS have appeared or are appearing in top MIS and HCI journals since 2003. Finally, an official organization of HCI in MIS, the AIS Special Interest Group on HCI (SIGHCI), was established in 2001 (Zhang, 2004).

BOUNDING HCI

A scientific field or discipline, such as MIS or physics, must have a boundary (which may or may not be well defined) that outlines matters of intrinsic interest to the field of inquiry. Over many years, the MIS discipline has gone through the process of clarifying its boundary. The same process has been occurring in the HCI sub-discipline (Zhang and Li, 2005). Based on the definition of HCI research in MIS given above (Zhang et al., 2002), Figure 1.1 represents a broad view of important HCI components that are pertinent to human interaction with technologies. Five components are identified: human and technology as the basic components, interaction as the core of interest, and task and context as the components making HCI issues meaningful. Several topics are listed inside each component to illustrate the components and the relationships among them.

The two basic components encompass human and technology. There can be many different ways of understanding humans in general and their specific characteristics pertinent to their interaction with IT. Figure 1.1 includes four categories: (1) demographics; (2) physical or motor skills; (3) cognitive issues; and (4) affective and motivational aspects. Personalities or traits can be examined within both the cognitive and affective categories. Many issues in the Human component fall into the ergonomics and psychology disciplines. HCI focuses, though, on the interplay between the human component and other components.

Technology can be broadly defined to include hardware, software, applications, data, information, knowledge, services, and procedures. Figure 1.1 indicates one way of examining technological

Figure 1.1   **An Overview of Broad HCI Issues**

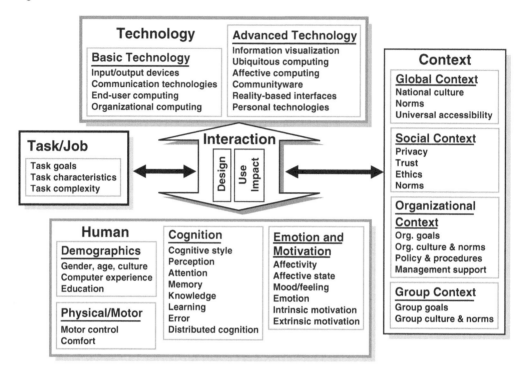

Source: Adapted and expanded from Zhang and Li (2005).

issues when studying HCI. Many of these technological issues have interested researchers in the HCI field for a long time (Shneiderman, 1987; Shneiderman and Plaisant, 2005). The figure was developed from the perspective of technology types often found in technical fields such as computer science or studies associated with the computer-human interaction (CHI) community.

The Interaction between Human and Technology represents the "I" in HCI. It is the core or the center of all the action in HCI studies. Interaction issues have been studied from two aspects of the IT artifact life cycle: during the IT development stage (before release), and during its use and impact stage (after release). Traditionally, HCI studies, especially research captured by ACM SIGCHI conferences and journals, were concerned with designing and implementing interactive systems for specified users, including usability issues. The primary focus has been the issues prior to the technology's release and actual use. Ideally, concerns and understanding from both points of view—human and technological—should influence design and usability issues.

The "Use/Impact" box on the right side inside the Interaction in Figure 1.1 is concerned with actual IT use in real contexts and its impact on users, organizations, and societies. Design studies can be and should be informed by what we learn from the use of the same or similar technologies. Thus, use/impact studies have implications for future designs. Historically, use/impact studies have been the focal concern of MIS, along with human factors and ergonomics, organizational psychology, social psychology, and other social science disciplines. In the MIS discipline, studies of individual reactions to technology (e.g., Compeau et al., 1999), IS evaluation from both individual and organizational levels (e.g., Goodhue, 1997; Goodhue, 1998; Goodhue, 1995; Goodhue and Thompson, 1995), and user technology acceptance (e.g., Davis, 1989; Venkatesh and Davis, 2000; Venkatesh et al., 2003) all fall into this area.

Humans use technologies not for the sake of those technologies, but to support tasks that are relevant or meaningful to their jobs or personal goals. In addition, people carry out tasks in settings or contexts that impose constraints on doing and completing the tasks. Four contexts are identified: group, organizational, social, and global. The Task and Context boxes add dynamic and essential meanings to the interaction experience. In this sense, studies of human-computer interaction are moderated by tasks and contexts. It is these broader task and context considerations that separate the primary foci of HCI studies in MIS from HCI studies in other disciplines. Later, we will discuss more disciplinary differences.

Based on a literature assessment of HCI studies in seven prime MIS journals between 1990 and 2002, Zhang and Li (2005) further provided a classification of the HCI subject topics. Table 1.1 adapts this classification, adding descriptions and examples.

The organization of the collected papers for Volume 1 is guided by the classification in Table 1.1. Although the papers in this volume do not cover all the topics listed in Table 1.1, due to limited space and the unavailability of prospective researchers, the scholars who contribute to this collection do provide a rich understanding of state-of-the-art HCI issues. Next, we discuss the topical themes covered in this volume and preview the collected papers within the broad HCI framework provided in Figure 1.1. Readers interested in discussions of other topics can read (Zhang and Li 2005) to find out what is demonstrated by the MIS literature on those topics.

FOUNDATIONS OF HCI RESEARCH

Disciplinary Perspectives and the Users

HCI started as an interdisciplinary field, has stayed interdisciplinary, and can be predicted to continue to be interdisciplinary. This is because no single discipline can completely cover the complex, extensive issues involved; as Dillon states: "There is no one field that can cover all the issues worthy of study" (in this volume). Given their relevance to many aspects of our lives and societies, HCI issues have attracted researchers, educators, and practitioners from many different fields. Interdisciplinary tension, as Carroll calls it, "has always been a resource to HCI, and an important factor to its success" (in the second volume). The key to success is to keep an open-minded attitude and to facilitate dialogues among various related disciplines, thus making the best of each discipline's unique perspectives and strengths. With this in mind, we collected papers from well-known authors that reflect several HCI-related disciplines and their relationships with each other. The contributors reveal different disciplinary views across the entirety of the two volumes. In this section, we highlight two specific papers on this subject.

MIS as a discipline has a lengthy and strong interest in information, and in the role information plays in business decision making and organizational effectiveness. For example, Banville and Landry (1989) concluded that the original perspective of MIS centered on either management, information, systems, or on a combination of these. A number of disciplines share this strong interest in information; these include MIS, HCI, and information science. As such, information can be used as a bridge among these related disciplines. An emphasis on information should also allow MIS and other disciplines to examine shared concerns, common approaches, and potential for collaboration. Dillon provides just this perspective. He examines how different disciplines treat

Table 1.1

HCI Topic Classification

ID	Category	Description and Examples
A	IT development	Concerned with issues that occur during IT development and/or implementation that are relevant to the relationship between human and technology. Focus on the process where IT is developed or implemented. The artifact is being worked on before actual use
A1	Development methods and tools	Structured approaches, object-oriented approaches, CASE tools, social-cognitive approaches for developing IT that consider roles of users and IT personnel
A2	User-analyst interaction	User involvement in analysis, user participation, user-analyst differences, user-analyst interaction
A3	Software/hardware development	Programmer/analyst cognition studies, design and development of specific or general applications or devices that consider some human aspects
A4	Software/hardware evaluation	System effectiveness, efficiency, quality, reliability, flexibility, and information quality evaluations that consider people as part of the mix
A5	User interface design and development	Interface metaphors, information presentations, multimedia
A6	User interface evaluation	Instrumental usability (e.g., ease of use, low error rate, ease of learning, retention rate, satisfaction), accessibility, information presentation evaluation
A7	User training	User training issues or studies during IT development (prior to product release or use)
B	IT use and impact	Concerned with issues that occur when humans use and/or evaluate IT; issues related to the reciprocal influences between IT and humans. The artifact is released and used in a real context
B1	Cognitive belief and behavior	Self-efficacy, perception, eBelief, incentives, expectation, intention, behavior, acceptance, adoption, resistance, use
B2	Attitude	Attitude, satisfaction, preference
B3	Learning	Learning models, learning processes, training in general (different from user training as part of system development)
B4	Emotion	Emotion, affect, hedonic quality, flow, enjoyment, humor, intrinsic motivation
B5	Performance	Performance, productivity, effectiveness, efficiency
B6	Trust	Trust, risk, loyalty, security, privacy
B7	Ethics	Ethical belief, ethical behavior, ethics
B8	Interpersonal relationship	Conflict, interdependence, agreement/disagreement, interference, tension, leadership, influence
B9	User support	Issues related to information center, end-user computing support, general user support

Source: Adapted from Zhang and Li (2005).

information in order to identify the similarities and differences between MIS and HCI. From an informational basis, "MIS can be considered to be primarily concerned with identifying, abstracting, and supporting the data flows that exist in organizations, and developing or supporting the technological (broadly conceived) means of exploiting the potential to serve organizational ends.

Similarly, HCI seeks to maximize the use of information through the design of humanly accept-able representational and manipulatory tools." Based on such analyses, Dillon outlines a number of research areas that can bridge the disciplines of MIS and HCI.

MIS scholars have built their HCI research on a large number of diverse disciplines, including information systems, business and management, psychology, philosophy, and communications, among others (Zhang and Li, 2005). Accordingly, HCI issues have been examined from the differ-ent analytical perspectives inherited from these disciplines. Kutzschan and Webster argue that MIS researchers, with their big-picture perspective, strong theories, and rigorous methodologies, are distinctively positioned to address HCI issues. Due to the increased sensitivity of HCI issues to businesses and marketplaces, MIS now benefits from a great opportunity to study HCI. Therefore, MIS is the natural home of HCI research.

The human is an important component in HCI studies, regardless of the researcher's discipli-nary perspective. Because studies of humans as users rely heavily on ideas about human psychol-ogy, both HCI and MIS have been able to connect directly with a basic science; this connection, in turn, gives its research depth and credibility. Historically, MIS research has studied humans at both stages of the IT life cycle: the IT development stage and the IT use and impact stage (Zhang and Li, 2005). MIS studies that have direct impact on IT development and use also examine humans' different roles—as developers, analysts, and designers of IT; as users or end users of IT; and as managers and stakeholders.[1] Tables 1.2 and 1.3 list some of the MIS research topics that explicitly consider humans as individuals or groups during the IT life cycle. They are meant to be illustrative rather than exhaustive.

Users or end users have been studied from at least the following perspectives in the MIS discipline:

- Users with individual differences such as general traits, IT-specific traits, cognitive styles, and personalities (e.g., Agarwal and Prasad, 1998; Benbasat and Taylor, 1978; Huber, 1983; Webster and Martocchio, 1992). Banker and Kauffman (2004) provided a detailed summary of MIS studies in this area.
- Users as social actors in the design, development, and use of information and communica-tion technologies (ICT) (Lamb and Kling, 2003). Lamb and Kling argued that most people who use ICT applications use multiple applications, in various roles, and as part of their efforts to produce goods and services while interacting with a variety of other people, often in multiple social contexts. Only if we take such a view of users can we better understand how organizational contexts shape ICT-related practices, and what complex and multiple roles people fulfill while adopting, adapting, and using ICT.
- Users as economic agents whose preferences, behaviors, personalities, and ultimately eco-nomic welfare are intricately linked to the design of information systems (Bapna et al., 2004).

It is noteworthy that supporting individuals or groups is not the only concern of HCI research in MIS. As noted by many, the mobile and pervasive nature of modern computer use by various peo-ple and organizations call for new challenges and opportunities (Lyytinen et al., 2004). Overall, the views of users have been broadened significantly. In this volume, DeSanctis examined how the concept of user has evolved from an individual user to a group of people, then to an entire firm or organization, and finally to a diffuse community with dynamic membership and purpose. This inevitable evolution challenges the design and research issues MIS scholars face, but also provides opportunities to advance their understanding of broad HCI issues.

Table 1.2

Some MIS Studies on Individuals During the IT Life Cycle

	IT Development	IT Use and Impact
Developers, Designers, Analysts	• Programmer/analyst cognition (Kim et al., 2000; Zmud et al., 1993) • Novice and expert system analysts (Pitts and Browne, 2004; Schenk et al., 1998) • Developers' intention of using methodologies (Hardgrave et al., 2003)	• Power relations between users and IS professionals (Markus and Bjørn-Andersen, 1987) • Analysts' view of IS failure (Lyytinen, 1988)
Users, End Users	• User participation and user involvement (e.g., Barki and Hartwick, 1994; 1989; Saleem, 1996) • Customer-developer links in system development, and Joint Application Design and Participatory Design (Carmel et al., 1993; Keil and Carmel, 1995) • User-developed applications (Rivard and Huff, 1984)	• Cognitive styles and individual differences (Benbasat and Taylor, 1978; Harrison and Rainer, 1992; Huber, 1983; Webster and Martocchio, 1992) • Individual reactions to IT (Compeau et al., 1999) • IT acceptance (Davis, 1989) • Individual IT performance and productivity (Goodhue and Thompson, 1995) • User training and computer self-efficacy (Compeau and Higgins, 1995)
Managers, Stockholders	• Building systems people want to use (Markus and Keil, 1994)	• Challenges to management on a personal level (Argyris, 1971) • Users' resistance (e.g., Dickson and Simmons, 1970) • Raising intrinsic motivation (Malhotra and Galletta, 2005) • Duality of technology (Orlikowski, 1992)[1]

[1]In this paper, Orlikowski considered all types of human agents: technology designers, users, and decision makers. She also considered both stages of the IT life cycle, looking at technology as a product of human action and technology as a medium of human action, with institutional consequences. Therefore, this study should not just fit this cell but all six cells.

IT Development: Theories of Individual and Group Work

In the context of promoting user-centered design of collaborative technology to support group work, Olson and Olson (1991) identified the different design approaches that existed at the time:

- Technology-driven design: a technology was proposed before anyone fully understood the problem or the best way to solve it;
- Rational design: design by prescription, in that a system is designed to change the way people behave;
- Intuitive design: a designer builds something because it seems intuitive that it will work well;
- Analogical design: systems are built to resemble people's present use of similar objects; and
- Evolutionary design: systems are built to expand the capabilities of current systems already in use.

Table 1.3

MIS Studies on Groups During the IT Life Cycle

	IT Development	IT Use and Impact
Developers, Designers, Analysts	• User-centered design of collaborative technology (Olson and Olson, 1991) • Global software team coordination (Espinosa and Carmel, 2005)	
Users, End Users	• The user interface design issues for GDSS (Gray and Olfman, 1989)	• Group performance and productivity (Dennis and Garfield, 2003; Dennis et al., 2001) • Collaborative telelearning (Alavi et al., 1995) • Cognitive feedback (Sengupta and Te'eni, 1993) • Behavior in group process (Massey and Clapper, 1995; Zigurs et al., 1988) • The effect of group memory on individual creativity (Satzinger et al., 1999) • On the development of shared mental models (Swaab et al., 2002) • Satisfaction with teamwork (Reinig, 2003)
Managers, Stockholders	• Developing Systems for Management of Organizational Knowledge (Markus et al., 2002) • GDSS design strategy (Huber, 1984)[1]	• Organizational Learning (Senge, 1990)

[1]In this paper, Huber actually covered both the development/design and use/implementation stages of the GDSS life cycle.

Olson and Olson note that in a user-centered design strategy, a design begins with detailed considerations of users' tasks and capabilities: Who are the potential users? How varied are they? What is their current work like? Which aspects of their work are difficult? What are their needs? There are three key aspects to this design strategy: involving users, iterative design, and the role of theory about users (Olson and Olson, 1991).

As we can see, several of these approaches still exist today; they can be applied to designing individual-based technologies as well as to collaborative work. Design is more than art. Theoretically informed design goes a long way to advance research and practice. As Baecker and colleagues pointed out, "Many empirical studies of interactive computer use have no theoretical orientation. Data is collected, but no underlying model or theory of the process exists to be confirmed or refuted. Such a theory would be very helpful because with many design decisions there are too many alternative proposals to test by trail and error. A strong theory or performance model could reduce the set of plausible alternatives to a manageable number of testing" (Baecker et al., 1995, p. 573). In the MIS literature, much theoretical work guides designers on developing information systems that support individuals and groups. In this section, we introduce three streams of such work to demonstrate the importance of such design theories.

Two papers cover research on designing systems for individual support. Given a long history of developing decision support systems (DSS) to help decision makers make a specific decision or choose a specific course of action, the issue of decision makers' confidence in decision quality becomes an important one. Kasper and Andoh-Baidoo present an extension of the DSS design theory for user calibration, which is defined as the correspondence between one's prediction of the quality of a decision and the actual quality of the decision. In a related paper, Silver broadens the original work published a decade ago on how a DSS enlightens or sways its users as they choose among and use the system's functional capabilities. The broadened theoretical work can be used to study not only DSS but a variety of other interactive information systems.

In a group setting, coordination becomes an important activity to ensure group success. Coordination activities relate to organizing and coordinating group activities, both during the course and over the course of a project. They include such activities as goal stating, agenda setting, history keeping, floor control, activity tracking, and project management (Olson and Olson, 1991). Coordination theory (Malone and Crowston, 1994) provides a detailed theoretical understanding of the dependencies between the tasks the different group members are carrying out and how the group coordinates its work. Built on research in several different disciplines, such as economics, organizational theory, and computer science, coordination theory has influenced many studies since its initial publication in 1994. In this volume, Crowston and his colleagues provide a ten-year retrospective on the development, use, and impact of coordination theory.

IT Development: Theories of Fit

The theoretical works in this section continue to shed light on developing effective information systems that can benefit individuals, groups, and organizations. The section comprises three papers on fit that, taken together, cover a broad range of aspects important in designing information systems.

The first two papers built and expanded on two important MIS models by their original creators: cognitive fit by Iris Vessey and task-technology fit by Dale Goodhue. Cognitive fit (CF) theory (Vessey, 1991; Vessey and Galletta, 1991) was initially introduced to explain the inconsistent results in the area of information presentations, where graphs and tables are used to support information acquisition and information evaluation tasks. In this volume, Vessey surveys the broad applications of CF, discusses the fundamental theoretical framework of CF theory, and points out future directions (Vessey, 2005).

Task-technology fit (TTF) (Goodhue and Thompson, 1995) studies the causal chain connecting information technology with its performance impact. The key idea of TTF is that a technology can have a positive performance impact only if it fits the task that is being supported. In this regard, TTF may sound very similar to cognitive fit theory. Yet, the granularity of analysis and the scope of considerations taken by these two models are different: Cognitive fit focuses more on the cognitive processes during individual problem solving, while TTF emphasizes the relationships among the various factors that influence the fit of the technology under analysis. TTF also analyzes the impact of the fit on other factors, such as system utilization, user attitude, and user performance—where users can be both individuals and groups (Zigurs and Buckland, 1998). TTF's focus moves beyond technology acceptance or utilization to analyze how technology impacts actual task performance. Despite the obvious importance of this construct, Goodhue argues that it is often neglected in major MIS models on information systems and performance.

An organizational information system does more than simply supporting productivity. Expanding the cognitive-affective model of organizational communication with IT support (Te'eni, 2001), and building on both cognitive fit and task-technology fit, Dov Te'eni presents a well-rounded and much broader concept of fit that has to do with physical, cognitive, and affective fit between human and computer. All three authors conclude that there is much to do to advance studies on fit in HCI and MIS disciplines. This further confirms the call for research in this area (Zhang et al., 2002).

IT Use and Impact: Beliefs and Behavior

The ultimate goal of developing IT is to support and positively impact individuals, groups and organizations. Human interaction with technology is goal-oriented behavior that constitutes two main questions: what causes users to use technology, and why the use of technology is different (Zhang et al., 2005). IS researchers have built heavily on psychological research into motivations and goal-oriented behaviors to understand how people behave around computers. In particular, IS researchers are interested in understanding how and why a computer-related behavior develops and how it influences future behavior. Influenced heavily by the theory of reasoned action and theory of planned behavior (Ajzen, 1991; Ajzen and Fishbein, 1980; Fishbein and Ajzen, 1975), a significant amount of IS research has been conducted in identifying relevant cognitive beliefs that lead to certain behavior.

One important belief that is related to computer use is computer self-efficacy (CSE) (Compeau and Higgins, 1995). CSE is defined as "an individual judgment of one's capability to use a computer" (Compeau and Higgins, 1995, p. 192). CSE has been found to influence user acceptance of technology and user learning about technology. Through a thorough review of MIS literature on CSE, Compeau and colleagues find that the formation of CSE, along with its careful conceptualization and measurement, is much less studied. Therefore, their paper focuses on these issues. Specifically, they present the state of the research on CSE, including its conceptualization, influence, and formation. Then they introduce a number of ongoing research programs in addressing the gaps and opportunities in this area. Finally, they conclude with an agenda for future research on CSE.

Among the many studies of behaviors related to information technology, behavioral information security has become an important area of research in recent years. Stanton and colleagues define behavioral information security as the human actions that influence the availability, confidentiality, and integrity of information systems. They note that despite the multibillion dollars spent on information security by commercial, nonprofit, and governmental organizations around the world, the success of security appears to depend upon the behavior of the individuals involved. Appropriate and constructive behavior by end users, system administrators, and others can enhance the effectiveness of information security while inappropriate and destructive behaviors can inhibit its effectiveness. Stanton and colleagues use social, organizational, and behavioral theories and approaches, and conduct a series of empirical investigations in developing a taxonomy of security behaviors and identifying the motivational predictors of such behaviors.

Information security is also heavily engineering and technology oriented, because much of the information security spending is in these areas. Just how are the human and technological aspects of security issues different and related? Dhillon and May use a semiotic framework to illustrate the holistic nature of information security issues. Such a semiotic framework has six layers: physical, empiric, syntactic, semantic, pragmatic, and social. The first three are technically oriented, and the last three are human issues. Besides identifying the role of each layer, it is important to understand the impact each layer has on other layers. Based on existing studies on using semiotic research in IS, Dhillon and May argue that when HCI or IS research considers only some layers when studying and designing information security, the results can be dysfunctional and dissatisfactory. The semiotic framework proves to be a useful tool, given that it can be used to analyze existing security principles. For example, Stanton and colleagues' paper on behavioral information security places more emphasis on the pragmatic and social layers of the semiotic framework.

IT Use and Impact: Affect, Aesthetics, Value, and Socialization

Other researchers investigate why people use technology and examine aspects of technology use that lie beyond cognitive reasoning. These include affect and emotion, aesthetics, human values, and social influence, which are covered by four papers in this volume.

Affect (mood, emotion, feeling) has been found to influence reflex, perception, cognition, and behavior (Norman, 2002; Russell, 2003; Zhang and Li, 2005) and has been studied in psychology, marketing, organizational behavior, and other disciplines. Although it has received less attention than cognitive approaches, affect has been covered in the IS literature for a long time and to quite some extent. Sun and Zhang examine the theoretical advancement of affect studies in several IS reference disciplines and propose an abstract model of an individual interacting with objects; they then develop an IT-specific model by applying the abstract model to integrate and interpret affect studies in the MIS discipline.

A specific aspect of affect is the pleasantness or unpleasantness that may be generated by visual attractiveness, or aesthetics, as Tractinsky puts it. Tractinsky makes a strong argument that aesthetics has become a major differentiating factor between IT products in that many products now provide the same functionality and meet the same needs; this has happened because aesthetics satisfies basic human needs and because human needs are increasingly supplied by IT. Perceived aesthetics (Tractinsky et al., 2000), perceived visual attractiveness (van der Heijden, 2003), and first impressions (Schenkman and Jonsson, 2000) have all been found to influence people's judgment of IT, as they regard what is beautiful is usable (Tractinsky et al., 2000). As Norman stated, beautiful things work better (Norman, 2004).

Values refer to what people consider important in life; they include trust, privacy, human welfare, freedom from bias, and autonomy, to name a few. According to Friedman and colleagues, an important and long-standing interest in designing information and computational systems should be to support enduring human values. Value sensitive design is a theoretically grounded approach to the design of IT that accounts for human values in a principled and comprehensive manner throughout the design process. Friedman and colleagues give detailed descriptions of the approach and some examples in their paper.

Forever social, we humans live in social environments and behave socially. Consequently, we treat everything in our environment, including other humans and even artifacts, socially. The media equation theory (Reeves and Nass, 1996) predicts and explains why people respond unconsciously and automatically to communication media (or artifacts in general) as if they were human. Computers are continuously regarded as social actors. How can HCI design help? In this volume, Nass and colleagues present abundant investigations to explore social consistency issues that are at the center of the more socially demanding interfaces of today's technology. The studied social responses to computers include personality, gender, emotion, and the use of "I."

Reflections

To conclude the first volume, we include two reflective pieces. In the first, Fred Davis, the creator of the technology acceptance model (TAM), deals with the relationship between TAM and HCI. In the second, Jonathan Grudin offers a historical cross-examination of three related disciplines.

Long established as a research topic, user acceptance of technology is considered "one of the most mature research areas in the contemporary IS literature" (Venkatesh et al., 2003). Organizations that spend millions of dollars on information technologies (IT) are primarily concerned with how their investments will influence organizational and individual performance (Torkzadeh and Doll, 1999). However, the expected productivity gains and organizational benefits delivered by IT cannot be realized unless IT is actually accepted and used (Hackbarth et al., 2003).

Due to its importance, several theoretical models have been developed in this research. For example, Venkatesh and colleagues (Venkatesh et al., 2003) reviewed eight models that have gained MIS scholars' attention in recent decades. Among the many efforts and models, the technology acceptance model (TAM) (Davis, 1989; Davis et al., 1989) is considered the most studied model and has generated much research interest and effort in the MIS community. Since the publication of TAM in late 1980s (Davis, 1989; Davis et al., 1989), abundant studies have been done to test the model (Adams et al., 1992; Davis, 1989; Davis, 1993; Davis et al., 1989), extend it (Igbaria et al., 1997; Venkatesh, 2000; Venkatesh and Davis, 2000; Venkatesh and Davis, 1996), or compare it with other models (Davis et al., 1989; Dishaw and Strong, 1999; Mathieson, 1991; Taylor and Todd, 1995; Venkatesh and Davis, 2000). In this volume, Fred Davis discusses how early HCI research inspired him during his dissertation work on TAM. He also discusses the evolution and current status of TAM research.

A historical view can be informative, enlightening, and intriguing. Because historical interpretations depend on the views taken by a researcher, they may yield unique results. Taking a historical perspective, Grudin compares three closely related disciplines that all have an intrinsic interest in HCI issues: human factors and ergonomics, computer-human interaction (CHI), and management information systems (MIS). He examines a rich set of historical events for each discipline. One frustration Grudin mentions is the terminologies used by MIS and CHI. On the surface, the different uses of the same terms do seem overwhelmingly confusing, as noted by Grudin repeatedly (Grudin, 1993). Yet, if we examine these differences more deeply, we can actually identify some fundamental differences among the different disciplines, such as the level of analysis in MIS and CHI: MIS emphasizes the macro level of IT development and use that is relevant and meaningful at the organizational level (Zhang et al., 2002); CHI, on the other hand, emphasizes the micro level of humans directly interacting with technology, with limited consideration of organizational meaningfulness. For example, Grudin mentions that "task analysis" has different meanings in MIS and in CHI: the word "task" in CHI would mean "move text" or "select-copy-paste," while the word "task" in MIS would usually refer to an organizational task. We think this difference arises because of the different levels of analysis these two disciplines take. "Moving text" or "selecting an object in GUI" is less meaningful in an organizational context than "finding a new location for the new branch of the business." To support the latter, IS designers need to go through the user's cognitive processes— i.e., they must conduct a cognitive task analysis by understanding how an organizational-level task can be supported by "tool-level" tasks that are, in turn, more directly supported by a computer system (such as a Decision Support System). Organizational-level tasks contextualize the interaction the user has with the computer when he or she is carrying out tool-level tasks. Therefore, although both studies in CHI and MIS may seem to be conducted at the level of the individual user, the tasks involved take place at different levels of abstraction (Zhang et al., 2005).

SUMMARY

HCI research in the MIS discipline has a long and an extensive history. Many different disciplines contribute to the development and enrichment of HCI research within the MIS discipline. There are also shared concerns and commonalities among MIS and other disciplines that have an interest in humans interacting with technologies. By the time a reader reads all the papers in this volume, it may become evident that MIS scholars emphasize organizational and business tasks and concerns, consider broad organizational and social contexts in their studies, and draw implications that are meaningful to organizations and management. The collected papers may also demonstrate the richness of HCI research topics in the MIS discipline. This can be further complemented by the collection on specific research topics in the second volume, *HCI and MIS: Applications.*

It may also become evident that the interest in HCI research in MIS will continue, just as Banker and Kauffman (2004) predicted. This has a lot to do with the recent advancement of technologies and relatively easy development of many sophisticated applications. More people are creating computer applications that affect many more people than ever before. User interfaces and human factors become the bottlenecks of acceptance and deployment of many promising technologies. In addition, being more productive and efficient are but two of several goals of technology users (Reinig et al., 1996; Te'eni, 2001; Zhang et al., 2002). We want to enhance not only our work, but also our life outside work, our connection with friends and families, and our capability to be more creative (Shneiderman, 2002). Because users are diverse and use technology in many different ways, the need for universally accessible IT (Shneiderman, 2000) affects more than just challenged people. Overall, human-centeredness has become more critical than ever before (Zhang et al., 2005). We hope HCI research in MIS will continue to grow. Together with other aspects of MIS research and with other disciplines related to HCI, we hope to make human experiences with technologies more pleasant, interesting, rewarding, and fulfilling, thus generating more business value for organizations and more social value for societies (Zhang and Li, 2005).

ACKNOWLEDGMENTS

We thank Drs. Alan Dennis and Joe Valacich for providing insight and pointers on some materials. Drs. Izak Benbasat, Gerry DeSanctis, Andrew Dillon, Jonathan Grudin, Ben Shneiderman, and Vladimir Zwass commented on early drafts, which enhanced the final paper considerably. We are responsible for any omissions, errors, or biases in this paper.

NOTE

1. In the MIS discipline, there are many studies on the management of IT where managers, CIOs, stakeholders, and other people play important roles that can be in both IT development and IT use stages in an organizational context. Their interaction with IT is most often at a higher level rather than at a direct hands-on level, so there are few sample studies of behavioral, cognitive, or affective impacts. Most often, managers deal with user resistance, raise intrinsic motivation of users, or "reengineer" a task to raise user productivity with IT support.

REFERENCES

Adams, D.A.; Nelson, R.R.; and Todd, P.A. Perceived usefulness, ease of use, and usage of information technology: a replication. *MIS Quarterly*, 16, 2 (1992), 227–247.

Agarwal, R., and Prasad, J. A conceptual and operational definition of personal innovativeness in the domain of information technology. *Information Systems Research*, 9, 2 (1998), 204–215.

Ajzen, I. The theory of planned behavior. *Organizational Behavior & Human Decision Processes*, 50, 2 (1991), 179–211.

Ajzen, I., and Fishbein, M. *Understanding Attitudes and Predicting Social Behavior*. Englewood Cliffs, NJ: Prentice-Hall, 1980.

Alavi, M.; Wheeler, B.C.; and Valacich, J. Using IT to reengineer business education: an exploratory investigation of collaborative telelearning. *MIS Quarterly*, 19, 3 (1995), 293–312.

Argyris, C. Management information systems: the challenge to rationality and emotionality. *Management Science*, 17, 6 (1971), B275–B292.

Baecker, R.; Grudin, J.; Buxton, W.; and Greenberg, S. *Readings in Human-Computer Interaction: Toward the Year 2000*. San Francisco: Morgan Kaufmann Publishers, 1995.

Banker, R.D., and Kauffman, R.J. The evolution of research on information systems: a fiftieth-year survey of the literature in management science. *Management Science*, 50, 3 (2004), 281–298.

Banville, C., and Landry, M. Can the field of MIS be disciplined? *Communications of the ACM*, 32, 1 (1989), 48–60.

Bapna, R.; Goes, P.; and Gupta, A. User heterogeneity and its impact on electronic auction market design: an empirical exploration. *MIS Quarterly*, 28, 1 (2004), 21–43.

Barki, H., and Hartwick, J. Measuring user participation, use involvement, and user attitude. *MIS Quarterly*, 18, 1 (1994), 59–82.

Barki, H., and Hartwick, J. Rethinking the concept of user involvement. *MIS Quarterly*, 13, 1 (1989), 53–63.

Baskerville, R., and Pries-Heje, J. Short cycle time systems development. *Information Systems Journal*, 14 (2004), 237–264.

Baskerville, R.L., and Myers, M.D. Information systems as a reference discipline. *MIS Quarterly*, 26, 1 (2002), 1–14.

Benbasat, I., and Taylor, R.N. The impact of cognitive styles on information systems design. *MIS Quarterly*, 2, 2 (1978), 43–54.

Bostrom, R.P., and Heinen, J.S. MIS problems and failures: a socio-technical perspective. Part I: The causes. *MIS Quarterly*, 1, 3 (1977), 17–32.

Bostrom, R.P.; Olfman, L.; and Sein, M.K. The importance of learning style in end-user training. *MIS Quarterly*, 14, 1 (1990), 101–119.

Carey, J.; Galletta, D.; Kim, J.; Te'eni, D.; Wildermuth, B.; and Zhang, P. The role of HCI in IS curricula: a call to action. *Communications of the AIS*, 13, 23 (2004), 357–379.

Carmel, E.; Whitaker, R.; and George, J.F. Participatory design and joint application design: a transatlantic comparison. *Communications of the ACM*, 36, 6 (1993), 40–48.

Chan, S.S.; Wolfe, R.J.; and Fang, X. Issues and strategies for integrating HCI in masters level MIS and e-commerce programs. *International Journal of Human-Computer Studies*, 59, 4 (2003), 497–520.

Compeau, D.R., and Higgins, C. Application of social cognitive theory to training for computer skills. *Information Systems Research*, 6, 2 (1995), 118–143.

Compeau, D.R., and Higgins, C.A. Computer self efficacy: development of a measure and initial test. *MIS Quarterly*, 19, 2 (1995), 189–211.

Compeau, D.R.; Higgins, C.A.; and Huff, S.L. Social sognitive theory and individual reactions to computing technology: a longitudinal study. *MIS Quarterly*, 23, 2 (1999), 145–158.

Culnan, M.J. The intellectual development of management information systems, 1972–1982: a co-citation analysis. *Management Science*, 32, 2 (1986), 156–172.

Culnan, M.J. Mapping the intellectual structure of MIS 1980–1985: a co-citation analysis. *MIS Quarterly*, 11, 3 (1987), 341–353.

Davis, F.D. Perceived usefulness, perceived ease of use, and user acceptance of information technology. *MIS Quarterly*, 13, 3 (1989), 319–342.

Davis, F.D. User acceptance of information technology: system characteristics, user perceptions and behavioral impacts. *International Journal of Man-Machine Studies*, 38, 3 (1993), 475–487.

Davis, F.D.; Bagozzi, R.P.; and Warshaw, P.R. User acceptance of computer technology: a comparison of two theoretical models. *Management Science*, 35, 8 (1989), 982–1003.

Dennis, A., and Garfield, M. The adoption and use of GSS in project teams: toward more participative processes and outcomes. *MIS Quarterly*, 27, 2 (2003), 289–323.

Dennis, A.R.; Wixom, B.H.; and Vandenberg, R.J. Understanding fit and appropriation effects in group support systems via meta-analysis. *MIS Quarterly*, 25, 2 (2001), 167–193.

Dickson, G.W., and Simmons, J.K. The behavioral side of MIS. *Business Horizons*, 13, 4 (1970), 59–71.

Dishaw, M.T., and Strong, D.M. Extending the technology acceptance model with task-technology fit constructs. *Information & Management*, 36, 1 (1999), 9–21.

Espinosa, A., and Carmel, E. The impact of time separation on coordination in global software teams: a conceptual foundation. *Journal of Software Process Improvement and Practice*, 8, 4 (2005), 249–266.

Fishbein, M., and Ajzen, I. *Belief, Attitude, Intention and Behavior: An Introduction to Theory and Research*. Reading, MA.: Addison-Wesley, 1975.

Gerlach, J., and Kuo, F.-Y. Understanding human computer interaction for information systems design. *MIS Quarterly*, 15, 4 (1991), 257–274.

Goodhue, D. The model underlying the measurement of the impacts of the IIC on the end-users. *Journal of the American Society for Information Science*, 48, 5 (1997), 449–453.

Goodhue, D.L. Development and measurement validity of a task-technology fit instrument for user evaluations of information systems. *Decision Sciences*, 29, 1 (1998), 105–137.

Goodhue, D.L. Understanding user evaluations of information systems. *Management Science*, 41, 12 (1995), 1827–1844.

Goodhue, D.L., and Thompson, R.L. Task-technology fit and individual performance. *MIS Quarterly*, 19, 2 (1995), 213–236.

Gorgone, J.T.; Gray, P.; Stohr, E.A.; Valacich, J.S.; and Wigand, R.T. MSIS 2006 curriculum review. *Communications of the AIS*, 15 (2005), 544–554.

Gray, P., and Olfman, L. The user interface in group decision support systems. *Decision Support Systems*, 5, 2 (1989), 119–137.

Grudin, J. Interface: an evolving concept. *Communications of the ACM*, 36, 4 (1993), 110–119.

Hackbarth, G.; Grover, V.; and Yi, M.Y. Computer playfulness and anxiety: positive and negative mediators of the system experience effect on perceived ease of use. *Information & Management*, 40, 3 (2003), 221.

Hardgrave, B.C.; Davis, F.; and Riemenschneider, C.K. Investigating determinants of software developers' intentions to follow methodologies. *Journal of Management Information Systems*, 20, 1 (2003), 123–151.

Harrison, A.W., and Rainer, R.K. The influence of individual differences on skill in end-user computing. *Journal of Management Information Systems*, 9, 1 (1992), 93–112.

Hefley, W.E.; Buie, E.A.; Lynch, G.F.; Muller, M.J.; Hoecker, D.G.; Carter, J.; and Roth, J.T. Integrating human factors with software engineering practices. In G. Perlman, G.K. Green, and M.S. Wogalter (eds.), *Human Factors Perspectives on Human-Computer Interaction: Selections from the Human Factors & Ergonomics Society Annual Meetings 1983–1994.* (Santa Monica, CA: Human Factors and Ergonomics Society, 1995), 359–363.

Hirschheim, R., and Klein, H.K. Four paradigms of information systems development. *Communication of the ACM*, 32, 10 (1989), 1199–1216.

Huber, G. Cognitive style as a basis for MIS and DSS designs: much ado about nothing? *Management Science*, 29, 5 (1983), 367–379.

Huber, G. Issues in the design of group decision support system. *MIS Quarterly*, 8, 8 (1984), 195–204.

Igbaria, M.; Zinatelli, N.; Cragg, P.; and Cavaye, A.L.M. Personal computing acceptance factors in small firms: a structural equation model. *MIS Quarterly*, 21, 3 (1997), 279–305.

Jarvenpaa, S.L. The effect of task demands and graphical format on information processing strategies. *Management Science*, 35, 3 (1989), 285–303.

Keil, M., and Carmel, E. Customer-developer links in software development. *Communications of the ACM*, 38, 5 (1995), 33–44.

Kim, J.; Hahn, J.; and Hahn, H. How do we understand a system with (so) many diagrams? Cognitive integration processes in diagrammatic reasoning. *Information Systems Research*, 11, 3 (2000), 284–303.

Lamb, R., and Kling, R. Reconceptualizing users as social actors in information systems research. *MIS Quarterly*, 27, 2 (2003), 197–235.

Lucas, H.C. Performance and the use of an information system. *Management Science*, 21, 8 (1975), 908–919.

Lyytinen, K. Expectation failure concept and systems analysts' view of information system failures: results of an exploratory study. *Information & Management*, 14 (1988), 45–56.

Lyytinen, K.; Yoo, Y.; Varshney, U.; Ackerman, M.; Davis, G.; Avital, M.; Robey, D.; Sawyer, S.; and Sorensen, C. Surfing the next wave: design and implementation challenges of ubiquitous computing environments. *Communication of the AIS*, 13, 40 (2004), 697–716.

Malhotra, Y., and Galletta, D.F. A multidimensional commitment model of volitional systems adoption and usage behavior. *Journal of Management Information Systems*, 22, 1 (Summer 2005), 117–151.

Malone, T.W., and Crowston, K. The interdisciplinary study of coordination. *Computing Surveys*, 26, 1 (1994), 87–119.

Mantei, M., and Teorey, T. Incorporating behavioral techniques into the system development life cycle. *MIS Quarterly*, 13, 3 (1989), 257–274.

Markus, L.M., and Björn-Andersen, N. Power over users: its exercise by system professionals. *Communication of the ACM*, 30, 6 (1987), 498–504.

Markus, M.L., and Keil, M. If we build IT, they will come: designing information systems that people want to use. *Sloan Management Review*, 35, 4 (1994), 11–25.

Markus, M.L.; Majchrzak, A.; and Gasser, L. A design theory for systems that support emergent knowledge processes. *MIS Quarterly*, 26, 3 (2002), 179–212.

Massey, A.P., and Clapper, D.L. Element finding: the impact of a group support system on a crucial phase of sense making. *Journal of Management Information Systems*, 11, 4 (1995), 150–176.

Mathieson, K. Predicting user intentions: comparing the technology acceptance model with the theory of planned behavior. *Information Systems Research*, 2, 3 (1991), 173–191.

Norman, D.A. Emotion and design: attractive things work better. *Interactions: New Visions of Human-Computer Interaction*, IX, 4 (2002), 36–42.

Norman, D.A. *Emotional Design: Why We Love (Or Hate) Everyday Things*. Cambridge, MA: Basic Books, 2004.

Olson, G., and Olson, J. User-centered design of collaboration technology. *Journal of Organizational Computing*, 1, 1 (1991), 41–60.

Orlikowski, W.J. The duality of technology: rethinking the concept of technology in organizations. *Organization Science*, 3, 3 (1992), 398–427.

Pitts, M.G., and Browne, G.J. Stopping behavior of system analysts during information requirements elicitation. *Journal of Management Information Systems*, 21, 1 (2004), 203–226.

Poole, M.S.; Holmes, M.; and DeSanctis, G. Conflict management in a computer-supported meeting environment. *Management Science*, 37, 8 (1991), 926–953.

Reeves, B., and Nass, C.I. *The Media Equation: How People Treat Computers, Televisions, and New Media as Real People and Places*. New York: Cambridge University Press, 1996.

Reinig, B.A. Toward an understanding of satisfaction with the process and outcomes of teamwork. *Journal of Management Information Systems*, 19, 4 (2003), 65–83.

Reinig, B.A.; Briggs, R.O.; Shepherd, M.M.; Yen, J.; and Nunamaker, J.F., Jr. Affective reward and the adoption of group support systems: productivity is not always enough. *Journal of Management Information Systems*, 12, 3 (1996), 171–185

Rivard, S., and Huff, S.L. User developed applications: evaluation of success from the DP department perspective. *MIS Quarterly* (1984), 39–50.

Russell, J.A. Core affect and the psychological construction of emotion. *Psychological Review*, 110, 1 (2003), 145–172.

Saleem, N. An empirical test of the contingency approach to user participation in information systems development. *Journal of Management Information Systems*, 13, 1 (1996), 145–167.

Satzinger, J.W.; Garfield, M.J.; and Nagasundaram, M. The creative process: the effects of group memory on individual idea generation. *Journal of Management Information Systems*, 15, 4 (1999), 143–160.

Schenk, K.D.; Vitalari, N.P.; and Davis, K.S. Differences between novice and expert systems analysts: what do we know and what we do. *Journal of Management Information Systems*, 15, 1 (1998), 9–50.

Schenkman, B.N., and Jonsson, F.U. Aesthetics and preferences of web pages. *Behaviour & Information Technology*, 19, 5 (2000), 367–377.

Sein, M.K., and Bostrom, R. The influence of individual differences in determining the effectiveness of conceptual models in training novice users. *Human-Computer Interaction*, 4 (1989), 197–229.

Senge, P. *The Fifth Discipline: The Art & Practice of the Learning Organization*. New York: Doubleday, 1990.

Sengupta, K., and Te'eni, D. Cognitive feedback in GDSS: improving control and convergence. *MIS Quarterly*, 17, 1 (1993), 87–113.

Shneiderman, B. *Designing the User Interface: Strategies for Effective Human-Computer Interaction*. Reading, MA: Addison-Wesley, 1987.

Shneiderman, B. *Leonardo's Laptop: Human Needs and the New Computing Technologies*. Cambridge, MA: MIT Press, 2002.

Shneiderman, B. Universal Usability. *Communications of the ACM*, 43, 5 (2000), 84–91.

Shneiderman, B., and Plaisant, C. *Designing the User Interface: Strategies for Effective Human-Computer Interaction*. New York: Addison-Wesley, 2005.

Swaab, R.I.; Postmes, T.; Neijens, P.; Kiers, M.H.; and Dumay, A.C.M. Multiparty negotiation support: the role of visualization's influence on the development of shared mental models. *Journal of Management Information Systems*, 19, 1 (2002), 129–150.

Swanson, E.B. Management information systems: appreciation and involvement. *Management Science*, 21, 2 (1974), 178–188.

Taylor, S., and Todd, P.A. Understanding information technology usage: a test of competing models. *Information Systems Research*, 6, 2 (1995), 144–176.

Te'eni, D. A cognitive-affective model of organizational communication for designing IT. *MIS Quarterly*, 25, 2 (2001), 251–312.

Torkzadeh, G., and Doll, W.J. The development of a tool for measuring the perceived impact of information technology on work. *Omega-International Journal of Management Science*, 27, 3 (1999), 327–339.

Tractinsky, N.; Katz, A.S.; and Ikar, D. What is beautiful is usable. *Interacting with Computers*, 13 (2000), 127–145.

van der Heijden, H. Factors influencing the usage of websites—the case of a generic portal in the Netherlands. *Information & Management*, 40, 6 (2003), 541–549.

Venkatesh, V. Determinants of perceived ease of use: integrating control, intrinsic motivation, and emotion into the technology acceptance model. *Information Systems Research*, 11, 4 (2000), 342–365.

Venkatesh, V., and Davis, F. A theoretical extension of the technology acceptance model: four longitudinal field studies. *Management Science*, 46, 2 (2000), 186–204.

Venkatesh, V., and Davis, F.D. A model of the antecedents of perceived ease of use: development and test. *Decision Science*, 27, 3 (1996), 451–481.

Venkatesh, V.; Morris, M.G.; Davis, G.B.; and Davis, F.D. User acceptance of information technology: toward a unified view. *MIS Quarterly*, 27, 3 (2003), 425–478.

Vessey, I. Cognitive fit: a theory-based analysis of the graphs versus tables literature. *Decision Sciences*, 22 (1991), 219–240.

Vessey, I. The effect of information presentation on decision making: A cost-benefit analysis. *Information & Management*, 27, 2 (1994), 103–119.

Vessey, I., and Galletta, D.F. Cognitive fit: an empirical study of information acquisition. *Information Systems Research*, 2, 1 (1991), 63–84.

Vessey, I.; Ramesh, V.; and Glass, R.L. Research in information systems: An empirical study of diversity in the discipline and its journals. *Journal of Management Information Systems*, 19, 2 (2002), 129–174.

Webster, J., and Martocchio, J.J. The differential effects of software training previews on training outcomes. *Journal of Management*, 21, 4 (1995), 757–787.

Webster, J., and Martocchio, J.J. Microcomputer playfulness: development of a measure with workplace implications. *MIS Quarterly*, 16, 1 (1992),

Yoo, Y., and Alavi, M. Media and group cohesion: relative influences on social presence, task participation, and group consensus. *MIS Quarterly*, 25, 3 (2001), 371–390.

Zhang, P. AIS SIGHCI three-year report. *AIS SIGHCI Newsletter*, 3, 1 (2004), 2–6.

Zhang, P. An image construction method for visualizing managerial data. *Decision Support Systems*, 23, 4 (1998), 371–387.

Zhang, P.; Benbasat, I.; Carey, J.; Davis, F.; Galletta, D.; and Strong, D. Human-computer interaction research in the MIS discipline. *Communications of the AIS*, 9, 20 (2002), 334–355.

Zhang, P.; Carey, J.; Te'eni, D.; and Tremaine, M. Integrating human-computer interaction development into the systems development life cycle: a methodology. *Communications of the AIS*, 15 (2005), 512–543.

Zhang, P., and Li, N. The importance of affective quality. *Communications of the ACM*, 48, 9 (2005), 105–108.

Zhang, P., and Li, N. The intellectual development of human-computer interaction research in MIS: a critical assessment of the MIS literature (1990–2002). *Journal of the Association for Information Systems*, 6, 11 (2005), 227–292.

Zhang, P.; Nah, F.H.F.; and Preece, J. HCI Studies in MIS. *Behaviour & Information Technology*, 23, 3 (2004), 147–151.

Zigurs, I., and Buckland, B.K. A theory of task/technology fit and group support systems effectiveness. *MIS Quarterly*, 22, 3 (1998), 313–334.

Zigurs, I.; Buckland, B.K.; Connolly, J.R.; and Wilson, E.V. A test of task-technology fit theory for group support systems. *Database for Advances in Information Systems*, 30, 3/4 (1999), 34.

Zigurs, I.; Poole, S.; and DeSanctis, G. A study of influence behavior in computer-mediated group decision making. *MIS Quarterly*, 12, 4 (1988), 625–644.

Zmud, R.W.; Anthony, W.P.; and Stair, R.M. The use of mental imagery to facilitate information identification in requirements analysis. *Journal of Management Information Systems*, 9, 4 (1993), 175–191.

PART I

DISCIPLINARY PERSPECTIVES
AND THE USERS

CHAPTER 2

INFORMATION INTERACTIONS

Bridging Disciplines in the Creation
of New Technologies

ANDREW DILLON

Abstract: *Designing information tools that meet human and organizational requirements involves skills, methods, and theories that are beyond the scope of one field. While the human-computer interaction (HCI) community draws on several disciplines to advance the state of the art, key concepts in the area remain undefined and the image of the user that drives various approaches is often overly limited or unarticulated, rendering communication among researchers problematic and education of future researchers and practitioners unfocused. However, rather than starting with definition at the user or interface level, the concept of information is potentially the most important one for us to agree upon. The present chapter presents a view of information as "product with purposive process" that aims to offer a representation of information that can be shared across MIS and HCI as both disciplines seek to inform interaction design.*

Keywords: *Information, Interdisciplinary Work, Design*

INTRODUCTION

The design of digital information systems has been studied formally and informally for decades. Throughout this time, the intellectual ownership of the process has never been settled. Certainly Management Information Systems (MIS) has taken the issue as its core focus, but the same could be said, with varying degrees of justification, of disciplines such as computer science, software engineering, and information science, among others. It might plausibly be argued that as information systems have become such a regular feature of contemporary working life, the need to study their design within the broader context of meaning in people's lives ensures that no one field can cover all the issues worthy of study here.

Human-computer interaction (HCI) is approaching, if it has not already arrived at, legitimacy as a field of inquiry at least as delineated as MIS, if measured by such criteria as number of dedicated journals, conferences, and professional societies. But where MIS research has tended to be located largely within business school environments, HCI programs have sprung up in computer science, psychology, information studies, or informatics departments (or some combination thereof). This lack of agreed disciplinary location has both advantages and disadvantages, depending on one's perspective, but it contributes to the impression that the field is novel or transitory, as opposed to having the departmental status of other disciplines on campus.

The general recognition of information systems design as a legitimate field of inquiry may be based on an interpretation that this is a form of computing research, broadly conceived. In conducting such work, a university is seen to traffic in contemporary scholarship of importance to society and its economic drivers. However, to many of us, what is really interesting about information systems is less the technological component and more the human or social aspects that underlie the study of systems use and impact. The very ubiquity that makes disciplinary ownership of information research so difficult to pinpoint becomes, in another light, the motivator for studying human behavior in this context, offering perhaps the greatest potential for building bridges between MIS and HCI.

Interdisciplinary sharing is no easy matter. Concepts that are familiar and routinely used in one discipline may trigger confusion or misunderstanding in another. Expectations or standards of evidence or theory building differ, and what constitutes an important question in one area may be deemed irrelevant or of secondary concern in the other. MIS is arguably more theoretically advanced than HCI, where there has been a longstanding debate about the real value of theory to designers (e.g., Landauer, 1991), though one might counter that the form of theory most used in MIS is heavily borrowed from elsewhere and makes few original contributions to the science of human activities. Perhaps most difficult to overcome is the publishing trajectory of each discipline's researchers. Scholars tend to populate publishing niches: a fixed set of journals, conferences, and networks where familiarity breeds communicative styles for inclusion and exclusion. These niches serve as powerful gatekeepers that render both bridge building and bridge crossing difficult. The reward structure in academia can lead to very narrow views of appropriate outlets for work (e.g., Mylonopoulos and Theoharakis, 2001). MIS departments tend to have more conservative publishing expectations than their HCI equivalents, frequently hiring and promoting on the basis of publication record in a rather narrow but specified range of "A" journals. The low cross-citation pattern one observes between these and other fields is evidence of this. For real intellectual synergy to occur, the common ground must be readily apparent and allow recognition to follow.

FINDING COMMON GROUND

Emphasis within MIS is given to planning, designing, and implementing technical systems, examining the human acceptance and use of these systems, and then evaluating the consequences of use for the organization involved. This is a broad terrain, especially as information systems have evolved and their uses have expanded. Current MIS research covers topics that twenty years ago were nonexistent (e.g., Galletta et al. [2004] on user tolerance of Web site delays, a paper that would be seen by many as mainstream HCI research). As a result, there are multiple outlets for MIS papers and distinct emphases within certain MIS schools on areas or types of IS research. The core literature suggests the existence of a robust discipline, so much so that Baskerville and Myers (2002) argue that it should serve as a model for other disciplines, even if MIS departments occupy a unique space in terms of the lack of pressure on faculty to fund their research through competitive grants. But even when a discipline's arrival seems agreed upon, there may always be an identity crisis, as Benbasat and Zmud (2003) now claim exists in MIS as a result of over-diversification. Indeed, Lyytinen and King (2004) argue that feelings of inadequacy within MIS are almost as old as the discipline itself.

The terrain covered by MIS is at least partly mirrored by research in HCI, which involves itself with the design and use of interactive technologies with a view to supporting the development of more usable and humanly acceptable systems (Shackel, 1997). Indeed, HCI research over the last twenty years has demonstrated wide-ranging interest in myriad technologies, often far from the commercial or industrial heart of most MIS work. The design process, the implementation of systems, and the human response to information technologies are all key to work in HCI, so much so that, at first glance, the unaligned researcher might easily confuse HCI with MIS. But there is no such confusion within the ranks. Developments such as the emergence of an HCI track at the AMCIS conference, or the publication of special issues of HCI journals dealing with MIS issues, are a very recent phenomenon (Zhang and Dillon, 2003), a formal acknowledgement of the existence of shared concerns, but with no commensurate doubts as to which way the ideas may flow.

One might propose a direct fit between HCI and MIS whereby those in MIS could exploit the relevant ideas and findings of HCI work on interface design when such design activities become part of their process. This would be a simple recommendation for bridge building, but not one that would necessarily lead to any conceptual cross-fertilization. MIS would draw on HCI much as computer science does, for insight or assistance at the point where users meet the tool. In return, HCI could exploit MIS as a specific application domain for its work, a context of use involving specific user types (managers) with a fairly bounded set of tasks (though it should be acknowledged that many MIS researchers would object to such a classification of their work).

In this vein, Dillon and Morris (1999) examined the relationship between MIS and HCI disciplines through a comparison of two key areas of research: acceptance theory in MIS and usability evaluation (UE) in HCI. They argued that these approaches were complementary, but rarely combined, and pointed to a lack of awareness in each camp of the value of the other approach.

> Obviously, both approaches have utility, but they do not cleanly complement each other. The operational definitions of effectiveness, efficiency, and satisfaction in UE are *not* equivalent to TAM's "ease of use" construct. Indeed it is possible that measuring usability in the UE manner might produce findings that are contradicted by TAM, since part of UE's definition of usability is more likely measured by usefulness in TAM. UE measures behavior of users with the system, while TAM measures affect, and, unfortunately, the relationship between the two is complicated. What seems to be missing from the current literature in this area is a unified model of use that supports both the process of design early on and clarifies the relationship between usability and acceptability. (Dillon and Morris, 1999, p. 232)

In a preliminary comparison of data obtained from both usability and acceptability measures, these authors noted that acceptance scores correlated highly with satisfaction, but neither were particularly good predictors of *effective* use. In other words, research could usefully explore both approaches to develop a more informed model of why people use and adopt certain information technologies. These authors advocated broadening the range of measures employed to include not only perceptual or attitudinal (e.g., TAM) and performance (e.g., task completion) measures, but objective analysis of a system's technical power or functionality (a characterization of what utility it objectively provided) to produce a hybrid model of use that drew equally from both traditions.

However, it is not clear that such an approach is ultimately the best way forward. To truly build bridges across disciplines, there needs to be a deeper sharing of key ideas and core concepts. But the obvious candidates for conceptual sharing are probably not, as might first appear, interfaces and users, since neither of these carry with them sufficient theoretical power on their own (though see DeSanctis). Attributes of interfaces or of users cannot alone explain sufficiently well how and why information systems work or fail. Research studies of users are contingent on addressing what is being used where, how, and why. Attempts to divorce user studies from these contextual issues show little prospect for revealing significant design insights (Dillon and Watson, 1996). The same is true for interfaces, which beg to be analyzed not as stand-alones, but as boundaries between activities and agents. Handbooks of design guidelines have been proposed over the last two decades, but few, if any, have had significant impact on practice, partly because guideline application is so context-dependent. Indeed, a typical design exercise for HCI students in my classes is to develop a highly unusable interface that conforms to such guidelines, a task that often proves quite easy to complete. Obviously there is no silver bullet here, but it seems that one potentially fruitful area for exploration, beyond users and interfaces, is the concept of information, wherein clarification of its nature and purpose for human activities might indicate more fundamental issues of relevance to both fields.

INFORMATION, NOT INTERACTION, AS A THE BASIS OF A SHARED PERSPECTIVE

Although the term "information" is ubiquitous, its definition as a meaningful concept in research on systems design remains somewhat vague. But how can this be? For researchers in MIS, information is a resource to be managed systematically to serve a common purpose; its impact on organizations and users can be reliably measured (e.g., McLeod and Schell, 2004). The emphasis therefore is on resource management, and, in particular, on creating better tools to support this activity. Travica (1999) argues that the use of information in this field tends to reduce the term to whatever technological application is being discussed, rendering it machine-processed data imbued with a business purpose. The emphasis of the field therefore is more on the processing, not on the concept, of information.

Within HCI, the term "information" is rarely, if ever, dealt with systematically. By its very name, HCI supposes that humans are using computers, and whatever it is that computers traffic in presumably defines information sufficiently well for this purpose. But the picture is more complicated than this. The term "interaction" in HCI may in fact be a historical anomaly. In early work, the acronym "HCI" was often taken to refer to the "human-computer interface" (for a thorough historical overview of the field up to the turn of the century, see Shackel 1997). By the 1980s "interaction" had replaced "interface" in common usage, even though many people remained uncomfortable with the idea that humans and computers ever interacted (Suchman, 1987). Nevertheless, computers were seen as information processors and the goal of HCI research was to help ease the processing of information and to render computers more usable for their intended user population.

But information as a concept still has only vague status within HCI and MIS, oddly enough. Despite the term's prominence, reflected in titles and publications, critical treatment of the information concept is not the norm. The most recent edition of the *Handbook of Human-Computer Interaction* (Helander et al., 1997), a standard reference within the field, contains multiple listings of the term in its index, but these are references to other areas where the term itself is employed conjointly, such as "information visualization," "information superhighway," "information retrieval," or "information filtering." Information alone is not defined, and certainly is not a central focus of writings on HCI. For HCI researchers, the goal of their work is more to understand how devices that manipulate and present "information" can be designed for ease of use; this has led to an emphasis on usability, with its attendant focus on efficiency of user performance. Yet information is central to HCI since the very goal of design is to create tools that get out of the way of users and their tasks, to create transparency in their workings so as to facilitate smoother interaction. A similar exercise in a current MIS textbook by Laudon and Laudon (2003) also lacks a detailed definition of the concept; indeed, the index to the 8th edition of this well-regarded text mentions the term "information" by itself only twice.

Even though defining commonsense terms is something of a thankless task, "information" has been subject to several attempts at definition over the years. Most noticeably, within the broad information studies realm (e.g., Williams and Carbo, 1997), a strong theme has been the need to draw firm lines between raw data and information. Accordingly, data is seen as the base material that conveys little in and of itself unless ordered, processed, or otherwise made useful to its recipients. Once given meaningful form, data becomes information. Given the strong ties between psychology and both MIS and HCI, it is odd that this distinction has little or no currency in cognitive psychology, where data and information are typically treated synonymously.

Conceptualizing information does not end with its demarcation from data. Information can itself be distinguished from knowledge, which in turn can be distinguished from wisdom, and more than a few books have been written on these terms and their putative relationships. In their classic text *Working Knowledge*, Davenport and Prusak (1997) articulate a view of information as "data that makes a difference" to the receiver, thereby highlighting the problems associated with extracting the important elements of a data set or the need to avoid being overwhelmed by too much data. Information, thus construed, has relevance or purpose, and is extracted or transformed from data by what these authors refer to as "the five C's": contextualization, categorization, calculation, correction, or condensation.

One does not have to accept the "five C's" approach to recognize that technology clearly plays a role in adding value to data. Thus, one can envisage an MIS- or HCI-style analysis of information tools or systems built on this view. Visualization tools can categorize data to be viewed in new ways, enhancing the emergence of information from complex data sets. Calculation is the backbone of computing, the defining triumph of what Landauer (1995) described as the first stage of computing, where technologies performed information tasks at a level impossible for humans to match. But technological support for Davenport and Prusak's methods is not the full story here, as these authors themselves acknowledge. More crucially, distinctions between data, information, and knowledge bring a significant human factor into the discussion, implying that data becomes information only when a user (a knowing human) makes sense of it and when it makes a difference for him or her. Making sense is itself multiply determined and context-dependent (Dervin, 1989), but the crucial distinction rests on the extraction of meaning or the imposition of order through human processing of some kind.

It is precisely because of this human factor that we cannot simply equate information with objects such as books or DVDs, no matter how appealing such a usage is at first. Buckland (1991) wrote a much-cited article on this in which he referred to the objectification of "information-as-thing." My reading of his argument is not that information *is* an object, but that once information is viewed as the potential for intelligent reading of data, there are few objects in our world that cannot serve as information, under some set of conditions.

Equating information to data that makes a difference for certain people is certainly a start, but is it a sufficiently strong basis for a field of study? There are alternatives, most noticeably the mathematical conceptualization of information that defines information in terms of the confidence levels in receivers of the conditions that exist at the source. Put another way, this defines information as the reduction of receiver uncertainty (e.g., Gharhamani, 2003), which is clearly a difference that is meaningful. This view of information has had significant impact on the design of computing systems, and both informed and drew on classic information processing theories of human cognition. However, I cannot see a way forward for our present concerns by utilizing this approach since it scales weakly to real-world tasks involving humans and information systems.

Dillon (2004) proposed a view of information as product with *purposive* process, arguing that information does not reside in objects or entities, but emerges from the engagement of such objects with humans as they go about their tasks in situ. In other words, books, DVDs, and databases do not contain information; they contain data. But information can result or emerge from the interaction of the data-carrying entity with a human. Humans can exploit the information potential of data objects only if they have the intelligence or capability to do so, and some of this capability is technological, though the majority of it is probably psychological. A book in a language you cannot read has significantly less data that you can exploit for information purposes than a book in your own language. But note that even such a book has some information potential for you, since your experience of books will undoubtedly lead you to conclude that this artifact possesses the capability to inform by virtue of its scriptlike qualities and ordered structure.

By extension, the information potential of any one data source will vary tremendously across the user population. Different users' different needs for the same data set will drive their examination and interpretation processes in distinct ways. This is the classic task effect with which we are all so familiar in systems design and evaluation. But beyond task differences, the psychological makeup of any one user is unique, so, at a very personal level, there will always be many different ways in which information is viewed, even by users performing the same tasks with the same data set and artifact. Furthermore, users are not isolated beings. There is always a strong contextual element to data exploration and interpretation, which ensures that information must be conceived of in terms of its occurrence of use, and the organizational, social, and cultural milieu in which use is made.

RETHINKING INFORMATION AS PRODUCT WITH POTENTIAL

Product with purposive process might be more neatly thought of as "product with potential," an approach that aims to overcome the forced separation of information into objects (products) or acts (processes) by advancing a view of information as the emergent property resulting from the purposing of these two elements into a meaningful context.

Equating information with products is an old habit, enforced by years of emphasis within the information world on collecting and storing data. While this has given rise to established methods and procedures in the collection and management realm, there has been a lack of commensurate theoretical and methodological development in the process aspects of information making. What are labeled in Figure 2.1 as the "arc of interpretation" and "arc of exploration" are fundamentally psychological phenomena that can be difficult to measure. Indeed, despite the routine use of "comprehension" as a measure of student performance in our universities, cognitive scientists do not even agree that the process can be defined. The point here though, is that our views of information have tended to be heavily one-sided, led by an objectification of the concept coupled with a weakly articulated assumption of the necessary human processing involved.

The term "mediation" is used in Figure 2.1 to highlight the often-essential role of some mechanism for translation between data and a human. Information technology is one such mediator, but it is not the only kind. Other experts, information specialists, coworkers, and the like can all serve as mediators in some contexts. However, for purposes of the present discussion, information technology is the primary mediator of interest. Thus, such technology carries, stores, retrieves, and presents data. It can provide a physical instantiation of data or the mechanism for making visible or audible the data of interest. Without this, it is not clear that we truly have an instance of information exchange. This is an important distinction. People can communicate directly with each other and we often talk of this as the exchange of information, but it is not clear that information has truly been exchanged. Data has certainly passed between the communicants, but this is not alone a sufficient basis for us to consider the process informational in a form that we would

Figure 2.1 **Information as Product with Purposive Process**

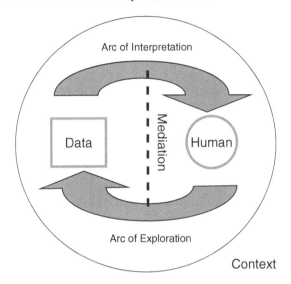

wish to study for systems design. This is not to say that meaning cannot be made in such exchanges, or more likely, that these exchanges, in the context of discussions about some objectified data set, are not informational, but that simple conversation between people is not the fundamental unit of information studies. The field of information studies properly involves artifacts involved in the acts of interpretation and exploration of data sets.

What this does imply is that an informational analysis of human activity is not the same as a communicational study or a sociological study, even though all may share many similarities of method and purpose. An informational analysis is built on a representation of some data first and foremost. Where the data is not represented in some form observable by a third party not present at the initial exchange, then the informational perspective, in the formal sense implied by a field of information studies (MIS or HCI) is not invoked.

So studies of information systems rest on data artifacts (technologies) of some type, which we may define to include the very artifacts and objects many take as information itself, as noted by Buckland. The term "technology" is used here to include the abstracted and embodied forms of data that are accessible to us when removed (temporally or physically) from the initial events or contexts of creation. Humans have created an elaborate set of such technologies to capture, manipulate, store, retrieve, and transfer data sets. This is the province of information and the design of information systems. In this light, the distinctions between MIS and HCI really do seem trivial, and are really ones of emphasis on specific details. This difference of emphasis is insufficient, in my mind, to warrant very formal distinctions between the fields of the kind we currently see within academia.

INTERACTION THROUGH INFORMATION

If we consider information, as product with potential, to be the basis for sharing ideas between MIS and HCI, how may we proceed? One option is to recast MIS and HCI within an enriched emphasis on information. In the first instance, this view recognizes the fields as sharing considerable intellectual overlap without them being equivalent. This lack of equivalence should not be seen as indicative of much more than natural differentiation resulting from institutionalized activities at the university department level. Although MIS and HCI can certainly be compared and contrasted in terms of core theory and major venues of activity, a large source of difference naturally emerges from the academic homes in which they exist and this source of difference will always affect the development and shaping of the discipline.

That aside, from an information perspective, MIS can be considered to be primarily concerned with identifying, abstracting, and supporting the data flows that exist in organizations, and developing or supporting the technological (broadly conceived) means of exploiting the potential to serve organizational ends. Similarly, HCI seeks to maximize the use of information through the design of humanly acceptable representational and manipulatory tools. These characterizations clearly emphasize commonality but also highlight aspects or facets of interest that are more properly thought of as belonging more in one discipline than in others.

An informational basis for comparing MIS and HCI could lead us to several interesting positions. First, is MIS just a bounded context of inquiry for tackling HCI problems? Given its industrial and organizational application zone, the emphasis in much MIS work might be taken as a sign of disinterest in some of the broader areas of inquiry pursued by certain mainstream HCI researchers, e.g., work in hypermedia design for education, or the significant body of HCI work that has addressed problems in aviation or vehicle interfaces (e.g., Wickens, 1991). There seems to be no fundamental reason why much of what has emerged from MIS could not be of use in this broader arena, but it is still the case that a typical MIS conference contains research that originates in or is applied to a more constrained set of usage environments or contexts than would be found at an HCI conference. This may be changing as MIS researchers begin to consider online education and computer-mediated consumer behavior more broadly, but blurred or not, the boundaries still remain.

A second interesting aspect of an informational analysis concerns the relative strengths of theory in MIS and HCI. It is probably the case that theoretical structures have been more keenly erected in MIS than in HCI. It is not obvious why this should be the case, since one might argue that HCI's focus on human psychology would have enabled it to borrow easily from well-established social science work in cognition. The problem, more likely, is that borrowing from cognitive psychology has proven to be more problematic for HCI than borrowing from social psychology has been for MIS, since the theoretical models driving work in perception, categorization, decision making, etc., have limited generalizability when seeking guidance for design outside of decisions that affect rapid aspects of interaction (keypresses, layout, image quality, etc.). There is little direct guidance in cognitive psychology for designers interested in usability, with the result that empiricism trumps rationalism in HCI literature.[1]

Like any applied field, MIS has also borrowed heavily from outside, although in doing so, it has tended to emphasize more social psychological perspectives than cognitive ones. Social psychological models have two distinct advantages: first, they tend to traffic in more observable human actions; second, they place greater emphasis on the environment in which human action occurs than do most cognitive approaches. As a result, the level of discourse that underlies MIS can more easily transpose social psychological models to meaningful issues in the application domain. In part this has been recognized in later HCI work, where concerns with collaboration and computer-supported work have caused a shift in that field towards more socially informed theorizing.

If we can see HCI and MIS as highly overlapping, but differing mainly in terms of contexts studied and theoretical borrowings, it may be possible to identify research problems that both share or could inform. A point of overlap for both MIS and HCI is the establishment of the purpose, the reason that the system for information handling and transfer is being constructed. This is the basis for most work in systems design, but can be lost, certainly in HCI, once concerns for usability lead to a focus on interface features. HCI researchers tend to talk in terms of tasks when thinking about usability, but tasks are not the basic unit of analysis within MIS research.

Usability has become rather narrowly understood to mean effectiveness, efficiency, and satisfaction for specified users, tasks, and contexts (e.g., Bevan and Macleod, 1994). Work in this area focuses on determining the criteria for usability and then measuring an interface against them in a user test. Such work has often been criticized for emphasizing performance outside of normal usage patterns and situations. Indeed, usability, as a formal concept, has barely made a move from the HCI world to other areas such as MIS where its relevance is, at first blush, obvious.

Determining criteria for effectiveness, efficiency, and satisfaction, to use the major ISO 9241 outline of usability, could actually be a real shared concern for MIS and HCI researchers. Understanding the forces that shape expectations for task performance with a system will open up areas of management, ownership, responsibility, and organizational expectations that are not typical of usability-oriented research. Indeed, a more socio-technical form of analysis of computer use has embraced usability in this manner with some success (e.g., Eason, 1989; Dillon, 2000), but it remains the exception rather than the norm in HCI work. By adopting a view of context more typical of MIS work in considerations of usability, there may be a broadening of the typical HCI approach that could benefit both communities and lead to a clearer articulation of what makes people use information systems. Such an articulation would possibly have greater potential for application to design than survey- or a user test–based approaches.

There are pockets of research in HCI on interface design, navigation in information space, or task performance in non-work-related activities that have developed strong empirical research findings and even some well-developed articulation of theoretical frameworks (e.g., Carroll, 1999; Dillon, 2004). While predictive modeling in HCI is limited (and has something of a bad reputation in this field) these areas are well enough understood for us to be able to predict user response with great accuracy in some circumstances. This is, again, one more area in which shared approaches can yield gains.

By turning our collective attention to information as product with purposive process or potential, we can start to articulate a more unified view of what problems we share and what methods we may use to solve them. Seeking a greater perspective than a user and a task, HCI could gain much from the organizational emphasis embraced by MIS, while yielding significant findings itself to the MIS concern with end-user response. But to get there we need a basis for sharing ideas that goes beyond the general terminology and concepts currently employed independently by each discipline. A shared view of information seems a plausible first candidate for developing a common platform for exchange.

WHY DO WE CARE?

The goals of research into information system design are many, including practical application of the results to real organizations, the formulation of better theories of human activities, and the design of new innovative products that can extend our capabilities as humans. No one discipline has a monopoly on the issues or can claim to be the birthing ground for invention and design. Yet disciplines such as MIS and HCI do have legitimate inputs that can help shape better systems. Harnessing the insights and perspectives of more than one field is problematic but, if successful, would likely yield real benefits to scholars and practitioners.

Information systems design has been characterized as an area that emerged in response to a phenomenon (King, 1993), but the concern with designing tools or products for users has a longer history than the computer, with associated sets of values and approaches that warrant a significant historical analysis in their own right to untangle. Talk of interdisciplinary exchanges is comparatively popular and easy; the practice is somewhat more complicated. A commonly understood set of terms is a necessary first step, and my argument here is that the key term for us all to become comfortable with is "information." Moving beyond data is important, but we need to move together to build the bridge. Foundation or keystone, information is our common concern.

NOTE

1. This is not to say that cognitive psychology is not relevant, only that it requires significant translation to take lab findings and apply them meaningfully so as to guide interface design effectively.

REFERENCES

Baskerville, R.L., and Myers, M.D. Information systems as a reference discipline. *MIS Quarterly*, 26, 1 (2002), 1–14.

Benbasat, I., and Zmud, R. The identity crisis within the IS discipline: defining and communicating the discipline's core properties, *MIS Quarterly*, 27, 2 (2003), 183–194.

Bevan, N., and Macleod, M. Usability measurement in context. *Behavior and Information Technology*, 13, 2 (1994), 132–145.

Buckland, M. Information as thing. *Journal of the American Society for Information Science*, 42, 5 (1991), 351–360.

Card, S.; Moran, T.; and Newell, A. *The Psychology of Human Computer Interaction*. Norwood, NJ: LEA, 1983.

Carroll, J. (ed.) *Minimalism: Beyond the Nurnberg Funnel*. Cambridge MA: MIT Press, 1999.

Dervin, B. Users as research inventions: how research categories perpetuate inequities. *Journal of Communication*, 38, 3 (1989), 216–232.

Dillon, A. Group dynamics meet cognition: applying socio-technical concepts in the design of information systems. In E. Coakes, D. Willis, and R. Lloyd-Jones (eds.), *The New SocioTech: Graffiti on the Long Wall*. London: Springer Verlag, 2000, pp. 119–125.

Dillon, A. What is this thing called information? In H. van Oostendorp, L. Breure, and A. Dillon (eds.), *Creation, Use and Deployment of Digital Information*. Norfolk: LEA, 2005, pp. 307–316.

Dillon, A., and Morris, M. P3: modeling and measuring the human determinants of information systems usage. *Proceedings of the 43rd Annual Meeting of the Human Factors and Ergonomics Society*. Santa Monica, CA: HFES, 1999, pp. 231–237.

Dillon, A., and Watson, C. User analysis in HCI: the historical lessons from individual differences research. *International Journal of Human-Computer Studies*, 45, 6 (1996), 619–637.

Davis, F.D. Perceived usefulness, perceived ease of use, and user acceptance of information technology. *MIS Quarterly*, 13, 3 (1989), 319–334.

Davenport, T., and Prusak, L. *Working Knowledge: How Organizations Manage What They Know*. Cambridge, MA: Harvard Business School Press, 1997.

Galletta, D.; Henry, R.; McCoy, S.; and Polak, P. Web site delays: how tolerant are users? *Journal of the Association for Information Systems*, 5, 1 (2004), 1–28.

Gharhamani, Z. Information theory. In *Macmillan Encyclopedia of Cognitive Science*, vol. 2. London: Nature Publishing Group, 2003, pp. 551–555.

Helander, M.; Landauer, T.; and Prabhu, V. *Handbook of Human-Computer Interaction*, 2nd ed. Amsterdam: North Holland, 1997.

Hobart, M., and Schiffman, Z. *Information Ages: Literacy, Numeracy and the Computer Revolution*. Baltimore, MD: Johns Hopkins University Press, 1998.

King, J.L. The IS field—what's in a name? *Information Systems Research*, 4, 4 (1993), 291–298.

Landauer, T. Let's get real: a position paper on the role of cognitive psychology in the design of humanly useful and usable systems. In J. Carroll (ed.) *Designing Interaction: Psychology at the Human-Computer Interface*. New York: Cambridge: University Press, 1991, pp. 60–73.

Landauer, T. *The Trouble with Computers*. Cambridge, MA: MIT Press, 1995.

Laudon, J., and Laudon, K. *Management Information Systems*, 8th ed. Upper Saddle River, NJ: Prentice Hall, 2003.

McLeod, R., and Schell, G. *Management Information Systems*, 9th ed. New York: Prentice Hall, 2004.

Mylonopoulos, N., and Theoharakis, V. Global perceptions of IS journals. *Communications of the ACM*, 44, 9 (2001), 29–33.

Shackel, B. Human-computer interaction—whence and whither? *Journal of the American Society for Information Science*, 48, 11 (1997), 970–986.

Suchman, L. *Plans and Situated Action: The Problem of Human-Machine Communications*. Cambridge: Cambridge University Press, 1987.

Travica, B. *New Organizational Designs: Information Aspects*. Stamford, CT: Ablex Publishing, 1999.

Williams, J., and Carbo, T. *Information Science: Still an Emerging Discipline*, Pittsburgh, PA: Cathedral Publishing, 1997.

Zhang, P., and Dillon, A. HCI and MIS: shared concerns. *International Journal of Human-Computer Studies*, 59, 4 (2003), 397–522.

CHAPTER 3

HCI AS MIS

ADRIENNE OLNICK KUTZSCHAN AND JANE WEBSTER

Abstract: *Human-computer interaction has traditionally been studied within computer science, engineering, psychology, and, to a much smaller degree, business. Each area brings its own unique contributions to the field. Nevertheless, this paper presents the argument that management information systems (MIS) researchers in business schools are distinctively positioned to address HCI issues, as they focus on people, information technologies, and wider contextual issues. MIS researchers' big-picture perspective, combined with related theory and rigorous methodologies, support this position. In addition, they have the unique ability not only to study applications during development, but to follow them through to market. For instance, there is a current void within HCI research of large-scale studies that include employee interactions with actual technologies; this represents a substantial opportunity for MIS researchers. This paper identifies issues that may be inhibiting MIS's ability to take full advantage of this opportunity, and makes suggestions for speeding up the progress of research in this area.*

Keywords: *Human-Computer Interaction, Management Information Systems, Reference Discipline, Undergraduate Education*

INTRODUCTION

> "HCI often falls in the cracks between university departments, such as Psychology, Computer Science, and perhaps Business."
>
> (survey respondent quoted in Singer et al., 2003)

This paper argues that business schools need to take the lead to ensure that HCI no longer falls between the cracks. With many computer-based systems now accessible not only by employees but by consumers and the general population, human-computer interaction (HCI) has come to represent a key topic for businesses. Well-designed software can result in business benefits such as decreased development costs, fewer user difficulties in finding desired information on Web sites, increased return visits and sales from e-commerce sites, and higher user satisfaction (UsabilityNet, 2003). For example, navigation features for product lists have been found to reduce the time to purchase ratio, and ultimately to account for variance in monthly sales (Lohse and Spiller, 1999).

While these findings are important, the adoption of HCI design principles, such as those for navigation, has been a slow process and to date these principles are still not fully implemented within the marketplace. Jakob Nielsen argued that the "first ten years of commercial web sites were a lost decade with very few designs that truly worked for customers" (Neal, 2003). According to Norman Nielson Group researchers, the average e-commerce Web site followed only 49 percent of NNG e-commerce usability standards in 2002, and this was up from only 45 percent in 2000 (Lang, 2002). In fact, the highest scoring e-commerce Web site followed only 66 percent of the e-commerce standards in 2002 (Nielsen, 2002). This was further substantiated by Webster and Ahuja (2006), who found that only 34 percent of the popular Web sites had site maps; 77 percent had navigation links on all pages; and 70 percent had consistent displays.

Given that even the most popular Web sites fail to consistently follow design guidelines, one can argue that HCI research is not currently informing organizational applications at an acceptable rate. There may be two reasons for this phenomenon. Developers of applications and/or products may not find HCI research to be helpful or relevant. For example, if the research suffers from weak methodology and/or theoretical foundations, then it may be difficult to interpret its results. Second, organizational members, such as marketers and application developers, may not know enough about HCI to follow development standards or even know that development standards exist. Therefore, there appears to be a disconnection between HCI researchers, HCI knowledge and training in organizations, and marketplace needs.

In today's fast-paced economy, HCI and usability practitioners are calling for relevance in HCI research (Czerwinski et al., 2003) and the marketplace continues to call for well-designed interfaces. HCI has been criticized for its lack of sensitivity to business issues, and this has been credited with holding HCI back from realizing its potential as a discipline (Gray and Salzman, 1998; Zolli, 2004). It is now becoming clear that HCI research and education are not regularly producing research that is tied to business and/or marketplace needs and are not developing HCI curricula that are sufficiently applied in organizations.

In response to these concerns, this paper makes the simple argument that human-computer interaction's natural home is not within psychology or computer science, but within business schools. To justify this argument, this paper will: first, review the differences between discipline-specific conceptualizations of HCI; second, describe the current state of HCI research and education; third, discuss how business disciplines, and more specifically management information systems (MIS), can contribute to HCI; and, finally, review the potential factors that may be holding MIS back from making these contributions, concluding with a list of suggested solutions to these challenges.

MULTIPLE CONCEPTUALIZATIONS OF HCI

Computer science and psychology are viewed as the intellectual foundations of HCI. Both areas study the interaction of the person and the technology, but incline toward their strengths in these respective areas. For instance, psychologists tend to focus more on individual characteristics and behaviors. An example of such an article would be one examining extroverts' and introverts' reactions to computer-generated speech on Web sites (Nass and Lee, 2001). In psychology, HCI is often called "human factors,"[1] and HCI researchers are supported by the American Psychological Association's division of "Applied Experimental and Engineering Psychology." This division describes human factors as the "psychological principles relating human behavior to the design and use of environments and systems within which people work and live" (APA, 2004).

Conversely, computer scientists focus more on developing technologies for the computer interface. An example would be a recent study that examines different types of diagrams for information structures, but does not take into account individual characteristics (Irani and Ware, 2003). Computer scientists are supported by the Association for Computing Machinery's (ACM) special interest group on computer-human interaction (SIGCHI) that describes CHI as "the design, evaluation, implementation, and study of interactive computing systems for human use."

Figure 3.1   **Human-Computer Interaction in Business**

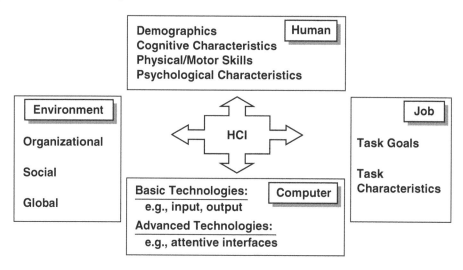

Source: Adapted from Zhang and Li (2004).

Although each of these HCI perspectives contributes to our understanding of the roles of the individual and technology, neither computer science nor psychology emphasizes the importance of other crucial variables such as information, tasks, and/or varying contexts (Dillon, chapter 2 in this volume). We feel that the lack of emphasis on these variables creates an incomplete definition of HCI. By contrast, business researchers, supported by the Association for Information Systems' (AIS) special interest group on human-computer interaction (SIGHCI), define HCI as "the inter-action between humans, information, technologies, and tasks, especially in the business, manage-rial, organizational, and cultural contexts" (AIS, 2004). In addition to the noticeable fact that MIS researchers put the "human" before the "computer" (while this is reversed for computer scientists' SIGCHI), MIS researchers also take a more contextual view of HCI, considering wider task, orga-nizational, and international issues. Thus, MIS researchers view HCI as the interplay not only between the human and the computer, but among other factors such as job characteristics and environmental issues (see Figure 3.1); in other words, HCI in MIS concerns the human use of technologies to support tasks within particular contexts (Zhang and Li, 2004). This results in MIS researchers working at a wide range of levels of analysis, from individual to cross-cultural issues.[2]

THE CURRENT STATE OF HCI RESEARCH AND EDUCATION

With the wider contextual strengths of MIS, one would expect HCI to reside mainly in business schools. HCI has represented a small, but core, element of MIS since its inception as a discipline (e.g., Mason and Mitroff, 1973). It regularly shows up in summaries of research areas within MIS (e.g., Banker and Kauffman, 2004; Swanson and Ramiller, 1993), and it continues to grow in impor-tance in MIS research (Carey et al., 2004; Chan et al., 2003). However, HCI has many homes, with, as we demonstrate next, the majority of HCI research and teaching occurring outside of business schools.

HCI Research

To date, HCI research has been credited with drawing attention to the importance and benefits of well-designed interfaces. However, HCI has also been criticized for not grounding its research in theory, not including contextual variables (i.e., variables beyond the person and the technology, such as organizational characteristics), using small sample sizes, and including methods and analysis techniques that are not always appropriate (Galletta et al., 2003; Gray and Salzman, 1998). For example, a review of an emerging area of HCI research, instant messaging (IM), noted that many of the studies do not draw from a theoretical base, do not include representative samples (rather they draw on the developers' colleagues in their own organizations or investigate teenagers or university students), are conducted by the developers of the systems themselves, and are presented at conferences, rather than published in journals (Cameron and Webster, 2005). Further, examining the home department of the IM articles' authors, we see that more than 80 percent are located either in technology-based industry research labs or in computer science.

To examine a more mature stream of HCI research, we also reviewed research on user disorientation, a topic that has been studied at least since the days of hypertext (e.g., Conklin, 1987). This topic was chosen because it has been referred to as one of the most important issues in hypertext navigation (Otter and Johnson, 2000), and because navigation has been identified as the fourth most frequently researched area by HCI practitioners (Singer et al., 2003). Furthermore, difficulty in finding features is among the most frequently cited reason for user frustration (Ceaparu et al., 2002). Within this older stream of research, we see more researchers outside of the computer science area. However, many of the weaknesses described above were still demonstrated. For example, most of the studies did not include contextual variables, did not provide strong theoretical justifications, and studied university students. Consistent with Gray and Salzman's (1998) critique of HCI experiments, we saw studies that could have been designed better: for example, some of the studies that were called experiments were actually studies that included no comparison or control groups (similar to "usability" studies). Furthermore, over half of the studies included sample sizes of thirty or less and almost half presented simple analytic findings, such as frequencies and correlations (see Table 3.1).

Both IM and disorientation research provide areas where MIS researchers can and do contribute. For example, within the disorientation literature, the majority of business researchers include much larger sample sizes and employ more rigorous methodologies. Furthermore, they are positioned to be more aware of wider contextual variables and current business and market needs. Therefore, we believe that MIS researchers in business schools have the unique capabilities to provide not only business sensitivity, but also methodological and theoretical rigor.

HCI Teaching

To examine where HCI education currently resides, we collected information from the Web on undergraduate HCI courses offered in the English language.[3] In order to be included here, the terms of HCI, human computer interaction, human-computer interaction, computer-human interaction, human factors, and/or usability had to be listed in either the course title or, when available, the course description. On occasion, only the program descriptions were included on the Web and the courses associated with each program were not specifically listed. When this occurred, the program levels were often described in detail. If the program level description included any of these same terms, then it was included as an HCI course. Alternatively, if the program did not provide a description of levels and/or a list of courses, it was not included in this summary.

Table 3.1

An Analysis of Disorientation Research

Authors	Schools	Theory Base	Journal
Ahuja and Webster (2001)	Both authors were from business—University of Waterloo	(1) 3 (2) 4	*Interacting with Computers*
Benbunan-Fich (2001)	Business—Seton Hall	(1) 3	(1) *Information & Management*
Bernard and Hamblin (2003)	Both authors were from psychology—Wichita State University	(1) 1	*Usability News*
Chen and Wells (1999)	One author was from the School of Journalism and Communication—University of Minnesota One author was from advertising within the School of Journalism and Communication—University of Minnesota	(1) 3	*Journal of Advertising Research*
D'Ambra and Rice (2001)	One author was from the School of Information Systems—University of New South Wales One author was from the School of Communication, Information and Library Studies—Rutgers University	(1) 3 (2) 3 (3) 3	*Information & Management*
Danielson (2002)	Symbolic Systems (multidisciplinary)—Stanford University	(1) 3	*Interacting with Computers*
Danielson (2003)	Symbolic systems (multidisciplinary)—Stanford University	(1) 3	*IT and Society*
Head et al. (2000)	All authors were from business—McMaster University	(1) 4	*International Journal of Human Computer Studies*
Jarvenpaa and Todd (1996)	Both authors were from business—University of Texas, Austin, and Queen's University	(1) 3	*International Journal of Electronic Commerce*
Kim and Yoo (2000)	Both authors were from business—Yonsei University	(1) 3 (2) 3	*International Journal of Human Computer Studies*
Lazar et al. (2003)	Three authors were from computing science—University of Maryland (First author from computing science) One author was from the HCI Institute—Carnegie Mellon University One author was from sociology—University of Maryland	(1) 3 (2) 3	*IT and Society*

Method	Participants	Sample Size	Statistical Analysis	Contextual Variables
(1) Survey	(1) Undergraduate and graduate students	(1) 135	(1) Confirmatory factor analysis	(1) No
(2) Experiment	(2) Undergraduate and graduate students	(2) 207	(2) Regression	(2) No
(1) Protocol analysis	(1) Undergraduate, graduate, and employees	(1) 8	(1) Frequencies/ qualitative data	(1) No
(1) Search tasks	(1) Not indicated	(1) 18	(1) Within subject ANOVA	(1) No
(1) Survey	(1) Undergraduate and graduate students	(1) 120	(1) Factor analysis, regression, and correlations	(1) No
(1) Focus group	(1) Undergraduate and graduate students	(1) 26	(1) Qualitative–content analysis	(1) Yes
(2) Survey	(2) Undergraduate students	(2) 295	(2) Factor analysis and regression	(2) Yes
(3) Survey	(3) Undergraduate students	(3) 178	(3) Factor analysis and regression	(3) Yes
(1) Experiment	(1) Does not specify	(1) 20	(1) T-test and correlations	(1) No
(1) Experiment	(1) University students	(1) 30	(1) Correlations	(1) No
(1) Experiment	(1) Business students (graduate and undergraduate)	(1) 24	(1) Analysis of variance	(1) No
(1) Open-ended survey, structured questionnaire and focus group	(1) Primary household shoppers	(1) 220	(1) Frequencies/ qualitative data	(1) Yes
(1) Experiment	(1) Undergraduate students	(1) 172	(1) Analysis of variance	(1) No
(2) Experiment	(2) Undergraduate students	(2) 67	(2) Analysis of variance	(2) No
(1) One-hour time diary	Not indicated	(1) 111	(1) Analysis frequencies	(1) No
(2) Search task		(2) 15	(2) Analysis of frequencies	(2) No

(continued)

Table 3.1 (*continued*)

Authors	Schools	Theory Base	Journal
Lederer et al. (1998)	Business—University of Kentucky	(1) 3	Conference: ACM Computer Personnel Research
Otter and Johnson (2000)	One author was from industry— Icon Media Lab, Classic House, London	(1) 3	*Interacting with Computers*
	One author was from the department of mathematical science—University of Bath	(2) 3 (3) 3	
Park and Kim (2000)	Both authors were from the Human-Computer Interaction Lab, department of cognitive science— Yonsei University	(1) 3 (2) 3	*International Journal of Human-Computer Interaction*
Watts-Perotti and Woods (1999)	Both authors were from Cognitive Systems Engineering Laboratory— Ohio State University	(1) 3 (2) 3	*International Journal of Human Computer Studies*
Wen (2003)	Computing and information systems—University of Sunderland, England	(1) 1	*IT & Society*
Yu and Roh (2002)	Both authors were from education— Seoul National University and Indiana University	(1) 4	*Journal of the American Society for Information Science and Technology*

Theory base scale (based on authors' judgment):
1: No theory
2: Empirical work as justification but no theoretical justification
3: Empirical work as justification and some theoretical justification
4: Both empirical and theoretical justification
If a research article contains multiple studies, each study is identified by "(1)" for study 1,
"(2)" for study 2, and so on.

The list of courses identified is not meant to be a completely comprehensive listing, but should provide the reader with some insight into the general distribution and location of current undergraduate HCI courses being offered in English. In order to identify these courses, a key word search with the Google search engine was conducted using combinations of the HCI terms listed above. The first one hundred Web sites returned for each search were investigated. In addition, if a Web site suggested additional Web sites, these were also searched and all relevant courses from these sites were captured. Finally, HCI courses known to the authors, but that did not show up in the Web search, were also included.[4]

Although this method of collecting course information was meant to be without bias, it is recognized that business courses are occasionally taught within a for-profit environment and this increasingly competitive marketplace may reduce the frequency with which detailed course information is offered on the Internet. Therefore, it is recognized that HCI courses taught out of business schools may be underrepresented within the list of course offerings. However, we choose to accept this potential bias as the Web search still reflects how people new to HCI may learn

Method	Participants	Sample Size	Statistical Analysis	Contextual Variables
(1) Survey and questionnaire	(1) Employees	(1) 163	(1) Regression	(1) No
(1) Questionnaire	(1) Young people	(1) 22	(1) Frequency	(1) No
(2) Search task	(2) Young people	(2) 12	(2) One-way ANOVA	(2) No
(3) Search task	(3) Young people	(3) 12	(3) T-tests	(3) No
(1) Experiment	(1) Undergraduate students	(1) 40	(1) Analysis of variance	(1) No
(2) Experiment	(2) Undergraduate students	(2) 64	(2) Analysis of variance	(2) No
(1) Structured interviews and observations	(1) Employees	(1) 7	(1) Qualitative data and frequencies	(1) No
(2) Experiments	(2) Employees	(2) 7	(2) Frequencies	(2) No
(1) Search task	(1) Students and employees	(1) 12	(1) Frequencies	(1) No
(1) Experiment	(1) Graduate and undergraduate students	(1) 17	(1) One-way ANOVA	(1) No

about the field. If HCI courses taught within business schools are difficult to find, then the chances that students and/or organizational members may learn about them decreases and this ultimately reduces the number of potential organizations able to apply HCI principles and research findings.

Table 3.2 lists about 150 undergraduate HCI courses that we identified through our search and Table 3.3 summarizes our findings by school and country. As these tables demonstrate, almost half of the HCI courses take place in computer science departments, with the remaining portion being offered in a wide variety of other areas, including engineering and psychology. In addition to department-level HCI courses, a few universities have created HCI institutes that are not tied to particular faculties or schools—such as Carnegie Mellon's Human-Computer Interaction Institute. These institutes tend to cross the disciplines of computer science and psychology.

These results suggest that HCI remains on the periphery of MIS teaching. This may result in a failure to reach all individuals who may potentially benefit from HCI training. Computer science currently dominates HCI education, and while this may be helpful to computer science professionals, it

Table 3.2

Sample of Undergraduate HCI Courses

School/Faculty	Number of Courses	Percentage
Business	6	4%
Computer science	68	45.6%
Engineering	32	21.5%
Fine arts	6	4%
Information science	11	7.4%
Psychology	16	10.7%
Other	10	6.8%
Total	149	100%

Note: Course descriptions are also available from the authors.

Table 3.3

HCI Course Offerings by Geographic Location

	Location						
	Asia	Australia	Canada	Other	UK	U.S.	Total
Faculty							
Business			1		3	2	6
			16.7%		50%	33.3%	100%
Computer science		4	7	3	18	36	68
		6.2%	10.8%	4.6%	27.7%	50.8%	100%
Engineering	3	1	5	3	5	15	32
	9.4%	3.1%	15.6%	9.4%	15.6%	46.9%	100%
Fine arts					3	3	6
					50%	50%	100%
Information science						11	11
						100%	100%
Other					1	9	10
					10%	90%	100%
Psychology	1		2			13	16
	6.3%		12.5%			81.3%	100%
Total	4	5	15	6	30	89	149
	2.7%	3.4%	10.1%	4%	20.1%	59.7%	100%

reduces the chances that business professionals will learn about HCI and ultimately request that HCI-related findings be incorporated in their technology-based projects.

HCI Challenges

Why do computer scientists dominate HCI research and teaching? This may be because computer scientists are uniquely situated to develop the latest HCI tools and techniques, and therefore get the attention of technology-based industries. These researchers thrive on creating the latest technologies, and need to continue to do so. However, this strength can also represent a weakness for the HCI field for several reasons. First, researchers often do not follow their tool development to market in terms of research; that is, they generally do not conduct large-sample tests on their technologies. Quite the opposite, these technologies are "moving targets" that are continually being extended and improved. Second, much of the research is atheoretical, with researchers appearing to "come up" with reasons for their technologies. For instance, they may draw on "common knowledge" of human behaviors or even theories from psychology to "justify" applications for their tools post hoc. Third, researchers generally do not test out their assumptions regarding appropriate applications through controlled studies such as experiments or large-scale field studies. By contrast, they often demonstrate their technologies to like-minded computer scientists. Fourth, the developers themselves and their colleagues frequently act as the "testers" for these applications. Therefore, the domination of computer science within HCI contributes to its current challenges and perceived lack of business sensitivity.

HOW CAN MIS HELP?

HCI in both computer science and psychology focuses on the individual's interaction with the technology. Although each group makes a valuable contribution to the field, MIS is posed to make an equal, if not more important, contribution. This is because MIS researchers attempt to truly bring together the context, the technology, and the individual in their studies.[5] For instance, research on computer self-efficacy has focused on the individual, the type of technology, and the organization (e.g., Compeau and Higgins, 1995). More generally, HCI studies in MIS tend to investigate organizationally relevant issues, go beyond micro human-computer issues, provide theoretical justifications and contributions, use solid methodologies, and provide implications for both research and practice (Zhang et al., 2002). Thus, MIS provides a unique perspective for HCI research (Zhang et al., 2002). Consequently, we propose that MIS researchers could address many of the weaknesses found in past HCI research by contributing a multidisciplinary view of research, a rich theoretical base, and strong methodological and analytical techniques.

The Big Picture

HCI is a multidisciplinary area, but this can represent a weakness for departments such as psychology and computer science. By contrast, MIS researchers draw on research not only from traditional areas within business such as organizational behavior and marketing, but also from fields outside of business such as sociology, engineering, and computer science. MIS is a multidisciplinary field, and MIS researchers have an understanding of the wider management literature, such as theories concerning job characteristics (e.g., Thatcher et al., 2003), groups (e.g., DeSanctis and Gallupe, 1987), strategy (e.g., Sabherwal and Chan, 2001; Sambamurthy et al., 2003), and cross-cultural issues (e.g., Walsham, 2003). This multidisciplinary perspective, examined at multiple levels of analysis, is key to HCI practice.

Theory

One weakness of HCI is a lack of "a good taxonomy" of HCI research (Zhang et al., 2002). For instance, when we examine the research investigating cognitive load as it relates to interface design, we see different terms for similar constructs, such as cognitive overhead (Conklin, 1987; Ransom et al., 1997), memory load (Vaughan, 1998), and information overload (Hiltz and Turoff,

1985), with little cross-fertilization across areas. MIS is more theoretically advanced (Dillon, chapter 2 in this volume), and this is where MIS researchers can make another important contribution. Theories can help structure and organize the field, allow knowledge to accumulate, and provide opportunities to share knowledge across disciplines. MIS can draw on theory to provide a common language and to help to integrate the multiple HCI disciplines.

Methods and Analytic Techniques

MIS researchers are trained in qualitative methods (such as ethnographies) and quantitative methods (such as controlled experiments). Because of their knowledge of measure development, including reliability and validity issues, they can provide valuable contributions to the HCI community by enhancing HCI measures (Zhang et al., 2002). They also value large-scale sampling.

MIS researchers have been trained to use a variety of analytical techniques, ranging from qualitative analyses (such as NVivo) to quantitative analyses (such as structural equation modeling). For instance, quantitative techniques that take into account multiple levels of analysis, such as WABA (within-and-between analyses) and HLM (hierarchical linear modeling), are particularly appropriate for HCI research.

WHAT'S HOLDING MIS BACK?

Given that MIS appears to be in an excellent position to contribute to the development and growth of HCI, one key question remains: What is holding HCI back from taking advantage of this opportunity? Several potential reasons have been suggested.

First, MIS is a young field itself, and not long ago it faced many of the same criticisms that HCI currently faces concerning issues such as methodological rigor. This, combined with the fact that it would be one of the first times for MIS to act as a reference discipline, forces us to struggle with the question of whether MIS is really ready for this challenge. However, MIS's ability to come so far in such a short period of time is testament to its growth and ability to learn from previous mistakes. In addition, its recent successes in developing theories and utilizing rigorous methods demonstrate its ability to address important research issues (Baskerville and Myers, 2002).

Second, HCI has been criticized for "testing, rather than inventing, new ideas. It looks at what has been, not what could be" (Zolli 2003, p. 65). One could argue that this is even more true of MIS research. Much MIS research is based on a behavioral, rather than a design, science paradigm (Hevner et al., 2004). MIS researchers are not the developers of emerging HCI technologies, and large-scale field applications of emerging interfaces are not available for testing. Therefore, some MIS researchers are willing to simply wait to evaluate technologies after implementation. However, years of software and technology development indicate that simply testing after development will not ensure that products meet end user needs. End-user needs must be considered from requirement gathering through to implementation. Therefore, if we recognize that computer science focuses more on the technology and does not consistently develop products to meet market needs, then simply testing products from an MIS perspective after development will only continue to facilitate the current concerns regarding HCI's research relevance and business sensitivity. MIS's influence on HCI must be felt well before the testing phase. Ultimately, MIS should assist in deciding which technology-related projects are important and which research questions are relevant to practitioners and future researchers.

A third issue relates to MIS's identity. One may question if the discipline of MIS has bought into Carr's argument that IT (and thus, by extension, HCI) is a commodity and does not matter (Carr, 2003). According to Carr (2003), the new rules governing IT management include a decrease in IT expenditures, the reduced importance of leading in development/research, and finally, the need to focus on vulnerabilities rather than IS opportunities. However, in order to accept the validity of these rules, one must assume that there is no room for competitive advantage due to advances in interaction and interface design. In a marketplace that continues to be very competitive and where technology has progressed from being necessary to being mandatory for business, this assumption is questionable. In many cases, a well-designed system is required just to maintain a position in the market. Therefore, it is still very important to consider HCI issues in order to ensure systems are well designed and meet market needs. Therefore, we believe HCI will continue to be an important topic within MIS research.

Finally, some would say that HCI has little importance, as we already know enough about humans and instead should be focusing more on technologies. In other words, we already know the basics about individuals, and it is impossible to meet every individual's needs. Therefore, some would question whether the technology can really change enough to meet the person's needs and interests. In addition, some would argue that if a person really wants an application, he or she will learn how to use it (i.e., the person will adapt to the technology). While we do not disagree that these arguments have some validity, we would rather see end users concentrate less on learning technologies and more on simply doing their work-related tasks. Furthermore, in a competitive marketplace, where consumers are demanding interfaces that minimize disorientation and are pleasurable to use, the need to ensure that interfaces meet consumer expectations is crucial to survival. Thus, this perspective fails to recognize the potential benefit of improved human-computer interaction in today's competitive marketplace.

CAN WE SPEED PROGRESS IN HCI?

With the sharp increase in consumer-based systems, HCI will continue to become more important to organizations. Thus, one view would be that HCI will progress on its own, with no assistance needed to accelerate its progress. This option has the advantage of drawing on the unique strengths of Computer Science and Psychology that may not be matched by researchers in other areas, like Business departments. With this option, MIS could stay in its traditional role of evaluating technologies in organizational contexts, once computer scientists have developed these systems. However, we propose that MIS researchers should not remain at the back end of development but need to help guide development.

Another option would be to create cross-disciplinary educational programs. Undergraduate majors in academic areas signal the importance and maturity of an area, bring in alumni funding, and help meet the demands of the marketplace. Because HCI is multidisciplinary, perhaps all that needs to be done to speed progress of HCI as a discipline is to create educational programs that cross disciplines. Therefore, one option would be to create undergraduate partnerships between computer science and psychology. A few universities have set up such programs: for example, the psychology department of Rutgers-Newark has partnered with the computer and information science (CIS) department at New Jersey Institute of Technology to jointly offer an HCI undergraduate program. They clearly ground HCI at the individual level of analysis: *"The main purpose of this field is to understand the nature of human-computer interaction and the constraints on design of such systems from understanding perceptual and cognitive aspects of humans"* (HCI, 2004). Although this partnership represents a positive step, we argue that such programs require an even wider contextual focus.

A third option, providing this wider contextual training, would be a three-way teaching partnership. One could envisage a typical undergraduate business school degree with a concentration in MIS, strengthened with HCI courses as well as specialized courses in cognitive psychology and computer science. As the starting point for developing such a curriculum, Hewett et al. (1996) present a model HCI curriculum for MIS, and Carey et al. (2004) describe a variety of alternatives for incorporating HCI into MIS curricula.

Another option for speeding HCI progress would be to create more research partnerships across disciplines. Encouraging trends in this area are recent HCI conference panels that included participants with backgrounds in computer science, psychology, information science, and business (e.g., Galletta et al., 2003). However, creating research partnerships may be even more difficult than teaching partnerships, as different reward structures are in place across the disciplines (e.g., standards of evidence, the suitability of conferences versus journal publications, journals considered to be highly rated, and so on: Dillon, chapter 2 in this volume). Perhaps partnerships through graduate students who major in MIS and minor in psychology and/or computer science would help to speed this process.

HCI opportunities are being driven by the needs of business and government, including recent calls for more HCI research on accessibility, group communications, and collaborative software (e.g., NCO/ITR&D, 2003; NCO/PITAC, 2000). To encourage progress as a field, we believe that focusing on MIS's distinctive behavioral strengths around task, group, organizational, and cross-cultural issues—that go beyond the human and the computer—will help to spur needed HCI research. For example, MIS researchers are familiar with theories that can help to inform e-commerce, such as those around the assimilation of Web technologies (e.g., Chatterjee et al., 2002). However, ways of pairing these behavioral science strengths with design science strengths need to be developed.

CONCLUSION

The void in the large-scale study of actual technologies with employees and consumers represents a substantial opportunity for MIS researchers. Further, with the continuing development of Web-based applications, we believe that HCI research and teaching will continue to grow in MIS departments. Optimistic signs of this have been recent HCI special sections and themes in journal issues by MIS researchers (e.g., *JAIS*, 2004; *JMIS*, 2005) and a forthcoming HCI textbook written specifically for an MIS audience (Te'eni et al., 2006). Therefore, we expect and hope to see HCI move from the periphery of MIS to a more central role in the near future. This move will benefit both HCI research and practice.

ACKNOWLEDGMENTS

We would like to thank Izak Benbasat, Andrew Gemino, Milena Head, and two anonymous reviewers for their comments on an earlier version of this paper. We presented some of these ideas in a panel (Galletta et al., 2003) and have benefited from discussions with the panel participants.

NOTES

1. Or, alternatively, "Engineering Psychology," "(Cognitive) Ergonomics," "Cognitive Engineering," or "Software Ergonomics."

2. One could then ask what is *not* HCI in MIS? We suggest that the interaction of the person and the technology must be part of the equation—and thus, studies investigating such issues as information systems for strategic advantage or outsourcing of IT—without considering the human interacting with the technology—would not be classified as HCI.

3. As undergraduate teaching often drives faculty hiring, we believe that this provides a suitable representation of HCI focus in universities. Additionally, an earlier review of masters programs found a similar pattern of results to those we present below, with Computer Science dominating HCI offerings (Chan et al. 2003).

4. Interestingly, the undergraduate HCI courses from universities that we have been associated with did not show up in our original searches (nor the HCI courses offered by the editors of this volume). It may be that Business Schools tend to keep their course offerings private, in an attempt to help maintain their competitive edge.

5. More recently, with the development of Web-based applications and so-called customer relationship management systems, marketers in Business Schools have also started to conduct research in this area.

REFERENCES

Ahuja, J.S., and Webster, J. Perceived disorientation: an examination of a new measure to assess web design effectiveness. *Interacting with Computers*, 14, 1 (2001), 15–29.

AIS Special interest group on human-computer interaction (SIGHCI). 2004 (available at http://melody.syr.edu/hci/index.cgi).

APA Division 21—applied experimental and engineering psychology. 2004 (available at http://www.apa.org/about/division/div21.html).

Banker, R.D., and Kauffman, R.J. The evolution of research on information systems: a fiftieth-year survey of the literature in management science. *Management Science*, 50, 3 (2004), 281–298.

Baskerville, R., and Myers, M. Information systems as a reference discipline. *MIS Quarterly*, 26, 1 (2002), 1–14.

Benbunan-Fich, R. Using protocol analysis to evaluate usability of a commercial website. *Information & Management*, 39 (2001), 151–163.

Bernard, M., and Hamblin, C. Cascading versus indexed menu design. 2003 (available at http://psychology.wichita.edu/surl/usabilitynews/51/menu.htm).

Cameron, A.F., and Webster, J. Unintended consequences of emerging communication technologies: instant messaging in the workplace. *Computers in Human Behavior*, 21, 1 (2005), 85–103.

Carey, J.; Galletta, D.; Kim, J.; Te'eni, D.; Wildemuth, B.; and Zhang, P. The role of human-computer interaction in management information systems curricula: a call to action. *Communications of the Association for Information Systems*, 13 (2004), 357–379.

Carr, N. IT doesn't matter. *Harvard Business Review*, 81, 5 (May 2003), 41–49.

Ceaparu, I.; Lazar, J.; Bessiere, K.; Robinson, J.; and Shneiderman, B. Determining causes of end-user frustration. Working Paper, University of Maryland, United States (2002).

Chan, S.; Wolfe, R.; and Fang, X. Issues and strategies for integrating HCI in masters level MIS and e-commerce programs. *International Journal of Human-Computer Studies*, 59 (2003), 497–520.

Chatterjee, D.; Grewal, R.; and Sambamurthy, V. Shaping up for e-commerce: Institutional enablers of the organizational assimilation of web technologies. *MIS Quarterly*, 26, 2 (2002), 65–89.

Chen, Q., and Wells, W. Attitude toward the site. *Journal of Advertising Research*, September/October (1999), 27–37.

Compeau, D., and Higgins, C.A. Computer self-efficacy: development of a measure and initial test. *MIS Quarterly*, 19, 2 (1995), 189–211.

Conklin, J. Hypertext: An introduction and survey. *IEEE Computer*, 20, 9 (1987), 17–41.

Czerwinski, M.; Benbasat, I.; Ratner, J.; Santhanam, R.; and Todd, P. Panel on HCI research transfer to practice: better together. In *Proceedings of the Second Annual Workshop on HCI Research in MIS, International Conference on Information Systems*, Seattle, WA: 2003, pp. 52–54.

D'Ambra, J., and Rice, R.E. Emerging factors in user evaluation of the world wide web. *Information & Management*, 38, 6 (2001), 373–384.

Danielson, D.R. Transitional volatility in web navigation. *IT & Society*, 1, 3 (2003), 131–159.

Danielson, D.R. Web navigation and behavioral effects of constantly visible site maps. *Interacting with Computers*, 14, 5 (2002), 601–618.

DeSanctis, G., and Gallupe, B. A foundation for the study of group decision support systems. *Management Science,* 33, 5 (1987), 589–609.

Galletta, D.; Lazar, J.; Olson, J.S.; Te'eni, D.; Mantei Tremaine, M.; and Webster, J. Finding common ground among HCI reference disciplines. In *Proceedings of the Second Annual Workshop on HCI Research in MIS*. Seattle, WA: International Conference on Information Systems, 2003, pp. 100–103.

Gray, W., and Salzman, M. Damaged merchandise? A review of experiments that compare usability evaluation methods. *Human-Computer Interaction*, 13, 3 (1998), 203–261.

HCI. Human-computer interaction. 2004 (available at http://psychology.rutgers.edu/hci).

Head, M.; Archer, N.; and Yuan, Y. World wide web navigation aid. *International Journal of Human-Computer Studies*, 53 (2000), 301–330.

Hevner, A.R.; March, S.T.; Park, J.; and Ram, S. Design science in information systems research. *MIS Quarterly*, 28, 1 (2004), 75–105.

Hewett, T.; Baecher, R.; Card, S.; Carey, T.; Casen, J.; Mantei, M.; Perlman, G.; Strong, G.; and Verplank, W. Curricula for human computer interaction. 1996 (available at http://www.acm.org/sigchi/cdg/cdgA.html).

Hiltz, S.R., and Turoff, M. Structuring computer-mediated communication systems to avoid information overload. *Communication of the ACM*, 28, 7 (1985), 680–689.

Irani, P., and Ware, C. Diagramming information structures using 3D perceptual primitives. *ACM Transactions on Computer-Human Interactions*, 10, 1 (2003), 1–19.

Jarvenpaa, S.L., and Todd, P.A. Consumer reactions to electronic shopping on the World Wide Web. *International Journal of Electronic Commerce*, 1, 2 (1996), 59–88.

JAIS editors. *Journal of the Association for Information Systems* special theme on HCI in MIS. 2004 (available at http://melody.syr.edu/hci/jais04/index.cgi).

JMIS editors. *Journal of Management Information Systems* special section on HCI in MIS, 22, 3 (2005–2006).

Kim, J., and Yoo, B. Toward the optimal link structure of the cyber shopping mall. *International Journal of Human Computer Studies*, 52, 3 (2000), 531–551.

Lang, P. Ecommerce websites are getting (slowly) better. 2002 (available at http://sellitontheweb.com/ezine/news0576.shtml).

Lazar, J.; Bessiere, K.; Ceaparu, I.; Robinson, J.; and Shneiderman, B. Help! I'm lost: User frustration in web navigation. *IT & Society*, 1, 3 (2003), 18–26.

Lederer, A.; Maupin, D.; Sena, M.; and Zhuang, Y. The role of ease of use, usefulness and attitude in the prediction of www usage. In *Proceedings of the ACM SIGCPR Conference on Computer Personnel Research*, Boston, MA: ACM Press, 1998, pp. 195–204.

Lohse, G., and Spiller, P. Internet retail store design: How the user interface influences traffic and sales. *Journal of Computer-Mediated Communication*, 5, 2 (1999) (available at http://jcmc.indiana.edu/vol5/issue2/lohse.htm).

Mason, R.O., and Mitroff, I.I. A program for research on management information systems. *Management Science*, 19, 5 (1973), 475–487.

Nass, C., and Lee, K.M. Does computer-synthesized speech manifest personality? Experimental tests of recognition, similarity-attraction, and consistency-attraction. *Journal of Experimental Psychology: Applied*, 7, 3 (2001), 171–181.

NCO/ITR&D Human-computer interaction and information management research needs. 2003 (available at http://www.hpcc.gov/pubs/hci-im_research_needs_final.pdf).

NCO/PITAC Transforming access to government through information technology. 2000. (available at http://www.itrd.gov/pubs/pitac/pres-transgov-11sep00.pdf).

Neal, D. Interview: good design pays off. 2003 (available at http://www.itweek.co.uk/Features/1141003).

Nielsen, J. Jakob Nielsen's alertbox: improving usability guideline compliance. 2002 (available at http://www.useit.com/alertbox/20020624.html).

Otter, M., and Johnson, H. Lost in hyperspace: Metrics and mental models. *Interacting with Computers*, 13 (2000), 1–40.

Park, J., and Kim, J. Contextual navigation aids for two world wide web systems. *International Journal of Human Computer Interaction*, 12, 2 (2000), 193–217.

Ransom, S.; Wu, X.; and Schmidt, H. Disorientation and cognitive overhead in hypertext systems. *International Journal of Artificial Intelligence Tools*, 6, 2 (1997), 227–253.

Sabherwal, R., and Chan, Y. Alignment between business and IS strategy. *Information Systems Research*, 12, 1 (2001), 11–33.

Sambamurthy, V.; Bharadwaj, A.; and Grover, V. Shaping agility through digital options: reconceptualizing the role of information in contemporary firms. *MIS Quarterly*, 27, 2 (2003), 237–263.

Singer, J.; Patrick, A.; and Vinson, N. Canadian human computer interaction research profile. 2003 (available at http://www.andrewpatrick.ca/hciprofile/).

Swanson, E.B., and Ramiller, N. Information systems research thematics: submissions to a new journal, 1987–1992. *Information Systems Research*, 4, 4 (1993), 299–330.

Te'eni, D.; Carey, J.; and Zhang, P. *Human-Computer Interaction: Developing Effective Organizational Information Systems*. New York: John Wiley & Sons, Inc., 2006.

Thatcher, J.; Stepina, L.; and Boyle, R. Turnover of information technology workers: examining empirically the influence of attitudes, job characteristics, and external markets. *Journal of Management Information Systems*, 19, 3 (2003), 231–261.

UsabilityNet Commercial Advantages. 2003 (available at http://www.usabilitynet.org/management/commercial.htm).

Vaughan, M. Testing the boundaries of two user-centered design principles: metaphors and memory load. *International Journal of Human-Computer Interaction*, 10, 3 (1998), 265–282.

Walsham, G. Cross-cultural software production and use: A structural analysis. *MIS Quarterly*, 26, 4 (2003), 559–380.

Watts-Perotti, J., and Woods, D.D. How experienced users avoid getting lost in large display networks. *International Journal of Human Computer Interaction*, 11, 4 (1999), 269–299.

Webster, J., and Ahuja, J.S. Enhancing the design of web navigation systems: the influence of user disorientation on engagement and performance. *MIS Quarterly*, 30, 3 (2006).

Wen, J. Post-valued recall web pages: user disorientation hits the big time. *IT & Society*, 1, 3 (2003), 184–194.

Yu, B.M., and Roh, Z.R. The effects of menu design on information seeking performance and user's attitude on the world wide web. *Journal of the American Society for Information Science and Technology*, 53, 11 (2002), 923–933.

Zhang, P.; Benbasat, I.; Carey, J.; David, F.R.; Galletta, D.; and Strong, D. AMCIS 2002 panels and workshops I: human-computer interaction research in the MIS discipline. *Communications of the Association for Information Systems*, 9 (2002), 334–355.

Zhang, P., and Li, N. An assessment of HCI research in MIS: topics and methods. *Computers in Human Behavior*, 20, 2 (2004), 125–147.

Zolli, A. Can HCI deliver on its promise? *Interactions*, XI, 2 (2004), 65.

CHAPTER 4

WHO IS THE USER?
INDIVIDUALS, GROUPS, COMMUNITIES

GERARDINE DESANCTIS

Abstract: *The progress of management information systems over the last fifty years has brought an ever-expanding notion of computer "user." We have witnessed the evolution of computer user from a single person to an interacting group, from a group of people to an entire firm or other organization, and from an organization to a diffuse community with dynamic membership and purpose. The result is a profound expansion in the scope of human-computer interaction (HCI) design and an explosion in the mandate for HCI research. This essay highlights some of the major design and research challenges associated with today's broad notion of computer user. These challenges do not reduce the earlier HCI agenda. Instead, they expand it and imply a continued need for the study of HCI at multiple levels of analysis.*

Key Words: *User-Computer Interaction, User Behavior, Research Directions*

INTRODUCTION

A paradox of our time is that computers have become at once personal and communal, less visible yet ubiquitous, mobile yet entrenched in the dense fabric of information and communications technologies that permeate our lives. At the interface between human and computer, this paradox unfurls in an ongoing transformation of computer "user" from an individual to an interacting group, from a group of people to an entire firm or other organization, and from an organization to a diffuse community with dynamic membership and purpose.

Although information systems have long been designed for use by many people, the conceptualization of "end user" by HCI designers has broadened over time. During the past fifty years, information technology has migrated from offering limited types of computational support in relatively confined organizational settings to providing intelligent mediating devices that connect large groups of people and business processes on a global scale. In the early days of mainframe computers, system developers conceived of end users as a relatively homogeneous lot. The user of an information system was an individual at a keyboard, or perhaps a manager or technical specialist reading a computer-generated report. Either way, the user was presumed to be "the decision maker" who used system outputs to make a judgment, select a choice, or formulate a plan (Alter, 1980; Davis and Olson, 1984).

In the early days of computing, the boundaries of the user, technology, and task were fairly obvious. Systems design focused on satisfying the needs of distinctive user groups, such as financial analysts, accountants, or general managers, confronted with fairly bounded decision tasks. HCI researchers assessed the success of an information system in terms of user acceptance, the

Table 4.1

Shifts in the Conceptualization of Computer User Over Time

Who Is the User?	Scope of Work	Technology	Systems Support
Individual	Worker-based	Terminal or personal computer	Decision support systems (DSS)
Group	Team-based	Networked computers	Group systems (GDSS, GSS)
Organization	Distributed work	Web-based platforms; multimedia	Enterprise-wide systems (e.g., EIS)
Community	Globalization	Ubiquitous computing	Electronic commerce, online forums, and communities

quality and efficiency of user decision processes, and user perceptions of the technology. In the early days of organizational computing, designers attempted to accommodate variations in user preferences where possible, but for the most part users were treated as common collectives. Indeed, individual differences and their implications for design were not center stage in systems design for several decades; research focused instead on designing technology to fit work task demands and assuring user motivation and acceptance (e.g., see Huber, 1983).

Though not to be underestimated, this relatively confined world of HCI was a comforting setting for systems designers and IS researchers until collaborative systems (i.e., groupware) came along. Suddenly the user became the group, tasks became multi-party, and decision processes became entwined with computer-mediated communication systems (Applegate, 1991; Gray and Olfman, 1989; Hiltz and Turoff, 1981; Olson and Olson, 1991). So-called advanced information technologies offered the potential to dramatically impact the social dynamics of organizational life (Huber, 1990; Rice, 1992). The complexity of the HCI setting increased dramatically. Systems designers and IS researchers, with their roots in psychology and organizational behavior, quickly became students of organizational communication and sociology. Issues of collaboration, coherence, conflict management, group decision processes, and so on, were added to the more traditional HCI concerns (e.g., Jessup and Valacich, 1993; Galegher, Kraut, and Egido, 1990; Malone and Crowston, 1994).

Today we are witness to a further explosion in the complexity of HCI as information systems are developed to support dynamic groups and communities, and work moves across the traditional boundaries of task, locale, and corporation. On the surface it may be the individual who types, talks, and looks at a computing device; but the presence and participation of others is near omnipresent. Further, the parties involved and nature of the work that people are doing together via computer is likely not fully specified. Groups are scattered and transient. Tasks are murky, and the organizational context is a shifting ground of business units, partners, or other entities—not all of which are completely clear or known. In sum, we are witness to a confluence of changes in technology and the nature of work that are expanding our notion of "user" and the essentials of human-computer interaction. Computers may be easier to use today than in the past, in the sense that machines are more intelligent and interfaces are more multimedia-based and friendly; however, human-computer systems are also more challenging to design, because they must accommodate collections of people from a multitude of backgrounds with diverse personal and professional needs who are interacting across organizational, geographic, and task boundaries. Thus, today we are witness to a profound expansion in the scope of HCI design and an explosion in the mandate for HCI research. Table 4.1 summarizes how the conceptualization of computer user in HCI design has broadened over time.

The remainder of this essay highlights some of the important design and research challenges brought about by today's explosion in HCI complexity. These challenges are largely related to the HCI needs of transient groups and communities, which increasingly serve as hotbeds for knowledge creation and information acquisition and transfer in modern life (Barab, Kling, and Gray, 2004). The challenges mentioned here are not mutually exclusive, nor are they exhaustive; rather, they are meant to be illustrative of the vast set of challenges confronting HCI design and research today and into the future.

HCI DESIGN CHALLENGES

Virtuality

Perhaps the most fundamental challenge for HCI systems design stems from the virtual nature of work which, although made possible by technology, simultaneously increases demand on the part of users for information access at any time and in any place (DeSanctis and Monge, 1999; Lipnack and Stamps, 1997; Mowshowitz, 2002). Increasingly, information access requires access to other people—colleagues, coworkers, friends, anyone in an appropriate knowledge network who can supply needed resources to the user. HCI design, therefore, must facilitate identification of appropriate parties, support for information sharing, and, in general, the ability to "be together" while apart (Hinds and Kiesler, 2002). Virtuality implies boundary spanning of all sorts: "edgeless, with permeable and continuously changing interfaces between company, supplier, and customers . . . offices, departments, and operating divisions constantly reforming according to need" (Davidow and Malone, 1992, p. 6).

For the past decade or so, supporting virtuality has meant that HCI needs to pay attention to collaboration processes (Malone and Crowston, 1994). Lateral coordination has been the emphasis. As we look to the future, this emphasis will likely expand to include targeted support for vertical relationships as well, since today's users require not only rapid response but also high security, learning, and tight organizational control. For example, teams and firms have an interest in using status differences and reputational or other social assets for strategic advantage (Benjamin and Poldony, 1999; Cummings, 2004; Earley and Mosakowski, 2000).

The implication is that support for status, power, leadership, and hierarchy may move to the foreground of HCI concern, supplementing support for collaboration (e.g., see Barab et al., 2004; Saunders, Robey, and Vavarek, 1994). As we look to the future, information systems will not only bring people together across boundaries but also selectively manage who can say what to whom, who should listen to what, and what information will be given priority and under what circumstances.

Dynamism

Concomitant with the expansion of the computer user to include diffuse groups, organizations, and communities is greater difficulty in specification of user needs and system requirements. There are two aspects to this dynamism. First is the changing composition of the collectives themselves (see Huber, 2004). How can an information system support a team when team members come and go? How can a system support members of an organization if employees turn over or the customer base is in flux? How can a community be supported when its participants are transient, or are as yet undefined? The issue is more than one of scalability, or supporting both large and small groups. Overall group needs and preferences vary as individuals move in and out of the target user group. The needs of a group include its members' communication with one another, their collective dreaming, goal setting, scheming, and actions. These collective needs change as unanticipated parties enter and leave the HCI experience, presenting challenges for systems designers.

Second, and potentially more challenging for designers, is the dynamic nature of the goals and tasks in which users today engage even if the composition of the user set is stable. Groups, organizations, and communities act within volatile markets and sociopolitical environments, so the nature of a group's (or any collective) work is likely to be highly changeable both in its components and in the interdependencies that link those components (Ilinitch, Lewin, and D'Aveni, 1998). The increasing trend toward knowledge work exacerbates this effect. Fluctuating task needs make systems specification arduous, to say the least, impacting not only the design of user-computer interfaces but also construction of databases, infrastructure, and other related system components.

The dynamic nature of work and who conducts it has always presented a challenge for systems designers, but the point is that today such dynamism is far more likely and the impacts more far-reaching. Why? Users and the computers they use are interconnected through a vast and distributed web of social relationships. Thus, unanticipated bottlenecks or deficiencies in an HCI experience can quickly ramify, spreading problems beyond any one person or task.

Background Participation

Traditionally designers thought of users as the parties having direct interaction with a computer through touch, speech, or some other direct means. The user was one who entered and retrieved information, or at least viewed reports. As computers advanced to support work teams, the notion of user broadened to include all members of a designated group, that is, the set of parties who send and receive information to and fro. Today this conception of user is limited because it presumes that all group members are interacting with each other when, in fact, there are also users who play a passive role, observing group members rather than directly interacting with them. As examples, we have Web cams to view meeting rooms and lurkers who read online discussions without contributing to them.

Today it is possible for users of group, organizational, or community systems to operate online in the background rather than in the foreground, choosing to observe or glimpse group activities without contributing or otherwise interacting with people (see Smith and Kollock, 1999). Background participants may not be readily identifiable as belonging to a given user group, but they are computer users nonetheless, in that they can retrieve and in some cases manipulate information. They can pass information retrieved from one group or organization to people outside that target group; and they can be observed and tracked while they do these things. Background participants may have somewhat different needs with regard to computer technology than traditional users. For example, background users may desire features to support observation and search, whereas foreground users prefer support for contribution, influence, and exit. One can also imagine situations where individuals or groups of users may move from foreground to background, or vice versa. The HCI needs of background participation have yet to be fully understood.

Transparency

Concurrent with the capability for background participation in IS environments is the increasingly public nature of computer use (Dutton, 1999). In our Internet age, information is not only stored and processed by computers but also linked, distributed, rearranged, translated, analyzed, annotated, blogged, and so on. User-computer interaction threatens to be less intimate (i.e., confined) if others observe or have later access to what users do—or do not do—online. As examples, consider the privacy surrounding an electronic transaction between a bank and its customer that later may be visible to a third party as part of an audit or legal action. Similarly, the contents of electronic conversations within a work team may be copied and posted to other electronic spaces; or the sidewalk conversation of a romantic couple may be recorded and then pod-cast. HCI experiences have the potential to extend far beyond the time and space confines of when and how a user interacts with a particular system.

Electronic trails provide traces of user activities long into the future. In this context, privacy is desirable yet elusive—especially if the user consists of an amorphous group of people from unknown, far-flung places (see Gurak, 1997). The challenge of transparency is to design systems that allow users to anticipate and trace HCI experiences within an extensive fabric of information and communication systems. Transparency is important not only as it relates to user privacy but also for user search, anticipation, and exploration of systems, for accountability and control, and for learning. In sum, whereas the technical functioning of the computer may be accepted by users of today as a black box, the data modification and network sharing capabilities of computers will require visibility and clarity so that users can "see into" HCI experiences of past, present, and future.

Cultural Transcendence

Cultural transcendence refers to design demands for information systems to incorporate the cross-cultural needs of multinational work teams, offshore workers, distributed communities, and, in general, the cultural diversity of user groups. The HCI design challenge is to provide multilingual capabilities and, even more, to support the more subtle needs associated with varying customs, preferences, and cognitive perspectives of user groups. Te'eni (2001) describes this as the challenge of communication complexity, that is, the need to provide a sense of context for users in order to facilitate mutual understanding during HCI experiences. Cultural transcendence requires reduction in complexity, creating a sense of common ground among a diverse set of participants. It may be that the time has come to revisit the study of individual differences, including demographic and other background characteristics, and how they shape HCI needs within diverse user communities.

HCI RESEARCH CHALLENGES

The transformation of user from sole individual to interacting groups, organization, and community implies a broader, more diffuse agenda for HCI research. The HCI field is exploding in the range of its concerns, creating a conundrum regarding the locus of research attention. What are the boundaries of the field in the new, amorphous arena of human-computer interaction? Where should research energies be directed? Insights into these questions are provided in the emerging literature, including the papers contained in this volume. Given the complex and dynamic needs of users, research boundaries are probably best left open and flexible. At the same time, each researcher should take care to scope the bounds of particular projects so that contributions of any one study to cumulative knowledge are clear. Three vital scoping challenges are briefly described here. These illustrate some of the important choices that researchers must address when participating in today's HCI research landscape.

Variation Across Collectives

Users as collectives, whether groups, organizations, or communities, vary in their properties and thus their particular HCI needs. The dimensions that distinguish these collectives include more than structural properties such as size of membership and demographic makeup. Collectives differ along other important dimensions that may affect their HCI needs, such as their participation patterns, extent of shared history, degree of social identity, and commonality in mental models. These kinds of social and cognitive dimensions should be identified by the researcher and carefully assessed since they are known to be critical to group processes such as information search, knowledge exchange, and learning (Jones, 1997; Reagans and Zuckerman, 2001). For example, we might anticipate the HCI needs of looser collectives (those with less frequent interaction) to differ from collectives with stronger ties (those with more frequent interaction among members). Lack of familiarity among individuals, unfamiliar language, status differences, physical differences, distinctive thought words, and emotional disparities can all make information sharing difficult (see Okhuysen and Eisenhardt, 2002; Sun and Zhang, this volume; Weisband, Schneider, and Connolly, 1995). Accounting for these types of variation across collectives will help researchers to design interventions and explain differences in system effects. To date, substantial research attention has been given to the dimensions of size and member diversity, but many more dimensions that distinguish among collectives are in need of study.

Cross-Level User Behavior

Individual, group, organization, and community are not distinct levels of analysis. Instead, they are inherently intertwined spheres in which people interact with one another, and distinctions in the levels can be arbitrary. As examples, the individual user may operate in and out of multiple group contexts. The groups making up an organization may include members both inside and outside of that organization. Communities, such as communities of experts, may be subsets of organizations or operate outside of organizational boundaries altogether. The researcher has the challenge not only of incorporating multilevel data in studies but also of specifying or bounding those levels in a meaningful way.

Traditionally, boundary specification was done by researchers based on formal membership, such as assignment to teams by an employer, or registration of membership by individuals in a professional association. Though still relevant, such boundary setting is limiting in a world where collectives are defined by many attributes other than formal structure and where research concerns include cognitive and emotional phenomena such as knowledge creation or information acquisition and transfer—phenomena that can take place across fuzzy boundaries rather than clear-cut ones (Foreman and Whetten, 2002). Researchers are advised to set levels of analysis using indicators other than formal structure and to establish boundaries that are meaningful to the phenomena being studied, even if such boundaries are fuzzy.

Hackman (2003) suggests "bracketing" when studying multiple levels of analysis; this means including in conceptual and empirical analyses constructs that exist one level lower and one level higher than those targeted for study. The reductionistic tendency of science may make it easier to move down rather than up a level; but, as Hackman points out, more insight often lies in higher-level factors. This is especially true in HCI settings where social context can have powerful impacts on cognition, affect, and behavior (Benbasat and Lim, 1993; Nardi, 1996; Orlikowski et al., 1995). Spiraling up to a higher level of analysis may be more important than drilling down since information that lies with individual users or groups can take on major impact as it moves up or out to other organizations and communities where it may be exploited for learning or goal achievement (see Okhuysen and Eisenhardt, 2002). Once levels of analysis are bounded, the researcher can follow "informed induction" (Hackman, 2003), which is the process of bootstrapping to ever better explanations of a phenomenon by drawing upon all the information one can capture—qualitative and archival data as well as quantitative measures.

HCI Evaluation Criteria

Perhaps the greatest challenge for HCI researchers is to select a meaningful measure of HCI success. Expansion of the boundaries of the field implies less clarity regarding how HCI outcomes should be evaluated. Usability, user satisfaction, and performance—the hallmarks of HCI evaluation—remain important, but many other criteria become relevant when users consist of groups, organizations, and communities. For groups, criteria such as mutual understanding, problem-solving effectiveness, commitment, and creative thinking are often relevant (Hollingshead and McGrath, 1995). For organizations and communities, criteria such as sustainability, competitive advantage, growth, and flexibility are of interest today (Huber, 2004; Preece, 2000). At all levels, matters of status, power, trust, leadership, network relations, time management, and learning are important (Barge and Hirokowa, 1989; Bernard, 1973; Butler, 2001; Harasim, 1993; Scott, 1995). Selection of evaluation criteria depends, of course, on the specific research question and the theoretical model used to drive the research. More than likely, multiple criteria are important and integrated theoretical models are needed that provide explanatory power brought on by multifactor explanations of user behavior (see Trevino et al., 2002).

A major challenge in developing and applying theoretical models is incoherence of system objectives and user needs in today's computing environment. Some groups or organizations may have focused tasks and goals; but others interact without clear or specified reasons. The goals of learning and entertainment may be mixed with those of efficiency or effectiveness. Greater diversity within groups and communities compound the evaluation challenge (e.g., see Kim, this volume). Further, differing preferences and needs of individuals within a group or other collective make selection of precise and meaningful evaluation criteria all the more difficult. In this research context, researchers would do well to consider multiple theoretical lenses and multiple measures of HCI success. Hubona, Straub, and Truex (in the second volume) describe how researchers can integrate multiple theories to yield multiple measures for HCI evaluation.

CONCLUSION

The expanded conceptualization of computer user from individual to group, organization, and community implies significant design and research challenges. Major design challenges are to incorporate the following capabilities into HCI systems: (1) virtuality, (2) dynamism, (3) background participation, (4) transparency, and (5) cultural transcendence. Major research challenges are to address questions such as: (1) What dimensions beyond structure (size and demographic makeup) can account for variations in HCI needs and impacts within and between groups, organizations, and communities? (2) How can boundaries between individual, group, organization, and community as levels of analysis be meaningfully distinguished for research purposes? (3) What criteria should be used to evaluate HCI success for groups, organizations, and communities? The HCI field is exploding in its scope and ambition. Many more challenges wait on the horizon. To the extent that HCI design and research can meet the unfolding challenges ahead, the field promises to take center stage in the ongoing study of management information systems.

ACKNOWLEDGMENTS

This paper is based upon work supported by the National Science Foundation Grant No. SES-0135602. The opinions, findings, and conclusions expressed here are those of the author and do not necessarily reflect the views of the National Science Foundation.

EDITORS' NOTE

At the time this book was in the copyediting stage, author Gerardine DeSanctis lost a battle with cancer, on August 16, 2005, at the young age of fifty-one. As many MIS scholars can testify, her contributions to the MIS field are numerous, significant, and long lasting. She was instrumental in several studies of group decision support systems at the University of Minnesota, and later, at Duke, and continued to focus her formidable attention and research skills on areas such as using tables and graphs for decision making, organizational learning, distributed teams, virtual communities, and electronic communication. She began her career with a PhD dissertation using an experiment, and later returned again and again to experiments over her exceptionally rich yet all-too-brief career. As a key arrow in the quiver of the HCI subdiscipline of MIS, her contributions in and support of experimental techniques were invaluable to HCI researchers. The loss to the community is incalculable and profound.

Beyond her obvious scholarly pursuits and achievements, which directly influenced the two editors' own research, the editors are particularly saddened at the loss of a great mentor, supporter, and friend. Her unselfish and caring nature is illustrated by her always prompt and enthusiastic responses to every one of our requests for work and advice on matters sometimes unrelated to these volumes. We were unaware of her health condition when we made these requests and she responded in spite of her situation. We were tremendously uplifted by her excitement for, and support of, these two volumes: by her promised short commentary that turned into a full chapter; by her thoughtful review of two other chapters that helped the authors very much; by her constant and uplifting encouragement about this project; and by her caring comments to help us as colleagues and friends. As recently as May 2005, she returned a review of the introductory chapter of this book. After what was obviously a very careful reading of the manuscript, she provided her typical encouraging comments along with suggestions and even typographical corrections. When a sincere apology reached her for not knowing her health condition and for burdening her with this work while she was in a hospital bed, she replied, "Ping, it was not a burden but a pleasant distraction! I enjoyed reading the chapter. I hope to get out of the hospital tomorrow or the next day, so I am on the upswing!" This was the Gerry we will always remember: so uplifting, so positive and encouraging, so full of hope! Many of us have benefited so much from Gerry's thoroughly upbeat, unselfish, and caring character. We will miss her greatly but at the same time we thoroughly celebrate how she touched our lives.

This chapter is one of the last publications produced by Gerry DeSanctis. We believe that just like many of her articles that have played important roles in diverse areas of MIS research, this chapter will continue Gerry's legacy for decades to come.

REFERENCES

Alter, S. *Decision support systems: Current practice and continuing challenges.* New York: Addison-Wesley, 1980.

Applegate, L.M. Technology support for cooperative work: a framework for studying introduction and assimilation in organizations. *Organizational Computing* 1, 1 (1991), 11–39.

Barab, S.A.; Kling, R.; and Gray, J.H. *Designing for Virtual Communities in the Service of Learning.* Cambridge: Cambridge University Press, 2004.

Barge, J.K., and Hirokawa, R.Y. Toward a communication competency model of group leadership. *Small Group Behavior* 20, 2 (1989), 167–189.

Benbasat, I., and Lim, L.H. The effects of group, task, context, and technology variables on the usefulness of group support systems: a meta-analysis of experimental studies. *Small Group Research* 24, 4 (1993), 430–462.

Benjamin, B.A., and Podolny, J.M. Status, quality, and social order in the California wine industry. *Administrative Science Quarterly* 44, 3 (1999), 563–590.

Bernard, J. *The Sociology of Community.* Glenview, IL: Scott, Foresman, 1973.

Butler, B.S. Membership size, communication activity, sustainability: a resource-based model of online social structures. *Information Systems Research* 12, 4 (2001), 346–362.

Cummings, J. Work groups, structural diversity, and knowledge sharing in a global organization. *Management Science* 50, 3 (2004), 352–364.

Davidow, W.H., and Malone, M.S. *The Virtual Corporation.* New York: Edward Burlingame Books/Harper Business, 1992.

Davis, G.B., and Olson, M.H. *Management Information Systems: Conceptual Foundations Structure and Development,* 2nd ed. New York: McGraw Hill, 1984.

DeSanctis, G., and Monge, P. Communication processes for virtual organizations. *Organization Science* 10, 6 (1999), 693–703.

Dutton, W.H. The virtual organization: tele-access in business and industry. In G. DeSanctis and J. Fulk (eds.), *Shaping Organization Form: Communication, Connection, and Community.* Newbury Park, CA: Sage, 1999, pp. 473–495.

Earley, P.C., and Mosakowski, E. Creating hybrid team cultures: an empirical test of transnational team functioning. *Academy of Management Journal* 43, 1 (2000), 26–50.

Foreman, P., and Whetten, D.A. Members' identification with multiple-identity organizations. *Organization Science* 13, 6 (2002), 618–635.

Galegher, J.; Kraut, R.E.; and Egido, C. (eds.) *Intellectual Teamwork: The Social and Technological Bases of Cooperative Work.* Hillsdale, NJ: Lawrence Erlbaum Associates, 1990.

Gray, P., and Olfman, L. The user interface in group decision support systems. *Decision Support Systems* 5, 2 (1989), 119–137.

Gurak, L. *Persuasion and Privacy in Cyberspace: The Online Protests over LotusMarketPlace and the Clipper Chip.* New Haven, CT: Yale University Press, 1997.

Hackman, J.R. Learning more by crossing levels: evidence from airplanes, hospitals, and orchestras. *Journal of Organizational Behavior* 24, 8 (2003), 905–923.

Harasim, L. *Global Networks: Computers and International Communication.* Cambridge, MA: MIT Press, 1993.

Hiltz, S.R., and Turoff, M. The evolution of user behavior in a computerized conferencing system. *Communications of the ACM* 24, 11 (1981), 739–751.

Hinds, P., and Kiesler, S. (eds.) *Distributed Work: New Research on Working Across Distance Using Technology.* Boston: MIT Press, 2002.

Hollingshead, A.B., and McGrath, J.E. Computer-assisted groups: A critical review of the empirical research. In R.A. Guzzo and E. Salas (eds.), *Team Effectiveness and Decision Making in Organizations.* San Francisco: Jossey-Bass, 1995, pp. 46–78.

Huber, G.P. Cognitive style as a basis for MIS and DSS designs: much ado about nothing? *Management Science,* 29 (1983), 567–579.

Huber, G.P. A theory of the effects of advanced information technologies on organizational design, intelligence, and decision making. *Academy of Management Review* 15, 1 (1990), 47–71.

Huber, G. *The Necessary Nature of Future Firms.* Thousand Oaks, CA: Sage, 2004.

Ilinitch, A.Y.; Lewin, A.Y.; and D'Aveni, R. *Managing in Times of Disorder: Hypercompetitive Organizational Responses.* SAGE, Thousand Oaks, CA, 1998.

Jessup, L.M., and Valacich, J. (eds.) *Group Support Systems: New Perspectives.* New York: Macmillan, 1993.

Jones, S. (ed.) *Virtual Culture: Identity and Communication in Cybersociety.* Thousand Oaks, CA: Sage, 1997.

Lipnack, J., and Stamps, J. *Virtual Teams: Reaching Across Space, Time and Organizations with Technology.* New York: John Wiley & Sons, 1997.

Malone, T.W., and Crowston, K. The interdisciplinary study of coordination. *Computing Surveys* 26, 1 (1994), 87–119.

Mowshowitz, A. *Virtual Organization: Toward a Theory of Societal Transformation Stimulated by Information Technology.* Westport, CT: Quorum Books, 2002.

Nardi, B.A. *Context and Consciousness: Activity Theory and Human-Computer Interaction.* Cambridge, MA: MIT Press, 1996.

Okhuysen, G.A., and Eisenhardt, K.M. Integrating knowledge in groups: how formal interventions enable flexibility. *Organization Science* 13, 4 (2002), 387–401.

Olson, G.M., and Olson, J.S. User-centered design of collaboration technology. *Journal of Organizational Computing* 1, 1 (1991), 41–60.

Orlikowski, W. J.; Yates, J.; Okamura, K.; and Fujimoto, M. Shaping electronic communication: the metastructuring of technology in the context of use. *Organization Science* 6, 4 (1995), 423–445.

Preece, J. *Online Communities: Supporting Usability, Supporting Sociability.* New York: John Wiley & Sons, 2000.

Reagans, R., and Zuckerman, E.W. Networks, diversity, and productivity: the social capital of corporate R&D teams. *Organization Science* 12, 4 (2001), 502–517.

Rice, R.E. Task analyzability, use of new media, and effectiveness: a multi-site exploration of media richness. *Organization Science* 3, 4 (1992), 475–500.

Saunders, C.S.; Robey, D.; and Vaverek, K.A. The persistence of status differentials in computer conferencing. *Human Communication Research* 20, 4 (1994), 443–472.

Scott, W.R. *Institutions and Organizations.* Menlo Park, CA: Sage, 1995.

Smith, M.A., and Kollock, P. *Communities in Cyberspace.* New York: Routledge, 1999.

Te'eni, D.A cognitive-affective model of organizational communication for designing IT. *MIS Quarterly* 25, 2 (2001), 251–312.

Trevino, L.K.; Webster, J.; and Stein, E.W. Making connections: complementary influences on communication media choices, attitudes, and use. *Organization Science* 11, 2 (2002), 163–182

Weisband, S.P.; Schneider, S.K.; and Connolly, T. Computer-mediated communication and social information: status salience and status differences. *Academy of Management Journal* 38, 4 (1995), 1124–1152.

PART II

IT DEVELOPMENT: THEORIES OF INDIVIDUAL AND GROUP WORK

CHAPTER 5

ADVANCING THE THEORY OF DSS DESIGN FOR USER CALIBRATION

GEORGE M. KASPER AND FRANCIS K. ANDOH-BAIDOO

Abstract: *This paper extends, revises, and reports a partial test of the theory of decision support systems (DSS) design for user calibration. The theory prescribes properties of a DSS needed for the users to achieve the goal of perfect calibration. Properties of expressiveness, visibility, and inquirability are posited as requisite components of the DSS dialog. We extend the original theory of DSS design for user calibration to address the issues of meta-design and critiquing. A test of components of the theory is reported that compared the effects on user calibration of problems depicted using either expressiveness in the form of text or visibility in the form of diagrams. The results of the study support the theory. When problems are new and novel, visual depiction improves calibration. As problems became more familiar and problem novelty decreased, no difference was found in user calibration between subjects exposed to visibility diagrams and those exposed to a traditional text paradigm.*

Keywords: *Decision Support Systems, Dialog, Design, Design Theory, User Calibration*

> "From the . . . users' point of view, the Dialog is the System."
> —Sprague and Carlson (1982, p. 29)

> "It's not what we don't know that gives us trouble, it's what we know that ain't so!"
> —Will Rogers

INTRODUCTION

The decision selection process is influenced by one's belief in the quality of the decision (Russo and Schoemaker, 1992). Decision support system designers and researchers have to appreciate users' perception of the quality of a decision to ensure that good decisions are implemented and that poor decisions are properly hedged. For the purposes of this discussion, the term decision support systems includes all forms of information systems and technologies designed to assist one or more decision makers in making a specific decision or choosing a specific course of action (Scott Morton, 1984). Although the nature of the support provided by DSS ranges from passive to intelligent (Henderson, 1987; Humphreys, 1986; Keen, 1987; Luconi et al., 1986; Manheim, 1988; Remus and Kottemann, 1986) and from individual to group (Olson and Olson, 1991), the primary goal in designing all DSS is to improve decision quality (Keen and Scott Morton, 1978; Scott Morton, 1984).

In fact, the focus on decision quality distinguishes DSS dialog (interface) design work from the human-computer interface (HCI) research done by computer scientists. HCI research by computer scientists has focused on efficient performance or on the minimization of time or errors in completing a task (Shneiderman, 1992). By contrast, DSS researchers investigating interface design issues focus on effective performance, typically in the form of improved decision quality, with decision time and decision confidence as secondary outcomes (Speier and Morris, 2003).

In differentiating between confidence, trust, predictability, and decision accuracy, Muir (1987, p. 1915) states:

> *Predictability* is a basis for trust, which, in turn, is the basis for an operator [user/decision maker] to make a *prediction* about the future behaviour of a referent. The *accuracy* of that prediction may be assessed by comparing it with the actual behavioural outcome. In addition, an individual who makes a prediction may associate a particular level of *confidence* with the prediction. Thus, *confidence* is a qualifier which is associated with a particular prediction, it is not synonymous with trust.

Realism in confidence is essential for good decision making; the ruinous consequences of unrealistic confidence litter the business decision-making landscape (Russo and Schoemaker, 1992). Indeed, the literature on "escalation to commitment" and the adage "throwing good money after bad" testify to the recurrence and cost of overconfidence (Staw, 1981), as people are often unrealistically confident in the quality of their decisions (Brown and Gould, 1987; Einhorn and Hogarth, 1978).

The best-known measure of the accuracy of one's confidence in a decision is calibration, the correspondence between one's prediction of the quality of a decision and the actual quality of the decision (Clemen and Murphy, 1990; Keller and Keller, 1993; Lichtenstein et al., 1982). Perfect calibration exists when the ascribed confidence equals the accuracy of the predicted outcome; otherwise, miscalibration is present, reflecting either underconfidence or overconfidence. Because action precedes outcome, decision confidence plays an essential role in both selecting and implementing a decision. When implementing a decision, overconfidence can be beneficial in helping overcome the inevitable setbacks and challenges. When selecting a decision, however, perfect calibration is preferred so that an alternative can be chosen untainted by unrealistic enthusiasm or trepidation (Fazlollahi and Vadihov, 2001).

Evidence from the DSS literature suggests that existing DSS can produce "illusory benefits" (Aldag and Powers, 1986; Davis et al., 1991) resulting in miscalibration, thereby distorting the decision selection process. Almost three decades had passed when Keen and Scott Morton (1978, p. 1342) recognized this and wrote, "Even though the . . . [decision aided] subjects [in their study] did better, their increased average time and reduced average confidence lead to the tentative conclusion that they did not have a 'handle' on the problem." By now, almost everyone can recount from personal experience a situation where computer-generated output produced an aura of exactness and reliance bordering on blind acceptance, even in the presence of compelling evidence to the contrary. For many, if the "computer says it's so," it is taken to be fact, even if the output flies in the face of logic. In these cases, user miscalibration may be amplified by the design of the DSS artifact. If DSS are to improve decision making, DSS designers and researchers must be concerned with user calibration.

The goal of DSS dialog design is to architect a two-way exchange of symbols and actions that produce holistic performance—performance that exceeds the sum of the parts. If this level of performance is to be achieved, a DSS must not only improve decision quality, it must also facilitate the decision maker's interpretation of the quality of decisions made using the DSS technology.

This paper extends, revises, and reports a partial test of the theory of DSS design for user calibration originally posited by Kasper (1996). Using Walls et al.'s (1992) framework for building IS design theory (ISDT), Kasper (1996) developed a DSS design theory for user calibration. In a recent review of literature, Walls et al. (2004) reported that Kasper (1996) was one of the few researchers who made extensive use of the ISDT concepts. However, two important components of the framework were not adequately addressed by Kasper. In this paper we extend the original theory of DSS design for user calibration to address all the components specified in Walls et al.'s framework. Further we report a partial test of the theory by comparing the user calibration efficiency of the visual computing paradigm with that of the conventional text paradigm over two levels of problem novelty. A preliminary version of these results is reported elsewhere (Ashford and Kasper, 2003). Here we clarify that reporting and provide more detail and discussion regarding the study and further studies of user calibration.

To frame the discussion within the broader notion of DSS, we begin by reviewing the general concepts and components of DSS. This properly frames the theory of DSS design for user calibration as a dialog design theory. Next, we draw extensively upon Kasper (1996) to describe the theory. We begin by describing the kernel theories. Next we present the properties needed to achieve the goal of perfect calibration, including meta-design. The laboratory test and test results follow. Finally, we summarize the paper, highlighting the contributions.

BACKGROUND

The works of Gorry and Scott Morton (1971), Keen and Scott Morton (1978), Bonczek, Holsapple, and Whinston (1981), Ginzberg and Stohr (1982), and Sprague and Carlson (1982) define the conceptual and theoretical foundations of DSS. Coined by Gorry and Scott Morton (1971), decision support systems are motivated by decisions and decision making, as opposed to systems supporting problem or opportunity identification, intelligence gathering, performance monitoring, communications, and other activities supporting organizational or individual performance.

If we use Simon's (1955) classic four phases of the decision-making process—intelligence, design, choice, and implementation and control—DSS concentrate on the design and choice phases (Fazlollahi and Vadihov, 2001). As a field of study, DSS argues that systems built to support the design and choice phases of decision making present unique challenges, both in theory and in practice. The term "decision making" implies judgment, personal assessment, and evaluation. In the DSS literature, the amount of decision-making judgment needed to solve a problem reflects the problem's structure. Problem structure is the degree to which aspects of design or choice are subject to computerization (Gorry and Scott Morton, 1971). If for any decision, all aspects of design and choice are structured and therefore computerizable, then no situational judgment is needed and the problem is said to be structured. DSS are not designed to play a role in structured problem environments; other forms of information systems, such as transaction processing systems, serve these situations. At the other extreme, if no structure can be applied to any part of the design or choice phases, then what is to be computerized? If nothing can be specified, what role can the computerized part of the DSS play in the overall human-machine system?

For DSS to be of any use, there must be some part of design or choice that can be computerized while other parts are left to the decision maker's expertise, judgment, and cognition. This partnership of human and machine dates to the work of Licklider (1960), who envisioned a man-machine symbiosis in which the human-computer decision-making whole would produce holistic results where the performance of the human and computer combination would exceed

Figure 5.1   **Decision Support Systems**

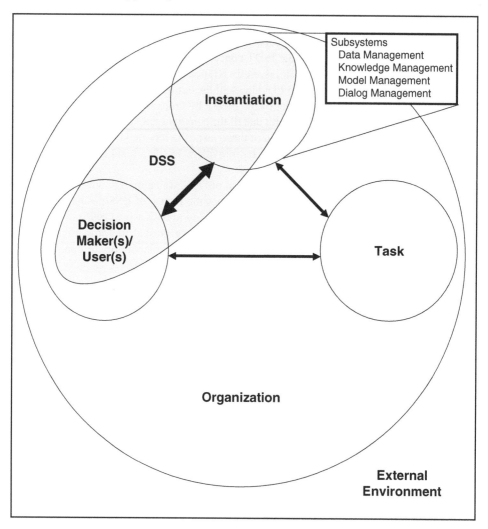

that possible by the simple sum of the parts. The goal of DSS dialog design is to architect an effi-cient and effective two-way exchange of symbols and actions to achieve holistic performance.

COMPONENTS OF DECISION SUPPORT SYSTEMS

Figure 5.1 shows the components of a DSS instantiation and those factors affecting both DSS instantiation and decision making. A DSS integrates decision maker and information technology into a synergistic unit to improve decision making. The decision maker and information technol-ogy combine to address a specific task within an organization and its environment. The interplay among decision maker, task, and information technology is the DSS and is a well-known triad in the information systems and technology literatures (Mason and Mitroff, 1973; Newell and Simon,

1972). This user(s)-task-technology triad exists within the contexts of both an organization and its external environment.

Data from a data subsystem (e.g., data warehouse/mart), models from a model subsystem (e.g., OLAP), and judgment from the decision-maker "subsystem" combine to form the DSS that addresses a specific task at a specific time within a specific organization impacted by a specific set of external environmental conditions. These data, model, and decision-maker subsystems combine to form the DSS through a dialog subsystem. All capabilities of the data, model, and decision-maker subsystems are joined through a dialog subsystem. "All capabilities of the system must be articulated and implemented through the Dialog" (Sprague and Carlson, 1982, p. 28). If the technology and decision maker are to combine to produce holistic outcomes, the dialog must be designed to orchestrate an effective symphony of data, models, and decision maker.

Model and Data Subsystem

The model subsystem consists of a model base and model management. A model base is a collection of computer-based decision models (Liang, 1988). The functions of a model base are similar to that of a database except that the objects stored in a model base are models. A model can be considered as a mathematical abstraction of a specific problem or a class of problems. Model management insulates the decision maker from the physical details of model base activities so that the decision maker can concentrate on decision-making logic (Blanning, 1993).

The development of online analytic processing (OLAP) represents the current instantiation of the model subsystem (Thomsen, 2002, pp. 8–10). A review of the pioneering work on model management subsystems can be found in Blanning (1993). The notion of data systems includes both data and knowledge, as first envisioned for DSS by Bonczek, Holsapple, and Whinston (1981, pp. 70–71). This merging of data and knowledge is occurring in data warehouse technology. The conceptualization of a data warehouse is evolving into a federated warehouse that includes both data and knowledge (Kerschberg, 2001). Ma (1997) argues that data management has received extensive treatment in the DSS literature, citing maturity of database technology and associated database design and database management systems as the reason.

Decision Maker

User differences have been and continue to be the focus of much discussion and research on interface design and system performance (Bickmore and Cassell, 2001; Curl et al., 1988; Huber, 1983; Markus et al., 2002). Indeed, user modeling—the encoding of knowledge about the user to improve human-computer interaction—has become a well-recognized topic in intelligent systems research (Kass and T., 1988; Moulin et al., 2002). Particularly relevant to the DSS design theory for user calibration, "[a] system may have several models of the same user who may be expert in one domain and novice in another" (Moulin et al., 2002, p. 177). Moreover, user acceptance and calibration of system output requires an explanation customized and adapted to the user during problem solving (Moulin et al., 2002). We discuss the development of user modeling, especially in the form of critiquing systems, below.

Dialog Subsystem

From the decision makers' perspective, the dialog is the system (Sprague and Carlson, 1982, p. 29). Dialog is an observable two-way exchange of symbols and actions (Hartson and Hix, 1989, p. 8).

Figure 5.2   **Decision-Making Usefulness of Different Means of Symbolic Representation in Relation to Problem Novelty**

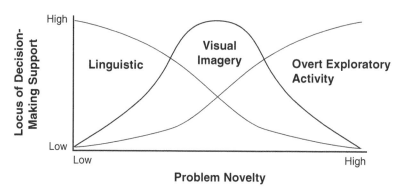

Source: Kaufmann (1980, 1985, 1996).

DSS dialog symbols and actions must promote both physical and cognitive interaction. In other words, a DSS dialog must contribute to enhancing the decision maker's cognitive problem-solving/decision-making activities in a convivial manner. The DSS design theory for user calibration contends that this will require designing the symbols and actions of the DSS dialog to reflect those of the decision maker's natural system of symbolic representation. In this regard we draw upon the work of Kaufmann (1980, 1985). Based on this work, the theory of DSS design for user calibration argues that DSS dialog symbols and actions can be conceptualized as those pertaining to expressiveness (linguistics reasoning), visibility (visual-imagery reasoning), and inquirability (overt-exploratory reasoning).

THEORIES RELEVANT TO USER CALIBRATION

The relationship between mental representation and decision making is articulated in the theory of symbolic representation in problem solving. Developed by Kaufmann (1980, 1985) and Helstrup (1987), the theory of symbolic representation in problem solving/decision making contends that problem solving/decision making is based on symbolic reasoning. Arguing that cognition cannot be separated from its symbols and reasoning, the theory uses the term "symbolic representation" to include both static internal coding(s) and active reasoning (Kaufmann, 1985). According to the theory, the symbols and actions in problem solving/decision making are: linguistic, visual imagery, and overt exploratory activity. Figure 5.2 provides a schematic illustration of the relationships proposed by the theory of symbolic representation in problem solving. It also shows the decision-making usefulness of the different symbols and actions in relation to problem novelty. The theory holds that the locus of symbolic representation for problem solving varies from linguistic to visual imagery representation to exploratory reasoning with problem novelty.

If the novelty of the problem is low, the usefulness of linguistic symbols as means of decision making is high. As problem novelty increases, the usefulness of both visual imagery and overt exploratory increase as means of decision making. As the degree of novelty exceeds the usefulness of one's linguistic and visual imagery symbols, one must resort to overt exploratory reasoning to construct a mental image of the problem. According to the theory, the quality of mental acts (decision quality, decision confidence, etc.) depends upon matching the appropriate symbols and actions to the needs dictated by the novelty of the problem.

Problem novelty, according to the theory, is based on both the degree and type of abstraction needed to generate an appropriate representation of the problem. The type of abstraction ranges from analytic to holistic. Familiar to MIS/DSS researchers as individual cognitive styles, the analytic type of abstraction requires decomposition and detail whereas the holistic type of abstraction requires aggregate and heuristic processing.

The degree of abstraction ranges from none to extensive. When no abstraction is needed, a problem can be solved by directly applying the decision maker's memory-based knowledge. At the other extreme, problems eliciting a high degree of abstraction require extensive reasoning and inference for the decision maker to formulate a mental representation of a problem. The degree of abstraction reflects the proportion of memory contained in one's representation of a problem. If the degree of abstraction is low, a very high proportion of one's mental representation of a problem is based on memory. Conversely, if the degree of abstraction is high, a very low proportion of one's mental representation of a problem is based on memory. The degree and type of abstraction combine to define problem novelty.

Problem novelty also plays a role in decision-confidence and decision-maker calibration. The current evidence suggests that decision-maker calibration is directly related to the degree of problem novelty. As the degree of problem novelty increases (the degree and type of abstraction increase), the likelihood of miscalibration increases (Juslin, 1993; Wagenaar, 1988).

The role of decision confidence in outcomes makes it clear that an effective DSS design must not only improve the quality of decisions; it must also facilitate the user's interpretation of the quality of decisions he or she makes using the aid. The effect of DSS design alternatives on the user's interpretation of the quality of decisions has been ignored by the IS research community, despite warnings of the dangers inherent in this neglect (Mason, 1969; Weizenbaum, 1966). To begin to consider the effects of DSS design on decision-confidence and decision-maker calibration, a theory is needed to guide the research. To provide this guidance, a DSS dialog design theory is needed.

A THEORY OF DSS DESIGN FOR USER CALIBRATION

The theory of DSS design for user calibration presented in this paper follows Walls et al.'s (1992) framework. The goal, the conceptual properties, and the interaction among the properties in specific situations needed to achieve the goal are introduced and developed below.

Goal of the Theory

Because the focus of DSS is decision quality, the DSS design theory for user calibration is primarily concerned with the realism needed for deciding on a decision. Perfect calibration requires that the decision maker's belief in the quality of a decision equal the quality of the decision (Russo and Schoemaker, 1992). Hence, the goal of the theory of DSS design for user calibration is to prescribe the DSS properties needed for users to achieve perfect calibration.

Properties of the Theory

The conceptualizations of symbolic representations in problem solving/decision making as developed by Kaufmann encourage proposing a design theory of symbols and actions for DSS design for user calibration consisting of linguistic expressiveness, visibility of imagery, and overt exploitation of inquiry. Expressiveness is the manner or tone of the exchange conveyed by the dialog symbols (e.g., condescending, matter-of-fact, supportive, directive, etc.). Expressiveness recognizes that the manner in which dialog symbols are expressed can engender feelings and beliefs. Visibility refers to dialog symbols and symbols in action (e.g., icons and animation) that facilitate the decision maker's image of the problem and solution. Inquirability defines both the nature of the act of inquisition and the acts of discovery and resolution through investigation. Collectively, expressiveness, visibility, and inquirability define basic research and development concepts for designing the symbols and actions of a DSS dialog. Expressiveness, visibility, and inquirability are developed in more detail below.

Expressiveness

The expressiveness dimension recognizes that the manner or tone in which dialog symbols are presented can engender feelings and beliefs. The tone of expressiveness can be condescending, matter-of-fact, supportive, and directive, among others. Expressiveness is currently conveyed to the user either through presentation or through audio media. In the latter case, expressiveness can also be monotone and monotonous or melodic and overly melodramatic, each engendering different feelings in the user.

> "One computer system may be capable of sophisticated reasoning but so limited in what it can . . . express that to a human user it appears to be only the simplest of dialog partners. Another computer may be severely limited in its reasoning abilities but may give the impression of considerable intelligence through sophisticated forms of expression. Examples of the former are expert systems . . . An example of the latter is the ELIZA program . . ." (Edwards and Mason, 1988, p. 141).

Using the human as a metaphor, it is often difficult for a listener to separate a speaker's dialect from his or her message and intelligence. One's choice of words and dialect often define the impression others have of the quality of the message and the speaker's intelligence. Dialog plays a similar role in DSS, and it is often quite difficult for a user to distinguish the quality of the decision made using the DSS from his or her impressions about the quality of the DSS themselves.

The expressiveness dimension includes the overall rhetorical strategy for eliciting and presenting symbols. Rhetorical strategy engenders feelings such as "credibility" (Brown and Yule, 1983, p. 148). The expressiveness properties of a DSS dialog can affect one's belief in the quality of a decision made using the aid. Examples of expressiveness dimensions that may affect user calibration include framing, connectiveness, and message construction.

Framing refers to the phrasing used to elicit and present dialog symbols. An example of a positive presentation frame is: "Under these conditions, 95 percent of the time X happens"; the corresponding negative presentation frame would be: "Under these conditions, 5 percent of the time X does not happen." Even though these convey equivalent information, the latter elicits a different response from the decision maker than does the former.

In addition to framing, the expressiveness dimension includes connectiveness. Connectiveness refers to the cohesion of the dialog. Connectiveness includes endophoric reference and resolution. Two forms of endophoria exist: reference back to material already presented (anaphoric) and reference forward to material to be presented (cataphoric) (Brown and Yule, 1983, pp. 192–193). A dialog that exhibits connectiveness engenders credibility because it gives the user the impression that the DSS are intelligent. In fact, much of ELIZA's ability to engender overconfidence was attributed to the connectiveness of its dialog (Weizenbaum, 1966).

Expressiveness also includes message construction. The frustration that can result from messages that are too cryptic is well known to all users of computer-based systems. On the other hand, some evidence suggests that anthropomorphic phrasing is counterproductive because users feel threatened and intimidated by messages that they feel are condescending and wordy (Buchheit and Moher, 1990; Shneiderman, 1987, pp. 322–325; Shneiderman, 1992, pp. 312–314). Rather than proving engaging, dialogs that exhibit anthropomorphic phrasing have been shown to distance the user from the decision by decreasing the decision maker's feeling of responsibility for the decision (Quintanar et al., 1982). According to Shneiderman (1992, p. 313), "the anthropomorphic interface . . . deceives, misleads, and confuses."

Collectively, it is clear that ". . . the words and phrases used in designing a computer dialog can make important differences in people's perceptions, emotional reactions, and motivations" (Shneiderman, 1987, p. 323; Shneiderman, 1992, p. 312). In this way, the expressiveness of a DSS's dialog can affect decision making. How user calibration is affected by rhetorical strategy, presentation frame, connectiveness, phrasing, message construction, and other aspects of a dialog's expressiveness characteristics remains to be investigated.

Visibility

"Seeing is believing." Recognition of the importance of visibility characteristics in problem solving is increasing. Visibility aspects are also receiving increasing attention in the human-computer interaction literature (Keller and Keller, 1993; Shneiderman, 1992; Veryard, 1986). Through visibility characteristics, the decision maker "sees" both the specific problem and the DSS better. Shneiderman recognizes the need for increased visibility capability in DSS when he writes, "Expert systems . . . tax the user with complexity, lack of visibility of the underlying process, and confusion about what functions the system can and cannot handle" (Shneiderman, 1992, p. 169).

Visibility requires that the user see the DSS work, and at work, that the user see the logical operations performed by the DSS and their application to a specific problem (Veryard, 1986). This requires increasing the observability of the DSS and their behavior. To improve decision making and user calibration, DSS must not only work; they must be seen working. This means that the DSS must facilitate the user's understanding of their logical behavior by effectively depicting their behavior. Indicators that the DSS work can be found in descriptive, outcome indicators such as information about the system's domain of competence, its history of performance, its performance over a range of tasks within its domain of expertise (Muir, 1987), and personal tests and benchmarks, among others. Depicting the DSS doing work is the challenge of information visualization and other forms of visual computing.

The notion of visibility characteristics also includes the user's mental imagery of the problem—that is, the visual imagery of the problem as discussed in the theory of symbolic representation in problem solving. In this sense, there is increasing recognition of the importance of visualization for creativity and problem solving. Information technologies are playing an increasingly important role in the visual depiction of complex problems (Keller and Keller, 1993). "A technical reality today and a cognitive imperative tomorrow, . . . the ability to visualize (information) is absolutely essential to ensure the integrity of analysis, to provoke insights, and to communicate those insights to others" (McCormick et al., 1987, p. 7). The need to support the user's cognitive abilities and visual imagery makes information visualization central to the development of graphical user interfaces.

Information visualization, according to Keller and Keller (1993), consists of exploration, analysis, and presentation. Exploration requires interactive forms of imaging to identify new relationships in the information. Analysis requires precise and rigorous techniques for comparing images to study known relationships in information. Presentation requires images that effectively convey the meaning of information. In this way, exploration involves "seeing" the problem, analysis involves seeing the DSS at work, and presentation involves seeing the work of the DSS.

For many problems, user calibration depends upon the user's ability to visualize the problem and to see the DSS at work and working through an effective presentation. The more visible the problem and observable and understandable the aid's behavior, the better is the user able to assess the quality of his or her decision, resulting in better calibration. The emerging technology of information visualization promises to provide the DSS tools to enable users to explore, analyze, and present information in order to improve user calibration.

Inquirability

In his well-known book on the subject, Churchman (1971, p. 275) concluded that the design of an inquiring system must consider both "knowing" and the "feeling of knowing." Knowing is the essence of decision quality and the feeling of knowing is decision confidence. By recognizing the importance of both decision quality and decision confidence, Churchman implies that the design of an inquiring system should consider user calibration. The term inquirability is used here to indicate how the actions of a DSS dialog engender an accurate feeling of knowing.

Inquirability characteristics define how well the dialog actions support the act of discovery, revealing and resolving. Inquirability characteristics comprise a continuum of dialog actions, ranging from the servile and illusory that lull to the contrarian that engage and continuously challenge. Dialog actions that are servile and illusory are designed to please, to unquestioningly respond by providing data that supports the decision maker's position(s) and assumption(s). Little, if any, new knowledge is revealed or resolved by a DSS dialog that is servile and illusory. At the other extreme, DSS dialog actions designed to be contrarian can engage and challenge the decision maker's positions and assumptions to reveal and resolve new knowledge through the dialectic process of debate and resolution.

Near the servile end of the inquirability continuum, the actions of a DSS dialog can be designed to generate data that justifies or supports a position, a set of assumptions, or a decision that the user has already made. According to survey data reported by Alter (1977), a major reason for using a DSS is to justify a decision that has already been made. Unfortunately, this adds nothing to holistic performance. The limited evidence suggests that decision makers who surrounded themselves with servile systems, "yes men" that voice no criticism, fail to make good decisions in crisis situations (Dunbar and Goldberg, 1978). Servile inquirability fails to inform because it simply presents data that accords with the decision maker's position. As might be expected, data that accords with one's decision does not affect decision confidence (Koriat et al., 1980) or improve decision-maker calibration. This suggests that inquirability designed or used to justify or support a position, set of assumptions, or a decision that the decision maker has already made has no effect on user calibration, cannot improve decision quality, and fails to produce holistic, synergistic outcomes.

Between servile and contrarian, designs of inquirability include highlighting, prompting, and other actions that direct, give advice, and suggest choices. Using these dialog actions, the DSS recommends a response to the user, providing varying degrees of explanation to support its recommendation. In the extreme, but not uncommon case, the DSS is incapable of providing any evidence to support its recommendation. Even in some of the most sophisticated systems, the DSS seem incapable of providing the user with anything more than a very superficial explanation for their recommendation. In general, dialog designs that simply recommend a response with little or no justification do not support user calibration because they fail to expose assumptions or bring to the user's attention information on the criticality of assumptions, nor do they suggest to the decision maker new and alternative views of the situation. Advice-giving systems encourage miscalibration because they place the user in the paradoxical and extremely difficult role of monitoring, and overruling when appropriate, the recommendations of a machine whose competence is presumed to exceed that of the user (Muir, 1987). In fact, the evidence suggests that ratification of a recommended action, such as occurs when a dialog highlights, prompts, or otherwise directs or gives advice to the user, not only increases overconfidence but also results in poorer decisions.

Research indicates that when evaluating another's answers, humans are both less correct and more overconfident than the original respondent (Block and Harper, 1991; Sniezek et al., 1990). In other words, those cued to a particular response or decision are likely to be more overconfident about the correctness of the decision than was the person who made the decision in the first place. Block and Harper (1991) found similar results: subjects who judged the quality of someone else's answers were both more overconfident and less correct than those not cued to a particular answer. These results suggest that for DSS dialog design, the actions of highlighting and prompting, and perhaps even the recommendation of specific decisions by expert systems, may actually contribute to miscalibration. This is because they place the user in the position of having to evaluate the quality of a recommendation that he or she has had little or no part in developing and that was made by a machine touted as having more expertise.

Near the contrarian end of the inquirability continuum, the actions of a DSS dialog are designed to engage and challenge the decision maker's positions and assumptions to reveal and resolve meta-knowledge through the dialectic process of debate and resolution. Because of this, inquirability based on the dialectic model of reasoning is perhaps the most effective for user calibration and decision performance. In dialectic inquirability, the actions of a DSS dialog are designed to reveal and resolve metaknowledge by debating a plan (thesis) and counterplan (antithesis) (Mason, 1969). Conceptually, the revealing and resolving of metaknowledge, characteristic of the dialectic method, is essential for user calibration when problem novelty is greatest. Cosier and Schwenk (1990) review the literature on disagreement in decision making and conclude that dialectic reasoning may be the best method to use when problem novelty is great. Likewise, Cosier and Schwenk (1990) and Mason (1969) demonstrate that dialectic reasoning results in better decisions, and Buyukkurt and Buyukkurt (1990) show that dialectic reasoning affects decision confidence.

The literature suggests that dialectic reasoning improves calibration. Central to Faust's (1986) suggested rules for improving calibration is the generation of evidence that disconfirms, challenges, and refutes one's position (i.e., dialectic reasoning). Koriat et al. (1980) found that memory-based knowledge that challenges or contradicts one's decision improves calibration. The need to justify one's decision to others has also been shown to improve calibration (Arkes et al., 1987). Each of these variants of dialectic reasoning improves decision-making performance and user calibration by revealing and resolving inconsistencies, by challenging, refuting, and or disconfirming one's prior mental representation.

Ultimately, effective outcomes depend upon the user's interpretation of the quality of decisions he or she makes using the DSS. For user calibration, this means that the DSS must support and facilitate the user's interpretation of the quality of decisions made using the aid. At a minimum, the symbols and actions of the DSS dialog should coincide with those of the user's natural system of problem solving. Expressiveness, visibility, and inquirability define DSS dialog categories of symbols and actions that parallel those theorized to constitute the user's mental system of problem solving/decision making. DSS design requires the judicious and effective application of the DSS dialog symbols and actions of expressiveness, visibility, and inquirability characteristics.

PROBLEM NOVELTY AND THE COMPONENTS OF THE THEORY

In addition to defining the components, a design theory must consider how the components work in a specific situation to achieve the desired goal (Walls et al., 1992). The DSS dialog design theory contends that the functional usefulness of expressiveness, visibility, and inquirability characteristics depend upon the novelty of the problem. This contention is supported by the literatures that suggest a relationship between problem novelty and one's knowledge, and the role of knowledge in decision making and user calibration. Recall that according to the theory of symbolic representation in problem solving, problem novelty is based on both the degree and type of abstraction needed to generate a solution to a problem. The type of abstraction is a reflection of the decision maker's cognitive style, and the degree of abstraction reflects the proportion of memory-based information contained in the decision maker's mental representation of the problem. Also recall that as problem novelty increases, the degree (and perhaps type) of abstraction needed to conceptualize the problem increases, as does the likelihood of miscalibration.

Problem novelty is also a characteristic of problem structure, a well-known concept in the DSS literature (Gorry and Scott Morton, 1971; Simon, 1960). Problem structure connotes something about the problem. Problem novelty on the other hand, as defined earlier by degree and type of abstraction, reflects something about the decision maker(s) in relation to the problem. Because decision-maker calibration is based on one's belief in the quality of a decision, it reflects something about the decision maker, and therefore problem novelty seems to be a more accurate descriptor than problem structure of the nature of the role played by the problem in user calibration. However, problem novelty and problem structure are closely aligned.

Problem novelty, according to DSS dialog design theory, determines the functional usefulness of expressiveness, visibility, and inquirability for decision making and user calibration. Problem novelty reflects the degree (and type[1]) of abstraction needed to develop a mental representation of the problem. Problem novelty is not an indication of one's perception of familiarity. Usually problems that seem "familiar" are in fact the ones most susceptible to inference-based mental reasoning that is illusory (Kaufmann, 1980; Mahajan, 1992). If the degree of problem novelty is low, a very high proportion of one's mental representation of the problem is based on direct memory. Conversely, if the degree of novelty is high, a very low proportion of one's mental representation of the problem is based on direct memory. As the degree of problem novelty increases, the proportion of memory in one's mental representation of the problem decreases and the likelihood of miscalibration increases (Juslin, 1993; Wagenaar, 1988). The relationships between the degree of problem novelty and the functional usefulness of the different dialog symbols and actions proposed by the DSS dialog design theory are illustrated in Figure 5.3.

Figure 5.3 proposes that the usefulness of expressiveness, visibility, and inquirability depend upon the degree of problem novelty. If the degree of problem novelty is low, the functional usefulness of expressiveness for user calibration is high. In other words, for problems where the user's mental symbols and methods of reasoning are naturally linguistic, a DSS dialog based on expressiveness alone, when properly designed, may be sufficient to support effective decision making. However, as the degree of problem novelty increases, the usefulness of the expressiveness dimension decreases relative to visibility and inquirability characteristics. When the novelty of a problem requires that the decision maker employ a mental representation based on visual imagery to solve the problem, the DSS must provide the decision maker with effective visibility capabilities. Likewise, when the novelty of a problem requires that the user(s) employ overt exploratory reasoning to build a mental representation of the problem, effective support requires the DSS dialog to deliver necessary inquirability capabilities.

Figure 5.3   Functional Usefulness of DSS Dialog Symbols and Actions for Decision-Maker Calibration in Relation to the Degree of Problem Novelty

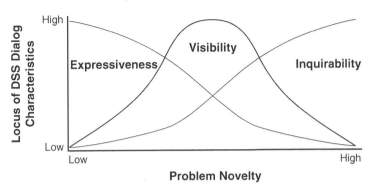

META-DESIGN AND DESIGN

Two aspects not discussed in the original presentation of the theory are meta-design and design (Walls et al., 2004). "Meta-design characterizes activities, processes, and objectives . . . that allow 'owners of problems' to act as designers and be creative" (Fischer et al., 2004, p. 35). In this way, design, learning, and development become part of every user's decision-making process. Moreover, for both practical and decision-making reasons, ". . . no matter how much designers and programmers try to anticipate and provide for what users will need, the effort always falls short because it is impossible to know in advance what may be needed. . . . End users should have the ability to create customizations, extensions, and applications . . ." to respond to their decision-making needs (Nadir, 1993, p. 3). The control inherent in this depiction of meta-design is essential to user calibration. One way to balance the illusory benefits of this control is through critiquing systems. "[A] critiquing system tests the credibility of a user's solution by examining the knowledge and judgment that she used to reach the solution" (Moulin et al., 2002, p. 182). Indeed, Vahidov and Elrod (1999) propose DSS that have two software agents, an "angel" and "devil," acting respectively as opponent and proponent of a user-suggested proposition. This dialectic process of debate is essential for perfect calibration.

EXAMPLES OF THE THEORY'S COMPONENTS

Examples of expressiveness, visibility, and inquirability abound, and several prototype systems already exist in various forms and stages of development. ELIZA (Weizenbaum, 1966) is perhaps the best-known example of the potential of expressiveness affects. Although dated, and crude by today's standards, ELIZA's expressiveness was very effective. A more futuristic example of expressiveness was depicted by the ultraintelligent computer system HAL in Arthur C. Clarke and Stanley Kubrick's 1968 classic science fiction screenplay *2001: A Space Odyssey*. HAL's anthropomorphic expressiveness was central to much of the movie's effectiveness.

Visual computing has rapidly become the standard for designing human-computer interfaces. One example known to many spreadsheet users is Palisade Corporation's @Risk, a risk analysis add-in for Microsoft Excel that displays output in graphic form. According to Palisade, @Risk allows one to "view" the results of their what-if analyses. Arena, another example of visualization, is simulation software that uses graphical images to improve user understanding by providing visual representations of the actual problem and operations.

Development of inquirability capabilities based on the dialectic method is not new (Nelson, 1973). However, very little research has been conducted on the effects of the different dialog actions of inquirability. Because of this, inquirability is the least developed of the three components of the theory.

In terms of a human metaphor, perhaps Helen Keller provides the best-known analogy for expressiveness, visibility, and inquirability capabilities. Left deaf and blind by an illness as a child, Keller's inquirability capabilities were intense and challenging, but she lacked the symbols to express herself (expressiveness) and "see" (visibility) the world until she was taught sign language.

The computer industry itself has proposed a number of futuristic systems that depict various combination and forms of expressiveness, visibility, and inquirability capabilities. One of the best known is *The Knowledge Navigator: Technologies to Get Us There and Beyond*, produced by Apple Computer in 1990. Another film that depicts several futuristic forms of the theory's components is *Multimedia Technology*, produced by Southwestern Bell Telephone in 1991. Both of these films depict very advanced levels of expressiveness, visibility, and inquirability by portraying ultraintelligent systems capable of asking challenging questions, anticipating and suggesting alternatives, and recognizing and synthesizing spoken language with multimedia visual display capabilities.

PARTIAL TEST OF THE THEORY OF DSS DESIGN FOR USER CALIBRATION

A design theory should be testable for it to be useful (Walls et al., 1992). Design theories predict that an artifact will achieve its goal to the extent that it possesses the properties prescribed by the theory (Walls et al., 1992). In the following we present a partial test of the theory of DSS design for user calibration.

Research Hypothesis

If users are to achieve perfect calibration, expressiveness and visibility must accurately convey the functioning and functionality of the DSS in relation to problem novelty, and expressiveness, visibility, and inquirability must accurately reflect and respond to problem novelty. For example, if the DSS are capable of sophisticated, dialectic reasoning, but problem novelty is low, user calibration is primarily dependent upon expressiveness accurately conveying the functioning and functionality of the DSS in relation to problem novelty, not in relation to the sophistication of the DSS. Conversely, if problem novelty is high but the DSS have limited inquirability, expressiveness and visibility may help the user recognize the limitations of the DSS, but they cannot compensate for the needed inquirability. In this way, expressiveness, visibility, and inquirability work together as a system in response to problem novelty, and are equally important for user calibration, either because they accurately convey the applicability or inapplicability of the DSS, or because they accurately reflect and respond to problem novelty.

Problem novelty, according to this design theory, determines the functional usefulness of expressiveness, visibility, and inquirability, for decision-making user calibration. Depicted in Figure 5.3, the theory of DSS design for user calibration posits that when problems are somewhat novel and unfamiliar (the midpoint along the x-axis), visibility is a more significant contributor to perfect calibration and expressiveness and inquirability play important but lesser, supporting roles. As problems become more familiar and problem novelty decreases, the theory posits that the contribution of expressiveness increases, equals, and eventually exceeds visibility as the primary contributor to user calibration. Stated in the null form, it is hypothesized that:

H_0: There is no difference in user calibration between subjects exposed to expressiveness and those exposed to visibility at either higher or lower levels of problem novelty.

In a perfect experiment, operationalizing the expressiveness treatment and visibility treatment would also have included some level of inquirability because according to the theory, inquirability is never completely absent from the mix of properties except perhaps at very low levels of problem novelty. Nevertheless, the basic experiment conducted in this research looks at expressiveness and visibility and for simplicity excludes inquirability and no treatment contains a mix of expressiveness and visibility. Also, the high and low levels of problem novelty lie to the left of the midpoint along the x-axis. This research merely claims that the treatments of problem novelty are reasonably different relative to each other to the left of the midpoint along the x-axis, with no specific indication of where precisely the treatments would lie. A research program is needed to properly assess the theory. What is being tested in this research is only the relative left part of the axis, and any theoretical claims from this research only apply to that part of the axis.

Experimental Design

To investigate this hypothesis, a laboratory experiment was conducted. The main effect studied was properties of DSS dialog design, and the dependent variable was user calibration. Specifically, the differential effect of expressiveness and visibility on user calibration was investigated. The experiment's design included two different problems to increase the generalizability of the findings and to build upon earlier related research, in particular, that of Bauer and Johnson-Laird (1993).

This research reports the results of a 2 × 2 × 2 laboratory experiment, looking at design (visibility diagrams vs. expressive text depictions) and problem novelty (higher or lower) in two different problem domains (people-and-places and electrical circuits). Four independent groups of participants were studied based on two factors: whether the problem format was verbal or diagrammatic, and whether the problem domain was people-and-places or electrical circuits.

After participants had completed the experimental task, two calculations of problem novelty, higher and lower, were defined by dividing each subject's responses into earlier and later decisions, again based on the work of Bauer and Johnson-Laird (1993) and Kaufmann (1980). The ten responses from each subject were divided into the first four that each subject answered and his or her last six responses. Bauer and Johnson-Laird (1993) used only four questions in their study. A calibration score was then computed for each of these two subsets for each subject. These subsets defined the two levels of problem novelty. Calibration based on the first four responses defined the higher category of problem novelty and calibration computed on the subject's last six responses defined the lower category of problem novelty.

Participants

A total of fifty-four students participated as subjects in the study. Most subjects were adult, non-traditional students reporting an average age of 30.3 years. Forty-seven percent of the subjects were female and 80 percent reported that English was their native language. Subjects were recruited from students enrolled in upper-division, undergraduate courses in information systems and psychology.

Seventy percent of the subjects in the study were information systems majors and the remainder was psychology majors. All participants volunteered for the study and were rewarded with course credit as required by American Psychological Association guidelines.

Forty subjects, ten in each group, completed all aspects of the experiment, followed all the instructions, and answered all the questions. To describe the groups' visual acuity, the sixteen-question Vividness of Visual Imagery Questionnaire (Marks, 1973) was administered.[2] As a group, subjects also reported average to above average (mean = 32.4, s.d. = 9.62) visual acuity as measured by the Vividness of Visual Imagery Questionnaire and self-reported "average" facility with logic and math problems. Although subjects were not given a specific time restriction, on average, they took about thirty-five minutes to complete all aspects of the study.

Experimental Decision Support System

The treatment combinations used in this study were borrowed directly from those developed by Bauer and Johnson-Laird (1993) to study deductive reasoning and inference.[3] They depicted logically identical problems as either people-and-places or electric circuit scenarios, and presented them as either text, a form of expressiveness, or diagrams, a form of visibility. An example of a people-and-places scenario presented as text is:

While the event is occurring:
Julia is in Atlanta or Ralph is in Tacoma (or both)
Julia is in Seattle or Paul is in Philadelphia (or both)
Ralph is in Tacoma or Paul is in Philadelphia (or both)
The event is occurring. What follows?
1.   Julia's in Seattle/Paul's in Philadelphia
2.   Paul's not in Philadelphia/Ralph's not in Tacoma
3.   Julia's not in Atlanta/Ralph's not in Tacoma/Paul's in Philadelphia
4.   Julia's in Atlanta/Paul's not in Philadelphia/Ralph's in Tacoma

A complete listing of the expressiveness treatments for the people-and-places scenario and the electrical circuits scenario are presented in Appendix A. Figure 5.4 shows the same problem as the example, but depicted as a visibility diagram. As can be seen, the shapes corresponding to the person fit only into a similarly shaped slot corresponding to a place. Subjects selected an alternative from a list of multiple-choice answers to the right of either the text or the diagram. To investigate the hypothesis of the study reported here, subjects also recorded their decision confidence in their selection.

The second problem representation, also borrowed from Bauer and Johnson-Laird, is an electric circuit scenario. An example of this scenario as text is:

While the light is on:
Switch A or B is on (or both)
Switch B is off or C is on (or both)
The light is on.
What follows?
1.   Nothing
2.   Close switch B and C

Figure 5.4   **Spatial-Visual Depiction of People-and-Places Scenario**

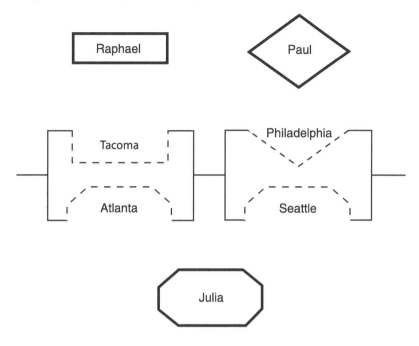

3. Close switch A and B
4. Close switch A and C

Note: B can be in one of three positions: on, off, or standby.[4]

The same problem is presented using a visibility diagram shown in Figure 5.5, with the same multiple choice options available from which to choose. The reader interested in a more detailed discussion of the problems used in this study is directed to original material presented in Bauer and Johnson-Laird (1993).

The Experiment's Procedure

Upon arrival, each subject was randomly assigned to one combination of the two treatment levels: the expressiveness or visibility, and people-and-places or electric circuits problem scenarios. A balanced number of subjects was assigned to each cell. The subject then read a two-page handout of instructions that included an example of the expressiveness or visibility display and the problem scenario, depending upon the treatment combination assigned. A description of the navigation procedures and operations they would be using to answer the multiple-choice questions was also presented. The instructions included a detailed discussion of the scoring rule, including a table of all possible scoring-rule outcomes that could be referred to throughout the study. The subject was then guided through a demonstration. Next, questions regarding the procedures and objectives of the study were answered. Each subject completed a consent form, a short, eleven-item questionnaire designed to collect descriptive demographic and background data, and the Vividness of Visual Imagery Questionnaire (Marks, 1973). The subject then began answering the

Figure 5.5   **Spatial-Visual Depiction of Electric Circuit Scenario**

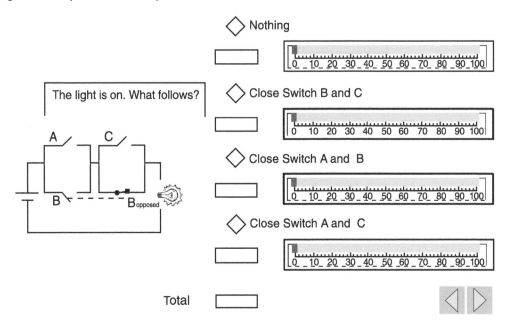

ten questions presented either as visibility diagrams or as expressive text, again as directed by the experiment's design.

To minimize any ordering effect, the ten questions in each treatment combination were counter-balanced with each question presented in each order position once. This resulted in ten different primary orderings of the ten questions in each treatment. Additionally, it was determined statistically that each of the ten questions presented were of the same level of difficulty. Each question was displayed and data collected using Dell II machines with 17″ monitors. The application was written in Assymetrix's ToolBook 4.0. An example of the display used in the study is shown in Figure 5.5.

For both the expressiveness and visibility problem representations, the problems were displayed on the left half of the screen and the potential answers on the right half of the screen. Figure 5.5 shows an example using the visibility diagram for the electric circuit scenario. The subject indicated his or her choice by clicking on the diamond next to the alternative. A v was placed in the diamond to indicate the selection. The subject used the slider just below each alternative to report his or her belief in the correctness of the selected alternative and other alternatives. The corresponding numerical value was displayed in the window to the left of the slider, and the sum of the four values was displayed in the Total window at the bottom of the screen. If the sum was not 100 ± .05, the subject was instructed to adjust the inputs. To proceed to the next question, the subject clicked on the arrow → at the bottom of the screen. This action also recorded the question data. By clicking on the ← arrow, the subject could return to the prior question. After answering all ten questions, the subject was debriefed, thanked, and dismissed.

Measuring User Calibration

To measure user calibration requires selecting a method and means for recording both decision quality and the subject's belief in the quality of each decision, a scoring rule and procedure that discourage gaming so that subjects are encouraged to report their beliefs honestly, and a formula for calculating calibration. Each of these requirements is discussed in the next sections.

Recording Beliefs and Decisions

Following the most common approach in calibration research for collecting data, subjects in this study answered a series of multiple-choice questions (such as those shown earlier) by reporting both their decisions and their confidence in the correctness of each decision. Each subject answered a total of ten multiple-choice questions. Four questions were the same questions used in Bauer and Johnson-Laird (1993) and the same truth table used by Bauer and Johnson-Laird (1993) was used to generate all questions used in this study. For each of these ten questions, the subject selected one alternative as the correct alternative, and then assigned a confidence value to that alternative and other alternatives, as desired. Analysis of pilot study data showed that assigning confidence values to multiple alternatives improved user calibration, a finding consistent with that of Sniezek, Paese, and Switzer (1990).

Recording Scales

Confidence is typically recorded on a scale ranging from 0 to 1 or some subset. In this study, this range was divided into increments of five-hundredths (i.e., 0.0, 0.05, 0.10, 0.15, . . . , 1.0) because research suggests that this is consistent with the respondent's "natural scaling" of decision confidence (Winkler, 1971).[5]

Scoring Rules

The purpose of a scoring rule is to encourage respondents to report their confidence honestly in each decision by eliciting values that reflect the respondent's actual belief in the quality of his or her selection. For this to occur, a scoring rule must (1) be understood by the subject so that its implications and the correspondence between beliefs and numerical values can be fully appreciated, and (2) maximize the subject's expected total score only when the subject reports values that correspond to his or her actual beliefs (Stael von Holstein, 1970). Assume that a subject's true decision confidence is expressed by the probability vector $P = (p_1, p_2, . . . , p_n)$ for a mutually exclusive and collectively exhaustive set of events, $\{E_1, E_2, . . . , E_n\}$. Assume further that the confidence values an assessor reports are represented by $R = (r_1, r_2, . . . , r_n)$. A proper scoring rule S exists if S is maximized only when $r = p$.

   This requirement is satisfied only by a very few somewhat complex scoring rules that require the respondent to perform high-level operations such as exponential, root, or log calculations (Murphy and Winkler, 1970). These complex operations make it almost impossible for subjects to quickly compute and fully appreciate the implications of their decisions and the correspondence between their actual beliefs and the values they report. In other words, these scoring rules confuse and may actually interfere with the subject's reporting values reflecting his or her actual beliefs.

   A scoring rule that meets the criterion of understandability is the well-known simple linear scoring rule $S_k(r) = r_k$, where k refers to the event that actually occurred and r_k is the confidence probability assigned by the subject to the kth response. Unfortunately, in its simplest form, this scoring rule is not strictly proper because $S(r,p) = \Sigma p_k r_k$ is maximized by setting one r_i (i.e., the r_i corresponding to the largest p_i) equal to 1.0 and the other r_is equal to 0.0. If $r_{i=k}$, then the subject appears to have complete confidence in the answer that turns out to be correct. On the other hand, if $r_{i \neq k}$, the subject appears totally wrong, but loses nothing because the scoring rule imposes no penalty for being wrong. In other words, a subject maximizes his or her score by assigning a confidence of 1.0 to one answer, despite his or her true belief in the quality of any answer.

Despite this limitation, most calibration research has used some variation of this simple linear scoring rule. In fact, comparing three complex proper scoring rules to the simple linear scoring rule, Rippey (1970) reported that the simple linear scoring rule actually produced more reliable results. Likewise, reviewing a number of these studies, Phillips (1970) concluded that the complex proper scoring rules did not yield significantly different values than those collected using a simple linear scoring rule, but, as expected, subjects found simple linear scoring rules more realistic and easier to understand.

Considering these tradeoffs, this study used a variant of the simple linear scoring rule that discouraged gaming and guessing by penalizing wrong answers. The scoring rule used here was:

$$S = r_k - [(\text{largest } r_{i \neq k})/2]$$

where S is the score, k refers to the correct alternative, r_k is the confidence probability assigned to that alternative, and $r_{i \neq k}$ are the confidence probabilities assigned to the alternatives that turn out to be incorrect. This variant of the simple scoring rule is easily understood because its implications can be more readily appreciated and the respondent can better understand the correspondence between her beliefs and the numerical values she reports. Yet, subjects are encouraged to report numerical values that correspond to their actual beliefs because of the penalty of one-half the largest confidence value assigned to an incorrect alternative choice. This results in a scoring rule that, for a four-alternative multiple-choice question, has a random guess expected value of .125 and a scoring range from 1.0 to −0.5.

Computing Calibration

The dependent variable for this study is calibration, the correspondence between an individual's confidence in a decision and the actual quality of the decision. The most popular calculation for calibration is:

$$\text{calibration} = \frac{1}{N} \sum_{t=1}^{T} n_t (r_t - c_t)^2$$

where N is the total number of responses, n_t is the number of times the confidence value r_t is used, c_t is the proportion correct for all items assigned confidence value r_t, and T is the total number of different response categories used (Clemen and Murphy, 1990). Using this formula, perfect calibration is a score of 0.0. The worst possible score, 1.0, can only be obtained when the responses are completely and consistently wrong, that is, $r_t = 1.0$ is always assigned to the wrong answer and $r_t = 0.0$ is always assigned to the answer that turns out to be correct.

Data Analysis

Analysis of this data shows that the content of the problem, electrical circuit or people and places, had no effect on either percentage correct (questions 1–4, $F_{(1,36)} = .08$, $p = 0.7$ and questions 5–10, $F_{(1,36)} = .01$, $p = 0.9$) or user calibration (questions 1–4, $F_{(1,36)} = .07$, $p = 0.7$ and questions

Figure 5.6   **Mean Calibration of Expressiveness (E) and Visibility (V) for Higher and Lower Problem Novelty**

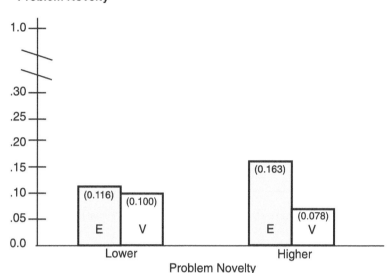

(Lower = mean calibration trials 5-10; Higher = mean calibration trials 1-4)

5–10, $F_{(1,36)}$ = .01, p = 0.9), so the data was collapsed over the problem content scenarios. In terms of percentage correct, these results are identical to those found by Bauer and Johnson-Laird (1990) who also collapsed the data over the same people-and-places and electric circuit scenarios. The mean of user calibration of this pooled data is shown for expressiveness and visibility for the two problem novelty categories in Figure 5.6, with the calibration mean printed in each bar. Recall that perfect calibration is zero, thus, the shorter the bar, the better the performance. Likewise, problem novelty is categorized from lower, calibration based on the last six questions answered by each subject, to higher, where the first four questions were used to compute calibration.

For the visibility (V) treatment, Figure 5.6 shows that average user calibration was overall the best, closest to zero, at the higher category of problem novelty (.078). The next best level of user calibration was at the visibility (V) lower category of problem novelty (.100). Comparing these results, the data suggest that the same subjects exposed to the visibility (V) treatment produced better user calibration in the first four tries (.078), when problem novelty was highest, than they did over the last six tries (.100) when problem novelty was lower.

For the expressiveness (E) treatment, the results in Figure 5.6 show that subjects exposed to the expressiveness (E) treatment had on average poorer calibration than did those exposed to visibility. Expressiveness produced the poorest average user calibration at both the higher and lower categories of problem novelty (.163 and .116). However, comparing the two expressiveness (E) bars shows that there was a marked improvement in user calibration from the higher to the lower category of problem novelty for those exposed to expressiveness (.163 to .116). In this regard, the change in user calibration for those exposed to the expressiveness treatment was as might be expected: user calibration improved as problem novelty decreased.

To assess the statistical significance of the differences in user calibration suggested by the means depicted in Figure 5.6, a multivariate analysis of variance (MANOVA) was computed using the two dependent variables, user calibration at the higher and lower groupings of problem novelty,

Table 5.1

Analysis of Variance of User Calibration for Higher (questions 1–4) and Lower Problem Novelty (questions 5–10)

a. ANOVA Results of User Calibration by Linguistic-Verbal and Spatial-Visual for Higher Problem Novelty (questions 1–4)

Source	d.f.	Type III SS	F-value	p-value
Expressiveness/Visibility	1	.073	5.232	.028*
Error	38	.528		
Corrected Total	39	.601		

$R^2 = .121$
*p < .05

b. ANOVA Results of User Calibration by Linguistic-Verbal and Spatial-Visual for Lower Problem Novelty (questions 5–10)

Source	d.f.	Type III SS	F-value	p-value
Expressiveness/Visibility	1	.002	.229	.635
Error	38	.405		
Corrected Total	39	.407		

$R^2 = .006$

and the independent variable of DSS locus of design, either expressiveness or visibility, for each subject. This model produced a Wilks Lambda treatment effect of $F_{(2,37)} = 2.8, p = 0.07$. Although not significant at the $\alpha = 0.05$ level, this result suggests significant univariate effects. Indeed, in the case of strong positive correlation between the dependent variables ($r = 0.45, p = 0.0031$), and interaction consistent with that hypothesized in Figure 5.3, the multivariate test is less powerful than it would be if the data were negatively correlated. In other words, the Wilks Lambda F-value may be confounded by the nature of the interaction between dependent variables.

To clarify the MANOVA results, analysis of variance (ANOVA) was computed for the higher and lower groupings of problem novelty separately. The results of these analyses are presented in Table 5.1.

The first ANOVA, Table 5.1a, shows results for data from the higher category of problem novelty. Subjects using the visibility (V) treatment were much better calibrated (0.078), had calibration scores closer to zero, than were those assigned to the expressiveness (E) treatment (0.163). These data show that subjects exposed to visibility produced user calibration that was significantly better than those subjects exposed to expressiveness ($F_{(2,37)} = 5.23, p = 0.028$). The Bonferroni minimum significant difference of 0.0755 confirms that the difference between 0.163 and 0.078 is significant at the $\alpha = 0.05$ level. For this data, H_0 can be rejected. The evidence shows that for the higher category of problem novelty (i.e., when the problems were the most novel), the average calibration of subjects using visibility diagrams was significantly better than it was for those subjects using expressive text.

The results of the ANOVA for the lower category of problem novelty are presented in Table 5.1b. There seems to be little difference between the average calibration of those exposed to expressiveness (E) (0.116) and those exposed to visibility (V) (0.100). These data show no significant difference in user calibration as a result of visibility and expressiveness treatment levels ($F_{(2,37)}$ = .229, p = 0.635). The Bonferroni minimum significant difference of 0.0661 exceeds the 0.016 difference in means (0.116–0.100). In this case, H_0 cannot be rejected. The data indicate that when problem novelty was lower and problems were more familiar and less novel, there was no difference in user calibration between subjects using visibility diagrams and those using expressive text.

Analyses also showed no significant difference in user calibration due to VVIQ subject differences (questions 1–4, $F_{(1,37)}$ = 2.57, p = 0.12, questions 5–10, $F_{(1,37)}$ = .14, p = 0.71) or decision time. These results add to the generalizability of the main finding that visibility improves user calibration when problems are new and somewhat novel.

SUMMARY AND CONCLUSIONS

To frame the theory of DSS design for user calibration as a dialog design theory, this paper began by reviewing the general concepts and components of DSS. Next, we drew extensively upon Kasper (1996) to describe the theory. We began by describing the kernel theories. Next we present the properties needed to achieve the goal of perfect calibration, including meta-design and critiquing.

Based on these ideas a hypothesis was posited. A test of this hypothesis provided a partial test of the theory of DSS design for user calibration. Specifically, the laboratory study compared the effects of expressiveness and visibility on user calibration at two levels of problem novelty. The results of this study supported the theory. When problems were new and novel, visibility diagrams significantly improved user calibration compared to expressive text. Later, when problems became more familiar, less novel, there was no difference in user calibration between visibility and expressiveness treatment levels.

IMPLICATIONS FOR FUTURE DSS RESEARCH AND PRACTICE

Although the research reported here is a beginning, focused on relatively simple forms of expressiveness and visibility, the long-term goal of this research program is to identify and investigate the effect of forms of expressiveness, visibility, and inquirability on user calibration under differing levels of problem novelty. At a minimum, this finding of a significant result encourages more empirical research into these effects.

At this first-study stage in this research program, recommendations and generalizations are a stretch. However, it can be said that developers of DSS must be increasingly conscious of visual imagery and visual computing as both influence decision quality (Gonzalez and Kasper, 1997; Speier and Morris, 2003) and user calibration, and that these effects have been demonstrated when the problems being addressed are episodic, new and novel to the decision maker. These results help move the visual computing paradigm from one of engaging and entertaining the user to one of decision supporting and improving user calibration in which the decision maker gains a better appreciation for the quality of the decision he or she is making using the DSS (Shneiderman, 1992).

How the DSS itself should shift among forms and depictions of expressiveness, visibility, and inquirability in consideration of problem novelty to achieve perfect calibration is an essential research stream. A DSS dialog could be a static architecture with fixed forms of the three modes corresponding to a static level of problem novelty, or the dialog could consist of a dynamic architecture that would shift among the three modes varying its presentation with respect to the level of problem novelty involved. Wood, reported by Johnson-Laird (1993), confirmed experimentally that subjects attack problems through imagery in the initial phase of problem solving, and as a consequence of increasing familiarity with the problems, they subsequently switch over to linguistic representation. Whether it is optimal for decision makers to choose among forms and depictions based on their assessment of problem novelty or to have this done without user input using within subjects experiments is also worthy of investigation.

This research presents two treatments for problem novelty based on dividing the problems into the first four and the next six problems. But this treatment is actually a combination of task-system treatment, since both the task and the system are more novel in the first four problems than in the next six. More complex experiments, where treatments are divided into four, with the task and/or system systematically varied among the subjects, could be conducted. These would further comment on the task-system aspect of decision making, and on how it affects decision-maker calibration, by determining how task and system combinations can affect problem novelty—which, in turn, will alter the properties of the optimal DSS dialog design to achieve perfect calibration.

Larkin and Simon (1987), Bauer and Johnson-Laird (1993), and Speier and Morris (2003) report that diagrams improved decision quality. The results reported here demonstrate that visibility diagrams also improve user calibration. Collectively, these studies suggest that visibility results in better decisions and that decision makers are better calibrated as to the quality of their decisions, at least in the environment in which the experiments were carried out. Specifically, when problems are new and novel, visibility improves user calibration.

The process of refutation is central to science, and this experiment is but one of many with varying methods, designs, instantiations, and mixes of expressiveness, visibility, and inquirability required to provide sufficient evidence of the theory's utility. It is in the collective that greater understanding emerges. As a first study, the treatments used in this study are modest approximations of the theory. However, before great time and effort is expended, this first study seems prudent. Researchers can now invest their time, effort, and resources with greater confidence.

Further research is needed to investigate the theory with much greater specificity, including variations on the mix of expressiveness, visibility and inquirability. Follow-up studies will necessarily be more detailed, incorporate more of the theory—especially in terms of an "effective mix" of expressiveness, visibility, and inquirability—and will eventually need to move out of the laboratory and into the real world. No matter how "realistic," all laboratory studies are contrived approximations of reality. Nevertheless, this first study is a necessary step in substantiating the theory of DSS design for user calibration.

APPENDIX 5.1. PEOPLE AND PLACES QUESTIONS IN EXPRESSIVENESS TREATMENT

1. When the event is occurring:
    Sally is in Ann Arbor or Jack is in Pittsburgh (or both)
    Jack is not in Pittsburgh or Jason is in New York (or both)
    The event is occurring. What follows?
    a. Sally's in Ann Arbor/Jason's not in New York
    b. Sally's in Ann Arbor/Jack's not in Pittsburgh
    c. Sally's not in Ann Arbor/Jack's in Pittsburgh
    d. Jason's in New York/Sally's not in Ann Arbor

2. When the event is occurring:
    Jack is in Pittsburgh or Carmen is in Chicago (but not both)
    Jason is in New York or Carmen is in Chicago (but not both)
    The event is occurring. What follows?
    a. Jack's in Pittsburgh/Carmen's in Chicago

    b. Carmen's in Chicago/Jason's in New York
    c. Jason's in New York/Jack's in Pittsburgh
    d. Jack's not in Pittsburgh/Jason's in New York

3.   When the event is occurring:
    John is in Boulder or Sally is in Ann Arbor (or both)
    Sally is in Ann Arbor or Joe is in Orlando (or both)
    The event is occurring. What follows?
    a. Sally's in Ann Arbor/John's in Boulder
    b. Sally's in Orlando/John's in Boulder
    c. Joe's in Orlando/Sally's not in Ann Arbor
    d. Joe's in Boulder/John's in Orlando

4.   When the event is occurring:
    Karl is in LA or Lydia is in Baltimore (but not both)
    Marcie is in Minneapolis or Lydia is in Detroit (but not both)
    The event is occurring. What follows?
    a. Karl's in LA/Lydia's in Baltimore
    b. Lydia's in Detroit/Karl's in LA
    c. Marcie's in Minneapolis/Lydia's in Detroit
    d. Karl's not in LA/Lydia's in Detroit

5.   When the event is occurring:
    Julia is in Atlanta or Ralph is in Tacoma (or both)
    Julia is in Seattle or Paul is in Philadelphia (or both)
    Ralph is in Tacoma or Paul is in Philadelphia (or both)
    The event is occurring. What follows?
    a. Julia's in Seattle/Paul's in Philadelphia
    b. Paul's not in Philadelphia/Ralph's not in Tacoma
    c. Julia's not in Atlanta/Ralph's not in Tacoma/Paul's in Philadelphia
    d. Julia's in Atlanta/Paul's not in Philadelphia/Ralph's in Tacoma

6.   When the event is occurring:
    Jack is in Pittsburgh or Julia is in Atlanta (but not both)
    Jason is in New York or Julia is in Seattle (but not both)
    Julia is in Atlanta or Jason is in Seattle (but not both)
    The event is occurring. What follows?
    a. Julia's in Atlanta/Jason's in Seattle
    b. Jack's in Pittsburgh/Jason's in New York
    c. Julia's in Seattle/Jack's in Pittsburgh
    d. Jack's not in Pittsburgh/Jason's not in New York

7.   When the event is occurring:
    Sally is in Ann Arbor or John is in Boulder (or both)
    Sally is in Ann Arbor or Joe is in Orlando (or both)
    John is in Boulder or Joe is in Orlando (or both)
    The event is occurring. What follows?
    a. Sally's in Ann Arbor/John's in Boulder
    b. Sally's not in Ann Arbor/Joe's in Boulder/John's in Orlando
    c. Joe's not in Orlando/Sally's not in Ann Arbor
    d. John's not in Boulder/Joe's not in Orlando

8. When the event is occurring:
   Lydia is in Baltimore or Karl is in LA (but not both)
   Lydia is in Detroit or Marcie is in Minneapolis (but not both)
   Lydia is in Baltimore or Marcie is in Detroit (but not both)
   The event is occurring. What follows?
   a. Lydia's in Detroit/Marcie's in Minneapolis
   b. Marcie's in Detroit/Karl's in LA
   c. Karl's in LA/Lydia's in Baltimore
   d. Marcie's in Detroit/Lydia's in Baltimore

9. When the event is occurring:
   Julia is in Atlanta or Ralph is in Tacoma (or both)
   Julia is in Seattle or Paul is in Philadelphia (or both)
   Ralph is in Tacoma or Paul is in Philadelphia (or both)
   The event is occurring. What follows?
   a. Ralph's in Tacoma/Paul's in Philadelphia
   b. Ralph's in Tacoma/Julia's in Atlanta
   c. Paul's in Philadelphia/Ralph's in Seattle
   d. Julia's not in Atlanta/Paul's in Philadelphia

10. When the event is occurring:
    Carmen is in Chicago or Ralph is in Tacoma (but not both)
    Carmen is in Chicago or Paul is in Philadelphia (but not both)
    The event is occurring. What follows?
    a. Carmen's in Chicago/Ralph's in Tacoma
    b. Carmen's in Chicago/Paul's in Philadelphia
    c. Paul's in Philadelphia/Ralph's not in Tacoma
    d. Paul's in Philadelphia/Ralph's in Tacoma

NOTES

1. See Dalal and Kasper (1994) for discussions of type of abstraction as it relates to the interaction of DSS, user, and problem.

2. The Vividness of Visual Imagery questionnaire produces an index on the quality of mental images formed by a respondent. Based on ratings from 1 (the mental image is clear and vivid) to 5 (no mental image is formed at all) for sixteen descriptions, the instrument's reliability is reported to range from 0.85 to 0.94, and it has been used in over one hundred studies (Marks, 1973; McKelvie, 1995).

3. We wish to thank Malcolm Bauer and P. N. Johnson-Laird for providing us with copies of their material.

4. Bauer and Johnson-Laird introduced the standby position of the switch (in which it is neither on nor off) so that the circuit problems would be equivalent to the three people-and-places problem possibilities: A may be in X, or A may be in Y, or A may be in neither X nor Y.

5. Based on 34,425 two-digit, self-reported responses, Winkler (1971) reported that 85 percent of the estimates ended in either zero or five (i.e., .05, .10, .15, .20 .25, etc.), and that these tendencies remained virtually constant over thirteen trials. In other words, given a choice, respondents tend to report their decision confidence in increments of 0.05.

REFERENCES

Aldag, R.J., and Powers, D.J. An empirical assessment of computer-assisted decision analysis. *Decision Sciences*, 17, 4 (1986), 572–588.

Alter, S. Why is man-computer interaction important for decision support systems? *Interfaces*, 7, 2 (1977), 109–115.

Arkes, H.R.; Christensen, C.; Lai, C.; and Blumer, C. Two methods of reducing overconfidence. *Organizational Behavior and Human Decision Processes*, 39, 1 (1987), 133–144.

Ashford, B., and Kasper, G.M. A test of the theory of DSS design for user calibration. In *Proceedings of the Second Annual Workshop on Human-Computer Interaction Research*, Seattle, WA, 2003, pp. 27–31.

Bauer, M.I., and Johnson-Laird, P.N. How diagrams can improve reasoning. *Psychological Science*, 4, 6 (1993), 372–378.

Bickmore, T., and Cassell, J. Relational agents: a model and implementation of building user trust. In *Proceedings of the SIGCHI Conference on Human Factors in Computing Systems*, Seattle, WA, 2001, pp. 396–403.

Blanning, R.W. Model management systems: an overview. *Decision Support Systems, Special Issue on Model Management Systems*, 9, 1 (1993), 9–18.

Block, R.A., and Harper, D.R. Overconfidence in estimation: testing the anchoring-and-adjustment hypothesis. *Organizational Behavior and Human Decision Processes*, 49, 2 (1991), 188–207.

Bonczek, R.H.; Holsapple, C.W.; and Whinston, A.B. *Foundations of Decision Support Systems*. New York: Academic Press, 1981.

Brown, G., and Yule, G. *Discourse Analysis*. London: Cambridge University Press, 1983.

Brown, P.S., and Gould, J.D. An experimental study of people creating spreadsheets. *ACM Transactions on Office Information Systems*, 5, 3 (1987), 258–272.

Buchheit, P., and Moher, T. Response assertiveness in human-computer dialogue. *International Journal of Man-Machine Studies*, 32, 1 (1990), 109–117.

Buyukkurt, B.K., and Buyukkurt, M.D. An experimental study of the effectiveness of three debiasing techniques. *Decision Sciences*, 22, 1 (1990), 14–31.

Churchman, C. *The Design of Inquiring Systems*. New York: Basic Books, 1971.

Clemen, R.T., and Murphy, A.H. The expected value of frequency calibration. *Organizational Behavior and Human Decision Processes*, 46, 1 (1990), 102–117.

Cosier, R.A., and Schwenk, C.R. Agreement and thinking alike: ingredients for poor decisions. *Academy of Management Executive*, 4, 1 (1990), 69–74.

Curl, S.; Olfman, L.; and Satzinger, J. An investigation of the roles of individual differences and user interface on database usability. *The DATA BASE for Advances in Information Systems*, 29, 1 (1988), 50–65.

Dalal, N.J., and Kasper, G.M. The design of joint cognitive systems: the effect of cognitive coupling on performance. *International Journal of Man-Machine Studies*, 40, 4 (1994), 677–702.

Davis, F.D.; Kottemann, J.E.; and Remus, W.E. What-if analysis and the illusion of control. In *Proceedings of the Twenty-Fourth Annual Hawaii International Conference on Systems Sciences*, Kauai, Hawaii, 1991, 452–460.

Dunbar, R.L.M., and Goldberg, W.H. Crisis development and strategic response in European corporations. In C.F. Smart and W.T. Stanbury (eds.), *Studies on Crisis Management*. Toronto: Butterfield and Company, 1978, pp. 140–149.

Edwards, J.L., and Mason, J.A. Evaluating the intelligence in dialog systems. *International Journal of Man-Machine Studies*, 28, 2/3 (1988), 139–173.

Einhorn, H.J., and Hogarth, R.M. Confidence in judgment persistence of the illusion of validity. *Psychological Review*, 85, 5 (1978), 395–416.

Faust, D. Learning and maintaining rules for decreasing judgment accuracy. *Journal of Personality Assessment*, 50, 4 (1986), 585–600.

Fazlollahi, B., and Vadihov, W.S. Method for generation of alternatives by decision support systems. *Journal of Management Information Systems*, 18, 2 (2001), 229–250.

Fischer, G.; Giaccardi, E.; Ye, Y.; Sutcliffe, A.G.; and Mehandjiev, N. Meta-design: a manifesto for end-user development. *Communications of the ACM*, 47, 9 (2004), 33–37.

Ginzberg, M.J., and Stohr, E.A. Decision support systems: issues and perspectives. In M.J. Ginzberg, W. Reitman, and E.A. Stohr (eds.), *Decision Support Systems*. Amsterdam: North Holland, 1982, 9–31.

Gonzalez, C., and Kasper, G.M. Animation in user interfaces designed for decision support systems: the effects of image abstraction, transition, and interactivity on decision quality. *Decision Sciences*, 28, 4 (1997), 793–823.

Gorry, G.A., and Scott Morton, M.S. A framework for management information systems. *Sloan Management Review*, 13, 1 (1971), 55–70.

Hartson, H.R., and Hix, D. Human-computer interface development: concepts and systems for its management. *Computing Surveys*, 21, 1 (1989), 5–92.

Helstrup, T. One, two, or three memories? A problem-solving approach to memory for performed acts. *Acta Psychologica*, 66 (1987), 37–68.

Henderson, J.C. Finding synergy between decision support systems and expert systems research. *Decision Sciences*, 18, 3 (1987), 333–349.

Huber, G. Cognitive style as a basis for MIS and DSS design: much ado about nothing. *Management Science*, 29, 5 (1983), 567–579.

Humphreys, P. *Intelligence in Decision Support.* B.V. (North-Holland): Elsevier Science Publishers, 1986.

Juslin, P. An explanation of the hard-easy effect in studies of realism of confidence in one's general knowledge. *European Journal of Cognitive Psychology*, 5, 1 (1993), 55–71.

Kasper, G.M. A theory of decision support systems for user calibration. *Information Systems Research*, 7, 2 (1996), 215–232.

Kass, R., and Finin, T. Modeling the user in natural language systems. *Computational Linguistics*, 14, 3 (1988), 5–22.

Kaufmann, G. The many faces of mental images. In C. Cornoldi, R.H. Logie, M.A. Brandimonte, G. Kaufmann, and D. Reisberg (eds.), *Stretching the Imagination: Representation and Transformation in Mental Imagery.* New York: Oxford University Press, 1996, pp. 77–118.

Kaufmann, G. *Imagery, Language and Cognition: Toward a Theory of Symbolic Activity in Problem-Solving*, Universitetsforlaget, Norway: Columbia University Press. 1980.

Kaufmann, G. A theory of symbolic representation in problem solving. *Journal of Mental Imagery*, 9, 2 (1985), 51–70.

Keen, P.G.W. Decision support systems: the next decade. *Decision Support Systems*, 3 (1987), 253–265.

Keen, P.G.W., and Scott Morton, M.S. *Decision Support Systems: An Organizational Perspective.* Reading, MA: Addison-Wesley, 1978.

Keller, P.R., and Keller, M.M. *Visual Cues: Practical Data Visualization.* Los Alamitos, CA: IEEE Computer Society Press, 1993.

Kerschberg, L. Knowledge management in heterogeneous data warehouse environments. In *Proceedings of the International Conference on Data Warehousing and Knowledge Discovery*, Munich, Germany, (2001), 1–10.

Koriat, A.; Lichtenstein, S.; and Fischhoff, B. Reasons for confidence. *Journal of Experimental Psychology: Human Learning and Memory*, 6, 2 (1980), 107–118.

Larkin, J., and Simon, H. Why a diagram is (sometimes) worth 10,000 words. *Cognitive Sciences*, 11 (1987), 65–99.

Liang, T.P. Model management for group decision support. *MIS Quarterly*, 12, 4 (1988), 667–680.

Lichtenstein, S.; Fischhoff, B.; and Phillips, L. Calibration of probabilities: the state of the art to 1980. In D. Kahneman, P. Slovic, and A. Tversky (eds.), *Judgment Under Uncertainty: Heuristics and Biases.* Cambridge: Cambridge University Press, 1982, pp. 306–334.

Licklider, J.C.R. Man-computer symbiosis. *IRE Transactions on Human Factors in Electronics*, 1, (1960), 4–11.

Luconi, F.L.; Malone, T.W.; and Morton, M.S.S. Expert systems: the next challenge for managers. *Sloan Management Review*, 27, 4 (1986), 3–14.

Ma, J. Type and inheritance theory for model management. *Decision Support Systems*, 19, 1 (1997), 53–60.

Mahajan, J. The overconfidence effect in marketing management predictions. *Journal of Marketing Research*, 29, 3 (1992), 393–342.

Manheim, M.L. An architecture for active DSS. In *Proceedings of the Twenty-First Annual Hawaii Conference on System Sciences*, Honolulu, Hawaii, 1988, 356–365.

Marks, D.F. Visual imagery differences in the recall of pictures. *Journal of Psychology*, 64, 1 (1973), 17–24.

Markus, M.L.; Majchrzak, A.; and Gasser, L. A design theory for systems that support emergent knowledge processes. *MIS Quarterly*, 26, 3 (2002), 179–212.

Mason, R.O. A dialectical approach to strategic management. *Management Science*, 15, 8 (1969), B-403–B-414.

Mason, R.O., and Mitroff, I.I. A program for research on management information systems. *Management Science*, 19, 5 (1973), 475–487.

McCormick, B.H.; DeFanti, T.A.; and Brown, M.D. Visualization in scientific computing. *Computer Graphics*, 21, 6 (1987), entire issue.

McKelvie, S. *Vividness of Visual Imagery: Measurement, Nature, Function and Dynamics.* Bronx, NY: Brandon House, 1995.

Moulin, B.; Irandoust, H.; Belanger, M.; and Desbordes, G. Explanation and argumentation capabilities: towards the creation of more persuasive agents. *Artificial Intelligence Review*, 17 (2002), 169–222.

Muir, B.M. Trust between humans and machines, and the design of decision aids. *International Journal of Man-Machine Studies*, 27, 5 (1987), 527–539.

Murphy, A.H., and Winkler, R.L. Scoring rules in probability assessment and evaluation. *Acta Psychologica*, 34 (1970), 273–286.

Nadir, B. *Perspectives on End User Computing*. Cambridge, MA: MIT Press, 1993.

Nelson, J.A. Dialectic information systems: a methodology for planning and decision making. PhD Dissertation, University of Pittsburgh, 1973.

Newell, A., and Simon, H.A. *Human Problem Solving*. Englewood Cliffs, NJ: Prentice Hall, 1972.

Olson, G.M., and Olson, J.S. User-centered design of collaborative technology. *Organizational Computing*, 1, 1 (1991), 61–83.

Phillips, L.D. The "true probability" problem. *Acta Psychologica*, 34 (1970), 254–264.

Quintanar, L.R.; Crowell, C.R.; Pryor, J.B.; and Adamopoulos, J. Human-computer interaction: a preliminary social psychological analysis. *Behavior Research Methods and Instrumentation*, 14, 2 (1982), 210–220.

Remus, W.E., and Kottemann, J. Toward intelligent decision support systems: an artificially intelligent statistician. *MIS Quarterly*, 10, 4 (1986), 403–418.

Rippey, R.M. A comparison of five different scoring functions for confidence tests. *Journal of Educational Measurement*, 7 (1970), 165–170.

Russo, J.E., and Schoemaker, P.J. Managing overconfidence. *Sloan Management Review* (1992), 7–17.

Scott Morton, M.S. *The State of the Art of Research*. Cambridge, MA: Harvard Business School Press, 1984.

Shneiderman, B. *Designing the User Interface: Strategies for Effective Human-Computer Interaction*. Reading, MA: Addison-Wesley, 1987.

Shneiderman, B. *Designing the User Interface: Strategies for Effective Human-Computer Interaction*, 2nd ed. Reading, MA: Addison-Wesley, 1992.

Simon, H.A. *The New Science of Management Decision*. New York: Harper and Row, 1960.

Sniezek, J.A.; Pease, P.W.; and Switzer, F.S., III. The effect of choosing on confidence in choice. *Organizational Behavior and Human Decision Processes*, 46, 2 (1990), 264–282.

Speier, C., and Morris, M.G. The influence of query interface design on decision-making performance. *MIS Quarterly*, 27, 3 (2003), 397–423.

Sprague, R., and Carlson, E. *Building Effective Decision Support Systems*. Englewood Cliffs, NJ: Prentice Hall, 1982.

Stael von Holstein, C.A. Measurement of subjective probability. *Acta Psychologica*, 34 (1970), 146–159.

Staw, B.M. The escalation of commitment to a course of action. *Academy of Management Review*, 6 (1981), 577–587.

Thomsen, E. *OLAP Solutions-Building Multidimensional Information Systems*. John Wiley & Sons, 2002.

Vahidov, R., and Elrod, R. Incorporating Critique and Argumentation in DSS. *Decision Support Systems*, 26 (1999), 249–258.

Veryard, R. The role of spatial-visual in systems. *Human Systems Management*, 6, 2 (1986), 167–175.

Wagenaar, W.A. Calibration and the effects of knowledge and reconstruction in retrieval from memory. *Cognition*, 28 (1988), 277–296.

Walls, J.G.; Widmeyer, G.R.; and El Sawy, O.A. Assessing information systems design theory in perspective: how was our 1992 initial rendition? *Journal of Information Technology Theory and Application*, 6, 2 (2004), 43–58.

Walls, J.G.; Widmeyer, G.R.; and El Sawy, O.A. Building an information systems design theory for vigilant EIS. *Information Systems Research*, 3, 1 (1992), 36–59.

Weizenbaum, J. ELIZA—a computer program for the study of natural language communication between man and machine. *Communications of the ACM*, 9, 1 (1966), 36–45.

Winkler, R. Probabilistic predictions: some experimental results. *Journal of the American Statistical Association*, 66, 336 (1971), 675–685.

CHAPTER 6

DECISIONAL GUIDANCE

Broadening the Scope

MARK S. SILVER

Abstract: *Decisional guidance was introduced as a design feature of decision support systems (DSS) more than a decade ago. It was originally defined as how a DSS enlightens or sways its users as they choose among and use the system's functional capabilities. Unlike mechanical guidance, the interface feature that helps users with the technicalities of invoking and using functionality, decisional guidance provides more substantive support for exercising discretion when choosing which functions to employ and while employing them. During the years since its introduction, decisional guidance has been used to study not only DSS but also a variety of other information systems, including group support systems, executive information systems, and CASE tools. This paper begins by summarizing the basic concepts of decisional guidance and reviewing how it has been studied empirically over the years. The paper revises the original definition in light of the review and broadens it to apply to information systems more generally. The typology of guidance is also updated. The paper concludes by presenting a more focused agenda for research based on the refined typology.*

Keywords: *Decisional Guidance, System Restrictiveness, System Design, System Effects, System Features, System Flexibility*

Decisional guidance refers to the features of an information system that affect the choices people make when interacting with that system. Users of an interactive system typically confront numerous choices, such as what to do next, which option to select, or what input value to provide. System features can guide these choices either deliberately, when guidance is intentionally built into a system, or inadvertently, as an unplanned consequence of the system's design. Even guidance that is deliberate is not necessarily directive; decisional guidance may sometimes attempt to influence the user's choice but other times may only enable a more informed choice.

Consider a few examples:

- A user of a statistical package is about to run a regression analysis. The software asks him if he wants to transform the data first. The user does not know why he would want to do this, but when he presses the Help button the system explains the implications of autocorrelation.
- An electronic spreadsheet supports ten different chart types, each with ten subtypes. A user is about to plot time series data and must select one of the one hundred possible chart types. The system recognizes that the data represent a time series and recommends the chart type and subtype the user used for time series data in the past.
- An architect is designing a building with CAD software. After he makes a series of design choices, the system warns him that the building is structurally unsound.

- A user is configuring a computer that she plans to purchase online. She is asked how much RAM she wants. The Web site provides information to help her choose.
- A user is shopping for a DVD player at an e-commerce Web site. The site asks her a series of questions about her preferences and then recommends three models.
- A word processor supports seventy-five different fonts, listed alphabetically. After going through about twenty of them, the user tires of the process and picks Century Gothic. Had he gone through the whole list, he would have selected Verdana. The order of the items played a role in which font was chosen.

These examples differ in many ways, but each represents a situation where the system affords the user an opportunity to exercise discretion and also contains a feature—decisional guidance—that could affect the choice the user makes.

The study of decisional guidance was motivated more than a decade ago by the observation that all but the most restrictive of interactive systems afford their users a range of behaviors. Understanding how the users of an interactive computer-based system behave—arguably the central issue in designing and studying those systems—therefore depends on understanding (1) the choices the system affords its users and (2) how the system's design features affect the choices users make. The former issue—how a system allows or constrains user discretion—is referred to as "system restrictiveness." The latter—how a system affects user behavior subject to those constraints—is referred to as the system's "decisional guidance" (Silver, 1990, 1991a, 1991b).

The modifier "decisional" is significant because it distinguishes decisional guidance from the "mechanical guidance" much more commonly found in interactive systems. While mechanical guidance helps users with the mechanics of how to invoke and use a system's functionality—for example, by providing help screens or tool tips—decisional guidance addresses the more substantive issue of how users exercise their discretion: which functions they select and how they behave while using them. For instance, mechanical guidance might provide a list of available functions, whereas decisional guidance might provide information about each function. Mechanical guidance might identify what to click to invoke a particular function, whereas decisional guidance might help determine which function to invoke. Mechanical guidance might indicate that a given input must be non-negative, but decisional guidance might help the user determine the most appropriate input value.

Decisional guidance was first studied in the context of decision support systems (DSS)—systems that affect, or are intended to affect, how people make decisions (Silver, 1991b). DSS constituted the first venue for exploring this attribute, in part, because DSS were among the first interactive computer-based systems studied by the information systems field. More significantly, decisional guidance was introduced in the DSS context because the concept is essential for truly understanding DSS. Computer-based decision support focuses on the processes through which users make decisions and the outcomes of those processes. The many choices that users make when selecting among and interacting with the system's functionality—the decision aids—determine the process and outcomes. Understanding how a system's features affect those choices—that is, which decision aids users employ and what inputs they supply—is therefore central to studying or designing DSS. And that is precisely what decisional guidance is about.

In the context of DSS, decisional guidance was defined as follows:

Decisional Guidance: How a Decision Support System enlightens or sways its users as they structure and execute their decision-making processes—that is, as they choose among and use the system's functional capabilities. (Silver, 1991a, p. 107).

Although this definition is expressed in the language of DSS—and decisional guidance may be especially significant in the DSS realm—the underlying concept applies to any interactive system that affords its users discretion. Use of such systems is intended to accomplish some task, so each point of interaction that allows users discretion represents a point at which decisional guidance might be in play, affecting the outcome of the task. Over the years researchers have applied decisional guidance not only to individual decision support but also to such other domains as group decision support systems (GDSS), executive information systems, CASE tools, and conceptual data modeling. Moreover, in the time since decisional guidance was introduced, use of applications software has grown dramatically with the popularity first of productivity tools (spreadsheets, word processors, presentation graphics, and the like) and now of browser-based applications for e-business and other activities on the Internet. These applications, too, demand analysis in terms of decisional guidance.

My previous work on decisional guidance (Silver, 1991a, 1991b) was intended to serve several purposes:

- To make researchers and practitioners aware of a set of design issues that were largely being ignored
- To provide researchers and practitioners with a structure for thinking about the design issues
- To pose a set of questions—mostly behavioral, but some engineering—whose answers would enlighten the substantive aspects of design

This paper's purpose is to move forward our understanding of decisional guidance in three ways:

- To apply what has been learned about decisional guidance in the DSS and other domains to clarify and refine the concept
- To broaden the scope of decisional guidance so it can be applied to any interactive computer-based system
- To produce a more focused agenda for further decisional guidance research

The original work raised a great many questions about the design, deployment, and effects of decisional guidance. The most central of these questions, to which all the others connect in some way, is this:

- How does decisional guidance affect user behavior?

This question's apparent simplicity conceals its complexity. The question does not have a singular answer. Decisional guidance comes in many varieties and each may have a different effect. Tasks, the people performing the tasks, and the environments within which they work also vary in many ways, and the same guidance mechanism may affect each differently. Moreover, a given guidance mechanism may produce a variety of effects (for instance, effects on performance, confidence, satisfaction, and so forth). This paper will not try to answer the central question but to position us better to address it.

The effects of an information system on user discretionary choices are not necessarily deliberate. They may be inadvertent—unintended consequences of the design of some feature. For instance, the order of items in a menu may affect the likelihood of a given item being selected. Although some human factors researchers have examined issues that might be classified as inadvertent guidance, information systems researchers studying guidance have focused almost exclusively on deliberate guidance. Indeed, decisional guidance is often described in the literature as a means of building a better or more effective system. So in common usage decisional guidance has implicitly referred to deliberate guidance. But both forms of guidance are important if researchers are to understand system

Table 6.1

The Original Deliberate Decisional Guidance Typology

Targets (which aspects of decision making the guidance addresses)
* Structuring the decision-making process (choosing functional capabilities)
* Executing the decision-making process (using functional capabilities)

Forms (what the guidance offers decision makers)
* Suggestive guidance
* Informative guidance

Modes (how the guidance mechanism works)
* Predefined
* Dynamic
* Participative

Scope (how much of the process is affected)
* Short range
* Long range

Source: Silver (1991b).

effects and practitioners are to design better systems. In fact, one reason for building deliberate guidance into a system is to preempt any unintended design consequences. Notwithstanding the importance of studying both types of decisional guidance, this paper focuses on the deliberate variety.

My previous work on decisional guidance in the DSS context consisted of a definition, a discussion of various issues, a typology for deliberate decisional guidance, and a large set of questions that we need to answer. This paper begins by first reviewing the original typology. Then it reviews the most prominent empirical studies of the effects of decisional guidance, focusing more on the issues the studies raise than on specific findings. These issues are then analyzed more fully to produce a revised and broadened definition and typology. The paper concludes with an agenda for research.

Because this paper focuses on revising and broadening the treatment of decisional guidance, it omits some of the ideas and much of the depth—especially in the realm of DSS—contained in the original works on this subject (Silver, 1991a, 1991b, 1990). These sources are recommended to the reader planning to work in the decisional guidance arena.

THE DIMENSIONS OF DELIBERATE DECISIONAL GUIDANCE: A TYPOLOGY

Deliberate decisional guidance—hereafter referred to simply as decisional guidance—is an umbrella term covering a wide array of system features that guide users. Silver (1991b) identified a four-dimensional typology for categorizing decisional guidance (Table 6.1). Reviewing the four dimensions is a prerequisite for examining the literature.

Targets: Structuring Versus Executing the Process

Deliberate decisional guidance targets the discretionary opportunities users encounter when working with a system. In general, people using a system make choices at two levels: (1) they choose which activity to perform (which functional capabilities to invoke) and (2) they make choices while engaging in a given activity (while interacting with the given function's features). Each level of choice represents a potential target for decisional guidance. When the system is a DSS, the first level is often called *structuring* or formulating the decision-making process. It involves "selecting a problem representation and then defining and ordering the set of information-processing and problem-solving activities to be performed" (Silver, 1991a, p. 111). The second level, referred to as *executing* the process, "entails actually performing the various information-processing and problem-solving activities" (Silver, 1991a, p. 111). More generic identifiers than "structuring" and "executing" will be useful in moving beyond DSS. The target of guidance for structuring the process can be viewed as support for *choosing* among the system's functional capabilities. Guidance for executing the process is guidance while *using* a given functional capability, which includes controlling the function, selecting among the options it offers, and supplying the inputs it requires.

Forms: Suggestive Versus Informative Guidance

In everyday speech, "guidance" most often refers to steering someone or something in a given direction. Decisional guidance, however, may be directive or may be non-directive, informing users without steering them toward a given choice. By analogy, consider guidance for a motorist. Directive guidance would be of the form, "Bear right at the fork!" But a signpost showing "North" to the left and "South" to the right would also be a guide.

Decisional guidance that is directive is referred to as *suggestive guidance*, defined as guidance that "makes judgmental recommendations (what to do, what input values to use) to the decision maker" (Silver, 1991a, p. 112). The term "suggestive" emphasizes that it is non-restrictive; the user may follow the suggestion or not. Non-directive guidance is referred to as *informative guidance,* defined as providing "pertinent information that enlightens the decision maker's judgment without suggesting how to act" (Silver, 1991a, p. 112). With informative guidance, the user draws his or her own conclusions about the most desirable action to take. Table 6.2 provides examples of each form of guidance for each target (structuring and executing the process).

Some researchers have characterized decisional guidance only as a means of directing users. From the perspective of understanding how system features affect behavior, both suggestive and informative guidance require study. And from the perspective of practice, each represents a feature that might be appropriate for a given design. So identifying and distinguishing the two forms of guidance seems best.

Modes: Predefined, Dynamic, and Participative

From where does the substance of guidance come? "Guidance mechanisms operate in one of three modes: predefined, dynamic, or participative. In the first case, the designer predefines the specific suggestions or the particular information displays and builds them into the guidance mechanism. In the other two cases, the designer constructs the guidance mechanism only; the mechanism then generates the suggestions and informational displays either itself by learning dynamically over time or with the active participation of the decision maker" (Silver, 1991a, p. 115).

Scope: Short- and Long-Range

Decisional guidance is usually delivered when the user confronts a choice—that is, when he or she is about to exercise discretion. This guidance, focused on the immediate issue, is referred to as *short-range guidance.* But sometimes, especially when the user is structuring a decision-making process, the user may want to plan ahead and formulate the whole process, or at least, several steps of the process. Guidance that supports a series of judgments is called *long-range guidance.*

Table 6.2

Examples of Deliberate Decisional Guidance

| | | **Form of Guidance** | |
		Suggestive Guidance	**Informative Guidance**
Structuring the Process (Choosing Functions)		Recommended operator	Description/Analysis of operators
		Set of recommended operators	Comparison of operators
		Ordered list of recommended operators	Map of relationships among operators
		Set of operators not recommended	Record of behavior in similar contexts
			History of activity this session
Executing the Process (Using Functions)		Recommended values	Description of required input values
		Set of recommended values	Descriptions of how inputs will be used
		Ordered list of recommended values	Tables, graphs, or analyses of data
		Set of values not recommended	Record of behavior in similar contexts
			History of activity this session

Target of Guidance is the overall vertical label spanning both row groups.

Source: Originally published in Silver, M.S. Decisional guidance for computer-based decision support. *MIS Quarterly*, 15, 1 (1991), 113. Copyright © 1991, Regents of the University of Minnesota. Reprinted by permission.

REVIEWING THE BEHAVIORAL RESEARCH ON DELIBERATE DECISIONAL GUIDANCE

Not surprisingly, most empirical studies of guidance have been in the domain of individual decision support. Behavioral studies have also applied the concept to group support and support for conceptual data modeling. Table 6.3 summarizes the most prominent empirical work on decisional guidance, and Figure 6.1 shows the studies organized by target and form of guidance. In selecting studies, only empirical studies of user behavior that explicitly refer to decisional guidance were included. Studies that focused on other system features that might be renamed or reframed as decisional guidance were not included.

What can be learned from these studies? While a number of specific empirical findings are reported that shed light on the effects of decisional guidance, these studies collectively teach us that the definition of decisional guidance and the typology of deliberate decisional guidance require clarification and modification. Because the studies differ in how they interpret the definition and operationalize the typology, we must be careful to construe the findings of each study in light of its own interpretation of decisional guidance. In particular, great care must be taken in attempting to generalize from the studies or to make comparisons across them. The foremost

Table 6.3

Empirical Studies of Deliberate Decisional Guidance

Study	Target of guidance	Forms of guidance	Dependent variables
Parikh, Fazlollahi, and Verma (2001)	Structuring	Suggestive Informative	• Quality • User satisfaction • Time • Learning
Wilson and Zigurs (1999)	Structuring	Suggestive	• Accuracy • Response time • Consistency • Willingness to accept guidance
Mahoney, Roush, and Dandy (2003)	Structuring	Suggestive	• Accuracy • Response time
Montazemi, Wang, Nainar, and Bart (1996)	Elements of structuring and executing	Suggestive Informative	• Performance
Huguenard and Ballou (2001)	Executing	Suggestive	• Performance • Satisfaction
Wang and Benbasat (2004)	Executing	Informative	• Trust (integrity)
Antony, Batra, and Santhanam (2005)	Executing	Suggestive	• Performance • Usability
Jiang and Klein (2000)	Structuring	Suggestive Informative	• Decision strategy • Choice
Limayem and DeSanctis (1993, 2000)	Structuring and executing	Suggestive Informative	• Group consensus • Decision time • Perceptions of process and outcomes • Perceptions of MCDM technology

contribution of these pioneering works is to help us refine and clarify, thus creating a sound foundation for the studies of the future.

The set of nine empirical studies provides an interesting range of tasks and guidance mechanisms. These are summarized in Table 6.4, which also includes several papers that did not qualify for inclusion in Table 6.3 but that broaden the set of tasks and guidance mechanisms.

Here are the significant findings of the nine empirical studies of deliberate decisional guidance.

On-Demand or Automatic	Principal Findings
On-demand	• Guidance outperformed no guidance for decision quality, user satisfaction, learning, and decision time (not total time) • Suggestive guidance outperformed informative guidance for decision quality and decision time • Informative guidance outperformed suggestive guidance for learning • Dynamic guidance outperformed predefined guidance for decision quality, learning, and decision time
Automatic	• Guidance outperformed no guidance • Most subjects preferred to make their own choices vs. using "good pre-selected displays" • Most subjects preferred to have the software advise them vs. choosing their own displays without advice • Effects on response time depended on task type
Automatic	• Matched displays outperformed mismatched displays • With guidance, field dependent individuals and field independents performed equally well
Automatic	• Less complex tasks: suggestive guidance outperformed informative guidance outperformed no-DSS • More complex tasks: informative guidance outperformed suggestive guidance and no-DSS, which tied
Automatic	• Guidance outperformed cognitive feedback (CF) and no guidance/feedback • Users of guidance and CF equally satisfied, more satisfied than users without guidance and CF
On-demand	• Guidance increased trust in integrity
Automatic	• Guidance outperformed no guidance/no restrictiveness • Guidance and restrictiveness performed equally well • Restrictive system perceived easier to use than one with guidance
Automatic	• Users employed different choice strategies when given different forms of guidance (suggestive vs. informative)
Automatic	• Groups with guidance had greater model understanding and greater decision time • Groups with guidance had better perceptions of the group decision process and outcomes, except for confidence • Groups with guidance had better perceptions of the MCDM GDSS

Performance

Eight of the studies addressed individual support, while the remaining one focused on group support. Six of the eight studies of individual support used some measure of outcome quality. Four of the six (Wilson and Zigurs, 1999; Parikh et al., 2001; Huguenard and Ballou, 2001; Antony et al., 2004) reported comparing various kinds of decisional guidance with computer-based systems containing no guidance. All four found significant, positive contributions of decisional guidance to performance quality.

Figure 6.1   **Studies of Decisional Guidance by Target and Form of Guidance**

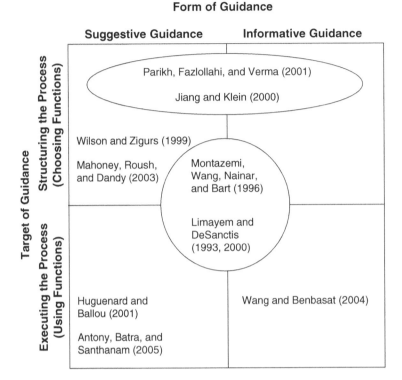

In studying performance, several of the studies considered not only quality but also the time required to complete the task. The findings were mixed. Parikh et al. (2001) found that users with decisional guidance spent significantly less time making decisions than those without, although their total system time increased due to the need to cope with the guidance. Wilson and Zigurs (1999) found that for spatial tasks, but not symbolic tasks, subjects given displays fitting the tasks required less time than subjects who selected their own displays. Mahoney et al. (2003) found that subjects responded significantly faster when given displays fitting the task than when given displays that did not fit. Limayem and DeSanctis (2000) found that groups given decisional guidance required significantly more time to complete their tasks.

Other Effects of Interest

Researchers have found a number of statistically significant guidance effects other than just performance effects. Parikh et al. (2001, 2002) studied user satisfaction and user learning, finding that decisional guidance contributed positively to both. More specifically, informative guidance contributed more than suggestive guidance to user learning, and dynamic guidance contributed more than predefined guidance. Limayem and DeSanctis (2000) studied similar outcomes in the context of groups. Decisional guidance led to better learning (model understanding) and higher perceptions of several types, including perceptions of decision quality and decision scheme satisfaction. Huguenard and Ballou (2001) found that users of suggestive guidance not only performed better but also were also more satisfied than those without the guidance. Wang and Benbasat

(2004) found that guidance contributed positively to the "integrity" component of trust. Jiang and Klein (2000) found that decisional guidance affected the strategies users employed.

Targets

The nine studies were fairly evenly spread over the two targets of guidance (Figure 6.1), with three targeting the structuring of the decision-making process (selecting a forecasting method and selecting an appropriate data display), three focusing on the execution (assigning jobs to machines, answering questions posed by an e-commerce recommendation agent, and designing databases), and two doing some of each (Table 6.3). This dimension of the typology seemed fairly straightforward, with the various studies easily placed in categories. Nonetheless, a potential ambiguity arises in a study not framed in terms of decisional guidance that could be recast as such. The paper (Singh, 1998) studied two cognitive aids that support the "strategy execution process" by helping users select the proper next step in an already structured decision-making process. Since the process was already formulated, referring to the invoking of each step as "executing the process" seems entirely appropriate. The typology, however, would characterize this activity as structuring the process rather than executing it, since structuring the process refers to the selection of functional capabilities and executing it refers to controlling or interacting with those capabilities *once invoked.* Given the conflict between the formal definitions and the intuitive usage in this study, the formal definitions should be revisited.

Forms of Guidance: Informative Versus Suggestive

Three of the empirical studies compared the effects of informative guidance with those of suggestive guidance. Parikh et al. (2001), in the most extensive study of decisional guidance thus far, constructed a DSS for a forecasting task, finding that suggestive guidance outperformed informative guidance in terms of decision quality and decision time (not total time), but informative guidance led to greater user learning. The task required users to choose a forecasting method for a time series. In predefined mode, informative guidance for a given forecasting method provided information such as the following:

```
Least-square regression model
When you plot the data with time on x-axis and a variable
(sales, profit, cost, etc.) on y-axis, if you see a linear trend,
this model should be used. A linear trend gives same slope any
point on the trend line. Least-square regression technique
identifies the trend and gives us slope and intercept.
```

Suggestive guidance in this mode included the same information plus such additional content as this:

```
Your data has . . .
  A linear trend
  Low fluctuation
  No seasonal change
```

Under the current typology, the study's suggestive guidance does not fit comfortably in either category. It does not strictly qualify as suggestive guidance because it does not explicitly recommend a

Table 6.4

Studies of Decisional Guidance: Tasks and Guidance Provided

Study	Task
Parikh, Fazlollahi, and Verma (2001) Parikh and Fazlollahi (2002)	Choosing a forecasting method for time series analysis
Wilson and Zigurs (1999) Mahoney, Roush, and Dandy (2003)	Answering questions about quantitative data
Montazemi, Wang, Nainar, and Bart (1996)	Problem formulation (for judgmental tasks)
Huguenard and Ballou (2001)	Job scheduling—assigning mail to sorting machines
Wang and Benbasat (2004)	Answering questions asked by a rule-based e-commerce recommendation agent
Antony, Batra, and Santhanam (2005)	Conceptual data modeling
Jiang and Klein (2000)	Choosing a forecasting method (as a multi-attribute task)
Limayem and DeSanctis (1993, 2000)	Group decision making (for a multi-criteria decision-making task)
Vessey, Jarvenpaa, and Tractinsky (1993) Jankowski (1997) Scott, Horvath, and Day (2000)	CASE tools
Wheeler and Valacich (1996)	Group decision making
Rai, Stubbart, and Paper (1994)	Executive information systems

course of action to the user. It provides two pieces of information that together imply that least squares should be used, but stops short of making a recommendation, leaving the user to draw that conclusion from the information. The system thus provides rich informative guidance but no suggestions. Nonetheless, although this guidance does not meet the precise standard for suggestive guidance, it is clearly in that spirit. The guidance was intended at least to nudge the user in the direction of least squares, and many users would likely be nudged. So this guidance mechanism—which was found to be beneficial to users—seems to sit between informative and suggestive guidance.

This lack of fit motivates contemplating the following hypothetical system. Suppose a different forecasting system provides guidance consisting of two elements: a statement about the dataset (for instance, that it has a linear trend) and a menu with highlights on those methods consistent with the statement. Here, too, the current typology would require classifying the mechanism as informative guidance, but it clearly has a suggestive or directive element.

Guidance Provided

Informative guidance included information about the various methods. Suggestive guidance included conclusions about the datasets and recommendations for which methods to use or not. Four different classes of guidance were provided by crossing informative and suggestive guidance with predefined and dynamic guidance.

Guidance provided displays (tables or graphs) that matched the task type (symbolic or spatial).

Suggestive guidance for one task helped "decision makers develop the 'correct' causal map of their decision environment" and for another helped "decision makers assess relevant dimensions and to develop the correct SWAT grid." Much of the suggestive guidance was in the form of feedback that corrected users. Informative guidance provided the same basic information but did not offer suggestions concerning the correct answers and did not guide the user to select relevant strategies.

Guidance made assignment suggestions based on a decision rule.

Guidance provided information about "the usefulness of different product features, as well as the potential cost of having them." General advice about how to approach a given question was also provided, but specific suggestions were not.

Guidance provided suggestions, and corrected errors, to facilitate following rules for good database design.

Informative guidance provided scores for each forecasting method on six attributes. Suggestive guidance allowed users to weight the attributes, calculating an overall score for each method.

Guidance provided feedforward and cognitive feedback to support group cognition and breakpoints in group interaction.

Guidance of various forms for steering an analyst through a specific systems development methodology.

Guidance for the faithful adoption of heuristics through GDSS features, training, and facilitation, instantiating and testing adaptive structuration theory (DeSanctis and Poole, 1994).

Informative and suggestive guidance for structuring and for executing executive decision-making processes with a focus on reducing human information-processing biases.

These two examples—and finding more is easy—suggest that categorizing guidance as informative or suggestive may be overly simplistic. This dimension of the typology needs a third category defining a middle ground between informing and suggesting.

Why does it matter if we have two or three categories? For practitioners, the typology represents a set of design choices, and making the distinction shows more fully the set of options. For researchers, the primary goal is to understand the behavioral effects of guidance. Guidance that explicitly recommends might be more likely to be followed than that which more subtly implies. But the explicit approach might lead to less user learning. These are conjectures, but the distinction needs to be made so the questions can be studied empirically. Forcing the in-between cases into one category or the other would likely be problematic when we try to generalize from a collection of studies. For instance, we can conclude from this study that one of these guidance mechanisms led to more learning than the other, but given the classification issue, we would not want to conclude that informative guidance leads to more learning than suggestive guidance.

Montazemi et al. (1996) compared suggestive guidance, informative guidance, and no computer-based support for two tasks, one with low complexity and the other with high complexity. For the task with low complexity, users given suggestive guidance outperformed those with informative guidance, who outperformed those without DSS. For the high complexity task, those with informative guidance still outperformed those without DSS, but users who received suggestive guidance performed comparably to those without DSS. The provocative findings concerning suggestive guidance are discussed in the next section on task differences. The findings with respect to informative guidance are less surprising, but analyzing the paper raises questions about defining and operationalizing informative guidance. Determining the value-added content of the informative guidance is a bit difficult without seeing the system, especially since the study did not have a DSS without any guidance. But as described in the paper, the informative guidance seems to be not so much guidance, as defined here, as a decision aid in the classical sense. Since many decision aids do provide people with information to enlighten their decisions, drawing the line between a powerful decision aid without guidance and an aid with informative guidance may be difficult.

Consider the hypothetical case of a simple decision aid that supports an elimination by aspects strategy for renting an apartment or buying a television set. The aid provides a matrix of alternatives and their attributes. Users are prompted to identify an attribute and cutoff value, which the aid uses to eliminate some of the alternatives. The information provided by the system would not be considered guidance. The matrix contains the basic information associated with the task. And the information is not focused on the discretionary choices the user makes (selecting an attribute and cutoff). Indeed, if the data matrix qualifies as informative guidance, then virtually every decision aid in the world would be considered informative guidance. Yet, some users might use this information in selecting a cutoff value, scanning the values of a particular attribute to choose an appropriate cutoff. So this information might well enlighten or sway the user in executing the process. And what if the decision aid were enhanced to provide statistical summaries of the values for each attribute (maximum, minimum, mean, median, and quartiles) to facilitate arriving at cutoffs? It would be easy to view this derived data, too, as part of the aid's basic functionality. But this feature has also been characterized as informative guidance (Silver, 1991b, p. 177). Where does one draw the line between basic functionality (and its information base) and informative guidance? The typology requires clarification of this issue.

Jiang and Klein (2000) studied decisional guidance for choosing a forecasting method where the choice among methods was structured as a multi-attribute choice problem. Informative guidance provided ratings for each of the four forecasting methods with respect to six attributes such as consistency and simplicity. Suggestive guidance allowed users to provide weights for each attribute and generated weighted scores for each forecasting method so users could see which scored highest. The study found that the form of guidance had a significant effect on which multi-attribute strategy users followed to select a forecasting method. Moreover, shifts in which multi-attribute selection strategy was employed often were accompanied by shifts in which forecasting method was selected. As with Montazemi et al. (1996), this study also highlights the possible blurriness in distinguishing between basic functionality and decisional guidance. Since the immediate task was a multi-attribute problem, the guidance provided—attribute scores and a weighting mechanism—might be seen as part of the decision aid rather than as additional guidance. But from the perspective of the ultimate task of performing a forecast, support for choosing a forecasting method can be seen as guidance.

Task and Individual Differences

Only two of the studies address individual or task differences that may affect the consequences of guidance. The limited attention is not surprising given the relative newness of guidance studies overall. Studying guidance more generally seems reasonable before taking on the contingencies. But the contingencies may be the keys to understanding guidance effects, which might wash out at higher levels of analysis. One would expect individual, task, and environmental differences to be fertile research areas in the future.

Montazemi et al. (1996) compared the effects of guidance for tasks with high and low complexity. Their surprising result was that with low task complexity suggestive guidance led to the best performance, but with high task complexity suggestive guidance was inferior to informative guidance and no better than solving the problem without a DSS. They attribute the finding to differences in the type of suggestive guidance provided, since the complexity of the more complex task prevented inclusion of feedback in the form of "task information." Analyzing the study raises two significant matters. First, the study suggests that finding a means of supplying effective suggestive guidance may be challenging for highly complex tasks. Second, since different suggestive guidance mechanisms were employed for the low and high complexity tasks, one might ask if the study is truly comparing the same form of guidance across two task types. Some might argue that the findings are as much a statement about differences in the guidance mechanisms as about differences in the tasks. Others might claim that the differences in task types drive the differences in guidance mechanisms so the comparison and conclusions are appropriate. Either way, one wonders how often the issue of different guidance mechanisms will arise when trying to compare guidance effects across different task types. And it presages the difficulties yet to be encountered when trying to generalize findings from individual studies of guidance.

Mahoney et al. (2003) compared the effects of decisional guidance for selecting displays between field independent subjects and field dependents, finding that with guidance the two groups performed equally well. Because field independents outperformed dependents when displays and tasks were mismatched, they see decisional guidance as a means of improving the performance of the field dependents. More generally, this study's finding suggests that individual differences may be important for understanding the effects of decisional guidance.

Restrictiveness

System restrictiveness and decisional guidance are two different system features that affect user behavior. But while they are distinct system attributes, they have an important relationship: They are alternative means to an end. Systems intended to direct user behavior can do so by restricting or by guiding. Several of the studies have implications for understanding the restrictiveness–guidance relationship.

Antony et al. (2005) implemented two versions of their knowledge-based system for database design. One was restrictive, forcing users to comply with the rules, and the other was guiding, facilitating and encouraging, but not requiring, rule compliance. The two approaches were equally effective in contributing to user performance. But the restrictive system was perceived as easier to use. Although this study is just one data point, it raises the possibility that—at least in some situations—restricting may be more desirable than guiding as a means of directing users. This possibility is especially important given the emphasis some DSS commentators place on flexibility (non-restrictiveness).

Wilson and Zigurs (1999), as well as Mahoney et al. (2003), used the theory of cognitive fit (Vessey and Galletta, 1991) to direct decision makers to data displays fitting the tasks they were performing. The findings of both studies support the theory of cognitive fit. Wilson and Zigurs (1999) found that subjects given only displays matching the task were more accurate than those who chose their own displays. Mahoney et al. (2003) found that subjects given only displays matching the task outperformed those given only mismatches. Both studies referred to giving users only displays that fit the task as suggestive guidance, and both found merit in such guidance.

These two studies raise questions about how suggestive guidance should be operationalized. Providing only displays that fit the task seems more restrictive than guiding, since users do not have a choice. Including a treatment that recommended the matching display but still allowed users to choose for themselves would be interesting and more closely match the definition of suggestive guidance.

Wilson and Zigurs (1999) gained insight into the restrictiveness–guidance design issue by asking their subjects about their preferences. Most subjects indicated they would prefer making their own choices over being restricted, but most also would prefer suggestive guidance over none. These preferences are intuitively appealing, yet intriguing, given that Antony et al.'s (2005) subjects perceived the restrictive system as the more usable.

These studies highlight a pair of issues: First, restrictiveness must be sharply distinguished from guidance, both definitionally and operationally. Second, the design trade-off between the two demands further empirical study. Studying system restrictiveness and suggestive guidance in a single study seems highly beneficial.

Invocation and Timing

Seven of the nine studies provided guidance automatically, while two (Parikh et al., 2001; Wang and Benbasat, 2004) provided it on demand, requiring users to request guidance. How guidance is invoked has been discussed in the literature (Silver, 1991b), but was not included in the typology. When studying the effects of decisional guidance, distinguishing those systems where guidance is always delivered to the user from those where the user may request it seems important. Moreover, for those systems providing guidance on demand, one would like to distinguish those users who requested guidance from those who did not. Just as Wilson and Zigurs (1999) asked users about their preferences for being restricted and being advised, researchers might want to solicit users' preferences for automatic versus on-demand guidance. Even better than asking users would be to observe their behavior and its consequences under each condition.

Several researchers have adopted decisional guidance as part of their efforts to classify CASE tools. Vessey et al. (1992) were the first to do so, distinguishing three approaches to supporting a given design methodology: a restrictive philosophy that forces users to follow the methodology's rules, a guiding philosophy that is suggestive, and a flexible approach that does not try to influence users. Jankowski (1997) further divided the guided approach into four cases based on two dimensions. His first dimension addresses the invocation issue, capturing the difference between unsolicited (automatic) and solicited (on-demand) guidance. He refers to these as active and passive feedback guidance, respectively. Scott et al. (2000) make a similar distinction. Jankowski's (1997) second dimension distinguishes guidance provided while the user is performing a task from guidance provided after the task is complete. This second distinction, which addresses the timing of guidance, also seems useful outside the realm of CASE tools.

Timing is implicitly or explicitly an issue in four of the nine empirical studies of decisional guidance. Several of the studies provided users with corrective feedback *after* they had already exercised their discretionary power. For instance, much of the suggestive guidance provided by Montazemi et al. (1996) was in the form of corrections to conclusions the user had drawn. Similarly, much of the guidance offered by Antony et al. (2005) reflected corrections to rule violations made by the user when designing the database. The guidance provided by Limayem and DeSanctis (2000) included several types of cognitive feedback given when various problems were detected in the group's progress. And, in addition to studying suggestive guidance versus no guidance, Huguenard and Ballou (2001) studied a version of the system that offered cognitive feedback, informing users when they violated the optimal decision rule. So, three studies include feedback within the domain of decisional guidance while a fourth explicitly contrasts feedback with decisional guidance. These observations suggest that the timing of guidance is another area where definitions and operationalization require clarification.

Summation

The one overall conclusion that can be fairly drawn from this set of studies is that guidance of various sorts can improve performance in various realms. Given the many definitional and operational issues raised by these studies, however, great care must be taken in interpreting and comparing the findings of individual studies. We are best served at this time by gaining insights about the specific features each study considered rather than trying to draw broad conclusions about particular kinds of guidance. The set of studies also suggests that even with more standardization of definitions and operationalization, generalizing from empirical studies of guidance will likely be difficult. This very small set of studies showed great diversity. With so many relevant dimensions and so many ways that guidance mechanisms can differ even within a single cell of the typology, drawing generalizable conclusions will be a significant challenge for future research to embrace. We must use what we have learned from these studies to refine the definition and typology in a manner that will help us confront that challenge.

REVISING THE DEFINITION AND TYPOLOGY

The foregoing observations lead to the following as a revised and broadened definition of decisional guidance (including inadvertent and deliberate guidance):

> **Decisional Guidance:** The design features of an interactive computer-based system that have, or are intended to have, the effect of enlightening, swaying, or directing its users as those users exercise the discretion the system grants them to choose among and use its functional capabilities.

Since this revision extends the concept beyond the domain of DSS, some researchers may find value in reparticularizing the definition to their own domains. For instance, DSS researchers may find value in identifying the choosing of functional capabilities as structuring the process and the using of them as executing the process, as in the original definition.

In addition to making decisional guidance more broadly applicable, the revised definition also makes explicit two points implicit in the original. First, the new definition clarifies the focus of decisional guidance on "design features." The original definition less sharply delineated whether guidance refers to the features, the effects, or both. The revision makes clear that the term decisional guidance refers to the features, and that the study of decisional guidance is the study of a set of system features and their effects. This shift in formal definition is consistent with the way the term has been applied in the literature, which typically discusses "the effects" or the "effectiveness" of decisional guidance, implying that the guidance itself is a system feature. Note that a given system may have many instances of decisional guidance—that is, many different features that enlighten, sway, or direct its users as they choose among and use its functional capabilities.

Table 6.5

Revisions to the Definition of Decisional Guidance

- Broadened scope
- Focus on system features
- Explicit contrast with restrictiveness

Second, the new definition makes explicit that decisional guidance does not intersect system restrictiveness. These distinct concepts refer to two different sets of system features that can affect a user's behavior and the outcome of a computer-based task. One way that a system can affect user behavior is by constraining it. This is restrictiveness. Another way is by enlightening, swaying, or directing users as they exercise the discretion the system affords them—in other words, within the constraints imposed by the system's restrictiveness. That is decisional guidance. A system that forces users into a particular behavior, therefore, is not guiding them (in the sense of decisional guidance). It is restricting them. The revised definition of decisional guidance includes the phrase "as those users exercise the discretion the system grants them" to make this distinction clear.

Some researchers have applied the term guidance to what is formally defined here as restrictiveness. Doing so is understandable since one might see a system that constrains users from doing certain things as "guiding" them to do others. Indeed, in casual usage, we often refer to forces that limit us as "guiding." We might say that a train is guided by the track, while in actuality the track restricts the train's path. Decisional guidance could have been defined differently to include such cases. But for the sake of advancing theory and practice we require a consistent use of terminology that differentiates two distinct phenomena: features that restrict and features that guide. This distinction is especially important given that in many cases restrictiveness trades off against guidance in designing systems, since the two represent alternative means to the same end. We are best served, therefore, by rigorously maintaining and adhering to the formal definitions and distinctions. To avoid confusion, we must be vigilant both in our writing and our reading of the literature.

Table 6.5 summarizes the differences between the original and revised definitions of decisional guidance. Given the broadened definition, here are a few illustrative opportunities for providing and studying guidance in realms other than decision support.

- Word Processing: We do not typically think about word processors in terms of user discretion, but authors do make many choices when editing their documents. Selecting an appropriate font, for instance, is a discretionary task. Given dozens of possible fonts, decisional guidance could help an author identify his or her preferred font for a given purpose. Moreover, since sans serif fonts are generally found to be less readable than those with serifs, guidance could help authors avoid using them in situations where they may significantly degrade readability. Such features as synonym finders and grammar checkers can also be examples of decisional guidance in word processing.
- Searching the Web: Finding information on the Web can be a challenging task. One way that search engines can help their users find what they need is by providing decisional guidance for specifying the search parameters. Enabling users to search for "similar pages" to a given page is another way to guide search. The order in which results are presented is yet another design feature that can influence user behavior.

- Internet Security and Privacy: Web browsers, virus checkers, and firewalls typically allow users to determine how strict the software should be in protecting against threats to security and privacy. Since increased vigilance in protecting against possible attacks can limit or interfere with useful functionality, setting the levels of security and privacy is a discretionary task requiring users to balance potential benefits and risks. Given the many complex options these programs generally offer, decisional guidance could help users arrive at the appropriate settings given their desired levels of risk and the functionality they need.
- B-to-C E-Commerce: Consumers confront numerous choices when purchasing goods online, including what to buy (brand, model, size, color, and so forth), where to buy it, how to ship it, and what extras (options, accessories, and warranties) to purchase. Decisional guidance could play a role in informing, swaying, or even directing these various choices. For instance, many Web sites currently provide features that either help users choose appropriate options and accessories or encourage users to add on extra options and accessories. But richer guidance mechanisms could be offered.

Having seen several examples of the broadened applicability of the revised definition, it is now time to revisit the typology of deliberate decisional guidance. Examining the typology's intended role may be useful before attempting to revise it. For system designers, the typology is a structured way to think of their options when creating guidance. Each dimension represents a design choice. For researchers, the typology implicitly identifies a set of research questions. Each element of the typology (for instance, suggestive guidance), or combination of elements (predefined on-demand suggestive guidance for structuring the process), needs to be studied to understand the consequences of this kind of guidance. And comparisons within a dimension (on-demand versus automatic guidance or suggestive versus informative guidance) present another set of researchable issues. The typology facilitates more focused studies that have greater hopes of being compared with other, equally focused studies, thus enabling more meaningful generalizations and broader conclusions. And, of course, these research activities in turn provide value to practitioners employing the typology.

So the challenge is to develop a set of dimensions that identify significant differences in the types of deliberate decisional guidance. Given how different guidance mechanisms can be—as seen in the small set of existing studies—we would like the cells of the typology to be relatively small, to allow for greater homogeneity. But we cannot have so many cells that the typology overwhelms researchers and practitioners alike. With this in mind, let us turn now to the elements of the revised typology (Table 6.6).

Guidance Targets: Choosing Versus Using Functional Capabilities

The original definitions of structuring the decision-making process and executing it worked well in classifying the empirical studies of guidance. The labels, however, need to be refined so that the dimension can be applied to systems other than DSS. Guidance for structuring the process in the new typology is therefore referred to as "guidance for choosing functional capabilities" and guidance for executing the process is called "guidance while using functional capabilities." Guidance for choosing the function is not part of the function itself; it is part of the broader system that facilitates choosing among functions. Guidance while using the function is embedded in the function and comes into play only once the function has been invoked. Note that both types of guidance address how users exercise the discretion the system affords them; the difference is whether the discretion is in choosing functions or in using those functions.

Table 6.6

A Revised Typology of Deliberate Decisional Guidance

Targets
- Choosing functional capabilities
- Using functional capabilities

Directivity
- Suggestive guidance
- Quasi-suggestive guidance
- Informative guidance

Modes
- Predefined
- Dynamic
- Participative

Invocation Styles
- Automatic
- On-demand
- Hybrid

Timing
- Concurrent
- Prospective
- Retrospective

Dropping the terms structuring and executing, and adhering to the distinction just made, also solves the semantic problem with classifying Singh's (1998) study of cognitive aids for "executing the process." At issue was whether invoking the next step in an already formulated decision process constituted structuring or executing the process. With the new terminology, invoking the next preformulated step, when other functions are available for selection, represents guidance for choosing a functional capability, not guidance while using it. DSS researchers may find value in retaining the more DSS-specific terms, but doing so will require care in applying them in a manner consistent with the distinctions and terminology of the new typology. In other words, Singh's cognitive aids for "executing the process" would need to be classified formally as guidance for structuring the process.

Directivity: Informative, Quasi-Suggestive, and Suggestive Guidance

Examining the roles of informative and suggestive guidance in the empirical studies brought to light two ambiguities in how they are operationalized: (1) some guidance features go beyond simply informing but stop short of suggesting and (2) some informative features might not be considered guidance at all. This dimension must be revised to resolve these concerns. Since the dimension's purpose is to distinguish guidance features that are directive from those that are non-directive, the first step is to rename the dimension "directivity."

Adding a middle category to the directivity dimension should solve the first problem, guidance mechanisms that do not make explicit recommendations but do have an implicit directedness to them. The examples we have encountered are situations where users can infer a course of action from the information provided but are required to "connect the dots," combining the information provided and drawing a logical conclusion. One might think of this category as a weaker form of directivity than suggestive guidance.

The second problem with the directivity dimension is that since most functional capabilities (for instance, decision aids) provide their users with information as part of their capabilities, distinguishing informative guidance for using a given function from non-guiding information offered by that function may be difficult. Indeed, guidance of any kind for using a functional capability is built into that function, so informative guidance is part of the function. The question becomes whether or not to characterize part of what that function offers as informative guidance. Note that this ambiguity is not an issue for guidance that supports choosing a capability, since such guidance is outside any individual function.

Research and practice are best served by drawing the line liberally, including more rather than less in the guidance category. The study of guidance is the study of how system features affect discretionary behavior. Defining what might otherwise be ambiguous cases as guidance ensures that they are focused upon as features that affect behavior. So what are the minimum requirements for a feature qualifying as deliberate decisional guidance? The feature must be focused at a point of interaction between the person and the system, because these interaction points are where users have the opportunity to exercise discretion. And the feature must offer information that is non-essential to the basic operation of the functional capability. If the information in question is essential to the functionality—that is, if the function would not work, would not be meaningful, or would be substantially different without the information—the feature should be viewed as part of the functionality and not guidance. But any additional information provided beyond this basic functionality should be characterized as guidance. This approach may tend to characterize as guidance some features that have been taken for granted in the past, but doing so is beneficial, not harmful. This approach views functions as containing basic features as well as, possibly, additional features that guide the interaction. To the extent that these added features enlighten, sway, or direct users in their interaction with the function, then considering them as guidance will help better understand the function's effect.

Formally, these revisions lead to the following definitions for the "directivity" dimension:

- *Suggestive guidance*: Deliberate decisional guidance that makes explicit recommendations to the user on how to exercise his or her discretion. The recommendation need not identify a single choice; suggestive guidance might endorse a set of alternative actions or might advise against one or more actions.
- *Quasi-suggestive guidance*: Deliberate decisional guidance that does not explicitly make a recommendation but from which one can directly infer a recommendation or direction.
- *Informative guidance*: Deliberate decisional guidance that provides pertinent information that enlightens the user's choice without suggesting or implying how to act. In the case of guidance within a specific functional capability, such information must be focused on a point of interaction between the person and the system and must go beyond the basic information essential to the function.

In all three cases, the discretion remains with the user. For instance, the user is free to accept or reject any suggestions. The difficulty in formalizing and operationalizing this dimension highlights the difficulty in building a cumulative research base in this area.

Modes: Predefined, Dynamic, or Participative

The mode of guidance received limited attention in the empirical studies. Jiang and Klein's (2000) informative guidance was predefined while their suggestive guidance was participative, but the study did not formally compare these two modes. Only Parikh et al. (2001) specifically studied the mode of guidance, comparing predefined guidance with dynamic guidance and finding that dynamic guidance significantly increased decision quality and user learning while significantly decreasing decision time. The study did not confirm the hypotheses that users of dynamic guidance would be more satisfied or would take less total time to make their decisions. Given the limited empirical testing of this dimension, refining it at this time has no basis.

Invocation Style: Automatic, On-Demand, or Hybrid

Two of the empirical studies required users to request guidance; the others provided it automatically. This difference is likely to affect outcomes, both because guidance on demand may in many cases not be demanded and because guidance given automatically might irritate more than it guides. Invocation style therefore seems a desirable dimension to add to the typology. Indeed, some guidance mechanisms may lend themselves to one invocation style more than the other. One can also conceive a hybrid style that combines automatic and on-demand invocation. For instance, invocation might be made "switchable," allowing users to choose for themselves between automatic and on-demand guidance. Or invocation might be primarily on-demand, with certain conditions triggering the guidance automatically.

Timing: Concurrent, Prospective, or Retrospective

Perhaps the greatest surprise in the empirical studies is the number of cases where the guidance was delivered as feedback after users had made their choices rather than as guidance prior to choosing. Following the lead of Limayem and DeSanctis (1993) for GDSS and Jankowski (1997) for CASE tools, distinguishing these two types of guidance makes sense. Dhaliwal and Benbasat (1996) made a similar distinction in studying explanations for knowledge-based systems. Limayem and DeSanctis (1993), as well as Dhaliwal and Benbasat (1996), used the terminology feedforward and feedback, but since feedforward and feedback have formal definitions that not all guidance may satisfy, alternative phrases are preferred here. Guidance that applies to a choice at the point of interaction is termed concurrent guidance, since it is provided concurrently with the choice point, whereas guidance that refers back to a choice already made is termed retrospective guidance.

Why would a system designer build retrospective guidance into a system? If a user is performing a task repeatedly (Huguenard and Ballou, 2001), feedback on what was just chosen can guide subsequent choices. In other cases (Limayem and DeSanctis, 2000; Montazemi et al., 1996; Antony et al., 2004), the guidance may be corrective, giving users a chance to change their choices. These observations suggest that the timing of guidance merits further study and is worth including in the typology.

Concurrent guidance would seem to be the most timely guidance. One can imagine situations where the guidance might occur even earlier. Guidance for a series of inputs might be provided at one time when a tool is first invoked. Guidance for planning a series of activities would guide users in advance of actually invoking and using each tool. Situations such as these, where guidance is provided significantly prior to the choice point, constitute a third case of timing: prospective guidance.

The original typology had a dimension distinguishing the scope of the guidance: short-range versus long-range. This is the only dimension of the original typology that none of the decisional guidance studies addressed. This dimension can now be dropped, since it is covered by the new "timing" dimension. Long-range guidance is now a form of prospective guidance, and short-range guidance is now concurrent guidance.

The topics of feedforward (Bjorkman, 1972) and feedback—especially, cognitive feedback (Te'eni, 1991)—have been receiving increasing attention in the information systems literature. How do they relate to the various types of guidance? Feedforward, which provides information about a task before the person begins to perform it, would most likely be prospective guidance or possibly concurrent guidance, depending on how it was implemented. Feedback, defined as "information about the decision-making process and its outcome" (Te'eni, 1991, p. 644) is a bit trickier. If the feedback is given for the reasons suggested already—to allow the user to correct an entry or to guide the user in an iterative task—the feedback would qualify as retrospective guidance. But much feedback is intended not to influence present system use at all, rather to enable user learning for the future. Such feedback would lie outside the realm of guidance, which informs, sways, or directs the user in exercising discretion within the system. So not all feedback is decisional guidance. But research in cognitive feedback could be a good source of mechanisms for retrospective guidance.

Guidance for Groups

Decisional guidance for groups seems to be an especially fertile area for research. Although there can be some crossover—for instance, some of the MCDM guidance included in Limayem and DeSanctis's (2000) system drew upon individual techniques—single-user guidance and group guidance are likely to be largely independent bodies of knowledge. A variant of this typology with added dimensions may be needed for group research and practice, since much of GDSS guidance focuses on the special needs of group interaction. For example, most of the guidance provided by Limayem and DeSanctis (2000) was targeted at three types of "group breakpoints." Similarly, Wheeler and Valacich (1996) distinguish between active and passive appropriation mediators—here, we can think of these as guidance features—noting that the multiple channels of group interaction may weaken the power of the computer-based system to guide. A prominent topic in GDSS research is the role of the human facilitator. Research on guidance for groups may help understand if and how a human facilitator can be replaced by computer-based features. Other topics of interest would likely include the role of guidance when groups are not co-located or when they meet asynchronously.

RESEARCH AGENDA FOR DELIBERATE DECISIONAL GUIDANCE

With the revised typology in place, we return to the question with which the paper began:

• How does decisional guidance affect user behavior?

Although Decisional Guidance is focused on user discretionary behavior, fully understanding guidance and its effects requires also studying user perceptions and user learning. People's perceptions may influence if and how they use a system and its guidance. Improved or degraded user learning may be a side effect of guidance that is of concern to designers and users. All told, three sets of consequences are of interest: effects on (1) behavior, (2) perceptions, and (3) learning. My purpose here is not to create an exhaustive set of issues to be studied but to pare the possible issues down to a manageable size, allowing us to focus on the most important. Even so, the list is substantial.

User Behavior

Since decisional guidance is defined in terms of features that affect users' discretionary behavior as they interact with a computer-based system, the most fundamental question is this:

- How does guidance affect the discretionary choices people make—that is, how does it affect the way they choose and use the system's functional capabilities?

This is not an outcome issue but a process question. What is the substantive connection between a system's decisional guidance mechanisms and the actions people take in choosing and using the system's functional capabilities? Answering this question fully will require addressing these more specific questions:

- When do people invoke guidance that is not provided automatically?
- Do people follow the recommendations of suggestive guidance? Of quasi-suggestive guidance? Are people more likely to follow suggestive guidance than quasi-suggestive guidance?
- Does informative guidance succeed in enlightening people's discretionary choices? If so, does such enlightenment alter their choices?

While decisional guidance may focus on choices, the consequences of those choices—the outcomes—do matter. Even within the DSS realm, defining task performance is sometimes difficult. As one moves to interactive systems other than DSS, defining task performance may be still more difficult or may not even be meaningful. Where possible, however, the effects of guidance on task performance need to be studied. This leads to the next question:

- For tasks where one can identify a measure of quality, does guidance improve performance quality? Do the effects on user choices—if any—lead to improved performance quality?

Finally, questions of efficiency are probably the least important for our agenda, but nonetheless have value:

- How does guidance affect the amount of time people spend performing a task with the system?

Together, these questions identify the primary research agenda for studying deliberate decisional guidance.

User Perceptions

Dhaliwal and Benbasat (1996) make an important point in their discussion of explanations in knowledge-based systems: "While perceptions are weak surrogates for decision effectiveness or efficiency, they also represent an important set of effects in their own right" (p. 357). In particular, negative perceptions of one kind or another about any information system may lead to non-use. For instance, Davis (1989) identified perceived usefulness and perceived ease of use as factors that contribute to intent to use an information system. In the case of decisional guidance, negative perceptions might lead to non-use at three levels: (1) users may eschew the entire system, (2) users may use the system but disregard the guidance, or (3) users may fail to demand guidance in systems where it is not given automatically. So perceptions about the guidance may play a role in determining the behavioral effects discussed in the preceding section.

This is not the place to review or debate the substantial literature on user perceptions. Here, two perceptions that seem especially important for decisional guidance are presented. Others are no doubt also worth investigating.

Perceived Ease of Use

The technology acceptance model (Davis, 1989) posits that perceived ease of use is an important contributor to intention to use an information system. Decisional guidance might therefore increase or decrease the likelihood of system use depending on whether the guidance increases or decreases the perceived usability of the system. Similarly, the perceived ease of use of a given guidance mechanism might influence whether or not that guidance is used, especially in cases where the guidance must be invoked on demand. Does guidance increase or decrease perceived usability? Plausible arguments can be made for both positions. If users see dealing with the guidance as an added burden, perceived usability may decline, reducing the chances of use. But guidance may make it easier for users to exercise their discretion. Informative guidance may put information needed for a choice at the user's fingertips. And suggestive guidance may make choosing even easier, by handing the user a recommendation. Both possibilities are consistent with Todd and Benbasat's (1999) conclusion in the DSS realm that users appear to use a system "in such a way as to maintain a low overall level of effort expenditure." Which perception applies in a given situation may be a function of the specific guidance mechanism and the individual user.

Trust

Dhaliwal and Benbasat (1996) as well as Wang and Benbasat (2004) assert that explanations in knowledge-based systems can affect the trust users place in such systems and that trust is an important determinant of use or of whether users follow the system's recommendations. Trust may be similarly important for suggestive and quasi-suggestive guidance. Trust in the guidance is likely to determine whether users follow the suggestions and whether they invoke guidance when it is not automatic.

User Learning

Deliberate decisional guidance is intended to affect the choices people make when exercising the discretion a system gives them. Its purpose is not to affect their learning for future tasks or system use. But user learning may be a consequence of concern to a system's designers and some forms of guidance likely do affect what people learn from using the system. In some sense, user learning might be seen as a side effect of guidance that demands our attention. Consequently, the research agenda needs to consider the following question:

- How does guidance affect user learning?

The Challenge of Generating Meaningful Findings

How meaningfully can any of the questions about guidance effects be answered? At what level of generality can worthwhile answers be given? Can we generalize to all decisional guidance? To a given class of guidance—for example, suggestive guidance? Or can we draw conclusions only about specific guidance mechanisms? Generalizing is always a challenge, but it looks to be especially difficult in the arena of decisional guidance.

Consider research on decision support systems, which faces a similar problem. The studies of whether or not DSS improve decision making have shown mixed results (Sharda et al., 1988; Benbasat and Nault, 1990). A number of explanations have been offered for the conflicting findings, and there may be various mediating variables, but when two different studies with two different decision aids reach two different conclusions, might the explanation simply be that one aid is helpful and the other is not? Put differently, might each study be making a statement not about computer-based decision aids generally but about the particular aid? Researching DSS at any level of generality is a challenge because there is such a wide variety of decision-aiding technology. Of course, two conclusions can be drawn from the conflicting studies: (1) In some cases, DSS help. (2) In some cases, they do not.

Guidance mechanisms present the same problem, since so many different mechanisms can be constructed. Of the nine empirical studies, only two studied essentially the same mechanism. The other mechanisms all varied greatly, even when they belonged to the same cell of the typology. Indeed, Montazemi et al. (1996) compared guidance for two types of tasks within a single study, but task differences necessitated studying a different guidance mechanism for each task.

Given the diversity of guidance mechanisms, what does it mean when a study concludes that "users of the system with decisional guidance outperformed those of the one without"? The statement is not that decisional guidance always, or even often, outperforms. The statement is about the one instance of guidance examined in the study. To what extent, then, is the conclusion about guidance in general and to what extent is it only about a given guidance mechanism? Suppose we designed a terrible guidance mechanism—for example, suggestive guidance that systematically makes poor recommendations. How meaningful would it be to claim that non-guidance outperformed guidance? Indeed, claiming that decisional guidance outperformed non-guidance is a statement about the possible: Constructing guidance that outperforms is possible. As such the conclusion has value, validating that the invention of guidance mechanisms and the study of their effects are worthwhile pursuits. But it does not provide a generalized answer to any of the questions.

What should be done? First, we should acknowledge that studying isolated guidance mechanisms for their own sakes and not with the intent to generalize has value. A given guidance mechanism that performs well in one system may be applicable to a variety of situations. Any promising mechanism needs to be understood well, not only so that others can implement it appropriately, but also to improve upon it or to refine it for other environments. Researchers must describe clearly the features of the guidance mechanisms they study—clearly enough that someone else can implement the same features in another system. This requires sharper and more detailed descriptions than we often find today. Moreover, comparing variants of a given guidance mechanism is valuable for improving the mechanism. In some cases, these variants might all reside within the same cell of the typology. In other instances, differences across cells might motivate alternative implementations of a guidance mechanism. For instance, the same guidance might be offered automatically or on demand. In short, inventing and studying guidance mechanisms are valuable activities as they add to the collection of mechanisms available.

But what about generalizing? Generalizing is an important research activity. Broadly applicable findings can guide researchers trying to invent broadly applicable guidance mechanisms. Broad conclusions can also benefit practitioners building guidance into their systems. But the very nature of the typology suggests that few findings will apply to all forms of guidance. In many ways, decisional guidance—even just the deliberate variety, as in the typology—is an umbrella covering a broad range of features. And generalizing is likely to be made even more difficult as differences in tasks, people, and environments introduce contingencies that matter. So few findings are likely to be universal.

As a starting point, researchers should carefully position the guidance mechanisms they study within the cells of the typology so that we can compare similarly focused studies to draw broader conclusions about a given kind of guidance. Doing so should also facilitate generalizing or making useful comparisons across cells of the typology. Studies that compare guidance mechanisms that differ only on a single dimension are especially useful as we look to generalize beyond individual mechanisms. The empirical studies reviewed here were limited to those explicitly defined in terms of decisional guidance. Many other existing studies of system features could have been framed as studies of guidance. Had they been expressed in terms of guidance and positioned within the typology, those studies could have contributed not only to our understanding of the given features but also to our cumulative understanding of decisional guidance.

Studies whose guidance is theory-based and whose effects are explained by the theory are especially valuable and likely sources of generalization. Using DSS research again as an analogy, Todd and Benbasat (1999) conducted a program of research focusing on essentially the same set of decision aids for one class of problems—multi-attribute decision making. Their designs and their findings draw on behavioral decision theory pertaining to the way decision makers trade off effort and accuracy. Positioning their work this way makes their findings applicable to a much broader range of systems and problems than just this specific set of aids or class of problems. Their findings about how people trade off effort and accuracy in the context of computer-based decision aids can be applied to studying other decision-making problems and implementing other support systems. Similarly, Wilson and Zigurs (1996) and Mahoney et al. (2003) both based their guidance on the theory of cognitive fit (Vessey and Galletta, 1991). One can therefore investigate the applicability of their findings to tasks and displays other than the ones they studied.

Studying the Typology

Before concluding, there is value in identifying the most promising issues to study for each dimension of the typology:

Targets

The targets dimension distinguishes two very different kinds of guidance: guidance for choosing and guidance for using the system's functional capabilities. These are not alternative types of guidance for a given discretionary opportunity. Rather they correspond to two different points of interaction with the system: points at which one chooses what to do and points along the way of doing it. Comparing the two would not make much sense and one should take care in applying findings concerning one target to the other. It may be interesting, however, to see if such factors as automatic versus on-demand guidance produce the same findings for both targets.

Directivity

Informative guidance seems fundamentally different from the two directive forms of guidance (quasi-suggestive and suggestive), since the motivations are different: Informative guidance reflects a desire to enlighten without influencing, whereas directive guidance points users in a given direction. Given the difference in motivations, it would seem that designers do not need to choose one type of guidance over the other. They could simply implement the type of guidance that is consistent with their motives and the means available to them. One might conclude, therefore, that informative guidance should be studied separately from quasi-suggestive and suggestive guidance. Similarly, one might conclude that making comparisons across these forms of guidance would not likely be fruitful and that applying conclusions from one form to the other would be risky.

But this need not be the case. At least three factors could cause a designer to implement informative guidance despite having the motive and means to direct the user. These are (1) concerns that users will reject suggestions if they feel their independence is compromised, (2) concerns that users will have negative perceptions about overly directive systems, and (3) concerns that users may learn less about the task when handed a solution. The same three concerns might explain why a designer might choose quasi-suggestive guidance over suggestive guidance. So comparing informative guidance with the more directive forms of guidance in terms of these concerns is worth pursuing. In short, directivity may be the key dimension to consider when studying all three types of effects: behavioral, perceptual, and learning.

A related question designers face is whether to guide or restrict users. Studies such as Anthony et al.'s (2004) that compare suggestive and restrictive approaches to directing users may be especially valuable.

Invocation Style

This dimension represents a basic design choice and should be relatively straightforward to study. The main question is how the various effects depend on whether guidance is given automatically or invoked by users on demand. Whether we should expect the findings to be unique to specific guidance mechanisms, to vary by cell in the typology, or to generalize across various types of guidance is unclear a priori. Two related issues of interest are (1) the effects of allowing people to select the invocation style for themselves and (2) whether people are more likely to follow quasi-suggestive and suggestive guidance when they request it.

Timing

Of the three options for timing guidance, the most typical case is guidance addressing a discretionary opportunity the user currently confronts. Most studies of guidance will likely focus on this case. But a sizable portion of the empirical studies did provide retrospective guidance, making one wonder why a system would correct users after the fact rather than making suggestions when the issue is initially on the table. Among the possible explanations are (1) that users may learn more by first grappling with the issue themselves or (2) that the range of acceptable choices may sometimes be so great that the system cannot advise in advance but can detect errors after the fact. Retrospective guidance may therefore be an interesting topic to study.

Modes

This is the most engineering-oriented of the dimensions, addressing how the guidance is generated. Technologically, providing predefined guidance is relatively easy (although the provision of guidance does not guarantee its success). Creating effective guidance mechanisms that dynamically generate customized guidance for the user or interact with the user to generate guidance is technologically more challenging. Comparing the effects of the three modes seems less fruitful than inventing new dynamic or participative guidance mechanisms and studying their effects.

CONCLUSION

After presenting the original definition and typology, this paper reviewed a set of empirical studies of the behavioral effects of decisional guidance as the starting point for updating and broadening the concept. The revised definition of decisional guidance and the revised typology of deliberate decisional guidance are intended to apply to a broad range of interactive computer-based systems. A research agenda was presented, identifying three sets of effects that need to be studied (user behavior, user perceptions, and user learning) as well as indicating the key research issues for each of the typology's dimensions. Along the way, several ideas were presented that are important for studying decisional guidance effectively and for building a cumulative knowledge base. The paper concludes by reemphasizing three of these points.

Generalization

The revised typology is intended to serve two purposes. One is to distinguish among different types of guidance, focusing researchers and helping practitioners select the most appropriate type of guidance. The other purpose is to facilitate meaningful generalization by identifying the underlying differences that may matter. Even with the revised typology, drawing broad generalizations about the effects of decisional guidance will be difficult because guidance mechanisms can vary greatly and because the unique features of a given mechanism may matter most. Researchers can improve our ability to generalize by describing well the guidance mechanisms they study and by locating them clearly within the typology. Studying theory-based guidance may be especially valuable.

Inadvertent Guidance

This paper—like all the studies of decisional guidance to date—concentrated on deliberate decisional guidance. But inadvertent guidance, situations where system features influence users in ways not intended by the designer, is also an important design concern. Subtle nuances in how features are implemented may have significant consequences for how users exercise discretion. Research on these features is greatly needed and practitioners need to be aware of this design issue.

Deliberate Guidance and Directivity

Just because guidance is deliberate does not mean it is intended to be directive. Directive guidance generally is implemented as quasi-suggestive or suggestive guidance, whereas non-directive guidance is generally implemented as informative guidance. Since a given system may have many guidance features, some may be directive and some may not. Designers need to be attuned to their design philosophies and motives when implementing guidance. Moreover, even directive guidance still allows users discretion, since they can reject the guidance's recommendations. An alternative approach to directing users is through restrictiveness, which forces users in a given direction. At a minimum, researchers need to be explicit about the restrictiveness–guidance distinction and clear as to which they are studying. Studying the trade-offs between these two directive approaches would be especially valuable.

Summation

Decades ago, forward-thinking practitioners and researchers recognized that the passive, batch-oriented, one-size-fits-all management information systems (MIS) of the day did not meet the needs of managers, who required more focused interactive tools that they could manipulate personally to support their specific managerial tasks. These revolutionaries similarly rebelled against overly rigid interactive systems that provided their users with little flexibility and discretion. Today, flexible interactive systems that afford users significant discretion are the norm in many application domains, not just in the realm of managerial support. But flexibility and discretion raise new questions: How will users behave given such flexibility? How will they exercise their discretion?

The study of decisional guidance promises an answer. Studying inadvertent decisional guidance can help practitioners limit the unintended consequences of the features they design. Studying deliberate decisional guidance—directive or not—can help practitioners develop and deploy guidance mechanisms that enable users to cope more effectively with the flexibility and discretion they are afforded. Such guidance, for instance, might help users deal with the featuritis of today's word processors, electronic spreadsheets, and other productivity software. Such guidance might help users cope with the overload of information and links they encounter on the World Wide Web. Such guidance might help users avoid known pitfalls in their decision-making processes. It might help increase consistency across users performing the same task in an organization. And it might help groups avoid process losses in their interactions.

Providing deliberate decisional guidance successfully requires more than recognizing an opportunity for guiding and inventing a corresponding guidance mechanism. Designers need to consider the consequences of these mechanisms—including performance effects, user perceptions, and learning effects, which often conflict with one another. We have much to learn in these areas. Our understanding of decisional guidance is still relatively primitive, but we are well positioned to advance our understanding and our practice.

ACKNOWLEDGMENTS

This chapter is dedicated to the memory of Gerry DeSanctis, whose guidance was always gracious and invaluable. I appreciate the helpful comments of Lynne Markus, Sidne Ward, Mihir Parikh, and two anonymous reviewers on earlier versions of the chapter. I also appreciate the support and advice of Ping Zhang and Dennis Galletta.

REFERENCES

Antony, S.; Batra, D.; and Santhanam, R. The use of a knowledge-based system in conceptual data modeling. *Decision Support Systems*, 41, 1 (2005), 176–188.

Benbasat, I., and Nault, B.R. An evaluation of empirical research in management support systems. *Decision Support Systems*, 6, 3 (1990), 203–226.

Bjorkman, M. Feedforward and feedback as determiners of knowledge and policy: notes on a neglected issue. *Scandinavian Journal of Psychology*, 13 (1972), 152–158.

Davis, F.D. Perceived usefulness, perceived ease of use and user acceptance of information technology. *MIS Quarterly*, 13, 3 (1989), 319–340.

DeSanctis, G., and Scott Poole, M. Capturing the complexity in advanced technology use: adaptive structuration theory. *Organization Science*, 5, 2 (1994), 121–147.

Dhaliwal, J.S., and Benbasat, I. The use and effects of knowledge-based system explanations: theoretical foundations and a framework for empirical evaluation. *Information Systems Research*, 7, 3 (1996), 342–362.

Huguenard, B., and Ballou, D. You may feel better off than you are: usefulness evaluations of cognitive feedback. In *Seventh Americas Conference on Information Systems*, Boston, 2001, pp. 271–277.

Jankowski, D. How can CASE help? A look at the feasibility of supporting structured analysis with case. *The DATA BASE for Advances in Information Systems*, 28, 4 (1997), 33–47.

Jiang, J.J., and Klein, G. Side effects of decision guidance in decision support systems. *Interacting with Computers*, 12, 5 (2000), 469–481.

Limayem, M., and DeSanctis, G. Automating decision guidance in a group decision environment. In *Proceedings of the Fourteenth International Conference on Information Systems*, Orlando, FL, 1993, pp. 157–168.

Limayem, M., and DeSanctis, G. Providing decisional guidance for multi-criteria decision making in groups. *Information Systems Research*, 11, 4 (2000), 386–401.

Mahoney, L.S.; Roush, P.B.; and Bandy, D. An investigation of the effects of decisional guidance and cognitive ability on decision-making involving uncertainty data. *Information and Organization*, 13, 2 (2003), 85–110.

Montazemi, A.R.; Wang, F.; Nainar, S.M.K.; and Bart, C.K. On the effectiveness of decision guidance. *Decision Support Systems*, 18, 2 (1996), 181–198.

Parikh, M.A., and Fazlollahi, B. Analyzing user satisfaction with decisional guidance. In *Decision Sciences Institute 2002 Annual Meeting Proceedings*, San Diego, CA: Decision Sciences Institute, 2002, pp. 128–133.

Parikh, M.; Fazlollahi, B.; and Verma, S. The effectiveness of decisional guidance: an empirical evaluation. *Decision Sciences*, 32, 2 (2001), 303–331.

Rai, A.; Stubbart, C.; and Paper, D. Can executive information systems reinforce biases? *Accounting, Management, and Information Technology*, 4, 2 (1994), 87–106.

Scott, L.; Horvath, L.; and Day, D. Characterizing case constraints. *Communications of the ACM*, 43, 11es (2000), 232–238.

Sharda, R.; Barr, S.H.; and McDonnell, J.C. Decision support system effectiveness: a review and an empirical test. *Management Science*, 34, 2 (1988), 139–159.

Silver, M.S. Decisional guidance for computer–based decision support. *MIS Quarterly*, 15, 1 (1991a), 105–122.

Silver, M.S. *Systems That Support Decision Makers: Description and Analysis*. Chichester: John Wiley & Sons, 1991b.

Silver, M.S. Decision support systems: directed and nondirected change. *Information Systems Research*, 1, 1 (1990), 47–70.

Singh, D.T. Incorporating cognitive aids into decision support systems: the case of the strategy execution progress. *Decision Support Systems*, 24, 2 (1998), 145–163.

Te'eni, D. Feedback in DSS as a source of control: experiments with the timing of feedback. *Decision Sciences*, 22, 3 (1991), 644–655.

Todd, P., and Benbasat, I. An experimental investigation of the impact of computer based decision aids on decision making strategies. *Information Systems Research*, 2, 2 (1991), 87–115.

Vessey, I., and Galletta, D. Cognitive fit: an empirical study of information acquisition. *Information Systems Research*, 2, 1 (1991), 63–84.

Vessey, I.; Jarvenpaa, S.L.; and Tractinsky, N. Evaluation of vendor products: case tools as methodology companions. *Communications of the ACM*, 35, 4 (1992), 90–105.

Wang, W., and Benbasat, I. Impact of explanations on trust in online recommendation agents. Working Paper 04-MIS-002, MIS Division, University of British Columbia, Vancouver, Canada, 2004.

Wheeler, B.C., and Valacich, J.S. Facilitation, GSS, and training as sources of process restrictiveness and guidance for structured group decision making: an empirical assessment. *Information Systems Research*, 7, 4 (1996), 429–450.

Wilson, E.V., and Zigurs, I. Decisional guidance and end user display choices. *Accounting, Management and Information Technologies*, 9, 1 (1999), 49–75.

CHAPTER 7

COORDINATION THEORY

A Ten-Year Retrospective

KEVIN CROWSTON, JOSEPH RUBLESKE, AND JAMES HOWISON

Abstract: *Since the initial publication in 1994, coordination theory has been referenced in nearly three hundred journal articles, book chapters, conference papers, and theses. Coordination theory provides an approach to a core problem in HCI: It analyzes group work to suggest alternative approaches involving computer support. Coordination theory suggests identifying the dependencies between the tasks the different group members are carrying out and the coordination mechanisms the group uses to coordinate its work, and then considering alternative mechanisms. This chapter will analyze the contribution of this body of research to determine how coordination theory has been used for user task analysis and modeling for HCI. Issues that will be addressed include: (1) how the theory has been applied; (2) factors that led to the success of the theory; and (3) identification of areas needing further research.*

Keywords: *Coordination Theory, HCI, Process Analysis, Group Work*

An increasingly ubiquitous application of computer systems is to help a group of people work together better. To do so requires an appreciation of what the group is doing and how its members might work together in a more efficient or effective manner. Such user/group task analysis and modeling is at the core of MIS HCI research. A key issue in the analysis of group work is an understanding of the dependencies between the tasks the different group members are carrying out and the way the group coordinates their work. However, many studies describe dependencies and processes only in general terms, without characterizing in detail differences between dependencies, the problems dependencies create or how the proposed coordination processes address those problems (Grant, 1996; Medema, 1996). This vagueness makes it difficult or impossible to determine what alternative processes might be useful in a given circumstance. Similarly, it is hard to translate from dependencies to specifications of individual activities or to uses of information and communication technologies (ICT) to support a process—e.g., as part of system development during a business process redesign effort (Davenport and Short, 1990; Hammer, 1990; Harrington, 1991; Harrison and Pratt, 1993).

In 1994, Malone and Crowston described a new approach to these problems, an approach they called coordination theory (CT) (Malone and Crowston, 1994). Their 1994 paper presented examples of similar coordination problems encountered in a variety of disciplines and analyzed them as arising from dependencies. For example, approaches to sharing resources (i.e., ways to manage the dependency created when multiple tasks require the same resources) have been analyzed in economics, organization theory, and computer science, among others. Other dependencies identified by Malone and Crowston are producer/consumer dependencies, simultaneity constraints and task/subtask relations. Since its 1994 publication, nearly three hundred papers and dissertations have referred to or made use of the CT approach. The purpose of this chapter is to introduce CT, review the impact it has had for MIS HCI and its limitations, to discuss factors contributing to its level of impact and to identify areas needing further research.

Before introducing coordination theory in detail, we wish to respond to commentators who have objected to the name "coordination theory," arguing that it is not in fact a theory. This critique presumes a definition of theory such as:

"A set of statements or principles devised to explain a group of facts or phenomena, especially one that has been repeatedly tested or is widely accepted and can be used to make predictions about natural phenomena"

(American Heritage Dictionary, 2000).

Such statements are also known as scientific laws. Malone and Crowston chose the name "coordination theory" in part because many of the fields synthesized do have such laws and the hope was that coordination theory would develop to include them, even if it did not in its initial statement. However, the critique overlooks the fact that theories include scientific concepts as well as laws (Kaplan, 1998, p. 297). Theory in this sense helps make sense of data and makes observed events meaningful. Concept and theory generation go hand in hand, and an initial set of concepts guides the search for data and for laws. As we will see, coordination theory definitely includes a set of concepts that can be used to label phenomena and link them to others, and thus fulfills this important function of theory. In its current state though, we would describe coordination theory as a pattern model (Kaplan, 1998, p. 327), meaning that it seeks to explain phenomena by showing how they fit a known pattern.

CONTRIBUTIONS OF COORDINATION THEORY

The primary purpose of Malone and Crowston (1994) was to synthesize work done on coordination from a variety of fields. The work started with an interest in how groupware (i.e., software designed to support groups of people working together) might help people to coordinate their activities better. The paper made three key contributions.

First Contribution: Definition of Coordination

The first contribution of the paper was a concise definition of coordination as "managing dependencies between activities." Coordination has been a long-standing interest of organizational scholars, and, more recently, of computer scientists, so many definitions for this term had been proposed. Malone and Crowston (1994) and Weigand et al. (2003) list several, including:

- Structuring and facilitating transactions between interdependent components (Chandler, 1962)
- The protocols, tasks, and decision-making mechanisms designed to achieve concerted actions between interdependent units (Thompson, 1967)
- The integrative devices for interconnecting differentiated sub-units (Lawrence and Lorsch, 1967)

- Composing purposeful actions into larger purposeful wholes (Holt, 1988)
- The integration and harmonious adjustment of individual work efforts towards the accomplishment of a larger goal (Singh and Rein, 1992)
- Establishing attunement between tasks with the purpose of accomplishing that the execution of separate tasks is timely, in the right order and of the right quantity (Reezigt, 1995)

In contrast to the first three definitions, drawn from the organization studies literature, Malone and Crowston (1994) conceptualize dependencies as arising between tasks rather than individuals or units. This approach has the advantage of making it easier to model the effects of reassignments of activities to different actors, which is common in process redesign efforts. Compared to the final three definitions, taken from the computer-supported cooperative work (CSCW) literature, the Malone and Crowston (1994) definition focuses attention on why coordination is needed, rather than on the desired outcome of coordination. This focus has advantages again for modeling, as will be discussed below.

Second Contribution: Modeling Framework

The second contribution of the 1994 paper was to provide a theoretical framework for analyzing coordination in complex processes, thus contributing to user task analysis and modeling. Consistent with the definition proposed above, Malone and Crowston (1994) analyzed group action in terms of *actors* performing *interdependent tasks*. These tasks might require or create *resources* of various types. For example, in the case of software requirements development, actors include the customers and various employees of the software company. Tasks include translating aspects of a customer's problem into system requirements and checking requirements for consistency against other requirements. Finally, resources include information about the customer's problem, existing system functionality, and analysts' time and effort. In this view, actors in organizations face *coordination problems* arising from dependencies that constrain how tasks can be performed.

It should be noted that in developing this framework, Malone and Crowston describe coordination mechanisms as relying on other necessary group functions, such as decision making, communications, and development of shared understandings and collective sensemaking (Britton et al., 2000; Crowston and Kammerer, 1998). To develop a complete model of some process would involve modeling all of these aspects: coordination, decision making, and communications. In practice, our analyses have tended to focus on the coordination aspects, bracketing the other phenomenon, though clearly groups might face problems in all of these.

Third Contribution: Typology of Dependencies and Coordination Mechanisms

The main claim of coordination theory is that dependencies and the mechanisms for managing them are general; that is, any given dependency and the mechanisms to manage it will be found in a variety of organizational settings. Thus the final contribution of coordination theory is a typology of dependencies and related coordination mechanisms, as shown in Table 7.1. For continuity, in this paper we will use the original typology presented by Malone and Crowston (1994), though it has been refined in more recent work; see Malone et al. (1999) and Crowston (2003).

For example, a common coordination problem is that certain tasks require specialized skills, thus constraining which actors can work on them. This dependency between a task and an actor arises in some form in nearly every organization. CT suggests identifying and studying such

Table 7.1

Examples of Common Dependencies Between Activities and Alternative Coordination Processes for Managing Them

Dependency	Examples of Coordination Processes for Managing Dependency
Shared resources	"First come/first serve," priority order, budgets, managerial decision, market-like bidding
• Task assignments	(same as for "Shared resources")
Producer/consumer relationships	
• Prerequisite constraints	Notification, sequencing, tracking
• Transfer	Inventory management (e.g., "just in time," "economic order quantity")
• Usability	Standardization, ask users, participatory design
• Design for manufacturability	Concurrent engineering
Simultaneity constraints	Scheduling, synchronization
Task/subtask	Goal selection, task decomposition

Source: From Malone and Crowston (1994).
Note: Indentations in the left column indicate more specialized versions of general dependency types.

common dependencies and their related coordination mechanisms across a wide variety of orga-nizational settings.

Another common dependency is the *producer/consumer* (or *flow*) dependency, in which one task creates a resource that is needed by another. Malone and Crowston (1994) divided this dependency into three subdependencies, *usability*, *transfer*, and *precedence*. The *usability* sub-dependency means that the resource created by the first task must be appropriate for the needs of the second task. The *transfer* subdependency means that the resource must be moved from where it was created to where the consuming task will be performed. And finally, the *precedence* sub-dependency means that the actor performing the second task must learn when the resource is available and when the task can be started.

To overcome these coordination problems, actors must perform additional work, which Malone and Crowston (1994) called *coordination mechanisms*. For example, if particular expertise is neces-sary to perform a particular task (a task-actor dependency), then an actor with that expertise must be identified and the task assigned to him or her. There are often several coordination mechanisms that can be used to manage a dependency. For example, mechanisms to manage the dependency between an activity and an actor include (among others): (1) having a manager pick a subordinate to perform the task; (2) assigning the task to the first available actor; and (3) a labor market in which actors bid on jobs. To manage a usability subdependency, the resource might be tailored to the needs of the consumer (meaning that the consumer has to provide that information to the producer) or a producer might follow a standard so the consumer knows what to expect. Mechanisms may be useful in a wide variety of organizational settings. Conversely, organizations with similar goals achieved using more or less the same set of activities will have to manage the same dependencies, but may choose different coordination mechanisms, thus resulting in different processes.

CT suggests that, given an organization performing some task, one way to generate alternative processes is to first identify the particular dependencies and coordination problems faced by that organization and then consider what alternative coordination mechanisms could be used to manage them. In particular, we can look for processes supported by extensive use of ICT, thus contributing to system design for collaborative systems.

Summary of Contributions

To summarize, Malone and Crowston (1994) made several contributions in defining coordination theory. Substantively, their 1994 paper provided (1) a succinct and actionable definition of coordination; (2) a framework for task analysis and modeling for collective processes; and (3) the beginning of a typology of dependencies and coordination mechanisms. The paper also advanced the field by drawing attention to coordination as a topic for research and providing examples of coordination topics in multiple disciplines. Coordination mechanisms are now an integral topic in fields such as distributed artificial intelligence and multi-agent systems.

EXAMPLE: COORDINATION IN RESTAURANT SERVICE

In order to make the previous presentation of CT more concrete, we will present two examples of its use for MIS HCI, in restaurant service and in software development. The first example is a short analysis of the customer service aspects of a restaurant. Restaurants have long been studied as important forums for coordination. The essential characteristics of restaurants—many customers, many orders, frequent deliveries, continuous monitoring of customers and of personnel in accomplishing work, and perishable products—makes them particularly illuminating for studies of logistical flows, information flows, and resultant needs for coordination. As Whyte (1948, pp. 18–19) noted, "Failure of coordination is perhaps the chief enemy of job satisfaction for the worker. And the varying and unpredictable demands of customers makes this coordination always difficult to achieve." He noted further that in a small restaurant, everyone was in direct contact "and the problems of communication and coordination are relatively simple," while in a larger restaurant, "coordination must be accomplished through people who are not generally in face-to-face contact with each other" (p. 47). Finally, we assume that all readers are familiar with the basic process of restaurant service, allowing us to focus on the coordination aspects of the analysis.

The first step in a CT-based analysis is to develop a description of the activities involved in the process. A simple description of these steps is shown in Figure 7.1, which shows actors on the left and activities performed by each across the page in time-order. Activities performed jointly are connected by dotted lines. While there may be some disagreements about details (note in particular that the kitchen is modeled as a single collective actor and cooking as a single high-level activity), the sequence of activities is recognizable as representative of a traditional sit-down cook-to-order restaurant.

Dependencies in Restaurant Process

The next step in the analysis is to identify dependencies in the process. Particularly important in this case are the producer/consumer dependencies between activities. These dependencies can be easily identified by noting where one activity produces a resource required by another. The resource flows and resulting dependencies for the restaurant process are shown in Figure 7.2. For example, the activity of cooking creates food that can then be served and eaten; customers' departures produce a table ready for busing; and busing and resetting a table produces a table ready for another party. One could also analyze shared resource dependencies between customers needing the same table or attention in the kitchen, but for brevity, we will omit this discussion.

Figure 7.1   The Restaurant Service Process
Actors are shown down the left side, activities performed by each are shown in order across the page. Activities performed jointly are connected with dotted lines.

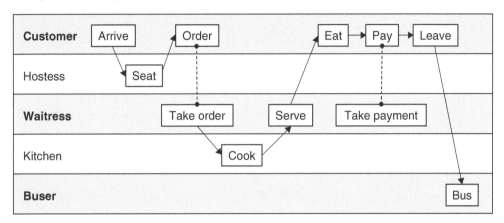

Figure 7.2   Flow of Resources Between Activities and Resulting Dependencies in the Restaurant Service Process

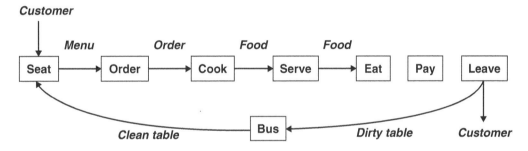

Viewing the process in terms of producer/consumer dependencies further suggests that the waitstaff act as intermediaries between the kitchen and the customer, taking an order and transmitting it to the kitchen, or taking food prepared by the kitchen and delivering it to the customer. In other words, there is a high-level dependency—between the cooking activities performed by the kitchen and the eating activities performed by the customer—that is managed by activities performed by the waitstaff. More specifically, the *usability* subdependency between cooking and eating is managed by taking an order (allowing the customer to select the most appropriate food and in some case, the kitchen to tailor the food to the customer). The *transfer* subdependency is managed by having the waitstaff move the food from the kitchen to the table. The *precedence* subdependency is managed by the customers' waiting for the food to be delivered. Similarly, activities performed by the host or hostess manage a dependency between customers needing tables and the activities involved in preparing tables. This model is shown in Figure 7.3.

The analysis can also be performed for dependencies that arise between the initial set of tasks and the tasks that comprise the chosen coordination mechanisms. In particular, for a traditional restaurant there is a producer/consumer dependency between serving and cooking that itself requires management, for the *precedence* subdependency in particular; that is, there must be some way for the waitstaff to know when the food is ready to be served.

Figure 7.3   **Model of High-Level Dependencies and Coordination Mechanisms for Restaurant Service**

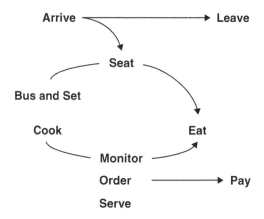

Alternative Processes

Having identified the dependencies, we can now use the taxonomies of dependencies and related coordination mechanisms to imagine alternative processes. In particular, we can look for processes that rely on ICT support, using the models to suggest the coordination functions that the systems need to perform.

For example, different actors might perform the order and transfer coordination mechanisms. In many busy restaurants, drinks and food are delivered by "runners" waiting in the kitchen rather than by the waiter or waitress who took the order. Similarly, rather than walking an order to the kitchen, waitstaff in many restaurants enter orders on a computer system that transmits them to the kitchen. Some restaurants even provide waitstaff with wireless terminals with which to transmit orders from table to kitchen. One could imagine providing such a terminal to the customer; orders would then be directly transmitted to the kitchen and delivered when they are ready, thus eliminating the role of the waitress or waiter, that is, disintermediation of the relationship between kitchen and customer (Benjamin and Wigand, 1995). (Indeed, we saw such a system in one Internet café: Customers visited the café's Web site to place orders for coffee and cakes, which were then delivered by the waitstaff.)

Restaurants have employed a large variety of information systems to manage the precedence subdependency between activities. In Malone and Crowston's (1994) analysis, a precedence dependency can be managed in one of two ways: either the person performing the first activity can notify the person performing the second that a resource is ready, or the second can monitor the performance of the first. A number of mechanisms have been devised to notify waitstaff that food is ready in the kitchen, ranging from a cook's shouting "Order up!" to bells, numbered lights on the wall, and, most recently, pagers. In the absence of a notification mechanism, actors must instead spend time monitoring the status of the previous activity. For example, a bused table, ready for customers, waits until the host or hostess notices it. A paging system can be used to let the buser notify the host or hostess that a table has been bused and is ready. Similarly, the waitstaff can monitor the kitchen to notice when an order is ready or the kitchen staff can page the wait staff to notify them that it is. Once a suitable notification system is available, it can be employed at all stages of the process. For example, waitstaff can be paged when new customers arrive at a table;

Figure 7.4 **Dependencies Between High-Level Tasks in Software Development**

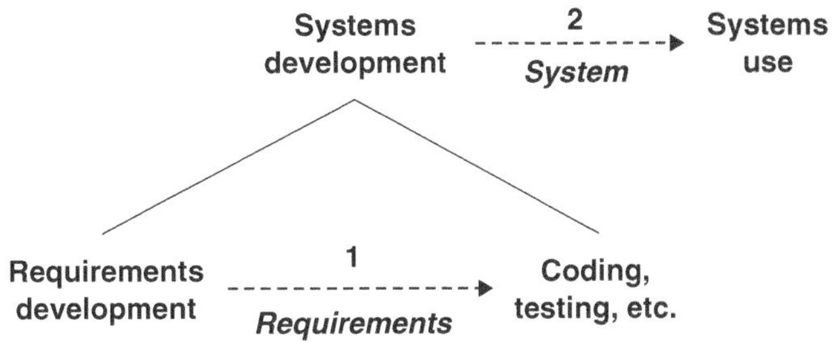

Note: Solid lines indicate decomposition of a task into subtasks. Dotted lines indicate a flow of resources and therefore a producer-consumer dependency.

a buser can be paged when the table has been vacated and is waiting to be bused. These changes can be employed in combination: for example, in a restaurant that employs runners, the waitstaff can be paged to meet the runner at tableside to make the final presentation of the food, thus maintaining the appearance of a single server.

In summary, this example illustrates the main uses of CT. A process can be analyzed in terms of the dependencies among resources and tasks and the current coordination mechanisms identified. This analysis can then be used to suggest alternative processes, created by substituting one coordination mechanism for another.

EXAMPLE: COORDINATION IN SOFTWARE REQUIREMENTS ANALYSIS

As a second more substantive example, we present a coordination theory analysis of the software requirements analysis process, drawn from Crowston and Kammerer (1998). Requirements analysis is the stage in the software development process of determining what functionality and interfaces a new system should have. Figure 7.4 places the requirements analysis process in the context of the overall software development process. This stage is especially important because it establishes the framework for the rest of the development effort. Early mistakes become increasingly more difficult and expensive to fix later in the process, so an inadequate requirements definition will have adverse effects throughout the development process and beyond (Pressman, 1982).

Dependencies in Software Requirements Analysis

A CT analysis involves identifying the dependencies that arise in this process and the coordination mechanisms being used to manage them. The primary tasks in requirements analysis are translating domain knowledge, such as customers' statements of their needs or descriptions of interacting systems, into requirements that can be used to develop software. In addition, these requirements need to be checked to ensure they are complete and consistent both with each other and with prior decisions about the system. Resources include the knowledge and effort of the analysts, other people whom the analysts consult and other sources of information. Between these tasks and resources, numerous dependencies are possible.

Task-Resource Dependencies

Most tasks require resources, if only the effort of the actor performing the task, and an important class of coordination processes manage the assignment of resources to tasks. Crowston (2003) suggests four steps to such resource assignments: identifying the type of resources needed, identifying available resources, selecting the resources and making the assignment. Most work on resource assignment (e.g., in economics, organization theory, or computer science) has focused on the middle steps, that is, techniques for identifying or selecting available resources. By contrast, in the requirements analysis process the first step—identifying what resources are needed to perform a particular task—seems equally important. Analysts can easily refer problems to one another, but they must somehow first determine who should be consulted for a particular problem based on the nature of the problem and the expertise and assignment of different developers. This problem is exacerbated by the potential for dependencies among requirements (i.e., between the products of these tasks), which increases the need for consultation.

Producer-Consumer Dependencies

A second major type of dependency is a producer-consumer dependency, where the output of one task is the input to another. Malone and Crowston (1994) note that such dependencies often impose additional constraints, in particular usability—ensuring that the output is of a form usable by the next task—and transfer—ensuring that the output is available to the consumer when needed. This type of dependency exists at a high level between the requirements process and further downstream software development processes. Although there are some transfer problems— e.g., making sure that the requirements are finished on schedule—usability seems to pose a key problem. Indeed, at the highest level shown in Figure 7.4, the requirements development process itself can be viewed as a coordination mechanism that ensures that the output of the software development process is usable by the eventual customers for the system. Malone and Crowston (1994) suggest alternative approaches to satisfying a usability dependency, including standardization (i.e., producing the output in an expected form), asking the users, and participatory design.

For the software developers who are the users of the requirements, the main approach to usability appears to be standardization. Most companies have standards for the format and content of requirements documents to ensure that they are easily usable by software developers. For the eventual customer of the software, though, a standard output is assumed to be unsatisfactory, since the companies studied developed customized systems. Making the system usable required the application of a lot of specialized knowledge about application domain (Walz et al., 1993), so that members of requirements development groups were often experts in their fields. However, gathering the information about the particular circumstances of the customer required considerable additional work.

Task-Subtask Dependencies

Third, some tasks are decomposable into subtasks. For example, the task of writing requirements must typically be decomposed into units of work that a single individual can perform. A key issue in any decomposition, however, is ensuring that the overall goal is satisfied by the performance of the subtasks. Without such a check, it is easy for analysts to focus on their component of the system and lose sight of the system's overall goals.

Feature and Requirement Interdependencies

Finally, there are dependencies between entities that need to be identified and managed, a dependency that Malone et al. (1999) labeled "fit." In particular, interactions among features are often a problem in large systems with many features. Analysts must determine how each feature interacts with every other feature in the system and control for undesirable interactions. When there are hundreds of features, each supported by different teams of people, these interactions may be extremely difficult to detect. Modifying the software for one feature may affect other features in very subtle ways that the analyst specifying the modification has not anticipated, with the result that those in charge of the affected feature might not become aware of the changes until their feature "breaks." In order to solve the feature-interaction problem, one must know how to get important information to the appropriate people without overloading everyone by broadcasting all information to all people. Additionally, the requirements themselves may have dependencies. Developing a consistent specification when many different people must write parts of the specification is difficult.

Coordination Mechanisms for Requirements Analysis

Many of the solutions proposed for requirements analysis correspond to the suggestions of CT, focusing on better ways to manage dependencies or even to reduce and eliminate them. An example of the second is the decomposition of a system into decoupled subparts with well-defined interfaces or using design methodologies that only allow certain kinds of interactions, with the goal of forcing dependencies along particular channels.

Strategies for managing dependencies focus on more efficient ways to transfer information among people, such as formal languages or prototyping, to surface dependencies. These include techniques for eliciting requirements from people, modeling techniques, requirements definition methods, and computer support tools (Brackett, 1990). Techniques for eliciting requirements include a variety of general techniques for information gathering, such as those surveyed by Davis (1983) and Powers, Adams, and Mills (1984). The joint application development technique (JAD), which was developed by IBM, allows analysts to get information from and negotiate with clients in intensive workshop sessions. Structured analysis and design technique (SADT) (Marca and McGowan, 1988) provides a method for iterative review of requirements by developer and client. Walk-throughs (Freedman and Weinberg, 1982) and technical reviews (Collofello, 1988) can be used to assess the quality and progress of the requirements definition process.

Modeling techniques are used to represent aspects of the information gathered. The methods are typically graphical, although physical and simulation models are occasionally used. Most modeling methods allow the system to be described in terms of several of the following in order to gain a sufficiently comprehensive view of the system: interfaces to external entities, functions to be performed, data transformations, structure of input/output data, relationships among information and system behavior (Brackett, 1990).

There are many computer-based tools to support requirements definition and model development. Most of these are method-specific tools. Non-method-specific tools also exist, with Problem Statement Language (PSL) and Problem Statement Analyzer (PSA), usually referred to as PSL/PSA (Teichroew and Hershey, 1977), being one of the most well known of these. The non-method-specific tools generally require either customization to the method used by the developer or translation from the developer's notation to the tool's notation. Finally, many tools have been developed to support prototyping. These include languages and packages designed for creating prototypes, fourth-generation languages, windowing system tool kits, and many others (Brackett, 1990).

In summary, a CT analysis of requirements analysis suggests viewing the requirements analysis process itself as a coordination mechanism for managing the usability of the software development process for the end user. Within the process, developers must identify and manage dependencies inherent in software requirements development, specifically dependencies between tasks and actors with the knowledge to contribute to the tasks, producer/consumer dependencies between requirements developers and programmers (especially with regards to usability), and dependencies among requirements and features themselves.

COORDINATION THEORY: IMPACT

In this section, we will discuss the impact that CT has had in general and on MIS HCI in particular. A common way to measure the impact of a theory is by counting citations to the seminal articles. By this measure, CT has had a moderate impact, as the CT articles—the 1994 Computing Surveys article (Malone and Crowston, 1994), an earlier conference paper (Malone and Crowston, 1990), and working-paper versions (Malone, 1988; Malone and Crowston, 1991)— have been cited in at least 287 journal articles, conference papers, and dissertations. This level of citations is well above the average, though not as high as a citation classic, such as TAM (Davis, 1989), which has closer to 800 citations.

To better understand the impact of CT, we examined the use of CT in these publications in more detail. In the remainder of this section, we will describe the method used to find and code citing articles, then discuss the factors that seem to have contributed to the success that CT has enjoyed. We conclude with a brief discussion of the progress that has been made on Malone and Crowston's (1994) research agenda and suggestions of areas for further research.

Method

Citations were found by searching for citations to the CT articles mentioned above in the ISI Social Science and Science Citation Indexes, which we accessed via Dialog. To find citations in conference papers and other sources not indexed by ISI, we also searched for citations in Citeseer (http://citeseer.psu.edu/). These two sources provided a total of 287 references between 1989 (a citation to the earliest working paper presentations of CT) through 2004. Note, though, that there is a delay between publication and indexing by citation databases, meaning that the data for recent years is likely incomplete. In addition, these two databases do not cover numerous sources, such as book chapters, such as those in Malone, Crowston, and Herman (2003), most of which cite Malone and Crowston (1994). As a result, the count of citations should be considered a lower bound.

We next obtained abstracts and full text for as many of the articles as we could. We were able to obtain the text for 232 of the articles. We then coded these articles according to the general topic of the work, how the research reported used CT, and if the research extended CT in some way. The coding system was developed through discussion among the authors to refine the definitions of the categories. Once we had come to agreement about how to code a subset of the articles, each author independently coded a portion of the remaining articles.

Findings: Uses of Coordination Theory

For how the research used CT, we coded articles into four categories, based on which of the three contributions of Malone and Crowston (1994) contributed to the research.

Figure 7.5   **Counts of Use of Articles Over Time**

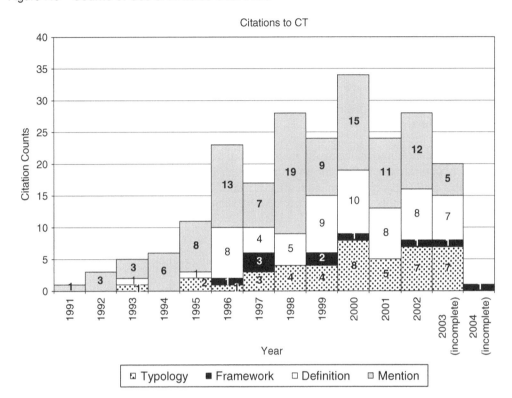

- The majority of articles (115/232 or about half) were coded as "mention," meaning that a CT article was cited (e.g., in a discussion of coordination), but that the research did not use the definition, modeling framework, or typology of dependencies and mechanisms proposed by Malone and Crowston (1994). (Indeed, a few articles included a CT reference without any discussion in the text of the paper.)
- The next largest group of articles (63/232 or just over a quarter) used the definition of coordination proposed by Malone and Crowston (1994) ("coordination is management of dependencies"), but not other aspects of the work.
- A small number of papers (10/232 or 4 percent) used the definition and the modeling framework (actors working on tasks that create or use resources) but not the typologies.
- The final set of articles (46/232 or 20 percent) made some use of the typology of dependencies and coordination mechanism. We focused most of our attention on these articles, since they represented the most substantive use of CT. Examples of the work in this group of articles are discussed below.

Figure 7.5 shows the count of articles by classification over time. The figure suggests a steady interest in CT over time (note that the citation counts for 2003 and especially 2004 are incomplete).

DISCUSSION: FACTORS IN THE IMPACT OF COORDINATION THEORY

In this section, we briefly discuss the factors involved in the level of adoption of CT. To analyze this success, we draw on work by Martens (2003). Based on a study of the life history of theories, she suggested eight factors important to the success of a theory, grouped into empirical, theoretical, and social factors.

Empirical Factors

Martens notes three empirical factors for the success of a theory: that the theory is applicable to a wide variety of phenomenon; that the phenomena are salient; and that the constructs are defined in a way that facilitates replication and testing. CT does generally well on these empirical criteria. First, our review of the citations discussed above shows that CT has been applied to a diverse range of settings. Major areas include:

- Software engineering (e.g., Crowston, 1997; Crowston and Kammerer, 1998; Faraj and Sproull, 2000; Krieger et al., 2003; e.g., McChesney, 1997),
- Systems design (e.g., Bernstein and Klein, 2002; e.g., Bernstein and Klein, 2002; Bui, 2000; Bui and Lee, 1999; Klein and Bernstein, 2004; Klusch et al., 2003; Ossowski and Omicini, 2002; Ricci et al., 2003; van Breemen and de Vries, 2001),
- Business processes (e.g., Albino et al., 2002; Lee and Lee, 1999; Lizotte and Chaib-draa, 1997; e.g., Sikora and Shaw, 1998),
- Supply chains (e.g., Bello et al., 2003; Britton et al., 2000; den Hengst and Sol, 2002; Kobayashi et al., 2003; e.g., Mehring, 2000), and
- Organizational simulations (e.g., Clancey et al., 1998).

For example, den Hengst and Sol (2002) focus on "interorganizational coordination structures" (IOCS) and the factors (such as ICTs) that influence them, and in particular, to assess how e-commerce will affect IOCS. The container-transport industry is used as a case study. Crowston (1997) uses CT to analyze the software problem fixing process of a large mini-computer manufacturer in order to identify sources of difficulties and possible alternative processes. CT has also been used to analyze the cataloguing processes of the *Flora of North America* digital library (Schnase et al., 1997), the benefits of active sick leave (Scheel et al., 2002), methods for organizational process change (Kim, 2000), knowledge management (Holsapple and Joshi, 2000; Holsapple and Joshi, 2002), and the use of genres for coordination (Yoshioka et al., 2001).

Second, as we noted in the introduction, in these diverse areas, many researchers have noted the importance of coordination problems and the potential for computer systems to help groups of people work together better, arguing for the salience of coordination as a research topic.

For the final factor though, testability, we note a negative result, since CT is not currently presented in a way that facilitates testing. Indeed, an early critique of CT, as mentioned above, was that it was not a theory at all, because it did not provide a list of hypothesized relationships. Martens's research suggests that it would be useful for the progress of CT to be able to state a set of testable propositions or hypotheses. These would likely be in the form of a process model, identifying factors that are necessary but not sufficient for better coordination of a process.

Theoretical Factors

Martens identifies two theoretical factors for the success of a theory: multiple uses for theory, and fit with other theories or approaches. Again, CT does well on these criteria. First, CT can be applied to several purposes, such as modeling a process to understanding how it works to suggesting improvements, or for designing new coordination mechanisms, particularly those that rely on information and communications technologies. A number of articles build on the modeling approach proposed by Malone and Crowston (1994). For example, Tolksdorf used the definition and modeling concepts from CT to develop an XML schema for describing business process models (Tolksdorf, 2000) and a dependency markup language (Tolksdorf, 2003).

Second, CT has been combined with other process modeling techniques. For example, Crowston and Osborn (2003) developed a six-step technique for documenting organizational processes by embedding CT in Checkland's (1981; 1990) soft systems methodology. They propose two general heuristics for identifying dependencies: dependency-focused analyses (identify dependencies then search for mechanisms) and activity-focused analyses (identify mechanisms then search for dependencies). Examples of each approach are provided in the form of a small marketing services company. Barbuceanu, Gray, and Mankovski (1999) offer a four-level model of social interaction and behavior into agent-based programming tools. In this model, an agent's request consists of a set of "obliged and forbidden behaviors." Social laws, expressed as obligations, are positioned at the highest level of this model. Below this level is a layer that considers each agent's unique priorities and authorities. The lowest levels of this model consist of scheduling and executing adopted behaviors, respectively.

Kim (2000) uses CT as a basis for organizational process change by applying the Massachusetts Institute of Technology Process Handbook (Malone et al., 1999) with a simulation technique. The handbook modeling approach extends the framework of CT described above by adding the notions of inheritance and decomposition. A process can be decomposed into smaller steps, which in turn can be decomposed further. Once the process has been decomposed, the dependencies among the steps can then be analyzed. A novel feature of the Process Handbook is the use of inheritance, adopted from object-oriented programming. A process in the handbook can be viewed as a specialization of a more general process (e.g., the processes for selling in a store or selling on an e-commerce Web site are both special cases of selling; the process the company Lands' End uses to sell using a Web site is still more specialized). This specialization can be done at any level of decomposition. The combination of the two approaches provides great flexibility in composing novel processes. Kim (2000) gives an example of this approach in a case of an organizational change in a hospital.

Several authors have developed new coordination mechanisms, particularly those in distributed artificial intelligence. For example, Decker in his PhD thesis designs and evaluates a "family" of coordination mechanisms for cooperative computational task environments. Chen and Decker describe seventeen coordination mechanisms to handle the dependency relationships among multiple agents' tasks. They describe these as components that can enable agents to adapt to changing environments. Each mechanism was catalogued into one of eight groups (p. 6):

- Avoidance
- Reservation schemes
- Simple predecessor-side commitments
- Simple successor-side commitments
- Polling approaches

- Shifting task dependencies (by learning or transferring mobile code)
- Various third-party mechanisms
- More complex multi-stage negotiation strategies

Schmidt and Simone (1996) focus on the use of artifacts for coordination purposes in cooperative settings. They suggest that coordination mechanisms "are characterized by a specific and crucial relationship between protocol and artifact," and consider computational coordination mechanisms, "in which the allocation of functionality between actor and artifact is changed in such a way that the coordination mechanism, as a software device, incorporates the artifact in a computational form as well as aspects of the protocol which, again in a computational form, operates on the artifact" (p. 185).

CT also has clear links to other theories of social behavior. The original presentation of CT indicated its reliance on theories of group decision making and communications. Englert et al. (1996) extend this layer framework to include and describe relationships among coordination, cooperation (modified from "group decision making"), communication, and selected communication media. Gittel (2000) notes the importance of human relations for successful coordination. Crowston and Kammerer (1998) combine CT and collective mind theory (Weick and Roberts, 1993) to identify sources of problems in managing teams of requirements analysts at two companies (extending the example presented above). The two theories complement each other in that CT assumes that individuals have shared understandings of the problems they face, while collective mind theory explains how those shared understandings develop. Weigand, van der Poll, and de Moor (2003) similarly note that the problem of coordination is aggravated by several factors, such as the information asymmetry between actors. They suggest that "when communicative action is aimed at mutual understanding, it is an integration mechanism indeed, and thus also a coordination mechanism" (p. 123).

Social Factors

Finally, Martens identifies three social factors for the acceptance of a theory: the theory is relatively easy to understand and to use; it first appears in a widely read journal; and it is communicated in a variety of settings (e.g., via students and lab members). CT scores generally well on the first and third criteria, but not as well on the second. The definition of coordination proposed by Malone and Crowston is quite simple and easy to understand, perhaps accounting for the high number of citations to the definition. The modeling framework is similar to many already in use, again suggesting that it is easy to use.

On the other hand, although *ACM Computing Surveys* is well known in the computer science field, it is hardly known outside of it. The choice of the original outlet explains the preponderance of citations in computer- and information-related fields and the relative paucity of citations in organizational-focused disciplines, even though CT was intended to unify these treatments of coordination. The article has recently been reprinted in two books, which may help in the dissemination of the ideas. Finally, CT has been picked up and further disseminated by several of Malone's students and colleagues (eleven of the forty-six substantive papers or about 25 percent were authored by Malone and his associates).

CONCLUSION

In the conclusion to their paper, Malone and Crowston set out a research agenda for CT. To conclude this paper, we will briefly discuss the progress that has been made in accomplishing this agenda and note places where more work is still needed.

Malone and Crowston's (1994) first agenda item was how to represent coordination processes. They note several possibilities, such as flow charts, Petri nets, and state transition diagrams. In more recent work, Malone et al. (1999) propose a representation technique (the "Process Handbook") that represents processes at various levels of abstraction, as described above. A further advantage of this approach is its ability to suggest new processes by navigating through the dual hierarchies, abstraction and composition. As well, the work reviewed above on modeling techniques shows that coordination can be incorporated into many modeling techniques.

The second agenda item was to determine what kinds of dependencies there are. Crowston (1994; 2003) conceptualized dependencies as arising from shared use of resources by multiple tasks, thus providing a conceptual basis for a typology of dependencies, though the resulting typology was nearly the same as shown in Table 7.1. Resources in this framework include anything produced or needed by a task. For example, Faraj and Sproull (2000) introduce the notion of expertise coordination ("the management of knowledge and skill dependencies") that "entails knowing where expertise is located, knowing where expertise is needed, and bringing needed expertise to bear."

The third agenda item was how to classify different coordination processes. The initial approach to this problem was to list coordination processes by the dependency they addresses. Malone et al. (1999) take this approach further by proposing a hierarchy of coordination processes from general to specific. Other authors have proposed different organizations. For example, Etcheverry, Lopisteguy, and Dagorret (2001a; 2001b) propose a catalog of coordination patterns. A pattern is defined as "a solution to a problem in a given context," so the catalog is organized by coordination contexts. More work could be done to bring together and organize the mechanisms that have been studied.

The fourth agenda item was about the generality of coordination mechanisms. Most of the work applying the typology of coordination mechanisms has assumed rather than tested the generality of the mechanisms. Nevertheless, the list of mechanisms does seem to have been useful in a variety of settings.

A final agenda item was how to analyze specific coordination practices, e.g., resource allocation. Malone and Crowston (1994) asked, "Can we characterize an entire 'design space' for solutions to this problem and analyze the major factors that would favor one solution over another in specific situations?" Most applications of CT are not very explicit about evaluation or factors that make particular coordination mechanisms more or less desirable. Some work has addressed specific metrics for coordination. For example, Frozza, and Alvares (2002) offer a list of criteria for comparing mechanisms: predictivity, adaptability, action control, communication mode, conflicts, information exchange, agents, applications, and advantages and disadvantages. Albino, Pontrandolfo, and Scozzi (2002) develop the notion of coordination load, "a quantitative index that measures the effort required to properly coordinate a given process," based on an analysis of the workflow in the process. The goal of this index is to allow a comparison of alternative coordination modes. Nevertheless, it is clear that we are far from characterizing the design space for any of the identified dependencies or coordination mechanisms.

In conclusion, the past ten years have seen considerable progress on the coordination theory agenda laid out by Malone and Crowston. The basic outlines of the theory are clear. Methods for capturing and documenting processes and coordination mechanisms and systematic typologies of dependencies and mechanisms have been developed. There are numerous examples of the application of CT in a variety of settings. Taken together, this body of work provides a solid basis for the application of CT. Challenges for future research include developing testable hypotheses (e.g., about the generality of coordination mechanisms) and more structured approaches to evaluate and choose between alternate coordination processes.

REFERENCES

Albino, V.; Pontrandolfo, P.; and Scozzi, B. Analysis of information flows to enhance the coordination of production processes. *International Journal of Production Economics*, 75 (2002), 7–9.

American Heritage Dictionary. Boston: Houghton Mifflin, 2000.

Barbuceanu, M.; Gray, T.; and Mankovski, S. Role of obligations in multiagent coordination. *Applied Artificial Intelligence*, 13, 1–2 (1999), 11–38.

Bello, D.C.; Chelariu, C.; and Zhang, L. The antecedents and performance consequences of relationalism in export distribution channels. *Journal Of Business Research*, 56, 1 (2003), 1–16.

Benjamin, R., and Wigand, R. Electronic markets and virtual value chains on the information superhighway. *Sloan Management Review*, Winter (1995), 62–72.

Bernstein, A., and Klein, M. Discovering services: towards high-precision service retrieval. In *Web Services, E-Business, and the Semantic Web* (Lecture Notes in Computer Science, vol. 2512), 2002, pp. 260–275.

Bernstein, A., and Klein, M. Towards high-precision service retrieval. In *Semantic Web—ISWC 2002* (Lecture Notes in Computer Science, vol. 2342), Springer, 2002, pp. 84–101.

Brackett, J.W. Software requirements, SEI curriculum module. In M. Dorfman and R.H. Thayer (eds.), *Standards, Guidelines, and Examples on System and Software Requirements Engineering.* Los Alamitos, CA: IEEE Computer Society Press, 1990, pp. 408–438.

Britton, L.C.; Wright, M.; and Ball, D.F. The use of co-ordination theory to improve service quality in executive search. *Service Industries Journal*, 20 (2000), 85–102.

Bui, T. Building agent-based corporate information systems: an application to telemedicine. *European Journal Of Operational Research*, 122, 2 (2000), 242–257.

Bui, T., and Lee, J. An agent-based framework for building decision support systems. *Decision Support Systems*, 25, 3 (1999), 225–237.

Chandler, A.D., Jr. *Strategy and Structure: Chapters in the History of the American Industrial Enterprise.* Cambridge, MA: MIT Press, 1962.

Checkland, P.B. *Systems Thinking, Systems Practice.* New York: Wiley, 1981.

Checkland, P.B., and Scholes, J. *Soft Systems Methodology in Action.* Chichester: Wiley, 1990.

Clancey, W.J.; Sachs, P.; Sierhuis, M.; and van Hoof, R. Brahms: simulating practice for work systems design. *International Journal Of Human Computer Studies*, 49 (1998), 831–865.

Collofello, J.S. *The Software Technical Review Process.* Pittsburgh, PA: Software Engineering Institute, Carnegie Mellon University, 1988.

Crowston, K. A coordination theory approach to organizational process design. *Organization Science*, 8, 2 (1997), 157–175.

Crowston, K. A taxonomy of organizational dependencies and coordination mechanisms. In T.W. Malone, K. Crowston, and G. Herman (eds.), *The Process Handbook.* Cambridge, MA: MIT Press, 2003, pp. 85–108.

Crowston, K. *A Taxonomy of Organizational Dependencies and Coordination Mechanisms.* Cambridge, MA: MIT Sloan School of Management, 1994.

Crowston, K., and Kammerer, E. Coordination and collective mind in software requirements development. *IBM Systems Journal*, 37, 2 (1998), 227–245.

Crowston, K., and Osborn, C.S. A coordination theory approach to process description and redesign. In T.W. Malone, K. Crowston, and G. Herman (eds.), *Organizing Business Knowledge: The MIT Process Handbook.* Cambridge, MA: MIT Press, 2003.

Davenport, T.H., and Short, J.E. The new industrial engineering: information technology and business process redesign. *Sloan Management Review*, 31, 4 (1990), 11–27.

Davis, F.D. Perceived usefulness, perceived ease of use and user acceptance of information technology. *MIS Quarterly*, 13 (1989), 319–340.

Davis, W.S. *Systems Analysis and Design.* Reading, MA: Addison-Wesley, 1983.

den Hengst, M., and Sol, H.G. The impact of electronic commerce on interorganizational coordination: A framework from theory applied to the container-transport industry. *International Journal Of Electronic Commerce*, 6, 4 (2002), 73–91.

Englert, J.; Eymann, T.; Gold, S.; Hummel, T.; and Schoder, D. *Beyond Automation: A Framework for Supporting Cooperation.* Freiburg, Germany: Institut für Informatik und Gesellschaft der Albert-Ludwigs-Universität, 1996.

Etcheverry, P.; Lopisteguy, P.; and Dagorret, P. Pattern-based guidelines for coordination engineering. In *Database and Expert Systems Applications* (Lecture Notes in Computer Science, vol. 2113), 2001a, pp. 155–164.

Etcheverry, P.; Lopisteguy, P.; and Dagorret, P. Specifying contexts for coordination patterns. In *Proceedings of Modeling and Using Context* (Lecture Notes in Computer Science, vol. 2116), 2001b, pp. 437–440.

Faraj, S., and Sproull, L. Coordinating expertise in software development teams. *Management Science*, 46, 12 (2000), 1554–1568.

Freedman, D.P., and Weinberg, G.M. *Handbook of Walkthroughs, Inspections, and Technical Reviews: Evaluating Programs, Projects, and Products*. Boston, MA: Little, Brown, 1982.

Frozza, R., and Alvares, L.O. Criteria for the analysis of coordination in multi-agent applications. In *Coordination Models and Languages, Proceedings* (Lecture Notes in Computer Science, vol. 2315), 2002, pp. 158–165.

Gittell, J. Organizing work to support relational coordination. *International Journal of Human Resource Management*, 11, 3 (2000), 517–534.

Grant, R.M. Toward a knowledge-based theory of the firm. *Strategic Management Journal*, 17, Winter (1996), 109–122.

Hammer, M. Reengineering work: don't automate, obliterate. *Harvard Business Review*, 68, July–August (1990), 104–112.

Harrington, H.J. *Business Process Improvement: The Breakthrough Strategy for Total Quality, Productivity, and Competitiveness*. New York: McGraw-Hill, 1991.

Harrison, D.B., and Pratt, M.D. A methodology for reengineering business. *Planning Review*, 21, 2 (1993), 6–11.

Holsapple, C.W., and Joshi, K.D. An investigation of factors that influence the management of knowledge in organizations. *Journal Of Strategic Information Systems* 9, 2–3 (2000), 235–261.

Holsapple, C.W., and Joshi, K.D. Knowledge management: a threefold framework. *Information Society*, 18, 1 (2002), 47–64.

Holt, A.W. Diplans: a new language for the study and implementation of coordination. *ACM Transactions on Office Information Systems*, 6, 2 (1988), 109–125.

Kaplan, A. *The Conduct of Inquiry: Methodology for Behavioural Science*. New Brunswick, NJ: Transaction Publishers, 1998.

Kim, H.W. Business process versus coordination process in organizational change. *International Journal Of Flexible Manufacturing Systems*, 12, 4 (2000), 275–290.

Klein, M., and Bernstein, A. Toward high-precision service retrieval. *IEEE Internet Computing*, 8, 1 (2004), 30–36.

Klusch, M.; Bergamaschi, S.; and Petta, P. European research and development of intelligent information agents: The AgentLink perspective. In *Intelligent Information Agents* (Lecture Notes in Computer Science, vol. 2586), 2003, pp. 1–21.

Kobayashi, T.; Tamaki, M.; and Komoda, N. Business process integration as a solution to the implementation of supply chain management systems. *Information & Management*, 40, 8 (2003), 769–780.

Krieger, M.; Vigder, M.; Dean, J.C.; and Siddiqui, M. Coordination in COTS-based development. In *Cots-Based Software Systems, Proceedings* (Lecture Notes in Computer Science, vol 2580), 2003, pp. 123–133.

Lawrence, P., and Lorsch, J. *Organization and Environment*. Boston, MA: Division of Research, Harvard Business School, 1967.

Lee, W.J., and Lee, K.C. PROMISE: A distributed DSS approach to coordinating production and marketing decisions. *Computers & Operations Research*, 26, 9 (1999), 901–920.

Lizotte, S., and Chaib-draa, B. Coordination in CE systems: An approach based on the management of dependencies between activities. *Concurrent Engineering—Research and Applications*, 5, 4 (1997), 367–377.

Malone, T.W. *What is Coordination Theory?* Cambridge, MA: MIT Sloan School of Management, 1988.

Malone, T.W., and Crowston, K. The interdisciplinary study of coordination. *Computing Surveys*, 26, 1 (1994), 87–119.

Malone, T.W., and Crowston, K. *Toward an Interdisciplinary Theory of Coordination*. Cambridge, MA: MIT Centre for Coordination Science, 1991.

Malone, T.W., and Crowston, K. What is coordination theory and how can it help design cooperative work systems? In D. Tatar (ed.), *Proceedings of the Third Conference on Computer-supported Cooperative Work*. Los Angeles, CA: ACM Press, 1990, pp. 357–370.

Malone, T.W.; Crowston, K.; and Herman, G. (eds.) *Organizing Business Knowledge: The MIT Process Handbook*. Cambridge, MA: MIT Press, 2003.

Malone, T.W.; Crowston, K.; Lee, J.; Pentland, B.; Dellarocas, C.; Wyner, G.; Quimby, J.; Osborne, C.; Bernstein, A.; Herman, G.; Klein, M.; and O'Donnell, E. Tools for inventing organizations: toward a handbook of organizational processes. *Management Science*, 43, 3 (1999), 425–443.

Marca, D.A., and McGowan, C.L. *SADT™: Structured Analysis and Design Technique*. New York: McGraw-Hill, 1988.

Martens, B.V.d.V. *Theories at Work: An Exploratory Study*. PhD Thesis, School of Information Studies, Syracuse University, Syracuse, NY, 2003.

McChesney, I.R. Effective coordination in the software process—historical perspectives and future directions. *Software Quality Journal*, 6, 3 (1997), 235–246.

Medema, S.G. Coase, costs and coordination. *Journal of Economic Issues*, 30, 2 (1996), 571–578.

Mehring, J.S. A practical setting for experiential learning about supply chains: Siemens brief case game supply chain simulator. *Production and Operations Management*, 9, 1 (2000), 56–65.

Ossowski, S., and Omicini, A. Coordination knowledge engineering. *Knowledge Engineering Review*, 17, 4 (2002), 309–316.

Powers, M.; Adams, D.; and Mills, H. *Computer Information Systems Development: Analysis and Design*. Cincinnati, OH: South-Western, 1984.

Reezigt, C. *Zicht op interne communicatie, ontwerp van een bedrijfseconomisch georiënteerd diagnose-instrument*. PhD Thesis, Faculty of Economics, University of Groningen, Groningen, Netherlands, 1995.

Ricci, A.; Omicini, A.; and Denti, E. Activity theory as a framework for MAS coordination. In *Engineering Societies in the Agents World III* (Lecture Notes in Computer Science, vol. 2577), 2003, pp. 96–110.

Scheel, I.B.; Hagen, K.B.; and Oxman, A.D. Active sick leave for patients with back pain—all the players onside, but still no action. *Spine*, 27, 6 (2002), 654–659.

Schmidt, K., and Simone, C. Coordination mechanisms: towards a conceptual foundation of CSCW systems design. *Computer Supported Cooperative Work: The Journal of Collaborative Computing*, 5, 2–3 (1996), 155–200.

Schnase, J.L.; Kama, D.L.; Tomlinson, K.L.; Sanchez, J.A.; Cunnius, E.L.; and Morin, N.R. The flora of North America digital library: a case study in biodiversity database publishing. *Journal of Network and Computer Applications*, 20 (1997), 87–103.

Sikora, R., and Shaw, M.J. A multi-agent framework for the coordination and integration of information systems. *Management Science*, 44, 11 (1998), 565–578.

Singh, B., and Rein, G.L. *Role Interaction Nets (RINs): A Process Definition Formalism*. Technical Report CT-083-92, Austin, TX: MCC, 1992.

Thompson, J.D. *Organizations in Action: Social Science Bases of Administrative Theory*. New York: McGraw-Hill, 1967.

Tolksdorf, R. Coordination technology for workflows on the Web: workspaces. In *Coordination Languages and Models, Proceedings* (Lecture Notes in Computer Science, vol. 1906), 2000, pp. 36–50.

Tolksdorf, R. A dependency markup language for Web services. In *Web, Web-Services, and Database Systems* (Lecture Notes in Computer Science, vol. 2593), 2003, pp. 129–140.

van Breemen, A.J.N., and de Vries, T.J.A. Design and implementation of a room thermostat using an agent-based approach. *Control Engineering Practice*, 9, 3 (2001), 233–248.

Walz, D.B.; Elam, J.J.; and Curtis, B. Inside a software design team: knowledge acquisition, sharing, and integration. *Communications of the ACM*, 36, 10 (1993), 63–77.

Weick, K.E., and Roberts, K. Collective mind in organizations: heedful interrelating on flight decks. *Administrative Science Quarterly*, 38, 3 (1993), 357–381.

Weigand, H.; van der Poll, F.; and de Moor, A. Coordination through communication. In *Proceedings of the 8th International Working Conference on the Language-Action Perspective on Communication Modeling*. Tilburg, The Netherlands, 2003, pp. 115–134.

Whyte, W.F. *Human Relations in the Restaurant Industry*. New York: McGraw-Hill, 1948.

Yoshioka, T.; Herman, G.; Yates, J.; and Orlikowski, W. Genre taxonomy: a knowledge repository of communicative actions. *ACM Transactions on Information Systems*, 19, 4 (2001), 431–456.

PART III

IT DEVELOPMENT: THEORIES OF FIT

CHAPTER 8

THE THEORY OF COGNITIVE FIT

One Aspect of a General Theory
of Problem Solving?

IRIS VESSEY

Abstract: *The theory of cognitive fit was first introduced in 1991 to explain the numerous equiv-ocal results from decades of studies on information presentation using graphs and tables. At that time, Vessey introduced cognitive fit as part of a general theory of problem solving based on the belief that the theory could be applied both across different domains and different concepts of fit. Here we examine what has happened to the theory since that time. Has the theory withstood the test of time? Has it been extended, deepened? To do so, we undertake an analysis of articles based on the core concept of cognitive fit, viz, matching problem representations to problem-solving tasks that have been published since 1991. We classified those studies according to whether they tested concepts found in the two foundational papers that present the theory, whether they applied the theory to new domains of investigation, and whether they used dimensions of fit other than the spatial-symbolic dichotomy addressed in the foundational studies.*

In addition to identifying studies similar to those on which the theory of cognitive fit was built, we found that the theory has been applied quite extensively to two other domains, that of multi-attribute judgments, largely in the domain of accounting, and that of multi-criteria decision making in map-related domains. The theory has also been applied to new dimensions of fit. Certain studies have investigated the traditional concept of fit, that is, the match-mismatch dichotomy, using new dimen-sions, while others have applied the notions of fit to the complexity of the relationship between the problem-solving task and the problem representation. Instead of addressing the match-mismatch dichotomy, therefore, the latter approach addresses the degree of match between task and problem representation. In all instances, the findings largely support the theory of cognitive fit. There are two provisos: (1) it appears that problem solvers may solve very simple spatial problems better with tables than with graphs because they are more familiar and therefore more effective with tables in those settings; and (2) accuracy/time trade-off remains equivocal due to the numerous factors that may influence the outcome. We then present recent extensions to the model of cognitive fit itself and to the situation in which the concurrent solution of two tasks is essential to problem solving. In the lat-ter, dual-task situation, we further distinguish between problem solving in well- and ill-defined tasks.

The analysis presented here supports the notion that the theory of cognitive fit is, indeed, one aspect of a general theory of problem solving.

Keywords: *Cognitive Fit, Task Complexity, Dimensions of Cognitive Fit, Extended Model of Cognitive Fit, Dual-Task Problem Solving, Ill-Structured Tasks, Well-Structured Tasks*

INTRODUCTION

The theory of cognitive fit was introduced in 1991 to explain the inconsistent results of numerous studies in the area of information presentation using graphs and tables (Vessey, 1991). Although Vessey referred to cognitive fit as a "paradigm," the research community has consistently accorded it the status of a theory, referring to it since its first appearance as "the theory of cognitive fit" or "cognitive fit theory." In keeping with these subsequent studies, we refer to cognitive fit as the "theory of cognitive fit."

Vessey introduced cognitive fit in 1991 as one element of a general theory of problem solving. This statement was intended to convey that the notions of cognitive fit applied across many domains and could be applied to many dimensions of fit. The notion of a general theory of problem solving was conceived early in the development process: Vessey developed the theory after observing similar problem-solving situations in the systems development domain (see Vessey and Weber, 1986). It was therefore clear when the theory first appeared that it had sufficient explanatory power to be applicable across domains.

The focus in the original paper on cognitive fit, in which Vessey analyzed prior studies as a basis for formulating the basic theory, was on the simple information acquisition and information evaluation tasks that almost exclusively made up the information presentation studies published at that time. Then, in 1994, Vessey published the extension to the basic theory that addressed problem solving in more complex tasks. That paper used cognitive cost-benefit theory as a unifying theory to explain cognitive fit in both simple and more complex tasks. The basic theory of cognitive fit is a special case of cost-benefit theory. Cost-benefit theory as applied to more complex tasks explains contingent decision-making behavior in which decision makers change strategy to accommodate even minor variations in the task or the task environment; for example, they trade off a slight loss in accuracy for a significant reduction in effort. Numerous factors influence the choice of strategy, among them the way in which information is presented.

Vessey and Galletta (1991) further extended the theory to include matching specific skills to problem representation and task, while Sinha and Vessey (1992) extended it to include matching a problem-solving tool to a problem representation and task. These studies revealed that, although matches of this type affect problem-solving performance, the key match remains that of matching a problem representation to a task.

Since their appearance in print, these papers on cognitive fit have been cited in numerous publications. As of April 28, 2004, for example, the original paper (Vessey, 1991) had been cited 102 times, as recorded by the ISI's Web of Science, and the empirical study based on it (Vessey and Galletta, 1991) had been cited sixty-eight times. Further, the extension of the theory to more complex tasks (Vessey, 1994) had been cited fourteen times, while the extension of CF to problem-solving tool (Sinha and Vessey, 1992) had been cited eleven times.

Our objective in this paper is to revisit the theory of cognitive fit at this point in time. We aim to determine whether the theory has stood the test of time, and, if so, examine the ways in which the theory has developed over time, that is, how it has been used and extended. At the same time, we attempt to trace a path for further evolution of the theory. For the purposes of this paper, we examine the core concepts of the theory, that is, the match between task and problem representation, in those articles that have examined cognitive fit in the domain of decision making. We do not examine, therefore, research on cognitive fit that appears in the software arena.

In the next section, we first present cost-benefit theory, which forms the overall theoretical framework for the theory of cognitive fit, the types of tasks to which it applies and the types of representations that support them, followed by the theory itself. It seems particularly important to present the extension of the theory to more complex tasks (Vessey, 1994) because it is clear that that material is relevant to many of the papers we analyze here, yet that paper has received significantly fewer citations than that presenting the basic theory. We next present the methodology used to determine studies for further examination and the way in which we classified those studies. In the next three sections, we present and evaluate studies identified as testing the theory of cognitive fit, extending it to new domains, and extending it to new dimensions of fit, respectively. We then present a number of recent extensions to the model of cognitive fit itself and to the situation in which the concurrent solution of two tasks is essential to problem solving. In the latter, dual-task, situation we further distinguish between problem solving in well- and ill-defined tasks. Finally, we discuss the findings of the study and present the implications for future research.

THEORY

Although, as noted above, the theory of cognitive fit was conceived as a general theory of problem solving, it was formally developed and justified using the numerous studies on graphs versus tables conducted over decades prior to the 1990s. We therefore present the theory and its implications within that context. We first present cost-benefit theory as the overall framework for the theory of cognitive fit, followed by the theory itself. We then highlight the fundamental aspects of the theory as applied to both simple and more complex tasks.

Cost-benefit theory is a framework within which decision making can be examined rather than a theory that presents well-articulated relationships among variables. In order to apply it to decision making using graphs and tables, we distinguish between strategy and process. Both are dynamic descriptions of decision making. We use the term "strategy" to describe a general approach to decision making that involves a number of steps or sub-tasks: Thus it most often describes a macro approach to solving a problem. We use the term "process" to refer to a specific approach or a micro operation that aids in accomplishing the task: Processes are used to address each of the sub-tasks that comprise the strategy. A major thesis of the theory of cognitive fit is that behavioral decision-making research has ignored the role processes play in the effectiveness of a particular display format (see, for example, Kleinmuntz and Schkade, 1993).

Cost-Benefit Theory as the Theoretical Framework

Researchers in behavioral decision making have observed that decision makers change strategy in response to what appear to be quite minor changes in the task and its environment. According to cost-benefit theory, decision makers trade off the effort required to make a decision vis-à-vis the accuracy of the outcome (Beach and Mitchell, 1978). Cost-benefit theory has been applied extensively to choice tasks.

A number of factors may influence the error and effort required to make a decision and may therefore induce decision makers to change strategy. These factors are usually characterized as relating to "task" and/or "context." According to Payne (1982), task variables are those "associated with the general structural characteristics of the decision problem." Those task variables most often examined in choice tasks are: (1) response mode (i.e., whether the task requires judgment or choice); (2) task complexity (number of alternatives, number of dimensions, and time pressure); (3) problem representation; and (4) agenda effects. Task variables have been shown to influence effort. Context variables are those related to the actual values of the objects under consideration. The most common context variables investigated are: (1) similarity of the alternatives and the overall attractiveness of the alternatives; (2) the variance in probabilities; and (3) the presence or absence of alternatives that are worse than others on both error and effort (Payne, Bettman, and Johnson, 1988). Context variables influence accuracy (Johnson and Payne, 1985).

Decision makers change strategy primarily in response to changes in task variables, which, as we have seen above, reduce effort. Numerous studies report strategy changes as the number of alternatives involved in choice decisions increases (see, for example, Payne, 1976; Olshavsky, 1979). Payne et al. (1988) have also demonstrated that strategy may change due to time pressure. Note, however, that cognitively simpler strategies can be almost as effective as the optimal strategies in many decision environments. Russo and Dosher (1983), for example, found that subjects in one experiment traded off a slight loss of accuracy (20 percent) for a substantial increase in speed (approximately seven times faster).

Studies reporting strategy changes due to context variables, and therefore a desire for accuracy, are much rarer. As we have seen above, the relative accuracy of a strategy varies across contexts, although the relative effort does not. Similar levels of accuracy can, however, be achieved across different contexts, although the effort required will vary. Accuracy considerations may therefore also lead to strategy shifts. Nonetheless, Todd and Benhasat (1991), in a study of decision aids for choice tasks, suggest that decision makers use aids only to reduce effort and not to improve accuracy.

Problem representation is one of the task characteristics that influences strategy shift. Cost-benefit theory can therefore be used to examine the effect of graphs and tables on decision-making performance. Certain other task effects, notably task complexity and time pressure, also appear to be particularly relevant to decision making using graphs and tables; factors such as these are also examined here.

Characteristics of Graph/Table Decision Making

To apply cost-benefit theory to decision making using graphs and tables, we first need to determine the characteristics of both the problem representations and the tasks they support. We view problem representation and decision-making task as independent, for two reasons. First, data and task can be presented independently. Second, solutions to the types of tasks examined here can be reached when the data are represented in either graphical or tabular format.

Characteristics of the Problem Representations

Let us assume we are considering graphs and tables derived from equivalent data, so that all information in one is inferable from the other, with a different type of information predominating in each. Our intuition quickly lets us see a meaningful distinction between graphs and tables similar to that characterized in the psychology literature as images and words (see Bettman and Zins, 1979; Paivio, 1971, 1978). We use the terms "spatial" and "symbolic" to characterize the differences between graphs and tables.

Graphs are spatial problem representations because they present spatially related information; that is, they emphasize relationships in the data. They do not present discrete data values directly. Spatial representations facilitate viewing the information they contain at a glance without addressing the elements separately or analytically; that is, the data in a graph are accessed using perceptual processes.

Tables are symbolic problem representations because they present symbolic information; that is, they emphasize discrete data values. They do not present data relationships directly. Symbolic representations, on the other hand, facilitate extracting specific data values; that is, the data in a table are accessed using analytical processes.

Characteristics of Relevant Tasks

Although there is no comprehensive theory of tasks (see, for example, Campbell, 1988; Fleishman, 1982; Wood 1986), we can examine tasks used in graph/table decision making to determine the abstract characteristics that might be facilitated by each type of representation. According to Einhorn and Hogarth (1981), decision making consists of three interrelated sub-tasks: information acquisition, evaluation, and feedback/learning. The first two sub-tasks are relevant to the analysis of graph/table decision making.

Information Acquisition Tasks.   Information acquisition tasks are those whose solution is achieved directly via information acquisition processes. Several researchers have identified two basic types of information acquisition tasks used in graphs versus tables studies (Umanath and Scammell, 1988; Umanath, Scammell, and Das, 1990; Washburne, 1927). One type of task, spatial, assesses the problem area as a whole rather than as discrete data values and therefore requires making associations or perceiving relationships in the data. The following example involves a comparison of trends and is therefore a spatial task:

> Between the years 1100 and 1438 whose earnings increased most rapidly, those of the wool, silk, or Calimala merchants? (Washburne, 1927)

Such tasks are best accomplished using perceptual processes.

The second type of task, symbolic, involves extracting discrete, and therefore precise, data values (Umanath and Scammell, 1988; Umanath, Scammell, and Das, 1990; Washburne, 1927). The following example requires a specific amount as the response and is therefore a symbolic task:

> How much did the wool merchants earn in the year 1100? (Washburne, 1927)

Such tasks are best accomplished using analytical processes.

Information Evaluation Tasks.   Certain evaluation tasks can be analyzed in a similar manner to tasks that involve information acquisition alone. In tasks involving fairly simple evaluation, the evaluation sub-tasks will be either spatial or symbolic in nature. For example, a task may require the extraction of given data values followed by a series of calculations. The critical point, here, is that we can infer the nature of both the information acquisition and the evaluation sub-tasks to be completed. With regard to the type of evaluation, we can again identify, as for information acquisition tasks:

(a) tasks that are basically spatial in nature; and
(b) tasks that are basically symbolic in nature.

Tasks involving information acquisition and well-defined information evaluation may therefore be accomplished via one of the two processes, spatial or symbolic, depending on the nature of each of the sub-tasks; that is, when the sub-tasks are well defined, so, too, are the processes that a problem solver will use to solve them. Hence, the distinction between process and strategy, highlighted in the introduction to the theory, is critical here.

When a task is sufficiently complex, however, its solution can be achieved via a number of different sets of sub-tasks, that is, strategies. Different strategies may have significant implications for the accuracy of the outcome and/or the effort involved. More complex tasks, for example, may vary substantially in both the amount and type of evaluation.

In general, more complex spatial tasks—forecasting, for example—involve perceptual evaluation. Because perceptual processes require less effort than analytical processes, the decision maker will have little incentive to use analytical evaluation processes to solve a spatial problem.

In general, more complex symbolic tasks involve analytical evaluation. The decision maker may, at some point, be induced to use perceptual rather than analytical evaluation processes to reduce the effort involved. Complex symbolic tasks may require a substantial amount of analytical processing; for example, they may require computations that are not difficult, but are tedious and time-consuming, and therefore error-prone. They may therefore place significant strain on the cognitive resources of the decision maker (Campbell, 1988). A complex symbolic task with even higher analytical demands may be a limiting task, that is, one that cannot be solved analytically without assistance of some kind. It may involve, for example, calculating trends from extremely complex functions. Such a task has further constraints placed on it from the viewpoint of its successful completion. Johnson and Payne (1985) speculate on the existence of this type of complex decision-making task in discussing the process of expected utility maximization. They state:

"Such processes, however, could well require inordinate amounts of time, and, in practice, be impossible for the unaided decision maker. Processing constraints, therefore, may impose severe limitations for the feasible region in which accuracy-effort trade-offs could be made."

The Theory of Cognitive Fit

The theory of cognitive fit applies cost-benefit theory to decision making using graphs and tables in two ways. First, the simple form of the theory, which addresses information acquisition and well-defined evaluation, is a special case of cost-benefit theory. Second, the more traditional view of cost-benefit theory involving strategy shift applies to decision making on more complex tasks where a number of appropriate strategies may be available. We first present the theory of cognitive fit followed by its application to both fairly simple as well as cognitively complex tasks. We also present the propositions that underlie the theory.

Fundamentals of Cognitive Fit

Figure 8.1 presents the model of decision making on which the theory of cognitive fit is based. When the types of information emphasized in the decision-making elements (problem representation and problem-solving task) match, the problem solver is able to use processes (and therefore formulate a mental representation) that also emphasize the same type of information. Consequently, the processes the problem solver uses to act both on the problem representation and on the task will match. The resultant, consistent mental representation will facilitate the decision-making process. Hence, cognitive fit leads to an effective (i.e., accurate or precise) and efficient (i.e., fast) problem solution.

Theoretical support for the relationships in the general problem-solving model comes from a variety of sources. The literature provides substantial support for problem solvers' use of processes that match the problem representation (Bettman and Kakkar, 1977; Kotovsky, Hayes, and Simon, 1985; Russo, 1977; Tversky and Kahneman, 1971, 1973, 1974). There is also substantial evidence that problem solvers use different processes for different types of tasks (Einhorn and Hogarth, 1981; Slovic and Lichtenstein, 1983; Tversky, Sattath, and Slovic, 1988; Vessey and Weber, 1986). Finally, there is evidence that matching the problem representation directly to the task has significant effects on problem-solving performance (Bettman and Zins, 1979; Simkin and Hastie, 1987; Wright, 1995).

Figure 8.1 **Cognitive Fit in Problem Solving**

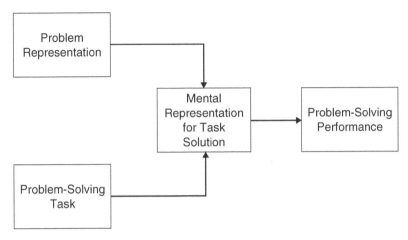

It is apparent, then, cognitive fit exists when spatial tasks are supported by spatial representations and when symbolic tasks are supported by symbolic representations. We state the following proposition.

Proposition 1: More effective and efficient decision making results when the problem representation matches the task to be accomplished.

Note that spatial tasks can be solved using symbolic representations, and vice versa. However, when the information in the problem representation and the task do not match, similar processes cannot be used both to act on the problem representation and to solve the problem, and the mental representation will have to be transformed. In terms of cost-benefit theory, the strategy, in this case the lower-level process, will require more effort and will most likely be less accurate. Hence, there is no incentive to use tables to support spatial tasks and vice versa.

Applying Cost-Benefit Principles to Tasks with Well-Defined Sub-Tasks

In this section, we examine the application of the theory of cognitive fit to tasks for which the subtasks are known. These are relatively simple tasks. They involve both information acquisition tasks and tasks that involve simple information evaluation.

Vessey (1991) assessed support for the theory of cognitive fit by analyzing in detail the effectiveness of graphs and tables in information acquisition studies published prior to the appearance of the theory of cognitive fit. She found that the theory could explain the findings of all prior studies with the exception of a limited number of studies that did not provide sufficient information to assess the nature of the representations and/or tasks used, and therefore the cognitive processes that would have been invoked.

Vessey also addressed the robustness of the theory by considering whether strategy shift occurred under any circumstances when cognitive fit existed. Perhaps the most common occurrence in decision making not considered by the basic theory is the effect of performance requirements (i.e., task demands of either time or accuracy) that are not consistent with the task type and the problem representation that best supports it: in general, perceptual processes lead to fast responses, while analytical processes lead to accurate responses. Hence a time requirement is consistent with the perceptual processes used to support spatial problem-solving elements. With a requirement for accuracy, however, decision makers may be induced to switch from perceptual to analytical processes. If this were so, a performance effect for graphs over tables would be unlikely, as processes would be uncontrolled. Similarly, decision makers using symbolic problem-solving elements may be induced to change to perceptual processes when a time requirement is imposed. Vessey (1991) found no evidence of strategy change occurring when cognitive fit existed. Hence the original study on cognitive fit provided substantial evidence to support the descriptive power and stability of the theory for information acquisition tasks.

Cognitive fit may also occur in tasks involving *well-defined evaluation*, that is, tasks that have just a few sub-tasks that are readily identifiable (Vessey 1991). Two situations may arise: (1) the processes required to support information acquisition and evaluation are similar; that is, both are perceptual or both analytical in nature, and therefore best supported by graphs and tables, respectively; or (2) the processes required to support information acquisition and evaluation do not match, in which case it is unlikely that use of either graphs or tables will result in performance advantages. Again, analysis of prior studies supported this assessment. Further, no support was observed for strategy change, which, in this case, is really process change.

Applying Cost-Benefit Principles to Complex Tasks with Numerous Ill-Defined Sub-Tasks

As we have seen, for tasks involving information acquisition and simple information evaluation, choosing a problem representation that matches the type of task being solved so as to achieve cognitive fit results in effective control of decision-making processes. Strategy shift may occur, however, in more complex tasks that require substantial evaluation. A number of different strategies might be used to address such tasks and there is scope for applying perceptual or analytical processes in the sub-tasks.

When complex spatial tasks are supported by spatial representations, and no undue emphasis is placed on accuracy, cognitive fit will exist and there will be no incentive to change strategy. Strategy shift may occur, however, on symbolic tasks as the inherent complexity of the task increases; that is, decision makers may prefer to use perceptual rather than analytical processes. At least two general situations may help to induce strategy shift during solution of complex symbolic problems. First, the high analytical demands of the task per se may induce the problem solver to expend less effort in decision making, resulting in the conscious choice of a less effortful strategy (Einhorn and Hogarth, 1981; Russo and Dosher, 1983). Second, performance constraints may be placed on the decision-making exercise, leading to strategy shift. Both of these factors are regarded as task variables and can be expected to lead to strategy shift largely through their influence on effort. As a result, in decision making using graphs or tables, the appropriate problem representation might not be a table, which supports analytical processes, but a graph, which supports the more parsimonious perceptual processes. We state the following propositions.

> *Proposition 2*:   As the amount of analytical evaluation required increases, decision makers choose between analytical processes resulting in high effort and accuracy and perceptual processes resulting in considerably lower effort and somewhat lower accuracy.

There may also exist the limiting case for which the use of perceptual processes alone is feasible. Again, perceptual processes are best supported with graphs.

> *Proposition 3*:   As the amount of analytical evaluation required increases, the problem can only be solved using perceptual processes.

Figure 8.2   **Cognitive Fit Extended to Include Performance Requirements**

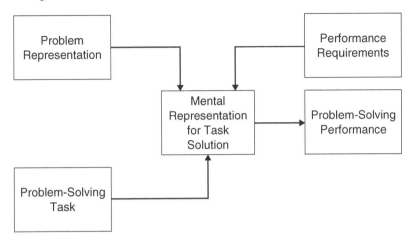

We can investigate in a little more depth strategy shift that is induced by complexity in solving symbolic tasks. A complex symbolic task at "moderate" levels of complexity should be solved more accurately and more quickly using tables rather than graphs. As task complexity increases, however, we expect that a level of complexity will be reached in which tables result in more accurate problem solving, while graphs result in quicker problem solving. Increasing complexity still further will result in graphs outperforming tables on both accuracy and time as decision makers find it increasingly difficult to use analytical processes. Hence there is a crossover point at which more complex symbolic tasks are better supported by graphs than by tables.

While complexity in and of itself may induce strategy shift, thereby favoring perceptual processing, environmental stresses such as constraints on time or accuracy are likely to exacerbate the situation, resulting in strategy shift at lower levels of task complexity. At that time, behavioral decision-making research had considered only time pressure in examining performance constraints. Nonetheless, because a desire for accuracy is known to result in strategy shift (albeit via context rather than task effects), it seems likely that a performance requirement of accuracy might also lead to a change in strategy. As we have seen, a requirement for speed encourages the use of perceptual processes, while a requirement for accuracy encourages the use of analytical processes. The model of cognitive fit can therefore be extended to include the effect of performance requirements on the formulation of the mental representation and therefore on decision-making performance (see Figure 8.2). We state the following propositions:

Proposition 4(a):   A performance requirement of speed encourages the use of perceptual evaluation processes.

Proposition 4(b):   A performance requirement of accuracy encourages the use of analytical evaluation processes.

A range of strategies will be possible depending on the sequence of sub-tasks chosen and the use of perceptual or analytical processes. It is likely, therefore, that no one strategy will be better on both error and effort than all others on more complex tasks. In this case, the decision maker will choose among the strategies based on the preferred trade-off between speed and accuracy of performance, a situation unlikely to result in advantages using either graphs or tables.

At the time of Vessey's second study on cognitive fit in more complex tasks (1994), the literature presented few examples of strategy shift in the graphs versus tables studies. Nonetheless, those studies identified supported the notion of strategy shift when performance requirements did not match (i.e., were inconsistent with) those emerging as a result of cognitive fit.

METHODOLOGY

In this section, we discuss how we obtained the sample of studies on cognitive fit that we used for further examination, followed by the way in which we classified the studies for our analyses.

Choice of Studies for Further Examination

To identify a set of articles that used, tested, or extended the theory of cognitive fit in some way, we engaged in the following series of steps.

Step 1.   The first step involved identifying an initial set of articles that reference the theory of cognitive fit. We first examined ISI's Web of Science to determine the studies published in journals referenced there that cited Vessey's 1991 paper. As noted earlier, on April 28, 2004 there were 102 such articles. It is interesting to note that Vessey and Galletta (1991) was not one of them, although it did, indeed, reference the article in question. This situation may have resulted from a timing issue because both articles appeared in spring of that year.

Step 2.   We then examined the 102 articles identified in Step 1 to determine those articles that referred to cognitive fit in the title, abstract, or the keywords. ISI generates what are known as Keywords Plus for many articles. These are "words or phrases that frequently appear in the titles of an article's references, but do not necessarily appear in the title of the article itself. Keywords Plus may be present for articles that have no author keywords, or may include important terms not listed among the title, abstract, or author keywords" (ISI Web of Science). In this way, we reduced the number of articles under consideration to twenty.

Step 3.   We then searched EBSCO, using "cognitive fit" in the title field, followed by system-generated plus author-supplied keywords, followed by author-supplied keywords alone to determine whether there were papers referenced there that were not included in the databases referenced by the Web of Science. Because the results obtained on April 28, 2004 were problematic, we used an earlier analysis conducted on November 26, 2003. This search revealed a further five articles. Initially, then, we identified in this way a total of twenty-five articles that referenced cognitive fit.

Step 4.   Although the principles that led to the formulation of the theory of cognitive fit were originally recognized in the domain of systems development (Vessey and Weber, 1986) and many studies have been conducted on cognitive fit in that area, this analysis addresses only those articles in which the theory is used to address decision-making issues. Hence, we eliminated studies conducted in the systems development domain. This step reduced the number of articles under consideration to nineteen.

Step 5.   Because the objective of this analysis is to examine the progress that has been made using the theory of cognitive fit, we further eliminated those articles that were conceptual in nature and did not test cognitive fit or extended concepts. Furthermore, certain of the conceptual papers did not address cognitive fit per se. Hence all the studies we examine here are empirical in nature. This step eliminated a further six articles, resulting in thirteen that addressed the desired issues.

Step 6.   As for the original derivation of the theory of cognitive fit in 1991, we examined only those articles that used pure problem representation formats. This step led to the elimination of an additional study.

Step 7.   We also eliminated three further studies on the grounds that they did not address core cognitive fit issues. Hence at this point, we had nine studies that did address such issues.

Step 8.   We identified a further five studies reported in the ISI Web of Science that also addressed core cognitive fit issues. We did this based on browsing certain promising articles identified in the Web of Science analysis and on references found in the initial set of core papers. We then had a total of fourteen papers that addressed the basic tenets of cognitive fit.

Step 9.   Finally, we added two recent papers of our own that illustrate points not demonstrated in the other studies identified to date.

Hence, in the analysis that follows we examine how sixteen studies addressed the theory of cognitive fit. Table 8.1 shows the disposition of the twenty-five studies identified by the end of Step 3 plus the seven studies identified following the derivation of the initial set of studies.

Classification of the Studies

We would like our classification system for cognitive fit studies to follow the premises of good classificatory design: (1) any taxonomy should have a well-defined purpose; (2) the criteria for classification should be well established; and (3) the method of classification should be unambiguous (Wheaton, 1973). From the viewpoint of taxonomic purpose, our goal in this research is to capture the characteristics of the use of the theory of cognitive fit in the HCI area since its first appearance in 1991. From the viewpoint of establishing classification criteria, we must specify the subject matter and then the criteria upon which the description, differentiation, and classification take place (Bailey, 1994). In our case, specifying the subject matter involves identifying the studies that have used cognitive fit substantively since that time (see prior section).

From the viewpoint of specifying a method for classification that assigns members to categories in a complete and unambiguous way, we must first provide operational definitions of the categories and, second, guidelines or definitions for placing objects into categories (Bailey, 1994; Wheaton, 1973). In developing a taxonomy of cognitive fit research, qualitative categories are appropriate. They are discrete categories with classes representing different kinds of things. Third, the classification method should include criteria for assessing the adequacy and utility of classification. In particular, it is generally agreed that a taxonomy should permit exhaustive classification and comprise mutually exclusive categories (Bailey, 1994).

We used an iterative process to determine an appropriate classification of published studies addressing the theory of cognitive fit. This approach was necessary due to the fact that studies could potentially have been classified in a number of different ways. For example, because the complexity of the task being addressed has theoretical significance, the studies could have been classified according to the types of tasks they address—for example, simple information acquisition and information evaluation tasks, more complex tasks, and limiting tasks. Studies could also have been classified according to the components of the cognitive fit model that they address—for example,

Table 8.1

Studies Cited as Being in Title and/or Abstracts/Keywords of ISI Web of Science and EBSCO

	Source	Disposition
Studies Examined from ISI Web of Science and EBSCO		
Beckman (2002)	Web of Science	Analyzed
Chan (2001)	Web of Science	Analyzed
Dennis and Carte (1998)	Web of Science	Analyzed
Dunn and Grabski (2001)	Web of Science	Analyzed
Hubona, Everett, Marsh, and Wauchope (1998)	Web of Science	Analyzed
Mahoney, Roush, and Bandy (2003)	Web of Science	Analyzed
Tuttle and Kershaw (1998)	Web of Science	Analyzed
Umanath and Vessey (1994)	Web of Science	Analyzed
Vessey and Galletta (1991)	EBSCO	Analyzed
Additional Studies Examined		
Borthick, Bowen, Jones, and Tse (2001)	Web of Science	Analyzed
Khatri, Vessey, Ram, and Ramesh (2006)	Author	Analyzed
Smelcer and Carmel (1997)	Web of Science	Analyzed
Speier and Morris (2003)	Web of Science	Analyzed
Speier, Vessey, and Valacich (2003)	Author	Analyzed
Wheeler and Jones (2003)	Web of Science	Analyzed
Wilson and Addo (1994)	Web of Science	Analyzed
Studies Not Further Examined		
Agarwal and Sinha (1996)	Web of Science	System development domain
Agarwal, De, and Sinha (1999)	EBSCO	System development domain
Agarwal, Sinha, and Tanniru (1996)	Web of Science	System development domain
Chandra and Krovi (1999)	Web of Science	Conceptual
Giordano (2002)	Web of Science	System development domain
Heliades and Edmonds (2000)	Web of Science	System development domain
Hung (2003)	Web of Science	Does not test core CF
Jahng, Jain, and Ramamurthy (2000)	Web of Science	Conceptual; not CF
Mennecke, Crossland, and Killingsworth (2000)	Web of Science	Does not test core CF
Meyer, Shamo, and Gopher (1999)	Web of Science	Conceptual
Ramarapu, Frolick, Wilkes, and Wetherbe (1997)	Web of Science	Conceptual
Sinha and Vessey (1992)	Web of Science	System development domain
Song and Salvendy (2003)	Web of Science	Conceptual; not CF
Swink and Robinson (1997)	Web of Science	Does not test core CF
Vessey (1994)	Web of Science	Conceptual foundation
Wright (1995)	Web of Science	Mixed representations

problem representation/task match, problem representation/problem-solving skill match, or problem-solving task/problem-solving tool match, and, indeed, three-way matches. Additionally, studies could have been classified by the domain in which they are applied.

From the viewpoint of classifying cognitive fit studies based on the theoretical distinction of task complexity, we found that the majority of the studies used more complex decision-making or problem-solving tasks, with very few studies addressing simple information acquisition and information evaluation tasks. Hence, this approach did not allow a sufficiently rich characterization of studies that addressed more complex tasks. From the viewpoint of classifying the studies based on which problem-solving elements were matched, we found that by far the majority of studies addressed matches between task type and problem representation, that is, the original formulation of the model (Vessey, 1991, 1994). Again, this basis for classification did not prove to be appropriate. Finally, classifying studies based on domain did not produce a sufficiently rich characterization of the studies. As a result of our experiences here, we can add a further criterion for a good classification system: A good classification system should result in balanced categories.

In the classification system presented here, we employed some aspects of the alternative bases for classification presented above. However, because our objective is to determine how the theory of cognitive fit has been used since its initial presentation, we classified studies based on the type of contribution that they make to the literature. Our taxonomy is based on mutually exclusive categories, each of which is divided into two sub-categories. Our first major category is based on studies that test the original formulations of cognitive fit (Vessey, 1991, 1994), with sub-categories based on task complexity. Our second major category is based on studies that extend the theory to new domains. Our subcategories are positioned in two specific domains, those of human judgment, and multi-criteria decision making. Our third major category is based on studies that use different dimensions of fit. In addition to studies that have investigated traditional notions of fit using new dimensions, a number of studies have applied the notions of fit to the complexity of the relationship between the task and the problem representation.

From the viewpoint of the process of classification, we first examined a study to determine whether it tested one of the original formulations of the theory. If it did not, then it was further examined to determine whether it addressed a new dimension of fit. If this category was not appropriate, either, then the study was examined to determine whether it displayed a new dimension of fit. In this way, we achieved a classification in which the categories are both mutually exclusive and have theoretical significance.

Table 8.2 presents the studies examined according to the classification system.

TESTING THE THEORY OF COGNITIVE FIT

In this section, we test the theory of cognitive fit as presented in Vessey's two conceptual papers (1991, 1994); that is, we examined studies of cognitive fit that involved quite simple information acquisition and information evaluation tasks, followed by those that investigated cognitive fit in more complex tasks.

Cognitive Fit in Simple Information Acquisition and Information Evaluation Tasks

We identified three studies that addressed the match of problem representation to task on simple information acquisition and information evaluation tasks. Table 8.3 presents the details. We first present the studies and then evaluate the findings.

Studies of Cognitive Fit on Simple Information Acquisition and Information Evaluation Tasks

Vessey and Galletta (1991) conducted a study to evaluate the characteristics of the basic theory of cognitive fit, several extensions to the basic theory, and several premises on which the theory is based. Here we present just those aspects of the study that evaluated the theory of cognitive fit. Because spatial and symbolic tasks cannot be compared in any meaningful way, the study used two experimental designs, one for each type of task. Problem representation was a between-subject variable, with five repetitions of the task type as a within-subject factor.

As expected, users made faster and more accurate decisions on symbolic tasks with tables than with graphs. However, users with graphs, though faster than those with tables on spatial tasks, as expected, were less accurate. Hence the authors found only partial support for cognitive fit on spatial tasks.

Table 8.2

Classification of Cognitive Fit Studies Examined

Testing the theory of cognitive fit
   Simple information acquisition and information evaluation tasks
      Vessey and Galletta (1991)
      Mahoney et al. (2001)
      Chan (2001)
   More complex tasks
      Wilson and Addo (1994)
      Speier and Morris (2003)
      Speier, Vessey, and Valacich (2003)
      Wheeler and Jones (2003)

Extending the theory of cognitive fit to new domains
   Human judgment tasks
      Umanath and Vessey (1994)
      Tuttle and Kershaw (1998)
   Multi-criteria decision making tasks
      Smelcer and Carmel (1997)
      Dennis and Carte (1998)

Extending the theory of cognitive fit to new dimensions
   Cognitive fit as traditional match-mismatch using new dimensions of fit
      Hubona, Everett, March, and Wauchope (1998)
      Beckman (2002)
      Khatri, Vessey, Ram, and Ramesh (2006)
   Cognitive fit based on the extent of fit between task and problem representation
      Borthick, Bowen, Jones, and Tse (2001)
      Dunn and Grabski (2001)

The second study in this category is that by Mahoney, Roush, and Bandy (2003). These researchers also conducted a study that investigated the effect of task type (spatial and symbolic) and presentation format (graphs and tables) on performance. Their results support cognitive fit for both accuracy and time on both spatial and symbolic tasks.

The third study in this category, that of Chan (2001), assessed the effect of graphs and information overload on decision quality. For the aspect of interest here, Chan hypothesized an interaction effect between presentation format and information load. He found neither a main effect for presentation format nor an interaction effect with information load (although he hypothesized both!), and summarizes his results by stating that "presentation format has little effect on decision quality for very simple or very complex tasks." Graphs and tables performed equally well in both conditions.

We can gain insight into why this finding occurred by examining the tasks Chan used. Chan's nominal task (low information load) consisted of predicting operating profit margin using a single variable—the operating profit margin. The associated displays presented this variable over the prior five years as a line graph and as values in a single row of a table. Hence the participants had just five data points with which to work. No mention is made of the data used for high information load. However, because no variable other than operating profit margin is mentioned in the article, one might infer that it also uses a single variable with more years of data. Hence it is perhaps not surprising that Chan's extremely simple information load conditions produced tasks that could be addressed equally well using either graphs or tables.

Table 8.3

Characteristics of Cognitive Fit Studies on Simple Information Acquisition and Information Evaluation Tasks

	Independent Variables		Dependent Variables			
			Accuracy		Time/Efficiency	
Study	Task Type	PR (matched with task type)	Expected	Actual	Expected	Actual
Vessey and Galletta (1991)	Spatial Symbolic	Spatial (G) Spatial Symbolic (T)	Spatial tasks: G > T Symbolic tasks: T > G	**Spatial tasks: T > G** Symbolic tasks: T > G	Spatial tasks: G > T Symbolic tasks:T > G	Spatial tasks: G > T Symbolic tasks: T > G
Mahoney et al. (2001)	Spatial Symbolic	Spatial (G) Symbolic (T)	Spatial tasks: G > T Symbolic tasks: T > G	Spatial tasks: G > T Symbolic tasks: T > G	Spatial tasks: G > T Symbolic tasks: T > G	Spatial tasks: G > T Symbolic tasks: T > G
Chan (2001)	Spatial	Spatial (G) Symbolic (T)	Interaction effect: At low info load: T > G At high info load: G > T	No interaction observed Further, G = T		

Note: Results in underlined type are not significant; results in bold type contradict expectations.

*Evaluation of Cognitive Fit in Simple Information Acquisition
and Information Evaluation Tasks*

The findings of these three studies largely support the theory of cognitive fit. The exceptions are the findings by Vessey and Galletta that tables are more accurate than graphs on spatial problems, and those of Chan that graphs and tables are equally effective in both their nominal and high information load conditions.

It appears likely that the lack of support for cognitive fit in spatial problem solving in Vessey and Galletta's (1991) study is due to the fact that the manipulation of spatial tasks was not sufficiently strong. A significant body of knowledge supports the notion that problem solvers are more familiar with tables than with graphs, including findings from this study itself. Hence, it is likely that participant performance, in general, is better with tables than graphs. On very simple tasks, the effects of cognitive fit may not be sufficient to overcome this effect. One would, however, expect to find the expected effects on somewhat more complex tasks. This situation would lead to some results supporting cognitive fit, those on the more complex tasks of this type, no effects in somewhat less complex tasks, and reverse effects on extremely simple tasks. It appears, then, that the overwhelming majority of studies analyzed by Vessey (1991) in formulating the basic theory of cognitive fit, which demonstrated that spatial representations were both more effective and more efficient in their support of spatial tasks than were symbolic representations, were somewhat more complex spatial tasks.

It also appears likely that Chan found no interaction effect between problem representation and information load also because the tasks were too simple, notwithstanding the fact that he investigated two levels of information load.

Cognitive Fit in More Complex Tasks

Many of the studies reviewed in this paper address more complex tasks. What distinguishes the studies presented in this section is that they represent direct tests of the effect of complexity on cognitive fit, hence testing certain aspects of the theory of cognitive fit presented in Vessey (1994). The studies examined, therefore, also include those that demonstrate the occurrence of strategy shift as complexity in symbolic tasks increases. We identified four studies that addressed the match of the problem representation to the task on more complex tests. Table 8.4 presents the details. We first present the studies and then evaluate the findings.

Studies of Cognitive Fit on More Complex Tasks

In the first experiment in this category, Wilson and Addo (1994) address some of the issues presented in Vessey (1994). They hypothesized that both task type and task complexity (in the form of question complexity) would influence performance with graphs and tables. In an experiment that varied display format (graphs and tables), task type (spatial and symbolic), and task complexity (low and high), the researchers tested two separate hypotheses related to the display format x question type interaction and the display format x question complexity interaction, respectively.

There were no significant differences in accuracy across any of the treatments. The researchers argue that their participants "set relatively inflexible accuracy standards and used the amount of time necessary to meet those standards" thereby causing the effects to be manifested in response time. They report that their findings for response time support both (1) the theory of cognitive fit, with graphs best supporting spatial tasks and tables best supporting symbolic tasks, overall; and (2) their task complexity notions; that is, irrespective of task type, low complexity problems are

Table 8.4

Characteristics of Cognitive Fit Studies on More Complex Tasks

| Study | Independent Variables | | Dependent Variables | | | |
| | Task Type | PR (matched with task type) | Accuracy | | Time/Efficiency | |
			Expected	Actual	Expected	Actual
Wilson and Addo (1994)	Spatial	Spatial (G)	For spatial questions: G > T	*Ceiling on accuracy; analyzed only effects on time*	For spatial questions: G > T	For spatial questions: G > T
	Symbolic	Symbolic (T)	For symbolic questions: T > G With low task comp: T > G With high task comp: G > T		For symbolic questions: T > G With low task complexity: T > G With high task comp: G > T	For symbolic questions: T > G With low task complexity: T > G With high task complexity: G > T
Speier and Morris (2003)	Symbolic	Spatial (visual interface) Symbolic (textual interface)	Low complexity: Textual > visual High complexity: Visual > textual	Low complexity: Textual > visual High complexity: Visual > textual	Low complexity: Textual > visual High complexity: Visual > textual	**Low complexity: Visual > textual High complexity: Textual > visual**
Speier, Vessey, and Valacich (2003)	Symbolic	Spatial (G) Symbolic (T)	Interaction effect: [Lower complexity (no interruptions): T > G Higher complexity (interruptions): T = G]	Interaction effect significant	Interaction effect: [Lower complexity (no interruptions): T > G Higher complexity (interruptions): G = T]	<u>Interaction effect non-significant</u>
	Spatial	Spatial (G) Symbolic (T)	No interaction effect: [Lower and higher complexity: G > T]	Interaction effect non-significant	No interaction effect: [Lower and higher complexity: G > T]	Interaction effect non-significant
Wheeler and Jones (2003)	Symbolic (High and low predictability environments are of low and high complexity, respectively.)	Symbolic (database—DB) Spatial (regression)	Low complexity: DB format > regr format High complexity: Rgr format > DB format	Low complexity: DB format > regr format High complexity: Rgr format > DB format		

Note: Results in underlined type are not significant; results in bold type contradict expectations.

better supported with tables and high complexity problems with graphs. Note that these findings are not necessarily consistent with all the tenets of cognitive fit.

To fully address cognitive fit, more finely grained analyses need to be conducted. The way in which the researchers present their findings does not allow us to go beyond their own statements because (1) they do not report analyses of pairwise comparisons; and (2) although they present graphs of their interactions, they do so with results averaged over the third factor, which are the low and high complexity conditions that we would like to analyze further. The researchers go on to state that: "Over some intermediate area, performance differences between tables and graphs are minimal." This statement echoes some of those in Vessey (1994). However, because the authors had a stronger concept of task complexity than of cognitive fit, they tended to overlook the role of task type.

The second study in this category is that of Speier and Morris (2003) who conducted an experiment to assess the effects of task complexity (problem-solving task) on the task of finding a home using an online system that had either a visual or a text-based query interface (problem representation). Task complexity was varied based on the number of alternatives in the low and high complexity conditions: five viable homes in the low complexity condition and approximately 200 in the high complexity condition.

The task is a multi-criteria decision making task that is essentially symbolic in nature. Each interface supported an elimination-by-aspects decision-making strategy, which requires multiple comparisons of alternatives, each of which is based on values of a single attribute. Although the authors acknowledge cognitive fit as the foundational theory supporting their work, they do not use cognitive fit to develop their hypotheses. Hence the role of the theory of cognitive fit in the paper is unclear. For example, they base their arguments for hypothesizing that the text-based interface will be better than the visual interface on an idiosyncrasy of the interface: The latter does not facilitate ready comparison of "a small number of feasible solutions simultaneously." They hypothesized that the text-based interface would be more accurate than the visual interface on relatively simple tasks, while the visual interface would be more accurate than the text-based interface on more complex tasks.

In referring to decision-making time, the researchers stated their hypotheses based on the correspondence of the task to "reality," with reality undefined and therefore impossible to measure. They argued that: "For most tasks, text-based characters on a screen are abstractions that result in only a loose correspondence between the system and reality, while visual interfaces provide a more direct mapping." They further state that the low complexity task has a greater correspondence with reality when supported by the text-based interface and that the high complexity task has a greater correspondence to reality when supported by the visual interface. Based on their reasoning, the text-based interface should result in faster decision making on simple tasks, while the visual interface should be quicker for complex tasks. Note that the theory of cognitive fit, while having nothing to do with arguments based on "reality," leads to similar conclusions, albeit for different reasons.

The researchers found that, as hypothesized, the text-based interface resulted in greater accuracy when task complexity was low, while the visual interface resulted in greater accuracy when task complexity was high. The findings for time, on the other hand, were contrary to expectations; decision time was lower for the visual interface on the low complexity task and lower for the text-based interface on the high complexity task. The authors offer no explanation for the fact that all five of their findings with respect to time were in the opposite direction to those hypothesized.

The findings of this study support the theory of cognitive fit for accuracy on complex symbolic tasks. Tables result in more accurate performance on simple tasks, those in which the number of alternatives is small, while graphs result in more accurate performance when the number of alternatives is large. Because symbolic processing becomes increasingly difficult as the number of alternatives increases, decision makers increasingly use perceptual processes that are supported by spatial representations instead of analytical processes supported by symbolic representations. Hence, the authors observed a change in processing strategy as complexity on the symbolic task increased. The type of task investigated here is therefore a limiting task (Johnson and Payne, 1985; Vessey, 1994). Hence, the hypotheses in this experiment can be explained by the theory of cognitive fit and the findings for accuracy support those notions.

With regard to their findings for time, in the high complexity condition, decision-making time using the text-based interface may have been lower than that for the visual interface simply because the participants could do little to respond to the task effectively using the text-based interface. Hence, whatever they did, they did very quickly. In the low complexity condition, tables, although more accurate than graphs, may have required more time because participants still had to review a significant amount of data, a task that can be achieved more quickly with a visual than with a text-based interface.

In the third study in this category, Speier, Vessey, and Valacich (2003) investigated the role of cognitive fit in the solution of both complex spatial and symbolic tasks in both the presence and absence of interruptions. In the case of spatial tasks, there were no interaction effects for either accuracy or time: As expected, graphs outperformed tables on complex spatial tasks on both accuracy and time. In the case of symbolic tasks, interruptions effectively increased the cognitive complexity of the task under investigation and were therefore expected to induce problem solvers to change to a more parsimonious strategy earlier than an environment without interruptions. In other words, with an appropriate choice of task complexity, the crossover effect described above can be observed. The researchers found that the effect was manifested in accuracy and not in time. Problem solvers were more accurate with tables than with graphs on their complex symbolic tasks when there were no interruptions. However, with interruptions, there was no difference in performance with graphs and tables. Hence, graphs permitted problem solvers to handle the increased cognitive complexity better than did tables.

The final study in this category is that of Wheeler and Jones (2003). In a study of bank loan decision making, the researchers address the choice, and suitability of the choice, of certain "decision aid features" in terms of performance on tasks of "high and low predictability." High and low predictability tasks were defined by the amount of data to be analyzed, which is, in essence, a measure of task complexity. The task is symbolic in nature and the data are discrete (debt ratio, cash flow, revenue trend—number of quarters out of the prior 20 that revenues increased). A database aid presented the history data in point form (symbolic problem representation), while a regression aid depicted the data visually (spatial problem representation). Hence both "decision aid features" shared the same history data; only the presentation of that data varied. These "aids" are referred to, henceforth, as "problem representations."

Wheeler and Jones (2003) hypothesized that participants would perform better with the database representation (symbolic) in high predictability (low complexity) environments, and better with the regression representation (spatial) in low predictability (high complexity) environments. Their findings support their hypotheses. Hence the study by Wheeler and Jones (2003) is a further example of strategy change on a symbolic task that occurs as complexity increases and the problem can no longer be solved analytically.

Evaluation of Cognitive Fit in More Complex Tasks

As noted above, the study by Wilson and Addo (1994) goes quite a way towards supporting the extended notion of cognitive fit based on task complexity (Vessey, 1994). However, their statement that, irrespective of task type, tables best support simple tasks and graphs best support complex tasks, is not borne out in the findings of their study. To fully test this statement, and therefore the theory, the researchers needed to conduct further analyses.

Based on analyses reported in the prior section, the results that Speier and Morris (2003) report support cognitive fit for accuracy on limiting tasks, that is, very complex symbolic tasks that cannot be solved using analytical processes.

The studies by Speier et al. (2003) and Wheeler and Jones (2003) both demonstrate strategy change, that is, a crossover effect, as more complex symbolic problems are better solved with spatial rather than with symbolic problem representations, foregoing, therefore, the more demanding analytical processes for the more parsimonious perceptual processes. In Speier et al., the effect was in accuracy and not in time. In Wheeler and Jones (2003), the effects were in both accuracy and time. On the other hand, in both of these studies graphs performed better than tables on complex spatial tasks on both time and accuracy.

Hence, the findings of these studies support the theory of cognitive fit for more complex tasks.

EXTENDING THE THEORY OF COGNITIVE FIT TO NEW DOMAINS

In this section, we discuss cognitive fit in two somewhat different types of tasks that have been examined in two well-defined domains: multi-attribute judgment tasks in the accounting domain and multi-criteria decision-making tasks in the map-related domains of maps, geographic information systems, and spatial decision support systems.

Cognitive Fit in Human Judgment Tasks

We identified two studies that were conducted on multi-attribute judgment tasks, both in the accounting domain, in our analysis of articles that used the theory of cognitive fit. Table 8.5 presents the details. We first present the studies and then evaluate the findings.

Studies of Cognitive Fit in Human Judgment Tasks

The first such study is by Umanath and Vessey (1994). These researchers examined information load and the ability of the theory of cognitive fit to explain the performance of certain display formats on the multi-attribute judgment task of bankruptcy prediction. They hypothesized that predicting bankruptcy required both holistic processes that aided in integrating large amounts of data (a number of financial indicators over a number of years), as well the ability to reference ranges and/or levels of individual financial indicators. Hence they hypothesized that graphs, which possess integrating capabilities as well as permitting access to the underlying data, are a more accurate display format than schematic (Chernoff) faces, which provide integrating capabilities but not access to the underlying data. They also predicted that there would be no differences in accuracy of performance between faces and tables because each provides only one of the two necessary types of data: Tables provide no integrating capabilities while faces do not preserve the underlying data. Similarly, they expected schematic faces to result in faster problem solving compared with tables and graphs, for which no differences were expected.

All hypotheses were supported, although the finding for the speed of faces over tables was marginal.

Table 8.5

Characteristics of Cognitive Fit Studies on Judgments in the Accounting Domain

Independent Variables			Dependent Variables			
			Accuracy		Time/Efficiency	
Study	Task Type	PR (matched with task type)	Expected	Actual	Expected	Actual
Umanath and Vessey (1994)	Holistic	Holistic (Chernoff faces) Spatial (G) (Symbolic) TT	G > F F = T	G > F F = T	F > G F > T G = T	F > G F > T (marginal) G = T
Tuttle and Kershaw (1998)	Holistic (Note: the researchers: • Manipulated strategy and • Ignored task type)	Spatial (G) Symbolic (T)	For holistic strategy: Jmt consistency: G > T Jmt model quality: G > T For analytical strategy: Jmt consistency: T > G Jmt model quality: T > G	For holistic strategy: Jmt consistency: G > T Jmt model quality: G > T For analytical strategy: Jmt consistency: T = G Jmt model quality: T = G	For holistic strategy: Jmt time: G > T For analytical strategy: Jmt time: T > G	For holistic strategy: Jmt time: G = T For analytical strategy: Jmt time: T > G

Note: Results in underlined type are not significant; results in bold type contradict expectations.

Tuttle and Kershaw (1998) conducted a multi-attribute judgment study based on the Umanath and Vessey study (1994). In this case, participants assessed performance of hypothetical plant managers, a holistic task, using both graphs and tables. The researchers make similar arguments to Umanath and Vessey, above, with respect to the effects of graphs and tables on both accuracy and speed of performance on their judgment task. With respect to processing strategy, Umanath and Vessey relied on an emergent property of the theory of cognitive fit with respect to the type of strategies that decision makers use when working with graphs and tables, a property that was shown to be valid in Vessey and Galletta's (1991) paper. Tuttle and Kershaw, on the other hand, manipulated strategy by encouraging their participants to use either a holistic strategy or an analytical strategy. Following completion of the judgment tasks, the researchers confirmed the effectiveness of their judgment strategy manipulation.

Participants used both holistic and analytical strategies to solve judgment problems using either graphs or tables; that is, strategy was a within-subjects variable, while presentation format was a between-subjects variable. All hypotheses involved between-subject issues; that is, analyses compared just the performance with graphs versus tables using holistic strategies and using analytical strategies. This approach is peculiar because within-subjects designs are generally used to increase the level of control (and therefore the statistical power) over the experimental variables of interest—in this case, processing strategy. No analyses were conducted, however, on the within-subjects factor of processing strategy.

The dependent variables were judgment accuracy (both consistency and "judgment model quality") and time. For the holistic strategy, graphs produced higher judgment accuracy manifested in both more consistent judgments and higher judgment model quality, than tables. There was no difference in judgment time between the two formats. The researchers concluded that display format impacted accuracy through both judgment consistency and judgment model quality, and not through judgment time.

For the analytical strategy, there was no difference in judgment accuracy, consistency of judgments, or judgment model quality between tables and graphs; tables, however, proved to be quicker than graphs. The researchers claim that participants achieved similar accuracy with graphs and tables by exerting more effort for the format that did not match the strategy (graphs).

By manipulating processing strategy across presentation format, the researchers created a match-mismatch situation of strategy with presentation format. However, they did not take into account the characteristics of the task they were addressing, one of the primary variables in the theory of cognitive fit. Use of the holistic strategy resulted in a match with the judgment task and the graphical format, and a mismatch with the table format. Hence, the findings for the holistic strategy are consistent with cognitive fit as the match between the task and the problem representation. Use of the analytical strategy resulted in a mismatch with both the judgment task and the graphical format and a match with the table format. With graphs, decision makers needed to transform spatial information into symbolic information, process that data analytically, and then make a holistic judgment. With tables, a similar process applies without the initial need to transform the data in the presentation format. Hence it is possible that decision makers with graphs expended considerable time to transform the data to a level comparable to that of the data presented in tables, which then resulted in no differences in accuracy between the two formats.

Evaluation of Cognitive Fit in Human Judgment Tasks

Given the above explanations of the findings of the study by Tuttle and Kershaw (1998), the findings of the two studies described in this section can be explained quite readily using the theory of cognitive fit.

Cognitive Fit in Multi-Criteria Decision-Making Tasks

Here we examine studies that evaluated cognitive fit in multi-criteria decision-making tasks. The studies investigated were in map-related domains. Table 8.6 presents the details of the studies identified. We first present the studies and then evaluate the findings.

Studies of Cognitive Fit in Multi-Criteria Decision-Making Tasks

We identified two studies related to multi-criteria decision making in map-based domains in our analysis of articles that used the theory of cognitive fit.

The first study is that of Smelcer and Carmel (1997) who assessed the effect of display format, maps and tables, on three different types of geographic relationships (proximity, adjacency, and containment), and three levels of task difficulty (high, medium, and low). Proximity refers to "how far apart" the objects of interest are; adjacency is used to indicate two objects that are "next to each other"; containment refers to the fact that a two-dimensional object "could contain other objects." Smelcer and Carmel argue that maps will support all three relationships better than tables because each contains spatial elements. The researchers used problem-solving time as the dependent variable because of the difficulties of simultaneously working with interval and ratio data in determining accuracy. The researchers report that there were no significant differences in error rates, and they include both correct and incorrect responses in the analysis of time. They found that proximity and adjacency tasks were indeed better supported by maps than by tables. Their findings for containment tasks were not supported, however: containment tasks resulted in equivalent performance (time) for graphs and tables.

The findings on containment tasks can be explained by the fact that containment is a symbolic rather than a spatial task and a map would not therefore aid this type of problem solving. Perusal of the researchers' table and map representations for the containment task (Table 6: tabular; Figure 5: map) reveals that the different objects contained in a space are represented as icons in both. In the table representation, the icons relevant to a space are located next to each other in the same row of the table. In the map representation, the icons are located in two-dimensional space within the specific area under investigation. Because of the essentially similar representation, it is not surprising that there was little difference in time to extract the required information from tables and maps.

The second study in this area is by Dennis and Carte (1998). In a study quite similar to that of Smelcer and Carmel, the researchers examined the effects of maps and tables on accuracy and time of completing both adjacency and containment tasks. However, they hypothesized that containment tasks are symbolic in nature rather than spatial, as noted above. Further, they examined participants' decision processes by examining the worksheets they used while conducting the two types of tasks. They hypothesized and found that: (1) map-based representations induced perceptual decision processes and that tabular representations induced analytical processes; (2) accuracy on adjacency tasks (spatial) was better with maps than with tables, while accuracy on containment tasks (symbolic) was better with tables than with graphs. On the other hand, while they found that time on adjacency tasks was better with maps than tables, they also found that time on containment tasks was also better with maps than with tables.

Comparing their findings with the original formulation of cognitive fit, Dennis and Carte state that "the predicted performance effects of CFT (... cognitive fit theory...) cannot be extended from elementary tasks to multi-criteria geographic tasks." This statement is correct. However, this experiment and its findings should be investigated in terms of the theory of cognitive fit extended

Table 8.6

Characteristics of Cognitive Fit Studies on Multi-Criteria Decision Making in Map-Related Domains

| | Independent Variables | | Dependent Variables | | | |
| | | | Accuracy | | Time/Efficiency | |
Study	Task Type	PR (matched with task type)	Expected	Actual	Expected	Actual
Smelcer and Carmel (1997)	Spatial (proximity)	Spatial (M)			Proximity tasks: M > T	Proximity tasks: M > T
	Spatial (adjacency)	Symbolic (T)			Adjacency tasks: M > T	Adjacency tasks: M > T
	Spatial (containment: claimed to be spatial; in reality symbolic)				Containment tasks: M > T	Containment tasks: <u>M = T</u>
Dennis and Carte (1998)	Adjacency (spatial)	Spatial (M)	Adjacency tasks: M > T	Adjacency tasks: M > T	Adjacency tasks: M > T	Adjacency tasks: M > T
	Containment (symbolic)	Symbolic (T)	Containment tasks: T > M	Containment tasks: T > M	Containment tasks: M > T	Containment tasks: M > T

Note: Results in underlined type are not significant; results in bold type contradict expectations.

to more complex tasks as presented in Vessey (1994).[1] The types of tasks investigated are not simple information acquisition and evaluation tasks and the simple version of cognitive fit does not apply in these circumstances. The symbolic containment task will be subject to time/accuracy trade-off as the complexity of the task increases. In the intermediate stages of complexity (i.e., prior to the level at which decision makers can no longer address the problem using analytical processes), accuracy may still be better with symbolic representations and speed will be faster with maps, as was found in this study.

Evaluation of Cognitive Fit in Multi-Criteria Decision-Making Tasks

Unlike the multi-criteria decision-making systems used in Speier and Morris (2003), GIS facilitate a broader range of possible tasks, some of which may be spatial in nature, while others may be symbolic. The two studies presented here address both spatial (proximity and adjacency) tasks and symbolic (containment) tasks. Proximity and adjacency tasks are best supported with maps rather than with tables of data (Smelcer and Carmel, 1997; Dennis and Carte, 1998). Smelcer and Carmel found the effect in speed of decision making, while Dennis and Carte found it by analyzing accuracy and time simultaneously. For Smelcer and Carmel's containment task, it appears likely that the spatial and symbolic problem representations were not sufficiently difficult to result in time differences, their measure of choice.

All of these findings support the theory of cognitive fit.

EXTENDING THE THEORY OF COGNITIVE FIT TO NEW DIMENSIONS

Certain studies of cognitive fit address dimensions of fit that are qualitatively different from those associated with spatial and symbolic processing. We characterize the first set of studies as using new dimensions in the context of the traditional match-mismatch form of fit and the second set of studies in terms of the extent of match between the problem-solving task and the problem representation.

Cognitive Fit Based on Traditional Match/Mismatch Using New Dimensions of Fit

We identified three studies that addressed the match of problem representation to task using new dimensions of fit, each of which is unique in its approach. One of the studies introduces a new dimension into an already-established domain of investigation; the second study is based in a new domain; and the third study establishes a new dimension of the task in the context of cognitive fit. Table 8.7 presents details of these studies. We first present the studies and then evaluate the findings.

Studies of Cognitive Fit Based on Traditional Match/Mismatch Using New Dimensions of Fit

The first study that extends the basic theory of cognitive fit to new dimensions is that of Hubona, Everett, March, and Wauchope (1998). The domain of investigation was that of "language-conveyed representations of spatial information." Their study used: (1) two types of spatial problem representations known as "survey" and "route" presented using natural language; and (2) two types of tasks that also emphasized the same types of information. The survey representation described the layout of a town as if one were picking out features on a map, while the route representation described the layout in terms of what one would observe on driving through it. Survey and route representations therefore emphasized declarative and procedural knowledge, respectively (Anderson, 1982, 1996). Hence, these dimensions represented a more in-depth differentiation of spatial representations than

Table 8.7

Characteristics of Cognitive Fit Studies in Different Domains

	Independent Variables		Dependent Variables			
			Accuracy		Time/Efficiency	
Study	Task Type	PR (matched with task type)	Expected	Actual	Expected	Actual
Hubona et al. (1998)	"Survey" inference	Survey description	For survey tasks: Survey PR > Route PR	For survey tasks: Survey PR = Route PR	For survey tasks: Survey PR > Route PR	For survey tasks: Survey PR > Route PR
	"Route" inference	Route description	For route tasks: Route PR > Survey PR	For route tasks: Route PR > Survey PR	For route tasks: Route PR > Survey PR	**For route tasks: Survey PR > Route PR**
Beckman (2002)	Rotation changes	Separate control over rotation and translation (simple vehicle controller [SVC])	Separate control required: SVC > JS	Separate control required: SVC > JS		
	Rotation and translation changes	Rotation and translation changes at the same time (joystick [JS])	Combination control required: JS > SVC	Combination control required: JS > SVC		
Khatri et al. (2006)	Internal representation of the task	One level (1-LA) Two level (2-LA) annotations	2-LA > 1-LA	2-LA > 1-LA		

Note: Results in underlined type are not significant; results in bold type contradict expectations.

had been apparent in prior research. Examples of survey and route inference questions, which required a true/false response, are, respectively: "The colorful maple trees are to the north and south of Maple Street"; and "If you turn left onto Pioneer Road from the Scenic Highway and drive straight ahead, you will eventually pass the Town Hall on your right."

The results for cognitive fit are as follows. For survey tasks, there was no difference in accuracy between survey and route descriptions; problem-solving time was, however, shorter when it was supported by a survey description. Hence, support for cognitive fit was manifested in time. For route tasks, accuracy was superior with the route description compared to the survey description, supporting cognitive fit. The finding for time, however, was in the opposite direction to that expected—a route description supporting a survey task was quicker than a route description supporting a route task. Examination of the route inference questions reveals that they are considerably longer and more difficult than the survey questions. For example: (1) they have at least two reference points compared with a single reference for the survey tasks; and (2) on occasion, the directions specified in the question are the reverse of those specified in the town description. Hence, although route questions were still answered more effectively with the route than with the survey description, it is perhaps not surprising that participants responded more quickly to route questions using the survey description than the route description. This observation highlights the importance of ensuring that task descriptions are comparable across treatments. In this case, complexity was not comparable across treatments.

Further, it is interesting to ponder the effect that drawing a map based on both survey and route descriptions might have on the comparisons made. A map would, in effect, be a survey description, from which it would be easier to respond to survey than to route questions. Although the researchers do not report on the numbers of participants who drew maps from each description, one might infer that few did because the accuracy for route tasks was better with route descriptions than survey descriptions; if all participants used "maps," there would have been no differences in performance with survey and route descriptions, irrespective of the task. In future research, it would be worthwhile to capture the way in which participants approached the problems.

The second study of this nature is that of Beckman (2002). This study extends the theory of cognitive fit to a domain that is quite unlike any other studied to date, that of human performance on motor tasks, specifically tasks involving physical control of ground vehicles. Studying cognitive fit in this new domain results in a new dimension of fit. The two task types addressed in the study are: (1) control of either rotation or translation changes, but not both concurrently; and (2) simultaneous control of combined rotation and translation changes. The virtual vehicle being controlled was the M1 tank, which can only move back and forth along the x axis (translation) and rotate around the y axis. The tasks were performed with physical user interfaces that either separated or combined translational and rotational control.

The user interface presents a "model" for viewing what the problem solver has to work with in order to complete the task (Norman, 1993). Hence, the user interface in these motor tasks corresponds to the problem representation in the theory of cognitive fit. The two interfaces were a simple vehicle controller and a joystick. The joystick allowed rotation and translation in the forward/reverse direction, both along the vertical axis. On the other hand, the simple vehicle controller had the same two degrees of motion freedom, with translational vehicle motion being controlled through the horizontal axis, and rotational vehicle motion through the vertical axis. Display characteristics for each interface were identical.

Hypotheses, which were based on the theory of cognitive fit, were tested using three "separation" tasks, which should be facilitated by the separate-control interface, the simple vehicle controller, and one "combination" task, which should be facilitated by the integrated-control interface, the joystick. The dependent measures, which were appropriate to the specific task, involved

Figure 8.3   **Cognitive Fit Model Extended to Include Internal Representation of the Task**

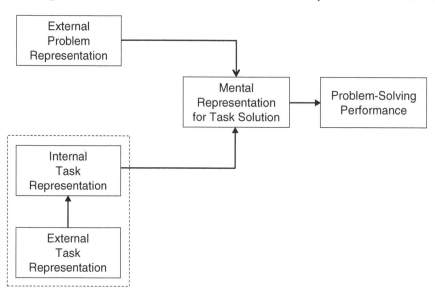

accuracy, or time, or a combination of the two. One of the separation tasks was facilitated by the separate control interface and the combination task was best supported by the joystick interface, as expected. Because ceiling effects were evident in the other two separation tasks, the experimental manipulations were ineffective. Hence, the two meaningful findings from this experiment support the theory of cognitive fit.

The third study of this nature is that of Khatri et al. (2006). This study provides an example of a further match that can be examined within the theory of cognitive fit, that between the internal representation of the task and the external problem representation used to address the task (Khatri et al., 2006). See Figure 8.3. Specifically, the researchers assessed whether geospatio-temporal extensions to traditional conceptual models—in this case, entity-relationship (ER) models—are best presented by annotating the conceptual schema or by providing the geospatio-temporal data as an additional external representation separate from the schema. The authors examined perform-ance on both syntactic and semantic schema comprehension tasks that were presented as questions in the form of English-language text.

The nature of the problem solver's internal representation of the task can be addressed by drawing on the theory of text comprehension (Kintsch, 1974; Rumelhart et al., 1972) and the related way in which text is stored in long-term memory. Text is viewed as being composed of propositions. In similar fashion, the knowledge acquired from the text is viewed as being stored in long-term memory as abstract conceptual propositions, consistent with Anderson and Bower's model of memory, that is, human associative memory (HAM) (1980).

In HAM, each proposition tree is divided into two sub-trees, one of which represents a fact, while the other represents a context; the tree therefore signifies that the fact is true in the given context. A fact can be subdivided into a subject and a predicate, and a predicate can be further subdivided into a relation and an object. Note that, in terms of the ER model, a relation and an object correspond to a relationship and an entity, respectively. The fact sub-tree therefore matches the information presented in the traditional ER model. The context sub-tree can be subdivided into location and time. Hence the context sub-tree represents geospatio-temporal data.

An ER model with geospatio-temporal data represented as annotations on the traditional conceptual schema, in which fact and context are stored together, therefore matches the way the problem solver structures the task in internal memory, while the representation of contextual geospatio-temporal data separate from the associated fact (i.e., entities and relationships) does not. The researchers' thesis that problem solvers using the annotated representation of geospatio-temporal data on conceptual schema would outperform those using the separate representation of geospatio-temporal data was supported in the experiment.

Evaluation of Cognitive Fit Based on Traditional Match/Mismatch
Using New Dimensions of Fit

With respect to the study by Hubona et al., on declarative and procedural dimensions of language-conveyed spatial information, the theory is supported for survey tasks on the basis of time, and for route tasks on the basis of accuracy, while the finding for speed was the opposite of that hypothesized. What is apparent here is that: (1) we need additional information to be able to assess the situation in more detail; (2) we need to ensure that tasks are comparable in all ways; and (3) we need to ensure that we use analyses that fully control for the possibility of accuracy/time trade-offs.

Beckman's study is quite a traditional study of the theory of cognitive fit in a significantly different domain, that is, tasks involving physical control of ground vehicles. The meaningful results from this study fully support the theory of cognitive fit. The study by Khatri et al. (2006) is also a traditional study of cognitive fit that recognizes the fact that the internal representation of the task itself can be matched to the problem representation. The results for accuracy in this experiment support the theory of cognitive fit.

Hence the analyses of the studies presented here suggest that the theory of cognitive fit can be extended to other dimensions of fit.

COGNITIVE FIT BASED ON THE EXTENT OF FIT BETWEEN
PROBLEM-SOLVING TASK AND PROBLEM REPRESENTATION

We identified two studies in which the extent of fit between the problem-solving task and problem representation varied. Table 8.8 presents details of these studies. We first present the studies and then evaluate the findings.

Studies of Cognitive Fit Based on the Extent of Fit Between Problem-Solving
Task and Problem Representation

The first study is by Borthick et al. (2001) who investigated "the effects of information request ambiguity and construct incongruence on query development." Although the researchers conducted a single experiment, their design of the ambiguity and construct congruence treatments and the results of the statistical analyses conducted can be conceived as testing what may be regarded as two cognitive fit models. What characterizes both of these studies is the notion of close and far matches between pairs of variables in the cognitive fit model. We do not further consider the first part of the study because it involves matching the problem-solving task to the problem-solving tool, which is outside the scope of this analysis.

The second set of results presented examines the effect of high and low congruence between problem-solving tasks (information requests) and the problem representation (in this case, an

Table 8.8

Characteristics of Cognitive Fit Studies Based on Extent of Fit Between Problem-Solving Task and Problem Representation

	Independent Variables		Dependent Variables			
			Accuracy		Time/Efficiency	
Study	Task Type	PR (matched with task type)	Expected	Actual	Expected	Actual
Borthick et al. (2001)	Close and far matches of problem representation to task	Spatial (ERD)	Simple (match) > Complex (mismatch)	Simple (match) > Complex (mismatch) (micro and macro errors)	Simple (match) > Complex (mismatch)	Simple (match) > Complex (mismatch) (# attempts; time n/s)
Dunn and Grabski (2001)	Localization of response based on REA model (strong moderate, no localization)	Spatial (REA accounting model); Symbolic (DCA accounting model)	Strong localization: REA > DCA Moderate localization: REA > DCA No localization: REA = DCA	Strong localization: REA > DCA Moderate localization: REA > DCA No localization: REA = DCA	Strong localization: REA > DCA Moderate localization: REA > DCA No localization: REA > DCA	**Strong localization: DCA > REA** **Moderate localization: DCA > REA** **No localization: DCA > REA**

Note: Results in underlined type are not significant; results in bold type contradict expectations.

entity-relationship diagram-ERD). High and low congruence was operationalized via the complexity involved in obtaining the required information from the ERD. In situations of high congruence, the information requested could be obtained by simple extraction from the ERD. In situations of low congruence, a number of transformations were required to obtain the required information. Such tasks involved, for example, creating temporary views, developing new relationships, or performing outer joins. Hence, the high congruency/low task complexity condition was matched to the presentation of the data in the form of the ERD, while the low congruency/high task complexity condition was mismatched with the data presentation. These results support the theory of cognitive fit for close versus far matches. In the authors' terms, congruency between the information request and the data representation leads to better performance than when the data representation and the information request are not congruent.

The second study, by Dunn and Grabski (2001), is also on database querying. The researchers conducted an experiment to determine the effects of varying levels of match between the problem (i.e., data) representation and the problem-solving task. The degree of match was operationalized as the extent of localization of the data, as presented in each of the accounting models used as the basis for data presentation. These models are the traditional DCA (debit-credit-account) approach, in which data is presented in list format—that is, the data are symbolic in nature—and the REA (resource-event-agent) accounting model, in which data are presented graphically. Supporting documentation for the DCA model adds details that cannot be represented within the model itself. Individual REA models are presented "in parts based on business processes" in the area under consideration. Use of this latter type of representation implies, therefore, that users may need to refer to many such diagrams in order to respond to a particular information request.

From the perspective of cognitive fit, the objective of the study was to assess the efficacy of varying degrees of match afforded by varying levels of localization of the required data in the REA model compared with the unlocalized data presented in the DCA model. The researchers proposed that the graphically oriented REA model would be more effective than the DCA model. They conducted a study that varied accounting model and problem-solving task, as well as experience. The participants were requested to explain how they would obtain an answer to a particular task (information request) from the available representations (accounting models).

In terms of accuracy, the researchers found support for the notion of fit in both the strong and moderate localization conditions (participants using the REA model outperformed those using the DCA model), with no difference between the two models in the no localization condition. Interestingly, REA model users took longer to complete the tasks than did DCA model users. The researchers suggest that this finding could have been due to the fact that, because the REA model presented more information, the participants may have suffered from information overload. Recall, however, that participants using the DCA model were required to refer to further documentation used to support that model, information that was not available directly from the chart of accounts; if participants did not do this sufficiently well, then a time/accuracy trade-off would occur and participants using the DCA model would be expected to be less accurate and to spend less time on solving the problems. Once again, we see that accuracy and time should be assessed simultaneously to detect the possibility of such effects.

Evaluation of Cognitive Fit Based on the Extent of Fit Between Problem-Solving Task and Problem Representation

These two experiments address somewhat similar dimensions of cognitive fit, termed "close and far" matches (Borthick et al., 2001), and "localization" of the data in the problem representation

(Dunn and Grabski, 2001). Both studies therefore address the needs of a specific task rather than a generic category of tasks. There are two major differences from the traditional formulation of cognitive fit. First, the dimension of fit presented here is not one of match-mismatch, as in the traditional form of cognitive fit. Instead, the dimension of fit in these experiments is related to the complexity of the relationship between the task itself and the problem representation. Hence the choice of problem representation is contextual in nature. Second, the difference is not absolute; it is, instead, one of degree.

In cognitive fit terms, to derive a consistent mental representation for a problem solution, a close match (or strong localization) requires fewer transformations than a far match (weak localization). Note the similarity of these arguments to that of the original derivation of the theory of cognitive fit; that is, that transformations are needed to develop a consistent mental representation when the processes acting on the problem-solving task and the problem representation do not match. Hence the theoretical arguments made for traditional cognitive fit apply to this type of match, also.

The results of these two experiments fully support the extension of cognitive fit to the new dimension of complexity in the interaction between problem representation and problem-solving task.

MORE RECENT THEORETICAL ADVANCES IN THE THEORY OF COGNITIVE FIT

Time does not stand still; nor does our knowledge or our theories. Our objective in this section is to present two theoretical advances to the theory of cognitive fit that have the potential, first, to deepen our knowledge of the underlying theoretical foundations of cognitive fit and, second, to extend the theory in order to explain much more complex phenomena.

Extending the Model of Cognitive Fit

The field of cognitive psychology has undergone changes since the theory of cognitive fit was first developed. We elaborate on the theory in light of those new developments.

The model of cognitive fit (Figure 8.1) views problem-solving performance as resulting from the interaction between the problem representation and the task. This model therefore views processing as taking place within the mental representation. To support the solution of the task, the problem solver develops a consistent mental representation that is based on the internalization of the information in the problem representation and in the task.

The basic problem-solving model used to describe cognitive fit can be enriched with a more recent formulation of problem solving. Zhang and Norman (1994), for example, suggest that a cognitive task be viewed as a "system of distributed representations with internal and external representations as two indispensable parts." The internal and external representational spaces form a "distributed representational space, which is the representation of the abstract task space" (Zhang, 1997). In this case, the "task space" is synonymous with Vessey's "mental representation." Hence we modify Figure 8.1 to reflect the fact that both the problem solver's internal representation of the problem domain and the external problem representation, as well as the interaction between them, contribute to the mental representation developed to solve the problem. Figure 8.4 presents the general model of problem solving that incorporates notions of distributed cognition that we call the extended model of cognitive fit. Note that this approach allows the researcher to consider independently the roles and nature of the internal representation of the domain of interest, the external problem representation, and the mental

Figure 8.4   **Extended Model of Cognitive Fit**

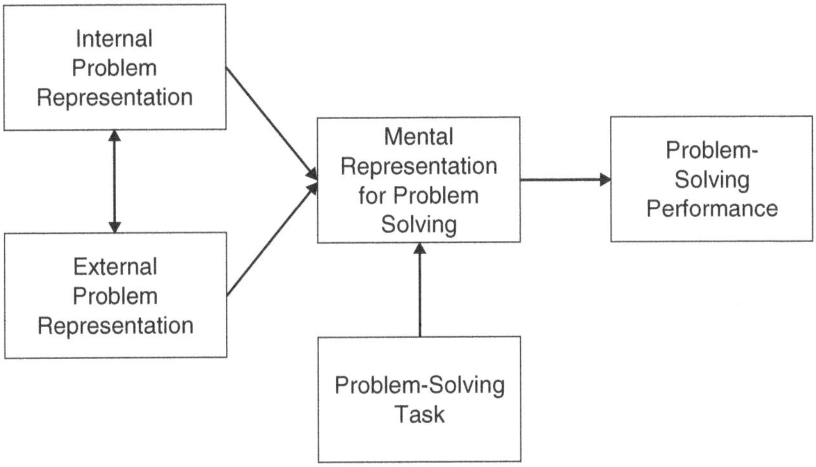

representation for task solution, hence overcoming the confounding of the internal representation of the problem with the mental representation for task solution in the prior model.

Extending the Theory of Cognitive Fit to Dual-Task Problem Solving

More recently, the theory of cognitive fit has been used in problem-solving situations involving dual tasks.

Many IS tasks can be viewed as involving dual tasks. We can conceive of this in two, related ways. First, all IS problem solving involves both the domain of IS and the domain of the application to which it is being applied. IS domain knowledge consists of representations, methods, techniques, and tools that form the basis for the development of application systems. Those application systems are developed to organize/structure solutions to real-world problems that exist in a given business area, or application domain; they could be in accounting, sales, or marketing, for example. It is clear, then, that knowledge of the IS and application domains go hand-in-hand in solving problems in IS. Second, many IS tasks themselves are, in fact, comprised of two types of tasks. For example, software comprehension is known to play a key role in debugging and in making changes to software (Hendrix et al., 2002; Robson et al., 1991). Note that, here, software comprehension is heavily based on application domain knowledge (see Shaft and Vessey, 1995); hence, in this instance, comprehension is synonymous with knowledge of the application domain.

Problem solving in these types of tasks can be conceptualized as the relationship between the two interacting sub-tasks. Figure 8.5 presents a general conceptualization of dual-task problem solving that views IS problem solving as involving both the domain of information systems and that of the application.[2]

The relationship between the dual tasks appears to be moderated by the type of task under investigation. The task characteristic that appears to influence problem solving is the extent to which the task solution is well understood, and therefore can be structured. (See Reitman's [1964] original conceptualization of tasks as being either well or ill structured in nature). When the task is ill structured, as in modifying computer software, both tasks are essential to effective problem

Figure 8.5   Dual-Task Model of Problem Solving in an IS Context

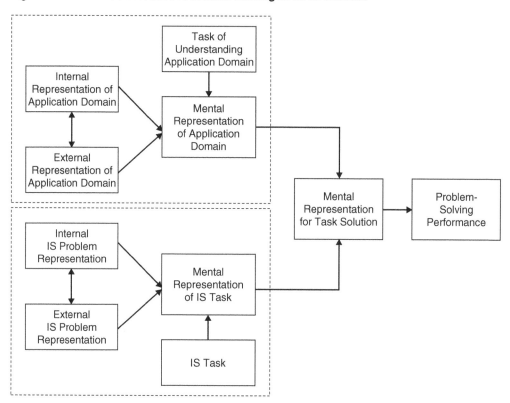

solution. Such a situation occurs, for example, in making a modification to a piece of software, a task that requires substantial software comprehension (Shaft and Vessey, 2006). In typical cognitive fit fashion, performance is enhanced when the mental representation of each of the sub-tasks emphasizes the same type of information. However, when the mental representation that a software maintainer has of a piece of software does not match the mental representation of the modification to be conducted, dual-task problem solving results in dual-task interference.

Shaft and Vessey conducted an experiment with professional programmers that showed that higher levels of software comprehension are associated with better performance on software modification tasks only when the maintainer's mental model of the software matched the type of modification to be conducted, in other words, when cognitive fit existed. However, when cognitive fit did not exist, problem solvers improved their knowledge of the software along dimensions with which they were already familiar and not those dimensions needed to conduct the modification task. Hence, increases in software comprehension that occurred during modification were inversely related to performance on the modification task, resulting in dual-task interference. Therefore in dual-task problem solving involving ill-structured tasks, cognitive fit moderates the relationship between the two tasks (in this case, modification and comprehension).

When the task is well structured, however, all of the information necessary for task solution is available via the problem representation alone. Such a situation occurs, for example, in comprehending a conceptual schema (Khatri et al., 2006; note that the dual-task context of this paper did not survive the review process. Nonetheless, the theory is appropriate, and the arguments on cognitive fit remain unchanged). The findings of this experiment show that when the schema comprehension tasks involve only data extraction (i.e., cognitive fit exists), knowledge of the application domain has no effect on problem-solving performance; problem solvers can address problems with reference only to the IS task materials. On the other hand, on more complex tasks for which problem solvers need to transform the data extracted from the conceptual schema (i.e., cognitive fit does not exist), knowledge of the application domain, although not essential, facilitates problem solution.

DISCUSSION AND IMPLICATIONS

The theory of cognitive fit was first introduced into the IS community in 1991 to explain the results of numerous studies that sought to address performance differences in the use of graphs versus tables. At the same time, the theory was thought to be one aspect of a general theory of problem solving, applicable across domains and possibly also across different dimensions of fit. In this study, therefore, we sought to determine how the theory of cognitive fit has been applied over time, whether the basic tenets of the theory are still applicable or whether the theory needs to be modified in some way, and, thereby, to assess whether it can be regarded as a general theory of problem solving.

This section discusses our findings and presents the contributions of our research. We conclude with the implications for future research into the theory of cognitive fit.

Discussion of the Findings

In this paper, we sought to address how the theory of cognitive fit has stood the test of time. The bulk of the paper is devoted to an analysis of published studies. Other recent studies are used to present theoretical advances that incorporate recent thinking in cognitive science into the basic model of cognitive fit and that extend the model to problem solving in situations involving two interacting tasks.

In our analysis of published studies based on the theory of cognitive fit, we classified studies according to whether they tested concepts found in the two foundational papers that present the theory (Vessey, 1991, 1994), whether they applied the theory to new domains of investigation, and whether they developed/used new dimensions of fit. By far the majority of studies in this analysis addressed more complex problem-solving tasks. We discuss each of these three situations in turn.

Studies of core cognitive fit conducted in both the realm of simple information acquisition and information evaluation tasks, and of more complex tasks, largely support expectations. There is one exception. According to the theory, graphs should result in more accurate and quicker solutions to simple spatial tasks than tables; this is the finding in the majority of studies examining simple spatial tasks (see Vessey, 1991; Mahoney et al., 2001). However, if the spatial task is too simple, the fact that problem solvers are not as familiar with graphs as they are with tables—see, for example, Vessey and Galletta (1991), among other authors—means that they incur some cognitive overhead in using graphs. In this case, the problem may be solved either more accurately using tables (Vessey, 1991) or equally as well (Chan, 2001).

The prediction that problem solvers will change strategy when requested to perform complex symbolic tasks using analytical processes, which are best supported by tables, to perceptual processes, which are best supported by graphs, is confirmed in this analysis. In fact, the complex symbolic task used by Speier and Morris (2003) was so complex that decision makers had little hope of using analytical processes to solve the problem. They therefore used perceptual processes. This type of task is referred to as a limiting task (Johnson and Payne, 1985; Vessey,

1994). This notion is supported in two further studies. The experiment by Speier et al. (2003) demonstrated that the increased complexity induced by interruptions in the work environment led problem solvers to change their problem-solving strategy on symbolic tasks from analytical processes (best supported by tables) to perceptual processes (best supported by graphs). In the experiment by Wheeler and Jones (2003), the solution of a symbolic task (both accuracy and time) was supported by a symbolic representation when there were few data points, and by a spatial representation when there were numerous data points.

A number of studies addressed new tasks in new domains. These were characterized as multi-attribute judgment tasks, in the accounting domain, and multi-criteria decision-making tasks in map-related domains. In general, these are tasks that are best addressed using analytical processes and holistic processes, respectively. In both of these sub-categories, the findings largely support the theory. Dennis and Carte (1998) call into question the formulation of the time component for cognitive fit, stating that graphs always result in quicker problem solving than tables. However, their arguments are based on the simple form of cognitive fit, which does not apply to the types of more complex tasks that they are addressing. In the intermediate stages of complexity (i.e., prior to the level at which decision makers can no longer handle the problem using analytical processes), accuracy may still be better with symbolic representations while speed may be faster with maps (i.e., spatial representations), as they found in their study. Hence it appears that the theory of cognitive fit applies equally well to more complex tasks of this nature.

Finally, we examined studies that used new/different dimensions of fit in applying the theory. The notion of fit occurring in studies addressed to date in this discussion is based on the match-mismatch between the problem representation and the task. Three studies examined in this category demonstrated the traditional match-mismatch form of fit, using new dimensions of fit (Beckman, 2002; Hubona et al., 1998; Khatri et al., 2006). In the two other studies in this category, fit is based on the degree of complexity in the relationship between the task and the problem representation (Borthick et al., 2001; Dunn and Grabski, 2001). Although this could be construed as task complexity, such a conceptualization would be somewhat misleading. In these tasks, the choice of problem representation is contextual in nature in that it relates to the task in the context of the problem representation used to support that task. The difference, therefore, is not absolute, but is, instead, one of degree. From the evidence presented here, the findings with new dimensions of fit appear to be essentially similar to those with traditional forms of fit.

Throughout all of these studies, the trade-off between accuracy and time remains undefined. It is clear that a number of other variables influence the problem-solving outcomes, such as a requirement for accuracy or time. Certain studies that find an effect in time but not accuracy attribute the findings to spending more time with a particular problem representation to achieve the same level of accuracy, and vice versa. Certain studies investigate either accuracy or time alone. Further, we have also seen that other environmental stresses such as interruptions influence the outcome. We can engage in some prescriptions with regard to the conduct of such studies: (1) Do not forget that performance instructions can bias the approach that participants take to solving the problem, and hence influence the findings of any study (see Vessey 1994, and Figure 8.2); (2) both time and accuracy should be measured so that if the effect does not appear in one of the variables it may be manifested in the other; not measuring either accuracy or time in these types of studies may be quite risky; (3) both time and accuracy should be measured simultaneously; (4) the effects of both the independent and dependent variables should be addressed during analysis—this can be done using the Messmer-Homans procedure (Vessey, 1987; Dennis and Carte, 1998).

Perhaps the major limitation of this analysis lies in the choice of studies for examination. Because numerous studies have cited the original papers on cognitive fit, it was essential to devise a systematic way of identifying studies for investigation. The approach used was based primarily on citations appearing in the ISI Web of Science. It is important to acknowledge, however, that the sample could have been developed in a number of ways. Nonetheless, there is no reason to suspect that bias was introduced in the approach used or that bias would have occurred using different approaches.

A related issue is the completeness of the sample of studies investigated. Because of time constraints it was not possible to examine all the studies that referenced the cornerstone cognitive fit paper (Vessey, 1991). However, it does appear likely that, had we done so, we would have identified further studies that fit the profile sought here. Not only do indexing services work in specific ways, so, too, do authors. It is possible that we did not identify studies because the authors did not signal sufficiently strongly their theoretical bases.

As an example of the vagaries of identifying desired articles, we cite an article we became aware of during our study, one that we do not examine here because it does not address the core issues. This empirical article cited Vessey and Galletta (1991) twenty-two times, indicating that this paper was very important to what the article was seeking to achieve. Yet the article did not acknowledge the theory of cognitive fit as its theoretical base, with the result that the paper would not have been identified in either an abstract or author-generated search for keywords. Further, Keywords Plus would not identify the paper as being based on cognitive fit had we sought studies that referenced Vessey and Galletta (1991) because keyword selection is based on "words and phrases that frequently appear in the titles of the article's references," and this paper cited just a single cognitive fit paper. This example illustrates the difficulties associated with determining a complete sample of relevant studies. Note, also, that the problems identified here present a problem for researchers who believe that identifying core theories is key to the success of our discipline (see, for example, Benbasat and Weber, 1996).

Another potential limitation lies in the classification system used to investigate the studies. As noted earlier, we considered numerous classification systems, and discarded the majority of them based on one of the three accepted tenets of such a classification system, plus our own fourth criterion, that of balance in the resulting categories. We found that studies could be classified most cleanly using the approach employed here. Yet a number of studies could have been classified according to more than one of the characteristics used. For example, Speier and Morris (2003), which we examined as an example of cognitive fit in more complex tasks because it illustrated strategy change, used a multi-criteria decision making problem, as did those studies examined under multi-criteria decision making in map-related domains. Nonetheless, the approach used here presents an interesting and potentially fruitful way of viewing the potential of the theory of cognitive fit.

Implications for Future Research

Our research has several implications for researchers.

First, to make the theory more explicit, it would be advantageous to be able to better define the relationship between accuracy and time. As we have seen, the effects may be apparent in one or the other of these dependent variables, depending on the emphasis placed on problem-solving outcome, or they may be apparent in both. There are some pointers in the literature as to how this issue could be addressed.

- Addo (1989), as presented in Wilson and Addo (1994), for example, presents a way of assessing task complexity associated with "graphics problem solving." Using this approach, Wilson and Addo address the complexity of tasks in graphics problem solving as follows: (1) the number and type of steps involved in acquiring information from a graph; the steps, in increasing order of complexity, are "identification, scan, comparison, and estimation"; (2) the effort required to isolate the relevant image from the rest of a data display; note that this issue is essentially one of proximity, a variable introduced in this article under multi-criteria decision making in map-related domains; and (3) polarity, which refers to questions that require yes or no responses. For their research, they emphasize the importance of proximity.

Note, however, that this approach begs the question of the processing strategy used for task solution. Applying cost-benefit principles to graph/table decision making shows unequivocally that problem solvers may use a number of different strategies to solve more complex problems. Processing strategy will therefore influence significantly the number of steps taken in the problem solution.[3] Hence any study that uses Addo's approach should also incorporate analyses of appropriate processing strategies.

- Smelcer and Carmel (1997) suggest applying the approach used by Card, Moran, and Newell (1980, 1983; keystroke-level model, GOMS) to evaluate the number of knowledge states for each task, "which helps to explain problem-solving times."[4] They point out that when problem solvers use maps, they can reduce the number of knowledge states needed for problem solution by using visual heuristics. On the other hand, those problem solvers using tables rely on exhaustive algorithms to find the correct solution from among the knowledge states in the mental representation. Note the similarity of these arguments to those for the use of perceptual and symbolic processes in the theory of cognitive fit. Smelcer and Carmel acknowledge that to apply Card et al.'s approach to determining the number of knowledge states that need to be traversed for effective task solution, one must understand the process used—for example, by conducting protocol analysis. Their analyses succeed in explaining problem-solving times quite well.

- Lohse (1993) advocates using a "computational cognitive engineering approach for quantifying the effectiveness, efficiency and quality of graphic designs," presumably based on eye movements. Lohse, however, tested his approach using very simple tasks, so simple, in fact, that he reports that "tables were always faster than graphs regardless of the task." It is not known whether Lohse's approach would scale to more complex tasks.

It is interesting to note that Lohse's claim about the speed of problem solving is the reverse of that made by Dennis and Carte (1998), who claimed that speed is always faster for graphs than for tables. The difference, of course, lies in the complexity of the tasks under examination.

Second, one of the more interesting directions of the research analyzed here is that involving new dimensions of fit. Future research could seek to determine new dimensions systematically. One might approach this task by first identifying different types of tasks or different characteristics of tasks that might be a target for matching. This approach could be difficult, however, because there is no theory of tasks on which such an investigation might be based. That may mean that new dimensions of fit will be uncovered by analyses of prior or existing research, as was done here, a tedious and time-consuming approach.

Third, recall that our extended model of cognitive fit (Figure 8.4) allows the researcher to consider independently the roles and nature of the internal representation of the problem domain, the external problem representation, and the mental representation for task solution. Hence, this model opens the way to investigating the nature of both the internal and mental problem-solving representations in cognitive fit. These representations may be investigated in two ways: (1) by examining the knowledge structures that problem solvers form during problem solving; and (2) by examining the processes problem solvers use during problem solving. Vessey and Galletta (1991) provided an example of investigating knowledge structures when they varied the sequence of presentation of task and problem representation in order to determine the importance of spatial and symbolic problem solving elements to problem solvers' mental representations. Dennis and Carte (1998) and Tuttle and Kershaw (1998) provide examples of investigating problem-solving processes. Dennis and Carte assessed the processes used by examining participants' worksheets ex post, while Tuttle and Kershaw (1998) informed participants of the process that they should use and checked the effectiveness of the manipulation by having participants respond to a set of questions.

Fourth, our recent identification of the importance of dual-task problem solving in the IS arena and its application to both well-structured and ill-structured tasks suggests that this is potentially a very fruitful way to look at a number of troublesome issues that have to date proved intractable. This theoretical formulation seems particularly important in ill-structured tasks where dual-task interference occurs when the contributing tasks do not manifest cognitive fit.

CONCLUSIONS

This research examined how the theory of cognitive fit has been applied in the area of human-computer interaction since its introduction in 1991. In particular, the research sought to investigate whether its promise to serve as one aspect of a general theory of problem solving has been substantiated over that timeframe. In order to do this, we classified relevant studies according to whether they tested concepts found in the two foundational papers that presented the theory (Vessey, 1991, 1994), whether they applied the theory to new domains of investigation, and whether they used dimensions of fit other than the spatial-symbolic dichotomy addressed in the foundational studies.

We found that such studies largely support the concepts originally presented, although there are some areas that need further investigation, particularly the accuracy/time trade-offs that can occur in response to performance requirements and when solving more complex symbolic problems that result in strategy change from more effortful analytical processes to more parsimonious perceptual processes. Under the latter circumstances, when presented with tasks of "medium" complexity, it appears that problems may be solved more accurately using tables, but more quickly using graphs. The theory of cognitive fit has been applied quite extensively to two domains in which considerable amounts of data are required for problem solving, those of human judgment and multi-criteria decision making using maps. The theory enjoys substantial support in these domains. Finally, the theory has been applied to dimensions of fit other than in the spatial-symbolic task environment in which it was formulated. One of the most prevalent forms of this type of fit that we identified was associated with the complexity of the relationship between the task and the problem representation. This notion of fit addresses the degree of match between task and problem representation rather than the familiar match-mismatch dichotomy typical of graph/table problem solving.

This paper also presents two recent theoretical developments that promise to significantly open up the basic area to further investigations. One development separates the problem solver's internal representation of the problem domain from the mental representation formed to solve the problem, thus facilitating investigations of other mechanisms underlying fit. The second development extends the theory of cognitive fit to problem solving that requires two sub-tasks to be addressed concurrently in arriving at the solution to the problem, a common occurrence in IS problem solving where, at a minimum, knowledge of both the application and IS domains influence problem solving. Current research suggests that dual-task problem solving is moderated by the degree of structure in the task under investigation.

We have demonstrated that the theory of cognitive fit applies to problems of varying complexity, to a number of problem domains, and to a number of dimensions of fit. Hence it is clear that it is, indeed, one aspect of a general theory of problem solving. When applicable, researchers should examine issues in the context of the theory, thereby adding to a substantial body of knowledge on its efficacy. System designers can use the theory as a substantive basis for designing more effective and efficient systems to support decision makers.

NOTES

1. Note that the authors may have been unaware of this paper—it did not appear among their references.
2. Note that this model uses the extended model of cognitive fit.
3. See Newell and Simon (1972) for an exposition of the relationship between knowledge states and problem-solving processes.
4. Recall that these researchers assessed only time in their experiment, and not accuracy.

REFERENCES

Addo, T.B.A. *Development of a Valid and Robust Metric for Measuring Question Complexity in Computer Graphics Experimentation.* Doctoral dissertation, Indiana University, 1989.

Agarwal, R.; De, P.; and Sinha, A.P. Comprehending object and process models: an empirical study. *IEEE Transactions on Software Engineering*, 25, 4 (1999), 541–556.

Agarwal, R., and Sinha, A.P. Cognitive fit in requirements modeling: a study of object and process methodologies. *Journal of Management Information Systems*, 13, 2 (1996), 137–162.

Agarwal, R.; Sinha, A.P.; and Tanniru, M. The role of prior experience and task characteristics in object-oriented modeling: an empirical study. *International Journal of Human-Computer Studies*, 45, 6 (1996), 639–667.

Anderson, J.R. Acquisition of cognitive skill. *Psychological Review*, 89, 4 (1982), 369–406.

Anderson, J.R. *The Architecture of Cognition.* Mahwah, N.J: Lawrence Erlbaum Associates, 1996.

Anderson, J.R., and Bower, G.H. *Human Associative Memory: A Brief Edition.* Hillsdale, NJ: Lawrence Erlbaum Associates, 1980.

Bailey, K.D. *Typologies and Taxonomies: An Introduction to Classification Techniques.* Thousand Oaks, CA: Sage Publications, 1994.

Beach, L.R., and Mitchell, F.R. A contingency model for the selection of decision strategies. *Academy of Management Review*, 3 (1978), 439–449.

Beckman, P.A. Concordance between task and interface rotational and translational control improves ground vehicle performance. *Human Factors*, 44, 4 (2002), 644–653.

Benbasat, I., and Weber, R. Rethinking "diversity" in information systems research. *Information Systems Research* 7, 4 (1996), 389–399.

Bettman, J.R., and Kakkar, P. Effects of information presentation format on consumer information acquisition strategies. *Journal of Consumer Research*, 3 (1977), 233–240.

Bettman, J.R., and Zins, M. Information format and choice task in decision making. *Journal of Consumer Research*, 6 (1979), 141–153.

Borthick, A.F.; Bowen, P.L.; Jones, D.R.; and Tse, M.H.K. The effects of information request ambiguity and construct incongruence on query development. *Decision Support Systems*, 32, 1 (2001), 3–25.

Campbell, D.J. Task complexity: a review and analysis. *Academy of Management Journal*, 13, 1 (1988), 40–52.

Card, S.K.; Moran, T.P.; and Newell, A. The keystroke-level model for user performance time with interactive systems. *Communications of the ACM*, 23, 7 (1980), 396–410.

Card, S.K.; Moran, T.P.; and Newell, A. *The Psychology of Human-Computer Interaction.* Hillsdale, NJ: Lawrence Erlbaum Associates, 1983.

Chan, S.Y. The use of graphs as decision aids in relation to information overload and managerial decision quality. *Journal of Information Science*, 27, 6 (2001), 417–425.

Chandra, A., and Krovi, R. Representational congruence and information retrieval: towards an extended model of cognitive fit. *Decision Support Systems*, 25, 4 (1999), 271–288.

Dennis, A.R., and Carte, T.A. Using geographical information systems for decision making: extending cognitive fit theory to map-based presentations. *Information Systems Research*, 9, 2 (1998), 194–203.

Dunn, C., and Grabski, S. An investigation of localization as an element of cognitive fit in accounting model representations. *Decision Sciences*, 32, 1 (2001), 55–94.

Einhorn, H.J., and Hogarth, R.M. Behavioral decision theory: processes of judgment and choice. *Annual Review of Psychology*, 32 (1981), 52–88.

Fleishman, E.A. Systems for describing human tasks. *American Psychologist*, 37, 7 (1982), 821–834.

Giordano, D. Evolution of interactive graphical representations into a design language: a distributed cognition account. *International Journal of Human-Computer Studies*, 57, 4 (2002), 317–345.

Heliades, G.P., and Edmonds, E.A. Notation and nature of task in comprehending design rationale. *Knowledge-Based Systems*, 13, 4 (2000), 215–224.

Hendrix, D.; Cross II, J.H.; and Maghsoodloo, S. The effectiveness of control structure diagrams in source code comprehension activities. *IEEE Transactions on Software Engineering*, 28, 5 (2002), 463–478.

Hubona, G.S.; Everett, S.; Marsh, E.; and Wauchope, K. Mental representations of spatial language. *International Journal of Human-Computer Studies*, 48, 6 (1998), 705–728.

Hung, S.Y. Expert versus novice use of the executive support systems: an empirical study. *Information and Management*, 40, 3 (2003), 177–189.

Jahng, J.; Jain, H.; and Ramamurthy, K. Effective design of electronic commerce environments: a proposed theory of congruence and an illustration. *IEEE Transactions on Systems, Man, and Cybernetics A*, 30, 4 (2000), 456–471.

Johnson, E., and Payne, J.W. Effort and accuracy in choice. *Management Science*, 31, 4 (1985), 395–414.

Khatri, V.; Vessey, I.; Ramesh, V.; Clay, P.; and Park, S-J. Understanding conceptual schemas: exploring the role of application and IS domain knowledge. *Information Systems Research*, 17, 1 (2006), 81–99.

Khatri, V.; Vessey, I.; Ram, S.; and Ramesh, V. Cognitive fit between conceptual models and internal problem representations: the case of geospatio-temporal conceptual schema comprehension. *IEEE Transactions on Professional Communication*, forthcoming.

Kintsch, W. *The Representation of Meaning in Memory*. Hillsdale, NJ: Lawrence Erlbaum Associates, 1974.

Kleinmuntz, D., and Schkade, D. Information displays and decision processes. *Psychological Science*, 4, 4 (1993), 1–7.

Kotovsky, K.; Hayes, J.R.; and Simon, H.A. Why are some problems hard? Evidence from Tower of Hanoi. *Cognitive Psychology*, 17 (1985), 248–294.

Lohse, G.L. Eye movement–based analysis of graphs and tables: the next generation. *International Conference on Information Systems* (1993), 213–224.

Mahoney, L.S.; Roush, P.B.; and Bandy, D. An investigation of the effects of decisional guidance and cognitive ability on decision-making involving uncertainty data. *Information and Organization*, 13 (2003), 85–110.

Mennecke, B.E.; Crossland, M.D.; and Killingsworth B.L. Is a map more than a picture? The role of SDSS technology, subject characteristics, and problem complexity on map reading and problem solving. *MIS Quarterly*, 24, 4 (2000), 601–629.

Meyer, J.; Shamo, M.K.; and Gopher, D. Information structure and the relative efficacy of tables and graphs. *Human Factors*, 41, 4 (1999), 570–587.

Newell, A., and Simon, H.A. *Human Problem Solving*. Englewood Cliffs, NJ: Prentice-Hall, 1972.

Norman, D.A. *Things That Make Us Smart*. Reading, MA: Addison-Wesley, 1993.

Olshavsky, R.W. Task complexity and contingent processing in decision making: a replication and extension. *Organizational Behavior and Human Performance*, 24 (1979), 300–316.

Paivio, A. Dual coding: theoretical issues and empirical evidence. In J.M. Scandura and C.J. Brainerd (eds.), *Structural Process Models of Complex Human Behavior*. Alpen aan den Rijn, The Netherlands: Sijthoff and Noordhoff, 1978, 527–550.

Paivio, A. *Imagery and Verbal Processes*. New York: Holt, Rinehart, and Winston, 1971.

Payne, J. Contingent decision behavior. *Psychological Bulletin*, 92, 2 (1982), 382–402.

Payne, J.W. Task complexity and contingent processing in decision making: an information search and protocol analysis. *Organizational Behavior and Human Performance*, 16 (1976), 366–387.

Payne, J.; Bettman, J.; and Johnson, E. Adaptive strategy selection in decision making. *Journal of Experimental Psychology: Learning, Memory, and Cognition*, 14 (1988), 534–552.

Ramarapu, N.K.; Frolick, M.N.; Wilkes, R.B.; and Wetherbe, J. The emergence of hypertext and problem solving: an experimental investigation of accessing and using information from linear versus nonlinear systems. *Decision Sciences*, 28, 4 (1997), 825–849.

Reitman, W.R. Heuristic decision procedures, open constraints, and the structure of ill-defined problems. In M.W. Shelly and G.L. Bryan (eds.), *Human Judgments and Optimality*. New York: John Wiley & Sons, 1964, pp. 282–315.

Robson, D.; Bennett, K. B.; Cornelius, B.; and Munro, M. Approaches to program comprehension. *The Journal of Systems and Software* 14 (1991), 79–84.

Rumelhart, D.; Lindsay, P.; and Norman, D. A process model for long-term memory. In E. Tulving and W. Donaldson (eds.), *Organization of Memory*. New York: Academic Press, 1972.

Russo, J.E. The value of unit price information. *Journal of Marketing Research*, 14 (1977), 193–201.

Russo, J.E., and Dosher, B.A. Strategies for multiattribute binary choice. *Journal of Experimental Psychology: Learning, Memory, and Cognition*, 9, 4 (1983), 676–696.

Shaft, T., and Vessey, I. The role of cognitive fit in the relationship between software comprehension and modification. *MIS Quarterly*, 30, 1 (2006), 39–55.

Shaft, T., and Vessey, I. The relevance of application domain knowledge: the case of computer program comprehension. *Information Systems Research*, 6, 3 (1995), 286–299.

Simkin, D., and Hastie, R. An information-processing analysis of graph perception. *Journal of the American Statistical Association*, 82, 398 (1987), 454–465.

Sinha, A., and I. Vessey. Cognitive fit in recursion and iteration: an empirical study. *IEEE Transactions on Software Engineering*, SE-18, 5 (1992), 386–379.

Slovic, P., and Lichtenstein, S. Preference reversals: a broader perspective. *American Economic Review*, 73 (1983), 596–605.

Smelcer, J.B., and Carmel, E. The effectiveness of different representations for managerial problem solving: comparing tables and maps. *Decision Sciences*, 28, 2 (1997), 391–420.

Song, G.F., and Salvendy, G. A framework for reuse of user experience in web browsing. *Behavior and Information Technology*, 22, 2 (2003), 79–90.

Speier, C., and Morris, M.G. The influence of query interface design on decision-making performance. *MIS Quarterly*, 27, 3 (2003), 397–423.

Speier, C.; Vessey, I.; and Valacich, J.S. The effects of computer-based interruptions, task complexity and information presentation on individual decision making performance. *Decision Sciences*, 34, 4 (2003), 771–797.

Swink, M., and Robinson, E.P. Complexity factors and intuition-based methods for facility network design. *Decision Sciences*, 28, 3 (1997), 583–614.

Todd, P., and Benbasat, I. An experimental investigation of the impact of computer based decision aids on decision making strategies. *Information Systems Research*, 2, 2 (1991), 87–115.

Tuttle, B.M., and Kershaw, R. Information presentation and judgment strategy from a cognitive fit perspective. *Journal of information Systems*, 12, 1 (1998), 1–17.

Tversky, A., and Kahneman, D. Judgment under uncertainty: heuristic and biases. *Science*, 185 (1974), 1124–1131.

Tversky, A., and Kahneman, D. Availability: a heuristic for judging frequency and probability. *Cognitive Psychology*, 5 (1973), 207–232.

Tversky, A., and Kahneman, D. Belief in the law of small numbers. *Psychological Bulletin*, 76 (1971), 105–110.

Tversky, A.; Sattath, S.; and Slovic, P. Contingent weighting in judgment and choice. *Psychological Review*, 95 (1988), 371–384.

Umanath, N.S., and Scammell, R.W. An experimental evaluation of the impact of data display format on recall performance. *Communications of the ACM*, 31, 5 (1988), 562–570.

Umanath, N.S.; Scammell, R.W.; and Das, S.R. An examination of two screen/report design variables in an information recall context. *Decision Sciences*, 21, 1 (1990), 216–240.

Umanath, N.S., and Vessey, I. Multiattribute data presentation and human judgment: a cognitive fit perspective. *Decision Sciences*, 25, 5/6 (1994), 795–824.

Vessey, I. The effect of information presentation on decision making: an analysis using cost-benefit theory. *Information and Management*, 27 (1994), 103–119.

Vessey, I. Cognitive fit: a theory-based analysis of the graphs versus tables literature. *Decision Sciences*, 22, 2 (1991), 219–240.

Vessey, I. On matching programmers' chunks with program structures: an empirical investigation. *International Journal of Man–Machine Studies*, 27 (1987), 65–89.

Vessey, I., and Galletta, D. Cognitive fit: an empirical study of information acquisition. *Information Systems Research*, 2, 1 (1991), 63–84.

Vessey, I., and Weber, R. Structured tools and conditional logic: an empirical investigation. *Communications of the ACM*, 29, 1 (1986), 48–59.

Washburne, J.N. An experimental study of various graphic, tabular and textural methods of presenting quantitative material. *Journal of Educational Psychology*, 18, 6 (1927), 361–376.

Wheaton, G.R. Development of taxonomy of human performance: a review of classificatory systems relating to tasks and performance. Technical Report, No. 726-12/68-TR-1 (December 1968), American Institute for Research, Washington, DC; abstracted in *JSAS Catalog of Selected Documents in Psychology*, No. 22, 1973.

Wheeler, P., and Jones, D.R. The effects of exclusive user choice of decision aid features on decision making. *Journal of Information Systems*, 17, 1 (2003), 63–83.

Wilson, E.V., and Addo, T.B.A. An investigation of the relative presentation efficiency of computer-displayed graphs. *Information and Management*, 26, 2 (1994), 105–115.

Wood, R.E. Task complexity: definition of the construct. *Organizational Behavior and Human Decision Processes*, 37 (1986), 60–82.

Wright, W.F. Superior loan collectibility judgments given graphical displays. *Auditing: A Journal of Theory and Practice*, 14, 2 (1995), 144–154.

Zhang, J. The nature of external representations in problem solving. *Cognitive Science*, 21, 2 (1997), 179–217.

Zhang, J., and Norman, D.A. Representations in distributed cognitive tasks. *Cognitive Science*, 57, 1994, 87–122.

CHAPTER 9

TASK-TECHNOLOGY FIT

A Critical (But Often Missing!) Construct in Models of Information Systems and Performance

DALE L. GOODHUE

Abstract: *This paper makes the case that task-technology fit is a critical construct that is often missing in models of information systems and performance. Its importance is deceptively obvious— a technology can have positive performance impacts only if it "fits" the task that is being supported. Unfortunately, not all technology does fit the tasks for which it is being used. However, some of the most frequently cited models in MIS individual research can be characterized as utilization focused, and are missing this key fit construct. Limitations of such models are explored, and the case is made for including both task-technology fit and utilization in models of performance. An approach for measuring task-technology fit is also described, followed by a selection of published empirical evidence involving task-technology fit. Finally, some potentially interesting new ways of conceptualizing task-technology fit are described.*

Keywords: *Task-Technology Fit, Performance Impacts, Information Systems, Utilization*

INTRODUCTION

Task-technology fit (TTF) is a construct that is part of the causal chain between information technology and performance impacts. On the surface, its importance is deceptively obvious—a technology can only have positive performance impacts if it "fits" the task that is being supported. The better the fit, the more positive the performance impacts. While the concept has been used to address both individual (e.g., Goodhue et al., 2000; Dishaw and Strong, 1999; Mathieson and Keil, 1998) and group (e.g., Zigurs and Buchland, 1998; Dennis et al., 2001) impacts, we will focus here primarily on the individual level.

Surprisingly, some of the most frequently cited models in MIS individual research (Delone and McLean's 1992 framework and Davis et al.'s 1989 technology acceptance model), focus only on utilization as the key requirement for performance, either ignoring, or including only implicitly, the fact that even when used equally, different technologies have a different impact on performance. Perhaps the lion's share of MIS research at the individual level could be characterized as "utilization focused," with a much smaller set that could be characterized as "task-technology fit focused." HCI research as well as MIS research needs to consider not only what aspects of a technology lead someone to choose to use it, but also the impacts on performance when the technology is used. This paper will first argue that to accurately reflect the relevant aspects of the impact of technology on performance, our models should incorporate aspects of both the utilization focus and the TTF focus. It will then go on to address the issue of measuring TTF. Finally, the paper summarizes some future directions for TTF research.

MODELS OF TECHNOLOGY IMPACT ON INDIVIDUAL PERFORMANCE: UTILIZATION VERSUS TTF

Before discussing specific models of IT and performance, it is important first to make two initial comments about conceptual models of information systems and performance. The first is that the link between information systems and performance is critical to the MIS field. If information systems do not have any ultimate practical benefits, then studying, learning about, and teaching about information systems also have no practical value. Certainly some researchers have failed to find empirical evidence of such an impact in particular situations (e.g., Pentland, 1989; Robey, 1979), and the discussion of the "productivity paradox" (e.g., Loveman, 1994) has suggested that there may be no such link in general. Other more recent research is more optimistic about the link, but the existence of that link is neither self-evident nor obvious. If it were, we would not see articles such as Nicholas Carr's "Information Technology Doesn't Matter" (2003) in the *Harvard Business Review*. The field of MIS will flourish only to the extent that society is convinced that information systems create performance benefits, and that MIS research and teaching can magnify those benefits.

A second initial comment is to emphasize how important conceptual models are. The models that we display in our papers and our classrooms and that we use as we think about and talk about information systems and performance benefits have a powerful effect on us. They both support and constrain our thinking. We cannot maintain one perspective on information systems, and at the same time display models that convey a different perspective. Therefore, a model that is missing a key construct can be dangerous to our ability to truly understand a phenomenon. Even if we acknowledge that key missing construct in one moment, if it does not appear in our models we will find ourselves ignoring it as we think about or explain the phenomenon in the next moment.

Two general models of the relationship between information systems and performance impacts are described below (what can be called the "utilization focus" and the "task-technology fit focus"). The argument is made that relying completely on either one of these has serious limitations.

Utilization Focus Research

The first, and most common, of the two general models is the "utilization focus" model. Research falling into this category employs user attitudes and beliefs to predict the utilization of information systems (e.g., Davis, 1989; Davis et al., 1989; Doll and Torkzadeh, 1991; Lucas, 1975, 1981; Robey, 1979; Swanson, 1987). Stated or unstated, the implication is that increased utilization will lead to positive performance impacts. Research in this category relies on well-defended theories of attitudes and behavior (Bagozzi, 1982; Fishbein and Ajzen, 1975; Triandis, 1980).

The model in Figure 9.1A is an approximation of how technology affects performance in this research. Aspects of the technology—for example, high quality systems (Lucas, 1975) or charge-back policies (Olson and Ives, 1982)—lead to user attitudes (beliefs, affect) about systems. These user attitudes—for example, perceived usefulness (Davis et al., 1989), or user information satisfaction (Baroudi et al., 1986)—as well as other non-attitudinal constructs such as social norms (Hartwick and Barki, 1994) and other situational factors then lead to intentions to utilize systems and ultimately to increased actual utilization. It is presumed that more actual utilization is uniformly

Figure 9.1   **Three Models of the Link From Technology to Performance**

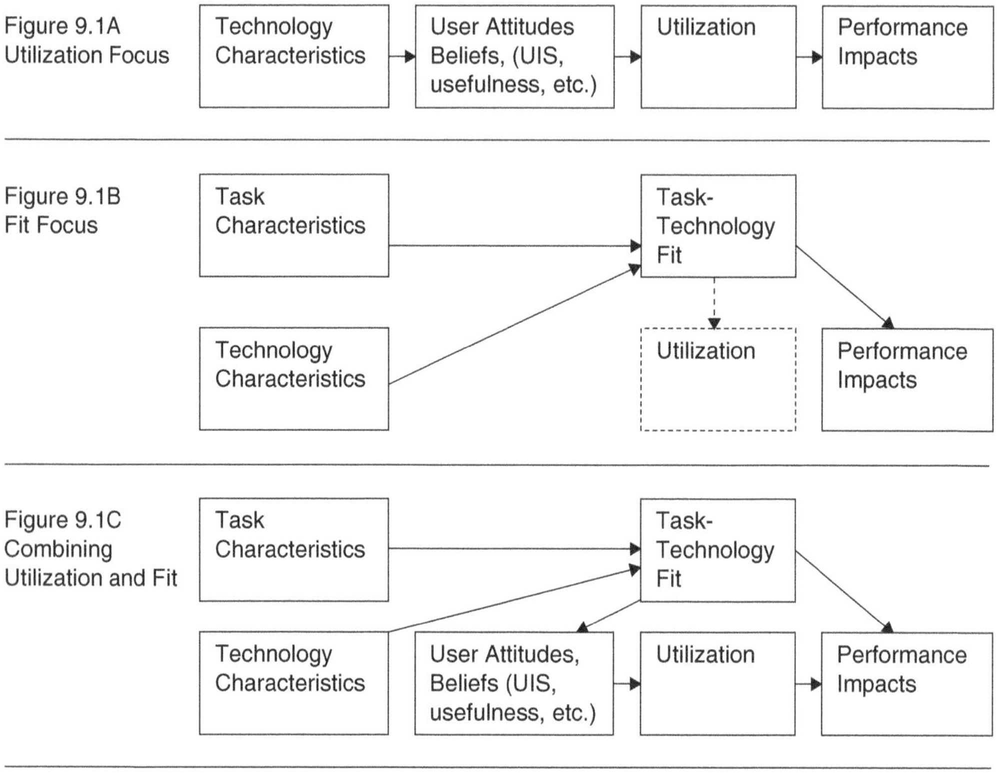

Figure 9.1A
Utilization Focus

| Technology Characteristics | → | User Attitudes Beliefs, (UIS, usefulness, etc.) | → | Utilization | → | Performance Impacts |

Figure 9.1B
Fit Focus

Task Characteristics

Technology Characteristics

Task-Technology Fit

Utilization

Performance Impacts

Figure 9.1C
Combining
Utilization and Fit

Task Characteristics

Technology Characteristics

Task-Technology Fit

User Attitudes, Beliefs (UIS, usefulness, etc.)

Utilization

Performance Impacts

Reprinted by permission from Goodhue and Thompson (1995). Copyright 1995, Regents of the University of Minnesota.

good because it will lead to more positive performance impacts. Grounded most importantly by Davis et al.'s (1989) technology acceptance model (TAM), a great deal of excellent MIS research has explored the factors leading to utilization of information technology.

The frequently cited Delone and McLean framework (1992) is generally consistent with this utilization focus view. Interestingly, as can be seen by looking at the original model (reproduced in Figure 9.2), Delone and McLean did not represent the causality between constructs in the usual way, by line arrows from one construct to another. Rather, the causal connections were represented by larger arrows that were not quite specific about exactly which constructs link to which other constructs. This is because at the time the article was published, there was still some ambiguity about exactly what the connections were. The diagram was intentionally made a bit vague about causality.

In providing researchers with a catalog or taxonomy of critical constructs related to IS success, Delone and McLean's framework is valuable beyond question. However, because the D&M model is generally consistent with the utilization focus model shown in Figure 9.1A, it reinforces the tendency of many IS researchers to think in terms of IS impact along these lines. As will be argued shortly, this has some important drawbacks. Further, since objective measures of individual performance are often hard to come by in organizational settings, researchers often focus only

Figure 9.2   **DeLone and McLean's Model of IS Success Constructs**

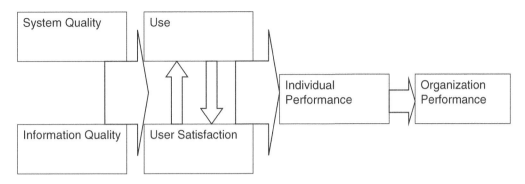

Reprinted by permission, DeLone, W.H., McLean, E.R., Information systems success: The quest for the dependent variable, *Information Systems Research*, **3**, number 1, March, 1992. Copyright 1992, the Institute for Operations Research and the Management Sciences (INFORMS), 7240 Parkway Drive, Suite 310, Hanover, MD 21076 USA.

on the first three boxes in Figure 9.1A, leaving as an untested assumption the link between use and individual performance (e.g., Venkatesh and Davis, 2000; Venkatesh et al., 2003).

Task-Technology Fit Focus Research

A smaller number of researchers have focused on situations where utilization can often be assumed, and have argued that performance impacts will result from task-technology fit—that is, when a technology provides features and support that "fit" the requirements of a task. This view is shown by the middle portion of Figure 9.1, Figure 9.1B.

The "fit" focus has been most evident in research on the impacts of graphs versus tables on individual decision-making performance. Two studies report that over a series of laboratory experiments, the impact of two different technologies for presenting data (a technology characteristic) on performance seemed to depend on the fit with the task (Benbasat et al., 1986; Dickson et al., 1986). Another study proposed that mismatches between data representations and tasks would decrease decision-making performance by requiring additional translations between data representations and decision processes (Vessey and Galletta, 1991). Some found strong support for this linkage between "cognitive fit" and performance in laboratory experiments (Jarvenpaa, 1989; Vessey and Galletta, 1991; Vessey, 1991).

There have also been links suggested between fit and utilization (shown as the dotted arrow in Figure 9.1B). At the organizational level, "fit" and utilization or adoption have been linked (Cooper and Zmud, 1990; Tornatzky and Klein, 1982). At the individual level, a "system/work fit" construct has been found to predict managerial workstation use (Floyd, 1988).

Limitations of Either Focus by Itself

Although each of these perspectives gives insight into the impact of information technology on performance, each alone has some important limitations. First of all, models focusing on fit alone (Figure 9.1B) do not give sufficient attention to the fact that systems must be utilized before they can produce performance benefits. Since utilization is a complex outcome, based on many other factors besides fit (such as habit, social norms, etc.), the TTF focus can benefit from the addition of the much richer understanding of utilization provided by the utilization focus research.

At the same time, the utilization focus alone (Figure 9.1A) also misses important aspects of the way information technology affects performance. First of all, for many users, utilization is more a function of how jobs are designed than the quality or usefulness of systems, or the attitudes of users toward using them. To the extent that utilization is not voluntary, performance impacts will depend increasingly on task-technology fit rather than utilization.

Secondly, there is little explicit recognition that more utilization of a poor system will not necessarily lead to higher performance. This is well illustrated by looking at findings in a study of auditors in the U.S.'s Internal Revenue Service (IRS) (Pentland, 1989). Pentland studied the implementation of a new end-user "automated examination system" (AES) to support field audits of completed tax returns. AES included a number of functionalities including database capabilities; word processing; spreadsheets; a tax calculator for taxes, interest, and penalties; and so on, all designed to help the IRS revenue agents. He captured user perceptions of the system, use, and objective measures of efficiency (average time per case) and effectiveness (average $ per hour). The IRS revenue agents generally rated the system as useful, consistent with the link between technology characteristics and user perceptions. Many of the agents used the system extensively, consistent with the link between user perceptions and use. Finally, Pentland found that there was no empirical link between the overall extent to which the system was used and either efficiency or effectiveness. This last finding is quite inconsistent with both Figure 9.1A and the D&M model.

What's Missing?

Of course, one study should not disconfirm a model, but it can raise questions. In fact, the interpretation of the findings by Pentland and the IRS pose a significant challenge for the utilization focus model. Pentland suggested that the reason overall use of the AES had no positive impact on performance was that it was a "poor fit" for most of the tasks the agents performed. In other words, use of a technology is not enough to improve performance—it is also necessary to take into account the "fit" of the technology to the tasks being performed.

Once surfaced, the importance of task-technology fit seems quite obvious. In fact, Pentland's more detailed analysis of his data suggests that utilization of two of the components of the system (spreadsheet and database) had a negative impact on efficiency, and use of two other components (word processing and the tax calculator) had a positive impact on effectiveness. In retrospect, it would appear that two of the four components had a good fit with the agents' tasks, and two had a poor fit. More use of the database and spreadsheet components degraded performance.

But if the importance of the fit between the technology and the task in this situation now seems obvious, it raises several pertinent questions: Is "good fit" almost always present in information technology implementations, or is it something that should not be assumed? The author's own experience from fifteen years of IS research is that more often than we would like to think, technology is applied to tasks for which it is a poor fit. If good fit cannot be assumed, where does the possibility of a "poor fit" to the required tasks enter into the utilization focus model of Figure 9.1A? There are two possible ways that fit might be assumed to be present in these models.

The first is the argument that when there is poor fit, individuals will not use the systems. In other words, utilization is a surrogate measure for fit. Unfortunately, this is not true in general. There are plenty of reasons why individuals use systems that are a poor fit to their tasks, or do not use systems that are a good fit to their tasks. Certainly some use is mandated, but that is not the only reason. Individuals might use a system because they do not realize it is a poor fit to their tasks

(Davis and Kotteman, 1994; Pentland, 1989). Or they might use or not use a system for a host of reasons (habit, social influences, politics, resistance to change, etc.) not related to performance impacts in their explicit tasks.

DeLone and McLean suggest a second way in which fit could be incorporated in the existing models in their retrospective look at the D&M model ten years after its first publication (DeLone and McLean, 2003). They suggest that "use" in general is not a predictor of performance (or *net benefits*, as they prefer to call it), but that we must move to consider "appropriate use." However, defining appropriate use is problematic. We could define it as that use which leads to net benefits, but this would make the link between use and net benefits tautological. Delone and McLean suggest that appropriate use might be the extent to which the full functionality of the system is used for the intended purposes (p. 16). However, in the context of the Pentland study, this would include use of the spreadsheet and database capabilities of the system, which we now know would reduce performance.

It could be argued that more recent utilization focus models incorporate the general concept of task-technology fit by including usefulness (Seddon, 1997) or performance expectation (Venkatesh et al., 2003) as a key predictor of utilization. Usefulness and performance expectation are probably closely related to task-technology fit, but even assuming that link, those models only include one of the two paths through which TTF contributes to performance. Even the modification suggested by Seddon (1997) shows the behavior of utilization as the only direct predictor of performance impacts. If we could assume that all systems were an excellent fit to the tasks they were used for, the utilization-focused models would be fine. But both Seddon (1997) and Venkatesh et al. (2003) completely ignore the reality that more use of a poorly fitting system (which can and does happen) will reduce performance.

The contention here is that both the utilization-focus model in Figure 9.1A and the DeLone and McLean models are lacking a critical construct—task-technology fit. The more straightforward approach to addressing the blind spot is to recognize that, for a technology to provide positive performance impacts, it must be used, *and* it must be a good fit for the tasks. Such a recognition must be reflected in our conceptual models. For example, in Figure 9.1C, the two perspectives are combined to show both the attitudes to behavior links and the impacts of task-technology fit. Of course, this solution carries the implication that one cannot ever predict performance impacts of information systems without an analysis of the tasks, and of the functionalities of the technology relevant to the tasks. But then how could one ever expect to predict performance impacts without such a consideration? While this produces its own set of conceptual and measurement issues, at least it focuses us on the critical constructs that will truly predict benefits.

A THIRD MODEL: TTF AND THE TECHNOLOGY TO PERFORMANCE CHAIN

Goodhue and Thompson (1995) have presented a more detailed model of the combination of the two theories applied to individuals, which they call the technology to performance chain (TPC), shown in Figure 9.3. By capturing the insights of both lines of research (recognizing that technologies must both be utilized *and* fit the task they support to have a positive performance impact), the TPC gives a more accurate picture of how technologies, user tasks, and utilization relate to changes in performance. The major features of the full model are described below.

Technologies are viewed as tools used by individuals in carrying out their tasks. In the context of information systems research, technology refers to computer systems (hardware, software, and data) and user support services (training, help lines, etc.) provided to assist users in their tasks. The model is intended to be general enough to focus on either the impacts of a specific system or the more general impact of the entire set of systems policies and services provided by an IS department.

Figure 9.3 **A Technology to Performance Chain**

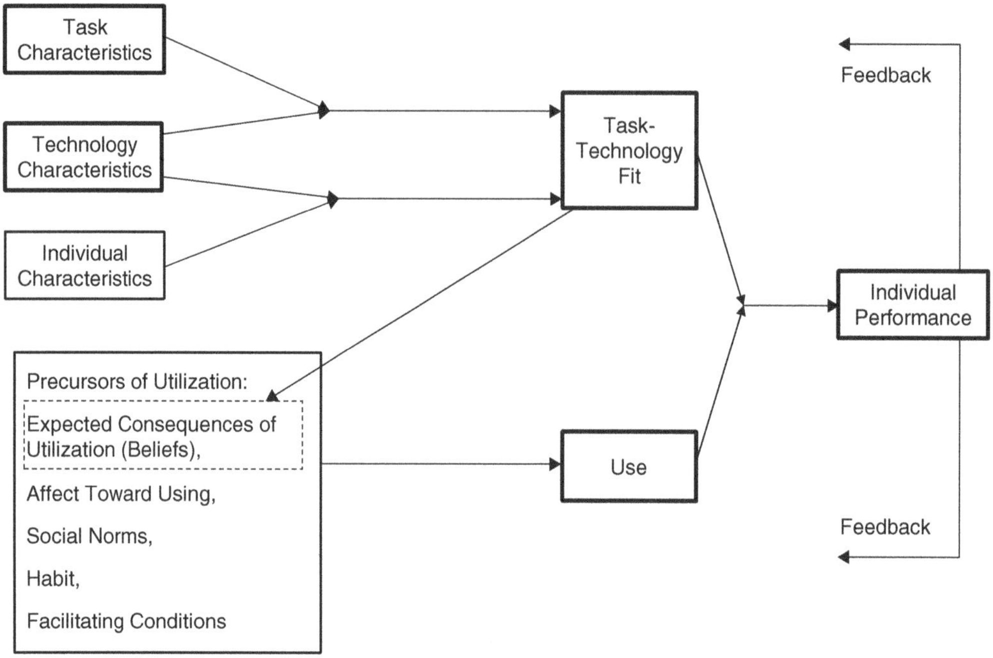

Reprinted by permission from Goodhue and Thompson, 1995. Copyright 1995, Regents of the University of Minnesota.

Tasks are broadly defined as the actions carried out by individuals in turning inputs into outputs. There is potential for some confusion in terminology here. Organizational researchers sometimes define technology quite broadly as actions used to transform inputs into outputs (e.g., Perrow, 1967; Fry and Slocum, 1984). Technologies are the tasks of individuals producing outputs. In MIS research, we tend to differentiate technologies from tasks. Task characteristics of interest include those that might move a user to rely more heavily on certain aspects of the information technology. For example, the need to answer many varied and unpredictable questions about company operations would move a user to depend more heavily upon an information system's capacity to process queries against a database of operational information.

Individuals may use technologies to assist them in the performance of their tasks. Characteristics of individuals such as training, computer literacy, or motivation could affect how easily and well the individuals will be able to utilize the technology to accomplish their tasks.

Task-technology fit (TTF) is the degree to which a technology assists an individual in performing his or her portfolio of tasks. More specifically, TTF is the correspondence between task requirements, individual abilities, and the functionality and features of the technology. Since TTF in this definition includes characteristics of the individual, a more accurate label for the construct might be task-individual-technology fit, but the simpler TTF label is easier to use.

The antecedents of TTF are the interactions between the task, technology, and the individual. Certain kinds of tasks (for example, interdependent tasks requiring information from many organizational units) require certain kinds of technological functionality (for example, integrated databases with much corporate data accessible to all). As the gap between the requirements of a task and the functionalities of a technology widens, TTF is reduced. Starting with the assumption that no system provides perfect data to meet complex task needs without any expenditure of effort (i.e., there is usually some non-zero gap), as tasks become more demanding or technologies offer less of the needed functionality, TTF will decrease.

Utilization is the behavior of employing the technology in completing tasks. Measures such as the duration of use, frequency of use, or the diversity of applications employed (Davis et al., 1989; Thompson et al., 1991, 1994) have been used. However, the construct is arguably not yet well understood, and efforts to refine the conceptualization should be grounded in an appropriate reference discipline (Trice and Treacy, 1988).

Since the lower portion of the TPC model in Figure 9.3 is derived from theories about attitudes (beliefs or affect) and behavior, a reference discipline such as the theory of reasoned action (Fishbein and Ajzen, 1975) would seem an appropriate choice. Consider the utilization of a *specific system* for *a single, defined task* in light of those theories. Beliefs about the consequences of use, affect toward use, social norms, etc., would lead to the individual's decision to use or not use the system. In this case, utilization should be conceptualized as the binary condition of use or no use. We would not be interested in *how long* the individual used the system at this single, defined task, since duration of use would be more a function of the size of the task and/or the TTF of the system, not the choice to use the system. When thinking about a single defined task, using the system longer is not indicative of improved performance—in fact the reverse! Longer duration of use in this case presumably means a poorer system (for this task), or less user familiarity with the technology.

If the focus is expanded to include a portfolio of some number of tasks (such as in a field study of information use), then the appropriate conceptualization would be the *proportion* of times the individual decided to use the system (the sum of the decisions to use the system, divided by the number of opportunities to use the system). Note that this is quite different from conceptualizing utilization as the duration or frequency of use. To illustrate problems with using duration as the measure of utilization, consider the following. A poor system might require a longer duration of use to accomplish the same portfolio of tasks; a good system might encourage more duration of use as new tasks are added to the portfolio (because of the effectiveness of the system). Likewise, this is quite different from using frequency of utilization. In this conceptualization, an individual who used the system three times out of four opportunities is a heavier user than one who used the system ten times out of twenty opportunities. Since this is not how utilization is usually measured, it points up the fact that conceptualizing and measuring utilization is more complicated than it might at first appear.

The antecedents of utilization can be suggested by theories about attitudes and behavior, as described above. Note that both voluntary and mandatory use can be reflected in the model. Mandatory use can be thought of as a situation where social norms to use a system are very strong and overpower other considerations such as the beliefs about expected task performance, consequences, and affect.

The impact of TTF on utilization is shown via a link between task-technology fit and beliefs about the consequences of using a system. This is because TTF as perceived by the user should be an important determinant of whether the system is believed to be more useful, more important, or more advantageous than the alternative. All of these three beliefs have been shown to predict utilization of systems (Davis et al., 1989; Hartwick and Barki, 1994; Moore and Benbasat, 1992), though they are not the only determinants, as the model shows.

Performance impact in this context is measured by how well an individual accomplishes a portfolio of tasks. Higher performance implies some mix of improved efficiency, improved effectiveness, and/or higher quality.

The impact of TTF on performance comes about through two very different pathways. First, as shown by the arrow from TTF to "Precursors to Utilization" in Figure 9.3, higher TTF will increase (in particular) beliefs about the positive consequences of utilization. These more positive beliefs should lead to stronger intentions to utilize the system, and ultimately to a greater likelihood of utilization.

Secondly, as shown by the arrow from TTF to Performance Impacts in Figure 9.3, at any given level of utilization, a system with higher TTF will lead to better performance, since it more closely meets the task needs of the individual. This second important link is completely missing in the utilization focus research illustrated in Figure 9.1A and Figure 9.2. This link explains why the IRS agents who used the database and spreadsheet capabilities of their new system more extensively had poorer performance (in the earlier example from Pentland, 1989).

Feedback is an important aspect of the model. Once a technology has been utilized and performance effects have been experienced, there will inevitably be a number of kinds of feedback. First, the actual experience of utilizing the technology may lead users to conclude that it has a better (or worse) impact on performance than anticipated, changing their expected consequences of utilization and therefore affecting future utilization. The individual may also learn from experience better ways of utilizing the technology, improving individual-technology fit, and hence overall TTF.

Relative Task-Technology Fit

Unless utilization is absolutely mandatory, there is always an alternative to the use of a new information technology. For example, one might continue to use the old technology, whatever it is. This alternative option is not typically described in the literature, but has a number of important consequences. Suppose that a new technology is introduced to support a particular type of managerial decision making. The likelihood of utilizing that new technology is not dependent upon the absolute task-technology fit of the new technology, but upon the relative TTF compared to the old technology (or to some third possible technology). Suppose the new technology has very good TTF, but it is only a little better than the old technology. In this situation, the impetus to use the new technology will be slight, and any performance gains will also be slight. Thus, it is important to consider the alternative technologies as one tries to predict or explain utilization and performance impacts of a new technology.

MEASURING TASK-TECHNOLOGY FIT

The above arguments for the impact of TTF on performance are made in general terms. As is often the case, as we begin to think about measuring a concept and testing its relationships to other constructs, we realize the need to define it more carefully. "Fit" can be conceptualized in a number of different ways, and this has important implications for measurement and testing (Schoonhoven, 1981; Van de Ven and Drazin, 1985; Venkatraman, 1989). The argument developed here is that the strength of the link between a technology characteristic and its task-technology fit is dependent upon how important that technology characteristic is, given the task demands and the capabilities of the user. For example, the more a task requires information from many different parts of the organization (a task characteristic), the stronger the link from the degree of organizational-wide data integration (a technology characteristic) is to TTF. On the other hand, if all information needs are local, then organizational-wide data integration may not be important to TTF. This corresponds exactly to one of Venkatraman's (1989) categories of fit (fit as moderation) and generally to Van de Ven and Drazin's (1985) interaction approach.

Because the concept of task-technology fit is so dependent upon the task, determining how to measure TTF requires at least some conceptualization of the task. A task may have several or many steps, and a given technology may "fit" or provide the needed functionality for some of those steps but not others. This suggests that before trying to measure task-technology fit, it is first necessary to be more explicit about exactly what the task is, and what the several steps are in carrying out that task. We can then ask to what extent the technology supports the user in carrying out each of those steps.

An Example of Developing a Task Model Before Measuring TTF

To give an example of how this might be done in practice, consider work by Goodhue (1995, 1998). He developed a task model for the task domain of "using quantitative information in managerial tasks," as described below.

The model includes three interacting steps of managerial use of information in their tasks: identifying information, accessing it, and interpreting it. Arrow (1974) and Ferrence (1970) have made a distinction between identifying needed information and acquiring it. Others (Cowan, 1986; O'Reilly, 1983; Saunders and Jones, 1990) have made a distinction between acquiring information and using it. Therefore, a rough process model of information use could consist of three interacting steps: identification of the data needed, acquisition of that data, and integration and interpretation of the data. These three steps are not necessarily sequential, and may be repeated.

To carry the example further, Goodhue was concerned with managers or knowledge workers for whom using quantitative information is only part of a larger business task. As these users attempt to identify, acquire, and interpret data, they will be frustrated in their efforts (and their overall performance) when the technology does not support them. For each subtask, there are several important dimensions of TTF on which systems and services might meet or fail to meet task needs. Enumerating these dimensions leads to a more detailed model of the task, which can be the basis for evaluating TTF at the detailed level.

Identifying Needed Data

There are at least five dimensions of TTF along which systems and services might be evaluated when users are identifying needed data. Users need information systems to contain the *right data* (Epstein and King, 1982; Bailey and Pearson, 1983), at the *right level of detail* (O'Reilly, 1982; Swanson 1987). The cognitive difficulty increases if the organization of the files is *confusing* (Bailey and Pearson, 1983), making it difficult to *locate* the needed data, if the *meaning* of the data elements is unclear (Epstein and King, 1982).

Accessing Identified Data

There are at least seven dimensions of TTF along which information systems and services might be evaluated for users accessing identified data. Users could be frustrated by poor *accessibility* of the data (Bailey and Pearson, 1983; Culnan, 1984) or if *authorization* is difficult. For those who use query languages or download data on their own, users will be frustrated if the hardware and software is not *easy to use* (Bailey and Pearson, 1983), they have received insufficient *training* (Bailey and Pearson, 1983), or systems are plagued by poor *reliability* (i.e., unexpected downtimes) (Bailey and Pearson, 1983; Swanson, 1987). When enlisting the aid of user support personnel, users will be frustrated by a lack of sufficient *assistance* (Swanson, 1987). Overall users will be frustrated by a lack of *flexibility* in meeting changing data needs (Bailey and Pearson, 1983).

Integrating and Interpreting Accessed Data

There are at least four more dimensions along which TTF could be evaluated as users attempt to make sense of accessed data and incorporate it into their decision processes. Data must be sufficiently *accurate* that it can be interpreted correctly (O'Reilly, 1982; Zmud, 1978); data from different sources that need to be integrated must be *compatible* (Epstein and King, 1982; Bailey and Pearson, 1983); the *presentation* of the data (on screens or reports) must be easily interpreted (Gallagher, 1978; Zmud, 1978); and the data must be sufficiently *current* (Swanson, 1987; Zmud, 1978). All together this suggests at least sixteen dimensions for evaluating the task-technology fit of information systems and services.

Who Should be the Judge?

Presumably, there is some "true" underlying TTF, perhaps relative to the best technology available for a given individual and task. But we may never know exactly what that true TTF is. An important question is: Who should make the evaluation of the task-technology fit of a given technology for a given set of users engaged in the given set of tasks? It would be possible to have "experts" make the evaluation, assuming they had a thorough knowledge of the tasks, the technology, and the users. This might be called an "engineering evaluation" of TTF. A second alternative is to ask the users who utilize a system in carrying out their tasks to evaluate its TTF for them personally. This could be called a "user-perception evaluation" of TTF. Each approach has its strengths and weaknesses. The real question is: Which group has a better understanding of the task, technology, and the individuals? Experts may miss important aspects of the task. There are plenty of cases where users ended up employing a technology in unexpected ways because the designers (experts) did not truly understand the tasks. On the other hand, there are certainly gaps between individual perceptions of a technology and its reality. Here we make the assumption that users are goal-directed individuals who are attempting to achieve good performance. In this light, we might expect that they are sensitive to aspects of the technology that lead to higher performance, and thus are capable of evaluating the TTF of systems. Under these assumptions, we can rely on user perceptions for our measures of TTF.

Generating Questions

It is important to realize that even though a construct similar to one of the TTF dimensions may be present in existing MIS questionnaires, these existing questionnaires often do not actually assess task-technology fit. For example, the typical questionnaire for user evaluations of IS—that is, user information satisfaction, or UIS (Bailey and Pearson, 1983)—asks users to rate the information system in the abstract, for the whole organization. For example, the UIS definition of accuracy is "the correctness of the output information"; respondents are asked to rate on a seven-point scale from accurate to inaccurate, high versus low, etc. (Bailey and Pearson, 1983, p. 541). First, data are rarely completely accurate, or need to be, but the questionnaire seems to ask respondents to evaluate whether the data are completely accurate. Second, one might question whether typical users are knowledgeable enough to answer this question in absolute terms, for the whole organization. The relevant question is whether the data are accurate enough for the tasks the user needs to accomplish. For example, to the statement "The data that I use or would like to use is accurate enough for my purposes," respondents are asked to agree or disagree on a seven-point scale (Goodhue, 1995, p. 1842). TTF questions need to clearly ask users to rate the systems and services they use, based on the fit with their personal task needs, something they are arguably capable of doing. Researchers must be careful in borrowing word for word from existing questionnaires.

The point is not that the measures developed by Goodhue are the way to assess task-technology fit, but rather that the approach used by Goodhue is one general way to develop a measure of task-technology fit in any task domain.

EMPIRICAL EVIDENCE

Here we will briefly summarize some of the findings from five empirical studies involving TTF at various levels of analysis: Goodhue (1995); Goodhue and Thompson (1995); Goodhue et al. (2000); Dennis et al. (2001); and Karimi et al. (2004).

The Moderating Effect of Task on the Impact of Technology

Goodhue (1995) investigated whether task characteristics moderated the impact of technology on user evaluations of TTF. For measures of the technology he looked at a number of aspects of information systems and services provided to users, including the extent of integrated common data, number of PCs per user, ratio of assistance personnel to users, and the decentralization of assistance personnel. Task characteristics included interdependence of user tasks with other parts of the organization, and the non-routineness of tasks. He also measured one individual character-istic, computer literacy. Finally he measured twelve dimensions of task-technology fit, based on the task model described earlier. Overall he found that for nine of the twelve dimensions of TTF, interactions between task characteristics and technology, or between individual characteristics and technology, explained a statistically significant amount of additional variance in TTF. In other word, people's assessments of whether the technology was meeting their needs was not just a function of the technology, or of the task, but was also a function of the interaction of the two.

For example, assessments of the accessibility of the data were not significantly explained by the main effect of the extent to which users had integrated databases, or by the main effect of whether they engaged in tasks that were interdependent with other areas of the organization. However, the *interaction* of integrated databases with interdependent tasks was statistically sig-nificant. For users with very little interdependence with other parts of the organization, increased data integration did not increase their perceptions of data accessibility. For users with high inter-dependence, increased data integration did increase their perceptions of data accessibility.

The Relative Importance of Utilization Versus TTF in Predicting Performance Impacts

Goodhue and Thompson (1995) investigated a number of aspects of the technology-to-performance chain, including the relative importance of TTF and utilization in predicting performance impacts. They measured eight dimensions of TTF, as well as utilization (the extent to which users had become dependent upon the major systems in their organization) and perceived performance impacts. Utilization alone produced an adjusted r-square of only .04 in explaining performance impacts. The eight TTF dimensions alone produced an adjusted r-square of .14. Together utilization and TTF produced an r-square of .16. The results were not different when utilization was measured as duration and frequency of use. Although not a lot of variance is explained, this certainly suggests that TTF may be more important than utilization in determining benefits. In other words, Figure 9.1C is a more accurate model of the relationship between technology and performance than Figure 9.1A, at least in this context.

Accurate Feedback to Users May be Important for Accurate User Evaluations of TTF

The argument that user evaluations of TTF are reasonable surrogates for the actual underlying TTF depends upon the assumption that users want to achieve good performance and thus are cognizant of how the technology affects performance at their tasks. Goodhue et al. (2000) accidentally discovered some possible limitations in this assumption when they asked laboratory subjects to retrieve answers to a series of managerial questions using queries on an information system. Half the subjects were presented with an integrated database, and half with a non-integrated database. Performance was measured in time to complete the tasks and accuracy. User evaluations of TTF did correlate significantly with time performance, but, contrary to expectations, not with accuracy performance. In hindsight, the authors recognized that subjects were well aware of the impacts of technology on time (since subjects themselves experienced any time delays caused by poor fit), but they were never made aware of accuracy problems in their answers, since they were never told the correct answers. Thus they had feedback in terms of time but not in terms of accuracy. Since the link between user perceptions of TTF and actual TTF depends upon users being aware of performance-related aspects of their use of the technology, this suggests that only with accurate feedback will user perceptions of TTF reflect actual TTF.

The Effect of TTF on the Impact of Group Support Systems

Though this paper has focused on TTF at the individual level, the concept is also clearly applicable at the group level. Dennis et al. (2001) conducted a meta-analysis of group support systems (GSS) to determine whether task-technology fit could help explain inconsistencies in GSS performance impacts from previous research. They proposed a model in which the fit between GSS capabilities and task type, along with appropriation support, should explain effectiveness, efficiency, and satisfaction. They looked at sixty-one studies that reported at least several of the key variables and also included direct comparison of GSS to non-GSS groups. They found that task-technology fit (matching task type with an appropriate GSS capability) improves effectiveness (decision quality and number of ideas generated), while appropriation support improves efficiency and process satisfaction. They concluded that although past GSS research lacks consistent findings when task-technology fit is not considered, that inconsistency is removed when TTF is taken into account.

The Relationship Between Environmental Uncertainty and User Evaluations of TTF

Goodhue (1995) and Goodhue and Thompson (1995) demonstrated the interaction effect of technology and task characteristics on evaluations of TTF, as described above. Karimi, Somers, and Gupta (2004) extended the focus further back and showed that organizational environmental characteristics (dynamism, hostility, and heterogeneity) heightened managers' perceptions of task non-routineness and interdependence with other parts of the organization. These heightened task characteristics in turn created more demanding information needs for managers, which lowered perceptions of the degree to which corporate data met those task needs. They thus demonstrated a strong link between organizational theories about environmental uncertainty and MIS theories about task-technology fit.

FUTURE DIRECTIONS

The basic idea behind the concept of task-technology fit is that a change in technology improves performance if the functionality of the new technology has a better "fit" with task requirements than the old technology. Despite TTF's intuitive appeal, there has been limited progress in defining precisely what "fit" is, how to measure it, and how exactly fit translates into better performance. Below some ongoing work (Goodhue et al., 2001) to advance the conceptualization of TTF is described.

Task, Technology, and Performance

Delineating how technology affects performance at a task is challenging. A search of the literature for formal definitions of "task" and "technology" suggests that organizational researchers often blur the distinction between the two. For example, Perrow (1967) and Fry and Slocum (1984) define technology broadly as actions used to transform inputs into outputs. Thompson's (1967) treatment of technology is also consistent with this view. Hackman (1969), Wood (1986), and Campbell (1988), who all did extensive reviews of the concept of task, define "task" as the collection of stimuli and instructions/goals that are presented to the task doer, and largely ignored the idea of technology as separate from task. For these researchers, the technologies are the tasks.

By contrast, because of their interest in the impact of information technology, task-technology fit researchers have sought to differentiate task from technology. For Jarvenpaa (1989) the task was choosing a restaurant, varied by changing the required choice rule, and the technology was the graphical format used to display the attribute values. Vessey and Galletta's (1991) task was information retrieval, varied by asking for symbolic information (point values) versus spatial information (relationships between values), and the technology was two-dimensional tables versus line graphs. For Goodhue (1995) and Goodhue and Thompson (1995),the task was meeting managerial information requirements that varied in terms of non-routineness and interdependence with other parts of the organization; the technology was different levels of MIS support. In fact, these task-technology fit researchers have tended to conceptualize tasks as existing *before* the application of technology, while organizational researchers have tended to conceptualize tasks *after* the application of technology. The former conceptualization of task can be called the "*underlying task*" and the latter the "*execution sequence*" utilized by the task doer to carry out the task.

To explain performance, all of the above TTF researchers focused their attention on the fit between the *underlying* task and the technology. Jarvenpaa looked at the "congruence" between task demands and information displays. Vessey and Galletta used the term "cognitive fit," which they defined as the degree to which the information representation and any tools or aids employed "match" the information required to perform a task. In this case "match" means that few transformations will be required to go from one to the other. Goodhue and Thompson defined task-technology fit as the "correspondence" between task requirements and the functionality of the technology. These are reasonable conceptualizations at a high level of abstraction, but there are problems in actually operationalizing general measures of "congruence," "cognitive fit," or "correspondence." Is there another way in which this problem of "fit" can be conceptualized? One approach is to go back and rethink how technology affects performance.

How Does Technology Affect Task Performance?

Technology can be thought of as affecting task performance in two ways. The first is by improving some non-human portion of the task, even while the task appears the same to the task doer (same process, same inputs and outputs, same interface). For example, the new technology might return an answer in less time, or give a higher-quality answer. In this case, the technology would not change the sequence of actions taken by the task doer (what might be called the execution sequence), but would result in better performance overall.

The second way technology affects task performance is by changing the possible execution sequences presented to the task doer. Each technology applied to a task enables a set of available execution sequences that could be used to carry out the task. These possible execution sequences are the different approaches or strategies that can be used for addressing the underlying task (e.g., Newell and Simon, 1972; Payne et al., 1996; Todd and Benbasat, 1999). To illustrate this point with an example, consider a task doer who is asked to report "sales minus returns and discounts" (an aggregate of several pieces of information from the organization's database). Even holding the technology constant, a task doer might opt either to create several simple queries, each one returning a small portion of the desired information (one possible execution sequence), to create fewer and more sophisticated queries, each one returning a greater portion of the desired information (a second possible execution sequence), or to guess at the approximate answer based on the task doer's general knowledge (a third possible execution sequence).

Parenthetically, we note that one could argue that there is a third way a technology could affect performance: It could completely carry out the task and eliminate the need for the task doer. However, there is always some other higher-level task doer in the background, carrying out some higher-level task and deciding to use the technology as opposed to a human. The technology has changed the task as presented to this latter task doer.

Changing the available technology generally means adding new possible execution sequences, removing old execution sequences, or changing the characteristics of existing execution sequences. Continuing with the example above, if the required "sales minus returns and discounts" information spanned several divisions and the available databases were not semantically integrated across the divisions, it would not be an option to use the execution sequence of retrieving all sales data for all divisions with one query, since fields might be defined differently for the different divisions. Rather, separate queries would be needed for each semantically distinct database. Switching to a semantically integrated database would change the execution sequences available to task doers, since now the entire task *could be* accomplished with a single more sophisticated query. Even so, there would still be several possible execution sequences beside the single large query. Regardless of which technology is available or which execution sequence is chosen, the underlying task of retrieving information on sales minus returns and discounts across divisions would remain the same.

This general relationship is shown in Figure 9.4. A change from technology 1 to technology 2 changes the possible execution sequences *presented to the task doer* for carrying out the same underlying task. In the figure, execution sequences A, B, and C are available with technology 1, while execution sequences C, D, and E are available with technology 2.

Presumably task doers choose a particular execution sequence based on their assessment of its "attractiveness" to them. In other words, they might take into account cognitive cost benefit considerations (Payne, 1982; Smith et al., 1982; Creyer et al., 1990) such as differences in expected performance and differences in effort required, as well as other non-cognitive costs such as the mechanical difficulties of walking to a different building to access a different database or bureaucratic difficulties of getting access to data. Finally, they may be affected by habit, social norms, or

Figure 9.4   **TTF as the "Attractiveness" of Various Possible Execution Sequences**

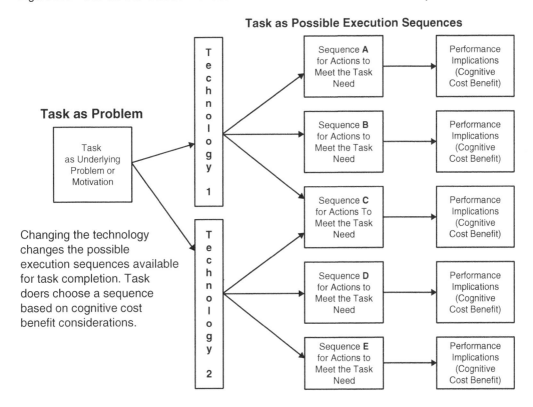

politics. Behavioral decision-making research has shown that, in general, selection of an execution sequence is sensitive to conditions such as task goals, time constraints, and task complexity (e.g., Bettman et al., 1998; Payne et al., 1996; Todd and Benbasat, 1999).

Figure 9.5 is a recasting of Figure 9.3 in terms of choices to use a particular execution sequence rather than choices to use a particular technology. Note that choosing an execution sequence is often tantamount to choosing a technology, but in this view it is not the technology that is chosen.

Further, to the extent that the task doer takes advantage of a new or changed execution sequence, a change in technology will lead to differences in the way the task process unfolds, which may lead to differences in task performance. This is because alternative execution sequences are not necessarily equally effective or efficient. For example, consolidating information from several small queries avoids having to write a sophisticated query, but creates the possibility of errors in consolidation. Guessing at the amount is quicker and easier than writing queries, but not as accurate as viewing corporate records.

Characterizing Execution Sequences Presented to the Task Doer

To understand the impact of technology on information retrieval performance we need to have some way of characterizing the relevant differences between execution sequences. First of all, there is the question of whether different available execution sequences have different performance outcomes, such as the accuracy of the reported number of "sales less returns and discounts," and

Figure 9.5   **Integrating the Concept of Execution Sequences into the Technology-to-Performance Chain**

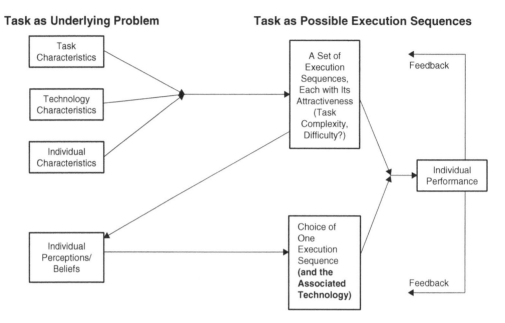

whether task doers will recognize and respond to those differences in their choice of execution sequence. O'Reilly (1982) has suggested that decision makers respond more to accessibility than to quality in their choice of information sources. Connelly and Thorn (1987) showed that decision makers do a less than optimal job of choosing when to access costly but more accurate information. However, Connelly and Thorn recognize that their data could be interpreted as a half-full rather than a half-empty glass (pp. 413–414). In other words, their study shows that decision makers do respond (though imperfectly) to benefit differences in information sources.

Beyond possible implications for the *quality of the output*, execution sequences may also differ in the effort required by the task doer (time, difficulty, effort) to carry out the execution sequence. As long as the possible execution sequences are roughly equivalent (i.e., include the same types of execution steps), the effort required for any execution sequence could be characterized by its computational complexity and its difficulty, as described below.

For computational complexity, both Campbell (1988) and Wood (1986) recognized that the computational complexity of the task as presented to the task doer is a major determinant of performance. Wood presents a useful breakdown for characterizing complexity in terms of required acts, information cues, and the relationship between acts and cues, and identifies three types of complexity (Wood, 1986, pp. 66–73):

Component complexity:	the number of distinct acts that are needed to complete the task and the number of distinct information cues that must be processed,
Coordinative complexity:	the number of precedence relationships related to the timing, frequency, intensity, and location requirements for carrying out the task processes and assimilating the information cues, and

Dynamic complexity: the degree to which relationships between task inputs and task products change over time.

For a collection of possible execution sequences that contain the same types of action steps, the computational complexity of each could be estimated using the framework above. Defined in this way, complexity is an objective characteristic of an execution sequence, independent of the task doer's characteristics.

The construct of difficulty suggested by Campbell (1988) also allows us to account for individual factors. Campbell proposed a useful distinction between task *complexity* and task *difficulty*, in which difficulty captures the commonsense observation that the same execution sequence may appear hard for some and easy for others because of their different levels of skills, abilities, and experience.

All this suggests a new way of thinking about task-technology fit. When considering applying a new technology to an existing underlying task, we need to consider the execution sequences currently being used, and the new execution sequences that will be enabled by the new technology. These new execution sequences can be characterized by their impact on the quality of the ultimate outcome, as well as by the cost born by the task doer in terms of complexity and difficulty. Task doers presumably choose an execution sequence based on their perceptions and weightings of these various factors.

As far as predicting performance impacts (as opposed to predicting use), a new technology has higher task-technology fit than the old technology when it enables an execution sequence that has some combination of lower complexity, lower difficulty, and an *a priori* prediction of higher output quality. The "*a priori* prediction of higher output quality" deserves a few word of explanation. In other words, it must be possible to recognize some difference in the execution sequence that logically ought to lead to higher output quality. It is important to stress the fact that one cannot define high TTF by an *a posteriori* experienced higher output quality—that would in effect define TTF as that which leads to higher quality output, creating a tautology.

Clearly, changing the weights attached to the three characteristics (*a priori* quality, complexity, difficulty) can change the determination of which execution sequence has the highest task-technology fit. This might seem like a disadvantage of looking at task-technology fit in this way, but in truth it is far more realistic and accurate. It is not possible to assess task-technology fit without taking into account the relative importance of output quality and effort. Altogether this moves us to a much more concrete conceptualization of task-technology fit than terms such as correspondence, congruence, or cognitive fit.

SUMMARY

The key concept of task-technology fit is that the value of a technology with a particular functionality depends on how much users need that functionality in the tasks they are doing. Task-technology fit is an important construct in the chain from technology to performance that is often ignored by MIS researchers and practitioners. This paper describes a model that includes two important but very different ways in which TTF can affect performance. First, by affecting user beliefs about the consequences of using a technology, TTF can change the likelihood that a technology will be used. Secondly, regardless of the reasons the technology is used, at any level of use (beyond no use!) greater TTF will deliver more performance impacts. This model is quite different from the most cited MIS models of technology impact on individual performance.

Finally, a new way of looking at task-technology fit suggests that technologies enable different execution sequences for carrying out an underlying task. Each execution sequence has a certain attractiveness that includes implications for final output quality as well as the burden to the task doer of carrying out the sequence. In a very real sense, task doers choose the execution sequence rather than the technology, and it is the execution sequence that has performance impacts. This way of thinking also allows us to view "unfaithful appropriations" of technologies in a non-negative way, as the discovery of an attractive execution sequence not anticipated by the technology designer.

ACKNOWLEDGMENTS

I thank Stefano Grazioli and Barbara Klein for their invaluable collaboration in developing the ideas described in the "Future Directions" section of this paper.

REFERENCES

Arrow, K.J. *The Limits of Organization*. New York: W.W. Norton, 1974.
Bagozzi, R.P. A field investigation of causal relations among cognitions, affect, intentions, and behavior. *Journal of Marketing Research*, 19, (1982), 562–584.
Bailey, J.E., and Pearson, S.W. Development of a tool measuring and analyzing computer user satisfaction. *Management Science*, 29, 5 (1983), 530–544.
Baroudi, J.J.; Olson, M.H.; and Ives, B. An empirical study of the impact of user involvement on system usage and information satisfaction. *Communications of the ACM*, 29, 3 (1986), 232–238.
Benbasat, I.; Dexter, A.S.; and Todd, P. An experimental program investigating color-enhanced and graphical information presentation: an integration of the findings. *Communications of the ACM*, 29, 11 (1986), 1094–1105.
Bettman, J.R.; Luce, M.F.; and Payne, J.W. Constructive consumer choice processes. *Journal of Consumer Research*, 25 (1998), 187–217.
Campbell, D.J. Task complexity: a review and analysis. *Academy of Management Review*, 13, 1 (1988), 40–52.
Carr, N. Information technology doesn't matter. *Harvard Business Review*, 81, 5 (2003), 41–49.
Connolly, T., and Thorn, B.K. Predecisional information acquisition: effects of task variables on suboptimal search strategies. *Organizational Behavior and Human Decision Processes*, 39 (1987), 197–416.
Cooper, R., and Zmud, R. Information technology implementation research: a technological diffusion approach. *Management Science*, 36, 2 (1990), 123–139.
Cowan, D.A. Developing a process model of problem recognition. *Academy of Management Review*, 11, 4 (1986), 763–776.
Creyer, E.H.; Bettman, J.R.; and Payne, J.W. The impact of accuracy and effort feedback and goals on adaptive decision behavior. *Journal of Behavioral Decision Making*, 3, 1 (1990), 1–16.
Culnan, M.J. The dimensions of accessibility to online information: implications for implementing office information systems. *ACM Transactions on Office Information Systems*, 2, 2 (1984), 141–150.
Davis, F.D. Perceived usefulness, perceived ease of use, and user acceptance of information technology. *MIS Quarterly*, 13 (1989), 319–342.
Davis, F.D.; Bagozzi, R.P.; and Warshaw, P.R. User acceptance of computer technology: a comparison of two theoretical models. *Management Science*, 35, 8 (1989), 982–1003.
Davis, F.D., and Kotteman, J.E. User perceptions of decision support effectiveness: two production planning experiments. *Decision Sciences*, 25, 1 (1994), 57–78.
DeLone, W.H., and McLean, E.R. Information systems success: the quest for the dependent variable. *Information Systems Research*, 3, 1 (1992), 60–95.
DeLone, W.H., and McLean, E.R. The DeLone and McLean model of information system success: a ten year update. *Journal of Management Information Systems*, 19, 4 (2003), 9–30.
Dennis, A.R.; Wixom, B.H.; and Vandenberg, R.J. Understanding fit and appropriation effects in group support systems via meta-analysis. *MIS Quarterly*, 25, 2 (2001), 167–193.
Dickson, G.W.; DeSanctis, G.; and McBride, D.J. Computer graphics for decision support: a cumulative experimental approach. *Communications of the ACM*, 29, 1 (1986), 40–47.

Dishaw, M.T., and Strong, D.M. Extending the technology acceptance model with task technology fit con-structs. *Information and Management*, 36, 1 (1999), 9–21.

Doll, W.J., and Torkzadeh, G. The measurement of end-user computing satisfaction: theoretical and method-ological issues. *MIS Quarterly*, 15, 1 (1991), 5–10.

Epstein, B.J., and King, W.R. An experimental study of the value of information. *Omega*, 10, 3 (1982), 249–258.

Ference, T.P. Organizational communications systems and the decision process. *Management Science*, 26, (1970), B83–B96.

Fishbein, M., and Ajzen, I. *Belief, Attitude, Intentions and Behavior: An Introduction to Theory and Research*. Addison-Wesley, Boston, (1975).

Floyd, S.W. A micro level model of information technology use by managers. In U.E. Gattiker, (ed.), *Studies in Technological Innovation and Human Resources, Vol. 1: Managing Technological Development*. Berlin: Walter de Gruyter, 1988, pp. 123–142.

Fry, C.R., and Slocum, J.W. Technology, structure, and workgroup effectiveness: a test of a contingency model. *Academy of Management Journal*, 27, 2 (1984), 221–246.

Gallagher, C.A. Perceptions of the value of a management information system. *Academy of Management Journal*, 17, 1 (1978), 46–55.

Goodhue, D.L. Understanding user evaluations of information systems. *Management Science*, 41, 12 (1995), 1827–1844.

Goodhue, D.L. Development and measurement validity of a task-technology fit instrument of user evalua-tions of information systems. *Decision Sciences*, 29, 1 (1998), 105–138.

Goodhue, D.L.; Grazioli, S.; and Klein, B.D. Beyond task/technology fit: how information technology affects performance by transforming the task. Working Paper, University of Georgia, 2001.

Goodhue, D.L.; Klein, B.D.; and March, S.T. User evaluations of IS as surrogates for objective performance. *Information & Management*, 38, 1 (2000), 87–101.

Goodhue, D.L., and Thompson R.L. Task-technology fit and individual performance. *MIS Quarterly*, 19, 2 (1995), 213–236.

Hackman, J.R. Toward understanding the role of tasks in behavioral research. *Acta Psychologica*, 31, 2 (1969), 97–128.

Hartwick, J., and Barki, H. Explaining the role of user participation in information system use. *Management Science*, 40, 4 (1994), 440–485.

Jarvenpaa, S.L. The effect of task demands and graphical format on information processing strategies. *Management Science*, 35, 3 (1989), 285–303.

Karimi, J.; Somers, T.M.; and Gupta, Y.P. Impact of environmental uncertainty and task characteristics on user satisfaction with data. *Information Systems Research*, 15, 2 (2004), 175–193.

Loveman, G.W. An assessment of the productivity impact of information technologies. In T.J. Allen and M.S. Scott Morton (eds.), *Information Technology and the Corporation of the 1990s: Research Studies*. Cambridge, MA: MIT Press, 1994, pp. 84–110.

Lucas, C.H., Jr. Performance and the use of an information system. *Management Science*, 21, 8 (1975), 908–919.

Lucas, C.H., Jr. *The Analysis, Design, and Implementation of Information Systems*, 2nd ed. New York: McGraw-Hill, 1981.

Mathieson, K., and Keil, M. Beyond the interface: ease of use and task/technology fit. *Information & Management*, 34, 4 (1998), 221–230.

Moore, G.C., and Benbasat, I. An empirical examination of a model of the factors affecting utilization of information technology by end users. Working Paper, University of British Columbia, 1992.

Newell, A., and Simon, H.A. *Human Problem Solving*. Englewood Cliffs, NJ: Prentice-Hall, 1972.

Olson, M.H., and Ives, B. Chargeback systems and user involvement in systems—an empirical investigation. *MIS Quarterly*, 6, 2 (1982), 47–60.

O'Reilly, C.A., III. Variations of decision makers' use of information sources: the impact of quality and accessibility of information. *Academy of Management Journal*, 25, 4 (1982), 756–771.

O'Reilly, C.A., III. The user of information in organizational decision making: a model and some proposi-tions. In *Research in Organizational Behavior*, 5. Greenwich, CT: JAI Press, 1983, pp. 103–139.

Payne, J.W. Contingent decision behavior. *Psychological Bulletin*, 92, 2 (1982), 382–402.

Payne, J.W.; Bettman, J.R.; and Luce, M.F. When time is money: decision behavior under opportunity-cost time pressure. *Organizational Behavior and Human Decision Processes*. 66, 2 (1996), 131–152.

Pentland, B.T. Use and productivity in personal computing: an empirical test. *Proceedings of the Tenth International Conference on Information Systems*. Boston, MA: International Conference on Information Systems, 1989, 211–222.

Perrow, C. A framework for the comparative analysis of organizations. *American Sociological Review*, 32, 2 (1967), 194–208.

Robey, D. User attitudes and management information systems use. *Academy of Management Journal*, 22, 3 (1979), 527–538.

Saunders, C., and Jones, J.W. Temporal sequences in information acquisition for decision making: a focus on source and medium. *Academy of Management Review*, 15, 1 (1990), 29–46.

Schoonhoven, C.B. Problems with contingency theory: testing assumptions hidden within the language of contingency theory. *Administrative Science Quarterly*, 26 (1981), 349–377.

Seddon, P.B. A respecification and extension of the DeLone and McLean model of IS success. *Information Systems Research*, 8, 3 (1997), 240–253.

Smith, J.F.; Mitchell, T.R.; and Beach, L.R. A cost-benefit mechanism for selecting problem-solving strategies: some extensions and empirical tests. *Organizational Behavior and Human Decision Processes*, 19 (1982), 370–396.

Swanson, E.B. Information channel disposition and use. *Decision Sciences*, 18, 1 (1987), 131–145.

Thompson, J.D. *Organizations In Action*. New York: McGraw-Hill, 1967.

Thompson, R.L.; Higgins, C.A.; and Howell, J.M. Towards a conceptual model of utilization. *MIS Quarterly*, 15, 1 (1991), 125–143.

Thompson, R.L.; Higgins, C.A.; and Howell, J.M. Influence of experience on personal computer utilization: testing a conceptual model. *Journal of Management Information Systems*, 11, 1 (1994), 167–187.

Todd, P., and Benbasat, I. Evaluating the impact of DSS, cognitive effort, and incentives on strategy selection. *Information Systems Research*, 10, 4 (1999), 357–376.

Tornatzky, L.G., and Klein, K.J. Innovation characteristics and innovation adoption-implementation: a meta-analysis of findings. *IEEE Transactions on Engineering Management*, 29, 1 (1982), 28–45.

Triandis, H.C. Values, attitudes and interpersonal behavior. In H.E. Howe (ed.), *Nebraska Symposium on Motivation, (1979): Beliefs, Attitudes and Values*. Lincoln, NE: University of Nebraska Press, 1980, pp. 195–259.

Trice, A.W., and Treacy, M.E. Utilization as a dependent variable in MIS research. *DataBase*, 19, 3/4 (1988), 33–41.

Van de Ven, A.H; and Drazin, R. The concept of fit in contingency theory. In L.L. Cummings and B.M. Staw (eds.), *Research in Organizational Behavior*, vol. 7. Greenwich, CT: JAI Press, 1985, pp. 333–365.

Venkatesh, V., and Davis, F. A theoretical extension of the technology acceptance model: four longitudinal field studies. *Management Science*, 46, 2 (2000), 186–205.

Venkatesh, V., et al. User acceptance of information technology: toward a unified view. *MIS Quarterly*, 27, 3 (2003), 425–478.

Venkatraman, N. The concept of fit in strategic research: toward verbal and statistical correspondence. *Academy of Management Review*, 14, 3 (1989), 423–444.

Vessey, I., and Galletta, D. Cognitive fit: an empirical study of information acquisition. *Information Systems Research*, 2, 1 (1991), 63–84.

Vessey, I. Cognitive fit: a theory-based analysis of the graphs vs. tables literature. *Decision Sciences*, 22, 2 (1991), 219–240.

Wood, R.E. Task complexity: definition of the construct. *Organizational Behavior and Human Decision Processes*, 37 (1986), 60–82.

Zigurs, I., and Buchland, B.K. A theory of task/technology fit and group support systems effectiveness. *MIS Quarterly*, 22, 3 (1998), 313–334.

Zmud, R.W. An empirical investigation of the dimensionality of the concept of information. *Decision Sciences*, 9, 2 (1978), 187–195.

CHAPTER 10

DESIGNS THAT FIT

An Overview of Fit Conceptualizations in HCI

DOV TE'ENI

Abstract: *It has been argued that fitting the human-computer interface to the user and the task enhances performance. This chapter reviews these claims and asks whether such claims have theoretical and practical value. It begins with an overview of three types of fit: physical, cognitive, and affective. Each type of fit is assessed for its value. The analysis then expands to consider dynamic aspects of fit to increase its value both in changing the practice of design and providing more powerful explanations of user behavior. The analysis concludes that there is value in the notion of fit in HCI design, yet the current fragmented and incomplete treatment of fit and the current shortcomings in its measurement hinder progress in this area.*

Keywords: *Fit, Design, Cognitive Fit, Affective Fit, Physiological Fit, HCI Metaphor, Communication, Personalization*

INTRODUCTION

Several researchers, using different conceptualizations and models of fit, claim that fitting the human-computer interface to attributes of the user and of the task at hand enhances performance. This chapter comments on these claims and asks whether such claims have theoretical and practical value. In particular, is the relationship between fit and performance nothing more than a tautology, too trivial to be of any value? Or put in another way: Is "good fit" nothing more than "good design"? Does the concept of fit facilitate better explanations or predictions of behavior? Do conceptualizations of fit offer practical insights into how to achieve a better design?

The paper demonstrates that the concept of fit has potential value in theory and practice, yet the current fragmented and incomplete treatment of fit and the current shortcomings in its measurement hinder progress in this area. In an attempt to judge the theoretical and practical value of fit, this chapter brings together several extant treatments of fit, providing a broad view that highlights existing, as well as missing, elements of fit. It ends with some unanswered questions left for future research.

The idea of fit in HCI is not new. In fact, it can be seen explicitly, but sometimes implicitly, in most metaphors of HCI. For instance, Kammersgaard (1988) characterizes four general perspectives that can be applied to HCI: the systems perspective, the dialog partner perspective, the tool perspective, and the media perspective. The systems perspective considers a phenomenon as consisting of similarly characterized components, all having a set of data types and a set of actions that enable the components to process and transfer data. The systems perspective is important in providing a comprehensive view of HCI. Inherent in the systems perspective is the idea of compatibility between subsystems in order to produce a concerted joint goal. Furthermore, the idea of compatibility between the human and computer subsystems implicitly assumes an efficient allocation of tasks that is based on the relative strengths and weaknesses of the subsystems. For example, computers should be designed to perform tasks that humans perform inaccurately or inefficiently. Fit between human and computer subsystems is therefore seen as a necessary condition for goal achievement.

In contrast to the systems perspective of HCI, the dialog-partner perspective regards the human and the computer as partners to dialog in a communication process in which both parties act as senders and receivers of messages. The major implication of this perspective is the pursuit of improving the dialog, mainly on the basis of how people communicate and how they fit the way they communicate to the prevailing circumstances. (Below I expand on the specific implications of this perspective on designing fit.)

The tool perspective regards the computer as offering a tool kit with which the user, who is in control, can produce some product using materials as inputs. This perspective is important in design because it underscores the need to fit the tool to the attributes and limitations of the users working in specified situations so that the user can work effectively, efficiently, and comfortably.

Finally, the media perspective treats the computer as a medium through which humans communicate. Importantly, this view stresses the collective context of use. The media perspective has implications for design at the level of the meaning communicated between people, emphasizing language and striving for perfect understanding between communicators. In particular, this perspective emphasizes the need to fit the medium to the context of the communication, to the type of information communicated, and to the communicators involved.

Thus, each of these perspectives can add, in general, to the design of HCI, and, in particular, to the role of fit in design. Depending on the perspective held (e.g., a tool perspective or a systems perspective), fit can be seen as the adaptation of the computer to characteristics and desires of the user or as the mutual adaptation of both the computer to the user through design and the user to the computer through training. Furthermore, depending on the perspective, different elements of the computer system are fitted to different attributes of the task and the user (the different emphases in each of the four perspectives are elaborated in the conclusion). I begin, however, with a demonstration of the implications on fit of the communication and media metaphors.

Borrowing from the world of communication is especially useful in setting the scope of our discussion. A significant part—some may argue all—of human-computer interaction has to do with communication between the user and the computer. It is therefore fruitful to learn from human-human communication. Effective communicators adapt their communication to their audience and the prevailing circumstances. In other words, they seek a fit among the different elements of communication: the message and medium of communication, the receiver of the communication, the goal of the communication, the physical and social context, etc. Consider several examples. Example 1: A speaker realizes the room is noisy so she raises her voice. Example 2: A speaker knows the message is sensitive and potentially embarrassing, so she seeks a private channel of communication. Example 3: Knowing the listener's young age, the speaker chooses bright colors and animation for her presentation. Example 4: A speaker knows that the listener needs the message in order to decide which direction to continue driving, so she provides the location of the destination relative to the listener's current location. Example 5: Seeing the listener frowning, the speaker explains the message in more detail with more concrete examples. Example 6: Seeing the listener's anguish at the bad news, the speaker expresses sympathy.

Projecting these ideas from human-human communication to human-computer interaction is straightforward. HCI examples that correspond to the six communication examples above could

Table 10.1

Potential Types of Fit in HCI

	Type of Guideline on Fit	Example of Guideline
1	Fit audio-visual output to the physical environment.	Fit screen brightness to light intensity.
2	Fit medium to affective considerations.	Choose a medium for conveying personal data that secures privacy.
3	Fit format to user characteristics.	Personalize fonts to user's age and taste.
4	Fit format to task characteristics.	Display quantitative information graphically for spatial tasks.
5	Fit information detail to complexity experienced by user.	Adjust level of explanations when user encounters difficulty.
6	Fit affective expressions to the user's emotional state.	Match colors, tone, and facial expressions to user's mood.

be (1) fitting the screen brightness to the light intensity in the room; (2) displaying sensitive messages only on a user's terminal rather than in less private media; (3) displaying bright colors and animation to young users; (4) displaying graphical data for spatial tasks; (5) providing more detailed feedback to students exhibiting difficulty in the task; and (6) computer-generated sympathetic messages to users encountering stressful information. Taking a relatively broad view of fit, I treat all these examples as incidents of fit. Table 10.1 generalizes the six examples as achieving different types of fit in HCI. This is not a comprehensive list of possibilities, but rather a demonstration of the scope of types of fit as they are discussed in this chapter.

Research on HCI in information systems (IS), as opposed to computer engineering, has traditionally concentrated on the design of software-based human-computer interfaces rather than hardware, treating the hardware as given. Ergonomic design of input and output devices has largely been left to other academic fields, e.g., human factors. The subset of HCI research in IS focusing on fit has similarly dealt primarily with the design of (software-based) information displays, relying on cognitive aspects of fit to direct design. In comparison with the broad range of types of fit demonstrated in Table 10.1, the review of research in this chapter has consequently more to say about cognitive aspects of fit than it does about physical aspects of fit. Furthermore, fitting designs to human characteristics has at least two levels: One is fit with the general (average) characteristics of users, and the second, more sophisticated, level is fit with particular characteristics of special tasks, special users, and other idiosyncrasies. In organizational settings, fitting designs to physical characteristics has usually been constrained to the "average" user engaged in a variety of tasks, making it possible to rely on ready-made ergonomic designs to fit all (with limited adjustments such as fitting the screen's position to the user's height). By contrast, fitting information displays to task idiosyncrasies has attracted considerable interest in IS research. Again, the organizational emphasis on task will be reflected in the discussions below that introduce the organizational task as a major influence in achieving cognitive, but not physical, fit.

In sum, the notion of fit in HCI design means different things to researchers taking different perspectives. Table 10.1 demonstrates a wide scope of possible guidelines for designing HCI to fit the user and the task in a given context. Indeed, this chapter attempts to take a broad view in order to review published research on various types of fit within an integrated framework; in so doing, it also attempts to identify unexplored areas. To this end, the chapter is organized around the framework depicted in Figure 10.1, which is developed gradually throughout the paper. For now,

Figure 10.1   **Framework for Understanding Fit in HCI**

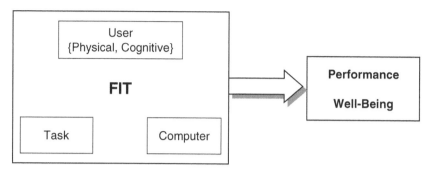

note that within the left-hand box of Figure 10.1, the label "fit" is located in between the three fac-tors: the user, the task, and the computer. In the right-hand box are two impacts of fit: the user's task-related performance and the user's overall well-being. Task-related performance has to do with the quality of the task output and the amount of resources consumed, e.g., the accuracy of the task and the effort and speed needed to complete the task. Overall well-being is the user's physi-cal, psychological, and social state impacted by the human-computer interaction, e.g., health haz-ards, emotions, and interpersonal relations. The general thrust of fit models is that fit enhances one or both results. Using this framework, I first review extant conceptualizations of fit in HCI and then examine what further aspects of fit should be studied.

EXAMPLES OF FIT IN HCI DESIGN

This section begins with a general call for "designs that fit human capabilities," continues with phy-sical fit, and then concentrates on cognitive fit. The next section adds affective fit and proposes a more general view with some possible extensions.

Design to Fit Users' Capabilities

Baecker et al. (1995) claim that "With a 'good' interface, human and computer should augment each other to produce a system that is greater than the sum of its parts" (p. 667). This claim assumes that the computer is designed in such a way that both the computer and the user perform the tasks that best suit their respective capabilities. The authors go on to emphasize that "a 'good' interaction technique maximizes human strengths, while a 'poor' one exposes [human] limita-tions" (p. 668). Following this line of thought, one can see why it is important to design for human error (an example of adapting the computer to user characteristics) and why it is important to train users (an example of adapting the user's knowledge to attributes of the computer). In general, the field of HCI has stressed designing far more than training.

   This view follows the systems perspective in proposing a design principle that strives to best fit the computer functionality to the user's capabilities. Such designs enable an efficient allocation of tasks to human and computer that is based on an understanding of the characteristics of both the user and the computer and of their relative strengths and weaknesses. Although the examples given are taken from the cognitive world, the same logic can be extended to the physiological aspects of the user and perhaps to the affective aspects, too. For example, our motor capabilities make it difficult to drag a figure on a computer screen so that it exactly aligns with another figure.

Letting the user indicate a general direction and location and leaving the exact alignment to the computer demonstrates the design principle of fitting the computer to the user's capabilities. Whether based on cognitive or motor capabilities, the strategy of achieving fit with user characteristics appears to be acknowledged by some leading HCI researchers as a useful guideline for practice. This may be considered as the most basic and general call for fit in designing HCI. I now turn to more specific treatments of fit in design.

Physical Fit

Although the term physical fit is not used widely, the connotation of matching the physical designs of input and output devices to the physiology of the user is at the heart of ergonomic design. For example, the popular flat keyboard is designed to fit the shape and size of the hands. Improved ergonomic designs that better fit the shape of the hand provide a tilted and curved keyboard that reduces the carpal tunnel stress that can result from lengthy typing sessions. Yet, overall, the fit of most input and output devices to the physiology of our entire body is rather limited, as evident in an amusing but very telling scenario introduced by Buxton (1986).

Imagine a futuristic situation in which all knowledge about our civilization has been lost and the only clues available were to be found in a computer equipment store that, by some unexplained miracle, had been preserved intact with all its equipment fully operable. A physical anthropologist was summoned to simulate the physiology of the (presumably) humans who used this equipment. What would they look like? One likely picture of a human would be of a creature "with a well-developed eye, a long right arm, a smaller left arm, uniform-length fingers and a 'low-fi' ear. But the dominating characteristics would be the prevalence of our visual system over our poorly developed manual dexterity" (Buxton, 1986). There would be hardly any clues in the computer store about our other senses, nor about our "other" eye and ear, not to mention our legs and feet. The difference between this human being and the one we know is amazing and, more importantly for designers of HCI, perplexing. In fact, had the physical anthropologist explored a driver's seat in a regular car, a more balanced view of our physiology would probably emerge.

Fortunately, new and improved ergonomic designs have emerged in the past twenty years (e.g., handheld devices and the click wheels on Apple's iPods). Nevertheless, Buxton's scenario is insightful. It highlights the extent to which the most popular input-output devices many people use on a daily basis (and some use them most of the day) are very poorly matched to our body. Using only a fraction of our faculties, current technology strains those it uses, and is so poorly fitted to our physiology that it often causes poor performance, frustration, fatigue, and long-term health hazards.

Ergonomic design of input and output devices concentrates on fitting the device to human physiology in performing generic, rather than specific, tasks, such as inputting numeric data to a computer or reading text from a computer screen. The general assumption is that good fit should require less effort, reduce health problems, and generate in the user a positive sensation or feeling of physical comfort. On the other hand, poor fit will usually require more muscular effort, result in physical strain during or after the activity, and generate uncertainty about the physical interaction with the computer.

Although anecdotal evidence suggests that health problems due to inadequate designs and poor work habits with computers cause significant damage to organizations, there is a paucity of research in the IS literature about the consequences of poor fit on performance and well-being. Indeed, the practical applications of fitting hardware to attributes of human physiology have stressed the impact on health and well-being, and only indirectly on performance, e.g., loss of working hours due to health problems (e.g., Sandsjo et al., 2003).

This limited view of physical fit and its impact on well-being may very well change with the advent of new input-output devices. In particular, virtual reality systems in the workplace will sense human behavior by means of physical devices, such as displays that track eye movement and gloves that track hand motion. The computerized system (i.e., the virtual environment) will be designed to react appropriately and communicate back to the user with haptic feedback, advanced graphics, and auditory cues. Thus, the physical aspects of human interaction will increase dramatically the diversity and complexity of the physical design, and, most likely, will produce a corresponding demand for a broader view of physical fit.

In sum, physical fit ensures minimal physical effort to accomplish the task and consideration for the user's overall well-being. The reliance on limited devices to enable input (primarily motor) and output (primarily visual and some auditory) has characterized computers in organizational settings. The general tendency to design hardware that fits all sizes and all tasks may, however, change with the advent of more advanced interactive technologies such as virtual reality systems that build on multiple senses. With it may come a stronger interest in physical fit and in the impact of fit on performance at the task level.

Cognitive Fit

In the IS literature, the most influential case of fit in HCI design is cognitive fit. In summarizing the design implications of cognitive fit, Vessey and Galletta (1991) state that "for most effective and efficient problem solving to occur, the problem representation and any tools or aids employed should all support the strategies required to perform that task." While the previous discussion emphasized the fit with user capabilities and implicitly assumed a set of tasks to be performed, cognitive fit emphasizes the fit with the user's model of the task demands. Moreover, cognitive fit proposes a theory that explains the link between fit and performance. Assuming the user has a mental model (representation) of the task demands, the computer representation displayed to the user can either match or not match the user's model. A match ensures consistency between the problem-solving processes that are appropriate for both representations, reducing the propensity for error and reducing the effort and time required. On the other hand, a mismatch between the two representations requires a transformation of one representation to suit the processes that fit the other representation, reducing accuracy and increasing time. Hence, fit is positively related to performance.

Cognitive fit theory was developed for the case of spatial and symbolic tasks that rely on perceptual and analytic problem-solving processes: Graphic displays fit spatial tasks, encouraging perceptual processes, and tabular displays fit symbolic tasks, encouraging analytic processes. Vessey (this volume) explains how the theory applies to simple tasks (Vessey, 1991) as well as complex tasks (Vessey, 1994). In complex tasks, the user chooses between alternative problem-solving processes on the basis of a cost-benefit analysis, in which a user balances the effort required to execute the process with the expected performance benefits. At some point, users judge the effort required to execute a more effortful problem-solving process such as analytic processes to be too high relative to the expected benefit and, therefore, shift to the easier perceptual processes. The theory cannot, however, predict the point at which a user will shift from one process to another. Nevertheless, the theory can predict the direction in which external influences, e.g., motivation to be accurate rather than fast, will influence the choice of problem-solving processes. Furthermore, fit is binary. The fit between representations is defined indirectly as positive when a graphic display is used for a spatial task or when a tabular display is used for a symbolic task. Other combinations result in no fit. This precludes intermediate levels of fit.

A review of empirical studies on cognitive fit (Vessey, this volume) concludes that the theory is generally supported, and, furthermore, that the predicted relationship holds for a broader view of fit than the original graph-table domain. Parallel research efforts (which do not use the term "cognitive fit") have also shown how incongruence between task demands and display hinders performance, e.g., Jarvenpaa (1989). However, several factors limit the strength of the evidence. First, there are no clearly defined measures of the main constructs (e.g., spatial-symbolic tasks) that researchers can adopt unambiguously. Second, as a result of the first problem, there is no objective measure of fit (beyond the binary fit relationship between pairs of spatial tasks—graphic display, etc.). Third, the experimental designs employed in most of the reviewed experiments do not observe directly the processes and representation assumed to be active in the user's mind. Finally, the cost-benefit trade-off is hard to measure directly; thus, conflicting results between experiments in terms of time spent and accuracy attained may be attributed to different priorities placed on accuracy and time. For example, a task involving containment, in which one spatial object is contained within another, is considered to be a spatial task in one study (Smelcer and Carmel, 1997) and a symbolic task in another study (Dennis and Carte, 1998). Accordingly, the studies predicted, respectively, that a map or a table would provide a better fit with the perceptual processes triggered by the map or analytic processes triggered by a table. There is however no direct observation of these processes and therefore no certainty that any one of these processes actually occurred. This point opens cognitive fit to criticism that the theory is not falsifiable.

Developing measures of fit is key to the development of cognitive fit for both theoretical and practical purposes. Measures are needed in order to test and compare applications of cognitive fit and to generalize the model to other types of tasks. Goodhue (this volume) underscores the need to develop measures for the higher-level concept of task-individual-technology fit. He raises two alternative judgments of fit: the "objective" judgment of the experts and the subjective judgment of the individual faced with the task. In both cases, judgment of fit must begin with a task analysis that produces the true informational requirements. (In Figure 10.1, the task demands would appear under the label Task.) However, having recognized the importance of defining task characteristics as the basis for computing fit with individual and technology characteristics, the usefulness of the measure to designers depends on its granularity. For example, a questionnaire with a user's evaluation of the task-technology fit based on perceptions of how well technology meets one's job requirements (Goodhue, 1998) can help predict job performance or technology acceptance, but it can only provide general feedback to the designer on the technology fit, with no direct input on the precise design. In contrast, a characterization of a task as one that requires certain perceptual processes (Vessey and Galletta, 1991) provides specific guidance on the choice of display. In other words, it is not only that measures of fit must be developed, they must be developed at the right level of granularity to be useful.

Norman (1991) advanced a very similar, yet broader, conceptualization of fit under the label of "naturalness." Naturalness is inversely related to the length of the translation between representations. The design implication is that the displayed representation "should allow the person to work with exactly the information acceptable to the task: neither more nor less" (ibid., p. 29). Unlike cognitive fit theory, this approach provides a basis for measures of fit, suggesting that fit can be measured by the length of the description of the mapping, given a decision on the terms used in the description. Norman proposes that researchers use psychological primitives to describe the mappings and thereby build a common ground for comparing measures of fit. Following this recommendation, Kennedy et al. (1998) computed the number of elementary information processes needed to perform a certain task based on quantitative displays of information. They used the number of steps as a measure of cognitive fit, showing how people prefer displays with high, rather than low, cognitive fit. The explanatory power, as well as the generality of this approach seems higher than the approach taken in the empirical work on cognitive fit. For example, Payne et al. (1988) used it to explain how decision behavior adapts to changes in information displays in order to minimize effort.

A classification of representations relevant to HCI advanced by Norman (1991) helps position cognitive fit in our discussion. First, there is the represented world of real objects and task demands. The represented world may be documented in various forms of public knowledge such as books, organizational memory, and culture. Second, there is the user's mental model of the represented world, that is, the representation of the task in its environment as the user sees it. This representation can be seen as part of the individual's cognitive characteristics. The third representation is the internal representation of the real world stored in the computer and the fourth representation is the representation displayed by the computer to the user. The last two representations would be part of the Computer in Figure 10.1. Cognitive fit theory refers to the match between the characteristics of the problem-solving strategy included in the user's mental model and the problem representation as it appears on the system display, e.g., a spatial task with a graphical display.

In sum, the cognitive fit theory has theoretical and practical value. Theoretically it can explain and predict performance, concentrating on the task level. Similar to physical fit, cognitive fit (naturalness) strives to minimize the cognitive effort needed to transform representations. In this sense, designs that fit are also those that impose minimal effort. Finally, cognitive fit rests on convincing theoretical grounds. Unfortunately, its potential is currently limited by measurement problems. Practically, cognitive fit calls attention to specific factors that should be taken into account when designing displays and can sometimes dictate the optimal designs. In particular, the idea of characterizing the task as symbolic or spatial and providing the most effective display (e.g., graphical or tabular) by fitting display to task is feasible and would appear to be important. This may be especially true in the organizational context that relies heavily on appropriate presentations for decision making. For cognitive fit to be of greater value it must, however, be generalized to enable analysis of tasks that relate to other cognitive aspects beyond perceptual versus analytic processes. Finally, as noted above, providing a sufficiently detailed analysis of the task is prerequisite to any computation of fit, but it must be complemented with a corresponding characterization of cognitive attributes such as memory, attention, and processing limitations.

SOME EMPHASES, EXTENSIONS, AND CONCERNS

Fit and the Allocation of Tasks

As noted above, Baecker et al. (1995) base their discussion of fit on the assumption that the computer and the user perform the tasks that best suit their respective capabilities. Early work on man-machine systems (during the 1960s and 1970s) adopted the systemic perspective in which a task would be allocated to the subsystem that could perform the task in the most effective and efficient way. In one of the earliest papers on task allocation, Fitts (1951) proposed a list of functions in which humans outperformed machines and vice versa. This list—and similar ones that emerged over time—e.g., Sanders and McCormick (1993)—could be used to allocate functions in the design of man-machine systems. For example, machine is better than man in computing arithmetic problems but man is better than machine in comprehending text. Advances in technology of course affect such lists; for example, computers may be able to analyze text in foreign languages better than humans. However, the basic principle of allocating tasks is one that should be part of the design. To facilitate this principle, Price (1985) built a decision matrix with two dimensions: human performance and machine performance. The intersection of both dimensions creates areas that reflect poor or good performance by each component and areas in which both or neither performs well. Tasks that fall into areas of distinct advantage to one component can be allocated directly. Tasks that fall into areas of ambiguity will be left to the designer's judgment or allocated contingently according to prevailing conditions. Such an allocation of tasks is also important in the design of flexible systems that allow dynamic adaptation according to changing conditions. For example, the layout of the screen may be adapted according to users' preferences that are learned gradually by the system. Initially, layout decisions are performed by the human, and then, if some pattern of behavior is detected, the task is performed automatically unless the user indicates otherwise.

Design for fit, therefore, can be seen to begin with an understanding of user and computer attributes, which in turn determine relative performance capabilities and limitations. As suggested above, the same line of thought could be applied for all dimensions of fit. To date, however, the "man is better than machine" analyses have concentrated on cognitive aspects and to some extent on physical aspects, especially in the design of robots. One of the practical contributions implied by the fit approach concerns, therefore, the starting point of HCI development; it suggest that the first stages of development should include a comparative analysis of human and computer attributes (Te'eni et al., 2006).

Affective Fit

Affect in HCI design is rapidly becoming an integral part of HCI research and teaching, in comparison to the past preoccupation with cognition in HCI (Picard and Klein, 2002). HCI researchers are now adopting a more balanced and integrated view of HCI in which both affective and cognitive aspects play a role in understanding user behavior and designing appropriately. A good example is Donald Norman's new emphasis on emotions in computing (Norman, 2003). As with physical and cognitive aspects of fit, I speculate (there is no evidence yet) that it is beneficial to fit the human-computer interaction to affective characteristics of the user or even of the task. Examples 2 and 6 in Table 10.1 follow from findings in human-human communication, suggesting that the computer system be designed to be sensitive to emotional aspects of the task (e.g., personal information that is potentially embarrassing) and the user's mood (e.g., bright colors may clash with an unhappy mood).

Affective fit may be seen as the design of the computer to fit the affective state that a user feels or would like to feel, or to fit the affective state most appropriate for the action the user needs to take. A consequence of poor affective fit is a negative feeling targeted at the computer, e.g., frustration and annoyance. Letting the user choose an emotion that best fits her feelings is a trivial example but it stresses the very common tendency to fit the icon or graphic in the message to match the receiver's and sender's moods. Projecting again from the practice of effective human-human communication to HCI, the system's appearance can be designed to exhibit empathy. For example, a software agent or personalized assistant could be designed to display either a smiling face or a perplexed face, depending on the user's mood. Inappropriately projecting a smiling face provokes negative reactions from the user. Affective fit can therefore also have practical value in improving design.

The measurement of affective characteristics, of affective fit and of the impact of affective fit is particularly difficult. Thus, measurement difficulties hinder both the study of affective fit and the practical possibility of gauging the emotion to be able to adapt to it. In particular, it is difficult to measure reactions to affective fit (or misfit), whether through psychological indicators, or observations of overt behavior. Some overt expressions of emotional reactions, such as swearing at the computer or hitting the display, are clearly evident to an observer, but they usually reflect extreme frustrations and are rare. In general, physiological indicators can gauge less extreme emotional reactions to affective fit. Moreover, in comparison with psychological indicators (e.g., questionnaire or observations), physiological indicators are less susceptible to misinterpretation (Wilson and Sasse, 2004). Examples of physiological measures include pupil size variation, electric brain potentials, heart rate and blood volume pulse, and facial muscles (Partala et al., 2003). Nevertheless, the measurement of affect, especially non-intrusive measurement, as a basis for studying and achieving fit by adaptive designs remains a major challenge (Cockton, 2004).

In sum, affective fit is identified as an unexplored territory, but one that may gain priority as research in the area of affect in HCI matures. Although there is no theory, or evidence at hand, it would appear that affective fit is a topic worthy of research. Drawing on the discussions of the impact of physical and cognitive fit, one can speculate that affective fit will impact the user's well-being and attitudes, and perhaps performance, too. The notion of negative energy generated in situations of frustration or the effort required to overcome negative emotions may lead to analyses of design that minimize such emotional effort. Such analyses would parallel the notions of minimizing physical and cognitive effort. Affective fit may therefore be an important complement to physical and cognitive fit in order to provide a holistic perspective of HCI.

When Good Fit Is Bad

Davern (1996) provides two important extensions to the study of cognitive fit. First, he shifts the emphasis from the state of fit (or misfit) resulting from the interaction between representations to the *process* of fitting the system and its actual use to the task demands. In other words, fit is not only the engineered solution offered to match the task demands but fit should also include the user's unintended (by the designer) appropriations of the system (DeSanctis and Poole, 1994).

Returning to communication metaphors, consider the following scenario that includes both an initial design as well as the user's adaptive behavior. Suppose there are theoretical grounds to suggest that rich media (such as video conferencing) best fit equivocal tasks, whilst lean media (such as e-mail) best fit unequivocal and routine tasks. Research has shown that fit results in higher task performance than situations of no fit. The dynamic treatment of fit requires the researcher (or designer) to further consider the users' adaptive behavior when they are faced with poor fit. For instance, users faced with lean media nevertheless adapt and find ways to overcome these limitations, e.g., by requiring more feedback (Te'eni, 2001). In this case, while task accuracy may not differ between rich and lean media, the user may invest more time and effort when using e-mail (poor fit) than when using video conferencing (good fit). Moreover, in situations of poor fit where the user faced with equivocal tasks is obliged to use lean media, designs that support feedback will be more effective. Thus, incorporating the user's reactions into the fit concept provides a more dynamic and more complete explanation of the user's task behavior and performance. This shift can therefore lead to a more valuable research framework of fit.

Davern's second contribution is to disentangle fit into four types (the names in parentheses are his): a) the correspondence between the computer representation and the real-world task demands ("representational fit"), b) the correspondence between the computer representation and the user's characteristics and mental model ("informational fit"[1]), c) the correspondence between the user's mental model and the real world ("reality fit"), and d) the correspondence between the user's mental model and the computer tools for manipulating representations ("tool fit").[2]

This classification of types of fit strengthens the value of the fit concept both theoretically and practically. Theoretically, even though one or two types of fit may be high, performance may decrease because reality fit or representational fit is poor (Goodhue, in this volume, makes a similar case).

For example, a user who models a given task as a spatial task interacts with a graphical display (good informational fit). However, the user has incorrectly modeled the task as a spatial task, while in fact it is symbolic (poor reality fit). This situation may result in poor performance, despite high satisfaction with the technology. As Davern notes, when users misperceive the situation to have a good fit with the task (overlooking, for example, the reality fit), they will have no incentive to learn and adapt, and as a result, their performance will decline rather than improve over time. Hence, a comprehensive treatment of fit clarifies why effective HCI needs to incorporate learning and training.

Practically, designers should be aware of all types of fit and their impact on performance because different designs are required to establish different types of fit. In particular, the distinction between informational fit and tool fit is a subtle one that is ignored in cognitive fit theory, in which the information and the (computerized) tool that manipulates the information are intertwined. I return to this point in the conclusion.

Davern's analysis indirectly raises another concern with the theories that build on mental models. Explaining the user's interaction with computers by relying on the central role of mental models is only one option, which is appropriate for controlled behavior found in complex or novel tasks. Another is to regard users' behavior in known situations as primarily perceptual reactions based on experience (Kahneman and Tversky, 1979). Obviously, a significant portion of human-computer interaction can be characterized as rote behavior. Don Norman argues that in such cases, mental models play no role (Parush, 2004). Fit would need to be conceptualized in relation to habits rather than mental models. Practically, this requires the designer to be sensitive to different modes of behavior (controlled and rote).

Fitting the design to the user's mental model is therefore not always good. In some cases, it may be better to train the user, that is, change the user's understanding or habits. In complex tasks that involve controlled behavior such as the interaction with decision support systems, the designer may attempt to restrict and guide decision behavior (Silver, 1991). In automatic or rote behavior, it is sometimes necessary to unlearn certain habits in order to retrain users on new devices rather than fitting the old device. For example, in the past, when experienced users of typewriters were asked to convert to computer keyboards, they first had to overcome some of their old typing habits (such as backspacing to underline or using the carriage return to advance a line), which interfered with working efficiently with computers. Fitting the keyboard to old habits was infeasible.

Davern's extensions to cognitive fit underscore the need to refine the concept of fit. First, striving for an optimal design that creates a good fit should be regarded only as the beginning of a good design. HCI design should also include the user's adaptive behavior as circumstances change and fit declines or rises. Second, the need to consider different types of fit and the interactions between them further expands the scope of research into fit. Both directions warrant further research.

Dynamic Fit and Personalization

The last two examples in Table 10.1 highlight the possibility of fitting the human-computer interaction to the way the dialog progresses. As in human-human communication, changes occur during a human-computer dialog, e.g., an unpleasant or incomprehensible message comes up, and both the computer and the user can react to maintain effective interaction: the computer can display the material at a slower rate or with more detail, or it can change the tone of voice to comply with a changing mood. This type of fit requires not only knowledge about the alternative designs and possible reactions but also a real-time detection and feedback mechanism that provides the necessary signals to direct and control adaptation. Achieving physical fit in advanced environments will require nearly continuous adaptations (as in the discussion above on virtual reality). Designers could also strive to achieve fit dynamically for complex cognitive operations in rich information environments (e.g., browsing large Web sites through adaptive views). In contrast, achieving affective fit dynamically has been met with skepticism, primarily because of sensing and measurement problems. A plausible solution may be adaptable systems in which the system is designed with the flexibility to let users adapt the system to their emotional state (Tractinsky, 2004).

Perhaps the most common manifestation of fit in practice is personalization. Displaying bright colors to young users, using French for the French-speaking user and using joyful expressions to communicate with the happy user are instances of fitting the human-computer interaction to the user characteristics, that is, personalizing the interface. Moreover, as noted above, human-computer interaction should be seen as a dynamic process in which designs adapt throughout the dialog. Indeed, adaptive and adaptable user interfaces are becoming an important area of development. In adaptable interfaces the user is given the tools to adapt the interfaces to his or her capabilities, level of knowledge, preferences, or physical setting. In adaptive interfaces the computer initiates the adaptation. A trivial example is the ability to adapt the brightness of the video terminal to fit the light in the room. A more complex example is the ability to adapt the content and presentation in a learning environment to the progress of a student (Papanikolaou et al., 2003).

A framework that integrates the various types of fit and their impact would provide a systematic basis for personalization. At present, the design of personalization concentrates on isolated aspects of fit. One interesting example of a more systematic approach is the user-centered approach to personalization at IBM (Karat et al., 2003). Although, personalization of a Web site connotes a broader form of adaptation than the HCI focus adopted in this chapter, the basic ideas are very similar. The researchers produced clusters of adaptable presentation features tailored both to known user characteristics (such as job type) and to the context implied (such as no graphics when response time is poor). They then sought to determine how personalization would impact effectiveness and ease of use. Finally, they recommended several policies for personalization, e.g., "adaptive presentation: The pages displayed are adapted based on my recent navigation path" (ibid., p. 698).

INTEGRATION

This chapter began with several examples of how researchers have conceptualized and advocated "fit" as a design goal. In particular, I took a critical view and commented on the value, and sometimes deficiencies, of these conceptualizations in contributing to theory and practice. The discussion went on to elaborate some of the concerns that have been voiced and some of the extensions offered. I now summarize and integrate the discussion by picking up again on some of the points made above and offering some new directions for studying fit.

Figure 10.2 refines and extends Figure 10.1, summarizing the aspects of fit discussed above. As already noted, broadening and generalizing some of the extant conceptualization of fit—e.g., from cognitive fit theory—will be important in enhancing the value of fit in HCI. Our definitions are accordingly very general. *User-computer fit* is achieved by matching the computer to the attributes and preferences of the user and is manifested in reduced effort and a better feeling found in designs of good fit in comparison to designs of poor fit. At the same time, designs should also allow for user learning and adaptation that achieve fit in ways unforeseen by the designer. One important element in deciding which direction to take is based on a reality check against the real world of either the user's mental model or the computer's internal representation.

Fit is multi-dimensional; the dimensions correspond to classes of human attributes. There are at least three types of fit that the designer needs to consider. *Physical fit* concerns fit with human

Figure 10.2 **Revised Framework for Studying Fit**

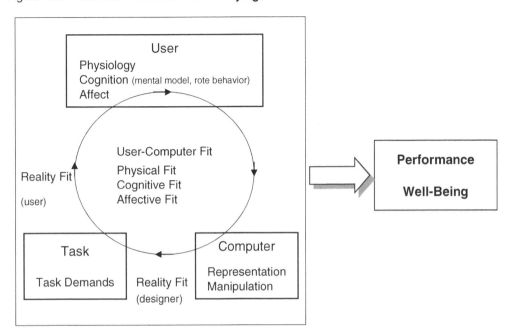

physiology, such as matching the keyboard to the shape and size of the hands. *Cognitive fit* concerns fit with human information processing. It may very well be that cognitive fit should be defined differently for rote behavior than it is for controlled behavior (only the latter relies on mental models). This distinction between rote and controlled behavior may relate to the differential impact on cognitive fit between complex and non-complex tasks (Vessey, this volume). *Affective fit* concerns fit with the affective state that the user feels or wants to feel. In Figure 10.2, the interaction among the user, the computer, and the task defines the three-dimensional user-computer fit (physical, cognitive, and affective).

The user-computer fit can be further refined to take account of the distinction between informational and tool level fit. The interaction between the user, the task, and the computer representation of the task is the informational level fit. In contrast, the interaction with the computer's manipulation facilities is the tool level fit. For example, the graphical representation may effect a perfect fit with the user's mental model, but procedural rather than direct manipulation tools may not fit the user's experience with manipulating graphical objects.

The discussion above further revealed the potential incongruity between the user's mental model of the task and the real-world task, and between the computer representation and the real-world task. Both relationships are labeled "reality fit" (Davern labeled them reality and representational fit, respectively). Reality fit must be examined in tangent with the user-computer fit.

Another important issue is the dynamic aspect of fit. Fit and adaptivity are two sides of the same coin. The circular effects relating the user, task, and computer suggest that fit must be reassessed and adjusted dynamically. Hence, systems that support human-computer interaction, as opposed to fully automatic systems, should be flexibly designed to support adaptive behavior (Te'eni, 2006).

Finally, fit is expected to enhance task performance (with respect to the goals set to or by the user) and the user's well-being. Although extant research shows only piecemeal relationships between different types of fit and their impact, future research will need to address the overall impact of fit. Given this conceptualization (Figure 10.2), I now return to the opening questions raised in the introduction.

Is fit useful for theory? Only if fit models can explain or predict performance and behavior will they be useful for research. Research in IS, particularly on cognitive fit, indicates a positive link between fit and task performance, yet more sophisticated and contingent models are needed to explain broader and more realistic situations. These advances in theory are also needed to address claims that fit theories are hardly falsifiable.

So what needs to be done? There is a need to substantiate some of the claims by more direct observations that would open up the black box of the "fitting" process. The development of valid and reliable measurement has been identified as a crucial step for further progress in all types of fit. In addition, broadening the scope of fit is essential. However, generalizing from very specific cognitive characteristics and processes to more general characteristics entails even more extensive development of measures. Indeed, we need to develop measures of fit at different levels of granularity according to the research question. Furthermore, while research on the link between cognitive fit and task performance seems promising, research in the IS literature and in some of the HCI journals on the link between physical fit and well-being is limited. Finally, the link between affective fit and both performance and well-being should be investigated.

Is there practical value in fit models? We have seen that "good fit" is not synonymous with "good design." In some cases it may lead to poor performance; thus, any conceptualization of fit must state explicitly when designers should and should not strive for fit. Fit has value as a general approach but also as a basis for more specific guidelines. The most basic contribution of fit is to enumerate the relevant aspects of fit based on user characteristics as a first step towards achieving fit. This step involves a task analysis in light of the relevant user's characteristics. It is then followed by an informed allocation of tasks to the computer and the user. As noted above, these steps are not usually included in common HCI methodologies.

A more specific contribution would be to map processes to tasks and displays (e.g., perceptual processes and graphic displays). Only after we learn more about individual aspects of fit should we also look at the interactions, for example, physical and cognitive. A third source of value to practice is the enumeration of types of cognitive fit between representations (see classifications by Norman and by Davern above). Knowing what to look for is a necessary first step in any practice. Moreover, understanding the sources of fit or misfit raises the question of whether to adapt the computer or train the user (or enable learning). Again, an explicit consideration of training is not usually included in common HCI methodologies. More generally, the view of fit in which adaptation is a two-way process will hopefully promote the practice of training and learning in HCI.

The skepticism about the feasibility of using fit models to enable adaptive systems is reminiscent of the cognitive style arguments in the early 1980s (Huber, 1983). One of the basic arguments for stopping all further research on cognitive style was that it is not feasible to design systems that could cope with all the possible combinations and variations one could expect in real-life situations. (Another argument was about poor measurement.) Even if the argument against systems that are adaptive to cognitive styles is correct, the research brings us closer to understanding what parameters should be incorporated into adaptable systems. Clearly, the last two examples in Table 10.1 on dynamic adaptation may be counterproductive in certain unpredicted conditions. Yet taking them as a starting point for designing adaptive systems is an important practical contribution of fit models.

Figure 10.2 is of course overly simplistic. In order to place fit within an HCI design paradigm, it would need to be evaluated alongside other general design principles. Here are some concerns that future research will need to address (in no particular order):

1. Fit comes at a cost: a cost to the user and a cost to the developer. The latter is straight-forward—fit demands more design and computing resources. The cost to the user is subtler. Consider the guideline recommended to IBM on adapting presentation according to previous navigations. The loss of consistency may reduce perceived control and cause a sense of discomfort (Te'eni and Feldman, 2001). Such trade-offs, as articulated convincingly in the case against consistency (Grudin, 1989), underscore the need to study fit in the context of other design principles.

2. The interaction between types of fit is unknown. Consider, for example, the relationship between informational fit and tool fit. Borrowing again from models of human-human communication, one could postulate that in normal conditions informational fit would be more important to the user, unless tool misfit crossed some threshold. If research could substantiate such claims, designers would be better informed in designing adaptive systems.

3. Fit implicitly assumes task allocation between computer and human (see discussion above). Past practices of ensuring effective task allocation are hardly considered today in HCI methodologies. Although fit brings this issue to the forefront, it offers little in understanding how to best allocate tasks. Research is needed to show how user characteristics should be taken into account when allocating tasks, at the outset of the interaction but perhaps also dynamically as the dialog evolves.

4. Computers are increasingly used to support communication and collaboration. Although the discussion of fit is limited to the individual, the social and organizational contexts should be considered in determining fit because the context may conflict or override the individual aspects discussed above. For example, linking colleagues through continuous video connections fits the cognitive need for realizing awareness and sensing the physical context that is lacking in virtual collaborations. However, in a field study in which continuous video connections were established in public spaces, too, some workers felt it conflicted with social needs such as privacy (Jancke et al., 2001). The challenge, therefore, is to learn how to study fit within a broader social and organizational context.

In conclusion, this commentary reviewed some isolated conceptualizations of fit and attempted to bring them together into one framework shown in Figure 10.2. In doing so it examined how current attempts can be complemented and their value to theory and practice strengthened. Hopefully, it will serve as a catalyst for future research on fit in HCI.

ACKNOWLEDGMENTS

I'm grateful to Noam Tractinsky, Jonathan Grudin, and Dennis Galletta for their insightful remarks.

NOTES

1. To avoid confusion, I do not use "cognitive fit," which is Davern's original label.
2. The four types are somewhat similar to Norman's classification of representations noted above.

REFERENCES

Baecker, R.M.; Grudin, J.; Buxton, W.A.S.; and Greenberg, S. Designing to fit human capabilities. In *Readings in Human-Computer Interaction: Towards the Year 2000*. San Francisco: Morgan Kaufman, 1995, pp. 667–680.

Buxton, W. There's more to interaction than meets the eye: some issues in manual input. In D.A. Norman and S.W. Draper (eds.), *User Centered Systems Design: New Perspectives on Human-Computer Interaction*. Hillsdale, NJ: Lawrence Erlbaum Associates, 1986, pp. 319–334.

Cockton, G. Doing to be: multiple routes to affective interaction. *Interacting with Computers*, 16, 4 (2004), 683–691.

Davern, M.J. (1996). When good fit is bad: the dynamics of perceived fit. *Proceedings of the Seventeenth International Conference of Information Systems. ICIS'96.* Cleveland, Ohio, 1996, pp. 112–120.

Dennis, A.R., and Carte, T.A. Using geographical information systems for decision making: extending cognitive fit theory to map-based presentations. *Information Systems Research*, 9, 2 (1998), 194–203.

Fitts, P.M. Human engineering for an effective air-navigation and traffic control system. *Ohio State University Research Foundation*, Columbus, OH, 1951.

Goodhue, D.L. Understanding user evaluations of information systems. *Management Science*, 41, 12 (1995), 1827–1844.

Goodhue, D.L. Development and measurement validity of a task-technology fit instrument of user evaluations of information systems. *Decision Sciences*, 29, 1 (1998), 105–138.

Grudin, J. The case against user interface consistency. *Communications of the ACM*, 32 (1989), 1164–1173.

Huber, G. Cognitive style as a basis for MIS/DSS: much ado about nothing. *Management Science*, 29 (1983), 567–579.

Jancke, G.; Venolia, G.; Grudin, J.; Cadiz, J.; and Gupta, A. Linking public spaces: technological and social issues. In *Proceedings of Conference Human Factors in Computing Systems, CHI2001*. New York: ACM Press, 2001, pp. 530–537.

Jarvenpaa, S.L. The effect of task demands and graphical format on information processing strategies. *Management Science*, 35, 3 (1989), 285–303.

Kammersgaard, J. Four different perspectives on human computer interaction. *International Journal of Man-Machine Studies*, 29 (1988), 343–362.

Karat, C.M.; Brodie, C.; Karat, J.; Vergo, J.; and Alpert, S.R. Personalizing the user experience on ibm.com. *IBM Systems Journal*, 42, 4 (2003), 686–701.

Kennedy, M.; Te'eni, D.; and Treleavan, J. Impacts of decision task, data and display on strategies for extracting information. *International Journal of Human Computer Studies*, 48 (1998), 159–180.

Long, J., and Whitefield, A. (eds.). *Cognitive Ergonomics and Human-Computer Interaction*. Cambridge: Cambridge University Press, 1989.

Papanikolaou, K.; Grigoriadou, M.; Kornilakis, H.; and Magoulas, G. Personalizing the interaction in a web-based educational hypermedia system: the case of Inspire. *User Modeling and User-Adapted Interaction*, 13, 3 (2003), 213–267.

Paratala, T., and Surakka, V. Pupil size variation as an indication of affective processing. *International Journal of Human-Computer Studies*, 59 (2003), 185–198.

Parush, A. Interview with Donald Norman on mental models. 2004 (available at http://www.carleton.ca/hotlab/hottopics/Articles/DonNormanInterview.html).

Payne, J.W.; Bettman, J.R.; and Johnson, E.J. Adaptive strategy selection in decision making. *Journal of Experimental Psychology*, 14 (1988), 534–552.

Picard, R.W. A society of models for video and image libraries. Tech. Report 360, MIT Media Laboratory Perceptual Computing, 1988.

Picard, R.W., and Klein, J. Computers that recognize and respond to user emotion: theoretical and practical implications. *Interacting with Computers*, 14, 2 (2002), 141–169.

Price, H.E. The allocation of functions in systems. *Human Factors*, 27 (1985), 33–45.

Sanders, M.S., and McCormick, E.J. *Human Factors in Engineering and Design*, 7th ed. New York: McGraw-Hill, 1993.

Sandsjö, L.; Kadefors, R.; Lundberg, U.; and the PROCID group. PROCID recommendations for healthier computer work. In D. Caldenfors, J. Eklund, and L. Kiviloog (eds.), *Humans in a Complex Environment: Proceedings of the 34th Annual Congress of the Nordic Ergonomic Society*. Kolmården, Sweden: Nordic Ergonomic Society, 2003, Vol. II, p. 683.

Silver, M.S. *Systems that Support Decision Makers: Description and Analysis.* New York: John Wiley & Sons, 1991.

Smelcer, J.B., and Carmel, E. The effectiveness of different representations for managerial problem solving: comparing tables and maps. *Decision Sciences,* 28, 2 (1997), 391–420.

Te'eni, D. A cognitive-affective model of organizational communication for designing IT. *MIS Quarterly,* 25, 2 (2001), 251–312.

Te'eni, D. Language action perspective as a basis for communication support systems. *Communications of the ACM* (2006).

Te'eni, D.; Carey, J.; and Zhang, P. *Human-Computer Interaction: Designing Effective Organizational Information Systems.* Chichester: John Wiley & Sons, 2006.

Te'eni, D., and Feldman, R. Performance and satisfaction in adaptive websites: a laboratory experiment on search tasks within a task-adapted website. *Journal of AIS,* 2, 3 (2001), 1–28.

Tractinsky, N. Tools over solutions? Comments on interacting with computers, *Interacting with Computers,* 16, 4 (2004), 751–757.

Tractinsky, N.; Shoval-Katz, A.; and Ikar, D. What is beautiful is usable. *Interacting with Computers,* 13 (2000), 127–145.

Vessey, I. The effect of information presentation on decision making: an analysis using cost-benefit theory. *Information & Management,* 27 (1994), 103–119.

Vessey, I; Cognitive fit: a theory-based analysis of the graphs versus tables literature. *Decision Sciences,* 22, 2 (1991), 219–240.

Vessey, I., and Galletta, D. Cognitive fit: an empirical study of information acquisition. *Information Systems Research,* 2, 1 (1991), 63–84.

Wilson, G.M., and Sasse, M.A. From doing to being: getting closer to the user experience. *Interacting with Computers,* 16, 4 (2004), 697–705.

PART IV

IT USE AND IMPACT:
BELIEFS AND BEHAVIOR

CHAPTER 11

COMPUTER SELF-EFFICACY

A Review

DEBORAH COMPEAU, JANE GRAVILL, NICOLE HAGGERTY, AND
HELEN KELLEY

Abstract: *Computer self-efficacy (CSE) has become an important construct in information systems research. CSE has been shown to influence both user acceptance of technology and user learning about technology in a variety of settings across a wide range of technologies. This paper first reviews existing studies in the MIS literature on CSE to present the current state of knowledge regarding this influential construct and key antecedents. The paper then identifies important issues facing researchers in this area, such as determining clarity in CSE definition and CSE measurement with respect to the context of the task and the technology domain. Several ongoing research programs aimed at furthering our understanding of the formation of CSE in phases of the computer software learning process within organizations are discussed, followed by suggestions regarding key avenues for future research on CSE. Review of the literature indicated that most studies on CSE have focused on the impact of CSE, paying relatively less attention to its formation. The ongoing research programs presented in this paper, and the future research directions suggested, focus on important steps we believe researchers must take if they are to begin filling the gaps in our knowledge of how CSE develops in the workplace, and understanding what influences this development. If our goal as researchers is to understand how and why a behavior develops and to extend an influence on future behavior, understanding the role of CSE (and other less immediate antecedents of behavior) remains important. This paper aims to assist in achieving this goal, and to provide important direction regarding future research on CSE.*

Keywords: *Computer Self-efficacy, Individual Technology Adoption and Use, Computer Training and Learning, Causal Attributions, Self-regulated Learning, Technical Support*

INTRODUCTION

Computer self-efficacy (CSE) has become an important construct in information systems research. First discussed by Davis et al. (1989), and Gist et al. (1989), CSE was seen as an important influence on training outcomes. Since then, CSE has also been shown to influence user acceptance of technology more broadly—as a direct influence on use (e.g., Compeau and Higgins, 1995b; Compeau et al., 1999), or through other cognitions such as perceived ease of use (e.g., Venkatesh and Davis, 1996; Venkatesh et al., 2003).

 Although a significant amount has been written about the impact of computer self-efficacy, relatively less attention has been paid to its formation. Compeau and Higgins (1995a) found that

Figure 11.1 **Social Cognitive Theory**

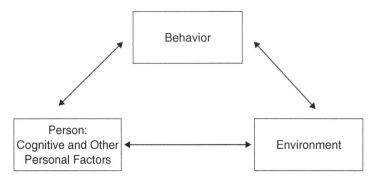

CSE was influenced by a behavior modeling training program. In another study, the same authors found that CSE was influenced by social influences in the organization (Compeau and Higgins, 1995b). Several authors have examined demographic and personality variables purported to influence CSE development (e.g., Henry and Stone, 1999; Thatcher and Perrewe, 2002).

At the same time, important questions about computer self-efficacy remain unanswered. Marakas et al. (1998), following Bandura, argue for the need for more domain specific measurement of CSE. Yet precisely where the domain should be defined is unclear. Is it a software package, a set of features in a software package, a computing platform (e.g., the PC)? How does task domain interact with technology domain in the definition of CSE? These are difficult questions about the very definition of the construct, which little research has addressed.

The purpose of this paper, then, is to review the state of research on computer self-efficacy in the information systems literature, with particular attention to its conceptualization, its influence, and its formation. We include a discussion of several research programs that we are undertaking that begin to address gaps and opportunities uncovered in our review of the computer self-efficacy literature. The paper concludes with an agenda for future research to further explore this important individual cognition.

THE NATURE OF COMPUTER SELF-EFFICACY

Computer self-efficacy is an adaptation of the broader notion of self-efficacy, which itself is conceptually situated within the broader context of social cognitive theory (Bandura, 1986). Within his notion of triadic reciprocality (Figure 11.1), Bandura lays a foundation for understanding the complexities of human functioning via the interactions that occur between the person (specifically his or her cognitions and emotions, including self-efficacy), his or her behaviors (including learning and performance), and the environment in which he or she is engaged. Accordingly, each of these three factors is seen as influencing the others while also being influenced by them. These complex interactions are difficult to study, yet Bandura's theorizing also provides us with the logic to tackle this complexity systematically. By theorizing and developing the causal sequence of a phenomenon within a specific and limited time frame, researchers can select a shortened and non-reciprocal causal chain to study—for example, that computer training design (an environmental factor) influences computer self efficacy (an individual factor) which in turn influences performance with computers (a behavior). The use of this strategy is implicit in much of the research on computer self-efficacy. We use this broad conceptualization of triadic reciprocality as an organizing framework throughout the paper to frame and illustrate the linkages between self-efficacy, other individual cognitive and personal factors, behavior, and the environment that have been investigated within various IS research streams and to suggest areas for future research. For each section of the paper we highlight the factors and directions of relationship implied by the body of research we review. Within this framework, self-efficacy (Bandura, 1997) represents an important individual factor whose adaptation, definition and measurement to the MIS field is explored next.

Definition and Measurement

Self-efficacy reflects a future-oriented belief about what one can accomplish, or according to Stajkovic and Luthans (1998), "an individual's convictions about his or her abilities to mobilize motivation, cognitive resources, and courses of action needed to successfully execute a specific task within a given context" (p. 62). In the context of IS research, computer self-efficacy is defined as "an individual judgment of one's capability to use a computer" (Compeau and Higgins, 1995b, p. 192). Thus, it is distinct from cognitive measures of competence, which reflect more on what one knows (Kraiger et al., 1993). It is also distinct from, albeit related to, outcome expectations, which reflect what one believes would occur if one were to complete some action.

A variety of views and measures of computer self-efficacy exist in the IS literature. They include both general computer self-efficacy (GCSE), focusing on the ability to use computers overall, and more specific computer self-efficacy measures (SCSE), tailored to the context of the study. For example, in a study of cooperative learning of database skills, SCSE was measured as an individual's expectation of achieving different grades on a data modeling assignment (Ryan et al., 2000). In other studies, SCSE was measured through a set of high-level statements about the individual's ability to use a particular system (e.g., Henry and Stone, 1994; Schmidt and Ford, 2003). For the sake of clarity, we use the term computer self-efficacy (CSE) throughout this paper when we discuss this important construct within the IS literature in general. We use the term general computer self-efficacy (GCSE) to refer to research studies and findings that utilize measures of an individual's assessment of his or her overall ability to use computers. We use the term specific computer self-efficacy (SCSE) with information on the specific IT task/context to refer to research studies and findings that utilize specific measures. Finally, we reserve the term self-efficacy (SE) to refer to the research and findings that we draw on from outside of the IT domain.

Most computer self-efficacy measures in the literature reflect the generative capacity of the individual to undertake some future behavior, as recommended by Bandura (1986, 1997). A few measures reflect more on the component skills of the behavior. For example, Torkzadeh and Koufteros (1994) measure SCSE through a series of thirty items that reflect the component skills of using a computer (e.g., moving a cursor around a worksheet, handling a floppy disk, and making selections from a menu) in addition to items that reflect task-oriented future behavior (e.g., using a computer to write a letter and writing simple programs).

Bandura (1986) argues that it is important to distinguish between these component skills and the ability to organize and execute courses of action:

> "In measuring driving self-efficacy, people are not asked to judge whether they can turn the ignition key, shift the automatic transmission, steer, accelerate and stop an automobile, blow the horn, monitor signs, read the flow of traffic and change traffic lanes. Rather they judge, whatever their subskills may be, the strength of their perceived efficaciousness to navigate through busy arterial roads, congested city traffic, onrushing freeway traffic, and twisting mountain roads." (p. 233)

The importance of task-focus relates, in part, to the distinction between computer self-efficacy and related constructs. Component skills, as reflected by the Torkzadeh and Koufteros items, are more difficult to separate from self-reports of cognitive user competence (Marcolin et al., 2000b). Thus, they might be seen as antecedent to the ability to use a computer for task-oriented behavior, but they lack the generative sense of being able to organize and execute courses of action. Sein et al. (1999) present a useful conceptualization of software knowledge levels that may be helpful in deciding on the types of questions to include in computer self-efficacy measures. They present a six-level hierarchy, with the first three levels representing various aspects of procedural knowledge.[1] The lowest is *command-based knowledge* (e.g., how to click on a button), followed by tool procedural knowledge (e.g., how to create a document or transaction), and *business procedural knowledge* (e.g., how to query a database for needed transactions). We maintain that a focus on either business procedural or tool procedural knowledge is preferable for measuring computer self-efficacy; such foci are also more closely aligned with Bandura's definition of self-efficacy, since the knowledge types focus on courses of action rather than on the component subskills required to complete the action.

A second issue with respect to the definition of computer self-efficacy relates to the dimensionality of the measure. Some recent studies suggest evidence of unreliability or multi-dimensionality in the Compeau and Higgins (1995b) measure of general computer self-efficacy. Gundlach and Thatcher (2000) argued that this was a multi-dimensional measure, reflecting "human assisted" and "individual" computer self-efficacy. Data presented by Thompson et al. (under review) supports an alternative view. It appears as though the items that reflect easier situations in which to use a system have become subject to a floor effect, and thus have different variance. In their study, the variances for the items on one factor were all smaller than those for the other factor (Table 11.1) and the distributions were markedly skewed for this factor as well. Thus, the existence of a second factor may reflect measurement issues rather than a conceptually different factor.

Interestingly, a comparison of the results from two studies, conducted in 1990 (Compeau and Higgins, 1995b) and 1999 (Marcolin et al., 2000a) do not show an increase in the means for the self-efficacy items, nor do they show large decreases in the variance (Table 11.2). The work of Gundlach and Thatcher and of Thompson et al. was conducted using student subjects, so perhaps the differences reflect those of different subgroups. Thompson et al. measured the construct on a seven-point scale, rather than using the two-part response recommended by Bandura, but this would not explain the variance difference. Moreover, data collected by Gravill et al. (2001) using managers and professionals used a seven-point scale but did not observe multi-dimensionality in the results. Thus, it seems important to ensure adequate variability in the response items, especially with student populations. Such variability may not be evident in all of the original questions developed by Compeau and Higgins.

Generality of Self-Efficacy

Bandura (1986, 1997) argues that self-efficacy (SE) judgments must be specific to the task in order to consistently predict behavior. He contrasts this domain-specific notion of SE with an overall general SE reflecting one's confidence in general (Bandura, 1997). Bandura argues that overall general SE is too broad to be of high predictive value, and that variations in domain specific confidence must be taken into account. This makes intuitive sense and has been discussed by several authors in information systems research. Yet the definition of "specific" remains relatively unexplored.

Marakas et al. (1998) provide an initial conceptualization of the domain for IS specific self-efficacy judgments. They suggest that GCSE is the weighted average of a collection of SCSE (defined at the software package level or the application environment level). They further argue

Table 11.1

Factor and Standard Deviation Scores

Item	Factor 1	Factor 2	Standard Deviation
...if someone showed me how to do it	0.835		0.936
...if someone helped me get started	0.815		1.114
...if I could call someone for help	0.813		1.121
...if I had seen someone using it	0.686	0.399	1.205
...if there was no one around		0.906	1.673
...if I had just the manuals		0.874	1.516
...if I had just the built-in help		0.633	1.689
...if I had a lot of time	0.449	0.562	1.235

Source: Data from Thompson et al. (2006).
Note: SE measured on a seven-point scale where 1 = not at all confident and 10 = totally confident.

Table 11.2

Mean and Standard Deviation Scores Across Studies

	Compeau and Higgins (1995a) (n = 394)		Marcolin et al. (2000) (n = 224)	
	Mean	Standard Deviation	Mean	Standard Deviation
...if there was no one around	5.16	2.79	4.34	2.61
...if I had just the manuals	5.85	2.69	5.02	2.71
...if I had seen someone using it	5.77	2.63	5.67	2.30
...if I could call someone for help	7.42	2.19	7.07	2.08
...if someone helped me get started	6.96	2.30	6.87	2.14
...if I had a lot of time	7.31	2.60	6.78	2.80
...if I had just the built-in help	5.58	2.55	5.52	2.82
...if someone showed me how to do it	7.71	2.24	7.77	2.05
	6.47	1.97	6.13	1.93

Source: Data from Compeau and Higgins (1995a); Marcolin et al. (2000).
Note: SE measured on an 11-point scale where 0 = could not use the computer under this circumstance, 1 = could do so, but not at all confident, and 10 = could do so and totally confident.

that GCSE is more resistant to influence in the short term, and may be a useful predictor of long-term behavior with respect to technology. SCSE judgments, on the other hand, are more susceptible to change, and are more important to understanding immediate task performance.

In IS research, we have almost always assessed SCSE at the software package level, assuming this to be the meaning of "specific" as defined by Bandura. Task considerations have been largely left out of our definitions, as noted by Marakas et al. (1998). Even where task is included in the CSE measure—for example, Compeau and Higgins's (1995b) measure asks about a task—the task is only vaguely defined as "something the user needs to accomplish." Thus, different respondents may reflect on very different kinds of tasks, resulting in a conceptual averaging across task domains that may be inappropriate. MIS researchers have, in effect, largely assumed that task is defined by the software. However, the challenge is that as software packages become increasingly comprehensive (e.g., MS Excel includes database management features; both Excel and PowerPoint include graphing features, etc.), there is less certainty that the task is defined by the software package. As software becomes more interrelated and interchangeable, it may become more removed from the work task. This suggests that it is perhaps necessary to be more precise in our CSE domain specificity, in order to reflect the tasks being performed by computer users that form the basis of their CSE judgments.

Thus, we need to think carefully about the domain of self-efficacy judgments and the relationship between task and technology in formulating our research and measurement contexts. Our definitions of GCSE and SCSE within IS have been, perhaps, too driven by technology considerations and not sufficiently driven by task considerations.

A second issue with regard to the definition of domain is the relationship between the general and specific computer self-efficacy judgments. Marakas et al. (1998) argue, as noted above, that GCSE can be thought of as a weighted average of a collection of SCSE judgments.

Agarwal et al. (2000) have examined the relationship between general computer self-efficacy and specific computer self-efficacy. They report on the relationship between GCSE and SCSE formed during computer training. They show that GCSE influences the initial development of SCSE (i.e., self-efficacy for the first software package learned) but not for SCSE developed for the second software package learned. They also showed the existence of cross-over effects between the specific software efficacies.

Compeau (1992) also discussed the evolution of GCSE and SCSE judgments throughout a classroom training program. In their program, students learned two application software packages (a word processor and a spreadsheet). This contrasts with Agarwal et al. (2000) whose subjects learned Windows followed by a spreadsheet, which can be thought of as a progression from beginning to more advanced topics (for novice computer users). But the Compeau study looked at software packages that did not explicitly build on one another. Their results, while similar to those of Agarwal et al. (2000) suggest a slightly different pattern.

Compeau (1992) reported the mean of GCSE, SCSE for word processing, and SCSE for spreadsheets at four different points in time (before training, after training in the first package, after training in the second package, and after the completion of the training program) for two groups of subjects. The first group learned the spreadsheet followed by the word processor; the second group learned the word processor followed by the spreadsheet. The results are reported in Table 11.3.

Repeated measures analysis of variance was conducted to see whether computer self-efficacy had changed through the course of training. Six one-way analyses of variance were conducted, for general self-efficacy, word processing self-efficacy, and spreadsheet self-efficacy for each of the two training groups. The overall tests showed significant differences for all of the self-efficacy measures. Follow-up tests were conducted using the Neuman-Keuls post hoc test.

For the group that learned the spreadsheet first, GCSE scores increased between the pre-training measure and the first post measure (after spreadsheet training), and then stayed constant from the first to the second post measure (after word-processing training) and to the follow-up conducted at the conclusion of the entire session. SCSE for word processing increased both following spreadsheet training and word processing training. It did not change from the second post measure to the follow up. SCSE for spreadsheets increased following spreadsheet training, and then stayed constant following word processing training through the follow-up measure. An equivalent pattern was observed for the group who learned word processing first.

These patterns suggest that training in either package influenced specific computer self-efficacy with respect to the package. SCSE regarding the other package in the study increased, but only if

Table 11.3

Self-Efficacy Scores Across Time

	Mean Scores for Self-Efficacy (Standard Deviation)			
	Pre-Training	Post 1	Post 2	Follow-Up
Group 1 (SS/WP: n = 35)				
General	4.11_a (1.98)	5.28_b (1.87)	5.47_b (1.91)	5.25_b (2.19)
WP	4.24_a (2.12)	5.21_b (1.97)	6.26_c (1.67)	6.20_c (2.44)
Spreadsheet	3.59_a (1.96)	5.93_b (1.44)	6.26_b (1.67)	5.44_b (2.65)
Group 2 (WP/SS: n = 40)				
General	4.14_a (2.36)	5.11_b (2.29)	5.25_b (2.26)	5.33_b (2.35)
WP	4.25_b (2.33)	5.54_b (2.22)	5.78_b (2.43)	5.74_b (2.31)
Spreadsheet	3.70_a (2.31)	4.34_b (2.35)	5.24_c (2.33)	5.52_c (2.61)

Source: From Compeau (1992).

$_{a,b,c}$ Means in the same row with the same subscript do not differ at the 0.001 level. No comparisons are made across rows.

the other training had not yet occurred. Thus crossover effects, such as those observed by Agarwal et al. (2000) seem to be more limited, perhaps moderated by proximal experiences. General computer self-efficacy beliefs showed some malleability through training, but were only affected by the first day of training (regardless of which software package was taught). This suggests that GCSE may not be simply an average of other SCSEs, since if it were, it would be expected to increase following both training sessions.

Summary

Based on this review of the nature of computer self-efficacy in terms of its definition, measurement, and domain specificity, several important conclusions can be drawn. First, it remains essential that IS researchers adapt the definition of computer self-efficacy to the task and context of study. Such definitional clarity should ensure that the domain of the task, and therefore the self-efficacy judgment, is clearly specified within the context of the research being undertaken. Understanding task considerations may be a particularly important area to consider. This specificity in definition should also ensure that the measure reflects a computer user's generative capacity to undertake a future computer-based task behavior and not a component sub-skill. Finally, with respect to measurement, it is essential that sample selection and measure adaptation attend to considerations of variability in response items so that underlying scales reflect the unidimensional nature of computer self-efficacy.

INFLUENCE OF COMPUTER SELF-EFFICACY

Bandura (1986) argues that self-efficacy influences a variety of individual behaviors and emotions. Within the framework of triadic reciprocality, computer self-efficacy is seen as influencing other cognitions and emotions of individuals, including perceived usefulness, ease of use, and anxiety. CSE is also seen as influencing individual behavior, including behavior choice (often operationalized as behavioral intention), performance, and effort/persistence.

Three of these four outcomes (behavior choice, performance, and anxiety) have been extensively studied in the information systems context. Effort/persistence has not been studied to date, though it is discussed later in our discussion of computer self-efficacy development in the context of self-regulated learning. The evidence on the influence of CSE in the remaining three areas is examined below. Table 11.A1 in the Appendix summarizes the studies and the effects observed.

Influence on Behavior Choice

Research in a variety of domains has clearly established the importance of CSE as an influence on people's decisions to use computers and on the extent of their use. As evidenced by the body of research highlighted in Table 11.A1 in the Appendix, CSE has been related to a multitude of behaviors, including computer adoption and use, various types of behavior intention (to behave ethically, to purchase) numerous job-related behaviors (such as absenteeism, career interests, job stress, knowledge sharing), resistance to change, and participation in systems development (see Table 11.A1 for specific references).

These studies provide clear evidence. Computer self-efficacy exerts an influence on individuals' choice behaviors with respect to information technology. Whether directly or indirectly, the degree of confidence possessed by an individual regarding some aspect of computing behavior (e.g., personal usage decisions, participation in systems development, knowledge sharing) exerts a strong influence on his or her ultimate choice to undertake these behaviors. Thus, when attempting to improve adoption and usage rates for IS applications, one key influence to examine is users' CSE. If non-users are low in CSE, then mechanisms to improve their confidence may be productively introduced in order to increase future usage.

Influence on Performance

Research on training, while less abundant, has been equally clear on the positive influence of computer self-efficacy. Table 11.A1 in the Appendix summarizes the studies investigating this aspect of the influence of CSE. In this research, CSE has been shown to influence the development of both declarative and procedural knowledge in training, performance in computer courses at university, task performance outside of training, and post-training motivation to learn. Further, the specific influence of SCSE (for spreadsheets) on performance was moderated by task complexity, with a stronger influence for high-complexity tasks. This suggests that individuals with greater SCSE attain higher performance when undertaking more complex tasks that those with lesser SCSE, which makes sense, since from a motivational standpoint, high self-efficacy is posited to influence choice behavior as well as persistence, thus leading to the development of greater capability.

Influence on Other Cognitions and Emotions

Within Bandura's notion of other individual cognitive and emotional factors (1986), MIS research has examined the influence of CSE on various other general and specific CSE judgments; other cognitions such as perceived usefulness, ease of use, outcome expectations (both personal and performance); and emotional responses such as playfulness, commitment, affect, and anxiety as outlined in Table 11.A1.

The results consistently show that CSE is related to other cognitive and emotional responses that influence choice behavior and/or performance. Interestingly, Venkatesh et al. (2003) suggested elimination of CSE from the antecedents of behavior in their unified theory of the acceptance and

Figure 11.2   **Influence of Computer Self-Efficacy**

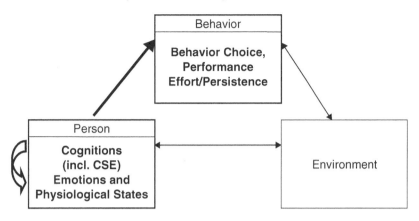

use of technology (UTAUT). They argued that if the influence of CSE is mediated by other factors, it is not necessary to include it in a model of technology acceptance. By contrast, we believe CSE should continue to be included, at least in some circumstances. Eliminating CSE makes sense if one's goal is prediction of behavior rather than understanding or influencing it. That is, if the goal is to predict who will use a computer, it is most efficient to measure the proximal antecedents, such as intention, perceived usefulness, etc. But if the goal is also to understand how and why a behavior develops and to exert an influence on future behavior, then understanding the role of CSE (and other less immediate antecedents) remains important.

Research involving CSE and anxiety has examined different directions of the relationship. Staples et al. (1999) viewed anxiety as an influence on self-efficacy, while Compeau and her colleagues (Compeau and Higgins, 1995b; Compeau et al., 1999) viewed self-efficacy as an influence on anxiety. In each of these studies, SE and anxiety were measured at the same point in time, so the direction of causality is somewhat arbitrary. Johnson and Marakas (2000) demonstrate in an experimental manipulation that anxiety is related to SCSE (for spreadsheets) and that the developed level of SCSE is related to subsequent anxiety that exists throughout the performance. Consequently, considering the ordering of these variables is important and consistent with Figure 11.2, which demonstrates the reciprocal relationship between anxiety and self-efficacy (Bandura, 1986). Furthermore, Lindsley et al. (1995) argue that emotional arousal (including anxiety) is a key reason for the existence of efficacy-performance spirals, and that such spirals—through mechanisms like SE and anxiety—become self-fulfilling prophecies.

Summary

Research in a variety of domains, and with a range of different populations, has shown computer self-efficacy to exert significant influences on a variety of individuals' computing-related behaviors and other cognitions and emotions. Directly or indirectly, individuals' confidence in their abilities influences the degree to which they use computers (given a choice), their interest in particular careers, the types of work-related tasks performed, and even their commitment to their jobs when technology usage is required (and particularly salient). Individuals' confidence also influences their level of performance, both in learning and in task-performance contexts. Although

Figure 11.3 **Antecedents of Computer Self-Efficacy**

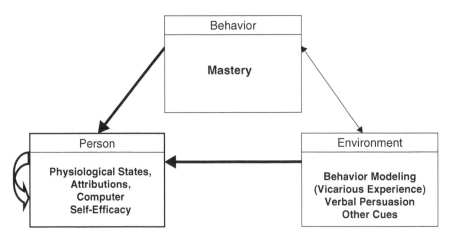

some research questions the importance of including CSE in studies of technology-related behavior (Venkatesh et al., 2003), we believe that the research evidence to date suggests CSE is an important factor that needs to be better understood.

DEVELOPMENT OF COMPUTER SELF-EFFICACY

Relatively less attention has been paid to the development of computer self-efficacy than to its influence. Yet the research does suggest important influences on CSE development. The authors' collective research also considers the various domains in which CSE is formed (training and learning, the introduction of new technology, support) and the ways in which the influences operate in these domains. Figure 11.3 depicts the scope of the influences of key antecedents on CSE development. Within the triadic reciprocality framework, physiological states and attributions are seen as individual cognitions and factors; enactive mastery is viewed as a behavior carried out by the individual; and vicarious experience (behavior modeling of others), verbal persuasion (by others), and other cues (i.e., tasks, resources, other situational factors) are viewed as environmental influences—all of which can influence an individual's development of CSE.

Antecedents

Bandura (1997) identifies four principal information sources, in order of strength of influence, which form efficacy beliefs over time: enactive mastery, vicarious experience, verbal persuasion, and physiological and affective states. According to Bandura (1997), these four primary sources of SE vary in the level of information they convey and their degree of interrelatedness. Furthermore, these four antecedents are very complex in nature (Gist et al., 1992). The patterns that emerge from this body of research suggest that several important antecedents directly influence CSE development, though overall we still explain relatively little of the variance in CSE through these variables. Table 11.A2 in the Appendix summarizes the studies examined in reviewing the research on the development of CSE.

Mastery

Enactive mastery is defined as information based on "authentic mastery experiences" (Bandura, 1986, p. 399), or past experiences with performing tasks. Bandura (1997) states that enactive mastery experiences are indicators of capability. These experiences are the most influential of the four sources, and provide the most direct information about performance accomplishments. According to Bandura (1997), successful experiences build strong self-efficacy beliefs, whereas failed experiences weaken especially less-established SE beliefs. The relationship between unsuccessful performance and mastery expectations is complicated, and depends partly on the timing of the task and the total pattern of experiences one has with the action (Bandura, 1986). Furthermore, Bandura stresses that "enactive mastery produces stronger and more generalized" (1997, p. 80) SE judgments than do the other three sources of information.

A variety of measurements for enactive mastery have been developed and tested. Enactive mastery has been measured using self-report measurements, demonstrations of performance via test results, and measures of computer experience (years of use, amount of training, number of packages learned). Regardless of the type of measurement instrument used to measure mastery, this source of information has been consistently reported to be strongly correlated with CSE. A higher level of enactive mastery leads to higher CSE beliefs (Table 11.A2).

Vicarious Experience

Bandura (1997) theorizes that "vicarious experiences mediated through modeled attainments" (pg. 86), which include either seeing or visualizing, are effective tools for the development of self-efficacy. Vicarious experience influences SE by providing competency information and through comparisons to the accomplishments of other individuals (Bandura, 1997). According to Bandura (1997), individuals compare their capabilities to the attainment of others because "there are no absolute measures of adequacy" (p. 86) for most activities and tasks. Individuals persuade themselves that they should also be able to achieve at least some similar performance achievements as others. By modeling another's behavior, the observer's self-efficacy is strengthened. However, the degree of influence of vicarious experience will depend upon the talents of the individual being observed. SE increases when one exceeds the attainments of associates/competitors, but SE decreases when associates/competitors outperform the observer. Moreover, vicarious experience has the strongest influence when model's traits (e.g., age and capability) are similar to the observer's characteristics, and the observer has little prior experience.

Modes of vicarious experience take different forms and influence SE in different ways depending on the type of information they convey (Bandura, 1997). These modes of modeling include actual modeling, symbolic modeling provided by various visual media, self-modeling, and cognitive self-modeling.

Most of the research investigating vicarious experiences, as outlined in Table 11.A2, has focused on the observational learning based on modeling the trainer and symbolic modeling mode (i.e., visual media). The positive effect of vicarious experience on CSE with regard to specific technology has been investigated by several IS researchers in both laboratory training settings and cross sectional surveys. Interestingly, this research has also highlighted variations in the influence of vicarious experience based on the type of vicarious experience observed and on the nature of the task. For example, Bolt et al. (2001) reported that task complexity moderated the influence of the type of vicarious experience (i.e., the type of training method—modeling vs. lecture) on spreadsheet SCSE. Compeau and Higgins (1995a) found support for the modeling videotape manipulation for one software package (spreadsheet) but not another (word processing). Yi and Davis (2003) have explored the four sub-processes of observational learning (Bandura, 1997), and found that observational learning, which consisted of attention, retention, production, and motivation dimensions, significantly influenced specific post-training computer self-efficacy.

Verbal Persuasion

Verbal persuasion refers to the use of suggestive persuasion by others to persuade an individual that one has a given level of capabilities (Bandura, 1997). Verbal persuasion can increase SE when positive, realistic persuasive information is conveyed, which in turn results in greater effort and persistence than if individuals have self-doubts when faced with difficulties. Individuals providing the persuasive feedback needed to possess the evaluative competencies to perform actions/tasks (Bandura, 1986), and the individuals must be viewed as credible and believable (Bandura, 1977a, 1977b). As suggested by Bandura (1978, 1986), verbal persuasion can increase one's self-efficacy, but is rarely enough to create enduring high levels of efficacy beliefs. The greatest benefit of verbal persuasion occurs in situations where individuals believe that they can produce effects through their behaviors (Bandura, 1997).

Verbal persuasion in the IS literature (Table 11.A2) has been either measured directly or manipulated in several studies. In studies using direct measures, verbal persuasion in combination with vicarious experience, when used to manipulate general computer self-efficacy, resulted in an increase in individuals' judgments of their capabilities to use computer technology (Hill et al., 1987; Smith, 1994) and the effects of verbal persuasion on GCSE held in another cross-sectional study (Compeau and Higgins, 1995b), but not in a longitudinal study of the same subjects (Compeau et al., 1999; Martocchio, 1994). Similar positive relationships between verbal persuasion and CSE have been found in experimental studies conducted in a training context (see Table 11.A2 for a list of studies in this area).

One's self-efficacy, according to Bandura (1997), can be influenced by the manner in which performance feedback is structured or framed. Attributional or evaluative feedback can be communicated in ways that enhance or undermine an individual's SE (Bandura, 1997). For example, Schunk and his colleagues (e.g., Schunk, 1982, 1983, 1984; Schunk and Cox, 1986; Schunk and Rice, 1986) investigated the effects of attributional feedback on SE judgments. They reported that attributional feedback highlighting effort and ability as reasons for success enhanced children's mathematical and reading SE judgments. From an IS perspective, Martocchio and Dulebohn (1994) reported that trainees who received feedback attributed to factors within their control, a causal dimension of attributions or causes of one's spreadsheet performance, demonstrated higher levels of SE, whereas trainees who received feedback attributed to factors outside their control had lower levels of SE.

Physiological States

According to Bandura (1997), physiological and affective states have an influence on self-efficacy judgments. The cognitive processing of emotional states is likely influenced by a variety of factors such as the level of action, appraisal of the sources of the arousal, prior experiences on how the arousal affects one's performance levels, and the conditions under which the arousal is elicited (Bandura, 1986). The optimal level of the emotional state is determined by the nature of the task plus the causal inferences concerning the arousal.

Certain negative emotional reactions such as fear, anxiety, and tenseness, or stressful situations, can lower computer self-efficacy. However, positive emotional states, such as excitement or enthusiasm, can enhance CSE. The few studies that have been undertaken in this area (Table 11.A2) have found a negative relationship between anxiety and CSE (Havelka, 2003; Johnson and Marakas, 2000; Martocchio, 1992; Staples et al., 1999).

In summary, a small number of studies have examined one or more of the primary sources of computer self-efficacy information. However, only one study, that by Kelley et al. (2000), has examined all four sources of CSE simultaneously. These investigations reported, for the most part, significant relationships between the four sources of information—enactive mastery, vicarious experience, verbal persuasion, and physiological and affective states—and CSE. Yet overall, we still explain relatively little of the variance in CSE through these variables.

Other Self-Efficacy Cues

Bandura focuses on the four principal sources of self-efficacy information. Yet Gist and Mitchell (1992) propose that the SE development process includes the assessment of a large number of external cues (e.g., tasks, and resources) and internal cues (e.g., motivation, and performance strategies). According to Gist and Mitchell (1992), internal cues comprise immediate affect or mood, personality factors (e.g., self-esteem, and personality types), and the general physical condition of an individual that produces arousal, whereas external cues include environmental factors (e.g., distractions, physical or psychological risk, physical conditions, and geographic settings), the complexity of the task, and the amount of resources required to complete the task successfully (e.g., material resources, time, and staff).

According to Schunk (1991), individuals cognitively filter the information conveyed by the four sources of SE by weighing, interpreting, and combining the contributions of personal factors (e.g., numbers and patterns of successful and unsuccessful performances) and situational factors (e.g., extent of external assistance received). For example, Type A personality (an internal cue) is generally associated with higher levels of psychological arousal. In addition, vicarious experience may provide external cue information on task ability and complexity or psychological strategies such as coping with anxiety (Gist and Mitchell, 1992). Each of these cues may then influence the development of self-efficacy.

As demonstrated in Table 11.A2, IS studies in this area have examined a wide range of internal and external cues outside of the four sources of SE information theorized by Bandura. In fact, our review of the literature reveals a range of antecedent cues (see table for specific studies) such as support, ease of use, task difficulty, complexity and novelty, physical conditions, teamwork, computer attitude, family income level, personal innovativeness, and more. Yet, little effort has yet been made to systematically explore the relationship of these internal and external cues to the four sources of CSE and the manner in which these cues operate through the four sources. Nevertheless, these studies provide early evidence that internal and external cues influence the formation of self-efficacy (Martocchio, 1994; Ryan et al., 2000; Sheng et al., 2003).

Summary

Our review indicates that CSE is influenced by all four of Bandura's sources of self-efficacy information. Moreover, consistent with Gist and Mitchell (1992), other influences also contribute to the formation of these judgments. However, the evidence on the antecedents of CSE remains less voluminous than that related to its outcomes, and we lack a holistic picture of how CSE judgments are formed and changed over time.

Figure 11.4   **Applying CSE Theory to Practice**

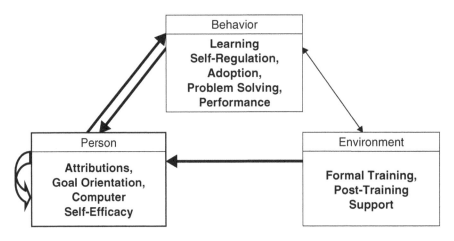

The following section describes our current attempts to understand how CSE judgments are formed, and how they influence behavior, by looking specifically at four contexts in which CSE plays a role. We draw primarily upon our own ongoing research, but also incorporate other findings that apply to the specific contexts, as a means of applying CSE theory to practice.

APPLYING CSE THEORY TO PRACTICE

Our ongoing programs of research adopt a holistic view of computer self-efficacy development by examining various events within the lifecycle of computer usage such as formal training to self-directed learning, new technology introductions, and everyday use. We are interested in understanding the different environments in which people develop confidence in their abilities during these events and in identifying the web of influences that drive CSE judgments across these different domains. Formal training settings are often the first, and generally the most obvious, context in which CSE is developed. But while formal training is an important place where CSE can be intentionally influenced, it represents only a small portion of the learning undertaken by individuals. Self-regulated learning is by far the more common means by which users learn (e.g., Nelson, 1991). Thus, we have also examined how CSE develops in this context. Even when learning is not the primary goal of the user, development of capability and CSE takes place. We also examined the development of CSE during the introduction of new technology, specifically enterprise-wide information systems, and during the resolution of technical problems with the aid of organizational support. The former represents a situation where work and learning are being managed simultaneously, as individuals adjust to a new technological domain while striving to maintain their task performance. The latter represents a situation where a technological problem during task performance has resulted in an inability to complete the task and where learning may be necessary to resolve the problem. Figure 11.4 depicts this theorizing within the framework of triadic reciprocality. Attributions, goal orientation, and self-regulation are seen as individual cognitions and factors influencing computer self-efficacy. Problem solving and self-regulated learning activities are seen as behaviors that influence computer self-efficacy, while learning, adoption, and performance are seen as behaviors that are influenced by computer self-efficacy. Environmental influences stem from the contexts of the various research streams, including attributes of formal training and post-training support provided to the individual.

The following sections review both our own research and relevant other research in each of these domains.

Formal Training

Computer self-efficacy is viewed as an important outcome of training. Given its influence on training performance, discussed above, and its influence on choice behaviors outside of training, recognizing formal training as an opportunity to improve users' judgments of their capability is critical. In fact, Marcolin et al. (2000b), following Kraiger et al. (1993), define CSE as an affective measure of a user's competence. This positions CSE as an important learning outcome in its own right.

Each of the four sources of efficacy information plays a role in formal training. Guided mastery is evident in the self-paced, customized experiences of computer-aided learning and in the practice sessions that are typically included in a training course. Verbal persuasion occurs through the feedback of the trainer, who advises the trainee about his or her level of capability and helps to enhance self-efficacy judgments. By reminding trainees of their level of progress and their capability relative to other novice learners, trainees can be encouraged to reflect more positively on their experiences. Thus, they develop confidence that, despite their current low performance, they will ultimately be able to learn the required behaviors. We have already discussed the relationship between CSE and physiological states. Behavior modeling remains the most investigated aspect of formal training from a self-efficacy perspective.

Behavior modeling can be part of the formal design of the training program (Compeau and Higgins, 1995a; Gist et al., 1989; Johnson and Marakas, 2000; Simon and Werner, 1996; Simon et al., 1996). It also occurs through every action of the trainer and through the behaviors of other training participants. Compeau and Higgins (1995a) acknowledged that the trainer in their study acted as a behavior model for all trainees, with a videotaped model as an additional modeling stimulus for their experimental groups. By demonstrating how to use the software, showing the resolution of her own mistakes if she made them, and explaining her approach to using the software, the trainer acted as a behavior model. One key difference between the trainer-as-model and the videotaped model was in the social comparison. Bandura (1986) and others argue that the most effective behavior models are those who are viewed as similar by the trainees, since modeling represents a process of social comparison. Thus, compared to a novice demonstrating his or her own use of the software (which is how Compeau and Higgins constructed their modeling intervention), the trainer, a software professional, was quite different from the novice trainees. Nonetheless, in their exposure to the trainer over the course of the training session, the trainees observed and modeled her behavior, with the result that their confidence increased, regardless of the training group. Consistent with social cognitive theory, however, SCSE increased more for those subjects who were exposed to the novice model.

Modeling is not limited to that provided by the trainer. Lim et al. (1997) found that subjects engaged in co-discovery learning learned more than those engaged in a learning alone protocol. While the authors do not assess computer self-efficacy, their results may also reflect the modeling that takes place between the learners in a co-discovery setting where each individual acts as a model for the other.

Models differ in the means through which they present information. Some models demonstrate flawless performance, executed easily. These masterful models demonstrate how it is done right, by those who are capable of doing it well. This is typical of many video-based training materials—a carefully rehearsed script is used to provide a demonstration, which is then edited to ensure that any errors are removed. The problem with these models is that they demonstrate a level of understanding so far beyond that of the learner that they can actually have a demoralizing effect.

An alternative—the coping model—demonstrates correct performance, but does so while also showing the likelihood of making errors and the coping strategies that one uses to deal with them when they occur. This sort of model is seen as more similar by the learner and their level of performance as more attainable. Thus, through the process of social comparison, a coping model typically exerts a greater effect than a masterful model (Meichenbaum, 1971).

The influence of different kinds of modeling has implications for how trainers structure their demonstrations. Often, demonstrators are reluctant to make errors as they view them as undermining their "expert" status in front of the trainee. Thus, when they make an error, they apologize, quickly recover while telling the trainees to ignore their mistake, and then proceed with the correct method. But by using mistakes that naturally occur, the trainer has the opportunity to persuade the trainee that "even the experts make mistakes" and, therefore, that making mistakes doesn't make one incapable of learning. This approach directly aims to improve self-efficacy, and Compeau (2002) found it to be characteristic of effective trainers, as rated by other trainers.

Yi and Davis (2003) explored the role of retention enhancement techniques in a modeling intervention. They found that their intervention, aimed at manipulating participants' retention enhancement abilities, significantly improved task performance through its effects on the retention processes dimension of observational learning. Observational learning processes were represented in this study as a second-order construct comprised of four dimensions of attention, retention, production, and motivation.

In conclusion, computer self-efficacy develops during formal training as an outcome of the training design, the formal behaviors of the trainer (including his or her modeling of appropriate performance and his or her verbal persuasion through feedback), and the informal, and perhaps unintentional, behaviors of the trainer and other training participants. CSE, in turn, influences training performance and choices about how to use the new skills after training, thus extending the influence of training to the workplace.

Self-Regulated Learning

Although formal training is one important context in which self-efficacy develops, it must be remembered that most user learning is self-directed (e.g., Gravill and Compeau, 2003; Nelson, 1991). There are several differences between the formal training setting and the self-directed setting that must be accounted for in our theorizing about CSE.

Self-regulated learning refers to a form of learning where individuals are required to control or manage their own learning experience. The process of self-regulation requires individuals to regularly monitor their learning progress, think about their abilities, evaluate how well they have understood the material they are learning, and to react accordingly (Bandura 1991; Kanfer and Ackerman 1989; Zimmerman 1989). The self-regulatory process, involving self-focused attention, provides individuals with the opportunity to evaluate their own performance that can influence their confidence in their abilities, or their self-efficacy. Individuals use self-regulated learning strategies such as determining what things they need to learn to accomplish a given task, determining what skills need more practice, determining the best learning approach to accomplish their learning goals, or monitoring their learning progress. The outcome of these strategic learning-related decisions can affect their confidence in their abilities to successfully perform tasks in the specific domain. If the feedback from this decision-making process is positive, individuals' confidence in their abilities may increase. However, if the feedback is negative, their confidence in their abilities, or their self-efficacy, may decrease.

The self-regulated learning context emphasizes the importance of individual differences, as individuals have control over their learning experience in this setting, and can make choices that directly influence their own learning. For example, individuals can choose to terminate their learning prematurely, can choose not to further practice a new skill if they believe they have mastered the skill, or can make other poor choices that limit their learning. Alternatively, in the classroom setting, learners' choices are largely influenced by the instructor in the form of classroom instruction or exercises and quizzes administered. Therefore, the influence of individual differences may be weaker in classroom settings where the instructor determines the amount of time learners spend on specific tasks (Brown, 2001), while their dependence on their self-evaluation, self-monitoring, self-control, and self-motivation skills is increased in the self-regulated learning context (Bandura, 1991). Two particular factors are being investigated in this research stream: goal orientation and self-awareness. Each of these is briefly discussed below.

Goal Orientation and Self-Efficacy

Researchers have identified goal orientation as an important factor to consider when examining the learning process (Bandura, 1987; Bandura and Cervone, 1983; Ford et al., 1998; Kanfer et al., 1994; Kanfer and Heggestad, 1999; Schmidt and Ford, 2003; VandeWalle et al., 1999). Mastery goal orientation refers to individuals' desire to develop new skills, understand tasks, and successfully achieve self-referenced standards for mastery of the learning objective. Individuals with a mastery orientation are interested in the learning process, understand that their mistakes are part of the learning process, and perceive mistakes as opportunities to learn and improve (Martocchio and Dulebohn, 1994). Therefore, these individuals, even if difficulties are encountered, tend to be resilient and demonstrate positive levels of self-efficacy (Bandura and Cervone, 1983). Mastery-oriented individuals are more likely to perceive mistakes as useful experiences for developing strategies to improve performance, as they believe they have the ability to organize the resources required to meet their learning objectives (Bandura and Cervone, 1983).

Performance goal orientation drives individuals' desire to achieve superiority in performing or achieving the goal compared to others, avoid negative judgments from others, to surpass normative-based standards, or to succeed with little effort (Kanfer et al., 1994). Performance orientation causes individuals to believe that their skill set or knowledge is fixed, and to therefore focus on demonstrating their competence (Brown, 2001).

The differences in individuals' goal orientation influence their approach to learning, their desire to set either learning-oriented or performance-oriented goals, or the persistence they choose to demonstrate during their learning experiences. As high mastery-orientation tends to cause individuals to believe they can improve their abilities, these individuals tend to demonstrate greater persistence in learning, perceive difficult tasks as challenges from which to learn, and perceive mistakes or negative feedback as learning experiences. High performance-orientation tends to cause individuals to avoid difficult tasks, as these tasks are viewed as potential for not performing well, or to terminate learning following negative feedback on performance. The "fixed skillset" view of individuals high in performance-orientation tends to cause them to interpret negative feedback in a self-diagnostic manner, as opposed to a task-diagnostic manner, thereby deflating their confidence in their abilities.

Interestingly, the interaction between goal orientation and self-efficacy within a particular domain can cause individuals to demonstrate a variety of behavioral patterns. Those high in performance orientation may show mastery-oriented behavior patterns in domains in which they have high confidence in their ability. Individuals high in performance-orientation and low in self-efficacy are much more likely to avoid challenging tasks, exhibit limited persistence in the face of difficulty or failure, and be easily distracted during their learning experiences. Individuals with low self-efficacy and high performance goal orientation are also more likely to engage in self-handicapping behaviors, such as introducing factors that reduce the likelihood of success and can serve as an excuse for poor performance (e.g., the computer training program hung, the computer accidentally rebooted), that serve to further limit their learning experiences.

Self-Awareness and Self-Efficacy

One's degree of self-attention is a second key factor to be considered when examining self-regulation (Bandura, 1977b; Carver and Scheier, 1981). As both self-awareness and self-efficacy play important roles in self-regulated learning, the relationship between the two needs to be examined in the self-regulated learning context (Gravill and Compeau, 2003).

Self-awareness is defined as the tendency to reflect upon one's own thoughts and abilities, or as self-understanding. Individuals' tendency toward self-awareness is believed to be associated with higher learning outcomes (e.g., Kruger and Dunning, 1999; Renner and Renner, 2001; Zimmerman and Martinez-Pons, 1988). Individuals' accurate assessment of their capabilities, or high self-awareness, is key to effective learning experiences, as those with high self-awareness, resulting in an increased understanding of their strengths and weaknesses, are in a better position to make effective learning choices. In addition to suggesting that greater self-awareness promotes greater self-efficacy, our research has found greater confidence in one's abilities can also promote greater self-awareness. Gravill et al. (2002) conceptualized self-awareness of abilities as the difference between individuals' self-reported and demonstrated knowledge of a spreadsheet computer software package, and found that those subjects with higher pretest GCSE had a smaller difference in these scores, or were more accurate in their self-assessments. This relationship was primarily attributed to the behavioral outcomes, or actions, caused by one's GCSE as they progress through the learning process. Bandura has established a theoretical link between self-efficacy and action and has conducted supporting studies, explaining that the central focus of self-efficacy theory is the dynamic interplay between self-referent thought, affect, and action (Bandura, 1986). SE has been shown to be related to the level of individuals' activity in their day-to-day learning activities and their interaction with their environment, from which they have the opportunity to become more self-aware of their capabilities.

As noted earlier, studies in MIS literature have examined the positive link between computer self-efficacy and individuals' participation in training, their performance in training, and their adoption of technology. This means that as individuals with high CSE advance through their day-to-day learning experiences, they tend to take advantage of opportunities (such as testing new software functionality or discussing new technology features with others) that provide them with important feedback regarding their current skills. The resulting increased awareness and ability to accurately self-assess one's skills is key to individuals' ongoing effective self-regulated learning, as effective identification of training needs is the first step in successful self-managed learning (Gravill et al., 2001). Ineffective self-assessment of ability has been shown to introduce problems in the learning process, or to limit learning outcomes (Kruger and Dunning, 1999; Renner and Renner, 2001).

Ultimately, this research initiative indicates that CSE plays a role in individuals' knowledge calibration, and suggests that CSE should be considered in situations where effective knowledge calibration is important, such as self-managed learning.

Summary

The self-regulated learning context is an important, yet under-researched, aspect of IS learning. Our preliminary investigations suggest a particularly important role for individual differences in this context, and demonstrate how two specific differences (goal orientation and self-awareness) influence the development of CSE, and thus other learning outcomes.

NEW TECHNOLOGY INTRODUCTION

Kelley et al. (1999, 2000) concentrate on the formation of specific computer self-efficacy in the context of post-system conversion of new enterprise systems. From a theoretical standpoint, the degree of behavioral change and learning required by complex computer technology such as enterprise systems makes them an ideal context for studying the formation of computer self-efficacy during the learning process. The implementation of complex computer technology creates an environment that is generally characterized by users as unpredictable, uncontrollable, and uncertain. Enterprise system users are motivated to gain a realistic causal understanding of their changing computer environment and to explain important computer-related performance events in order to predict their own behavioral actions, such as usage patterns and control events, in their new computer environments. Hence, the formation of CSE relies on a complex process of sense-making (i.e., attribution theory of motivation), which includes interpretation and attribution activities by individuals. During this sense-making process, individuals are attempting to identify the causes of actions and behaviors in order to determine how they should respond to the new enterprise system during present and future performance activities. Thus, users of recently implemented enterprise systems need to understand, and make sense of, events and behaviors in their radically changing work environments before they will effectively learn, adopt, and use this technology.

According to Bandura (1997), most motivation is cognitively generated through the exercise of forethought or retrospective reasoning. People "form beliefs about what they can do, they anticipate likely positive and negative outcomes of different pursuits, and they set goals for themselves and plan courses of action designed to realize valued future outcomes and avoid aversive ones" (p. 122). Outcome expectancies and cognized goals represent the key anticipatory mechanisms while causal attributions of past performance represent the key retrospective mechanism.

Kelley et al. (1999, 2000) focused on one specific type of motivational processes—causal attributions from the theoretical perspective of Weiner's (1985) attribution theory of motivation. The basic premise of Weiner's (1986) attribution model is that individuals' causal attributions of successful and failed performance influence future expectancies and affect, which in turn influence future behavior. These attributions may pertain to ability, effort, task difficulty, luck, mood, and help/hindrance from other individuals and differ along the dimensions of locus of causality (i.e., internal/external to attributer), stability (i.e., constant/varied over time), and controllability (i.e., changeable/unchangeable).

The temporal sequence of events for attributional judgments begins with a performance outcome that is interpreted by the individual as either successful or failed. Individuals then utilize available information (e.g., performance history and performance of others) to infer explanations specific to the events that caused the performance outcomes. The causal attributions of performance determine future behaviors by providing the basis for subsequent actions to either continue or discontinue the behavior.

The Kelley et al. (1999) study extends attribution theory by broadening the net of causal attributions that users attribute to computer performance and the related causal dimensions. They reported that enterprise system users attributed their successful computer-related performance to willingness to change applications, effort, and persistence. In contrast, enterprise system users ascribed their failed computer-related performance to lack of computer training, lack of computer support, and applications that were difficult to use. Of interest, post-survey interviews with enterprise system users and technical individuals highlighted two important findings. A small portion of the enterprise system users did not view their failed computer-related performance attainments as their individual performance; instead, they reported the performance failures as computer technology performance issues. Individuals' definitional views of the causal attributions of successful performance of computer technology varied depending on whether the interviewees were users of the enterprise system or technical individuals. Specifically, enterprise system users considered effort and persistence as positive causal attributions of their performance behaviors, whereas technicians perceived effort and persistence as very negative attributions that reflected possible design problems with the computer technology.

Enterprise system users viewed their causal attributions of successful performance as internal and self-controlled dimensions, whereas their causal attributions of failed performance were external and unstable dimensions. Respondents appeared to advance self-fulfilling perspectives (i.e., took personal credit) for successful performance, and offered self-protecting viewpoints (i.e., denied responsibility for their behavior by attributing failed performance to implementation factors such as lack of training and computer support) for unsuccessful performance.

Several implications follow from this research. Attributions ascribed to users' enterprise system performance and the causal dimensions are context-specific. Kelley et al. (1999) suggest that Weiner's four achievement causes do not comprehensively represent causal perceptions in all IS contexts. The context-specific findings reported by Kelley et al. (1999) are supported by other IS studies. Specifically, these IS studies found that computer-related performance levels are attributed to bad luck, system quality (Hufnagel, 1990), task difficulty, effort, and instructor support (Henry and Martinko, 1997; Henry et al., 1993).

One aspect of the research investigating users' retrospective reasoning of their new technology performance is the investigation of the influence of the causal attributions ascribed to both successful and failed performances on the formation of computer self-efficacy. Kelley et al. (1999) utilized a causal model to test the associations of attributions ascribed to successful performance and attributions attributed to unsuccessful performance on CSE. Their results indicated that 18.6 percent of the variance in CSE was explained by causal attributions of successful and failed computer performances. The path from attributions attributed to successful computer-related performance to CSE was positive and significant. Moreover, causal attributions ascribed to failed computer-related performance had a significant negative effect on CSE. These results suggest that successful causal attributions are associated with heightened self-efficacy beliefs and that failed causal attributions are associated with lower self-efficacy beliefs. As theorized by both Weiner (1985) and Bandura (1997), individuals' retrospective judgments of their performance attainments predict subsequent performance attainments and have motivational effects.

Bandura (1997) reported results from prior studies (e.g., Relich et al., 1986; Schunk and Rice, 1986) that showed that the influence of causal attributions on achievement outcomes is mediated by changes in self-efficacy judgments. Bandura (1997) stated that "the more the arbitrary reasons raise efficacy beliefs, the higher are the subsequent performance attainments" (p. 123). In a new computer technology environment, Kelley et al. (1999) found significant, indirect paths between successful and failed causal attributions and computer self-efficacy, which in turn significantly influenced enterprise system users' perceived overall PeopleSoft satisfaction, PeopleSoft performance, and PeopleSoft productivity.

Other research in this area examines the relationship between users' retrospective reasoning about their successful and failed computer performances and other behavioral and learning outcomes. Attribution theory has been applied in studies aimed at explaining IS adoption (e.g., Martinko et al., 1996), individuals' reactions to IS (e.g., Rozell and Gardner, 2000), and skill acquisition (e.g., Mitchell et al., 1994). In other empirical studies, attributions such as effort and luck (Henry et al., 1993) and attributional styles or traits (Henry et al., 1993; Rozell and Gardner, 1999, 2000) influence CSE and performance. Mitchell et al. (1994) reported that causal attributions such as task complexity and desire to do well influence subsequent computer performance. Collectively, these results suggest that implementers, managers, and enterprise system teams must be cognizant of the strong influence that users' attributional analyses of computer performance have on self-efficacy and usage behaviors. In order for organizations to derive the individual benefits of enterprise systems sooner, they must develop training and support mechanisms that incorporate the sense-making process, which includes attribution activities by individuals. Organizations need to provide attributional retraining when necessary, and to change their support and training mechanisms and strategies as users' enterprise system experiences increase. The efficaciousness of the interventions designed to positively influence users' self-efficacy will depend on the determinants that are affected by the intervention strategies and on their weighted contributions.

In conclusion, research initiatives that focus on developing a deeper understanding of the implementation of new computer technology domain provide early evidence that causal attributions conceived retrospectively for prior computer-related performance influence the formation of computer self-efficacy beliefs. Bandura (1997) theorizes that the causal attributions of users' successful and failed performances have motivational effects on present and future actions and behaviors. Organizations need, therefore, to influence the ways users mentally analyze stimuli to result in more successful attribution patterns and fewer failure attribution patterns in order to enhance CSE and increase IS usage patterns. From a research perspective there is a need to broaden our exploration of the attribution phenomenon to other IT domains and deepen our understanding of the myriad influences around attributions, self-efficacy, and human-computer interaction.

Everyday Problem Solving and Technical Support

Haggerty and Compeau (2001, 2002) have begun a program of research to examine the role of technical support as a key mechanism for developing users' ability to learn and use increasingly complex and interrelated technologies after training in everyday use (Brancheau and Brown, 1993). Support is defined for this research as the range of organizational actions taken to plan, organize, staff, support, and coordinate technology and services to assist end users (Brancheau and Brown, 1993). Thus, the goal of support has been to assist and help end users realize productivity and performance gains from their technology by providing them with knowledge, skills, and resources (Govindarajulu and Reithel, 1998; Govindarajulu et al., 2000; Speier and Brown, 1997; Trauth and Cole, 1992).

While IT support has been the subject of some research, the links between IT support and users' development of knowledge, skills, and abilities, including self-efficacy, has not received detailed research attention. Given the ongoing managerial challenges associated with enabling users to be productive with their technology, and given the role that IT support is assumed to have in that activity, the research recounted here focuses attention on the specific ways in which support enhances individual cognitive and personal factors, including user self-efficacy and learning.

This research program also draws on social cognitive theory (Bandura, 1986) because of its focus on individual behaviors (both choice and performance), and explanations of how individuals learn. This theoretical stance assists in conceptualizing the phenomenon of support and its role in user learning, including CSE development. An individual's use of technology to perform tasks (a behavior) leads to many outcomes, including technical problems. Problem-solving activities cause users to seek IT support as a valuable external resource (an environmental factor in SCT).

Interactions between the user and the support environment can be characterized by the vicarious capability of individuals to learn from observing and/or interacting with these support mechanisms to solve a technological problem (changed individual factors including the development of computer self-efficacy, satisfaction, and new computer knowledge and skills).

From an SCT perspective, interaction with support mechanisms can constitute an opportunity for people to learn through two processes, as influenced by the support mechanism chosen. By using support mechanisms that involve interactions with others (help desks, peers, etc.), the user can learn by observation of the performance and verbal explanations provided by others during the support event—a process referred to as observational learning in Bandura's theory (1986). By using support mechanisms in which the user performs his or her own problem solving using support resources (manuals, online help, multimedia simulations), the user can also learn through observational learning by observing and studying verbal modeling (including written text) and symbolic modeling (multimedia). In addition, he can learn through enactive learning processes as he experiments with implementing solutions provided by the support mechanism chosen (Bandura, 1986). Enactive mastery experiences are salient indicators of capability and produce strong information cues for CSE development. Theoretically, regardless of the mode selected, an incident of using technical support affords an everyday occasion, inevitably experienced by every computer user, wherein individual characteristics such as computer self-efficacy may be influenced.

Within this research, specific computer self-efficacy judgments play a role in a number of places, including selection of a technical support mechanism, and, after selection, the influence of the chosen support mechanism on the development of users' specific computer self-efficacy judgments about the problem experienced.

With regard to support resource choice, when users of technology experience a technical problem that they are unable to resolve on their own, they will be guided in their choice of support by a number of factors, including their attributional analysis of the problem, their motivation to maintain their self-image, and by their specific computer self-efficacy towards utilizing a particular mechanism (Wood and Bandura, 1989). In a given support event situation, an individual's SCSE beliefs about being able to use a particular support mechanism based on prior experience with it will influence his or her choice of which mechanism to use. For example, an individual with a strong sense of SCSE judgments towards using a self-discovery support mechanism such as an online help function will likely choose to use online support again. Also, SCSE judgments influence motivation and persistence with a support mechanism. For example, the individual with a strong sense of SCSE who uses the online help function for particular problems is more likely to use it thoroughly and persistently than someone with a lower sense of SCSE towards online help. SCSE beliefs of this type would be formed from the four sources mentioned previously— prior enactive mastery (prior use of the resource), vicarious observation (of others use of the resource), verbal persuasion (encouragement by others), and emotional arousal (level of anxiety or excitement experienced).

In addition to the role that SCSE beliefs play in support resource choice, individual computer self-efficacy continues to have a role once the choice has been made and the support event is under way. In our research, specific computer self-efficacy was seen as being formed via the use of support and SCSE was seen as influencing other support outcomes such as learning and satisfaction. More specifically, individuals learning observationally are accessing support mechanisms from which they can gain valuable performance information and feedback from models on which to construct and evaluate their own performances and specific computer self-efficacy judgments. Individuals learning experientially are accessing support mechanisms that enable them to obtain information and at the same time experiment with applying that information to solve their technical problems. Both of these processes (vicarious experience and enactive mastery) are acting together during a given support event because when users require technical help, they can observe both how the support resource is diagnosing and suggesting solutions to their problems and how they must enact those solutions to determine if they solve the problem. Thus, support and how it is provided during a given event is influential in the development of users' SCSE judgments towards resolving the same or a similar problem on their own in the future, along with other learning outcomes.

In turn, specific computer self-efficacy judgments in this research were theorized as influencing the thought patterns (Martocchio and Dulebohn, 1994) and emotional reactions (Compeau and Higgins, 1995b) of users. In other words, following a support event, individuals who develop higher levels of SCSE beliefs as a result of the support provided will be more motivated towards learning because they judge themselves as being more able (Martocchio and Dulebohn, 1994). Similarly, the influence of support events on user satisfaction is also seen as partially taking place through the mediating influence of users' SCSE judgments. Individuals who develop a lower sense of SCSE as a result of the support event are likely to judge themselves as less able and this will have a negative influence on their reactions to support events (Bandura, 1986; Gist and Mitchell, 1992). The evidence for this relationship is indicated by the study of negative emotions, such as fear, anxiety, and stress (Bandura, 1986, 1997). However, it is expected that the influence of CSE on more positively oriented affective reactions, such as satisfaction, will also exist. Thus SCSE is represented in the research as partially mediating the influence between the nature of support provided during the support event and user learning and user satisfaction. A mediating influence rather than moderating influence was judged as most accurately representing Bandura's theory of the role of self-efficacy on individual behaviors, learning, and affective reactions (Bandura, 1986, 1997) and is consistent with prior IS research (Agarwal et al., 2000b; Compeau and Higgins, 1995a, 1995b; Johnson and Marakas, 2000; Marakas et al., 1998).

On the basis of this theoretical development, and focusing specifically on support provided by organizational help desks, Haggerty (2004) developed a causal model via a detailed, qualitative study involving critical incident interviewing of support users and detailed observation of over one hundred support users and the help desk analysts they contacted. This facet of the research revealed how and why support influences users' specific computer self-efficacy development and other learning outcomes, validating and extending the theoretical stance discussed above. Further, the work utilized this understanding to develop empirical measures and test the causal model in a subsequent survey study of almost three hundred computer users in two different organizational settings. The findings provide significant insight into, among other outcomes, the development of SCSE in everyday computer usage settings, outside of formal training/study sessions.

In the qualitative study, we found that the use of a well-structured problem-solving process; detailed, yet non-jargon-filled, verbal explanations; and aspects of service quality such as patient, helpful, and knowledgeable analysts form the basis of effective support. Conversely, support providers who use trial-and-error approaches to diagnosis and solution attempts take too much time; provide little if any explanations, or explanations with too many technical terms; act impatiently or inexpertly; or are unhelpful by providing an ineffective support event.

We also found evidence as to how and why these characteristics of support influenced a user's specific computer self-efficacy. A user's SCSE—in this setting defined as his or her belief in his or her ability to resolve the same or a similar computer problem on his or her own in the future— was qualitatively related to attributes of the service quality demonstrated by the analyst and the language he or she used in providing explanations to the user. By acting impatiently, seeming to be unhelpful, failing to provide explanations or using technical jargon, the analyst could intimidate the user and make him or her feel "like an idiot." This was seen as having a strong potential to diminish the user's confidence in his or her own ability to solve the problem, which then prompted his or her call to the help desk. Users indicated that such support made them feel like they had caused the problem or lacked the capability to understand what the problem/solution was and therefore were demonstrating a low level of capability that diminished their confidence in handling the problem in the future.

Furthermore, findings from observation and analysis of actual support calls indicated a significant relationship between the user's development of SCSE and the proportion of the call spent in verbal modeling. The more time spent in explaining the situation or providing information to the user, the higher the user's reported confidence in his or her ability to resolve the problem in the future. This is because such support provides a better opportunity to transmit information, hold the user's attention, and enable the user to use more cognitive processes over a longer period of time to absorb the verbally modeled activities of the help desk analyst (Bandura, 1986). These types of support contexts allow users a greater opportunity to develop and change SCSE towards resolving the same or a similar problem on their own in the future.

Finally, various contextual aspects of support events were found to play a role in SCSE development and other learning outcomes. Problem context was examined, and qualitative findings indicate differences between calls involving technical problems (where analyst and user work together) versus routine service requests (where the user must call the help desk to get a service such as a password reset, activation of accounts, or setting up hardware repair appointments). During support events in which the user was calling with a problem requiring assistance, and the analyst and user worked together to resolve the problem, the user experienced higher SCSE development and learning outcomes. This finding indicates that not all support events are equally relevant to the development of user SCSE. Users are more likely to learn and develop SCSE from calls to the help desk in which the user is experiencing a more technical problem, rather than calls in which the user asks the help desk to perform a standardized task for him or her. Additionally, user competence plays a role: users who were assessed as higher in competence by those who observed their performances during support reported learning less from support events.

In previous research, the role of support has been limited to views of its availability (Guimaraes, 1996; Mirani and King, 1994; Rainer et al., 1989) with outcomes of support primarily related to satisfaction and the development of positive user beliefs and attitudes (Thompson et al., 1991; Venkatesh and Davis, 1996). This program has extended our understanding of support by revealing that is it not just the availability of support but the manner in which it is provided to users that holds the key to their SCSE development and learning.

More specifically, important support goals should go beyond satisfaction to incorporate the development of the user's confidence in his or her ability to solve the problem on his or her own in the future, and the new facts, information, and problem-solving strategies that the user can learn from the provision of support. In particular, it is important that managerial practice take note of the distinction here—support can lead to improved learning about problems and about technology, but user SCSE plays an important mediating role. It is important to develop users' self-confidence in their ability to resolve the same or similar problems on their own in the future, as that focus helps develop the user's motivational efforts to attend to support so he or she can learn. To do this, organizations should develop the problem-solving processes and verbal modeling skills used by the analysts. Support managers can develop analyst training programs that arm analysts with insight into efficient and well-structured problem-solving processes, and with insight into how to deliver their technical knowledge through easily comprehensible and detailed explanations during support. Finally, support organizations should expand their measurement practices so that they actively measure and manage users' self-efficacy development, learning, and satisfaction from support.

From a research perspective, other support resources (outside of the help desk) that are available and utilized by users require investigation. In everyday computer usage, specific attention needs to be paid to how CSE influences support resource choice when users experience technical problems or require assistance and in how CSE develops along with learning and other factors depending on the support resource used.

Summary

This section has recounted the range of research that explores the development of computer self-efficacy in various contexts related to users' computer software learning processes within organizations. The ongoing programs of research presented addressed the development of CSE in environments such as formal training, self-directed learning, new technology implementation, and enterprise-wide information systems support. Each of these learning opportunities within organizations represents a situation where CSE has been demonstrated to be an important influence to be considered. While still ongoing, and thus not conclusive, these programs of research present initial results that further our understanding of how CSE is developed, and how various organizational activities (such as training, support, technology introduction) ought to be designed and managed.

FUTURE DIRECTIONS

In undertaking this extensive review of computer self-efficacy within the IS field, we have uncovered a wide variety of fruitful areas for future research. In this section we summarize these avenues according to the key dimensions of this review.

Definition and Measurement of CSE

Our review concluded that opportunities exist for future research in the fundamental area of computer self-efficacy definition and measurement. Specifically, future research is required to empirically test the conceptual development in the work of Marakas et al. (1998). Their discussion of the generality and specificity of self-efficacy suggests the need to study the evolution of both and how they are related to each other. Given their theorization, the question remains, is GCSE a weighted average of a collection of SCSE, or is it something different? Also, how are these two levels of CSE related to individual technology performances and outcomes?

Furthermore, the relationship between the task that individuals are attempting to accomplish and their efficacy towards the technology that they use in its accomplishment requires further study. As this review highlights, Bandura (1997) argues that SE must be specific to the task. In MIS research we have largely assumed that the task and the technology used are undifferentiated. Thus we have tended to study the influence of, for example, Lotus 123 self-efficacy and Windows 95 self-efficacy (Agarwal et al., 2000a) as if these were the "tasks" that the user is attempting to accomplish rather than more task-oriented activities such as "creating a financial model" using Lotus 123 or "creating an effective file structure" using Windows 95. In today's world of increasingly integrated and multi-functional software programs, it seems particularly important to theorize and empirically examine the relationship between task and technology in the formation and influence of CSE. These arguments regarding task domain and technology domain are important to our future development of the CSE concept and our understanding of its influences on user behavior in organizations. They remind us of the need to carefully examine the definition of CSE and the domain in which it is measured.

Influence of CSE

Prior research has provided substantial insight into the manner in which CSE influences behavior choice, performance, other forms of CSE, affect, and anxiety. Nevertheless, substantial opportunities exist to continue research on the influence of CSE. First, we suggest a need to study the fourth outcome of SE suggested by Bandura (1986) which is under-researched in the MIS domain—effort/persistence, particularly in field-based settings.

This outcome is related to the second opportunity for future research with regard to the methodologies we use, namely that relevant phenomenon involving computer self-efficacy beliefs should be studied outside of cross-sectional approaches—including process-oriented or longitudinal research. Much more could be added to our understanding of the role of CSE by incorporating temporal considerations into our research designs. For example, it is difficult to imagine research on effort/persistence outcomes that does not incorporate a timing element that would be best served by process-oriented or longitudinal modes of observation. By focusing only on single aspects of the relationship between CSE and outcomes and relying on cross-sectional research, we may be missing opportunities to understand the spiraling relationships between self-efficacy, anxiety, and behavior. Given the fundamental view of social cognitive theory (Bandura, 1986) that behavior, environment, and individuals are engaged in a continuing reciprocal interaction (see Figure 11.2), the separation of research on self-efficacy's antecedents and outcomes is artificial, and risks missing important aspects of the phenomenon.[2]

Third, an opportunity exists to understand how computer self-efficacy interacts with task characteristics (Bolt et al., 2001) and technology characteristics (Hung and Liang, 2001) in producing various outcomes. Studying such interaction effects holds the promise of revealing the more subtle aspects of CSE influence.

Development of CSE

Generally, our review of the literature highlights that substantially less research has been undertaken to understand the development of CSE compared to research examining the influence of CSE. Yet, if our goal as researchers is not just to predict behavior and outcomes but also to lend insight to practice in how to influence them, then we must also research how individuals develop CSE so that managerial interventions can be designed to assist in strengthening CSE. Our review highlights several areas of opportunity for future research in this area.

As it relates to mastery experiences, investigation of the total patterns of mastery experiences appears to be absent in the literature. Additional research is needed in order to advance our understanding of how the overall patterns of mastery experiences influence CSE, which Bandura notes produces "stronger and more generalized" (Bandura, 1997, p. 80) SE judgments.

With regard to modeling, our review suggests that IS research is also needed to further investigate the complex relationship between vicarious experience and SE. For example, in practice, individual computer users are subject to a wide variety of concurrent vicarious experiences (others' computer use, online tutorials, local and help desk personnel) and more research is required to study the repertoire of vicarious experience that individuals draw on as their CSE develops. IS researchers have much to discover about the various modes of vicarious experience in a variety of IS settings and technology-related tasks and the four processes that govern observational learning.

Our review highlights that only a small number of studies have considered the influence of verbal persuasion on CSE development. Valuable research remains to be undertaken on the effects of verbal persuasion on CSE development in a wide variety of contexts, particularly outside of formal training settings. The attitudes of other trainees have been shown to influence attitudes and behaviors towards computer technologies. Galletta et al. (1994) found that trainees in an experiment where one of their classmates (who was, in fact, a confederate) criticized a software package and eventually stormed out of a training session developed poorer attitudes towards the technology and demonstrated lower declarative knowledge after training. While computer self-efficacy was not specifically examined by the authors, their results do suggest that the reactions of others in a group training setting bear further investigation as influences on CSE.

Since verbal persuasion is something that practitioners can quite easily undertake, research on this influence would be particularly useful to practice. For example, in an environment where new technology is introduced, further research is required on the effects of positive evaluative feedback on the development of individual CSE with the new technology.

Further, a complex area of verbal persuasion that needs investigation is the effect that appraisal disparity has on the formulation of CSE. Bandura (1997) theorizes that appraisal disparity, or the differences between the appraisals of people's capabilities conveyed by others and those individuals' own judgments of their current capabilities, will have different affects on the future development of self-efficacy. The optimal level of appraisal disparity (minimal, moderate, or maximum), according to Bandura (1997), will depend on the temporal proximity of the tasks (short-term vs. distant future) and the nature of the performance activity (basic skills deficits or misuse of preexisting skills). For example, the optimal level of appraisal disparity will be lower for short-term performance than for future performance (Bandura, 1997). Of interest to the field is whether the optimal level of appraisal disparity varies depending on the IS setting (e.g., formal training, introduction of new technology, or in a support environment), type of computer-related skills, and/or nature of tasks to be completed.

Physiological states (mainly anxiety), like verbal persuasion, have been relatively underresearched. Thus opportunities exist to explore other physiological states beyond anxiety in a broad array of IS contexts.

Finally our review notes that research into the influence that other SE cues may have is providing early evidence of the importance of studying efficacy information cues that are internal or external and their relationship to the four sources of efficacy information theorized by Bandura. First, efforts should be made to organize and make sense of the range of internal and external cues that have already been studied, as our review of the literature has identified via the lens of social cognitive theory. Furthermore, IS researchers need to investigate external cues and how they operate through the four sources of efficacy information. Environmental factors and the complexities of computer-related tasks investigated in training, self-directed learning, recent implementation of computer technology, and technology support environments would deepen our understanding of how SE is developed. Finally an opportunity exists to undertake more comprehensive studies of internal efficacy information cues with an emphasis on identifying which of the numerous cues highlighted by prior research is most influential in the formation of CSE.

CONCLUSIONS

Computer self-efficacy has been an important individual variable in studies of the interaction between people and technology for nearly two decades. Our understanding of its influence and its development has been significantly enhanced by the work of many researchers. This review shows that the antecedents of computer self-efficacy judgments have been less well researched than the outcomes, and describes how several ongoing programs of research are seeking to redress this imbalance.

Integrating and synthesizing the IS and related literature in order to identify and highlight unanswered questions about the formulation of computer self-efficacy was the genesis for this paper. A core body of knowledge regarding the roles of the four sources of information, cues, and attributions in the formation of CSE has been advanced. Yet many unanswered questions still remain.

Let's start by answering this question: "What do we know about the various antecedents and processes that influence the development of computer self-efficacy?" The four primary sources of self-efficacy—enactive mastery, vicarious experience, verbal persuasion, and physiological states—have received varying degrees of attention by IS researchers. A cumulative body of knowledge regarding the relationships of these four sources of information and computer self-efficacy has been established. The collective evidence that materializes from prior investigations of enactive mastery, vicarious experience, verbal persuasion, and physiological states demonstrates that these four sources of information consistently play important roles in the development of CSE in variety of IS contexts. In IS research, we have typically investigated the more straightforward nature of the formation of CSE, and through this examination we have concluded that the formation of CSE is a complex phenomenon and that its more complicated nature and methodological questions need to be addressed. Emerging in the literature are new streams of CSE research that are broadening our understanding of the formation of CSE. These new streams are focusing on understanding how different environments within the life cycle of computer usage (from formal training to self-directed learning to new technology introductions to everyday use) and various mediating processes, such as cognitive, motivational, affective, and selective, influence individuals' development of confidence in their capabilities during these events. The results so far are very promising and suggestive of additional work in the future.

As we have highlighted, however, several important questions remain unanswered. Definitional and measurement questions remain particularly focused on the relationship between general and specific computer self-efficacy judgments, the specification of the domain, and the incorporation of task, in addition to technology considerations in the specification of CSE measures. We believe the inclusion of interaction effects and the use of more longitudinal studies are, as noted earlier, particularly fruitful areas to pursue. This literature review has suggested numerous necessary steps for future research into attributional motivators in the formation of CSE, the important role of CSE in users' effective formal training and self-directed learning experiences, and the important role of support mechanism in the development of CSE. These synopses of examples are potential avenues for fruitful research in the formation of CSE.

We believe that the role of computer self-efficacy in human-computer interaction remains a fertile area for future research, and have outlined several opportunities based on our analysis of the field. We anticipate additional investigation in this area and foresee advancement and expansion of our core body of CSE knowledge.

APPENDIX 11.1

Table 11.A1

Summary of Outcomes: Behavior Choice, Performance Attainment, Other Cognitions and Emotions

Outcome	Specific Focus	References
Behavior Choice		
	Behavioral intention to use IT	Hill et al. (1987); Venkatesh et al. (2003)
	Desired participation in system development	Hunton and Beeler (1997)
	Early adoption	Burkhardt and Brass (1990)
	Intention to purchase IT products	Hill et al. (1986, 1987)
	Moderating relationship: CSE * source expertise → intentions to try new software	Hill et al. (1986)
	Use	Compeau and Higgins (1995b); Compeau et al. (1999)
	Intention to behave ethically	Kuo and Hsu (2001)
	Resistance to change	Ellen et al. (1991)
	Absenteeism	McDonald and Siegall (1996)
	Career interests	Smith (2002)
	Knowledge sharing	Bock and Kim (2002)
	Lateness	McDonald and Siegall (1996)
Performance Attainment		
	Academic goal	Smith (2002)
	Declarative knowledge and/or procedural knowledge	Compeau and Higgins (1995a); Gist et al. (1989); Gravill and Compeau (2003); Jawahar and Elango (2001); Johnson and Marakas (2000); Martocchio (1992, 1994); Martocchio and Dulebohn (1994); Rozell and Gardner (1999); Ryan et al. (2000); Stone et al. (1996); Webster and Martocchio (1993); Webster and Martocchio (1995)
	Motivation to learn	Webster and Martocchio (1993)
	Task or course grade expectations	Rozell and Gardner (1999, 2000)
	Performance	Kelley et al. (1999, 2000); McDonald and Siegall (1996); Staples et al. (1999)
	Task performance	Mitchell et al. (1994); Yi and Davis (2003) (immediate and delayed)
	Productivity	Kelley et al. (1999, 2000); Staples et al. 1999
	Over-estimation	
	Self-awareness	
	Self-reported knowledge	
	Moderating relationship: task complexity by SE → performance	Bolt et al. (2001)
	Post-training expectations of transfer of skill (covariate)	Shayo and Olfman (2000)

(continued)

Table 11.A1 (*continued*)

Outcome	Specific Focus	References
Other Cognitions and Emotions		
	Ability to cope	Staples et al. 1999
	Ease of use	Agarwal and Karahanna (2000); Agarwal et al. (2000); Dabholkar and Bagozzi (2002) (ease of use * SE → attitude); Igbaria and Iivari (1995); Venkatesh (2000); Venkatesh and Davis (1996)
	Expectations of outcomes	Compeau and Higgins (1995a, 1995b); Compeau et al. (1999); Henry and Stone (1994, 1995); Johnson and Marakas (2000); Smith (2002); Stone and Henry (2003)
	Perceived behavioral control	Taylor and Todd (1995)
	Post-training reactions	Webster and Martocchio (1995)
	Usefulness	Agarwal and Karahanna (2000); Chau and Hu (2001); Hung and Liang (2001)
	Moderating relationship: CSE by training approach → software SE	Gist et al. (1989)
	Affect	Compeau and Higgins (1995b); Compeau et al. (1999)
	Anxiety	Compeau and Higgins (1995b); Compeau et al. (1999); Henderson et al. (1995); Igbaria and Iivari (1995); Johnson and Marakas (2000)
	Job stress	Staples et al. (1999)
	Liking of product	Hill et al. (1986)
	Perceived microcomputer playfulness	Webster and Martocchio (1992)
	Organizational commitment	McDonald and Siegall (1996); Staples et al. (1999); Stone et al. (2003)
	Satisfaction with management	Staples et al. (1999)
	Satisfaction with job	Henry and Stone (1994, 1995); McDonald and Siegall (1996); Staples et al. 1999
	Satisfaction	Hung and Liang (2001) (moderating relationship: function by task type); Kelley et al. (1999, 2000)

Table 11.A2

Summary of Antecedents: Mastery, Vicarious Experience, Verbal Persuasion, Psychological States, Other Cues

Outcome	Specific Focus	References
Mastery		
		Agarwal et al. (2000); Bolt et al. (2001); Busch (1995); Compeau and Higgins (1995a); Delcourt and Kinzie (1993); Ertmer et al. (1994); Gist et al. (1989); Havelka (2003); Henry and Stone (1994, 1995, 1999); Hill et al. (1987); Igbaria and Iivari (1995); Johnson and Marakas (2000); Kelley et al. (2000); Kinzie et al. (1994); Martocchio and Dulebohn (1994); Mitchell et al. (1994); Miura (1987); Ogletree and Williams (1990); Schmidt and Ford (2003); Smith (2002); Staples et al. (1999); Stone et al. (2003)

(*continued*)

Table 11.A2 (*continued*)

Outcome	Specific Focus	References

Vicarious Experience

| | Manipulation in laboratory experiments | Bolt et al. (2001) (modeling video); Compeau and Higgins (1995a) (modeling video); Gist et al. (1989) (modeling video); Johnson and Marakas (2000) (modeling video); Lim et al. (1997) (co-discovery learning); Yi and Davis (2003) (model-based retention/enhancement intervention and observational learning process—attention, retention, production, and motivation) |
| | Measured directly | Busch (1995) (encouragement by friends); Compeau and Higgins (1995b) (others' use); Compeau et al. (1999) (encouragement of others); Smith (1994); Staples et al. (1999) (best practices by manager) |

Verbal Persuasion

| | Manipulation in field or laboratory experiments | Martocchio and Dulebohn (1994) (performance feedback to factors within control, dimension of attributions); Martocchio and Webster (1992) (positive/negative performance evaluation in handwritten form) |
| | Measured directly | Compeau and Higgins (1995b) (encouragement by others); Mitchell et al. (1994) (task feedback) |

Physiological States

| | Anxiety | Havelka (2003); Johnson and Marakas (2000); Kelley et al. (2000); Martocchio (1992); Staples et al. (1999); Thatcher and Perrewe (2002) |

Other Cues

| | External cues | Busch (1995) (PC ownership today); Compeau and Higgins (1995b) (organizational support); Haggerty and Compeau (2002) (technical support characteristics); Henry and Stone (1994, 1995) (ease of use and management support); Hill et al. (1986) (perceptions of product complexity); Igbaria and Iivari (1995) (organizational support); Kelley et al. (1999, 2000) (undesirable attributions); Martocchio (1994) (training intervention); Mitchell et al. (1994) (physical comfort, task difficulty, task complexity, task novelty, work disturbances, available resources, task feedback); Rozell and Gardner (1999) (computer training); Sheng et al. (2003) (information flow, involvement, teamwork); Staples et al. (1999) (physical conditions, connectivity); Stone et al. (1996) (software specific training and accounting training); Torkzadeh and Koufteros (1994) (computer training) |
| | Internal cues | Agarwal et al. (2000) (personal innovativeness in IT); Busch (1995) (gender); Delcourt and Kinzie (1993) (age, sex, education level, and attitudes); Gist et al. 1989 (level of education); Havelka (2003) (family income level, major); Kinzie et al. (1994) (computer attitude); Martocchio (1992, 1994) (pre-training expectations; age, pre-training expectations); Martocchio and Webster (1992) (age); Mitchell et al. (1994) (level of alertness, desire to do well); Miura (1987) (education level, gender, major); Murphy et al. 1989 (gender); Ogletree and Williams 1990 (gender, psychological sex-typing); Rozell and Gardner (1999) (computer attitude); Rozell and Gardner (2000) (computer attitude, attributional style); Schmidt and Ford (2003) (ability, metacognitive activity); Thatcher and Perrewe (2002) (personal innovativeness in IT) |

NOTES

1. The remaining levels are outside the scope of this discussion, but include tool conceptual (i.e., understanding what the tool can do), business motivational (understanding why the tool would be useful in a particular setting), and metacognition (learning to learn) levels.

2. We do recognize the irony of this statement, given our choice to separate our discussion of the research into the very categories that we critiqued. Our organization was deliberate, however as it is most consistent with the structure of the literature, and thus natural as a way of presenting its status. In our ongoing work (reviewed in the next section) we have begun to take a more holistic view of these relationships within the context of various events within the life cycle of computer usage, from formal training to self-directed learning to new technology introductions to everyday use.

REFERENCES

Agarwal, R., and Karahanna, E. Time flies when you're having fun: cognitive absorption and beliefs about information technology usage. *MIS Quarterly*, 24, 4 (2000), 665–694.

Agarwal, R.; Sambamurthy, V.; and Stair, R.M. Research report: the evolving relationship between general and specific computer self-efficacy—an empirical assessment. *Information Systems Research*, 11, 4 (2000), 418–430.

Bandura, A. Self-efficacy: toward a unifying theory of behavioral change. *Psychological Review*, 84, 2 (1977a), 191–215.

Bandura, A. *Social Learning Theory*. Englewood Cliffs, NJ: Prentice-Hall, 1977b.

Bandura, A. Reflections on self-efficacy. *Advances in Behaviour Research and Therapy*, 1 (1978), 237–269.

Bandura, A. *Social Foundations of Thought and Action: A Social Cognitive Theory*. Englewood Cliffs, NJ: Prentice-Hall, 1986.

Bandura, A. *Self-Regulation of Motivation and Action through Goal Systems. Cognitive Perspectives on Emotion and Motivation*. Dordrecht: Kluwer Academic Publishers, 1987.

Bandura, A. Social cognitive theory of self-regulation. *Organization Behavior and Human Decision Processes*, 50 (1991), 248–287.

Bandura, A. *Self-Efficacy: The Exercise of Control*. New York: W.H. Freeman and Company, 1997.

Bandura, A., and Cervone, D. Self-evaluative and self-efficacy mechanisms governing the motivation effects of goal systems. *Journal of Personality and Social Psychology*, 45, 5 (1983), 1017–1028.

Bock, G.W., and Kim, Y.G. Breaking the myths of rewards: an exploratory study of attitudes about knowledge sharing. *Information Resources Management Journal*, 15, 2 (2002), 14–21.

Bolt, M.A.; Killough, L.N.; and Koh, H.C. Testing the interaction effects of task complexity in computer training using the social cognitive model. *Decision Sciences*, 32, 1 (2001), 1–20.

Brancheau, J.C., and Brown, C.V. The management of end-user computing: status and directions. *ACM Computing Surveys*, 25, 4 (1993), 437–481.

Brown, K. Using computers to deliver training: which employees learn and why? *Personnel Psychology*, 54, 2 (2001), 271–296.

Burkhardt, M.E., and Brass, D.J. Changing patterns or patterns of change: the effects of a change in technology on social network structure and power. *Administrative Science Quarterly*, 35, 1 (1990), 104–127.

Busch, T. Gender differences in self-efficacy and attitudes toward computers. *Journal of Educational Computing Research*, 12, 2 (1995), 147–158.

Carver, C., and Scheier, M. *Attention and Self-Regulation: A Control-Theory Approach to Human Behavior*. New York: Springer-Verlag, 1981.

Chau, P.Y.K., and Hu, P.J.H. Information technology acceptance by individual professionals: a model comparison approach. *Decision Sciences*, 34, 4 (2001), 699–719.

Compeau, D. *Individual Reactions to Computer Technology: A Social Cognitive Theory Perspective*. PhD thesis, University of Western Ontario, 1992.

Compeau, D., and Higgins, C. Application of social cognitive theory to training for computer skills. *Information Systems Research*, 6, 2 (1995), 118–143.

Compeau, D., and Higgins, C. Computer self-efficacy: development of a measure and initial test. *MIS Quarterly*, 19, 2 (1995), 189–211.

Compeau, D.; Higgins, C.; and Huff, S. Social cognitive theory and individual reactions to computing technology: a longitudinal study. *MIS Quarterly*, 23, 2 (1999), 145–158.

Dabholkar, P.A., and Bagozzi, R.P. An attitudinal model of technology-based self-service: moderating effects of consumer traits and situational factors. *Academy of Marketing, Science Journal*, 30, 3 (2002), 184–201.

Davis, F.D.; Bagozzi, R.P.; and Warshaw, P.R. User acceptance of computer technology: a comparison of two theoretical models. *Management Science*, 35, 8 (1989), 982–1003.

Delcourt, M.A.B., and Kinzie, M.B. Computer technologies in teacher education: the measurement of attitudes and self-efficacy. *Journal of Research and Development in Education*, 27, 1 (1993), 35–41.

Ellen, P.S.; Bearden, W.O.; and Sharma, S. Resistance to technological innovations: an examination of the role of self-efficacy and performance satisfaction. *Journal of the Academy of Marketing Science*, 19, 4 (1991), 297–307.

Ertmer, P.A.; Evenbeck, E.; Cennamo, K.S.; and Lehman, J.D. Enhancing self-efficacy for computer technologies through the use of positive classroom experiences. *Educational Technology Research and Development*, 42 (1994), 45–62.

Ford, J.; Smith, E.; Weissbein, D.; Gully, S.; and Salas, E. Relationships of goal orientation, metacognitive activity, and practice strategies with learning outcomes and transfer. *Journal of Applied Psychology*, 83, 2 (1998), 218–233.

Galletta, D.F.; Ahuja, M.; Hartman, A.; Peace, A.; and Teo, T. An empirical study of peer influence on user attitudes, behavior, and performance. In J.I. DeGross, S.L. Huff, and M.C. Munro (eds.), *Proceedings of the Fifteenth Annual International Conference on Information Systems*, Vancouver, BC, December 14–17, 1994, pp. 229–242.

Gist, M.E., and Mitchell, T.R. Self-efficacy: a theoretical analysis of its determinants and malleability. *Academy of Management Review*, 17, 2 (1992), 183–211.

Gist, M.E.; Schwoerer, C.; and Rosen, B. Effects of alternative training methods on self-efficacy and performance in computer software training. *Journal of Applied Psychology*, 74 (1989), 884–891.

Govindarajulu, C., and Reithel, B. Beyond the information center: an instrument to measure end-user computing support from multiple sources. *Information & Management*, 33 (1998), 241–250.

Govindarajulu, C.; Reithel, B.; and Sethi, V. A model of end user attitudes and intentions toward alternative sources of support. *Information & Management*, 37 (2000), 77–86.

Gravill, J., and Compeau, D. Self-regulated learning strategies and computer software training. In S.T. March, A. Massey, and J.I. DeGross (eds.), *Proceedings of the International Conference on Information Systems*. Seattle, WA, December 14–17, 2003, pp. 788–793.

Gravill, J.; Compeau, D.; and Marcolin, B. Frame-of-reference effects on the accuracy of self-assessed user competence. In V. Storey, S. Sarkar, and J.I. DeGross (eds.), *Proceedings for International Conference on Information Systems*. New Orleans, LA: December 16–19, 2001, pp. 525–530.

Gravill, J.; Compeau, D.; and Marcolin, B. Metacognition and I.T.—the influence of self-efficacy on self-awareness. In J.I. DeGross, J.D. Becker, and J.J. Elam, *Proceedings for Americas Conference on Information Systems*, Dallas, TX, December 13–16, 2002, pp. 1015–1064.

Guimaraes, T. Assessing the impact of information centers on end-user computing and company performance. *Information Resources Management Journal*, 9, 1, 1996, 6–15.

Gundlach, M.J., and Thatcher, J.B. examining the multi-dimensionality of computer self-efficacy. Unpublished manuscript, Florida State University, Tallahassee, FL, 2000.

Haggerty, N. *Towards an Understanding of Post-Training User Learning through IT Support*. PhD thesis, Richard Ivey School of Business, University of Western Ontario, 2004.

Haggerty, N., and Compeau, D. Help! I need somebody: new directions in IT support. In D. Strong and D. Straub (eds.), *Proceedings of the Americas Conference on Information Systems*. Boston, MA, August 3–5, 2001, pp. 1693–1700.

Haggerty, N., and Compeau, D. A social cognitive view of technical support and its influence on user learning. In L. Applegate, R. Galliers, and J.I. DeGross (eds.), *Proceedings of the International Conference on Information Systems*. Barcelona, December 15–18, 2002, pp. 791–795.

Havelka, D. Predicting software self efficacy among business students: a preliminary assessment. *Journal of Information Systems Education*, 14, 2 (2003), 145–152.

Henderson, R.D.; Deane, F.P.; and Ward, M.J. Occupational differences in computer related anxiety: implications for the implementation of a computerized patient management information system. *Behavior and Information Technology*, 14, 1 (1995), 23–31.

Henry, J.W., and Martinko, M.J. An attributional analysis of the rejection of information technology. *Journal of End User Computing*, 9, 4 (1997), 3–17.

Henry, J.W.; Martinko, M.J.; and Pierce, M.A. Attributional style as a predictor of success in a first computer science course. *Computer Personnel*, 16, 4 (1993), 15–37.

Henry, J.W., and Stone, R.W. A structural equation model of end-user satisfaction with a computer-based medical information system. *Information Resources Management Journal*, 7, 3 (1994), 21–33.

Henry, J.W., and Stone, R.W. Computer self-efficacy and outcome expectancy: the effects on the end-user's job satisfaction. *Computer Personnel*, 16, 4, 1995, 15–34.

Henry, J.W., and Stone, R.W. The impacts of end-user gender, education, performance, and system use on computer self-efficacy and outcome expectancy. *Southern Business Review*, 25, 1 (1999), 10–16.

Hill, T.N.; Smith, D.; and Mann, M.F. Communicating innovations: convincing computer phobics to adopt innovative technologies. In R.J. Lutz (ed.), *Advances in Consumer Research*. Provo, UT: Association for Consumer Research, 1986, pp. 419–422.

Hill, T.; Smith, N.D.; and Mann, M.F. Role of efficacy expectations in predicting the decision to use advanced technologies: the case of computers. *Journal of Applied Psychology*, 72, 2 (1987), 307–313.

Hufnagel, E. User satisfaction—are we really measuring system effectiveness? In *Hawaii International Conference on System Sciences*. Kona, HI: Computer Society Press, 1990, pp. 437–446.

Hung, S.Y., and Liang, T.P. Effect of computer self-efficacy on the use of executive support systems. *Industrial Management +Data Systems*, 101, 5/6 (2001), 227–236.

Hunton, J.E., and Beeler, J.D. Effects of the user participation in systems development by end users: a longitudinal field experiment. *MIS Quarterly*, 21, 4 (1997), 359–388.

Igbaria, M., and Iivari, J. The effects of self-efficacy on computer usage. *OMEGA International Journal of Management Sciences*, 23, 6 (1995), 587–605.

Jawahar, I.M., and Elango, B. The effect of attitudes, goal setting and self-efficacy on end user performance. *Journal of End User Computing*, 13, 2 (2001), 40–45.

Johnson, R.D., and Marakas, G.M. Research report: the role of behavioral modeling in computer skills acquisition—toward refinement of the model. *Information Systems Research*, 11, 4 (2000), 402–417.

Kanfer, R., and Ackerman, P. Motivation and cognitive abilities: an integrative/aptitude-treatment interaction approach to skill acquisition. *Journal of Applied Psychology Monograph*, 74, 4 (1989), 657–690.

Kanfer, R.; Ackerman, P.; Murtha, T.; Dugdal, B.; and Nelson, L. Goal setting, conditions of practice, and task performance: a resource allocation perspective. *Journal of Applied Psychology*, 79, 6 (1994), 826–835.

Kanfer, R., and Heggestad, E. Individual differences in motivation: traits and self-regulatory skills. In P. Ackerman, P. Kyllonen, and R. Roberts (eds.), *Learning and Individual Differences*. Washington, D.C.: American Psychological Association, 1999, pp. 293–309.

Kelley, H.; Compeau, D.; and Higgins, C. Attribution analysis of computer self-efficacy. In W.D. Haseman and D.L. Nazareth (eds.), *Proceedings of the Fifth Americas Conference on Information Systems*. Milwaukee, WI, August 13–15, 1999, pp. 782–784.

Kelley, H.; Compeau, D.; and Higgins, C. Linking attribution theory and self-efficacy theory: a bridge for investigating IS success. In Y. Chan and A. Croteau (eds.), *Proceedings of the Administrative Science Association of Canada*. Montreal, July 8–11, 2000, pp. 57–66.

Kinzie, M.B.; Delcourt, M.A.B.; and Powers, S.M. Computer technologies: attitudes and self-efficacy across undergraduate disciplines. *Research in Higher Education*, 35, 6 (1994), pp. 745–768.

Kraiger, K.; Ford, J.K.; and Salas, E. Application of cognitive, skill-based, and affective theories of learning outcomes to new methods of training evaluation. *Journal of Applied Psychology*, 78, 2 (1993), 311–328.

Kruger, J., and Dunning, D. Unskilled and unaware of it: how difficulties in recognizing one's own incompetence lead to inflated self-assessments. *Journal of Personality and Social Psychology*, 77, 6 (1999), 1121–1134.

Kuo, F.-Y., and Hsu, M.-H. Development and validation of ethical computer self-efficacy measure: the case of softlifting. *Journal of Business Ethics*, 32, 4 (2001), 299–315.

Lim, K.H.; Ward, L.M.; and Benbasat, I. An empirical study of computer system learning: comparison of co-discovery and self-discovery methods. *Information Systems Research*, 8, 3 (1997), 254–272.

Lindsley, D.H.; Brass, D.J.; and Thomas, J.B. Efficacy-performance spirals: a multilevel perspective. *Academy of Management Review*, 20, 3 (1995), 645–678.

Marakas, G.M.; Yi, M.Y.; and Johnson, R.D. The multilevel and multifaceted character of computer self-efficacy: toward clarification of the construct and an integrative framework for research. *Information Systems Research*, 9, 2 (1998), 126–163.

Marcolin, B.; Compeau, D.; and Munro, M. Understanding the antecedents of user competence. In Y. Chan and A. Croteau (eds.), *Proceedings of the Administrative Science Association of Canada*, Montreal, 2000a, pp. 57–66.

Marcolin, B.; Compeau, D.; Munro, M.; and Huff, S. Assessing user competence: conceptualization and measurement. *Information Systems Research*, 11, 1 (2000b), 37–60.

Martinko, M.J.; Henry, J.W.; and Zmud, R.W. An attributional explanation of individual reactions to information technology in the workplace. *Behaviour and Information Technology*, 15, 5 (1996), 313–330.

Martocchio, J.J. Microcomputer usage as an opportunity: the influence of context in employee training. *Personal Psychology*, 45, 3 (1992), 529–552.

Martocchio, J.J. Effects of conceptions of ability on anxiety, self-efficacy, and learning in training. *Journal of Applied Psychology*, 79, 6 (1994), 819–825.

Martocchio, J.J., and Dulebohn, J. Performance feedback effects in training: the role of perceived controllability. *Personnel Psychology*, 47 (1994), 357–373.

Martocchio, J.J., and Webster, J. Effects of feedback and cognitive playfulness on performance in microcomputer software training. *Personnel Psychology*, 45 (1992), 553–578.

McDonald, T., and Siegall, M. Enhancing worker self-efficacy: an approach for reducing negative reactions to technological change. *Journal of Managerial Psychology*, 11, 2 (1996), 41–44.

Meichenbaum, D.H. Examination of model characteristics in reducing avoidance behavior. *Journal of Personality and Social Psychology*, 17, 3 (1971), 298–307.

Mirani, R., and King, W. The development of a measure for end-user computing support. *Decision Sciences*, 25, 4 (1994), 481–498.

Mitchell, T.R.; Hopper, H.; Daniels, D.; George-Falvy, J.; and James, L.R. Predicting self-efficacy and performance during skill acquisition. *Journal of Applied Psychology*, 79, 4 (1994), 506–517.

Miura, I.T. The relationship of computer self efficacy expectations to computer interest and course enrolment in college. *Sex Roles*, 16, 5/6 (1987), 303–311.

Murphy, C.A.; Coover, D.; and Owen, S.V. Development and validation of the computer self-efficacy scale. *Educational and Psychological Measurement*, 49, (1989), 893–899.

Nelson, R. Educational needs as perceived by IS and end-user personnel: a survey of knowledge and skill requirements. *MIS Quarterly*, 15, 4 (1991), 503–521.

Ogletree, S.M., and Williams, S.W. Sex and sex-typing effects on computer attitudes and aptitude. *Sex Roles*, 23, 11–12 (1990), 703–712.

Rainer, K.; Carr, H.; Snyder, C.; and Frolick, M. The information center career. *Journal of Management Information Systems*, 6, 2 (1989), 93–104.

Relich, J.D.; Debus, R.L.; and Walker, R. The mediating role of attribution and self-efficacy variables for treatment effects on achievement outcomes. *Contemporary Educational Psychology*, 11 (1986), 195–216.

Renner, C., and Renner, M. But I thought I knew that: using confidence estimation as a debiasing technique to improve classroom performance. *Applied Cognitive Psychology*, (15) 2001, 23–32.

Rozell, E.J., and Gardner, W.L. Computer-related success and failure: a longitudinal field study of the factors influencing computer-related performance. *Computers in Human Behavior*, 15 (1999), 1–10.

Rozell, E.J., and Gardner, W.L. Cognitive, motivation, and affective processes associated with computer-related performance: a path analysis. *Computers in Human Behavior*, 16 (2000), 199–222.

Ryan, S.D.; Bordoloi, B.; and Harrison, D.A. Acquiring conceptual data modeling skills: the effect of cooperative learning and self-efficacy on learning outcomes. *Database for Advances in Information Systems*, 31, 4 (2000), 9–24.

Schmidt, A., and Ford, K. Learning within a learner control training environment: the interactive effects of goal orientation and metacognitive instruction on learning outcomes. *Personnel Psychology*, 56 (2003), 405–429.

Schunk, D.H. Effects of effort attributional feedback on children's perceived self-efficacy and achievement. *Journal of Educational Psychology*, 74 (1982), 548–556.

Schunk, D.H. Ability versus effort attributional feedback: differential effects on self-efficacy and achievement. *Journal of Educational Psychology*, 75 (1983), 848–856.

Schunk, D.H. Sequential attributional feedback and children's achievement behaviors. *Journal of Educational Psychology*, 76 (1984), 1159–1169.

Schunk, D.H. Self-efficacy and academic motivation. *Educational Psychologist*, 79 (1991), 238–244.

Schunk, D.H., and Cox, P.D. Strategy training and attributional feedback with learning disabled students. *Journal of Educational Psychology*, 78 (1986), 201–209.

Schunk, D.H., and Gunn, T.P. Self-efficacy and skill development: influence of task strategies and attributions. *Journal of Educational Research*, 79 (1986), 238–244.

Schunk, D.H., and Rice, T.P. Extended attributional feedback: sequence effects during remedial reading instruction. *Journal of Early Adolescence*, 6 (1986), 55–66.

Sein, M.K.; Bostrom, R.P.; and Olfman, L. Rethinking end-user training strategy: applying a hierarchical knowledge-level model. *Journal of End User Computing*, 9 (1999), 32–39.

Shayo, C., and Olfman, L. The role of training in preparing end users to learn related software. *Journal of End User Computing*, 12, 1 (2000), 3–13.

Sheng, Y.P.; Pearson, J.M.; and Crosby, L. Organizational culture and employees' computer self-efficacy: an empirical study. *Information Resources Management Journal*, 16, 3 (2003), 42–58.

Simon, S.J.; Grover, V.; Teng, J.T.C.; and Whitcomb, K. The relationship of information system training methods and cognitive ability to end user satisfaction, comprehension, and skill transfer: a longitudinal study. *Information Systems Research*, 7, 4 (1996), 466–489.

Simon, S.J., and Werner, J.M. Computer training through behavior modeling, self-paced, and instructional approaches: a field experiment. *Journal of Applied Psychology*, 81, 6 (1996), 648–659.

Smith, J.M. The effects of education on computer self-efficacy. *Journal of Industrial Teacher Education*, 31, 3 (1994), 51–65.

Smith, S.M. Using the social cognitive model to explain vocational interest in information technology. *Information Technology, Learning, and Performance Journal*, 20, 1 (2002), 1–9.

Speier, C., and Brown, C. Differences in end-user computing support and control across user departments. *Information & Management*, 32, 1 (1997), 85–99.

Stajkovic, A.D., and Luthans, F. Self-efficacy and work-related performance: a meta-analysis. *Psychological Bulletin*, 124, 2 (1998), 240–261.

Staples, D.S.; Hulland, J.S.; and Higgins, C.A. A self-efficacy theory explanation for the management of remote workers in virtual organizations. *Organization Science*, 10, 6 (1999), 758–776.

Stone, D.N.; Arunachalam, V.; and Chandler, J.S. Cross-cultural comparisons: an empirical investigation of knowledge, skill, self-efficacy and computer anxiety in accounting education. *Issues in Accounting Education*, 11, 2 (1996), 345–376.

Stone, R.W., and Henry, J.W. The roles of computer self-efficacy and outcome expectancy in influencing the computer end-user's organizational commitment. *Journal of End User Computing*, 15, 1 (2003), 38–53.

Taylor, S., and Todd, P. Assessing IT usage: the role of prior experience. *MIS Quarterly*, 19, 4 (1995), 561–570.

Thatcher, J.B., and Perrewe, P.L. An empirical examination of individual traits as antecedents to computer anxiety and computer self-efficacy. *MIS Quarterly*, 26, 4 (2002), 381–396.

Thompson, R.L.; Compeau, D.; and Higgins, C. Intentions to use information technologies: an integrative model. *Journal of Organizational and End User Computing*, 18, 3 (2006), 25–43.

Thompson, R.L., Higgins, C.A., and Howell, J.M. Personal computing: toward a conceptual model of utilization. *MIS Quarterly*, 15, 1 (1991), 125–143.

Torkzadeh, G., and Koufteros, Z. Factorial validity of a computer self-efficacy scale and the impact of computer training. *Educational and Psychological Measurement*, 54, 3 (1994), 813–821.

Trauth, E., and Cole, E. The organizational interface: a method for supporting end users of packaged software. *MIS Quarterly*, 16, 1 (1992), 35–53.

VandeWalle, D.; Brown, S.; Cron, W.; and Slocum, J. The influence of goal orientation and self-regulation tactics on sales performance: a longitudinal field test. *Journal of Applied Psychology*, 84, 2 (1999), 249–259.

Venkatesh, V. Determinants of perceived ease of use: integrating control, intrinsic motivation and emotion into the technology acceptance model. *Information Systems Research*, 11, 4 (2000), 342–365.

Venkatesh, V., and Davis, F. A model of the antecedents of perceived ease of use: development and test. *Decision Sciences*, 27, 3 (1996), 451–481.

Venkatesh, V.; Morris, M.G.; Davis, F.D.; and Davis, G.B. User acceptance of information technology: toward a unified view. *MIS Quarterly*, 27, 3 (2003), 425–478.

Webster, J., and Martocchio, J.J. Microcomputer playfulness: development of a measure with workplace implications. *MIS Quarterly*, 16, 2 (1992), 201–226.

Webster, J., and Martocchio, J.J. Turning work into play: implications for microcomputer software training. *Journal of Management*, 19, 1 (1993), 127–146.

Webster, J., and Martocchio, J.J. The differential effects of software training previews on training outcomes. *Journal of Management*, 21, 4 (1995), 757–787.

Weiner, B. An attributional theory of achievement motivation and emotion. *Psychological Review*, 92, 4 (1985), 548–573.

Weiner, B. *An Attributional Theory of Motivation and Emotion.* New York: Springer-Verlag, 1986.

Wood, R., and Bandura, A. Social cognitive theory of organizational management. *Academy of Management Review*, 14, 3 (1989), 361–384.

Yi, M.Y., and Davis, F.D. Developing and validating an observational learning model of computer software training and skill acquisition. *Information Systems Research*, 14, 2 (2003), 146–169.

Zimmerman, B.J. A social cognitive view of self-regulated academic learning. *Journal of Educational Psychology*, 81, 3 (1989), 329–350.

Zimmerman, B.J., and Martinez-Pons, M. Construct validation of strategy model of student self-regulated learning. *Journal of Educational Psychology*, 3 (1988), 284–290.

CHAPTER 12

BEHAVIORAL INFORMATION SECURITY

An Overview, Results, and
Research Agenda

JEFFREY M. STANTON, KATHRYN R. STAM, PAUL M. MASTRANGELO,
AND JEFFREY A. JOLTON

Abstract: *Information security is a multibillion-dollar problem faced by commercial, non-profit, and government organizations around the world. Because of their adverse effects on organizational information systems, viruses, hackers, and malicious insiders can jeopardize organizations' capabilities to pursue their missions effectively. Although technology-based solutions help to mitigate some of the many problems of information security, even the best technology cannot work successfully unless effective human-computer interaction occurs. Information technology professionals, managers, and end users all play a significant role in determining whether the behavior that occurs as people interact with information technology will support the maintenance of effective security or undermine it. In the present paper we try to apply behavioral science concepts and techniques to understanding problems of information security in organizations. We analyzed a large set of interviews, developed a set of behavioral categories, and conducted three survey studies (N = 1167, N = 298, and N = 414) to explore whether and how behavioral science could apply to the complex set of organizational problems surrounding contemporary information security. We report these results and provide a future research agenda for researchers who wish to support organizations' efforts to ensure security of their information assets.*

Keywords: *Information Security, Organizational Psychology, Surveys*

INTRODUCTION

Over recent decades, most work organizations have come to depend on information technology. As connectivity among computers has increased, so has the likelihood of intrusion, theft, defacement, etc. Surprisingly, although organizations sometimes focus more on vulnerability to external attack, industry research by Ernst and Young (2002) indicated that well over half of the cost of security failures results from insider activity. Computer scientists, network engineers, information technology specialists, and others have developed technological solutions for these information security problems (e.g., Won, 2001), and a large software and hardware development industry is dedicated to the design and marketing of security-related devices such as firewalls and biometrics.

Many of these developments have resulted in positive business and economic outcomes (Dhillon, 2001), but a constraint appears throughout in the behaviors of the human agents who access, use, administer, and maintain information resources. The success of security appears to depend upon the effective behavior of the individuals involved in its use. Appropriate and constructive behavior by end users, system administrators, and others can enhance the effectiveness of information security, while inappropriate and destructive behaviors can inhibit its effectiveness. Human behavior is complex and multi-faceted, and this complexity defies the expectations for control and predictability that technology developers routinely assume for the technology with which they work. As the Organisation for Economic Co-Operation and Development's *Guidelines for the Security of Information Systems* state, "Each participant is an important actor for ensuring security. Participants, as appropriate to their roles, should be aware of the relevant security risks and preventive measures, assume responsibility and take steps to enhance the security of information systems and networks" (OECD, 2002, p. 8). This statement represents a shift in perspective from the guidelines that the OECD published ten years earlier: Whereas the earlier guidelines were technology centric, the current guidelines emphasize that the actions of individuals and organizations influence security.

This paper takes this perspective on information security to heart by focusing on "behavioral information security," which is defined as the human actions that influence the availability, confidentiality, and integrity of information systems. We have investigated these behaviors and their motivational antecedents through a linked series of studies. Our goal in the present paper lies in discussing the results from these studies and drawing out the implications of these results for future science and practice in organizations. With this paper we hope to continue the process started by other researchers of substantiating the claim that social, organizational, and behavioral scientists have much to contribute in addressing the problems of information security faced by contemporary work organizations. We expect that this contribution can come from applying researchers' established expertise in understanding and influencing the behaviors involved in the use of information technology. In the remainder of this paper we review some of the literature that we drew upon in framing this line of research. We then briefly overview the results of three studies we conducted that have explored this new research area. Finally, we describe our vision for future research in the behavioral aspects of information security.

Technology, Human Factors, Management, and the Behavioral Gap

At the low end, losses from security breaches have been estimated at approximately $20 billion per year across all U.S. organizations (Security Wire Digest, 2000). These losses have spurred increased spending on information security specialists and technology: According to a 2002 industry survey by *Information Security* magazine, very large organizations spend an average of $6 million per year apiece on information security. Smaller organizations spend on average nearly 20 percent of their overall information technology budgets on security-related products.

Product development in this new sub-industry has received ample intellectual backing from an array of academic research programs on cryptography, public key infrastructure, watermarking, access control, intrusion detection, and related topics. The CiteSeer automated indexing facility (http://citeseer.nj.nec.com) lists more than ten thousand academic science and engineering articles related to information security. Although relatively small by comparison, bodies of research in the human factors and business management have also developed in information security. In the next few pages, we provide overviews of the research in these areas and then discuss how new research might fit into the neglected gap between the different areas.

Engineering and Technology Approaches to Information Security

Clarke (2001) described five main areas of information security: service integrity, data integrity, data secrecy, authentication, and non-repudiation. Much research and many technologies reflect capabilities in subsets of these five areas (cf. Caelli et al., 1991). For example, academic research on cryptography provides theories and algorithms that help to ensure data secrecy, non-repudiation, and other capabilities (e.g., Rivest et al., 1978). As Bruce Schneier suggested in *Applied Cryptography* (1995), these tools give control over information privacy and security when, "planning a political campaign, discussing taxes, designing a new product [or] planning a marketing strategy" (p. xix). In short, cryptography is part of an essential tool kit for implementing some of the basic functions of information security.

Notably, however, in Schneier's (2000) follow-up book, *Secrets and Lies*, he also asserted that such tools provide insufficient information protection on their own: "If you think that technology can solve your security problems, then you don't understand the problems and you don't understand the technology" (p. xii). Schneier and others (e.g., Horowitz, 2001; Hull, 2002; Scanlon, 2002) have suggested that the vagaries of user behavior constitute one of the major "detrimental" influences on the usefulness of security technology (i.e., what one might term the "pesky humans" proposition).

With awareness of this idea, however, some computer scientists have recognized that understanding variability in user behavior may actually be an important lever for improving the effectiveness of security technology. For example, some researchers have used behavioral profiles as a strategy for authentication and intrusion detection (e.g., Monrose and Rubin, 1997; Yeung and Ding, 2002; Singh et al., 2001; Seleznyov et al., 2001). Such research exemplifies use of variability in human behavior as a starting point for improving the functions of information security.

Thus, in overview, engineering-focused information security research has provided theories, algorithms, and methods to support essential functions of security. Standards developers ensure interoperability among these methods, and a marketplace of information security products uses the academic research and the standards to provide technological approaches for supporting security. Although awareness of the user as a source of variance in system activity and performance appears in some research, this awareness has primarily been applied to information security problems related to authentication, rather than to larger issues of human-computer interaction. In the next subsection we examine how human factors research has helped to improve information security by focusing on what happens at the human-computer interface.

Human Factors Engineering

The field of human factors engineering, "is concerned with the role of humans in complex systems, the design of equipment and facilities for human use, and the development of environments for comfort and safety" (Salvendy, 1987, p. xvii). As such, the field has an important role in promoting information security by integrating an awareness of the capabilities of the human organism with knowledge of information systems to improve interfaces and overall performance of the "human-machine" system. Such improvements might focus on increasing the effectiveness of authentication interfaces, system maintenance interfaces, and any other task where a user must work directly with a device to promote security. Human factors researchers also specialize in understanding visualization tasks, human error in task performance, and the determinants of accidents and failures in human-machine systems.

As an example of human factors research, Yan et al. (2000) worked on improving authentication by conducting an experiment with four hundred university students comparing the "crackability" of passwords that users chose using different mnemonics. By building upon basic research on learning and memory to devise their experimental conditions, this article shows an imaginative strategy for using behavioral science as the basis of improving information security. Other researchers such as Proctor et al. (2002) and Wood (1996) have also taken a human factors approach in attempts to improve password authentication.

In a different approach, Gonzalez and Sawicka (2002) used their expertise in safety analysis to create a system dynamics model of behavioral compliance with information security measures. This research represents a notable example of bringing a systems perspective to bear on behavioral aspects of information security. Human factors engineers have also made indirect contributions to information security by providing basic research on visualizing network structures, examining failures in human-machine systems, and providing an understanding of the limits of vigilance and attention in danger situations (e.g., Parasuraman and Bowers, 1987).

Traditionally, human factors research focuses on what happens in complex systems at the junction between individual users and system interfaces. This perspective necessarily and rightly pays less attention to the larger business context in which behaviors occur. In contrast to the human factors perspective, management researchers examine information security in the context of risks to business processes, alternative methods of mitigating those risks, and cost-benefit analyses for choosing among those alternatives. In the following section, we briefly review the area of information security management.

Information Security Management

Management scholars sometimes view information security in terms of the risks that security problems present to the effective functioning of the business. In this light, one important job role of managers comprises managing information security risks. Tudor (2000) summarized information security management as working "to establish controls and measures to minimize the risk of loss of information and system resources" (p. 1). The control most frequently mentioned in this literature is organizational policy: analyzing the business environment and its risks to ascertain an optimal set of policies; communicating and implementing those policies; and promoting and assessing compliance with policies (Perry, 1985). Dhillon's (2001) edited book on information security management provides a cross-section of the research topics in this area.

Considerable research has occurred at the intersection of information security and organizational policy development (e.g., Anderson, 1996; Dhillon, 2001; Lichtenstein and Swatman, 1997; Lindup, 1995; Warman, 1992; Wood, 1995). One stream in this research defines the front end of the policy development process by focusing first on the analysis of business risk associated with information security. For example, Straub and Welke (1998) outlined general models for analyzing the risk inherent in information systems. Their efforts described how to link risk analysis with later managerial decision making. Ettredge and Richardson (2001) conducted a similar analysis targeted specifically at the risks of e-commerce.

David (2002) contrasted security policies that can be enforced through purely mechanical means and those that require human detection and judgment: "Enforcement of the first of these can be aided with automatic log off after some period of no keyboard activity, but the second requires supervisory action after policy violations are reported" (p. 507). This quote demonstrates a shared attitude among many who work on information security policy that detection of policy violations and enforcement of rules through administrative action provides a good connection between an organization's behavioral goals and actual worker behavior. One might label this the "traffic stop" approach: Give out tickets for "security violations" to maintain safety on the information highway.

In a different approach to the management of information security, Gordon and Loeb (2002) developed financial analysis frameworks for judging costs and benefits of information security. Wei et al. (2001) did the same, but specifically focused on financial analysis of intrusion detection systems. These financial analyses often estimate the costs of "cleanup" after an information security problem has occurred. Such estimates require a detailed understanding of what specific activities, procedures, and equipment the cleanup would require. Some authors have termed this "disaster recovery planning" (e.g., Hawkins et al., 2000), and this also constitutes a burgeoning new area of information security research, particularly following the events of September 11, 2001.

The Neglected Gap: Motivation, Behavior, and Information Security

The research landscape we have painted starts by foregrounding research on algorithms, methods, and standards that supports a variety of technology products for information security. Upon this technology foreground, human factors experts have worked to simplify and rationalize the interfaces of security-related systems. Because most such systems exist in the context of organizations, management experts have analyzed business risks associated with information systems and have drafted organizational policies to cope with these risks. We believe that an important missing layer in this assortment of approaches lies between the machine interface and the business-level concerns of management. In particular, we believe that information security research presently gives too little attention to the antecedents of behavior among the individuals whose actions and activities with information resources influence the status of information security.

As an example, despite the availability of encrypted e-mail products and organizational policies decreeing the importance of secure communications, few people use such products. Each research camp can offer an explanation: Technologists might lament the lack of a widely accepted industry standard, human factors engineers might criticize user interfaces used to secure e-mail as counterintuitive, and management scholars might say that the risk of costly disaster has historically been too low to bother enforcing the policies. A behavioral security perspective might offer a different scenario: Workers find encrypted e-mail inconvenient, particularly in light of the fact that they are under pressure to get a lot of work accomplished without delays. Additionally, workers may believe that their routine correspondence usually contains no information of real value; in those rare cases when they have a sensitive message to give to someone else, a phone call or face-to-face meeting will substitute. Finally, workers see that even top managers never use secure e-mail, never mention it as a high priority, never offer training on its use, and never reward those few who use the feature diligently.

All of these concerns comprise a "middle road" that plots a route between the low-level user interface and high-level business level issues. This middle road comprises the precursors, setting, and motivators of the behaviors that affect the security status of the firm's technology and information resources. Attitudes, beliefs, preferences, norms, social facilitators, and social constraints fall within this domain, as do some larger scale issues such as leadership, group dynamics, and coordination. Thus, a basic assumption inherent in a behavioral approach to security would suggest that security-related behavior can become more effective if the precursors, setting, and motivators change to facilitate desired behaviors and inhibit undesirable ones.

An existing model for the direction such research could take appears in the literature on computer misuse and abuse. For example, Straub (1990) investigated the impact of sanctions and other forms of obtaining compliance in organizations to ascertain the extent to which the severity and certainty of sanctions would influence "computer abuse." Other work in this area includes Loch and Conger (1996); Armstrong et al. (2000); Stanton (2002); and Morahan-Martin and Schumacher (2001). Interestingly, these projects and related work on the "insider threat" to information security (e.g., Anderson et al., 1999; Schultz, 2002; Shaw, Post, and Ruby, 2002) have all tended to focus primarily on the intentionally disruptive behavior enacted by a small proportion of the workers in any given organization. The few exceptions to this spotlight on troublesome actions have included some examinations of the importance of user awareness and training (e.g., Spurling, 1995; Thomson and von Solms, 1998), and analyses of the ethical guides that may influence security related behavior (e.g., Siponen, 2001; Trompeters and Eloff, 2001). We believe that these latter projects hold substantial promise for helping to shift behavior-focused research away from the common assumption that workers are wrongdoers whose behavior must be carefully circumscribed. In contrast to that common assumption, our own research program, as described below, focuses on understanding the origins and contexts of both positive and negative security-related behaviors.

RESEARCH PHASE 1: FRAMING THE PROBLEM

Over a period of about a year, we conducted longitudinal research in four organizations: a hospital, a manufacturing facility, a mental health services provider, and a private university. In each case, the institution was undergoing a series of organizational changes related to the deployment of new information technology, in most cases an enterprise resource system (a large, modular software system that provides information services for several functional areas). As one facet of our project we interviewed information security professionals about information security issues that they faced. We also queried regular employees about their perspectives on information security. In total, we interviewed fifty-nine individuals, of whom approximately 30 percent had work responsibilities in information security. In keeping with the exploratory nature of the study, we used "bottom up" thematic coding to understand common ideas expressed in the interviews.

Early on, information security professionals taught us that their most worrisome concerns lay with the internal employees who comprised their "user population," and not with technology issues per se. Although external attacks on computer systems were reportedly ubiquitous, technical controls existed in abundance to handle these problems (e.g., firewalls and antivirus protection). By contrast, internal employees often have extensive access to systems and data, along with specialized knowledge and expertise on the organizations' business practices, and these constitute important sources of vulnerability. A representative verbatim comment from an information security professional was:

> "Well, you know most of the most dangerous attacks come from inside the organization, the most damage that is going to occur is *not* the people from outside the organization. It probably is going to be someone working for you . . ."

Following up on this concern, we began to ask information security professionals about the specific kinds of employee behaviors that they considered most important with respect to information security. Many respondents mentioned password management (i.e., choosing a good password and changing it frequently), as well as logging out of unused systems, performing backups of critical data, avoiding illegal software use, and updating security software (e.g., antivirus signatures). A representative quotation here was:

> *Interviewer*:   I am going to change the focus here again, and ask about things . . . that non-IT professionals do that affect information security.

> *Respondent*:   Okay. What, like writing a password down, and using your dog or cat's name as your password, using the same password, never changing your password, those kinds of things, like we all do, you know, stick up notes on your PC? I mean giving your password to your friends, those are all things that everyone, IT professionals included, would do. You know I must have a couple of dozen passwords that I use for accounts that I try to use, and I have a hard time trying to keep track of all of that. Doesn't everybody?

As this quote suggests, both information security professionals and regular employees sometimes engage in inappropriate security-related behaviors without malign intent. Regular employees often mentioned that the reasons they circumvented security controls revolved around balancing productivity and security: Security controls were often perceived as inconvenient and counterproductive. Information security professionals also cited awareness and education of end users as a key issue that could either enhance or detract from security. We also ascertained that a wide range of behaviors and many variants on behaviors relevant to information security existed. Finally, we noted the presence of motivational conflicts in which the desire to "do the right thing" might become thwarted by other concerns such as productivity and convenience. Together, the results of this qualitative work suggested to us that an important next step might involve the development of a systematic and organized list of the important security-related behaviors that occur in organizational contexts.

RESEARCH PHASE 2: DEFINING THE BEHAVIORAL DOMAIN

Our goal for this phase was to construct and test a set of categories for information security behaviors. We hoped that this knowledge would support later research efforts that focus on understanding the antecedents and consequences of information security behavior. We began by conducting 110 additional interviews with managers, information technology professionals, and regular employees during which we asked respondents to describe both beneficial and detrimental behaviors that employees within organizations enact that affect information security. From the transcripts of these interviews we compiled a raw list of security related behaviors. Next, we prepared a card deck listing the eighty-two resultant behaviors. Ten individuals (graduate students and faculty in information technology) sorted the cards into self-generated categories. By collapsing across the many similarities among these independently generated categories, we developed a six-element taxonomy of security behavior that varied along two dimensions: intentionality and technical expertise. The intentionality dimension appeared to capture whether the behavior described on the card was intentionally malicious, intentionally beneficial, or perhaps somewhere in between (i.e., absent explicit intention to help or harm). The technical expertise dimension focused on the degree of computer or information technology knowledge and skill that the actor needed to have in order to perform the behavior described on the card.

The Six Categories

Figure 12.1 below depicts the six categories arranged on two dimensions. To illustrate with contrasting categories, "aware assurance" refers to positive security practices conducted by well-trained personnel, while "detrimental misuse" refers to the inappropriate and intentional behaviors of inexpert individuals who misuse information resources. An example of aware assurance would be when a well-trained end user discovers a back door on her desktop PC by using the task and

Figure 12.1 **Two-Factor Taxonomy of End-User Security Behaviors**

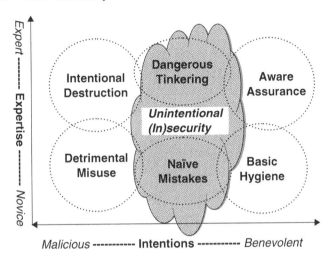

process list to investigate unusual hard drive activity. An example of detrimental misuse would be when a worker uses the company's e-mail to forward pornographic materials to a coworker. In Figure 12.1, each category shows a slight degree of overlap with its neighbors in recognition of the likely existence of behaviors near the borderlines. Note that the phrase "basic hygiene" is used here in analogy to personal hygiene: Like washing one's hands to prevent the spread of germs, we assume that simple and habitual information security practices like protecting one's password can, in the long run, improve security.

In Figure 12.1, the central "dark cloud" of unintentional (in)security suggests that sometimes individuals act without explicit intentions either to harm or help information security. Our experts' list of behaviors contained many examples of "naïve mistakes" (e.g., using one's social security number as a password) that suggested a lack of awareness of basic information security principles rather than an intention to cause harm. Similarly, dangerous tinkering suggests that an individual with a higher degree of technical expertise might affect information security as an unintended consequence of his or her ability to use complex technology with unintentional properties (e.g., by installing a remote access program for the sake of convenience, but forgetting to change the default passwords).

Testing the Categories

To provide some verification of these categories, we developed a paper and pencil instrument that included the full list of the behaviors. Based on feedback we had received in the first phase of the study, a small set of cards had their respective descriptions divided into two discrete behaviors. Also based on feedback from the initial study, we reworded each item so that it consistently referred to the actor by the impersonal pronoun "he" or "she." We presented these items in alternation to avoid bias based on the gender of the portrayed actor. The result was a series of ninety-four statements such as, "He brought a wireless gateway device into his office, and installed it on the network without authorization." For each of the ninety-four behaviors, we asked respondents to assign the behavior to one of the six categories appearing in Figure 12.1. We also asked the respondent to rate the apparent intentionality of the behavior, and the apparent degree of necessary technical know-how. We distributed a total of seventy-five surveys and received forty-nine completed surveys for a response rate of 65 percent. Respondents for this second phase of the study were forty-nine students in information technology bachelor's and master's degree programs.

Because our primary interest lay in the list of behaviors rather than in individuals' responses, we began our analysis of these data by aggregating category assignments and ratings across all forty-nine respondents. To aggregate the categorical variable that designated the six categories of behavior we took the modal response. In the case of three behaviors, there were ties (i.e., bimodality): In these cases, we chose one of the two modal categories at random. To aggregate the two rating variables, we calculated both the mean and the standard deviation across all forty-nine responses. The mean provided a single index of each behavior's standing on the intentionality scale and the expertise scale. The standard deviation provided an index of disagreement among raters about the status of intentionality and the degree of required expertise for each behavior.

We ran a two-factor MANOVA on the aggregated mean ratings, using individual behaviors as cases and mean scores on expertise and intentionality as the dependent variables. The multivariate omnibus tests were statistically significant for the expertise categorization factor, $F(2,87) = 92.5$, $p < .001$, and for the intentionality categorization factor, $F(4,174) = 98.8$, $p < .001$. The alert reader will recognize that the F-values for the main effects signify substantial effect sizes. Indeed, the eta-squared value for the main effect of expertise categorization was .68 and the eta-squared value for the main effect of intentionality was .69: Both values can be interpreted as large effect sizes (Cohen, 1992). These effect sizes support the success of the categorization scheme by demonstrating that the means for the two conditions of expertise appeared at substantially different points on our five-point scale and that the three conditions of intentionality did likewise. Further, the ordering of the means was, in all cases, as one would expect, with the means for low expertise and malicious intent near the bottom of their respective scales and the means for high expertise and benevolent intent near the top of their respective scales.

Possibly more interesting are the contents of Table 12.1. This table provides a view of the items that generated the most disagreements (i.e., a high standard deviation among the set of forty-nine ratings provided by the respondents on a particular item), with the top five items focusing on disagreements on expertise and the bottom five items focusing on disagreements on intentionality. Note that the smallest standard deviation for any item was .47, so the values in this table (up to three times as large) suggest substantial disagreements on the items highlighted here. Note that the three out of five expertise items pertain to training. Possibly, raters were unsure whether they should rate the actor's expertise prior to the training or following it. For intentionality, it is interesting to note that the stated behaviors may in some cases be legitimate for incumbents in certain roles (e.g., security specialists) while being inappropriate for other roles (e.g., regular employees), and the absence of information about the actor's position in the organization may have made judging intentionality more difficult in these cases. Another note of interest about the last five behaviors in Table 12.1 is that they are all actions with serious import: Their ultimate results or implications could have substantial negative effects on the organization.

To recap, our goal in this second phase of research was to transform a raw list of security-related behaviors into a more manageable taxonomy with recognizable dimensions that had logical and definitional appeal. Our results suggest that we achieved a degree of success in this goal. While just three of the ninety-four behaviors failed to generate a clear majority vote, for the remaining ninety-one behaviors a consensus emerged on where that behavior belonged in our six-element taxonomy. Further, when we used this consensus as a basis for comparing ratings of expertise and intentionality (the two dimensions of our taxonomy) statistical analysis of mean ratings clearly showed that as a group our raters assigned normative levels of expertise and intentionality

Table 12.1

Behaviors Generating Greatest Disagreement

Category	SD Expertise	SD Intentionality	Behavior Description
Detrimental Misuse	**1.60**	1.10	She mailed an encryption software CD to a foreign country in violation of international or regional export control laws.
Aware Assurance	**1.49**	.65	She did a training program to become familiar with indicators of virus infection and to learn how to report operational anomalies to resource administrators.
Aware Assurance	**1.44**	.86	He participated in advanced security training designated by the organization.
Basic Hygiene	**1.42**	.47	He did a training program to learn about the sensitivity/criticality of special company files so that he could apply appropriate protective measures when handling the information.
Basic Hygiene	**1.38**	1.17	She constructively criticized organizational security policies to her boss.
Detrimental Misuse	1.29	**1.42**	He found and saved trade secret information about other companies using the Internet.
Detrimental Misuse	.84	**1.34**	To assess how well the network was running, he set up a network monitoring device that intercepted data not intended for his system.
Intentional Destruction	1.03	**1.33**	He used an intrusion detection program on the company's network, even though that was not part of his job.
Detrimental Misuse	1.11	**1.28**	He used unsolicited e-mail to advertise a service offered by the organization.
Intentional Destruction	1.20	**1.21**	She deleted a colleague's account information so that he would not be able to access his files.

Note: SD refers to standard deviation, used here as an index of disagreement among raters. Values in boldface indicate which variable served as the sorting key. The first five behaviors were the most disagreed upon for the expertise variable, while the last five were the most disagreed upon for the intentionality variable.

consistent with the classification scheme. We expect that most security-related behaviors that occur in organizations could be positioned on this two-dimensional taxonomy.

From a practical perspective, this work simplifies the task of developing criterion measures that assess security-related behavior in organizations. Such criterion measures must attempt to capture, through observations, self-ratings, or other ratings, the occurrence of behaviors that require high and low expertise and the occurrence of behaviors whose apparent intentionality spans the malicious–benevolent spectrum. Another important characteristic of this two-dimensional taxonomy is that it provides clear indications of paths that organizations can take toward improving their security status. In general, any interventions that shift intentionality toward the benevolent end of the continuum ought to improve the organization's security status. Likewise, with the exception of those employees who may have malicious intentions toward the organization, providing training and other forms of expertise development appear to have the potential to benefit the organization's information security.

From a theoretical perspective, it would be interesting to pursue the question of how security personnel judge users' intentions differently based on whether they see the behavior as requiring a lot of expertise or a little expertise. This question ties in with the notion of trust as a fundamental component of security in organizations. Knowing whom to trust and under what circumstances to trust them can make an important difference in security personnel's ability to detect and respond to potential security problems. If security personnel misjudge the trustworthiness of another actor based on irrelevant information, this may 1) make it more difficult for certain employees to conduct a legitimate activities, and/or; 2) make it easier for individuals with malicious intentions to carry out detrimental tasks.

RESEARCH PHASE 3: SURVEYS OF NOVICE BEHAVIORS

We used the list of end-user security-related behaviors compiled in the previous phase of research as the basis for three subsequent survey studies. We focused on the positive or benign security-related behaviors that could be enacted by employees who did not possess specialized security training (e.g., regularly changing passwords). Because little systematic research exists concerning the occurrence of these behaviors in organizations, we believed that an important next step would be to screen the behaviors against a variety of plausible predictors. At the conclusion of this work we expected to ascertain a set of patterns relating personal and contextual factors to security behaviors that we could then use as a basis for proposing a conceptual framework of variables and processes to guide future research.

Survey Study 1

Genesee Survey Services, a consulting firm based in Rochester, NY, conducts an annual nationwide study of U.S. workers from a variety of industries. The National Work Opinion Survey (NWOS) serves as a source of normative data on measures of organizational concern. The NWOS is distributed by postal mail to a random sample of U.S. employees (using a professionally compiled sampling frame) along with a postage-paid return envelope. The 2003 version of the NWOS included nine items customized for the present study based on the list of security-related behaviors described above. The NWOS sample comprised regular managers and employees, so we sampled only from the "novice" items in our taxonomy because we expected to find relatively few individuals with professional security training in the sample. We used three items pertaining to password management (e.g., frequency of changing the password), three items pertaining to password sharing (e.g., sharing with others in the work group) and three items pertaining to organizational support of security-related behaviors (e.g., "My company/organization provides training programs to help employees improve their awareness of computer and information security."). The survey was distributed to N = 4000 individuals and N = 2011 usable surveys were returned for a response rate of approximately 50 percent. The survey was offered in several versions, and not all of the versions contained the customized items. After accounting for these variations and missing data we had N = 1167 surveys with usable data on the security-related items.

The NWOS captures information about the respondent's organization and demographics. We screened these organizational and demographic variables as possible predictors. We factor analyzed the security-related items using a principal components extraction and varimax rotation. The breakdown of items into factors reflected our original intentions for the items: three items indicating password sharing (alpha = .67), three items indicating organizational support of security-related behaviors (alpha = .77), and three items indicating password management (alpha = .56).

This low value of alpha led us to remove an item pertaining to writing down one's password, and this increased that latter alpha reliability estimate to .68. We analyzed the password-writing item separately.

Next we conducted analyses to explore the effects of organizational circumstances and personal demographics on the behaviors. In the first analysis we used MANOVA to examine effects of geographic location, size of company, and type of industry on password management, password writing, password sharing, and organizational support for security. Multivariate results indicated that company size, Wilk's lambda = .88, $F(40,1894) = 1.5$, $p < .05$, and company type, Wilk's lambda = .88, $F(56,1943) = 1.8$, $p < .05$, had statistically significant effects on the outcomes. In overview, results showed that employees in larger organizations reported better password management practices (more frequent password changing and selection of stronger passwords); employees from the military, financial institutions, and telecommunications/Internet companies reported better password management practices than employees in other organization types; and more security support was perceived in the military and public utilities than in other organizations.

Finally we examined demographic factors: Multivariate tests revealed that job type, job tenure, union membership, age, and income level had statistically significant effects on the outcome variables, with Wilk's lambda values ranging from .95 (job type) to .99 (union membership). Administrative personnel, managers, and technicians reported better password management than people in other job types, but administrative support personnel, managers, first-level supervisors, and sales/management personnel also tended to share their passwords with others more frequently than those in other job types. Individuals with longer service reported greater organizational support for secure behaviors (e.g., availability of training). Union members reported slightly less favorable password management practices than those not in unions. Those with higher incomes reported better password management practices and less password sharing than those with lower incomes.

The MANOVA and regression findings described above suggest that organizational and demographic factors relate to security behavior. Individuals in organizations that had "a lot at stake" (e.g., in military and financial institutions) had apparently received the training, tools, and incentives needed to enact more effective information security behavior. Likewise, individuals further up the organizational hierarchy may have both a greater personal investment in the organization as well as access to more resources (such as training) than those further down or with a shorter history in the organization.

Survey Study 2

As in the first survey study, we focused on asking about novice behaviors (e.g., choosing a hard-to-guess password). In addition to asking about password management, the eight security-related behaviors on this survey included several behaviors not assessed in survey study 1: three types of counterproductive computer usage, discussing security policies with coworkers, and abiding by acceptable use policies. The survey randomly sampled eight hundred employed adult respondents from the StudyResponse online panelist project (http://www.StudyResponse.org). We intentionally sampled individuals who reported their jobs as not in the military, utilities, financial institutions, or telecom so that we would not need to control for organization type in this research. Given the 298 usable responses we obtained, this procedure yielded a response rate of 37.25 percent. Participants completed a brief survey with measures of organizational commitment (Allen and Meyer, 1990), assessments of positive and negative feelings at work (Miles, Borman, Spector, and Fox, 2002), a self-assessment of technical know-how, demographic data, and a sample of eight of the novice behaviors from our security behavior list.

Table 12.2

Correlations of Security-Related Behaviors with Predictors

Behavior	Technical Know-How	Organizational Commitment	Positive Work Feelings	Negative Work Feelings
Tell password to other people in organization				.13*
Write down password				
Use work computer for personal Web surfing	.14*			
Use work computer for personal e-mail	.17**			
Use work computer for games, chat, or instant messaging	.12*			
Undergo training on organization's acceptable use policy	.12*			
Talk with coworkers about organization's acceptable use policy	.14*			.12*
Abide by organization's acceptable use policy		.24**	.22**	

Note: *p < .05; **p < .01.

As with the previous survey, we examined relations between organizational predictors and the individual security-related behaviors from our novice list. For this survey, however, the items each tapped different behaviors, so we did not form them into scale scores but instead analyzed correlations with each item individually. Table 12.2 displays the results of this correlation analysis. Results evident from Table 12.2 suggest that technical know-how served as the most consistent predictor of the novice behaviors. Note, however, that increased technical know-how was also associated positively with non-productive uses of workplace computers such as gaming and instant messaging. The attitude predictors performed poorly except with respect to the correlation with individuals' reports of their compliance with acceptable use policies. In this case, both organizational commitment and positive workplace feelings associated positively with policy compliance.

Survey Study 3

Given the relative importance of technical know-how in predicting both positive and negative novice security behaviors, we conducted a third study in which employees in ten different organizations responded to a brief survey inquiring about training they had received and their relative expertise in the use of computers. All ten of the organizations were for-profit firms and they varied in size from seven employees to seven hundred employees. A total of $N = 414$ employees responded to the survey. An exact estimate of the response rate was difficult to obtain because we did not have access to the complete lists of sampled respondents within each organization, but we estimated that a total of 750 employees received invitations to participate for an approximate response rate of 55 percent. In this study we added two items to assess self-efficacy (Cronbach's alpha reliability .62), because of the importance of self-efficacy in putting knowledge and skills to work. Individuals who lack self-efficacy tend to perform poorly on a task regardless of their skill or know-how with the task (e.g., Bandura and Wood, 1989). We also had a self-report of the number of individuals supervised by the respondent as a proxy for managerial status. In this study, the outcome variable was a self-report of positive password-related behavior.

Multiple regression results indicated that training, computer usage, self-efficacy, and number of individuals supervised all served as predictors of positive password behavior. The multiple R-squared in this analysis was .33, $F(4,408) = 44.4$, $p < .001$. The most influential predictor was self-efficacy, with a beta weight of .45, $p < .001$. Training (beta $= .11$, $p < .05$) and computer usage (beta $= .15$, $p < .05$) both had modest positive relations to password behavior. Finally, the number of employees supervised had a negative beta weight (beta $= -.09$, $p < .05$), indicating that the greater one's supervisory responsibilities, the worse one's reported password behavior was. Taken in overview, these results complement and extend the results of the first two surveys by suggesting that task knowledge and self-efficacy have meaningful associations with novice security-related behaviors. In the next section, we offer a framework for understanding these results and becoming prepared for next steps in behavioral research on information security.

PROPOSED RESEARCH FRAMEWORK AND NEXT STEPS

Looking back over the three phases of research, it appears evident that the research tools and techniques of behavioral science can provide a variety of data about security-related behaviors in organizations. Our qualitative work revealed the nature and scope of behavioral security problems faced by individuals with responsibility for information security. We used these insights to develop and test a categorized list of criterion behaviors for use in subsequent studies. Our subsequent survey work suggested that organizational, demographic, and attitudinal factors could predict some of the novice behaviors that information security professionals consider easy targets for improvement (e.g., password management). Taken together, these studies suggest that security behaviors relate to a combination of relevant organizational and personal factors and a variety of mediating influences (see Figure 12.2).

Figure 12.2 organizes our thinking about the groups of variables, processes, and resources likely to be relevant to understanding, predicting, and influencing security-related behaviors into a proposed set of causal processes. Three different types of elements in the figure include rectangles for variables or families of variables, ovals for activities or behaviors, and cylinders for "stocks" or resources that can be built or depleted over time. (Calling something a stock or resource elevates it beyond being simply a variable: A stock or resource can be measured using a variable, but it further signifies a real supply of something—such as disk space, money, caseload, morale, or inventory—that can be used up, depleted, and/or replenished. See Karnopp and Rosenberg, 1975, for further details.) The elements in the figure are numbered to match the following narrative description. Organizational factors (#1) appear in the upper left of the figure in recognition of results from the first survey. In the first survey, we found organizational predictors that set the stage for the behavioral repertoires of employees. For instance, in military settings the conditions may exist where the value of information security is continually reinforced through everyday practices, training, and socialization. We do not know, at this stage of the research, what specific organizational practices or characteristics may have the greatest effect on information security. At least three candidates exist, however. First, we propose that strong and visible leadership in an organization can contribute to setting the stage for positive security behaviors. When leaders publicly endorse, support, and abide by the organization's security policies, employees may internalize aspects of the organization's mission and values in their attitudes and beliefs (#2). Second, we propose that organizational factors such as the organization's mission and slack financial resources will influence the allocation of resources to processes of enforcing organizational policies (#3) and running security training and awareness programs (#4). Finally, we propose that organizational factors such the degree of bureaucratic centralization and hierarchical nature of the organization will influence the amount of policy knowledge

Figure 12.2   **Framework for Investigating Behavioral Information Security**

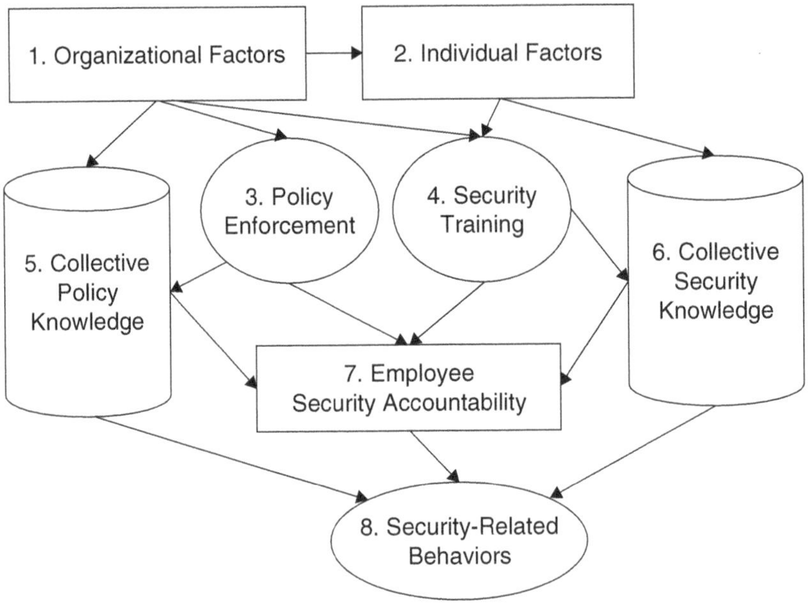

collectively possessed by all organization members (#5). This latter construct is portrayed as a stock or resource in recognition that collective knowledge can be built up through educational, documentary, and enforcement efforts, and can be depleted by neglect and employment attrition.

Next, we found evidence in survey study 2 suggesting that job-relevant attitudes and beliefs (#2) influence employees' willingness to become engaged with information security–related issues in the workplace. Organizational commitment, as well as positive and negative feelings about work, may influence employees' willingness to seek optional training or participate in mandatory training concerning information security (#4). It is likely that individual factors (#2) also comprise basic aptitudes and prior knowledge related to technical computer tasks and that these—as well as formal training—influence the amount of security knowledge collectively possessed by all organization members (#6). In a parallel construction to collective policy knowledge (#5), collective security knowledge is portrayed as a stock or resource in recognition that collective knowledge can be built up through ongoing efforts, and can be depleted by neglect and employment attrition. We recognize that conceptualizing these areas of collective knowledge as organizational "stocks" or resources is more speculative than some of the other propositions, but we believe the idea has significant potential for helping explain the course of security successes and failures at an organization. In our phase 1 qualitative research reported above, we found a large degree of heterogeneity with respect to the *maintenance* of policy at the research sites. In some organizations, policies were fresh in the sense that someone within the organization was paying attention to them, updating them, promoting them, and ensuring that employee training and awareness programs included consideration of policies. In other organizations, policies were stale: Printed binders full of dry boilerplate gathered dust on bookshelves throughout the facility. These findings led us to the belief that both security policy knowledge—what an employee is expected to do—and procedural security knowledge—how they can do it—may comprise critical resources in ensuring positive security behaviors.

Finally, survey studies 2 and 3 suggested that policy knowledge (#5) and employee security knowledge (#6) may each influence employees' security-related behaviors (#8). Policy knowledge (#5) provides the mechanism through which the organization's leadership communicates the priorities and preferences for security to employees. In effect, employees who have substantial awareness of the content of policies know what security goals are valued as well as the general repertoire of acceptable behaviors that lead to those goals. To enact those behaviors requires at least one more ingredient, however: Employees must know specifically what steps to take to achieve a certain security goal. Knowledge of these steps emerges from the security knowledge (#6) developed, in part, through training programs (#4).

In addition, however, we propose one additional intermediary construct suggested by our research: employee security accountability (#7). Taken as a whole, our studies suggest that knowledge by itself is insufficient to make sure that employees do the right thing. Employees must feel that they "should do it," in other words, that enacting the prescribed behaviors leads to valued outcomes and helps to avoid unpleasant ones. We propose that this security accountability (#7) arises primarily from the observation of examples of policy enforcement (#3) that show how the organization notices and punishes transgressions as well as from participation in training programs (#4) that show the organization's commitment to facilitating right behavior.

The elements depicted in Figure 12.2 along with the proposed interconnections among them represent our latest thinking about the influences of organizational circumstances and personal factors on security-related behaviors. It seems certain that the elements and interconnections do not represent an exhaustive list of the possibilities, but the program of qualitative and quantitative research we have conducted to date has provided supportive information that bolsters our choice of variables, resources, and organizational processes depicted in the figure.

CONCLUSION

Building on this research, we hope that other researchers can help us advance the application of behavioral science to problems of information security. Much work remains in order to facilitate future research in this area. In particular, the research community needs to develop appropriate protocols and instruments for assessing such variables as employee security accountability. Self-report instruments for measuring basic security knowledge, policy knowledge, and other constructs indicated in Figure 12.2 would also provide benefits for future research. After addressing measurement and assessment issues, the next pressing need lies in the area of access to organizations. Like many organizational issues, research on information security in organizations apparently requires a careful understanding of the context in which security-related behaviors take place. It is difficult to obtain this level of understanding without access to frank and detailed information from the various relevant stakeholder groups in the organization, i.e., leaders, technology and security specialists, and the end-user population. In turn, this access requires the painstaking development of individual relationships with organizations. A more efficient approach might include the formation of a research consortium, perhaps centered on cooperation with a professional organization of security personnel who would provide broad-based access to relevant information from a wide range of organizations. Finally, we believe that researchers can help to advance the state of theory in the area of behavioral information security, perhaps building upon some of the ideas offered in this paper. Relevant theory, focusing on motivation and behavior in organizational contexts, can provide guideposts that help with the formulation of future research as well as practical interventions.

We hope that researchers will see from our results that influencing information security-related behavior constitutes a complex and interesting set of problems worthy of extended programs of research. This research must incorporate a systemic model of the technology user in context, rather than focusing solely on intrapersonal issues such as knowledge or attitudes or purely organizational issues such as organization size or type. Information systems user behavior occurs within an organizational context, and full consideration of that context must include social, technological, and organizational influences in addition to the basic characteristics and proclivities of the individual users. We believe that ultimately such research can contribute practical solutions that improve the information security of contemporary organizations. Research and development in the area of technology-based security controls has a substantial lead on behavioral research, however. Behavioral researchers must catch up by demonstrating that the human side of the information security "problem" has measurements, models, explanations, and viable interventions for improving information security within organizations.

ACKNOWLEDGMENTS

This work was supported in part by a small grant from the SIOP Foundation and in part by award ITR-0312078 from the National Science Foundation. Neither the SIOP Foundation nor the National Science Foundation necessarily endorses the findings or conclusions of this work.

The authors appreciate the assistance of Isabelle Fagnot, Indira Guzman, Vibha Vijayasri, and Cavinda Caldera in the collection and preparation of the data for this paper.

REFERENCES

Allen, N.J., and Meyer, J.P. The measurement and antecedents of affective, continuance, and normative commitment to the organization. *Journal of Occupational Psychology*, 63 (1990), 1–18.

Anderson, R.H.; Feldman, P.M.; Gerwehr, S.; Houghton, B.; Mesic, R.; Pinder, J.D.; Rothenberg, J.; and Chiesa, J. *Securing the U.S. defense information infrastructure: A proposed approach.* Washington, DC: Rand, 1999.

Anderson, R. *A Security Policy Model for Clinical Information Systems.* Proceedings of the IEEE Symposium on Security and Privacy, Oakland, CA, May 6–8, 1996, pp. 30–43.

Armstrong, L.; Phillips, J.G.; and Saling, L.L. Potential determinants of heavier internet usage. *International Journal of Human-Computer Studies*, 53, 4 (2000), 537–550.

Bandura, A., and Wood, R. Effect of perceived controllability and performance standards on self-regulation of complex decision making. *Journal of Personality and Social Psychology*, 56 (1989), 805–814.

Caelli, W.; Longley. D.; and Shain, M. *Information Security Handbook,* New York: Stockton Press, 1991.

Clarke, R. *Introduction to Information Security.* Unpublished manuscript. Canberra, Australia: Australian National University, 2001 (available at http://www.anu.edu.au/people/Roger.Clarke/EC/IntroSecy.html).

Cohen, J. A power primer. *Psychological Bulletin*, 112, 1 (1992), 155–159.

David, J. Policy enforcement in the workplace. *Computers and Security*, 21, 6 (2002), 506–513.

Dhillon, G. (ed.) *Information Security Management: Global Challenges in the New Millennium.* Hershey, PA: Idea Group Publishing, 2001.

Ernst and Young LLP. *Global Information Security Survey.* London: Presentation Services, 2002.

Ettredge, M., and Richardson, V.J. *Assessing the risk in e-commerce.* Working Paper: University of Kansas, 2001 (available at: http://dlib2.computer.org/conferen/hicss/1435/pdf/14350194.pdf).

Gonzalez, J.J., and Sawicka, A. A framework for human factors in information security. Presented at the 2002 WSEAS Int. Conf. on Information Security, Rio de Janeiro, 2002 (available at http://ikt.hia.no/josejg/).

Gordon, L.A., and Loeb, M.P. The economics of information security investment. *ACM Transactions on Information and System Security*, 5, 4 (2002), 438–457.

Hawkins, S.M.; Yen, D.C.; and Chou, D.C. Disaster recovery planning: a strategy for data security. *Information Management & Computer Security*, 8, 5 (2000), 222–229.

Horowitz, A. Top 10 security mistakes. *Computerworld*, 35, 28,(2001).

Hull, S. People are the weak links in IT security. *The Argus*, April 16, 2002.

Karnopp, D., and Rosenberg, R.C. *System Dynamics: A Unified Approach*. New York: Wiley, 1975.

Lichtenstein, S., and Swatman, P.M.C. Internet acceptable usage policy for organizations. *Information Management & Computer Security*, 5, 5 (1997), 182–190.

Lindup, K.R. A new model for information security policies. *Computer & Security*, 14, 8 (1995), 691–695.

Loch, K.D., and Conger, S. (1996). Evaluating ethical decision-making and computer use. *Communications of the ACM, 39* (7), 74–83.

Miles, D.E.; Borman, W.E.; Spector, P.E.; and Fox, S. Building an integrative model of extra role work behaviors: a comparison of counterproductive work behavior with organizational citizenship behavior. *International Journal of Selection and Assessment*, 10 (2002), 51–57.

Monrose, F., and Rubin, A. Authentication via keystroke dynamics. In *4th ACM Conference on Computer and Communications Security,* Zurich, Switzerland. New York: ACM Press, 1997, pp. 48–56.

OECD. *OECD Guidelines for the Security of Information Systems and Networks: Towards a Culture of Security*. Organisation For Economic Co-Operation And Development, 2002 (available at: http://www.oecd.org/dataoecd/16/22/15582260.pdf).

Parasuraman, R., and Bowers, J.C. Attention and vigilance in human-computer interaction. In A. Gale and B. Christie (eds.), *Psychophysiology of the Electronic Workplace*. London: Wiley, 1987, pp. 163–194.

Perry, W.E. *Management Strategies for Computer Security*. Boston: Butterworth, 1985.

Proctor, R.W.; Lien, M.-C.; Vu, K.-P.L.; Schultz, E.E.; and Salvendy, G. Improving computer security for authentication of users: influence of proactive password restrictions. *Behavior Research Methods, Instruments & Computers*, 34, 2 (2002), 163–169.

Rivest, R.L.; Shamir, A.; Adleman, L.A. A method for obtaining digital signatures and public-key cryptosystems. *Communications of the ACM*, 21, 2 (1978), 120–126.

Salvendy, G. (ed.) *Handbook of Human Factors*. New York: Wiley-Interscience, 1987.

Scanlon, B. The weakest link. *ZDNet Australia News & Technology,* 2002 (available at: http://www.zdnet.com.au/newstech/security/story/0,2000024985,20241014–5,00.htm).

Schneier, B. *Applied Cryptography: Protocols, Algorithms, and Source Code in C*, 2nd ed. New York: Wiley, 1995.

Schneier, B. *Secrets and Lies*. New York: Wiley, 2000.

Schultz, E.E. A framework for understanding and predicting insider attacks. *Computers and Security,* 21, 6 (2002), 526–531.

Security Wire Digest. CSI/FBI study says: security breaches on the rise. 2000 (available at http://www.lexias.com/1.0/securitywiredigest_27MAR2000.html).

Seleznyov, A.; Mazhelis, O.; and Puuronen, S. Learning temporal regularities of user behavior for anomaly detection. In V.I. Gorodetski, V.A. Skormin, and L.J. Popyack (eds.), *Information Assurance in Computer Networks. Methods, Models and Architectures for Network Security*. St. Petersburg, Russia: International Workshop MMM-ACNS, 2001, pp. 143–152.

Shaw, E.D.; Post, J.M.; and Ruby, K.G. Inside the mind of the insider. 2002 (available at: http://www.securitymanagement.com/library/000762.html).

Singh, H.; Furnell, S.; Lines, B.; and Dowland, P. Investigating and Evaluating Behavioural Profiling and Intrusion Detection Using Data Mining. In V.I. Gorodetski, V.A. Skormin, and L.J. Popyack (eds.), *Information Assurance in Computer Networks. Methods, Models and Architectures for Network Security*. St. Petersburg, Russia: International Workshop MMM-ACNS, 2001, pp. 153–158.

Siponen, M.T. On the role of human morality in information systems security. *Information Resources Management Journal*, 14, 4 (2001), 15–23.

Spurling, P. Promoting security awareness and commitment. *Information Management & Computer Security,* 3, 2 (1995), 20–26.

Stanton, J.M. Company profile of the frequent internet user: web addict or happy employee? *Communications of the Association for Computing Machinery*, 45, 1 (2002), 55–59.

Straub, D.W. Effective IS security: an empirical study. *Information Systems Research*, 1, 2 (1990), 255–277.

Straub, D.W., and Welke, R.J. Coping with systems risk: security planning models for management decision making. *MIS Quarterly,* 22, 4 (1998), 441–464.

Thomson, M.E., and von Solms, R. Information security awareness: educating our users effectively. *Information Management & Computer Security*, 6, 4 (1998), 167–173.

Trompeter, C.M., and Eloff, J.H.P. A framework for the implementation of socio-ethical controls in information security. *Computers & Security*, 20 (2001), 384–391.

Tudor, J.K. *Information Security Architecture: An Integrated Approach to Security in the Organization*. Boca Raton, FL: CRC Press, 2000.

Warman, A.R. Organizational computer security policy: the reality. *European Journal of Information Systems*, 1, 5 (1992), 305–310.

Wei, H.; Frinke, D.; Olivia, C.; and Ritter, C. Cost-Benefit Analysis for Network Intrusion Detection Systems. In *Proceedings of the CSI 28th Annual Computer Security Conference*, Washington, DC, October 2001.

Won, D. (ed.) *Proceedings of the Third International Conference on Information Security and Cryptology (ICISC 2000)*. Berlin: Springer, 2001.

Wood, C.C. Writing infosec policies. *Computer & Security*, 14, 8 (1995), 667–674.

Wood, C.C. Constructing difficult-to-guess passwords. *Information Management & Computer Security*, 4, 1 (1996), 43–44.

Yan, J.; Blackwell, A.; Anderson, R.; and Grant, A. *The Memorability and Security of Passwords—Some Empirical Results*. Technical Report No. 500, Computer Laboratory, University of Cambridge, 2000 (available at http://www.ftp.cl.cam.ac.uk/ftp/users/rja14/tr500.pdf).

Yeung, D.-Y., and Ding, Y. (2002). User profiling for intrusion detection using dynamic and static behavioral models. In M.-S. Cheng, P.S. Yu, and B. Liu (eds.), *Advances in Knowledge Discovery and Data Mining 6th Pacific-Asia Conference, PAKDD 2002, Taipei, Taiwan, May 6–8, 2002. Proceedings*, 2002, pp. 494–505.

CHAPTER 13

INTERPRETING SECURITY IN HUMAN-COMPUTER INTERACTIONS

A Semiotic Analysis

GURPREET DHILLON AND JEFFREY MAY

Abstract: *Although there has been extensive research in the area of information systems security and human-computer interaction (HCI), security in the context of HCI has not been well understood. This paper proposes a framework for identifying and interpreting the deep-rooted human and technical issues that deal with security in the context of HCI. The concepts are grounded in semiotics. This paper argues that analyzing security in the context of HCI from the semiotic perspective transcends existing organizational and computer-technical knowledge, thus allowing HCI designers a better ability to incorporate a more rounded design solution that seeks to minimize actual security threats and maximize user satisfaction when it comes to feeling secure.*

Keywords: *HCI, Semiotics, Security*

INTRODUCTION

Several researchers have attempted to define the field of human-computer interaction (HCI) and the various research issues that are related to it. In the context of management information systems (MIS), Zhang et al. (2003) consider HCI to be concerned with how humans interact with information, technologies, and tasks, especially in business, managerial, organizational, and cultural contexts. In identifying HCI research issues, Zhang et al. (2003) discuss seven major areas: relationship building and management, task modeling and organizational fit, user acceptance, enhancing HCI measurement, emphasizing the holistic experience of humans interacting with technologies, emphasizing a broader range of users, and a new taxonomy of MIS/HCI.

Along similar lines, Olson and Olson (2003) define HCI as the study of how people interact with computing technology. In identifying HCI research issues, Olson and Olson (2003) discuss six major areas: the science of HCI (e.g., cognitive modeling, distributed cognition), user interface development, usability methods, the workplace, computer-supported cooperative work (e.g., voice and video conferencing tools, repositories of shared knowledge, social filtering, trust in people when communicating via technology), and the larger social context (e.g., psychological and social costs of the digital divide).

Traditionally, HCI has been the study of how people design, implement, and use interactive computer systems and how computers affect individuals, organizations, and society (Myers et al., 1996). In identifying HCI research issues, Myers et al. (1996) discuss five major areas of interest: universal access to distributed information, lifelong learning, e-commerce, information visualization, and computer-mediated communications.

Clearly the literature on HCI touches upon a broad spectrum of issues. Yet, management of information system security has not been considered as a topic area of interest to HCI researchers. However, when examining the major issues related to HCI and e-commerce, Nah and Davis (2002) do suggest that Web usability, interface design, and especially trust as key areas for future research. However, the research area of trust, defined as the willingness of a user to take risks, is not necessarily synonymous with the research area of security. In a survey conducted by Abrazhevich (2001), it was found that the major issues that concerned users of e-commerce sites were applicability, traceability, trust, security, convertibility, ease of use, and reliability; trust and security were found to be the most important areas of concern. As a result of this survey, there should be no doubt that interpreting security in the context of HCI is an important area of interest.

Obviously, much research has been conducted in the area of security for various implementations of information systems. This research has covered traditional topics such as authentication (passwords, biometrics), security operations (intrusion detection, vigilance, policies and practices), and development of secure systems (developing for security, understanding users, installation and operation support). These traditional topics are, no doubt, important in the context of HCI security. This paper, however, proposes a more complete analysis that deals with deep-rooted issues. A more complete analysis is required to uncover issues that deal more specifically with the human components of HCI security and how these human-level issues interact with technical issues.

As a result, this paper proposes a method, using a semiotics approach, for discovering and interpreting the deep-rooted issues that deal with security in the context of HCI. This paper is organized into three major sections. Section 2 discusses semiotic concepts along with research that applies the semiotic paradigm to other IS related issues. Section 3 then discusses actual security issues pertaining to HCI that require a more extensive and detailed analysis. Section 4 presents a method for conducting this extensive analysis using a semiotic framework. Finally, conclusions are drawn in Section 5.

MIS AND SEMIOTIC ANALYSIS

Semiotics is the study of signs where a sign is defined as anything that has meaning to somebody in some respect or capacity (Stamper, 1973). More specifically, semiotics is the discipline that helps in studying information, information flow (communication), and culture. This enables accurate interpretation of meanings through acts of signification (Barley, 1983; Manning, 1992; Falkenberg et al., 1998).

The semiotic ladder, an analytical tool developed in the field of semiotics, represents the study of signs at six different layers of abstraction (Stamper, 1973; Liebenau and Backhouse, 1990). The ladder (Table 13.1) consists of physical, empiric, syntactic, semantic, pragmatic, and social layers. The six layers can further be classified into two levels—technical and human issues—pertaining to information flows.

Braf (2001) suggests that the purpose of the semiotic ladder is to provide a framework for understanding the many different usages of information, from technical to human considerations. Clearly, HCI consists of both technical and human factors. Therefore it can be argued that developing an understanding at various levels of the semiotic ladder would serve to uncover the surface-level and deep-rooted issues that would be of interest to HCI system designers. Additionally, semiotic analysis could then serve as a starting point for uncovering the technical and human issues of security in the context of HCI.

As with any framework, much confusion is often found when one attempts to completely distinguish between the individual layers. Many issues could be interpreted at more than one layer,

Table 13.1

Semiotic Ladder

	Technical Level
Physics Layer (Physical World)	Signals, traces, physical distinctions, hardware
Empiric Layer	Noise, entropy, pattern, variety, noise variety, redundancy, codes, efficiency
Syntactic Layer	Formal structure, logic, data, records, files, computer language
	Human Level
Semantic Layer	Meanings, propositions, validity, truth, signification, denotation
Pragmatic Layer	Communications, conversations, negotiations, intentions
Social Layer (Social World)	Cultural norms, beliefs, expectations, functions, commitments, law, culture, contracts, values, shared models of reality, attitudes

Source: Based on Liebenau and Backhouse (1990).

indicating that distinct boundaries between the layers of the semiotic ladder do not always appear for every design issue, especially when one is dealing with the ladder's human layers (Kitiyadisai, 1991). Obviously, this confusion is merited because human layers are typically qualitative in nature and do not expose distinct boundaries like those produced by the quantitative technical layers. However, one must attempt to find some place in the semiotic ladder for all the concepts and issues that go into designing a system if one is planning to undertake a semiotic analysis. The rest of this section will address the distinctions between the layers of the semiotic ladder and will conclude with identifying research that applies the semiotic paradigm to other IS-related issues.

Technical Level

The technical platform of any information system includes hardware, telecommunications, and software (Falkenberg et al., 1998). When dealing with these three components of any IS technical platform, Falkenberg et al. state that generally hardware maps to the physical layer, telecommunications maps to the empiric layer, and software maps to the syntactic layer of the semiotic ladder. These three layers require research mainly from the mathematics and natural science perspective, and each individual layer of the technical level is well defined in the literature (Morris, 1964).

In short, the physical layer of the semiotic ladder is mainly concerned with modeling the properties of information as input to and output from any physical component of an information system. At the physical layer, the term "information" is generally defined as a collection of tokens that have both dynamic and static properties. A dynamic token is referred to as a signal and a static token is referred to as a mark. The physical layer is thus concerned with modeling these tokens in terms of their sources, destinations, and routes over which they are transmitted.

In contrast to the physical level, the empiric layer views information in terms of its availability and usability. The empiric layer is mainly concerned with the properties dealing with the transmission of tokens across channels of communication. Clearly the engineering principles of noise, entropy, pattern, variety, noise variety, redundancy, codes, and efficiency would all be addressed at the empiric layer (refer to Table 13.1).

In contrast to the empiric layer, the syntactic layer is not concerned with any empirical or statistical properties of information; concerned with the form and shape of this information, the syntactic layer is mainly concerned with the structure and form of tokens. This structure and form are generally expressed as syntax, and require generally agreed upon rules and formulations for consistency.

Human Level

Designers who limit themselves to technical considerations are capable of understanding the importance of each technical layer and how the layers interact with each other. However, these layers generally disregard any human considerations. As a result, any designer who confines his attention to these layers alone typically will not address the business requirements and human considerations of an information system. As a result, information systems that are designed solely based on technical requirements generally fail (Dhillon and Backhouse, 1996). Hence, understanding the human-level layers of the semiotic ladder is paramount to the success of any information system design.

As shown in Table 13.1, the semantic layer lies at the interface of the technical and human levels of the semiotic ladder. The semantic layer is mainly concerned with meanings and is not concerned with what language is used, how the message is encoded, or by what medium any message is transmitted. Meaning can be interpreted by two very different semantic principles (Falkenberg et al., 1998). The first principle, known as the objectivistic principle, assumes that meanings are mappings from syntactic structures onto objective features of a real world. The objectivistic principle assumes a perfect world scenario because it considers the real world to be the same for everyone and one that everyone knows independently of language. The second principle, the constructivist principle, has a more realistic orientation. It assumes that meanings are constructed and continuously tested and repaired. These repairs are made by the actions of people when using any syntactic structure. This involves an evaluation of language-action relationships. Of course, a well-thought-out semantic analysis would attempt to address and correct any potential failures before implementing any type of information system, thus limiting the repair work that would need to be done after implementation. Semantic analysis would then consider various concepts such as propositions, validity, truth, signification, and denotation to uncover a rich understanding of meaning to all concerned with a particular information system.

In contrast to the semantic layer, the pragmatic layer is not concerned with semantic meaning; pragmatics are concerned with placing the intentions of both the sender and receiver in context. In other words, the pragmatic layer recognizes that meanings do not provide accurate or intended actions or reactions when taken out of context. At the pragmatic level, communication is studied intensively and is considered to be successful when a meaningful utterance is passed by a sender with a certain intention and is interpreted by the receiver of this utterance with the same intention. As a result, pragmatic analysis tends to deal with conversations, negotiations, and intentions of the social arena of an information system. Pragmatic analysis also helps in interpreting the patterns of behavior and obligation afforded by different stakeholders.

In contrast to the pragmatic layer, the social layer of the semiotic ladder deals with the consequences or outcomes of pragmatic communication. When a meaningful utterance has occurred, the social layer would identify the social norms that would be changed, altered, or affected in some way. As shown in Table 13.1, some examples of these cultural norms might include beliefs, expectations, functions, commitments, law, culture, contracts, values, shared models of reality, and attitudes.

Previous Semiotic Research in IS

Several researchers have taken a semiotics approach to analyzing various issues related to information systems. For example, Nadin (1997) introduces using the semiotic paradigm for designing information systems and argues that regardless of whether or not system designers know it, they are in fact using various concepts of semiotics from designing user interfaces to programming. Yet, when attention is only given to the various parts of a system rather than the whole system, various interactions between the parts might fail. Nadin (1997) states, "Creating a coherent semiotic strategy is like creating a meta-program that unites program, data flow, I/O performance, connectivity, process and human interface, cultural and social acceptance, learning, and satisfaction."

Connolly and Phillips (2002) present another example of applying the semiotic paradigm to IS-related issues. In their research, Connolly and Phillips concluded that user interfaces should ideally be defined on the pragmatic and social layers, whereas the remaining four layers would be used for automating the design. Connolly and Phillips also conclude that special attention should be given to defining relationships between the different levels of the semiotic ladder. In other words, after the various layers of the semiotic ladder are identified for a particular design, further analysis should be conducted to identify how each layer affects the other. These relationships between the layers could further reveal deep-rooted issues that could add enrichment to the design experience.

Other recent works that apply the semiotic paradigm to IS-related issues include those of Anderson (2001), Liu (2002), and Sjöström and Goldkuhl (2003). Anderson (2001) discussed the role of semiotics in user interface design and stated that semiotics is helpful for positioning the design of computer systems in a broader theoretical and philosophical context. Liu (2002) argues that as a result of the inability of users to understand the meanings of words and the inability of analysts to understand user requirements, a method with an emphasis on semantics is needed to clarify meanings. And Sjöström and Goldkuhl (2003) presented a socio-pragmatic and semiotic concept of user interfaces and argue that conceptualizing user interfaces by using the semiotic paradigm allows for understanding IS use as social action and understanding how IS artifacts can be seen as communicative instruments in such social action.

SECURITY ISSUES IN THE CONTEXT OF HCI

As mentioned above, the purpose of this paper is to propose a semiotic approach for discovering and interpreting the deep-rooted issues that deal with security in the context of HCI. Before this approach can be introduced, general issues that pertain to security in the context of HCI must be identified. To uncover these security issues, this section will use already established general security frameworks as a basis for studying HCI.

Of course, general security of IS has been a topic area that has been well researched. Previous research has identified a range of security principles, mainly to ensure the technical security of systems. Such principles have related to managing the confidentiality, integrity, and availability (CIA) of information. However in recent years a number of social and organizational factors have also been considered important for managing IS security. Dhillon and Backhouse (2000) term these the RITE principles—principles that address issues related to responsibility structures, integrity of roles, trustworthiness of people, and general ethical conduct. Although it is important to understand the origin and scope of a range of security issues and principles, it is clearly beyond the scope of this paper. A more thorough review of CIA (Bishop, 2003) and RITE can be found in Backhouse and Dhillon (1996) and Dhillon and Backhouse (2001).

This paper will, however, use the principles of CIA and RITE as a lens to examine and thus generate general security issues that pertain to HCI. The security issues generated in this section will then be used along with the discussion in Section 2, to provide the basis for the semiotic analysis and proposed framework given in Section 4.

Applying the Principle of CIA to Security Issues in the Context of HCI

The principle of CIA refers to examining the issues of confidentiality, integrity, and availability from the perspective of data security. Dhillon and Backhouse (2000) state that confidentiality refers to restricting data access to those who are interested and who should be allowed to access such data. In the context of HCI, confidentiality is no doubt a very important issue. When dealing with confidentiality from the customer perspective, customers need to feel as if only those who require access are handling the sensitive data they pass over the Internet. Hence, the question of how this feeling of confidentiality can be conveyed to the user must be addressed. When dealing with confidentiality from the organizational perspective, organizations need to determine how to give access only to those permitted to view sensitive data, and how any access policies created will be implemented, maintained, and most importantly, secured.

Integrity refers to maintaining the values of the data stored and manipulated, such as maintaining the correct signs and symbols. When dealing with integrity in the context of HCI, there should be no doubt that organizations must address the question of how data can be maintained and secured in a consistent fashion. Data integrity is crucial to maintaining customer loyalty. For example, when dealing with an online banking scheme, what would be the consequences of incorrect account balances to both the customer and the organization? However, even if data integrity is maintained, organizations also need to address their ability to accurately secure the interpretation of data. Organizations must secure that interpretations of data are consistent with company rules and policies.

Availability refers to keeping data available when they are needed. When dealing with availability in the context of HCI, policies must be implemented that address the question of when data should be available to both customers and employees. For example, an online banking scenario would certainly require data to be available to customers twenty-four hours a day, yet the organization must also determine when various employees should be allowed to access data. Additionally, policies for handling system failures should be addressed when dealing with the concept of availability.

Applying RITE Principles to Security Issues in the Context of HCI

Dhillon and Backhouse (2000) note that the traditional principles of CIA apply to scenarios where information is seen as data, yet does not necessarily address the changing organizational context in which this data is interpreted and used. As a result, it can be argued that for organizations to meet the changing demands of the future, an organizational subculture needs to be formed that addresses the issues of responsibility, integrity, trust, and ethicality (RITE).

Responsibility refers not only to accountability for security issues but to handling future new security developments. In the context of HCI, responsibility would thus require an organization to determine who is accountable for various security operations and also policy formation that determines who will be responsible for new security threats that are not necessarily defined in the company hierarchy or some organizational chart. For example, an online banking Web site would be subject to new forms of outside threats that could not necessarily be predicted because of the increasing sophistication of hackers. Who in the organization is responsible for handling such threats?

Table 13.2

Design Issues for Security in the Context of HCI

Confidentiality	**I-1.** How can the sense of confidentiality be conveyed to the user?
	I-2. How will an organization determine access policies to sensitive data and how will these policies be implemented, maintained, and secured?
Integrity	**I-3.** How can data be maintained and secured in a consistent manner?
	I-4. How can organizations secure that interpretations of data are consistent with company rules and policies?
Availability	**I-5.** How does an organization determine when data should be available to both customers and employees, and how will these policies be implemented, maintained, and secured?
	I-6. What types of policies should be created for system failure?
Responsibility	**I-7.** What types of policies will be created that determine who is accountable for various security operations?
	I-8. What types of policies will be created that determine who will be responsible for new security threats that are not necessarily defined in the company hierarchy or by some organizational chart?
Integrity of Roles	**I-9.** What types of policies will be created that determine who in the organization should be trusted with sensitive data so that inside threats can be minimized?
Trust	**I-10.** How will policies define appropriate norms and patterns of behavior to ensure that that all members of an organization can be expected or trusted to implement these policies?
Ethicality	**I-11.** How will organizations convey ethical policies to employees about informal norms and behaviors that come about in daily operations?

Integrity (integrity of roles) refers to the issues that surround determining who in an organization should be given access to sensitive information to minimize inside threats. It is widely known that most security threats come from inside an organization. In the context of HCI such as online banking scenarios or sites that require customers to divulge credit card information, the question then becomes who in this type of organization is deemed to be trusted with sensitive data so that inside threats can be minimized.

Trust refers to defining the appropriate levels of norms and patterns of behavior that all members of an organization should be trusted to implement. In the context of HCI, this concept of trust is paramount because systems are often managed virtually in the absence of close supervision. Hence, levels of norms and patterns of behavior must be well defined and explained thoroughly in company policies. Perhaps such policies would also concentrate on conveying strict penalties for violations of company trust policies that go beyond termination and focus more on criminal penalties.

Ethicality refers to defining ethical practices that should be followed by employees when rules defining such practices cannot be predetermined due to new and dynamic situations. In the context of HCI, the issue of ethicality is crucial because the business that surrounds HCI-type systems is ever-changing. Hence ethical policies need to be adequately communicated to the employees. To a large extent, this can be made possible by formalizing the normative structures.

Summary

Table 13.2 summarizes the various design issues generated in the previous discussion that come from interpreting IS security in the context of HCI. As shown in Table 13.2, the design issues generated by CIA concentrate on how things can be done where both technical and human level considerations must be addressed. Issues generated by RITE concentrate on mostly human considerations that deal mainly with policy formation. The next section will be devoted to examining these design issues using the semiotic ladder as a framework for further analysis.

A SEMIOTIC FRAMEWORK FOR ANALYZING SECURITY IN THE CONTEXT OF HCI

As previously mentioned, the purpose of this paper is to propose a general semiotic framework for discovering and interpreting the deep-rooted human and technical issues relating to security in the context of HCI. This section proposes this framework, as shown in Table 13.3, and discusses the rationale behind this table.

Table 13.3 is a result of analyzing the various design issues shown in Table 13.2 and incorporating the semiotic principles discussed earlier in this paper. As shown in Table 13.3, CIA and RITE design issues are related in that they both require extensive human-level analysis. However, CIA design issues require a deeper technical analysis than RITE design issues. That is, design issues generated by CIA require an organization to determine the hardware, software, and telecommunication equipment needed for authentication, intrusion detection, vigilance, and maintaining consistent and available data. These technical requirements are illustrated in Table 13.3 at the physical, empiric, and syntactic layers. As previously mentioned, organizations are typically capable of determining these technical requirements rather easily. However, analyzing human-level considerations would require a much deeper analysis and is often times overlooked or disregarded.

Human Level Analysis

Conducting a deep-rooted analysis at the human level would require each individual layer to be thoroughly investigated. At the semantic layer, the organization would be required to validate various design issues shown in Table 13.2 that pertain to that organization. For example, an organization would be required to validate whether data is being maintained and secured in a consistent manner. That is, the organization must periodically determine if data integrity is being preserved after various security implementations are undertaken. As another example, an organization might also be required to validate if informal norms and behaviors that come about in the daily operations are being followed.

To confirm the pertinent issues in Table 13.2, validation procedures would need to be created and would obviously be organization specific. However, based on the constructivist principle discussed in Section 2, these validation procedures would probably indicate the need for repair work to be done. Hence, to ensure semantic meaning to all pertinent parties across the various design issues in Table 13.2, the organization must be prepared and willing to address repair needs. For example, if an organization determines that informal norms and behaviors are not being followed, then perhaps the organization might determine the need for creating additional company policies. These additional company policies would then serve to formalize or draw attention to the importance of following informal norms and behaviors that are created in the dynamic workplace.

Additionally, semantic layer analysis would require the organization to determine the meanings, propositions, and denotations required to convey the feeling of security to users. Of course, how to convey the feeling of security to a user would be specific to each organization and type of HCI system. For example, organizations might either rely on their reputation or provide documentation in the form of text or interactive GUI.

Table 13.3

Semiotic Framework for Analyzing Security in the Context of HCI

Semiotic Layer	CIA	RITE
Physical	Hardware needed for authentication, intrusion detection, vigilance, and maintaining consistent and available data	NA
	Storage of policies	
Empiric	Telecommunication equipment needed for authentication, intrusion detection, vigilance, and maintaining consistent and available data	NA
	Efficiency and redundancy of policies	
Syntactic	Software needed for authentication, intrusion detection, vigilance, and maintaining consistent and available data	NA
	Language and structure of policies	
Semantic	Validation of pertinent CIA design issues; meanings, propositions, and denotations required to convey the feeling of security to users (GUI)	Validation of pertinent RITE design issues (e.g., validation that informal norms and behaviors that come about in daily operations are being followed)
	Validation, meanings, propositions, truth, and denotations of policies	
Pragmatic	Communications, conversations, and negotiations required to implement pertinent CIA design issues; intentions of GUI	Communications, conversations, and negotiations required to implement pertinent RITE design issues (e.g., communications, conversations, and negotiations required to define employee accountability domains)
	Intentions of policies	
Social	Social impact of implementing pertinent CIA design issues (e.g., social impact of poor security reputation)	Social impact of implementing pertinent RITE design issues (e.g., social impact of allowing data access to specific individuals in an organization)
	Cultural norms, beliefs, expectations, functions, commitments, law, culture, contracts, values, shared models of reality, and attitudes that policy formation seeks to address or change	

At the pragmatic layer, the organization would be required to determine the necessary communications, conversations, and negotiations required to maintain pertinent CIA and RITE design issues, as shown in Table 13.2. For example, pragmatic analysis might uncover the types of communications and negotiations required to determine who in an organization is allowed to access various types of data. As another example, pragmatic analysis would seek to uncover the communications, conversations, and negotiations required to necessitate employee accountability for various security operations. In other words, pragmatic analysis might uncover and thus assign various security domains to specific employees so that questions about who is responsible for future security threats can be minimized. Additionally, since a GUI would probably be used as the communication medium to users, pragmatic analysis would uncover the true intentions of the various GUI components used by HCI systems.

At the social layer, the organization would be required to determine the social impact of implementing pertinent CIA and RITE design issues shown in Table 13.2. Determining the social impact of the various design issues would certainly signify the level of importance for each issue and would provide organizational goals that would govern operation and policy formation. For example, social layer analysis might determine the social impact of a poor security reputation, thus highlighting the real importance of various design issues or specific company policies. As another example, social layer analysis might discover that restricting data access to various individuals in an organization has a negative impact on employee morale. Hence, this negative impact would be measured against the underlying purpose of these restrictions to determine if access policies should be revised.

Policy Formation

As shown in Table 13.3, CIA and RITE design issues both require formation and upkeep of policies that govern the various design issues shown in Table 13.2. Additionally, Table 13.2 illustrates that the formation and upkeep of these policies need to be analyzed at both the technical and human levels of the semiotic ladder.

At the technical level, policy formation should be analyzed at the physical, empiric, and syntactic layers. At the physical layer, the organization needs to consider where the actual storage of policies will be located and who should be able to access these policies. Obviously, policies that should be made available to all members of an organization should be warehoused in a location that is easy to access. At the empiric and syntactic layers, the organization would be required to examine the efficiency of any policies. Policies should be written in a concise manner, carefully considering the language used, so that all employees are capable of understanding the major issues without having to sift through redundant and inefficiently structured documents.

At the human level, policy formation should be rigorously analyzed at the semantic, pragmatic, and social layers. At the semantic layer, the meanings, propositions, truth, and denotations of policies must be analyzed. Additionally, semantic analysis would require policy validation procedures to be implemented that would examine policy effectiveness in terms of reaching goals. At the pragmatic layer, the real intentions of any policies must be uncovered. And at the social layer, the cultural norms, beliefs, expectations, functions, commitments, law, culture, contracts, values, shared models of reality, and attitudes that policy formation seeks to address or change need to be thoroughly examined.

CONCLUSIONS

This paper thoroughly discusses semiotic concepts along with research that applies the semiotic paradigm to various IS-related issues. The discussion on semiotics was presented to argue that semiotics does indeed provide a rich means to interpret security in the context of HCI. This paper then uses principles of CIA and RITE to uncover actual security issues that pertain to HCI that require a more extensive and detailed analysis. These issues are then analyzed from a semiotic perspective to propose a general framework (Table 13.3) for discovering and interpreting the deep-rooted human and technical issues that deal with security in the context of HCI. We propose that analyzing security in the context of HCI from the semiotic perspective transcends existing organizational and computer-technical knowledge, thus allowing designers a better ability to incorporate a more rounded design solution that seeks to minimize security threats and maximize user satisfaction. It should be noted that further research in the form of case studies should be conducted that would entail a more extensive analysis by applying the framework presented in Table 13.3 to specific organizational situations.

REFERENCES

Abrazhevich, D. A survey of user attitudes towards electronic payment systems. In *The 15th Annual Conference of the Human Computer Interaction Group of the British Computer Socie*ty, vol. 2. Toulouse, France: Cepadues-Editions, 2001, pp. 69–71.

Andersen, P.B. What semiotics can and cannot do for HCI. *Knowledge-Base Systems*, 14 (2001), 419–424.

Barley, S.R. Semiotics and the study of occupational and organizational cultures. *Administrative Science Quarterly*, 28 (1983), 393–413.

Backhouse, J., and Dhillon, G. Structures of responsibility and security of information systems. *European Journal of Information Systems*, 5, 1 (1996), 2–9.

Bishop, M. *Computer Security: Art and Science*. Boston: Addison-Wesley, 2003.

Braf, E. Knowledge or information—what makes the difference? IFIP 8.1 Conference, Montreal. In *Proceedings of Organizational Semiotics: Evolving a Science of Information Systems*, 2001.

Connolly, J.H., and Phillips, I.W. User-system interface design—an organisation semiotic perspective. In K. Liu, R.J. Clarke, P.B. Andersen, and R.K. Stamper (eds.), *Organizational Semiotics—Evolving a Science of Information Systems*. Dordrecht, The Netherlands: Kluwer Academic Publishers, 2002, pp. 119–132.

Dhillon, G., and Backhouse, J. Risks in the use of information technology within organizations. *International Journal of Information Management*, 16, 1 (1996), 65–74.

Dhillon, G., and Backhouse, J. Information system security management in the new millennium. *Communications of the ACM*, 43, 7 (2000), 125–128.

Dhillon, G., and Backhouse, J. Current directions in IS security research: towards socio-organizational perspectives. *Information Systems Journal*, 11, 2 (2001), 127–153.

Falkenberg, E.; Hesse, W.; Lindgreen, P.; Nilsson, B.; Oei, H.; Rolland, C.; Stamper, R.; Van Assche, F.; Verrijn-Stuart, A.; and Voss, K. *Frisco Report: A Framework of Information System Concepts*. International Federation for Information Processing (IFIP), 1998.

Kitiyadisai, K. *Relevance and information systems*. PhD thesis, London School of Economics, University of London, 1991.

Liebenau, J., and Backhouse, J. *Understanding Information*. London: Macmillan, 1990.

Liu, K. Semiotics for information systems engineering—reduce the gap between specification, design, and implementation. *1st Int. Workshop on Interpretative Approaches to Information Systems & Computing Research* (SIG-IAM 2002). Brunel, UK: 2002, pp. 62–65.

Manning, P. *Organizational Communication*. New York: Aldine de Gruyter, 1992.

Morris, C. *Signification and Significance—a Study of the Relation of Signs and Values*. Cambridge, MA: MIT Press, 1964.

Myers, B.; Hollan, J.; and Cruz, I. Strategic directions in human-computer interaction. *ACM Computing Surveys*, 28, 4 (1996), 794–809.

Nadin, M. *A Semiotic Introduction to System Design*. Cambridge: Cambridge University Press, 1997.

Nah, F., and Davis, S. HCI research issues in electronic commerce. *Journal of Electronic Commerce Research*, 3, 3 (2002), 98–113.

Olson, G.M., and Olson, J.S. Human-computer interaction: psychological aspects of the human use of computing. *Annual Review of Psychology*, 54, 1 (2003), 491–516.

Sjöström, J., and Goldkuhl, G. The semiotics of user interfaces—a socio-pragmatic perspective. *6th International Workshop on Organizational Semiotics*, Reading, UK, July 11–12, 2003.

Stamper, R. *Information in Business and Administrative Systems*. London: Batsford, 1973.

Zhang, P.; Benbasat, I.; Carey, J.; Davis, F.; Galletta, D.; and Strong, D. Human-computer interaction research in the MIS discipline. *Communications of the Association for Information Systems*, 9, 20 (2002), 334–355.

PART V

IT USE AND IMPACT: AFFECT, AESTHETICS, VALUE, AND SOCIALIZATION

CHAPTER 14

THE ROLE OF AFFECT IN INFORMATION SYSTEMS RESEARCH

A Critical Survey and a Research Model

HESHAN SUN AND PING ZHANG

Abstract: *Most existing models or theories in IS focus on the cognitive and behavioral aspects of human decision-making processes and on individual reactions to using technologies in organizations and other contexts. The influence of affect or emotion is traditionally neglected. The affective aspect, however, is considered crucial, and has gained attention in psychology, marketing, organizational behavior, and other fields. Recently, affect and related concepts have attracted attention from researchers in information systems (IS) and human-computer interaction (HCI). Yet, studies of affect have been scattered and less systematic. This paper first examines the theoretical advancement of affect studies in several referencing disciplines to IS: psychology, organizational psychology, and marketing and consumer behavior. An abstract model of the individual interacting with an object (IIO) is developed to represent the important contributors to behavior intention and behavior of people interacting with objects. Then the chapter continues with a comprehensive survey of existing studies on affect in the IS discipline to demonstrate the current status of the research stream, some conceptual discrepancies and limitations, and some potential areas for future research. An IT-specific model of IIO, a model of individual interaction with IT (IIIT), is constructed as both a framework and a theoretical model to interpret and predict individual IT user behavior. This study is an attempt to highlight and systematically analyze the influence of affect in IS and therefore has great implications for both researchers and practitioners.*

Key words: *Affect, Emotion, Cognition, Information Systems, Personality Trait, Affective Reactions Toward Using IT, Cognitive Reactions Toward Using IT*

INTRODUCTION

Affect, a general word for several related but different concepts, normally refers to mood, emotion, and feelings (Russell, 2003). Affect is conceived as an umbrella for a set of more specific mental processes including emotions, moods, and attitudes (Bagozzi et al., 1999; Liljander and Mattsson, 2002). It is noteworthy that affect is too broad a class of events to be a single scientific category (Russell and Barrett, 1999). Affect's boundary is so blurry that it keeps being the most mysterious aspect of the psychology of human beings (Russell, 2003). Despite this, research on affect is of great interest to researchers in fields such as psychology, marketing and customer research, and organizational behavior, due to continuously recognized important impacts that affect has on people's everyday social judgments (Forgas, 1995).

In the information systems (IS) and human-computer interaction (HCI) fields, however, affect has historically received little attention. Most existing theories and models focus on cognitive aspects of human beings, presuming that users must discard their affective selves to work efficiently and rationally with computers (Brave and Nass, 2002). Affective factors seem at best marginally relevant to human-computer interaction and at worst oxymoronic (Brave and Nass, 2002). Studies on psychology, marketing and consumer research, and organizational behavior research, however, suggest that affect can help in explaining a significant amount of variance in users' behavior.

The advantages of studying affect are not limited to this. Affect has several features, some of which are somehow different from what we would expect them to be. For example, people often exhibit greater commonality in affective reactions toward stimuli than in the reason-based or cognitive assessments (Pham et al., 2001); knowing this is of great practical value (e.g., for systems design). It contradicts the widespread assumptions that affective judgments are inherently subjective and contextually labile, hence unreliable, and that cognitive, or reason-based judgments are more objective, which makes them a more dependable source of evaluative information. Pham et al. (2001) attributed the higher interpersonal consistency of affective feelings to the broad applicability and inherent stability of universal affective sensory-motor programs and culturally shared emotional schemata. Cognition, by comparison, leaves more room for idiosyncrasy. More importantly, affect can have more explanatory power than cognition does under certain circumstances, which is of great interest to both researchers and practitioners (Pham et al., 2001).

Affect's definitions vary in prior studies in IS field. It has been viewed as a personal trait (Agarwal and Karahanna, 2000; Webster and Martocchio, 1992; Yager et al., 1997), as a state (Venkatesh, 1999; Webster et al., 1993), as antecedent of cognition (Venkatesh, 2000), as consequence of cognition (Compeau et al., 1999), and as a positive thing (Csikszentmihalyi, 2000; Novak et al., 2003) or a negative thing (Compeau et al., 1999; i.e., Hackbarth et al., 2003; Thatcher and Perrewe, 2002). Together, these studies seem a bit confusing and less than comprehensive. So it is necessary to examine different views and roles of affect in IS research.

One of the motivations of this research lies in the inconsistent results of attitude, a concept closely related to affect, in prior IS empirical studies. A good example is the technology acceptance model (TAM) (Davis, 1989; Davis et al., 1989), which is viewed as the most well-known model of individual reactions towards technologies (Taylor and Todd, 1995). Attitude was hypothesized to be a predictor of users' behavioral intention towards using new technologies or actual usage of them, and is also the only affect-related factor in TAM. But attitude was omitted from the original TAM due to its weak mediating effects on the relationship between perceived usefulness and behavioral intention (Davis et al., 1989). Mixed results have been demonstrated by a number of TAM-related studies (Sun and Zhang, 2006). Triandis (1980) argued for the separation of the affective (which has a like/dislike connotation) and cognitive components of attitude. Triandis subsequently introduced the term "affect," defined as "the feelings of joy, elation, or pleasure, or depression, disgust, displeasure, or hate associated by an individual with a particular act" (Triandis, 1980). This study is, therefore, an attempt to examine and identify the major issues pertaining to affective concepts as well as their relationships to other related concepts.

This study started with an examination of the research on affective concepts in several reference disciplines of IS. Then, an abstract model of an individual interacting with an object (IIO) was developed based on this examination. The IIO model was then used as guidance to scrutinize affect-related studies in IS. A set of IT-specific affective concepts is identified, and their relationships to other factors are crystallized, resulting in a model of individuals' interaction with IT (IIIT) that can explain existing affect-related studies and guide future investigations and systems development practice.

THEORETICAL GROUNDS AND AN ABSTRACT MODEL

This section starts with a review of the basic concepts and relationships of affect that have been studied in three reference disciplines of IS: psychology, marketing and consumer research, and organizational and social psychology. Based on findings in these three fields, an abstract model of an individual interacting with stimuli is proposed, which provides a ground for further discussions of affect studies in IS.

Theoretical Background

Table 14.1 summarizes the important concepts to be introduced in this section and used in the rest of the paper. These concepts will be discussed in detail later.

Affect, Core Affect, Emotion, and Mood

Psychology has provided major theoretical bases for research on affect. In this field, affect-related concepts such as emotion and mood have been studied for a long time and continue to be a focal research area (Remington et al., 2000). For example, an examination of articles published between 1991 and 1997 in the *Journal of Personality and Social Psychology*, a primary psychology journal, shows a total of 359 (30 percent) articles in which emotion was assessed (Russell and Barrett, 1999). Recently, the concept of affect has been further analyzed and clarified (e.g., Russell, 2003), which greatly promotes the usability of this concept in other fields.

Basically, the structure of affect includes two independent dimensions, valence and arousal, which are also called the "big two" of affect (Yik and Russell, 2001). The circumplex model of affect was created by Schosberg (1952, 1941) and subsequently most extensively elaborated by Russell (1980). It is one of the most widely studied models (Remington et al., 2000). Figure 14.1 shows the two dimensions of affect. The horizontal dimension is pleasure-displeasure (or valence), ranging from one extreme (e.g., agony) to the other extreme (e.g., ecstasy) and the vertical dimension is arousal (or activation), ranging from sleepiness to excitement (Russell, 2003).

Recently, affect has been further clarified, and core affect was identified as a primitive concept upon which all other affective concepts, including emotions, are built (Russell, 2003; Russell and Barrett, 1999). Core affect is a continuous assessment of one's current state. Core affect is object free (free-floating) and depicts the affective state using valence and arousal (Russell, 2003).

Affective reaction toward interacting with an object is a person's subjective perception or judgment about whether such interaction will change his or her core affect or his or her emotion toward the object.

Cognitive reaction toward interacting with the object involves cognitive reasoning, or appraisal, and is a weighting of the implications of an event for one's well-being. Cognitive reaction and affective reaction to interacting with an object can be quite different: one might understand taking a medicine as useful and necessary for one's health; nevertheless, one can at the same time consider it unpleasant due to its smell and taste.

Another commonly seen concept and term is mood. Usually the concepts of emotion and mood are distinguished from each other by one of three criteria: duration, intensity, and diffuseness or globality (Frijda, 1993). In general, emotions have shorter duration and higher intensity than moods. Of more interest, emotion is usually toward a particular object or objects, while mood provides a "background." Specifically, emotions are intentional phenomena and usually involve a subject-object

Table 14.1

A Summary of General Concepts

Concepts	Definition	Sources
Core affect	A neurophysiological state consciously accessible as a simple, nonreflective feeling that is an integral blend of hedonic (pleasure–displeasure) and arousal (sleepy–activated) values.	Russell (2003, p. 149)
Affective quality	The ability to cause a change in core affect.	Russell (2003, p. 149)
Attributed affect	In an attributed affect, a change in core affect is linked to its perceived cause. Thus, attributed affect is defined by three necessary and, when together, sufficient features: (a) a change in core affect; (b) an object; and (c) attribution of the core affect to the object.	Russell (2003, p. 149)
Perceived affective quality	An individual's perception of an object's ability to change his or her core affect. It is a perceptual process that estimates the affective quality of the object.	Zhang and Li (2004)
Object	A person, condition, thing, or event at which a mental state is directed.	Russell (2003, p. 149)
Trait	An enduring predisposition to response to stimuli across situations.	Weiss (2002); Weiss et al. (1999)
State	A subjective characteristic of an experience.	(Ellis, 1973)
Mood	Prolonged core affect with no object (simple mood) or with a quasi-object; affective states without an object or without a specific object	Frijda (1993); Russell (2003, p. 149)
Emotion	There is little convergence on emotion's definition. Generally, it is an affective state directed toward a specific object or objects.	Forgas (1995); Russell (2003, p. 149)
Affect	An umbrella for a set of more specific mental processes including emotions, moods, and attitudes.	Bagozzi et al. (1999)
Attitude	An individual's positive or negative feelings (evaluative affect) about performing the target behavior.	Fishbein and Ajzen (1975, p. 216)
Affective reaction toward interacting with an object	A person's subjective perception or judgment on whether interacting with the object will change his or her core affect or his or her emotion toward the object.	This research/paper
Cognitive reaction toward interacting with an object	Cognitive reasoning, or appraisal, or weighting of the implications of interacting with an object for one's well-being.	This research/paper

relationship. Moods, however, are affective states without any specific target object(s) and are usually viewed as "background" factors (Lazarus, 1991).

Trait and State

The distinction between trait and state is well studied in psychology, marketing and consumer research, and organizational and social psychology. Incidentally, the last two decades have seen an increased interest in the study of relationships between transient affective states and enduring

Figure 14.1   **A Circular Structure of Affect**

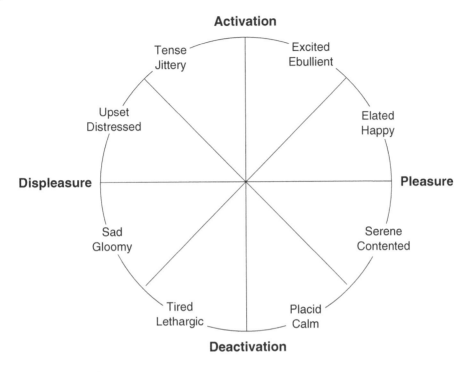

Source: Russell (2003).

personality characteristics (Ilies and Judge, 2002). Trait reflects the static aspect of information processing that impacts a broad range of variables. By contrast, affective states can be theorized as being "a product of variables such as stimuli reception context and individual differences" (Martin, 2003), and as varying over time and as having more dynamic influence on individuals' behavior (Schmukle et al., 2002). The trait is empirically confirmed to be a predictor of the average level of mood, a prolonged affective state (Weiss et al., 1999). From another perspective, state affect includes a "dispositional" component, which refers to the trait affect (Schmukle et al., 2002).

Trait variables have no direct influence on behavioral intention. Psychological research suggests that the influence of a trait variable on behavior is mediated by beliefs and affective factors (e.g., Fishbein and Ajzen, 1975).

The organizational behavior literature also supports the causal relationship between affective trait and state. For example, an individual's expression of affect at work could be strongly influenced by personality traits. Weiss (2002) argued that "affective state but not beliefs mediates the relationship between affective disposition (trait) and satisfaction" (p. 183). His argument is based on one of his earlier works (Weiss et al., 1999), in which he empirically suggested that daily mood levels mediate any effects of dispositional happiness on satisfaction. One mechanism through which affective trait exerts its influence is interpretation of job circumstances, which is considered a "stimulus" of affect change in the workplace. For example, Brief (1998) argued that affect traits determine how employees "interpret" the job circumstance, with "interpretation" referring to "how a person construes or apprehends the objective circumstances of his or her job" (p. 96).

Affect and Cognition

The distinction between affect and cognition has been studied extensively. A cognitive concept used in psychology research is appraisal, which refers to one's perception of an object's qualities such as its future prospects, its relevance to one's goals, its causal antecedents, and so on (Russell, 2003). Traditional psychological theories insist that affect is "post-cognitive"; that is, it occurs only when considerable cognitive operations have been accomplished (Zajonc, 1980). Zajonc (1980) drew a picture depicting a "typical information-processing model of affect," in which an affective reaction, such as liking, disliking, preference, evaluation, or the experience of pleasure or displeasure, is "based on a prior cognitive process in which a variety of content discriminations are made and features are identified, examined for their value, and weighted for their contribution" (p. 151). For example, a classic psychological theory, the theory of reasoned action (Fishbein and Ajzen, 1975), posits that cognitive beliefs predict individuals' attitude, which has an affective component.

The second paradigm on affect-cognition relationships, however, argues that affect and cognition are "separate and partially independent systems" (Zajonc, 1984). Affect could precede cognitive process in a behavioral chain. Or, in Zajonc's words, preferences need no inferences (1980). Berkowitz's three-step theory about how affect and cognition interact to influence behavior goes further and identifies two distinct types of affect: low-order affective reactions and high-order affective reactions (Berkowitz, 1993). While a low-order affective reaction is elicited by "relatively basic and automatic associative processes" (Berkowitz, 1993), a high-order affective reaction comes from a more deliberate cognitive processing. Therefore, affect may occur either before or after cognitive processing. Consistent with this theory, Epstein (1993) created cognitive-experiential self-theory (CEST), in which affect (called experiential system) and cognition (called rational system) operate in parallel.

All these theories share a single opinion that affect and cognition are interdependent. Even Zajonc's theory, which addresses affect's independence from cognition, admits that affect and cognition are just "partially" independent from each other and they usually "function conjointly" (1982). Similarly, Berkowitz (1993) argues in his theory that high-order affect arises from controlled, deliberate processes involved in thinking, reasoning, and consciousness. Leventhal (1984) suggests that affect arises from two sources, one of which is "a memory route" that involves cognitive and conceptual processing.

While the second paradigm seems more convincing and actually has become more and more accepted by researchers in psychology and other relevant fields, the first paradigm has also received theoretical and empirical support. Actually, we can regard the first paradigm on the cognition → affect causal flow as a part of the relationship between cognition and affect. Therefore, the next question is: How are affect and cognitive interdependent, and specifically, under what circumstance does affect influence cognition, or vice versa? Several theories tried to answer this question by introducing various moderators representing a variety of conditions.

Affect infusion model (AIM) (Forgas, 1995) identified four processing strategies, in which affect may have different influences on cognition, such as performance appraisal, reactions to feedback, and task perceptions. Affect infusion refers to "the process whereby affectively loaded information exerts an influence on and becomes incorporated into the judgmental process, entering into the judge's deliberations and eventually coloring the judgmental outcome" (p. 39). One mechanism of interest is affect priming, which implies that affect may indirectly influence judgments during substantive processing through its selective influence on attention, encoding, retrieval, and associative processes in a way similar to mood-congruence. Specifically, affect can selectively facilitate the learning of mood-congruent information, facilitate the recall of information encountered in a matching rather than a non-matching affect state, and bias the interpretation of ambiguous social information (Forgas and George, 2001).

It is noteworthy that the impact of affect on cognition is situational, depending on personal variables, task characteristics, and situational features. Specifically, Forgas (1995) identified the factors that determine processing choice. Familiarity (with the target or stimuli), complexity and typicality, personal relevance, specific motivation, and cognitive capacity have been found to influence an individual's choice of processing strategies. Several previous studies suggest that more prolonged, extensive, complex, atypical or unusual, personally relevant, and less motivated processing increases the degree of affect infusion (Forgas, 1995; Forgas and George, 2001).

Marketing and consumer research also shows that affect, such as emotion (Chaudhuri, 2002) and valence of experience (Chen and Dubinsky, 2003), influences cognitive concepts such as perceived risk (Chaudhuri, 2002), and perceived product quality (Chen and Dubinsky, 2003), to name a few. Affect has various effects on cognition, such as retrieval effects, encoding effects, and state-dependent learning effects (Bagozzi et al., 1999). But basically, affect influences cognition through a mood-congruence mechanism (Bagozzi et al., 1999; Chen and Dubinsky, 2003). From a process perspective, Mattila and Wirtz (2000) argued that pre-consumption affect can be translated into post-purchase evaluations. Specifically, consumers' initial affective reaction may lead them to mood-consistent information, which is used to form associated cognitive structures.

Mood-congruence has received much attention in the literature. Several theoretical and empirical studies provided support to the principle of mood-congruence as the mechanism through which affect influences cognition. For example, Wegener et al. (1995) discovered that happy (versus sad) moods lead to more information messages in persuasive communication when a "pro-attitudinal/uplifting" position is taken, and lead to fewer information messages when a "counter-attitudinal/depression" position is taken.

Cognition influences affect as well. A task that requires more cognitive effort to evaluate can lead to more negative affect (Garbarino and Edull, 1997). Therefore, perceived ease of use of the artifact (e.g., Web sites) was proposed and empirically confirmed as an antecedent of affective reactions such as valence of experience (Chen and Dubinsky, 2003). In their research on e-commerce, ease of use of the Web site is the most influential factor among the three antecedents of valence of experience (ease of use, relevant information, and customer service), with an affective factor defined as "a consumer's emotional or attitudinal state aroused by the pre-purchase on-line shopping experience" (p. 327).

Affect, Attitude, and Behavior

Attitude often has been a dependent variable in organizational psychology, marketing, and consumer research. Attitude is normally defined as and often measured by "an individual's positive or negative feelings (evaluative affect) about performing the target behavior" (Fishbein and Ajzen, 1975, p. 216). It is one of the few concepts that have an affective component. Thus, it is important to examine the relationships between affect and attitude.

Marketing and consumer research shows that a person's affect such as his mood (e.g., Garbarino and Edull, 1997) or valence of experience (Chen and Dubinsky, 2003), can influence various aspects of cognitive information processing, including encoding and retrieval of information about the products, brands, services, and promotions, the advertisements, and customer loyalty (Bagozzi et al., 1999; Dube et al., 2003; Kroeber-Riel, 1984; Lu and Lin, 2002; Zhou and Bao, 2002).

Marketing and consumer researchers have historically taken the view that consumers' evaluations are based primarily on reason-based assessments of the target's characteristics (see Bettman et al., 1998) and reason-based assessments of the target are often regarded as having higher normative/evidentiary status than feelings (Pham et al., 2001). However, affect sometimes provides judgmental responses that are potentially faster and more consistent across individuals, and subsequently more predictive (Pham et al., 2001). Pham et al.'s four empirical studies showed that affect performs better than cognition in predicting judgments. Similarly, Murry, Lastovicka, and Singh (1992) also suggest that affective state has a direct effect upon attitudes toward advertising.

Researchers in marketing and consumer research have identified several conditions under which affect has more influence. For example, Bagozzi et al. (1999) argued that when the processing of information in a communication is low (e.g., due to low motivation, distraction, low need for cognition, and weak arguments), emotional content in the communication gets processed directly and transfers to, or influences, attitude toward the product or advertisement. In other words, the consumer's affective mood has a direct effect on attitude when the likelihood of information processing is low. When the likelihood of information processing is high, the affective mood influences cognitive thoughts that are consistent with the mood.

Organizational behavior literature also demonstrates that affects such as mood (Weiss et al., 1999) and beliefs tend to independently predict attitude such as job satisfaction, defined as the overall evaluation one makes about one's job and measured by "like/dislike" and other criteria (Weiss, 2002; Weiss et al., 1999). First, several researchers empirically proved that affects and beliefs are distinct (Crites et al., 1994; Trafimow and Sheeran, 1998). Second, although they are independent, affects and beliefs jointly predict users' reactions toward stimuli (Abelson et al., 1982; Breckler and Wiggins, 1989; Crites et al., 1994). For example, Forgas (1995) argued that affects can influence evaluative judgments directly through the principle of "affect-as-information." Third, the relative importance of affects and beliefs varies. Sometimes, affect has higher regression coefficients for attitudes; at other times cognition has higher regression coefficients (Crites et al., 1994; Weiss, 2002).

The relationship between predictive capabilities of affect and cognition for behavioral intention is also reported in the literature. Trafimow and Sheeran (1998) conducted four analyses trying to figure out which one accounts for more variance in behavioral intention for smoking. Their results showed that affect accounts for significant unique variance in intention, but that cognition has no such impact on intention. However, in their studies, Trafimow and Sheeran (1998) further tested the impacts of affect and cognition on the study habits of college students. As expected, cognition, not affect, has significant impacts. Their findings suggest the strong moderating effects of the task.

An Abstract Model of the Individual Interacting with Objects

Based on the above discussions, we present a general or abstract model of various elements involved in the mental processes of an individual's interaction with an object (IIO) in his or her environment. Figure 14.2 depicts this model; all concepts used in the model were defined earlier in Table 14.1. The final dependent variables of the model are intention to interact with the object or/and the actual behavior during the interaction. Studies in psychology have demonstrated the strong relationship between these two dependent variables (Ajzen, 1985; Fishbein and Ajzen, 1975), which is beyond the scope of this paper.

The IIO model reflects the theoretical and empirical findings from existing literature discussed above such as those about (1) trait → affective reaction (Brief, 1998; Fishbein and Ajzen, 1975; Weiss, 2002; Weiss et al., 1999); (2) the interaction between affective and cognitive reactions (Bagozzi et al., 1999; Berkowitz, 1993; Chaudhuri, 2002; Chen and Dubinsky, 2003; Epstein, 1993; Fishbein and Ajzen, 1975; Forgas, 1995; Forgas and George, 2001; Garbarino and Edull,

Figure 14.2   **An Abstract Model of Individuals Interacting with Object (IIO)**

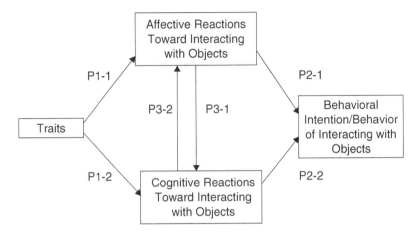

1997; Leventhal, 1984; Mattila and Wirtz, 2000; Wegener et al., 1995; Zajonc, 1980; Zajonc, 1984; Zajonc and Markus, 1982); and (3) trait → behavioral intention/behavior (e.g., Abelson et al., 1982; Bagozzi et al., 1999; Bettman et al., 1998; Breckler and Wiggins, 1989; Chen and Dubinsky, 2003; Crites et al., 1994; Dube et al., 2003; Fishbein and Ajzen, 1975; Garbarino and Edull, 1997; Kroeber-Riel, 1984; Lu and Lin, 2002; Murry et al., 1992; Pham et al., 2001; Trafimow and Sheeran, 1998; Weiss, 2002; Weiss et al., 1999; Zhou and Bao, 2002; Zigurs and Buckland, 1998).

The basic idea of the IIO model is that an individual's traits influence both affective reactions and cognitive reactions that he or she has toward interacting with the object. These two types of reactions influence each other, either at a different stage of the process or at the same time. These two reactions together determine the final behavioral intention or behavior of interacting with the object. We use the general term "interacting" to indicate different possible actions a person can have on objects. For example, in the IT context, interacting with objects can be using IT. In the consumer context, interacting with products can be buying products. We hope that this abstract model is general enough to be applied to a number of situations and contexts where individuals have to interact with objects in the environment.

The relationships in the model are represented in the form of propositions below. These propositions will be further verified or confirmed by studies in the IS field in the next section.

P1–1:   Traits have impacts on affective reactions
P1–2:   Traits have impacts on cognitive reactions
P2–1:   Affective reactions influence behaviors/behavioral intentions
P2–2:   Cognitive reactions influence behaviors/behavioral intentions
P3–1:   Affective reactions influence cognitive reactions
P3–2:   Cognitive reactions influence affective reactions

THE ROLE OF AFFECT IN IS

An extensive literature search through various databases and academic journals resulted in a total of fifty-one papers with affect and IS foci; these are reviewed in this research. Appendix 14.1 lists

Table 14.2

IT-Specific Concepts

Concepts	Definition	Sources
Microcomputer playfulness (CP)	A situation-specific individual characteristic representing a type of intellectual or cognitive playfulness and describing an individual's tendency to interact spontaneously, inventively, and imaginatively with microcomputers.	Webster and Martocchio (1992)
Personal innovativeness in IT (PIIT)	An individual trait reflecting a willingness to try out any new technology.	Agarwal and Karahanna (2000)
Computer anxiety	A "state anxiety" with computers, or, more generally, information technologies representing a personally threatening stimulus.	Coffin and MacIntyre (1999)
Flow	Holistic sensation that people feel when they act with total involvement.	Trevino and Webster (1992)
Cognitive absorption	A state of deep involvement with IT.	Agarwal and Karahanna (2000)
Perceived enjoyment	The extent to which the activity of using computers is perceived to be enjoyable in its own right, apart from any performance consequences that may be anticipated.	Davis et al. (1992)
Perceived playfulness	The strength of one's belief that interacting with the World Wide Web will fulfill the user's intrinsic motives.	Moon and Kim (2001)
Attitude toward using IT	An individual's positive or negative feelings (evaluative affect) about performing the target behavior.	Davis et al. (1989, p. 984)
Satisfaction with using IT	Users' affect concerning (feeling about) their prior IT use.	Bhattacherjee (2001)
Perceived usefulness (PU)	The degree to which a person believes that using a particular technology will enhance his or her performance.	Davis (1989, p. 320)
Perceived ease of use (PEOU)	The degree to which a person believes that using a particular system would be free of effort.	Davis (1989, p. 320)
Computer self-efficacy (CSE)	An individual's beliefs about his or her capabilities to use computers.	Compeau et al. (1999, p. 147)

these papers and the outlets. Before getting to the details of the examination, Table 14.2 summarizes the important concepts that are IS-specific and discussed in this section.

In this section, IS is identified as a unique discipline, distinct from other disciplines that have been reviewed in previous sections. Then, affect-related concepts are examined. Consequently, an IT-specific model of IIO is presented to predict the relationships among the affective concepts and other important concepts. A set of IT-specific propositions is listed along the discussion of the existing studies. It is hoped that the specific model and the propositions will guide additional theoretical and empirical studies on the role of affect on individual interactions with IT.

The Uniqueness of IS Concerns

While applying theoretical works from relevant disciplines, we need to take the uniqueness of the IS field into consideration.

Different from organizational behavior, marketing and consumer research, the IS discipline is concerned with individuals' behaviors toward particular types of objects: information and communication technology, or IT as we often use the term. In addition, such concerns are situated mostly in organizational, managerial, and business contexts. Such contexts make both the affective and cognitive reactions toward using IT unique as well.

In IS, work or job-oriented technologies are commonly studied. In other words, users are more likely to be extrinsically motivated. This argument can in part be proved by the salient importance of usefulness, which indeed is viewed as "extrinsic motivation" by some researchers (e.g., Davis et al., 1992) in determining users' behavioral intentions (Sun and Zhang, 2006). We notice that prior studies, however, are generally focused on effectiveness-related information technologies such as spreadsheets and word processors (Jackson et al., 1997), customer dial-up systems (Subramanian, 1994), database management systems (DBMSs) (Szajna, 1994), managerial systems (Venkatesh and Davis, 2000), telemedicine technology (Chau and Hu, 2002), and information retrieval systems (Venkatesh and Davis, 2000), all of which usually bring out extrinsic motivations (Sun and Zhang, 2006). Given the heavy emphasis on the effectiveness of IT in jobs and work, the question of whether affect plays a role in its use remains. To answer these questions, relevant concepts being studied in IS are examined next.

IT-Specific Concepts and a Model

Using different terms with different definitions and measures, prior researchers have explored affect from different perspectives. In order to facilitate discussion, the studied terms were "standardized" by relating them to the key concepts introduced in the section "Theoretical Grounds and an Abstract Model." When necessary to make the points clear, original definitions used in the studies are cited and their meanings in terms of the "standard" concepts are explained.

Traits

Two trait variables, microcomputer or computer playfulness (CP) and personal innovativeness in IT (PIIT), have gained considerable attention in IS research. The basic distinction between traits and states merits mention again. In general, traits refer to comparatively stable characteristics of individuals that are relatively invariant to situational stimuli (Webster and Martocchio, 1992). States, on the other hand, refer to affective or cognitive episodes that are experienced in the short run and that fluctuate over time (Webster and Martocchio, 1992).

Although affect can be either a trait or a state (Webster and Martocchio, 1992), computer playfulness is traditionally used as a trait variable. Microcomputer playfulness represents a type of intellectual or cognitive playfulness and describes an individual's tendency to interact spontaneously, inventively, and imaginatively with microcomputers (Webster and Martocchio, 1992). The computer playfulness scale (CPS) (Webster and Martocchio, 1992) consists of seven items: spontaneous, unimaginative, flexible, creative, playful, unoriginal, and uninventive. The seven-item construct is confirmed to have temporal stability (during the five weeks of the experiment's duration) and situational consistency, which implies that computer playfulness is a trait variable (Yager et al., 1997). This measurement is confirmed to be valid and reliable and therefore is widely used when trait affect is studied (Agarwal and Karahanna, 2000; Atkinson and Kydd, 1997; Venkatesh, 2000).

The other salient trait variable is personal innovativeness in IT (PIIT) (Agarwal and Karahanna, 2000). All four items measuring PIIT focus on individuals' willingness to try "new" information technologies.

It is noteworthy that both trait variables are IT-specific; that is, they are defined specifically for the IT-related situations. The studies we are aware of yield another two trait variables that are more general: negative affectivity, which is an aspect of neuroticism and is a broad stable trait that influences individuals' emotions and behavior (Thatcher and Perrewe, 2002), and trait anxiety, which refers to a general tendency to experience anxiety when confronted with problems or challenges (Thatcher and Perrewe, 2002). In their empirical study, Thatcher and Perrewe (2002) failed to confirm negative affectivity's influence on computer anxiety, giving rise to speculations that a broadly conceptualized trait such as neuroticism or extraversion may exert a less pervasive influence on situational individual difference than do situation-specific traits (Thatcher and Perrewe, 2002; Webster and Martocchio, 1992). Therefore, for the purpose of this study, we use IT-specific traits instead of general personality variables as trait indicators.

Affective Reactions

Although they have different names, the above concepts share some common characteristics; that is, they all have to do with perceived impact on users' core affect.

Computer anxiety is one of the relatively frequently studied affective reactions toward using IT. It is a "state anxiety," with the computer, or, more generally, information technology representing a personally threatening stimulus (Coffin and MacIntyre, 1999). Computer anxiety is proposed and confirmed to be important in forming users' behavioral intention or actual behavioral (Brosnan, 1999; Compeau and Higgins, 1995; Compeau et al., 1999) and cognitive reactions (e.g., Brosnan, 1999; Hackbarth et al., 2003; Venkatesh, 2000).

Flow represents an affective state, characterized by feelings of control, attention focus, and curiosity and intrinsic interest (Trevino and Webster, 1992). A person experiencing flow is motivated more by intrinsic needs than by extrinsic rewards. In contrast to those motivated by extrinsic rewards, individuals experiencing flow state focus more on the process than on the outcomes.

Flow is a multi-dimensional construct. Some researchers have defined it as possessing three dimensions—control, concentration, and enjoyment (e.g., Csikszentmihalyi, 1975; Csikszentmihalyi, 1988; Ghani et al., 1991; Trevino and Webster, 1992; Webster et al., 1993). Other researchers, however, have proposed different dimensions of flow (e.g., Trevino and Webster, 1992). Nonetheless, two dimensions, enjoyment and concentration, have been the cores of any flow definition. More explicitly, Ghani and Deshpande (1994) argued that two key characteristics of flow are: (1) total concentration on an activity; and (2) the enjoyment one derives from the activity. In the IT context or in computer-mediated environments, flow has been found to lead to increased communication, exploratory behavior, learning, positive affect, increased computer use, etc. (Finneran and Zhang, 2005; Finneran and Zhang, 2003).

A similar concept is cognitive absorption, referring to a state of deep involvement with IT (Agarwal and Karahanna, 2000). Five dimensions of cognitive absorption have been identified: temporal dissociation, focused immersions, heightened enjoyment, control, and curiosity. Compared with flow, cognitive absorption includes all the three dimensions of flow, enjoyment, concentration, and control. Researchers also noticed this overlap and viewed cognitive absorption as a "state of flow" (Agarwal and Karahanna, 2000).

Another set of affective reaction variables consists of perceived enjoyment and other similar concepts such as perceived fun (Brosnan, 1999; Igbaria et al., 1996), physical arousal and affective reward (Reinig et al., 1996), positive mood (Martocchio, 1992), computer liking (Al-Khaldi and Al-Jabri, 1998), perceived affective quality of IT (Zhang and Li, 2004), and affect (Cheung, 2000).

While their names imply affective components, attitude and satisfaction, which have been extensively studied within the last two decades, deserve further discussion. Borrowed mainly from Theory of Reasoned Action, attitude is defined as "an individual's positive or negative feelings (evaluative affect) about performing the target behavior" (Davis et al., 1989). The definition of satisfaction in the IS field is very similar to those used in marketing and organizational behavior research. Actually, researchers who study users' satisfaction directly refer to the definitions of satisfaction. Both attitude and satisfaction are considered affect factors; satisfaction is conceptually distinct from attitude in that satisfaction is a transient and experience-specific affect, while attitude is relatively more enduring. Thus, a user may have a positive attitude (with a pleasant experience) but may still feel dissatisfied if his or her actual experience is below expectation (Bhattacherjee, 2001 p. 607).

Table 14.3 lists the definitions, sources, and original measures of affective concepts studied in IS research, along with their reinterpretations using the affective and cognitive reaction concepts defined in the section "Theoretical Grounds and an Abstract Model." For affective reactions, the two dimensions (arousal and pleasure) are considered. Most of these original measuring items can be reinterpreted by the two reaction concepts. It is noteworthy that researchers sometimes use experiments to gain more accurate user descriptions of their affective reactions under the assumption the users may not recall their spontaneous affective reactions. For example, Venkatesh and Speier (2000) randomly assigned subjects to two different training interventions, game-based and traditional interventions respectively, each of which had three 2-hour sessions. After the last session, subjects were given a knowledge test.

Several interesting observations can be obtained from Table 14.3. First, there is little consistency or agreement between the terms used and their measures: the same term may mean different concepts or may be measured differently, and the same concept may be defined as different terms. Second, the meanings of the affective concepts do not always fall within the affective reaction dimensions. Some have to do with a mix of affective and cognitive reactions (Compeau and Higgins, 1995; Moon and Kim, 2001). Third, the measures of some concepts of affective reaction emphasize one dimension more than the other: Flow, perceived playfulness, and cognitive absorption have more measuring items for arousal than pleasure, while enjoyment (Igbaria et al., 1995) has more items for pleasure than for arousal.

Cognitive Reactions

Compared to trait and affective reaction variables, cognitive reaction variables are well studied in literature. Several major concepts have been proposed and tested, among which we identify three major concepts: perceived usefulness, perceived ease of use, and computer self-efficacy. Perceived usefulness (PU) and perceived ease of use (PEOU) are widely used in IS research when studying users' adoption of IT. Perceived usefulness has been confirmed as an important, if not the most important, factor that influences user technology acceptance and therefore has received a great deal of attention from prior researchers (Sun and Zhang, 2006). There is almost no doubt that usefulness is the most important issue in determining users' intentions. Because of its importance, almost all models or theories that we are aware of include similar (if not totally the same) concepts, with perceived usefulness such as outcome expectation in the computer self-efficacy model (Compeau and Higgins, 1995), extrinsic motivation in the motivational model (Davis et al., 1992), and performance expectancy in the united theory of acceptance and use of technology (UTAUT) (Venkatesh et al., 2003).

Another salient variable is perceived ease of use. Similar concepts are also found in several other theories or models such as effort expectancy in UTAUT, and perceived complexity in Thompson

Table 14.3

Affective Factors Studied in IS

Affective Factor Definition and Source	Original Measure Items	Affective Reaction?		Cognitive Reaction?	Note
		Arousal	Pleasure		
Affect: The feelings of joy, elation, pleasure, depression, disgust, displeasure, or hate associated by an individual with a particular act (Thompson et al., 1991). Also used in Al-Khaldi and Wallance (1999) and Cheung et al. (2000)	1. PCs made work more interesting.	✓			
	2. Working with PCs was fun.	✓	✓		
	3. PCs were all right for some jobs but not for the kind of job wanted (reverse scored).	✓			
Affect: Liking of particular behavior (Compeau and Higgins, 1995a, 1995b). Also used in Compeau et al. (1999)	1. I like working with computers.	✓			
	2. I look forward to those aspects of my job that require me to use a computer.	✓			
	3. Once I start working on the computer, I find it hard to stop.	✓			
	4. Using a computer is frustrating for me.	✓	✓		
	5. I get bored quickly when working on a computer.	✓	✓		
Affective reward: The positive emotional response sometimes associated with goal attainment (Reinig, 1996)	Would like to do again:				
	Stimulating	✓			
	Arousing	✓			
	Dull	✓			
	Fulfilling	✓			
	Efficient	✓			
	Accomplished	✓			
	Won	✓			
	Dissatisfying	✓			Unclear
	Excellent	✓			
	Enjoyable	✓			
	Gratifying	✓			
	Boring	✓			
	Motivated	✓			
	Satisfying	✓			Unclear
	Interesting	✓			

Attitude: An individual's positive or negative feelings (evaluative affect) about performing the target behavior (Davis, 1989; Davis et al., 1989)	Using the system is: A good idea / Pleasant/unpleasant / Beneficial to the task	✓ ✓		Summative
Attitude: (Moon, 2001) Defined the same way as defined by Davis et al. (1989)	Using a computer is: Good/bad / Wise/foolish / Pleasant/unpleasant / Positive/negative	Unclear ✓ ✓		Summative
Cognitive absorption: A state of deep involvement with software (Agarwal and Karahanna, 2000)	Temporal dissociation / Focused immersion / Heightened enjoyment / Control / Curiosity	✓ ✓ ✓ ✓	✓	
Computer anxiety: The tendency of individuals to be uneasy, apprehensive, or fearful about current or future use of computers (Brosnan, 1999; Coffin and MacIntyre, 1999; Compeau and Higgins, 1995b; Compeau et al., 1999; Durndell and Haag, 2002; Karahanna et al., 2002; Perry and Ballou, 1997; Thatcher and Perrewe, 2002; Webster et al., 1990)	Computer anxiety rating scale (CARS): 1. I feel insecure about my ability to interpret a computer printout. 2. I look forward to using a computer. 3. I do not think I would be able to learn a computer programming language. 4. Learning about computers is an exciting challenge. 5. I am confident that I can learn computer skills. 6. Anyone can learn to use a computer if he or she is patient and motivated. 7. Learning to operate computers is like learning any new skill—the more you practice, the better you become. 8. I am afraid that if I begin to use computers I will become dependent upon them and lose some of my reasoning skills. 9. I am sure that with time and practice I will be as comfortable working with computers as I am in working with a typewriter. 10. I feel that I will be able to keep up with the advances happening in the computer field. 11. I dislike working with machines that are smarter than I am. 12. I feel apprehensive about using computers. 13. I have difficulty in understanding the technical aspects of computers.			

(continued)

Table 14.3 (*continued*)

Affective Factor Definition and Source	Original Measure Items	Affective Reaction? Arousal	Affective Reaction? Pleasure	Cognitive Reaction?	Note
	14. It scares me to think that I could cause the computer to destroy a large amount of information by hitting the wrong key.				
	15. I hesitate to use a computer for fear of making mistakes that I cannot correct.				
	16. You have to be a genius to understand all the special keys contained on most computer terminals.				
	17. If given the opportunity, I would like to learn about and use computers.				
	18. I have avoided computers because they are unfamiliar and somewhat intimidating to me.				
	19. I feel computers are necessary tools in both educational and work settings.				
Computer anxiety: Fear of computers or the tendency of a person to be uneasy, apprehensive and phobic towards current or future use of computers in general (Al-Khaldi and Al-Jabri, 1998; Venkatesh, 2000)	Computers do not scare me at all.	✓			
	Working with a computer makes me nervous.	✓			
	I do not feel threatened when others talk about computers.	✓	✓		
	It wouldn't bother me to take a computer course.	✓	✓		
	Computers make me feel uncomfortable.	✓	✓		
	I feel at ease in a computer class.	✓	✓		
	I get a sinking feeling when I think of trying to use a computer.	✓			
Computer anxiety: The apprehension or fear that results when an individual is faced with the possibility of using an IS (Hackbarth et al., 2003)	I feel comfortable working with a computer.	✓			
	Computers make me feel uneasy.	✓			
	Does not scare me	✓	✓		
	Have lots of self-confidence	✓			
	Get a sinking feeling	✓	✓		
	Feel comfortable	✓	✓		
	Feel okay about trying a new problem	Evaluative			
	No good	Evaluative			
	Not the type to do well		✓		
	Do not feel threatened	✓	✓		

(continued)

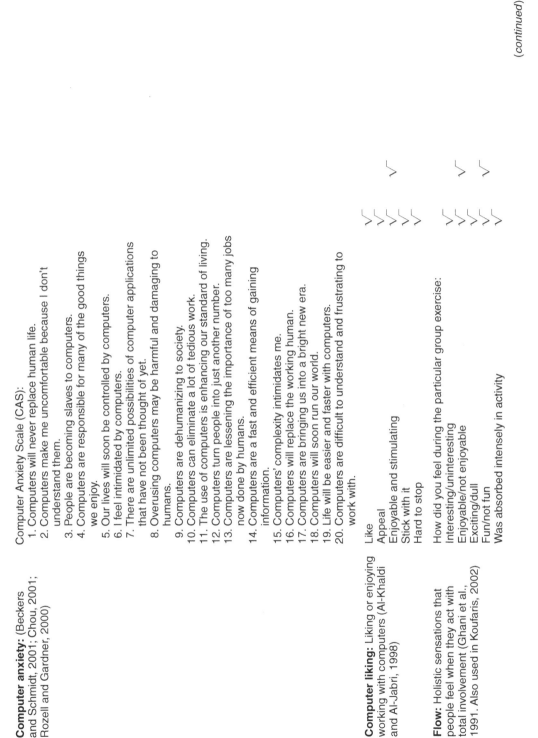

Computer anxiety: (Beckers and Schmidt, 2001; Chou, 2001; Rozell and Gardner, 2000)

Computer Anxiety Scale (CAS):
1. Computers will never replace human life.
2. Computers make me uncomfortable because I don't understand them.
3. People are becoming slaves to computers.
4. Computers are responsible for many of the good things we enjoy.
5. Our lives will soon be controlled by computers.
6. I feel intimidated by computers.
7. There are unlimited possibilities of computer applications that have not been thought of yet.
8. Overusing computers may be harmful and damaging to humans.
9. Computers are dehumanizing to society.
10. Computers can eliminate a lot of tedious work.
11. The use of computers is enhancing our standard of living.
12. Computers turn people into just another number.
13. Computers are lessening the importance of too many jobs now done by humans.
14. Computers are a fast and efficient means of gaining information.
15. Computers' complexity intimidates me.
16. Computers will replace the working human.
17. Computers are bringing us into a bright new era.
18. Computers will soon run our world.
19. Life will be easier and faster with computers.
20. Computers are difficult to understand and frustrating to work with.

Computer liking: Liking or enjoying working with computers (Al-Khaldi and Al-Jabri, 1998)

Like
Appeal
Enjoyable and stimulating
Stick with it
Hard to stop

Flow: Holistic sensations that people feel when they act with total involvement (Ghani et al., 1991. Also used in Koufaris, 2002)

How did you feel during the particular group exercise:
Interesting/uninteresting
Enjoyable/not enjoyable
Exciting/dull
Fun/not fun
Was absorbed intensely in activity

Table 14.3 (*continued*)

Affective Factor Definition and Source	Original Measure Items	Affective Reaction? Arousal	Affective Reaction? Pleasure	Cognitive Reaction?	Note
Flow: A temporary state of playfulness, characterized by feelings of control, attention focus, and curiosity and intrinsic interest (Webster and Martocchio, 1995; Webster et al., 1993)	Attention was focused on activity Concentrated fully on activity Was deeply engrossed in activity	✓ ✓ ✓			
Flow: An extremely enjoyable experience, where an individual engages in an online game activity with total involvement, enjoyment, control, concentration, and intrinsic interest (Hsu and Lu, 2003)	Lost control Absorbed Excited by my curiosity	✓ ✓ ✓			
	Do you think you have ever experienced flow in playing an online game?	✓	✓		
	In general, how frequently would you say you have experienced "flow" when you play an online game?	✓	✓		
Fun: (Perry and Ballou, 1997)	To what extent was the Excel training fun? How enjoyable was the Excel training? Most of the time I play an online game I feel that I am in flow.	✓ ✓ ✓	✓ ✓ ✓		
Perceived affective quality: An individual's perception of an object's ability to change his or her core affect (Zhang and Li, 2004)	1. Arousal quality 2. Sleepy quality 3. Pleasant quality 4. Unpleasant quality	✓ ✓ ✓ ✓			
Perceived enjoyment: The extent to which the activity of using computers is perceived to be enjoyable in its own right, apart from any performance consequences that may be anticipated (Davis et al., 1992). Also used in Igbaria et al. (1996); Atkinson and Kydd (1997);	1. I find using the system to be enjoyable. 2. The actual process of using the system is "unpleasant/pleasant." 3. I have fun using the system (likely/unlikely).	✓ ✓ ✓	✓ ✓		

Construct / Source	Items		
Venkatesh (2000); Venkatesh and Speier (2000); Venkatesh (2002); Yi and Hwang, (2003)			
Perceived enjoyment: A user's intrinsic motivation to use a technology (Igbaria et al., 1995). Also used in Teo et al. (1999)	Using a computer in my job is:		
	Fun-frustrating	✓	✓
	Pleasant-unpleasant	✓	
	Negative-positive	✓	
	Pleasurable-painful	✓	
	Exciting-dull	✓	
	Foolish-wise	Unclear	
	Enjoyable-not enjoyable	✓	✓
Perceived playfulness: The strength of one's belief that interacting with the World Wide Web will fulfill the user's intrinsic motives (Moon and Kim, 2001)	1. I do not realize the time has elapsed.	✓	✓
	2. I am not aware of any noise.	✓	
	3. I often forget the work I must do.	✓	✓
	Using the World Wide Web:		
	4. Makes my task enjoyable.	✓	✓
	5. Makes my task fun.	✓	✓
	6. Keeps me happy during my task.	✓	
	7. Stimulates my curiosity.	✓	
	8. Leads to exploration.	✓	
	9. Arouses my imagination.	✓	
Play: (Perry and Ballou, 1997)	To what extent do you expect the Excel training to be like "play"?	✓	✓
	To what extent do you expect it to feel like you are playing in the Excel training?	✓	✓
Playfulness: (Liu and Arnett, 2000)	Enjoyment	✓	✓
	Excitement	✓	
	Feeling of participation	✓	
	Charming	✓	
	Escapism	Unclear	
Physical arousal: (Beckers and Schmidt, 2001)	I feel like I am short of breath when I am in front of the computer.	✓	
	I have sweaty palms when I work with the computer.	✓	

(continued)

Table 14.3 (*continued*)

Affective Factor Definition and Source	Original Measure Items	Affective Reaction?		Cognitive Reaction?	Note
		Arousal	Pleasure		
Satisfaction: Service satisfaction (of an application service provider [ASP]): a positive affective state resulting from the appraisal of all aspects of a firm's working relationship with another firm (Susarla et al., 2003)	My company's senior management is satisfied with security and privacy offered by the ASP. My company's senior management is willing to share workload and information with an ASP. My company's management information systems (MIS) department is satisfied with the security and privacy offered by the ASP. Our MIS is willing to share workload and information with an ASP. Overall, I am satisfied with the ASP's way of implementing IS projects.				Unclear what "satisfied" means in this paper.
Satisfaction: Users' affect regarding (feeling about) prior online banking division use (Bhattacherjee, 2001)	Your overall experience of online banking division use is: Very dissatisfied/very satisfied. Very displeased/very pleased. Very frustrated/very contented. Absolutely terrible/absolutely delighted.	√ √ √	√	Unclear	

Figure 14.3   **A Model of Individual Interaction with IT (IIIT)**

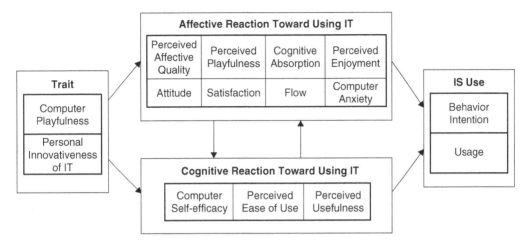

et al.'s model (1991). Although less important than PU, PEOU has been confirmed to significantly influence users' behavioral intention or actual usage behaviors (e.g., Davis, 1989; Taylor and Todd, 1995; Taylor and Todd, 1995; Venkatesh and Davis, 2000; Venkatesh et al., 2003).

PU and PEOU are two major cognitive determinants of users' adoption of information technologies, while other factors are supposed to influence users' behavioral intention or actual usage via these two factors (Davis, 1989). Computer self-efficacy (CSE) also is believed to play an important role in individuals' decision making. CSE is closely related to affect factors such as affect and anxiety, and other cognitive concepts such as PU (Compeau et al., 1999) and PEOU (Venkatesh, 2000).

A Model of Individual Interaction with IT (IIIT)

Based on the above examination, an IT-specific model of an individual's interacting with IT can be constructed by applying the abstract model IIO shown in the section "Theoretical Grounds and an Abstract Model." The final dependent variables are the same: behavioral intention to use IT and usage of IT. For the affective reactions, all existing terms but the two "affects" are relatively recognizable and studied in IS. These terms are used as they were defined. Figure 14.3 depicts the IT-specific model, which denotes individual interaction with IT (IIIT).

Our main goal here is to illustrate the big picture of important contributors to individual interaction with IT. Therefore, we focus on the relationships among the clusters of components such as traits, affective reaction, cognitive reaction and behavioral intention/usage. Due to the scope of this paper, we omit the specific relations among specific affective reactions and among cognitive reactions, even though existing studies provided empirical evidence showing the existence of these relations. For example, studies have identified that computer self-efficacy influences perceived ease of use and perceived usefulness (Compeau and Higgins, 1995; Compeau and Higgins, 1995).

The main idea of IIIT is that personal traits influence both affective and cognitive reactions toward using IT; affective and cognitive reactions influence each other, and together they determine IT use intention and behavior. The specific propositions in the abstract model of IIO should be applicable here in the IIIT model. In the next section, relationships among the related concepts are analyzed to confirm and validate the general propositions.

Table 14.4

The Impacts of Traits on Affective Reactions Toward Using IT

Article ID	Trait (IV)	Affective Reaction (DV)	P1–1 Supported?
Agarwal and Karahanna (2000)	CPS	Cognitive absorption	Yes
	PIIT	Cognitive absorption	Yes
Martocchio and Webster (1992)	CPS	Positive mood	Yes
Thatcher and Perrewe (2002)	Trait anxiety	Computer anxiety	Yes
	PIIT	Computer anxiety	Yes
Webster and Martocchio (1992)	CPS	Computer anxiety	Yes
Webster and Martocchio (1995)	CPS	Flow	Yes
Sun and Zhang (2004)	CPS	Perceived enjoyment	Yes

IV: Independent variable. DV: Dependent variable. CPS: Computer playfulness. PIIT: Personal innovativeness in IT.

Table 14.5

The Impacts of Traits on Cognitive Reactions

Article ID	Trait (IV)	Cognitive Reaction (DV)	P1–2 Supported?
Hackbarth et al. (2003)	CPS	PEOU	Yes
Karahanna et al. (2002)	PIIT	Relatively advantages of GSS	Yes
Venkatesh (2000)	CPS	PEOU	Yes
Sun and Zhang (2004, Model 2)	CPS	PEOU	Partial yes

CPS: Computer playfulness. PEOU: Perceived ease of use. PIIT: Personal innovativeness in IT.

Examination of the Relationships in IIIT

The Impacts of Traits

Table 14.4 summarizes empirical findings on relationships between traits and affective reactions; Table 14.5 shows relationships between traits and cognitive reactions. These results are compared to the general propositions derived from the IIO model. Developed based on the empirical evidence and the general propositions, these IT-specific propositions can guide additional empirical studies and practice on the role of affect in the IS field.

Table 14.4 posits that a user's trait variables, computer playfulness, and personal innovativeness in IT can predict his or her affective reaction. Agarwal and Karahanna (2000) tested the impacts of both of the two trait variables on the users' affective reaction named cognitive absorption using the World Wide Web as the target technology.

Computer playfulness may predict users' perceptions, especially PEOU, in that those people who are more playful with information technologies in general are expected to indulge in using a new IT just for the sake of using it, rather than for the specific positive outcomes associated with use (Venkatesh, 2000). These "playful" users tend to underestimate the difficulties of using a new technology since they quite simply enjoy the process and do not perceive it as requiring effort compared to those who are less playful (Venkatesh, 2000).

It is noteworthy that a recent study indicates the possible full mediating effect of perceived enjoyment between computer playfulness and perceived ease of use (Sun and Zhang, 2004). Computer playfulness has a significant effect on perceived ease of use. However, when perceived enjoyment is introduced as a mediator between computer playfulness and perceived ease of use, the relationship between computer playfulness and perceived ease of use becomes non-significant, and the relationship between computer playfulness and perceived enjoyment and that between perceived enjoyment and ease of use are significant. This result indicates a mediating effect of perceived enjoyment in the relationships between computer playfulness and perceived ease of use. More empirical studies are needed to further validate and generalize this argument about the linkage between traits and cognitive reactions.

Empirical studies (e.g., Karahanna et al., 2002) have found that PIIT can predict the formation of users' perceptions such as perceived usefulness. More innovative users have more positive perceptions of the usefulness of information technologies.

Tables 4 and 5 show some gaps in the current IS studies. For example, we found very few empirical studies focusing on the following relationships: CPS on perceived playfulness, perceived enjoyment (except Sun and Zhang, 2004), attitude and satisfaction, and PIIT on perceived playfulness, perceived enjoyment, flow, attitude, and satisfaction. Further explorations of these links may provide more insight into how individuals' traits influence their affective reactions toward using IT.

The Affective Antecedents of Behavioral Intention

For the purpose of this paper, we focus only on the affective antecedents of behavioral intention/usage. For the cognitive reactions as antecedents, please refer to other technology acceptance papers. Table 14.6 shows empirical evidence of affective reactions as antecedents of behavioral intention/usage. In general, these influences are direct ones, as hypothesized by P2–1. For example, Agarwal and Karahanna (2000) argued that contrary to the prediction that the influence of cognitive absorption on behavioral intention would be fully mediated by belief concepts, cognitive absorption has a direct significant impact on BI. Zhang and Li also find that perceived affective quality of a course management system has a direct impact on intention to use the system (Zhang and Li, 2004).

However, some exceptions do exist. For example, an affective reaction variable, named affect in Thompson et al.'s research, fails to precede users' actual usage behaviors (1991). Interestingly, Cheung et al. (2000) recently retested this model and again found the impact of affect on usage to be insignificant. Thompson et al. argue that the insignificant influence of affect on actual usage is a result of the "different theoretical structures" from other research on affect and implies that affect may have an indirect impact on usage via intention. Nevertheless, other research confirmed that affective reaction variables could have significant impacts on usage. We thus attribute the failure of affect to predict usage in Thompson et al.'s and following Cheung et al.'s research to poorly defined and ill-measured concepts. Actually, their measurements have a relatively low reliability (Cronbach's Alpha = 0.61), which at least partially supports our argument.

Using the same measurement in Davis et al. (1992) but a different name (intrinsic motivation), Venkatesh et al.'s (2002) finding of the impact of enjoyment is inconsistent with Davis et al.'s. The inconsistency is very likely to be a result of the different theorized relationships between ease of use and affect factors, named respectively intrinsic motivation and enjoyment in their studies. While Davis et al. argued that ease of use predicts the affect (enjoyment), Venkatesh et al. suggested another relationship: Affect (intrinsic motivation) predicts ease of use. From another

Table 14.6

Affective Reaction's Impacts on BI/Usage

Article ID	Affective Reaction (IV)	BI/B (DV)	P2–1 Supported?
Agarwal and Karahanna (2000)	Cognitive absorption	BI	Yes
Al-Khaldi et al. (1998)	Computer anxiety	Usage	Yes
	Computer liking	Usage	Yes
Al-Khaldi and Wallance (1999)	Affect	Usage	Yes
Atkinson and Kydd (1997)	Enjoyment	Usage	Yes
Brosnan (1999)	Computer anxiety	Usage	Yes
Cheung et al. (2000)	Affect	Usage	No
Compeau and Higgins (1995a)	Affect	Usage	Yes
	Anxiety	Usage	Yes
Compeau et al. (1999)	Affect	Usage	Yes
	Computer anxiety	Usage	No
Davis (1989)	Attitude	BI	Yes
Davis et al. (1989)	Attitude	BI	Yes
Davis et al. (1992)	Enjoyment	BI	Yes
Hsu and Lu (2003)	Flow	BI	Yes
Hu et al. (1999)	Attitude	BI	Yes
Igbaria et al. (1995)	Perceived enjoyment	Usage	Partially yes
Igbarai et al. (1996)	Perceived fun/enjoyment	Usage	Yes
Koufaris (2002)	Flow	BI	Partially yes
Moon and Kim (2001)	Perceived playfulness	BI	Yes
Rozell and III (2000)	Affective reaction	Future computer-related performance	Yes
Sun and Zhang (2004)	Perceived enjoyment	BI	No
Teo et al. (1999)	Perceived enjoyment	Usage	Partially yes
Thompson et al. (1991)	Affect	Usage	No
Venkatesh and Speier (2000)	Perceived enjoyment	BI	Yes
Venkatesh et al. (2002)	Intrinsic motivation (Perceived enjoyment)	BI	No
Zhang and Li (2004)	Perceived affective quality	BI	Yes
Zhang and Li (2005)	Perceived affective quality	BI	No

IV: Independent variable. DV: Dependent variable. BI: Behavioral intention.

perspective, this inconsistency reflects the interaction between these two concepts, which will be discussed in the next section.

In a different study investigating the effect of perceived affective quality (PAQ), Zhang and Li find that perceived affective quality of a university Web site does not have a direct impact on behavior intention of using the Web site (Zhang and Li, 2005), which is different from that in Zhang and Li (2004). One possible reason for the difference is the voluntariness of IT use: Participants were required to use the course management system in the study where PAQ has a direct impact on BI (Zhang and Li, 2004).

As for the cognitive reaction variables, much prior IS research has already confirmed a strong influence of cognitive reaction variables on behavioral intention or actual usage behavior. In another words, proposition 2–2 is supported by the literature. In this study, we haven't discussed these relationships in detail because it is not the focus of this research. (For more details, please refer to Sun and Zhang [2006]).

Table 14.7

Affective Reaction → Cognitive Reaction

Article ID	Affective Reaction (IV)	Cognitive Reaction (DV)	P3–1 Supported?
Agarwal and Karahanna (2000)	Cognitive absorption	PU	Yes
	Cognitive absorption	PEOU	Yes
Beckers and Schmidt (2001)	Physical Arousal	Beliefs	Yes
	Affective feeling	Beliefs	Partially yes
Brosnan (1999)	Perceived fun	CSE	Yes
	Computer anxiety	PU	Yes
	Computer anxiety	PEOU	Yes
Coffin and MacIntyre (1999)	Computer anxiety	CSE	Yes
Durndell and Hagg (2002)	Computer anxiety	CSE	Yes
Hackbarth et al. (2003)	Computer anxiety	PEOU	Yes
Rozell and III (2000)	Computer anxiety	CSE	No
Karahanna et al. (2002)	Computer anxiety	Relative advantage	No
Sun and Zhang (2004)	Perceived enjoyment	PEOU	Yes
Thatcher and Perrewe (2002)	Computer anxiety	CSE	Yes
Venkatesh (2000)	Computer anxiety	PEOU	Yes
	Enjoyment (state)	PEOU	Yes
Venkatesh et al. (2002)	Intrinsic motivation (Perceived enjoyment)	PU	Yes
	Intrinsic motivation (Perceived enjoyment)	PEOU	Yes
Yi and Hwang (2003)	Enjoyment	PU	Yes
	Enjoyment	PEOU	Yes
	Enjoyment	CSE	Yes
Zhang and Li (2004)	Perceived affective quality	PU	Yes
	Perceived affective quality	PEOU	Yes

IV: Independent variable. DV: Dependent variable. PU: Perceived usefulness. PEOU: Perceived ease of use. CSE: Computer self-efficacy.

The Relationship Between Affective and Cognitive Reactions

Examination of the IS literature indicates that affective reactions and cognitive reactions are quite distinguishable and have a reciprocal relationship (Tables 14.7 and 14.8). For example, while Davis et al. (1992) confirmed the effects of perceived ease of use on enjoyment, Venkatesh (2000) argued that perceived enjoyment also influenced perceived ease of use. Another example is the reciprocal impact between computer self-efficacy and affect and anxiety (Compeau and Higgins, 1995; Compeau et al., 1999; Thatcher and Perrewe, 2002). In fact, the theoretical basis of the computer self-efficacy model, social learning theory (SLT), suggests that self-efficacy and anxiety influence each other (Bandura, 1977). We will examine each direction separately.

Affective reactions → Cognitive reactions. Table 14.7 summarizes the impacts affective reactions have on cognitive reactions.

In general, the proposed influence of affective reaction on cognition reactions in IIO is confirmed in IS studies (Table 14.7) with few exceptions. While named differently and emphasizing different aspects, affective reaction variables have significant influence on cognitive reaction variables. Similar to the principle of mood-congruence, there is likely to be a natural propensity to overlook the affective aspects of an activity by attributing instrumental value (Agarwal and Karahanna, 2000). Users may rationalize that they are "voluntarily spending a lot of time on this activity and enjoying it, therefore, it must be useful" (Agarwal and Karahanna, 2000, p. 676). Venkatesh et al. (2002) also hypothesized and lately confirmed that intrinsic motivation increases the deliberation and thoroughness of cognitive processing and leads to enhanced perceptions of extrinsic motivation conceptualized as perceived usefulness. Similarly, Yi and Hwang (2003) tested and confirmed the effects of enjoyment on perceived usefulness. Perceived enjoyment also has a very strong effect on perceived ease of use. Actually researchers argued that it may be the strongest antecedent of perceived ease of use (Sun and Zhang, 2004). Computer anxiety is also confirmed to negatively influence PU (Brosnan, 1999). Generally speaking, less anxious computer users are more likely to perceive IT to be useful (Brosnan, 1999).

There are, however, some exceptions. Karahanna et al.'s research (2002) attributed the insignificant influence of computer anxiety on PU to users' experience, which makes the computer anxiety "not a significant consideration in their evaluation" (p. 337). The insignificant link between computer anxiety and computer self-efficacy in Rozell and Gardner's research (2000) may be due to the complexity of the proposed model used in their studies.

Affective reactions also influence PEOU. All articles (Agarwal and Karahanna, 2000; Sun and Zhang, 2004; Venkatesh, 2000; Venkatesh et al., 2002; Yi and Hwang, 2003) that discussed the effects of affective reaction variables on PEOU also empirically confirmed this relationship (Table 14.7). Positive affective reactions encourage more mental resources to be allocated to the task or to the interaction with the technologies of interest. High arousal, usually with "temporal dissociation," as suggested in flow theory, makes individuals perceive themselves as possessing ample time to complete a task, which in turn reduces the perception of workload associated with using the technologies (Agarwal and Karahanna, 2000). The above discussion indicates that both dimensions of affect, arousal and valence, lead to perceived ease of use. In Venkatesh et al.'s research (Venkatesh et al., 2002), intrinsic motivation is supposed to make individuals "underestimate" the difficulty associated with using the technologies since they enjoy the process itself and do not perceive it to be arduous compared to those people with less intrinsic motivation. Computer anxiety, negative affective state, also has influence on PEOU (Brosnan, 1999; Hackbarth et al., 2003; Venkatesh, 2000). Users with lower levels of computer anxiety tend to regard IT as being easier to use. Resource allocation theory argues that lower levels of computer anxiety can also be seen as a result of anxiety reduction by directing some of the attentional resources to an off-task activity, which usually increases the effort required to accomplish tasks (high PEOU) (Venkatesh, 2000).

Affective reaction factors are also related to CSE. Although not studied frequently, the impacts of affective reaction factors such as fun (Brosnan, 1999) and enjoyment (Yi and Hwang, 2003) on CSE are empirically found to be significant. Computer anxiety is also confirmed to have significant impacts on CSE (Coffin and MacIntyre, 1999; Durndell and Haag, 2002; Thatcher and Perrewe, 2002). Bandura's theory of self-efficacy argues that self-efficacy beliefs are strengthened by anxiety reduction (Bandura, 1977).

It is noteworthy that the literature review yields an impression that PEOU is more related to affect than PU. While PU is generally viewed as an extrinsic motivation, PEOU, together with affective factors, is viewed as an intrinsic motivation (Atkinson and Kydd, 1997). PEOU and affective reaction factors—e.g., enjoyment—show similar patterns that are different from that of PU. Specifically, Atkinson and Kydd's research (1997) indicated that intrinsic motivation variables, PEOU and enjoyment, are important in predicting use of the Web for entertainment purposes,

Table 14.8

Cognitive Reaction → Affective Reaction

Article ID	Cognitive Reaction (IV)	Affective Reaction (DV)	P3–2 Supported?
Beckers and Schmidt (2001)	Computer self-efficacy	Physical arousal	No
	CSE	Affective feeling	No
Bhattacherjee (2001)	PU	Satisfaction	Yes
Brosnan (1999)	CSE	Computer anxiety	Yes
	PEOU	Computer anxiety	Yes
	CSE	Perceived fun	Yes
Cheung et al. (2000)	Complexity	Affect	Yes
Chung and Tan (2004)	PU	Perceived playfulness	Yes
Compeau and Higgins (1995a)	CSE	Affect	Yes
	CSE	Computer anxiety	Yes
	Outcome expectation (PU)	Affect	Yes
Compeau et al. (1999)	CSE	Affect	Yes
	CSE	Computer anxiety	Yes
	Outcome expectation (PU)	Affect	Yes
Davis (1989)	PU	Attitude	Yes
	PEOU	Attitude	Yes
Davis et al. (1989)	PU	Attitude	Yes
	PEOU	Attitude	Yes
Davis et al. (1992)	PEOU	Enjoyment	Yes
Durndell and Hagg (2002)	CSE	Computer anxiety	Yes
Hsu and Lu (2003)	PEOU	Flow experience	Yes
Hu (1999, p. 2374)	PU	Attitude	Yes
	PEOU	Attitude	No
Igbaria et al. (1995)	PEOU	Perceived enjoyment	Yes
Igbarial et al. (1996)	Perceived complexity (PEOU)	Perceived fun/enjoyment	Yes
Moon and Kim (2001)	PEOU	Perceived playfulness	Yes
	PEOU	Attitude	Yes
Teo et al. (1999)	PEOU	Perceived enjoyment	Yes
Webster and Martocchio (1995)	CSE	Flow	No

IV: Independent variable. DV: Dependent variable. CSE: Computer self-efficacy. PU: Perceived usefulness. PEOU: Perceived ease of use.

while PU is not. On the other hand, PU, as an extrinsic motivation variable, is important in predicting Web use for course-related purposes, while PEOU and enjoyment don't have significant impacts. Venkatesh's research (Venkatesh, 2000) also empirically found the close association between enjoyment and PEOU. Our literature review yields the same results. Table 14.7 shows that all studies confirm the significant relationships between affect-related factors and PEOU.

Cognitive reactions → affective reactions. Table 14.8 indicates that the proposed impact of cognitive reactions on affective reactions in IIO (P 3–2) is generally supported, although some exceptions exist.

First, PU could influence users' affective reactions significantly. Generally the satisfaction derived from the positive perception of usefulness is attributed to the IT usage, causing an increasing affective reaction to IT (Compeau and Higgins, 1995).

Second, PEOU's impact on affective reaction variables receives substantial theoretical and empirical supports. In the motivational model created by Davis et al. (1992), ease of use is hypothesized to precede enjoyment since it is a source of information relevant to feelings of self-efficacy, competence, and self-determination; self-efficacy is one of the major factors theorized to underlie affective reactions (Bandura, 1982; Bandura, 1977). Flow theory also suggests that the feasibility of the activity for an individual encourages flow (Csikszentmihalyi, 1988). Information technologies that are threatening and difficult to use are less likely to be enjoyable for users. PEOU may also negatively relate to computer anxiety. Considering that PEOU is closely related to computer self-efficacy and that computer self-efficacy is confirmed to have significant effects on computer anxiety, it is very likely that PEOU is significantly related to computer anxiety. Brosnan (1999) empirically confirmed this effect.

Exceptions do exist. For example, Hu et al. (1999) failed to confirm the PEOU's anticipated impact on attitude. Hu et al. attributed this failure to their subjects, physicians, who have above-average general competence and therefore can "assimilate a new technology quickly and become familiar with its operation without as intense training as might be necessary for other user populations" (p. 105). This result actually echoes our argument in the first section that studies of attitude show mixed results. Consistent with our argument, the impact of perceived usefulness on BI is not totally mediated by attitude, which confirms the "independence" of affective and cognitive reactions.

CSE's impacts on affective reaction variables are also widely studied. The major work has been done by Compeau and Higgins (1995) who adapted Bandura's social cognitive theory to the IS field. Computer self-efficacy influences users' affective reactions in that users tend to enjoy using information technologies when they feel they are capable of mastering them successfully. Conversely, when they do not feel they can handle IT, users dislike it or have negative affective reactions to it (Compeau and Higgins, 1995). Bandura's self-efficacy theory also confirmed this relationship, arguing that individuals experience anxiety in attempting to perform certain behaviors that they do not feel competent to perform (Bandura, 1977). Those with higher self-efficacy are more likely to experience positive affect than those with lower self-efficacy. This causal relationship is empirically confirmed in IS literatures (Brosnan, 1999; Compeau and Higgins, 1995; Compeau et al., 1999; Durndell and Haag, 2002).

There are some exceptions. For instance, Beckers and Schmidt (2001) failed to confirm the impact of computer self-efficacy on affect, which was separated into physical arousal and affective feelings in their research. Their findings, however, indicated that contrary to their expectation, computer literacy, which refers to users' actual experience with computers, has a significant relationship with computer self-efficacy and affect factors (Beckers and Schmidt, 2001). In other words, computer literacy mediates CSE's influence on physical arousal and affective feeling. Therefore, they argued that self-efficacy might influence physical arousal and affective feelings only to the extent that it raises computer literacy (Beckers and Schmidt, 2001). So we still expect a significant relationship between CSE and affective reaction factors after controlling the computer literacy factor.

DISCUSSIONS AND CONCLUSION

Affect receives remarkably less attention from IS researchers than cognition. However, affect has been confirmed to be critical in understanding human behavior in fields such as psychology, marketing, and consumer and organizational behavior research. While studying affect-related concepts, IS researchers focus on different aspects of affect and its role in individual reactions toward using IT. The relationships between affective factors and other types of factors, such as cognitive or behavioral factors, are less consistent in the existing IS research. In addition, few studies have attempted to examine the role of affect systematically in order to guide research and practice.

Motivated by the advances in other fields, we try to establish a model of the individual interacting with IT where affect is an integral and important part. This model also holds existing findings together in a cohesive way, and thus is able to explain existing IS research. Further, it has potential for a better understanding of the role of affect in the IS field. The IIIT model is based on a general model of the individuals interacting with objects (IIO) in the environment, and draws upon solid research in three relevant disciplines: psychology, marketing and consumer research, and organizational behavior. Both the IIO and IIIT models are theoretically sound and can explain empirical evidence found in existing studies.

The proposed IIIT model draws on many prior studies, such as the technology acceptance model (Davis, 1989; Davis et al., 1989), computer self-efficacy model (Compeau and Higgins, 1995), cognitive absorption (Agarwal and Karahanna, 2000), and flow (Finneran and Zhang, 2003; Ghani et al., 1991), to name a few, and it reassembles them in a novel way by positioning clear relationships among the related concepts.

It is noteworthy that the IIIT model reflects only the key components and their relationships. In a complex world, more factors may come into play. For example, many IS studies have shown that social norms, facilitating factors, task natures, and user experience, among others, can influence user behavior intention and usage of IT. In other words, the relationships depicted in the IIIT model can be situational, and moderating factors could come into play. For example, Venkatesh (2000) found that experience moderates the effect of trait variable (computer playfulness) on users' perceptions of ease of use: trait influences PEOU only for inexperienced users. Experienced users' affective reaction of "perceived enjoyment" has more influence on PEOU. It was argued that with increasing experience, system use may become more routine, less challenging, and less discovery-oriented, and, therefore, perceived enjoyment derived from actual interaction with the system becomes more critical in forming users' perceptions of ease of use. A task's characteristics have also been confirmed to have significant moderating effects. For example, Atkinson and Kydd (1997) hypothesized and empirically confirmed the moderating effects of the task's purpose. Users of work-related tasks are more driven by extrinsic motivation, measured as PU, while users of entertainment-related tasks are more driven by intrinsic motivations, one of which is enjoyment. Task complexity has shown to have moderating effects. According to the affect infusion model, more complex tasks recruit more extensive processing strategies, increasing the scope of affect infusion, which means more influence of affect on cognition (Forgas, 1995). Another related concept is the task's novelty. The more complex a task, the more likely that individuals constantly receive novel information and have to interpret and assimilate it into a pre-existing representational system, a process in which affect is supposed to play an important role (Forgas, 1995). All these findings suggest the importance of moderating effects.

This research calls for more attention to affect-related factors. In this study, we mentioned several times that some of the deficiencies of existing theories and models in explaining users' behavior may be due to their ignoring the role of affect. This study goes further and confirms that affect does matter in determining users' behavioral intentions and actual usage behaviors. Affect also has significant influence on cognitive factors. Future researchers can go in several directions. First, the synthesis of the existing affect-related concepts may be helpful. As we can see in the IIIT model, several affect-related concepts that are correlated have been named and conceptualized differently in prior studies. Therefore, synthesis may be a good way to contribute to this stream of research. Second, the interactions between affect and other groups of factors deserve more attention. Third, as we suggested in a prior text, the distinctions between different types of affect (e.g., trait vs. state) should be identified. Fourth, the dimensions of affect deserve more attention. Psychological research could be a valuable reference source of affect dimensions. For example, Russell and colleagues produced the affect grid, which received lots of attention in psychology (Russell, 2003; Russell and Barrett, 1999). It may be a good starting point to study the dimensions of affect as well as their different relationships with other factors.

This study also has implications for practitioners. This research calls for their attention to IT users' affective reactions. Integrating IT with organizational and social environment, practitioners should not ignore users' affective reactions to their technologies, which are supposed to be related to their performance usage behavior. ITs are no longer "cold machines." More personalized ITs are needed to improve users' use and subsequent performance. This research suggests that affect can be influenced by users' traits and can influence users' cognition and behaviors through various mechanisms.

There are a few limitations of this study. First, we haven't considered the influence of users' demographic characteristics while focusing on the task and experience. The exclusion, however, does not mean that these factors are not important. Actually, several IS literatures noticed and tested the impact of gender on affect-related factors, especially computer anxiety. The second limitation of this study is the relative small pool of literature examined, due to time and space limits; this may bias our findings. Considering more previous studies may increase the validity of our findings.

APPENDIX 14.1. LIST OF IS STUDIES REVIEWED IN THIS PAPER

Table 14.9

Articles for Review

Article ID	Journal	Article ID	Journal
Agarwal and Karahanna (2000)	MIS Quarterly	Karahanna et al. (2002)	Decision Support Systems
Agarwal and Prasad (1998)	Information Systems Research	Koufaris (2002)	Information Systems Research
Al-Khaldi and Al-Jabri (1998)	Computers in Human Behavior	Liu and Arnett (2000)	Information & Management
Al-Khaldi and Wallace (1999)	Information & Management	Martocchio (1992)	Personnel Psychology
Atkinson and Kydd (1997)	DATA BASE	Moon and Kim (2001)	Information & Management
Beckers and Schmidt (2001)	Computers in Human Behavior	Perry and Ballou (1997)	DATA BASE
Bhattacherjee (2001)	MIS Quarterly	Reinig et al. (1996)	Journal of Management Information Systems
Brosnan (1999)	Computers in Human Behavior	Rozell and Gardner (2000)	Computers in Human Behavior
Cheung (2000)	Decision Support Systems	Sun and Zhang (2004)	Proceedings of The Third HCI/MIS Workshop
Chou (2001)	Computers in Human Behavior	Susarla et al. (2003)	MIS Quarterly
Chung and Tan (2004)	Information & Management	Teo et al. (1999)	Omega
Coffin and MacIntyre (1999)	Computers in Human Behavior	Thatcher and Perrewe (2002)	MIS Quarterly
Compeau and Higgins (1995a)	Information Systems Research	Thompson et al. (1991)	MIS Quarterly
Compeau and Higgins (1995b)	MIS Quarterly	Venkatesh (1999)	MIS Quarterly

(continued)

Table 14.9 (*continued*)

Article ID	Journal	Article ID	Journal
Compeau et al. (1999)	*MIS Quarterly*	Venkatesh (2000)	*Information Systems Research*
Davis (1989)	*MIS Quarterly*	Venkatesh and Speier (2000)	*International Journal of Human-Computer Studies*
Davis et al. (1989)	*Management Science*	Venkatesh et al. (2002)	*Decision Sciences*
Davis et al. (1992)	*Journal of Applied Social Psychology*	Webster et al. (1990)	*Proceedings of The Eleventh International Conference on Information Systems*
Durndell and Haag (2002)	*Computers in Human Behavior*	Webster and Martocchio (1992)	*MIS Quarterly*
Ghani et al. (1991)	*Proceedings of the Twelfth International Conference on Information Systems*	Webster et al. (1993)	*Computers in Human Behavior*
Gill (1996)	*MIS Quarterly*	Webster and Martocchio (1995)	*Journal of Management*
Hackbarth et al. (2003)	*Information & management*	Yager et al. (1997)	*DATA BASE*
Hsu and Lu (2003)	*Information & Management*	Yi and Hwang (2003)	*International Journal of Human-Computer Studies*
Hu et al. (1999)	*Journal of Management Information Systems*	Zhang and Li (2004)	*Proceedings of the Twenty-Fifth International Conference on Information Systems*
Igbaria et al. (1995)	*Information & Management*	Zhang and Li (2005)	*Communications of the ACM*
Igbaria et al. (1996)	*Journal of Management Information Systems*		

NOTE

1. It is worth noting that IT-related services have gained a great deal of attention in the IS field, and consequently a number of studies have focused on individual reactions toward utilizing services. In this paper, we use IT for parsimonious reasons and keep our discussions focused.

REFERENCES

Abelson, R.P.; Kinder, D.R.; Peters, M.D.; and Fiske, S.T. Effective and semantic components in political person perception. *Journal of Personality and Social Psychology*, 42 (1982), 619–630.

Agarwal, R., and Karahanna, E. Time flies when you're having fun: cognitive absorption and beliefs about information technology usage. *MIS Quarterly*, 24, 4 (2000), 665–694.

Ajzen, I. From intentions to actions: A theory of planned behavior. In J. Kuhl and J. Beckmann (eds.), *Action Control: From Cognition to Behavior*. New York: Springer Verlag, 1985, pp. 11–39.

Al-Khaldi, M.A., and Al-Jabri, I.M. The relationship of attitudes to computer utilization: new evidence from a developing nation. *Computers in Human Behavior*, 14, 1 (1998), 23–42.

Al-Khaldi, M.A., and Wallace, R.S.O. The influence of attitudes on personal computer utilization among knowledge workers: the case of Saudi Arabia. *Information & Management*, 36, 4 (1999), 185–204.

Atkinson, M.A., and Kydd, C. Individual characteristics associated with world wide web use: an empirical study of playfulness and motivation. *The DATA BASE for Advances in Information Systems*, 28, 2 (1997), 53–62.

Bagozzi, R.P., Gopinath, M., and Nyer, P.U. The role of emotions in marketing. *Journal of The Academy of Marketing Science*, 27, 2 (1999), 184–206.

Bandura, A. Self-efficacy mechanism in human agency. *American Psychologist*, 37 (1982), 122–147.

Bandura, A. Self-efficacy: towards a unifying theory of behavioral change. *Psychological Review*, 84 (1977), 191–215.

Beckers, J.J., and Schmidt, H.G. The structure of computer anxiety: a six-factor model. *Computers in Human Behavior*, 17, 1 (2001), 35–49.

Berkowitz, L. Towards a general theory of anger and emotional aggression: implications of the cognitive-neoassociationistic perspective for the analysis of anger and other emotions. In R.S. Wyer and T.K. Srull (eds.), *Advances in Social Cognition*, 6, Hillsdale, NJ: Erlbaum, 1993, pp. 1–46.

Bettman, J.R.; Luce, M.F.; and Payne, J.W. Constructive consumer choice processes. *Journal of Consumer Research*, 25 (1998), 187–217.

Bhattacherjee, A. Understanding information systems continuance: an expectation-confirmation model. *MIS Quarterly*, 25, 3 (2001), 351.

Brave, S., and Nass, C. Emotion in human-computer interaction. In J. Jacko and A. Sears (eds.), *Handbook of Human-Computer Interaction*. New York: Lawrence Erlbaum Associates, 2002, pp. 251–271.

Breckler, S.J., and Wiggins, E.C. Affect versus evaluation in the structure of attitudes. *Journal of Experimental Social Psychology*, 25 (1989), 253–271.

Brief, A.P. *Attitudes in and around Organizations*. Thousand Oaks, CA: Sage, 1998.

Brosnan, M.J. Modeling technophobia: a case for word processing. *Computers in Human Behavior*, 15 (1999), 105–121.

Chau, P.Y.K., and Hu, P.J. Investigating healthcare professionals' decisions to accept telemedicine technology: an empirical test of competing theories. *Information & Management*, 39, 4 (2002), 297–311.

Chaudhuri, A. A study of emotion and reason in products and services. *Journal of Consumer Behavior*, 1, 3 (2002), 267–279.

Chen, Z., and Dubinsky, A.J. A conceptual model of perceived customer value in e-commerce: a preliminary investigation. *Psychology and Marketing*, 20, 4 (2003), 323–347.

Cheung, W.; Chang, M.K.; and Lai, V.S. Prediction of internet and world wide web usage at work: a test of an extended Triandis model. *Decision Support Systems*, 30, 1 (2000), 83–100.

Chou, H.W. Effects of training method and computer anxiety on learning performance and self-efficacy. *Computers in Human Behavior*, 17, 1 (2001), 51–69.

Chung, J., and Tan, F.B. Antecedents of perceived playfulness: an exploratory study on user acceptance of general information-searching websites. *Information & Management*, 41, 7 (2004), 869–881.

Coffin, R.J., and MacIntyre, P.D. Motivational influences on computer-related affective states. *Computers in Human Behavior*, 15, 5 (1999), 549–569.

Compeau, D.R., and Higgins, C.A. Application of social cognitive theory to training for computer skills. *Information Systems Research*, 6, 2 (1995), 118–143.

Compeau, D.R., and Higgins, C.A. Computer self-efficacy: development of a measure and initial test. *MIS Quarterly*, 19, 2 (1995), 189–211.

Compeau, D.R.; Higgins, C.A.; and Huff, S. Social cognitive theory and individual reactions to computing technology: a longitudinal study. *MIS Quarterly*, 23, 2 (1999), 145–158.

Crites, S.L.; Fabrigar, L.R.; and Petty, R.E. Measuring the affective and cognitive properties of attitudes: conceptual and methodological issues. *Personality & Social Psychology Bulletin*, 20 (1994), 619–634.

Csikszentmihalyi, M. *Beyond Boredom and Anxiety*. San Francisco: Jossey-Bass, 1975.

Csikszentmihalyi, M. Happiness, flow and economic equality. *American Psychologist*, 55, 10 (2000), 1163–1164.

Csikszentmihalyi, M. Motivation and creativity: toward a synthesis of structural and energistic approaches to cognition. *New Ideas in Psychology*, 6, 2 (1988), 159–176.

Davis, F.D. Perceived usefulness, perceived ease of use, and user acceptance of information technology. *MIS Quarterly*, 13, 3 (1989), 319–342.

Davis, F.D.; Bagozzi, R.P.; and Warshaw, P.R. Extrinsic and intrinsic motivation to use computers in the workplace. *Journal of Applied Social Psychology*, 22 (1992), 1111–1132.

Davis, F.D.; Bagozzi, R.P.; and Warshaw, P.R. User acceptance of computer technology: a comparison of two theoretical models. *Management Science*, 35, 8 (1989), 982–1003.

Dube, L., Cervellon, M.C. and Jingyuan, H. Should consumer attitudes be reduced to their affective and cognitive bases? Validation of a hierarchical model. *International Journal of Research in Marketing*, 20, 3 (2003), 259–272.

Durndell, A., and Haag, Z. Computer self efficacy, computer anxiety, attitudes towards the Internet and reported experience with the internet, by gender, in an East European sample. *Computers in Human Behavior*, 18, 5 (2002), 521–535.

Ellis, M.J. *Why People Play*. Englewood Cliffs, NJ: Prentice-Hall, 1973.

Epstein, S. Emotion and self-theory. In M. Lewis and J.M. Haviland (eds.), *Handbook of Emotions*. New York: Guilford, 1993, pp. 313–326.

Finneran, C.M., and Zhang, P. Flow in computer-mediated environments: promises and challenges. *Communications of the AIS*, 15, 4, (2005), pp. 82–101.

Finneran, C.M., and Zhang, P. A person-artefact-task (PAT) model of flow antecedents in computer-mediated environments. *International Journal of Human-Computer Studies*, 59, 4 (2003), 475–496.

Fishbein, M., and Ajzen, I. *Beliefs, Attitude, Intention and Behavior: An Introduction to Theory and Research*. Reading, MA: Addison-Wesley, 1975.

Forgas, J.P. Mood and judgment: the affect infusion model (AIM). *Psychological Bulletin*, 117 (1995), 39–66.

Forgas, J.P., and George, J.M. Affective influences on judgments and behavior in organizations: an information processing perspective. *Organizational Behavior and Human Decision Processes*, 86, 1 (2001), 3–34.

Frijda, N.H. Mood, emotion episodes, and emotions. In M. Lewis and J.M. Haviland (eds.), *Handbook of Emotions*. New York: Guilford Press, 1993, pp. 381–403.

Garbarino, E.C., and Edull, J.A. Cognitive effort, affect, and choice. *Journal of Consumer Research*, 8 (1997), 241–243.

Ghani, J.A., and Deshpande, S.P. Task characteristics and the experience of optimal flow in human-computer interaction. *The Journal of Psychology*, 128, 4 (1994), 381–391.

Ghani, J.A., Supnick, R., and Rooney, P. The experience of flow in computer-mediated and in face-to-face groups. In J.I. DeGross, I. Benbasat, G. DeSanctis, and C.M. Beath (eds.), *Proceedings of the Twelfth International Conference on Information Systems*, New York, NY, 1991, pp. 229–237.

Hackbarth, G.; Grover, V.; and Yi, M.Y. Computer playfulness and anxiety: positive and negative mediators of the system experience effect on perceived ease of use. *Information & Management*, 40, 3 (2003), 221.

Hsu, C.L., and Lu, H.P. Why do people play on-line games? An extended TAM with social influences and flow experience. *Information & Management*, 41, 7 (2003), 853–868.

Hu, P.J., Chau, P.Y.K., Sheng, O.R.L., and Tam, K.Y. Examining the technology acceptance model using physician acceptance of telemedicine technology. *Journal of Management Information Systems*, 16, 2 (1999), 91–112.

Igbaria, M.; Iivari, J.; and Maragahh, H. Why do individuals use computer technology? A Finnish case study. *Information & Management*, 29, 5 (1995), 227–238.

Igbaria, M.; Parasuraman, S.; and Baroudi, J.J. A motivational model of microcomputer usage. *Journal of Management Information Systems*, 13, 1 (1996), 127–144.

Ilies, R., and Judge, T.A. Understanding the dynamic relationships among personality, mood, and job satisfaction: A field experience sampling study. *Organizational Behavior and Human Decision Processes*, 89 (2002), 1119–1139.

Jackson, C.M.; Chow, S.; and Leitch, R.A. Toward an understanding of the behavioral intention to use an information-system. *Decision Sciences*, 28, 2 (1997), 357–389.

Karahanna, E.; Ahuja, M.; Srite, M.; and Galvin, J. Individual differences and relative advantage: the case of GSS. *Decision Support Systems*, 32, 4 (2002), 327–341.

Koufaris, M. Applying the technology acceptance model and flow theory to online consumer behavior. *Information Systems Research*, 13, 2 (2002), 205–223.

Kroeber-Riel, W. Emotional product differentiation by classical-conditioning—with consequences for the low-involvement hierarchy. *Advances in Consumer Research*, 11 (1984), 538–543.

Lazarus, R.S. *Emotion and Adaptation*. New York: Oxford University Press, 1991.

Leventhal, H. A perceptual-motor theory of emotion. In L. Berkowitz (ed.), *Advances in Experimental Social Psychology*. Orlando, FL: Academic Press, 1984, pp. 118–182.

Liljander, V., and Mattsson, J. Impact of customer preconsumption mood on the evaluation of employee behavior in service encounters. *Psychology and Marketing*, 19, 10 (2002), 837–860.

Liu, C., and Arnett, K.P. Exploring the factors associated with web site success in the context of electronic commerce. *Information & Management*, 38, 1 (2000), 23–33.

Lu, H.P., and Lin, J.C.C. Predicting customer behavior in the market-space: a study of Rayport and Sviokla's framework. *Information & Management*, 40, 1 (2002), 1–10.

Martin, B.A.S. The influence of gender on mood effects in advertising. *Psychology and Marketing*, 20, 3 (2003), 249–273.

Martocchio, J.J., and Webster, J. Effects of feedback and cognitive playfulness on performance in microcomputer software training. *Personnel Psychology*, 45 (1992), 553–578.

Mattila, A., and Wirtz, J. The role of preconsumption affect in postpurchase evaluation of services. *Psychology and Marketing*, 17, 7 (2000), 587–605.

Moon, J.W., and Kim, Y.G. Extending the TAM for a world-wide-web context. *Information & Management*, 38, 4 (2001), 217–230.

Murry, J.P.; Lastovicka, J.L.; and Singh, S. Feeling and liking responses to television programs: An examination of two explanations for media-context effects. *Journal of Consumer Research*, 18 (1992), 441–451.

Novak, T.P.; Hoffman, D.L.; and Duhachek, A. The influence of goal-directed and experiential activities on online flow experiences. *Journal of Consumer Psychology*, 13, 1–2 (2003), 3–16.

Perry, E.L., and Ballou, D.J. The role of work, play, and fun in microcomputer software training. *The DATA BASE for Advances in Information Systems*, 28, 2 (1997), 93–112.

Pham, M.T.; Cohen, J.B.; Pracejus, J.W.; and Hughes, G.D. Affect monitoring and the primacy of feelings in judgment. *Journal of Consumer Research*, 28, 2 (2001), 167–188.

Reinig, B.A.; Briggs, R.O.; Shepherd, M.M.; Yen, J.; and Nunamaker, J.F., Jr., Affective reward and the adoption of group support systems: productivity is not always enough. *Journal of Management Information Systems*, 12, 3 (1996), 171–185.

Remington, N.A.; Fabrigar, L.R.; and Visser, P.S. Reexamining the circumplex model of affect. *Journal of Personality and Social Psychology*, 79, 2 (2000), 286–300.

Rozell, E.J., and Gardner, W.L., III. Cognitive, motivation, and affective processes associated with computer-related performance: a path analysis. *Computers in Human Behavior*, 16, 2 (2000), 199–222.

Russell, J.A. A circumplex model of affect. *Journal of Personality and Social Psychology*, 39 (1980), 1161–1178.

Russell, J.A. Core affect and the psychological construction of emotion. *Psychological Review*, 110, 1 (2003), 145–172.

Russell, J.A., and Barrett, L.F. Core affect, prototypical emotional episodes, and other things called emotion: dissecting the elephant. *Journal of Personality and Social Psychology*, 76, 5 (1999), 805–819.

Schlosberg, H. The description of facial expression in terms of two dimensions. *Journal of Experimental Psychology*, 44 (1952), 229–237.

Schlosberg, H. A scale for the judgment of facial expressions. *Journal of Experimental Psychology*, 29 (1941), 497–510.

Schmukle, S.C.; Egloff, B.; and Burns, L.R. The relationship between positive and negative affect in the Positive and Negative Affect Schedule. *Journal of Research in Personality*, 36, (2002), pp. 463–475.

Subramanian, G.H. A replication of perceived usefulness and perceived ease of use measurement. *Decision Science*, 25, 5–6 (1994), 863–874.

Sun, H., and Zhang, P. The role of moderating factors in user technology acceptance. *International Journal of Human-Computer Studies (IJHCS)*, 64, 2 (2006), 53–78.

Sun, H., and Zhang, P. An empirical study on the roles of affective variables in user adoption of search engines. In *Proceedings of the Third Pre-ICIS Human Computer Interaction (MIS/HCI) Workshop*, Washington, DC, 2004, pp. 25–29.

Susarla, A.; Barua, A.; and Andrew, BW. Understanding the service component of application service provision: an empirical analysis of satisfaction with ASP services. *MIS Quarterly*, 27, 1 (2003), 91–123.

Szajna, B. Software evaluation and choice: predictive validation of the technology acceptance instrument. *MIS Quarterly*, 18, 3 (1994), 319–324.

Taylor, S., and Todd, P.A. Assessing IT usage: the role of prior experience. *MIS Quarterly*, 19, 4 (1995), 561–570.

Taylor, S., and Todd, P.A. Understanding information technology usage: a test of competing models. *Information Systems Research*, 6, 2 (1995), 144–176.

Teo, T.S.H., Lim, V.K.G., and Lai, R.Y.C. Intrinsic and extrinsic motivation in internet usage. *Omega*, 27, 1 (1999), 25–37.

Thatcher, J.B., and Perrewe, P.L. An empirical examination of individual traits as antecedents to computer anxiety and computer self-efficacy. *MIS Quarterly*, 26, 4 (2002), 381–396.

Thompson, R.L.; Higgins, C.A.; and Howell, J.M. Personal computing: toward a conceptual model of utilization. *MIS Quarterly*, 15, 1 (1991), 125–136.

Trafimow, D., and Sheeran, P. Some tests of the distinction between cognitive and affective beliefs. *Journal of Experimental Social Psychology*, 34 (1998), 378–397.

Trevino, L.K., and Webster, J. Flow in computer-mediated communication. *Communication Research*, 19, 5 (1992), 539–573.

Triandis, H.C. Values, attitudes, and interpersonal behavior. In *Nebraska Symposium on Motivation, Beliefs, Attitudes, and Values*, Lincoln, NE: University of Nebraska Press, 1980, pp. 195–259.

Venkatesh, V. Creation of favorable user perceptions: exploring the role of intrinsic motivation. *MIS Quarterly*, 23, 2 (1999), 239.

Venkatesh, V. Determinants of perceived ease of use: integrating control, intrinsic motivation, and emotion into the technology acceptance model. *Information Systems Research*, 11, 4 (2000), 342–365.

Venkatesh, V., and Davis, F. A theoretical extension of the technology acceptance model: four longitudinal field studies. *Management Science*, 46, 2 (2000), 186–204.

Venkatesh, V.; Morris, M.G.; Davis, G.B.; and Davis, F.D. User acceptance of information technology: toward a unified view. *MIS Quarterly*, 27, 3 (2003), 425–478.

Venkatesh, V., and Speier, C. Creating an effective training environment for enhancing telework. *International Journal of Human-Computer Studies*, 52, 6 (2000), 991–1005.

Venkatesh, V.; Speier, C.; and Morris, M.G. User acceptance enablers in individual decision making about technology: toward an integrated model. *Decision Sciences*, 33, 2 (2002), 297–316.

Webster, J.; Heian, J.B.; and Michelman, J.E. Computer training and computer anxiety in the educational process: an experimental analysis. In *Proceedings of the Eleventh International Conference on Information Systems,* Copenhagen, Denmark, 1990, pp. 171–182.

Webster, J., and Martocchio, J.J. Microcomputer playfulness: development of a measure with workplace implications. *MIS Quarterly*, 16, 2 (1992), 201.

Webster, J., and Martocchio, J.J. The differential effects of software training previews on training outcomes. *Journal of Management*, 21 (1995), 757–787.

Webster, J.; Trevino, L.K.; and Ryan, L. The dimensionality and correlates of flow in human-computer interactions. *Computers in Human Behavior*, 9, 4 (1993), 411–426.

Wegener, D.T.; Petty, R.E.; and Smith, S.M. Positive mood can increase or decrease message scrutiny: the hedonic contingency view of mood and message processing. *Journal of Social Psychology*, 69 (1995), 5–15.

Weiss, H.M. Deconstructing job satisfaction separating evaluations, beliefs, and affective experiences. *Human Resource Management Review*, 12 (2002), 173–194.

Weiss, H.M.; Nicholas, J.P.; and Daus, C.S. An examination of the joint effects of affective experiences and job beliefs on job satisfaction and variations in affective experiences over time. *Organizational Behavior and Human Decision Processes*, 78, 1 (1999), 1–24.

Yager, S.E.; Kappelman, L.A.; Maples, G.A.; and Prybutok, V.R. Microcomputer playfulness: stable or dynamic trait? *The DATA BASE for Advances in Information Systems*, 28, 2 (1997), 43–52.

Yi, M.Y., and Hwang, Y. Predicting the use of web-based information systems: self-efficacy, enjoyment, learning goal orientation, and the technology acceptance model. *International Journal of Human-Computer Studies*, 59, 4 (2003), 431–449.

Yik, M.S.M., and Russell, J.A. Predicting the big two of affect from the big five of personality. *Journal of Research in Personality*, 35 (2001), 247–277.

Zajonc, R.B. Feeling and thinking: preferences need no inferences. *American Psychologist*, 35 (1980), 151–175.

Zajonc, R.B. On the primacy of affect. *American Psychologist* (1984), 117–123.

Zajonc, R.B., and Markus, H. Affective and cognitive factors in preferences. *Journal of Consumer Research*, 9, 2 (1982), 123–131.

Zhang, P., and Li, N. The importance of affective quality. *Communications of the ACM*, 48, 9 (2005), 105–108.

Zhang, P., and Li, N. Love at first sight or sustained effect? The role of perceived affective quality on users' cognitive reactions to IT. In *Proceedings of the International Conference on Information Systems (ICIS'04)*, Washington, DC, 2004, pp. 283–296.

Zhou, Z., and Bao, Y. Users' attitudes toward web advertising—effects of internet motivation and internet ability. *Advances in Consumer Research*, 29 (2002), 71–78.

Zigurs, I., and Buckland, B.K. A theory of task/technology fit and group support systems effectiveness. *MIS Quarterly*, 22, 3 (1998), 313–334.

CHAPTER 15

AESTHETICS IN INFORMATION TECHNOLOGY

Motivation and Future Research Directions

NOAM TRACTINSKY

Abstract: *Researchers in the fields of management information systems (MIS) and human-computer interaction (HCI) have largely ignored the aesthetic dimension of information technology. This paper argues that aesthetics should be conceived as an integral part of information technology just as it is in other aspects of our lives. Four reasons are provided for this premise: (1) In many cases, aesthetics becomes a major differentiating factor between IT products; (2) our evaluations of the environment, including IT, are primarily visual; (3) aesthetics satisfies basic human needs, and human needs are increasingly supplied by information technology; and (4) aesthetic considerations are becoming increasingly important in our society, in large part thanks to IT. The paper proposes research directions for the study of aesthetics in information technology and provides some examples of research questions to illustrate the viability of this topic.*

Keywords: *Aesthetics, Design, Human-Computer Interaction, Information Technology, Visual Appearance*

INTRODUCTION

Information systems are artifacts, made to serve individuals, organizations, and society. Early information processing artifacts were designed to support a small number of well-defined organizational activities (e.g., payroll processing). Over the years, information technologies have penetrated almost every aspect of human life. The roles of IT, the ways in which it services society, have changed considerably. Consequently, people's experiences with IT have changed as well, along with their expectations, demands, and evaluations of existing and new IT artifacts. These changes call for reevaluation of how researchers and practitioners alike approach the design of the IT artifact. Whereas past research and practical guidelines stressed avoiding negative user experiences, a new vision of IT sees opportunities for positive experiences. In line with these changes, the purpose of this paper is to highlight a neglected aspect of IT design, namely its visual aesthetics.[1]

Of the various design disciplines, none can match architecture in terms of practical experience and scholarly work. Previous research noted the analogy between architecture and various facets of IT such as software development (Beregi, 1984; Gamma et al., 1994) and the user interface (Hooper, 1986). Architecture is viewed as a potential reference discipline to MIS research and practice (Lee, 1991; Kim et al., 2002) and for Brooks (1975), the architect of an information system, "like the architect of the building, is the user's agent. It is his job to bring professional and technical knowledge to bear in the unalloyed interest of the user . . ." (p. 45). This paper, too, is anchored in some of the oldest notions in architecture, put forward by Vitruvius (first century B.C.), who enjoys a special place in architectural thought. Architectural theory from the Renaissance onward has been based on his thoughts or on a dialogue with his ideas (Kruft, 1994). Vitruvius argued that architecture must satisfy three distinct requirements: *firmitas* (strength), which covers the field of statics, construction, and materials; *utilitas* (utility), the use of the building and its functioning; and *venustas* (beauty), the aesthetic requirements (Kruft, 1994). Although architectural theories have since evolved considerably, Vitruvian principles still hold much intuitive and theoretical appeal to this date (Kruft, 1994).

It is easy to see the parallels between the Vitruvian principles and some of the principles governing the field of information systems. Much of the work in this field relates to the soundness and the robustness of the artifacts created by professionals (*firmitas*). Traditionally, the various IT disciplines have emphasized qualities related to the reliability, correctness, stability, and internal logic of their products.

The second Vitruvian principle, *utilitas*, is addressed by a certain stream in MIS research and by a large segment of the human-computer interaction (HCI) community. It deals with the ways in which information technology should be designed to meet individual and organizational needs in order to promote organizational efficiency and effectiveness (e.g., Ackoff, 1967; Keen and Scott Morton, 1978). A sizable body of empirical research in the field of MIS has dealt with the effects of IT on users. This stream of research can be traced back some three decades (e.g., Dickson et al., 1977), to a time when the utility of an information system was measured mainly by objective means (e.g., decision quality and speed). Subjective evaluations of the information system played a minor role in the Minnesota experiments, but gained more attention during the next decade with the introduction of the technology acceptance model (TAM) (Davis, 1989). Later researchers began including aspects of subjective experience that went beyond mere utility valuations (e.g., Webster and Martocchio, 1992). Almost in parallel, but with somewhat different emphases, the field of HCI emerged as a counterforce to the traditional *firmitas*-oriented computing disciplines. In HCI, understanding users, their tasks, and how the system can facilitate achieving users' goals were brought to the fore (Card et al., 1983). The main emphasis of these research efforts has been studying and promoting efficiency (e.g., Butler, 1996).

Until very recently, however, the third Vitruvian requirement, *venustas*, was almost completely absent from research in the various IT disciplines. This absence is particularly glaring in studies of interactive systems. MIS and HCI texts hardly make any reference to matters of aesthetics. Whenever aesthetic issues are discussed in the HCI literature, they are likely to be qualified with warnings against their potentially detrimental effects. There may be a couple of reasons why the computing disciplines have neglected aesthetics. One reason may stem from resentment of attempts by some in the computer industry to oversell glitz and fashion in lieu of substance and usefulness. Another reason may lie in the computing disciplines' origins in disciplines that emphasize hard science, efficiency, and utility. Thus, other aspects of the interaction were not recognized as belonging in the field.

However, other design disciplines have paid much attention to aesthetics and have spawned lively debates regarding its merits. The balance between the aesthetic qualities of artifacts and the other two Vitruvian dimensions has shifted through the years. The emphasis on mass production following the industrial revolution tilted the pendulum away from aesthetic considerations. In the early twentieth century, however, industrial designers began introducing aesthetic considerations to mass production, partially for marketing purposes (Petroski, 1993). From the consumer viewpoint, aesthetic quality can make engineering products more readily acceptable and can improve their commercial value. Yamamoto and Lambert (1994) suggest that people cannot arrange and weigh the factors in a complex decision with pure objectivity. A similar argument is advanced by Helander (2003), who found that people judge the comfort of chairs more by the chairs' aesthetics than by their ergonomics. Consequently, the product's aesthetics can act as a factor enhancing the desirability of that product. From a designer viewpoint, an aesthetic approach can also reveal solutions to hidden problems, because visual thinking leads to clarification of forms and to their organization into integrated patterns (Ashford, 1969). The contrary viewpoint saw aesthetics as irrelevant (or even detrimental) to the achievement of users' goals and as a gratuity that deflected the design effort from issues of substance to issues of style. Norman (1988) argued that the pendulum may have swung too much in favor of putting aesthetics ahead of usability. Recently, however, it has been claimed that modern design places too much emphasis on performance issues and not enough on aspects, such as aesthetics, that promote pleasure (e.g., Blythe et al., 2003; Green and Jordan, 2002; Norman, 2004a).

Few doubt that the aesthetic criterion is inseparable from effective design of interactive IT (Alben, 1996). The importance of beauty, or aesthetics—terms that are used interchangeably in this work—has been recognized since antiquity. In some ancient traditions, beauty, and the perception of beauty, were of cosmic importance (Feagin and Maynard, 1997). Following Vitruvius, Alberti defined beauty as the wholeness of a body, "a great and holy matter" (Johnson, 1994, p. 402). Modern social science has established the importance of aesthetics in everyday life. In a seminal paper, Dion, Berscheid, and Walster (1972) demonstrated that a person's physical appearance influences other aspects of the social interaction. A meta-analytical study found that "attractiveness is an advantage in a variety of important real-life situations" (Langlois et al., 2000, p. 399). We are affected not only by the beauty of other people but also by the aesthetics of nature and of architecture (e.g., Nasar, 1988; Porteous, 1996), and of artifacts (Postrel, 2002; Coates, 2003; Norman, 2004a). Aesthetics plays an important role in new product development, marketing strategies, and the retail environment (Kotler and Rath, 1984; Russell and Pratt, 1980; Whitney, 1988). Bloch (1995) concluded that the "physical form or design of a product is an unquestioned determinant of its marketplace success" (p. 16).

Interest in visual aesthetics (as distinguished from abstract elegance) is growing in the computing community as well. For example, the Aesthetic Computing community (Fishwick, 2002, 2003) is targeting the application of art theory and practice to computing, in an attempt to augment existing representations and notions of aesthetics in computing.

The robust findings regarding the ubiquitous importance of aesthetics make its absence from the agenda of the IT disciplines even more puzzling. Lately, evidence in support of its role in HCI has started to emerge. This evidence encompasses both hardware and software issues. For example, Apple's iMac was heralded as the "aesthetic revolution in computing," and an indication that the visual appearance of IT had become a major factor in buyers' purchasing decisions (Postrel, 2002). Recent empirical studies indicate that aesthetic design enhances perceptions of and attitudes toward various computing products, specifically in the context of the Web (Schenkman and Jonsson, 2000; Kim et al., 2002; van der Heijden, 2003). Other studies have found aesthetics to be of importance, though not in a dominant way, in affecting users' perceptions (Zhang and von Dran, 2000; Tarasewich et al., 2001). Although they did not measure aesthetics directly, some studies indicate that Web site design is a major determinant of perceived credibility and trustworthiness of e-commerce sites (Fogg et al., 2002; McKnight et al., 2002). Research suggests that aesthetics is an important determinant of the pleasure experienced by the user during the interaction (Jordan, 1998). It was found to be highly correlated with perceptions of systems' usability both before (Tractinsky, 1997) and after (Tractinsky et al., 2000) the interaction, and with user satisfaction (Lindgaard and Dudek, 2003).

Thus, despite the paucity of direct empirical evidence regarding the role of aesthetics in IT, the recent findings cited above, as well as considerable theoretical, empirical, and anecdotal evidence from other disciplines, indicate that this is an area worthy of closer examination. We present this evidence in the next section.

THE CASE FOR STUDYING AND PRACTICING AESTHETICS IN IT

The case for incorporating the aesthetic aspect into IT practice and research is based on four arguments: three theoretical and one practical. It should be clear that these arguments do not imply that aesthetic considerations are or should become the most important factor in the development or management of IT projects. Obviously, aesthetics matters differently for different types of systems, users, tasks, and contexts. Rather, the premise is that while aesthetic issues have thus far been ignored in IT research, there are compelling arguments as to why they should receive more attention in the future.

Level of Performance Exceeds Most Users' Needs

Advances in information technology have, to a large degree, exceeded the requirements and needs of many users and organizations. A growing body of literature indicates that this might be the case for both individuals (e.g., Norman, 1998) and organizations (e.g., Carr, 2003). Norman (1998) suggests that as the functionality of new IT products exceed users' needs, and as the price of systems decrease, the competition becomes more oriented towards enhancing the users' experience rather than towards improving functionality. Once IT provides all the required features at ever-decreasing prices, considerations of convenience and reliability, and, later, of appearance and symbolic ownership become more important. Norman compares this process to the state of the watch industry, which long ago passed users' technological requirements: watches are now often marketed as fashion accessories or so as to provoke emotion.

Carr (2003) indicates that similar developments occur at the organizational level: price reductions, sufficient functionality, and more sophisticated consumers lead to the commoditization of IT. While Carr's prescriptions for IT strategy have been heavily debated, his description of the developments in the field applies to many organizations. Many of Carr's critics indicate that it is not IT per se that creates strategic advantage; rather, it is how organizations harness its potential that helps differentiate them from the competition. This does not diminish the potential contribution of aesthetic design. To the contrary, aesthetics can become an important tool for differentiating IT products. A notable example of differentiating by aesthetics is the success of the iMac, which has been attributed to the shift in emphasis from performance and reliability to aesthetics and style (Postrel, 2002).

To a large extent, the use of aesthetics as a differentiating factor resembles similarly crowded markets where "aesthetics is often the only way to make a product stand out" (Postrel, 2002, p. 2). According to this view, aesthetics may not overcome bad usability, unreliable systems, or significant lack of features, but it matters when all else is equal. And, allowing for a slight overgeneralization, "all else is equal" is becoming the state of affairs in the rapidly commoditized IT market.

Many Aesthetically Based Evaluations Are Fast and Persistent

Previous research in MIS and in HCI largely presumed that human decision making relies entirely on cognitive processes. Current findings and theories, however, portray a different picture. Recent research indicates that the two human information processing systems, the affective and the cognitive, are intertwined (Bargh, 2004; Ortony et al., 2005; Russell, 2003). Norman and his colleagues (Norman, 2002, 2004a; Ortony et al., 2005), suggest a hierarchical three-level theory of human behavior that integrates the affective and the cognitive systems. At each level, the world is being evaluated (affect) and interpreted (cognition). At bottom, the visceral level surveys the environment and rapidly communicates affective signals to the higher levels. The routine (or behavioral) level is where most of our learned behavior takes place. Finally, the reflection level is where the highest-level processes occur. One important role of affect in human behavior stems from the fact that some of its reactions are very rapid (Pham et al., 2001; Norman, 2004a) it can color subsequent cognitive processes because our thoughts normally occur after the affective system has transmitted its initial information. Aesthetic evaluations may take place on all three levels of Norman et al.'s model, but there are some hints that the first aesthetic impressions are affective, are formed immediately at a low level, and thus precede cognitive processes (Zajonc and Markus, 1982; Pham et al., 2001; Norman, 2004a). Hence, the immediate affective reactions may color and potentially sway successive cognitive processes (Pham et al., 2001; Duckworth et al., 2002).

It should be noted that it is not necessary for aesthetic impressions to be extremely rapid in order to leave their traces on subsequent decision processes. This is because in many cases aesthetic evaluations of an object can be made faster than evaluations of other, more latent attributes of the object. The phenomenon of aesthetic perceptions of an object coloring other perceived attributes of the same object is familiar in the social sciences. Cowley (2000) suggests that "we're designed to care about looks, even though looks aren't earned and reveal nothing about character" (p. 193). Thus, in what is known as the "beautiful is good" stereotype, a person's attractiveness was found to affect how people perceive other attributes of that person (Dion et al., 1972; Eagly et al., 1991). The effects of the "beautiful is good" stereotype are pervasive and consequential. For example, beautiful people earn more in the marketplace (Hamermesh and Biddle, 1994), and better-looking university instructors receive higher teaching evaluations (Hamermesh and Parker, 2005).

Still, it is important to note that the effect of attractive objects is not restricted to first impressions and brief encounters. It is also worth emphasizing that aesthetic evaluations are made not only immediately but they are also based on more elaborated cognitive and affective processes (Csikszentmihalyi and Robinson, 1990; Norman, 2004). Those later evaluations may be based on different aesthetic criteria (e.g., symbolic references hidden in the artifact; fine details that escape first impressions; relations with other objects in the environment), but they, too, serve an important function in shaping our attitudes towards objects. Langlois et al. (2000) concluded that the "effects of facial attractiveness are robust and pandemic, extending beyond initial impressions of strangers to actual interactions with those whom people know and observe" (p. 404).

Similar results to those obtained in the social world were also observed in human-computer interaction. A strong evidence for the immediacy of first aesthetic impression in IT was provided by Fernandes et al. (2003). They found that attractiveness evaluations of Web pages to which participants were exposed for only 500 ms were very highly correlated with attractiveness evaluations of the same pages under unlimited exposure. We have recently replicated and validated these findings (Tractinsky et al., 2004). Then, aesthetic impressions may affect how people perceive other system attributes (Tractinsky et al., 2000). We still do not have direct evidence that the aesthetics of IT impacts users' decision processes, but evidence regarding the influence of affect on decision making exist in other fields (e.g., Isen, 2001).

Obviously, the fact that some aesthetic impressions are formed immediately does not imply any deterministic consequences in human-computer interaction, just as human-human interactions are not determined by aesthetic perceptions alone (Eagly et al., 1991). Many factors can potentially moderate the relations between aesthetic characteristics of an IT artifact and the attitudinal or behavioral consequences of the interaction (I refer to some of these moderators in the next section). Thus, some responses to aesthetic stimuli are innate and relatively invariant, but some are learned and depend on culture, education, and other experiences and acquired tastes.

Aesthetics Satisfies Basic Human Needs

The degree to which aesthetic considerations have gained (or should gain) importance in the industrial landscape remains a contested issue. Designing aesthetic information systems may be viewed by some as gratuitous or even manipulative. In his seminal book *The Psychology of Everyday Things*, Norman (1988) criticized designers' tendency to emphasize aesthetics at the expense of practical features of the artifact, such as usability and functionality. Early criticisms of what was perceived as overemphasizing aesthetics may reflect, in fact, a practical recognition that artifacts should primarily satisfy basic requirements, such as reliability and usability. Recently, however, with the increased recognition of the role of emotion in decision making the reverse has been argued: modern design has placed too much emphasis on performance issues and not enough on emotional aspects, such as pleasure, fun, and excitement, which are fundamental motivators of human behavior, and to which aesthetics is a major contributor (e.g., Green and Jordan, 2002; Norman, 2002, 2004a; Coates, 2003; Hassenzahl, 2003).

The notion that aesthetics satisfies human needs is not new. Maslow (1954) lists aesthetics as one of the basic needs in his theory of human motivation. Aesthetics may also be viewed as a motivator (as opposed to a hygienic) factor, to use Herzberg's terminology (Zhang and von Dran, 2000). Postrel (2002) suggests that aesthetic pleasure has intrinsic value: "People seek it out, they reward those who offer new-and-improved pleasures, and they identify with those who share their tastes" (p. 75). The need for aesthetics does not disappear in front of the computer. IT users strive for a more complete and satisfying interactive experience; an experience that not only achieves certain well-defined goals but also involves the senses and generates affective responses (Bly et al., 1998; Venkatesh and Brown, 2001).

Fogarty et al. (2001) claim that since computer technology has moved beyond the confinements of the work environment and into the rest of our lives, its use has expanded into wider aspects and its requirements have shifted as well. If the value of computing technology was once measured mostly by its usefulness for solving problems and by its ease of use, additional requirements, such as desirability, have now emerged. Issues of visual appeal and aesthetics have become an integral part of interactive system designs. Indeed, in striking contrast to the principles and the guidelines advocated by usability researchers and gurus, any random perusal of Web sites would suggest that aesthetic considerations are paramount in designing for the Web. One of the interesting phenomena of current IT usage is the personalization of the application's appearance. The growing demand for personalized user interfaces seems to spring from the quest for richer and more affective experience (Blom and Monk, 2003). The desire expressed by users to tailor the appearance of their applications to their tastes is epitomized by the proliferation of skins—alternative interfaces to commonly used applications. Skins allow users to change an application's appearance while preserving its functionality (but not necessarily its ease of use!). Recent trends in PC-based application design indicate that "skinnability" (the ability to tailor the application's appearance) has become a common feature in many types of personal computing applications. Our studies indicate that the choice of skins by individual users has much to do with the skins' aesthetic properties (Tractinsky and Lavie, 2002; Tractinsky and Zmiri, 2006).

Practically, Aesthetics Is Here to Stay

The idea that style overcomes substance or influences perceptions of seemingly unrelated attributes of people, objects, or interactive systems may sound appalling. We can argue the ethical/moral aspects of such an idea, but we cannot deny its existence, nor can we ignore the positive effects of aesthetics on our well-being (cf. Norman, 2004a; Isen, 2001). But, more importantly, we cannot ignore the fact that aesthetic issues have become more pervasive than they used to be. Postrel (2002) argues that "sensory appeals are everywhere, they are increasingly personalized, and they are intensifying" (p. 5). According to Postrel, today's aesthetics pleases and liberates the masses. Probably as a result of all of the previous arguments, aesthetics appears to be increasing in supply and demand, fueled to a large extent by information technology.

IT is increasingly becoming a vehicle to provide aesthetics; in fact, one of the unintended results of IT is that it is particularly friendly to aesthetic applications. Users can create, edit, transmit, and receive aesthetic designs in almost any imaginable domain. One of the major genres of visual aesthetics—photography—is gradually becoming dominated by information technology. Digital cinematography follows suit. The animation industry transformed itself from drawing flip books by hand to relying heavily on IT in less than ten years (Olsen, 2004), and the worldwide market for digital animation is worth about $70 billion, according to current estimates (Hiscock, 2004). Designers in industries such as fashion, mass media, art, business documents, and Web development are equipped with applications that offer many more design options, and much more time to explore them. In a sense, CAD applications are to the designer what DSS are to a decision maker: they relieve designers from tedious work, allowing them to explore, experiment, and finally implement new designs while considerably expediting the design life cycle. In other words, IT increases society's creative potential.

The role of IT in establishing the pervasiveness of aesthetics in today's business world is described by Schroeder (2002), who argues that "Web design has brought visual issues into the mainstream of strategic thinking … The Web mandates visualizing almost every aspect of corporate strategy, operations and communication" (p. 22). Moreover, Postrel (2002) suggests that "the computer-driven democratization of design has made more people sensitive to graphic quality. Bit by bit, the general public has learned the literal and metaphorical language of graphic design. Carried by computers, aesthetics has spread to places and professions that were formerly off-limits to any such frivolity" (p. 55). An aesthetic cycle is in the working, where aesthetic supply creates more demand, which in turn feeds even more supply. "Over time people learn. They discover more about what's aesthetically possible and more about what they like" (p. 55). And the more aesthetically aware people become, the greater their need for aesthetics.

TOWARD A RESEARCH AGENDA OF AESTHETICS IN INFORMATION TECHNOLOGY

Two broad approaches dominate the study of aesthetics: philosophical, or top-down, inquiries, and empirical, or bottom-up, studies. Both approaches have mostly relied on the studies of available contemporaneous stimuli such as works of art, natural and constructed landscapes, architectural work, and other artifacts. In line with this manuscript's reliance on mainly empirical evidence as a basis for its major premise, this section concentrates on measurable and testable research ideas. Lavie and Tractinsky (2004) classified much of the empirical research on aesthetics as belonging to either the "experimentalist" or the "exploratory" traditions (see also Porteous, 1996). To some extent, the two methods reflect a philosophical debate over whether aesthetics lies in the object or in the viewer. Traditionally, studies of the first type attempt to test hypotheses about the effects of isolated elements of an object or a form on human preferences. This type of research usually seeks to iden-tify general laws of aesthetic qualities and is most commonly associated with the "experimental aes-thetics" stream of research (e.g., Berlyne, 1974). As such, it reflects the objective approach to the study of aesthetics. Although Berlyne's theory was highly influential, subsequent research has ques-tioned its predictions (e.g., Martindale et al., 1990; Whitfield, 2000) as well as the entire experimen-tal aesthetics enterprise (Arnheim, 1992). The exploratory tradition tries to delineate higher-order factors that represent people's perceptions of the evaluated objects. This stream of research is con-cerned more with subjective perceptions of aesthetics than with the objective properties of things. It is also typified by the evaluation of complete and ecologically valid stimuli (e.g., works of art, build-ings, and landscapes) rather than manipulated, artificial stimuli in controlled settings.

Obviously, aesthetics has not, until very recently, been studied systematically in the context of IT. However, given the relevance of aesthetics to IT and keeping in line with the tradition of study-ing contemporaneous artifacts and phenomena, IT is a natural context for the study of aesthetics today and in the foreseeable future. I suggest below two general approaches to the study of aes-thetics in IT. The first approach is presented as a framework in the mold of traditional positivist research. This framework identifies constructs and variables that can be manipulated or measured in relatively controlled settings. The second approach is more open-ended, identifying issues and general research questions that are difficult to study within the former approach. This approach may be necessary if we wish to render a more comprehensive picture of IT aesthetics. Hopefully, this paper will stimulate research in both directions.

A Research Framework

The ubiquity of IT in today's world makes for abundant research questions and opportunities, which are only partially represented in this section. A general research framework is presented in Figure 15.1. It treats aesthetics as a variable on par with other frequently studied variables in IS: in its core is an evaluative construct that is affected by some design characteristics of the IT artifact; it may, in turn, affect other IT-related variables; and those effects are moderated by addi-tional variables that are often employed in IS research. The idea is to present the pervasive rele-vance of aesthetics to IT by including in the framework variables that have a demonstrated "track record" in IT research. Obviously, this approach restricts the framework and perhaps ignores some of the more distinct contributions of aesthetics. Thus, the next subsection will introduce some broader issues and other, more speculative research questions.

Design Characteristics

The framework begins with the design characteristics of the information technology artifact as inde-pendent variables. Researchers may study those characteristics as objective or perceived variables. The history of aesthetics and IT research is filled with studies of both types, and the choice of which type to use should be left for the researcher to decide. For example, research on graphics in MIS has concentrated on objective design features (e.g., Benbasat et al., 1986; Jarvenpaa and Dickson, 1988) whereas much of the research on technology acceptance is based on perceived sys-tem characteristics (e.g., Venkatesh and Davis, 2000). Obviously, researchers and designers are interested in the concrete, objective aesthetic design choices that cause predictable user reactions. An example of such objective design guidelines can be found in Kim et al. (2003), who recommend, for instance: "use colors with different hues between background and menu bar" as one of the guidelines to create a futuristic atmosphere in a Web page. However, the quest for meaningful

Figure 15.1 **A General Framework for the Study of Aesthetics in Information Technology**

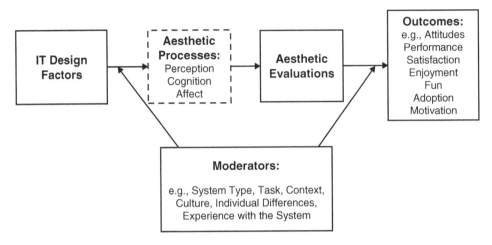

Note: The dashed box represents low-level processes that are generally not studied by IT researchers.

objective guidelines may run into some harsh realities. Thus far, with very few exceptions, extensive research has failed to come up with objective laws of aesthetics (Martindale et al., 1990; Boselie, 1992; Swede, 1994). In addition, design guidelines in HCI are notoriously sensitive to contextual variations. The more specific a guideline, the less generalizable it is; and as guidelines become less specific they lend themselves to more subjective interpretations. Thus, we might have to settle, at least in the short run, for identifying more subjective and general aesthetic design characteristics such as "classical" vs. "expressive" aesthetic dimensions of Web pages (Lavie and Tractinsky, 2004).

Aesthetic Processes

Based on the design characteristics of interactive systems, users perceive and evaluate various attributes of the system (e.g., ease of use, usefulness), including its aesthetics. As mentioned earlier, some of these aesthetic evaluations are likely immediate, strong, and may dominate the ensuing interactive experience. These perceptions and evaluations are tied to affective and cognitive processes that are not yet fully understood. While some progress is being made regarding the low-level (i.e., neurophysiological) nature of these processes (e.g., Cela-Conde et al., 2004), the specific details are only tangential to IT research in the sense that they increase the distance between the IT constructs and the final outcome variables of interest (Benbasat and Zmud, 2003). They are depicted in the framework, however, for their central role in eventually generating a range of IT-relevant outcomes: They may form (or change) users' attitudes towards the system; improve (or worsen) their performance; affect their satisfaction; and influence their willingness to buy or adopt the system. This group of variables is depicted in Figure 15.1 within a dashed box to indicate their auxiliary role in IS research.

Aesthetic Evaluations of IT

As mentioned above, all three levels of processing in Norman's (2004) model may participate in the processing of aesthetic information. Still, IT researchers may be interested less in the details of low-level mechanisms (i.e., biological, physiological) of those processes, and more in abstract, higher-level aesthetic evaluations. Such processes are more accessible to behavioral research methods and can convey a decent degree of information about the IT antecedents of aesthetic perceptions and evaluations and about the consequences of such perceptions. To date, most studies of aesthetics in IT have only measured a general aesthetic evaluation of the IT artifact. Such a measure can be a one- or a multiple-item scale assessing the system's aesthetics. For example, Kurosu and Kashimura (1995), Tractinsky (1997), Schenkman and Jonsson (2000), and Hassenzahl (2004a) have all used a single item asking about the beauty of the IT artifact, while Van der Heijden (2003) employed a three-item scale measuring perceived attractiveness. These broad measures were sufficient to demonstrate the relations between overall aesthetic perceptions and their IT antecedents and consequences. For example, Kurosu and Kashimura (1995) and Tractinsky (1997) found that manipulating the layout of objects on an ATM machine affects evaluations of the machine's beauty. In turn, the aesthetic perceptions influenced the evaluation of other system attributes, such as its ease of use (Tractinsky et al., 2000). Hassenzahl (2004a) found that perceived beauty was related to the perceived goodness of a system. Van der Heijden's (2003) composite measure of visual attractiveness was associated with perceived ease of use, usefulness, and enjoyment of a Web site, and in Schenkman and Jonsson (2000) perceived beauty was related to overall preferences of Web sites.

Perhaps of even greater interest is the ability to identify various sub-dimensions or nuances of aesthetic evaluations that are relevant to the IT context. This can help in finer-grain analyses of the associations between certain design characteristics of interactive systems and their behavioral consequences, and in providing richer accounts of HCI processes. There are already a few examples of research involving such higher-resolution measures. Kim et al. (2003) have identified specific elements of aesthetic design and were able to link them to various emotional dimensions experienced while browsing the Web. Similarly, specific (as opposed to general) aesthetic evaluations can improve our understanding of how design influences various outcome variables (e.g., Lavie and Tractinsky, 2004; Hassenzahl, 2004). I discuss this issue in more detail in the next subsection.

Outcome Variables

In the proposed framework, the range of potential outcomes can span virtually the whole gamut of outcome variables employed by behavioral IS researchers. For example, all of the categories of dependent variables identified by DeLone and McLean (1992) can serve as outcome variables in research on aesthetics: system quality, information quality, information use, user satisfaction, and individual and organizational impacts. In addition, aesthetics may influence outcomes that are more affective in nature and that were not considered at the time as highly pertinent to IT research, such as online consumer behavior (e.g., Tractinsky and Rao, 2001) and related constructs such as trust (Karvonen, 2000), pleasure (Jordan, 1998), or flow (Csikszentmihalyi, 1990; Csikszentmihalyi and Robinson, 1990). All of these and similar variables may mediate the effects of IT aesthetics on the type of variables proposed by DeLone and McLean.

Moderating Variables

Obviously, the effects of aesthetics are moderated by various factors. A partial list of potential moderators include the type of system used (e.g., a handheld entertainment system vs. a Web-based banking system); the task(s) to be performed with the system; the social context in which the system is used; cultural (organizational, societal, national) differences; motivational factors; and the degree of experience with, and exposure to, the system. One especially intriguing question is whether the impact of aesthetics is confined to voluntary use of IT. I am not familiar with direct evidence regarding the effect of aesthetics in mandated environments, but research suggests that such effect exists. For example, in reviewing the literature on the effects of positive affect, Isen (2001) found that decision makers' performance improves when positive affect is induced in various settings (e.g., medical decision making). In the context of mandated use of IT, Zhang and Li (2004) demonstrated that affective qualities of an information system influenced users' intentions to use it, both directly and indirectly. Thus, since aesthetics generates affective responses (Csikszentmihalyi and Robinson, 1990; Norman, 2004; Rafaeli and Vilnai-Yavetz, 2004), it would not be surprising to find that IT aesthetics influences decision making even when usage is mandatory.

Individual differences constitute a set of potentially important moderators in the study of aesthetics. At one extreme some people crave aesthetics so much that ugliness makes them physically ill (Maslow, 1954); at the other extreme, some remain relatively indifferent to aesthetic variations. People differ in terms of their aesthetic preferences. Research findings indicate that education moderates aesthetic preferences (Getzels and Csikszentmihalyi, 1969; Devlin and Nasar, 1989; Csikszentmihalyi and Robinson, 1990). Individual differences in aesthetic preferences may also be a by-product of cultural (e.g., organizational, societal, or national) differences. For example, Postrel (2002) suggests social affiliation as another major source of aesthetic differences due to the potential of aesthetic signals to establish group identity. At the same time, there is evidence for common cross-cultural aesthetic attitudes to humans (e.g., Langlois et al., 2000) or landscapes, whether urban or natural (Nasar, 1998). Thus, research can concentrate both on common preferences of IT aesthetics and on differentiating features.

Illustration

The framework identifies various types of relevant variables, but it is up to the researcher to generate specific research questions and hypotheses regarding how design elements of the IT artifact and the usage context affect the dependent variables of interest. To illustrate the type of studies that can be carried out, consider trust in Web stores. McKnight et al. (2002) found that consumers' perceptions of a Web site's quality (including design elements) were a very strong predictor of trusting beliefs in the retailer and of consumers' intentions to buy from the site. Similarly, in a survey of 2,684 Web users, Fogg et al. (2002) found that users use the design look of a site as the most prominent cue in evaluating the site's credibility. Unfortunately, neither of these studies obtained separate measures of visual attractiveness or aesthetics. However, given the prominence of visual stimuli in human judgment and the demonstrated effects of IT aesthetics on users' perceptions of other system attributes, it would not be an exaggeration to propose that the aesthetics of a Web site has an effect on the perceived credibility or trustworthiness of the Web store (Karvonen, 2000). An even more interesting question, perhaps, is what kind of aesthetics—or which aesthetic dimensions—affects trustworthiness. Following this path, we first need to tease out the aesthetic elements in IT as indicated previously. Some of these elements may be shared with other visual media or artifacts, some may be unique to IT, and some may be unique to certain types of IT (e.g., a Web page vs. a PDA application).

Methodological Issues

Although the study of aesthetics in IT is still in its infancy, a series of methodological issues has already been raised and others will probably emerge as more studies are conducted. These issues reflect both operational and measurement difficulties and philosophical differences. I will briefly mention three such issues. Firstly, conventional data-gathering instruments may not be enough to measure the range of responses associated with the aesthetic experience. This calls for the development of novel measures, whether behavioral (e.g., Desmet et al., 2000) or physiological (Cela-Conde et al., 2004). Secondly, it is difficult to operationalize and to manipulate the interface's aesthetics independently of other system attributes, such as usability. This is a problem regardless of whether we study objective or subjective attributes of the information technology. Finally, another issue of methodological importance is whether measures of aesthetics and of other system attributes should be taken within individuals or be averaged over individuals. We may use either method, but the conclusions to be drawn from each method are different. Some of these issues are discussed in more detail by Norman (2004b), Monk (2004), Tractinsky (2004), and Hassenzahl (2004b).

Beyond the Research Framework

There are many open-ended issues and research questions that do not fit neatly in the framework described above. Some of these issues are discussed below.

Consider, for example, the idea raised by Postrel (2002) of IT as a vehicle for aesthetic creation and communication. IT has considerably augmented our ability to copy, produce, reproduce, and distribute aesthetics. Digital photography, editing equipment, scanners, powerful and easy-to-use graphic applications, and Internet-based communication methods are just a few examples of how this is done. What are the psychological, organizational, economic, and societal impacts of this IT-based aesthetic revolution? Does the aesthetic use of IT promote self-presentation of individuals (Tractinsky and Meyer, 1999) or of organizations? How do organizations and industries use IT aesthetics to create value and to compete in increasingly crowded markets?

These questions are closely related to the value of IT aesthetics. How much are people willing to invest in improving the aesthetics of IT? What are they willing to trade off for more aesthetics? For illustrative purposes, consider the endowment effect, a situation in which owners of an object request more money to give it up than they would be willing to pay to acquire it (Thaler, 1980). In the context of evaluating mobile phones, Hassenzahl (personal communication) found that the endowment effect was stronger for hedonic qualities (e.g., beauty) relative to utilitarian qualities (e.g., functionality). If replicated in other IT contexts, such findings would suggest that the aesthetics of IT is perceived and is valued separately from other attributes of the IT artifact, and that quite often its effects on users are even more pronounced than the effects of the other attributes.

A related question centers on how individuals and organizations use aesthetics to create, change, or preserve their identities. Several studies have been conducted on this role of aesthetics in organizations (e.g., Rafaeli and Vilnai-Yavetz, 2004; Schroeder, 2002). On the individual level of analysis, one of the most fascinating behaviors on the Web is the downloading of skins in order to personalize one's applications, whether on desktops, PDAs, or cell phones. Koeppel (2000) estimates that by the year 2000, more than fifty million skins had already been downloaded from the major skin sites. Current research in this area suggests that aesthetics plays a significant role in this domain as well (Blom and Monk, 2003; Tractinsky and Zmiri, 2006). While the use of skins reflect individual differences, the emergence of aesthetic genres, mainly in Web design, suggests commonalities within, and differences between, groups of use. Postrel suggests that Web genres are formed according to horizontal social affiliations, rather than vertical, or even national, affiliations. Thus, an intriguing line of research relates to the study of aesthetic genres of IT: how they emerge and evolve, and how they influence the development and usage of IT.

The opening statement of this paper refers to theoretical notions from architecture, the oldest design discipline. The idea that architecture can serve as a reference discipline for MIS is not new (e.g., Lee, 1991), but it is quite surprising to note how little of an impact architectural theory has made on IT research. A study by Kim et al. (2002) demonstrates the viability of this research direction in explaining online customer satisfaction and loyalty by the three Vitruvian principles. Clearly, IT research can benefit considerably from judicious use of theories in architecture and its sub-disciplines (e.g., urban and landscape planning).

To improve our understanding of the role of aesthetics in IT, we should identify relevant constructs and dimensions. This can be done both empirically and conceptually. For example, Lavie and Tractinsky (2004) have empirically identified two aesthetic dimensions in the context of Web pages. The improved resolution (two aesthetic constructs instead of one) helped explain the results of previous studies that found high correlations between aesthetics and usability. In contrast to this bottom-up process, IT researchers may conceptually identify new constructs based on their own work or on work that has been done in other areas of aesthetic research. An example for the former is the work of Hassenzahl (2004a), who, based on his own model of the user experience (Hassenzahl, 2003), found that certain hedonic attributes affect perceptions of both beauty and goodness of a system. As an example of the latter type of work, consider the conceptual typology suggested by Hermeren (1988). The typology distinguishes between five aesthetic qualities: emotion qualities, behavior qualities, gestalt qualities, taste qualities, and reaction qualities. Future studies can examine aesthetics in IT from each of these five perspectives. A similar approach is offered by Löwgren (2006), who proposes five general clusters comprised of nineteen qualities of user experience of digital designs. Some of these qualities are directly related to visual aesthetics (e.g., elegance, identity, and seductivity).

Aesthetic considerations should eventually be translated into actual blueprints for design activities. This will not be easy. Organizations have invested much effort to transform design activities to accommodate *firmitas* and *utilitas* requirements. Methods and techniques to advance user-centered design have been proposed, but attempts to integrate them into mainstream development methodologies in industrial settings have met with only limited success (Stewart, 2003). Many still mistakenly treat interaction design as an afterthought and appropriately adding *venustas* to the mix will not be trivial.

Finally, let us consider a role reversal. Until now, we have mostly discussed how aesthetic concepts influence IT-related phenomena. Perhaps it is time to consider the opportunity provided by IT for the study of aesthetics. Despite being concerned with issues of beauty and aesthetics for so long, our scientific understanding of them and of their influence on humans remains very modest. However, IT's capability to manipulate and communicate designs and to collect data of various types can serve as a valuable research tool in the study of aesthetics per se. The inherent power of IT as a research tool and the fact that many real-world aesthetic designs are today based on IT create an opportunity for studies that are both ecologically valid and well controlled. IT's unique characteristics can facilitate the integration of both the experimentalist and the exploratory schools of research noted earlier in this section. IT can facilitate the manipulation of aesthetic stimuli, the transmission of the designs, the collection of data over the Internet, and the recording of various implicit measures (Cela-Conde et al., 2004; Tractinsky et al., 2004) that would help in gaining new insights about the aesthetic experience.

CONCLUSION

The study of aesthetics is "uncomfortable (to the scientist)" (Maslow, 1954, p. 97) and "fraught with difficulties" (Norman, 2004b, p. 316). Still, it has always been an exciting research area.

Now, it is even relevant! In this paper I tried to explain why it is appropriate to study aesthetics within the context of IT and to suggest some direction for research in this area. Evidence suggests that aesthetics matters in almost every aspect of human life. The rapid proliferation of IT and the increasing migration of applications from corporate and academic settings to everyday activities necessitate a much more rigorous attempt at understanding how IT and aesthetics relate. The research directions proposed here are far from being exhaustive. In the tradition of empirical research in IS, a research framework was presented, which identifies key variables and proposed relationships between antecedents and consequences of aesthetic evaluations of IT. However, many other research directions are also possible, some of which were also outlined. It is important to reiterate that the purpose of this work is not to suggest the predominance of aesthetic considerations over others. Rather, it is to advocate better balance of major design dimensions in IT, a balance that is much more pronounced in other design disciplines.

ACKNOWLEDGMENT

This is an extended version of a paper presented at the 25th International Conference on Information Systems (ICIS), Washington, DC, December, 2004.

NOTE

1. The term "aesthetics" was introduced into philosophical terminology in the eighteenth century by Baumgarten. It has evolved through the years and has different meanings for different schools of thought (cf., Lavie and Tractinsky, 2004). Here we are interested in its common meaning as "an artistically beautiful or pleasing appearance" (*The American Heritage Dictionary of the English Language*), or as "a pleasing appearance or effect: Beauty" (*Merriam-Webster's Collegiate Dictionary*). For broader perspectives on IT aesthetics see Laurel (1991) and Stolterman (1994).

REFERENCES

Ackoff, R.L. Management misinformation systems. *Management Science*, 14, 4 (1967), B147–B156.

Alben, L. Quality of experience: defining the criteria for effective interaction design. *Interactions* 3, 3 (1996), 11–15.

Arnheim, R. But is it science? In G.C. Cupchik and J. Laszlo (eds.), *Emerging Visions of the Aesthetic Process: Psychology, Semiology, and Philosophy*. Cambridge: Cambridge University Press, 1992.

Ashford, F.C. *The Aesthetic of Engineering Design*, London: Business Books, 1969.

Bargh, J.A. Bypassing the will: towards demystifying the nonconscious control of social behavior. In R.R. Hassin, J.S. Uleman, and J.A. Bargh (eds.), *The New Unconscious*. New York: Oxford University Press, 2004, pp. 37–58.

Benbasat, I.; Dexter, A.S.; and Todd, P. An experimental program investigating color-enhanced and graphical information presentation: an integration of the findings. *Communications of the ACM*, 29, 11 (1986), 1094–1105.

Benbasat, I., and Zmud, R.W. The identity crisis within the IS discipline: defining and communicating the discipline's core properties. *MIS Quarterly*, 27, 2 (2003), 183–194.

Beregi, W.E. Architecture prototyping in the software engineering environment. *IBM Systems Journal*, 23, 1 (1984), 4–18.

Berlyne, D.E. (ed.), *Studies in the New Experimental Aesthetics: Steps Toward an Objective Psychology of Aesthetic Appreciation*. Washington, DC: Washington Hemisphere Publishing Corporation, 1974.

Bloch, P. Seeking the ideal form: product design and consumer response. *Journal of Marketing*, 59, (1995), 16–29.

Blom, J.O., and Monk, A.F. Theory of personalization of appearance: why users personalize their PCs and mobile phones. *Human-Computer Interaction*, 18, 3 (2003), 193–228.

Bly, S.; Cook, L.; Bickmore, T.; Churchill, E.; and Sullivan, J.W. The rise of personal web pages at work. In *CHI 98 Conference Summary on Human Factors in Computing Systems*. New York: ACM Press/ Addison-Wesley, 1998, pp. 313–314.

Blythe, M.A.; Monk, A.F.; Overbeeke, K.; and Wright, P.C. (eds.), *Funology: From Usability to Enjoyment*. Dordrecht, The Netherlands: Kluwer Academic Publishers, 2003.

Boselie, F. The golden section has no special aesthetic attractivity! *Empirical Studies of the Arts*, 10, 1 (1992), 1–18.

Brooks, F.P. *The Mythical Man-Month*. Reading, MA: Addison-Wesley, 1975.

Butler, K.A. Usability engineering turns 10. *Interactions*, 3, 1 (1996), 59–75.

Card, S.K.; Moran, T.P.; and Newell, A. *The Psychology of Human-Computer Interaction*. Hillsdale, N.J.: Lawrence Erlbaum Associates, 1983.

Carr, N. IT doesn't matter. *Harvard Business Review*, 81, 5, (2003), 41–49.

Cela-Conde, C.J. et al. Activation of the prefrontal cortex in the human visual aesthetic perception. *Proceedings of the National Academy of Sciences (PNAS)*, 101, 16 (2004), 6321–6325.

Coates, D. *Watches Tell More than Time*. New York: McGraw-Hill, 2003.

Cowley, G. The biology of beauty. In W.A. Lesko (ed.), *Readings in Social Psychology: General, Classic, and Contemporary Selections*, 4th ed. Boston: Allyn and Bacon, 2000, pp. 188–194.

Csikszentmihalyi, M. *Flow: The Psychology of Optimal Experience*. New York: Harper and Row, 1990.

Csikszentmihalyi, M., and Robinson, R.E. *The Art of Seeing: An Interpretation of the Aesthetic Encounter*. Malibu, CA: The J. Paul Getty Trust, 1990.

Davis, F.D. Perceived usefulness, perceived ease of use and user acceptance of information technology. *MIS Quarterly* 13, (1989), 319–339.

DeLone, W.H., and McLean, E.R. Information systems success: the quest for the dependent variable. *Information Systems Research*, 3, 1 (1992), 60–95.

Desmet, P.M.A.; Hekkert, P.; and Jacobs, J.J. When a car makes you smile: development and application of an instrument to measure product emotions. In S.J. Hoch and R.J. Meyer (eds.), *Advances in Consumer Research*, vol. 27. Ann Arbor, MI: Association for Consumer Research, 2000, pp. 111–117.

Devlin, A.S., and Nasar, J.L. The beauty and the beast compared: Some preliminary comparisons of "high" versus "popular" residential architecture and public versus architect judgements of the same. *Journal of Environmental Psychology*, 9 (1989), 333–344.

Dickson, G.W.; Senn, J.A.; and Chervany, N.L. Research in management information systems: the Minnesota experiments. *Management Science*, 23, 9 (1977), 913–923.

Dion, K.; Berscheid, E.; and Walster, E. What is beautiful is good. *Journal of Personality and Social Psychology*, 24, 3 (1972), 285–290.

Duckworth, K.L.; Bargh, J.A.; Garcia, M.; and Chaiken, S. The automatic evaluation of novel stimuli. *Psychological Science*, 13, 6 (2002), 513–519.

Eagly, A.H.; Ashmore, R.D.; Makhijani, M.G.; and Longo, L.C. What is beautiful is good, but. . .: a meta-analytic review of research on the physical attractiveness stereotype. *Psychological Bulletin*, 110, 1 (1991), 109–128.

Feagin, S., and Maynard P. *Aesthetics*. Oxford: Oxford University Press, 1997.

Fernandes, G.; Lindgaard, G.; Dillon, R.; and Wood, J. Judging the appeal of web sites. In *Proceedings of the 4th World Congress on the Management of Electronic Commerce*. Hamilton, ON, Canada, 2003.

Fishwick, P.A. Aesthetic programming: crafting personalized software. *Leonardo*, 35, 4 (2002), 383–390.

Fishwick, P.A. Aesthetic computing manifesto. *Leonardo*, 36, 4 (2003), 255.

Fogarty, G.; Forlizzi, J.; and Hudson, S.E. Aesthetic information collages: generating decorative displays that contain information. *Proceedings of the 14th Annual ACM Symposium on User Interface Software and Technology*. New York: ACM Press, 2001, pp. 141–150.

Fogg, B.J.; Soohoo, C.; Danielsen, D.; Marable, L.; Stanford, J.; and Tauber, E.R. *How Do People Evaluate a Web Site's Credibility?* Report. Persuasive Technology Lab, Stanford University, 2002.

Gamma, E.; Helm, R.; Johnson, R.; and Vlissides, J. *Design Patterns: Elements of Reusable Object-Oriented Software*. New York: Addison-Wesley, 1994.

Getzels, J.W., and Csikszentmihalyi, M. Aesthetic opinion: an empirical study. *Public Opinion Quarterly*, 33, 1 (1969), 34–45.

Green, W.S., and Jordan, P.W. (eds.), *Designing Pleasurable Products*. London: Taylor and Francis, 2002.

Hamermesh, D., and Biddle, J. Beauty and the labor market. *American Economic Review*, 84 (1994), 1174–194.

Hamermesh, D., and Parker, A.M. Beauty in the classroom: professors' pulchritude and putative pedagogical productivity. *Economics of Education Review*, 24, 4 (2005), 369–376.

Hassenzahl, M. The thing and I: understanding the relationship between user and product. In M.A. Blythe, A.F. Monk, K. Overbeeke, and P.C. Wright (eds.), *Funology: From Usability to Enjoyment*. Dordrecht, The Netherlands: Kluwer Academic Publishers, 2003, pp. 31–42.

Hassenzahl, M. The interplay of beauty, goodness and usability in interactive products. *Human-Computer Interaction*. 19, 4 (2004), 319–349.

Hassenzahl, M. Beautiful objects as an extension of the self: a reply. *Human-Computer Interaction*, 19, 4 (2004), 377–386.

van der Heijden, H. Factors influencing the usage of websites: the case of a generic portal in the Netherlands. *Information & Management*, 40, 6 (2003), 541–549.

Helander, M.G. Forget about ergonomics in chair design? Focus on aesthetics and comfort! *Ergonomics*, 46, 13/14 (2003), 1306–1319.

Hermeren, G. The variety of aesthetic qualities. In M.H. Mitias (ed.), *Aesthetic Quality and Aesthetic Experience*. Amsterdam: Rodopi, 1988, pp. 11–23.

Hiscock, G. Indian animation finds digital niche. CNN, 2004 (available at: http://www.cnn.com/2004/WORLD/asiapcf/09/21/india.eye.animation/index.html, accessed on February 10, 2005).

Hooper, K. Architectural design: an analogy. In: D.A. Norman and S.W. Draper (eds.), *User Centered System Design*. London: Lawrence Erlbaum, 1986, pp. 9–23.

Isen, A.M. An influence of positive affect on decision making in complex situations: theoretical issues with practical implications. *Journal of Consumer Psychology*, 11, 2 (2001), 75–85.

Jarvenpaa, S.L., and Dickson, G.W. Graphics and managerial decision making: research based guidelines. *Communications of the ACM*, 31, 6 (1988), 764–774.

Johnson, P.A. *The Theory of Architecture: Concepts, Themes, and Practices*. New York: John Wiley & Sons, 1994.

Jordan, P.W. Human factors for pleasure in product use. *Applied Ergonomics*. 29, 1 (1998), 25–33.

Karvonen, K. The beauty of simplicity. In *Proceedings of the ACM Conference on Universal Usability (CUU 2000)*. New York: ACM Press, 2000, pp. 85–90.

Keen, P.G.W., and Scott Morton, M. *Decision Support Systems: An Organizational Perspective*. Reading, MA: Addison-Wesley, 1978.

Kim, J.; Lee, J.; and Choi, D. Designing emotionally evocative homepages: an empirical study of the quantitative relations between design factors and emotional dimensions. *International Journal of Human-Computer Studies*, 59 (2003), 899–940.

Kim, J.; Lee, J.; Han, K.; and Lee, M. Businesses as buildings: metrics for the architectural quality of internet businesses. *Information Systems Research*, 13, 2 (2002), 239–254.

Koeppel, D. GUIs just want to have fun: the faceless interface is dead. Long live skins, the hyper-personal edge of desktop computing. *Wired*, August 10, 2000 (available from http://www.wired.com/wired/archive/8.10/skins.html, accessed on February 10, 2005).

Kotler, P., and Rath A.G. Design a powerful but neglected strategic tool. *Journal of Business Strategy*, 5 (1984), 16–21.

Kruft, H.W. *A History of Architectural Theory: From Vitruvius to the Present*. New York: Zwemmer and Princeton Architectural Press, 1994.

Kurosu, M., and Kashimura, K. Apparent usability vs. inherent usability. In *CHI '95 Conference Companion*. New York: ACM Press, pp. 292–293.

Langlois J.H.; Kalakanis L.; Rubenstein A.J.; Larson A.; Hallam M.; and Smoot M. Maxims or myths of beauty? A meta-analytic and theoretical review. *Psychological Bulletin*, 126, 3 (2000), 390–423.

Laurel, B. *Computers as Theatre*. Boston, MA: Addison-Wesley, 1991.

Lavie, T., and Tractinsky, N. Assessing dimensions of perceived visual aesthetics of web sites. *International Journal of Human-Computer Studies*, 60 (2004), 269–298.

Lee, A.S. Architecture as a reference discipline for MIS. In H.E. Nissen, H.K Klein, and R. Hirschheim (eds.), *Information Research: Contemporary Approaches and Emergent Traditions*. North-Holland, Amsterdam, 1991, pp. 573–592.

Lindgaard, G., and Dudek, C. What is this evasive beast we call user satisfaction? *Interacting with Computers*, 15 (2003), 429–452.

Löwgren, J. Articulating the use qualities of digital designs. In P. Fishwick (ed.), *Aesthetic Computing*. Cambridge, MA: MIT Press, 2006.

Martindale, C.; Moore, K.; and Borkum, J. Aesthetic preference: anomalous findings for Berlyne's psychobiological theory. *American Journal of Psychology*, 103, 1 (1990), 53–80.

Maslow, A.H. *Motivation and Personality*. New York: Harper & Row, 1954.

McKnight, D.H.; Choudhury, V.; and Kacmar, C. Developing and validating trust measures for e-commerce: an integrative typology. *Information Systems Research*, 13, 3 (2002), 334–359.

Monk, A. The product as fixed-effect fallacy. *Human-Computer Interaction*, 19, 4 (2004), 371–375.

Nasar, J.L. *The Evaluative Image of the City*. Thousand Oaks, CA: Sage Publications, 1998.

Nasar, J.L. (ed.), *Environmental Aesthetics: Theory, Research, and Applications*. Cambridge: Cambridge University Press, 1988.

Norman, D.A. *The Psychology of Everyday Things*. New York: Basic Books, 1988.

Norman, D.A. *The Invisible Computer: Why Good Products Can Fail, the Personal Computer Is So Complex, and Information Appliances Are the Solution*. Cambridge, MA: MIT Press, 1998.

Norman, D.A. Emotion and design: attractive things work better. *Interactions*, 9, 4 (2002), 36–42.

Norman, D.A. *Emotional Design: Why We Love (or Hate) Everyday Things*. New York: Basic Books, 2004.

Norman, D.A. Introduction to the special issue on beauty, goodness and usability. *Human Computer Interaction*, 19, 4 (2004), 311–318.

Olsen, S. Hollywood whistles a high-tech 'toon. CNET Networks, 2004 (available at http://news.com.com/Hollywood+whistles+a+high-tech+toon/2100–1025_3–5431677.html, accessed on February 10, 2005).

Ortony, A.; Norman, D.A.; and Revelle, W. The role of affect and proto-affect in effective functioning. In J.-M. Fellous and M.A. Arbib (eds.), *Who Needs Emotions? The Brain Meets the Machine*. New York: Oxford University Press, 2005.

Petroski, H. *The Evolution of Useful Things*. New York: Alfred A. Knopf, 1993.

Pham, M.T.; Cohen, J.B.; Pracejus, J.W.; and Hughes, G.D. (2001) Affect monitoring and the primacy of feelings in judgment. *Journal of Consumer Research*, 28 (2001), 167–188.

Porteous, J.D. *Environmental Aesthetics: Ideas, Politics and Planning*. London: Routledge, 1996.

Postrel, V. *The Substance of Style*. New York: HarperCollins, 2002.

Rafaeli, A., and Vilnai-Yavetz, I. Emotion as a connection of physical artifacts and organizations. *Organization Science*, 15, 6 (2004), 671–686.

Russell, J.A. Core affect and the psychological construction of emotion. *Psychological Review*, 110, 1 (2003), 145–172.

Russell, J.A., and Pratt, G.A. Description of the affective quality attributed to environments. *Journal of Personality and Social Psychology*, 38, 2 (1980), 311–322.

Schenkman, B.N., and Jonsson, F.U. Aesthetics and preferences of web pages. *Behavior and Information Technology*, 19, 5 (2000), 367–377.

Schroeder, J.E. *Visual Consumption*. London: Routledge, 2002.

Stewart, T. Design and development. In J. Jacko and A. Sears (eds.), *The Human-Computer Interaction Handbook*. Mahwah, N.J.: Lawrence Erlbaum Associates, 2003, pp. 987–990.

Stolterman, E. "The Aesthetics of Information Systems." Department of Informatics, Umeå Universitet, 1994.

Swede, G., 1994. Basic theoretical issues. In G. Swede (ed.), *The Psychology of Art: An Experimental Approach*. Toronto: Canadian Scholars' Press Inc., 1994.

Tarasewich, P.; Daniel, H.Z.; and Griffin, H.E. Aesthetics and web site design. *Quarterly Journal of Electronic Commerce*, 2, 1 (2001), 67–81.

Thaler, R. Toward a positive theory of consumer choice. *Journal of Economic Behavior and Organization*, 1 (1980), 39–60.

Tractinsky, N. A few notes on the study of beauty in HCI. *Human-Computer Interaction*, 19, 4 (2004), 351–357.

Tractinsky, N. Aesthetics and apparent usability: empirically assessing cultural and methodological issues. In *CHI 97 Conference Proceedings*. New York: ACM Press, 1997, pp. 115–122.

Tractinsky, N.; Cokhavi, A.; and Kirschenbaum, M. Using ratings and response latencies to evaluate the consistency of immediate aesthetic perceptions of web pages. In *Proceedings of the Third Annual Workshop on HCI Research in MIS*. Association for Information Systems Special Interest Group on Human-Computer Interaction (AIS SIGHCI), pp. 40–44.

Tractinsky, N., and Lavie, T. Aesthetic and usability considerations in users' choice of personal media players. *Proceedings Volume 2 of the 16th British HCI Conference*. London: BCS, pp. 70–73.

Tractinsky, N., and Meyer, J. Junkchart or goldgraph? Effects of presentation objectives and content desirability on information presentation. *MIS Quarterly*, 23, 3 (1999), 397–420.

Tractinsky, N., and Rao, V.S. Social dimensions of internet shopping: theory-based arguments for web-store design. *Human Systems Management*, 20, (2001), 105–121.

Tractinsky, N.; Shoval-Katz, A.; and Ikar, D. What is beautiful is usable. *Interacting with Computers*, 13 (2000), 127–145.

Tractinsky, N., and Zmiri, D. Exploring attributes of skins as potential antecedents of emotion in HCI. In P. Fishwick (ed.), *Aesthetic Computing*. Cambridge, MA: MIT Press, 2006.

Venkatesh, V., and Brown, S.A. A longitudinal investigation of personal computers in homes: adoption determinants and emerging challenges. *MIS Quarterly*, 25, 1 (2001), 71–102.

Venkatesh, V., and Davis, F.D. A theoretical extension of the technology acceptance model: four longitudinal field studies. *Management Science*, 46, 2 (2000), 186–204.

Webster J., and Martocchio J. Microcomputer playfulness: development of a measure with workplace implications. *MIS Quarterly*, 16, 2 (1992), 201–225.

Whitfield, T.W.A. Beyond prototypicality: toward a categorical-motivation model of aesthetics. *Empirical Studies of the Arts*, 18, 1 (2000), 1–11.

Whitney, D.E. Manufacturing by design. *Harvard Business Review*, 66, 4 (1988), 83–91.

Yamamoto, M., and Lambert, D.R. The impact of product aesthetics on the evaluation of industrial products. *Journal of Product Innovation Management*, 11 (1994), 309–324.

Zajonc, R.B., and Markus, H. Affective and cognitive factors in preferences. *Journal of Consumer Research*, 9, 2 (1982), 123–131.

Zhang, P., and von Dran, G.M. Satisfiers and dissatisfiers: a two-factor model for website design and evaluation. *Journal of the American Society for Information Science*, 51, 14 (2000), 1253–1268.

Zhang, P., and Li, N. Love at first sight or sustained effect? The role of perceived affective quality on users' cognitive reactions to information technology. In *Proceedings of the 25th Annual International Conference on Information Systems (ICIS)*, pp. 283–295.

CHAPTER 16

VALUE SENSITIVE DESIGN AND INFORMATION SYSTEMS

BATYA FRIEDMAN, PETER H. KAHN, JR., AND ALAN BORNING

Abstract: *Value Sensitive Design is a theoretically grounded approach to the design of technology that accounts for human values in a principled and comprehensive manner throughout the design process. It employs an integrative and iterative tripartite methodology, consisting of conceptual, empirical, and technical investigations. We explicate Value Sensitive Design by drawing on three case studies. The first study concerns information and control of Web browser cookies, implicating the value of informed consent. The second study concerns using high-definition plasma displays in an office environment to provide a "window" to the outside world, implicating the values of physical and psychological well-being and privacy in public spaces. The third study concerns an integrated land use, transportation, and environmental simulation system to support public deliberation and debate on major land use and transportation decisions, implicating the values of fairness, accountability, and support for the democratic process, as well as a highly diverse range of values that might be held by different stakeholders, such as environmental sustainability, opportunities for business expansion, or walkable neighborhoods. We conclude with direct and practical suggestions for how to engage in Value Sensitive Design.*

Keywords: *Computers and Society, Cookies, Design Methods, Ethics, Human Values, Informed Consent, Interface Design, Interaction Design, Privacy, Simulation, Security, Social Computing, Surveillance, Urban Development, Value Sensitive Design, Values in Design, Web Browsers*

INTRODUCTION

There is a long-standing interest in designing information and computational systems that support enduring human values. Researchers have focused, for example, on the value of privacy (Ackerman and Cranor, 1999; Agre and Rotenberg, 1998; Fuchs, 1999; Jancke et al., 2001; Palen and Grudin, 2003; Tang, 1997), ownership and property (Lipinski and Britz, 2000), physical welfare (Leveson, 1991), freedom from bias (Friedman and Nissenbaum, 1996), universal usability (Shneiderman, 1999, 2000; Thomas, 1997), autonomy (Suchman, 1994; Winograd, 1994), informed consent (Millett et al., 2001), and trust (Fogg and Tseng, 1999; Palen and Grudin, 2003; Riegelsberger and Sasse, 2002; Rocco, 1998; Zheng et al., 2001). Still, there is a need for an overarching theoretical and methodological framework with which to handle the value dimensions of design work.

Value Sensitive Design is one effort to provide such a framework—for example, Friedman (1997a), Friedman and Kahn (2003), Friedman and Nissenbaum (1996), Hagman et al. (2003), Nissenbaum (1998), Tang (1997), and Thomas (1997). Our goal in this paper is to provide an account of Value Sensitive Design, with enough detail for other researchers and designers to critically examine and systematically build on this approach.

We begin by sketching the key features of Value Sensitive Design, and then describe its integrative tripartite methodology, which involves conceptual, empirical, and technical investigations, employed iteratively. Then we explicate Value Sensitive Design by drawing on three case studies. One involves cookies and informed consent in Web browsers; the second involves HDTV display technology in an office environment; the third involves user interactions and interface for an integrated land use, transportation, and environmental simulation. We conclude with direct and practical suggestions for how to engage in Value Sensitive Design.

WHAT IS VALUE SENSITIVE DESIGN?

Value Sensitive Design is a theoretically grounded approach to the design of technology that accounts for human values in a principled and comprehensive manner throughout the design process.

What Is a Value?

In a narrow sense, the word "value" refers simply to the economic worth of an object. For example, the value of a computer could be said to be two thousand dollars. However, in the work described here, we use a broader meaning of the term wherein a value refers to what a person or group of people consider important in life.[1] In this sense, people find many things of value, both lofty and mundane: their children, friendship, morning tea, education, art, a walk in the woods, nice manners, good science, a wise leader, clean air.

This broader framing of values has a long history. Since the time of Plato, for example, the content of value-oriented discourse has ranged widely, emphasizing "the good, the end, the right, obligation, virtue, moral judgment, aesthetic judgment, the beautiful, truth, and validity" (Frankena, 1972, p. 229). Sometimes ethics has been subsumed within a theory of values; at other times, conversely, ethical values have been viewed as just one component of ethics more generally. Either way, it is usually agreed (Moore, 1903/1978) that values should not be conflated with facts (the "fact/value distinction") especially insofar as facts do not logically entail value. In other words, "is" does not imply "ought" (the naturalistic fallacy). In this way, values cannot be motivated only by an empirical account of the external world, but depend substantively on the interests and desires of human beings within a cultural milieu. In Table 16.1 in "Human Values (with Ethical Import) Often Implicated in System Design," later in this chapter, we provide a list of human values with ethical import that are often implicated in system design, along with working definitions and references to the literature.

Related Approaches to Values and System Design

In the 1950s, during the early periods of computerization, cyberneticist Norbert Wiener (1953/1985) argued that technology could help make us better human beings, and create a more just society. But for it to do so, he argued, we have to take control of the technology. We have to reject the "worshiping (of) the new gadgets which are our own creation as if they were our masters" (p. 678). Similarly, a few decades later, computer scientist Joseph Weizenbaum (1972) wrote:

What is wrong, I think, is that we have permitted technological metaphors . . . and technique itself to so thoroughly pervade our thought processes that we have finally abdicated to technology the very duty to formulate questions . . . Where a simple man might ask: "Do we need these things?," technology asks "what electronic wizardry will make them safe?" Where a simple man will ask "is it good?," technology asks "will it work?" (pp. 611–612)

More recently, supporting human values through system design has emerged within at least four important approaches. Computer ethics advances our understanding of key values that lie at the intersection of computer technology and human lives—for example, Bynum (1985), Johnson and Miller (1997), and Nissenbaum (1999). Social informatics has been successful in providing socio-technical analyses of deployed technologies—for example, Kling, Rosenbaum, and Hert (1998), Kling and Star (1998), and Sawyer and Rosenbaum (2000). Computer-supported cooperative work (CSCW) has been successful in the design of new technologies to help people collaborate effectively in the workplace—for example, Fuchs (1999), Galegher, Kraut, and Egido (1990), Olson and Teasley (1996), and Grudin (1988). Finally, participatory design substantively embeds democratic values into its practice—for example, Bjerknes and Bratteteig (1995), Bødker (1990), Carroll and Rosson (in this volume), Ehn (1989), Greenbaum and Kyng (1991), and Kyng and Mathiassen (1997). (See Friedman and Kahn [2003] for a review of each of these approaches.)

THE TRIPARTITE METHODOLOGY: CONCEPTUAL, EMPIRICAL, AND TECHNICAL INVESTIGATIONS

Think of an oil painting by Monet or Cézanne. From a distance it looks whole; but up close you can see many layers of paint upon paint. Some paints have been applied with careful brushstrokes, others perhaps energetically with a palette knife or fingertips, conveying outlines or regions of color. The diverse techniques are employed one on top of the other, repeatedly, and in response to what has been laid down earlier. Together they create an artifact that could not have been generated by a single technique in isolation from the others. So, too, with Value Sensitive Design. An artifact or design emerges through iterations upon a process that is more than the sum of its parts. Nonetheless, the parts provide us with a good place to start. Value Sensitive Design builds on an iterative methodology that integrates conceptual, empirical, and technical investigations; thus, as a step toward conveying Value Sensitive Design, we describe each investigation separately.

Conceptual Investigations

Who are the direct and indirect stakeholders affected by the design at hand? How are both classes of stakeholders affected? What values are implicated? How should we engage in trade-offs among competing values in the design, implementation, and use of information systems (e.g., autonomy vs. security, or anonymity vs. trust)? Should moral values (e.g., a right to privacy) have greater weight than, or even trump, non-moral values (e.g., aesthetic preferences)? Value Sensitive Design takes up these questions under the rubric of conceptual investigations.

In addition, careful working conceptualizations of specific values clarify fundamental issues raised by the project at hand, and provide a basis for comparing results across research teams. For example, in their analysis of trust in online system design, Friedman, Kahn, and Howe (2000), drawing on Baier (1986), first offer a philosophically informed working conceptualization of trust. They propose that people trust when they are vulnerable to harm from others, yet believe those others would not harm them even though they could. In turn, trust depends on people's ability to make three types of assessments. One is about the harms they might incur. The second is about the goodwill others possess toward them that would keep those others from doing them harm. The third involves whether or not harms that do occur lie outside the parameters of the trust relationship. From such conceptualizations, Friedman et al. were able to define clearly what they meant by trust online. This definition is in some cases different from what other researchers have meant by the term—for example, the Computer Science and Telecommunications Board, in their thoughtful publication *Trust in Cyberspace* (Schneider, 1999), adopted the terms "trust" and "trustworthy" to describe systems that perform as expected along the dimensions of correctness, security, reliability, safety, and survivability. Such a definition, which equates "trust" with expectations for machine performance, differs markedly from one that says trust is fundamentally a relationship among people (sometimes mediated by machines).

Empirical Investigations

Conceptual investigations can only go so far. Depending on the questions at hand, many analyses will need to be informed by empirical investigations of the human context in which the technical artifact is situated. Empirical investigations are also often needed to evaluate the success of a particular design. Empirical investigations can be applied to any human activity that can be observed, measured, or documented. Thus, the entire range of quantitative and qualitative methods used in social science research is potentially applicable here, including observations, interviews, surveys, experimental manipulations, collection of relevant documents, and measurements of user behavior and human physiology.

Empirical investigations can focus, for example, on questions such as: How do stakeholders apprehend individual values in the interactive context? How do they prioritize competing values in design trade-offs? How do they prioritize individual values and usability considerations? Are there differences between espoused practice (what people say) compared with actual practice (what people do)? Moreover, because the development of new technologies affects groups as well as individuals, questions emerge about how organizations appropriate value considerations in the design process. For example, regarding value considerations, what are organizations' motivations, methods of training and dissemination, reward structures, and economic incentives?

Technical Investigations

As discussed in "Value Sensitive Design's Constellation of Features," later in this chapter, Value Sensitive Design adopts the position that technologies in general, and information and computer technologies in particular, provide value suitabilities that follow from properties of the technology. That is, a given technology is more suitable for certain activities and more readily supports certain values while rendering other activities and values more difficult to realize.

In one form, technical investigations focus on how existing technological properties and underlying mechanisms support or hinder human values. For example, some video-based collaborative work systems provide blurred views of office settings, while other systems provide clear images that reveal detailed information about who is present and what they are doing. Thus the two designs differentially adjudicate the value trade-off between an individual's privacy and the group's awareness of individual members' presence and activities.

In the second form, technical investigations involve the proactive design of systems to support values identified in the conceptual investigation. For example, Fuchs (1999) developed a notification service for a collaborative work system in which the underlying technical mechanisms implement a value hierarchy whereby an individual's desire for privacy overrides other group members' desires for awareness.

At times, technical investigations—particularly of the first form—may seem similar to empirical investigations insofar as both involve technological and empirical activity. However, they differ markedly on their unit of analysis. Technical investigations focus on the technology itself. Empirical investigations focus on the individuals, groups, or larger social systems that configure, use, or are otherwise affected by the technology.

VALUE SENSITIVE DESIGN IN PRACTICE: THREE CASE STUDIES

To illustrate Value Sensitive Design's integrative and iterative tripartite methodology, we draw on three case studies with real-world applications, one completed and two under way. Each case study represents a unique design space.

Cookies and Informed Consent in Web Browsers

Informed consent provides a critical protection for privacy, and supports other human values such as autonomy and trust. Yet currently there is a mismatch between industry practice and the public's interest. According to a recent report from the Federal Trade Commission (2000), for example, 59 percent of Web sites that collect personal identifying information neither inform Internet users that they are collecting such information nor seek the users' consent. Yet, according to a Harris poll (2000), 88 percent of users want sites to garner their consent in such situations.

Against this backdrop, Friedman, Felten, and their colleagues (Friedman et al., 2002; Friedman et al., 2000; Millett et al., 2001) sought to design Web-based interactions that support informed consent in a Web browser through the development of new technical mechanisms for cookie management. This project was an early proof-of-concept project for Value Sensitive Design, which we use here to illustrate several key features of the methodology.

Conceptualizing the Value

One part of a conceptual investigation entails a philosophically informed analysis of the central value constructs. Accordingly, Friedman et al. began their project with a conceptual investigation of informed consent itself. They drew on diverse literature, such as the Belmont Report, which delineates ethical principles and guidelines for the protection of human subjects (Belmont Report, 1978; Faden and Beauchamp, 1986), to develop criteria for informed consent in online interactions. In brief, the idea of "informed" encompasses disclosure and comprehension. "Disclosure" refers to providing accurate information about the benefits and harms that might reasonably be expected from the action under consideration. "Comprehension" refers to the individual's accurate interpretation of what is being disclosed. In turn, the idea of "consent" encompasses voluntariness, comprehension, and agreement. "Voluntariness" refers to ensuring that the action is not controlled or coerced. "Comprehension" refers to possessing the mental, emotional, and physical capabilities needed to be capable of giving informed consent. "Agreement" refers to a reasonably clear opportunity to accept or decline to participate. Moreover, agreement should be ongoing; that is, the individual should be able to withdraw from the interaction at any time. See Friedman, Millet, and Felten (2000) for an expanded discussion of these five criteria.

Using a Conceptual Investigation to Analyze Existing Technical Mechanisms

With a conceptualization for informed consent online in hand, Friedman et al. conducted a retrospective analysis (one form of a technical investigation) of how the cookie and Web browser technology embedded in Netscape Navigator and Internet Explorer changed with respect to informed consent over a five-year period, beginning in 1995. Specifically, they used the criteria of disclosure, comprehension, voluntariness, competence, and agreement to evaluate how well each browser in each stage of its development supported the users' experience of informed consent. Through this retrospective analysis, they found that although cookie technology had improved over time regarding informed consent (e.g., increased visibility of cookies, increased options for accepting or declining cookies, and access to information about cookie content), as of 1999 some startling problems remained. For example: (a) Although browsers disclosed to users some information about cookies, they still did not disclose the right sort of information—that is, information about the potential harms and benefits from setting a particular cookie. (b) In Internet Explorer, the burden to accept or decline all third-party cookies still fell to the user, placing undue burden on the user to decline each third-party cookie one at a time. (c) Users' out-of-the-box experience of cookies (i.e., the default setting) was no different in 1999 than it was in 1995: to accept all cookies (i.e., the novice user installed a browser that accepted all cookies and disclosed nothing about that activity to the user). (d) Neither browser alerted a user when a site wished to use a cookie and for what purpose, as opposed to when a site wished to store a cookie.

The Iteration and Integration of Conceptual, Technical, and Empirical Investigations

Based on the results from these conceptual and technical investigations, Friedman et al. then iteratively used the results to guide a second technical investigation: a redesign of the Mozilla browser (the open-source code for Netscape Navigator). Specifically, they developed three new types of mechanisms: (a) peripheral awareness of cookies; (b) just-in-time information about individual cookies and cookies in general; and (c) just-in-time management of cookies (see Figure 16.1). In the process of their technical work, Friedman et al. conducted formative evaluations (empirical investigations) that led to a further design criterion, minimal distraction, which refers to meeting the above criteria for informed consent without unduly diverting the user from the task at hand. Two situations are of concern here. First, if users are overwhelmed with queries to consent to participate in events with minor benefits and risks, they may become numbed to the informed consent process by the time participation in an event with significant benefits and risks is at hand. Thus, the user's participation in that event may not receive the careful attention that is warranted. Second, if the overall distraction to obtain informed consent becomes so great as to be perceived to be an intolerable nuisance, users are likely to disengage from the informed consent process in its entirety and accept or decline participation by rote. Thus undue distraction can single-handedly undermine informed consent. In this way, the iterative results of the above empirical investigations not only shaped and then validated the technical work, but impacted the initial conceptual investigation by adding to the model of informed consent the criterion of minimal distraction.

Thus, this project illustrates the iterative and integrative nature of Value Sensitive Design, and provides a proof-of-concept for Value Sensitive Design in the context of mainstream Internet software.

Room with a View: Using Plasma Displays in Interior Offices

Janice is in her office, writing a report. She's trying to conceptualize the report's higher-level structure, but her ideas won't quite take form. Then she looks up from her desk and rests her eyes on the fountain and plaza area outside her building. She notices the water bursting upward, and that a small group of people are gathering by the water's edge. She rests her eyes on the surrounding pool of calm water. Her eyes then lift toward the clouds and the streaking sunshine.

Figure 16.1.   **Screen shot (a) of the Mozilla implementation shows the peripheral awareness of cookies interface (at the left) in the context of browsing the Web. Each time a cookie is set, a color-coded entry for that cookie appears in the sidebar. Third-party cookies are red; others are green. At the user's discretion, he or she can click on any entry to bring up the Mozilla cookie manager for that cookie. Screen shot (b) was taken after the user had clicked on an entry to bring up the just-in-time cookie management tool (in the center) for a particular cookie.**

 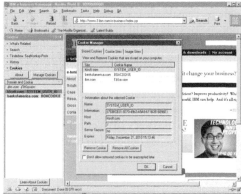

(a) Peripheral awareness mechanism.   (b) Just-in-time cookie management tool.

Twenty seconds later she returns to her writing task at hand, slightly refreshed, and with an idea taking shape.

What's particularly novel about this workplace scenario is that Janice works in an interior office. Instead of a real window looking out onto the plaza, Janice has a large-screen video plasma display that continuously shows the local outdoor scene in real time. Realistic? Beneficial? This design space is currently being researched by Kahn, Friedman, and their colleagues, using the framework of Value Sensitive Design.

In Kahn et al.'s initial conceptual investigation of this design space, they drew on the psychological literature that suggests that interaction with real nature can garner physiological and psychological benefits. For example, in one study, Ulrich (1984) found that post-operative recovery improved when patients were assigned to a room with a view of a natural setting (a small stand of deciduous trees) versus a view of a brown brick wall. More generally, studies have shown that even minimal connection with nature—such as looking at a natural landscape—can reduce immediate and long-term stress, reduce sickness of prisoners, and calm patients before and during surgery. (See Beck and Katcher [1996], Kahn [1999], and Ulrich [1993] for reviews.) Thus Kahn et al. hypothesized that an "augmented window" of nature could render benefits in a work environment in terms of the human values of physical health, emotional well-being, and creativity.

To investigate this question in a laboratory context, Kahn et al. are comparing the short-term benefits of working in an office with a view out the window of a beautiful nature scene versus an identical view (in real time) shown on a large plasma display that covers the window in the same office (Figure 16.2a). In this latter condition, they employed a High Definition TV (HDTV) camera (Figure 16.2b) to capture real-time local images. The control condition involved a blank covering over the window. Their measures entailed (a) physiological data (heart rate), (b) performance data (on cognitive and creativity tasks), (c) video data that captured each subject's eye gaze on a

Figure 16.2.   **Large Display Technology Studies**

(a) "The Watcher"   (b) The HDTV Camera   (c) "The Watched"

second-by-second level so that analyses can determine whether physiological benefits accrued immediately following an eye gaze onto the plasma screen, and (d) social-cognitive data (based on a fifty-minute interview with each subject at the conclusion of the experimental condition wherein they garnered each subject's reasoned perspective on the experience). Data analysis is in progress. However, preliminary results are showing the following trends. First, participants looked at the plasma screen just as frequently as they looked out the real window, and more frequently than they stared at the blank wall. In this sense, the plasma-display window was functioning like a real window. But, when participants gazed for thirty seconds or more, the real window provided greater physiological recovery from low-level stress than the plasma-display window.

From the standpoint of illustrating Value Sensitive Design, we would like to emphasize five ideas.

Multiple Empirical Methods

Under the rubric of empirical investigations, Value Sensitive Design supports and encourages multiple empirical methods to be used in concert to address the question at hand. As noted above, for example, this study employed physiological data (heart rate), two types of performance data (on cognitive and creativity tasks), behavioral data (eye gaze), and reasoning data (the social-cognitive interview). From a value-oriented perspective, multiple psychological measures increase the veracity of most accounts of technology in use.

Direct and Indirect Stakeholders

In their initial conceptual investigation of the values implicated in this study, Kahn et al. sought to identify not only direct but also indirect stakeholders affected by such display technology. At that early point, it became clear to the researchers that an important class of indirect stakeholders (and their respective values) needed to be included: namely, the individuals who, by virtue of walking through the fountain scene, unknowingly had their images displayed on the large display in the "inside" office (Figure 16.2c). In other words, if this application of projection technology were to come into widespread use (as Web cams and surveillance cameras have begun to) then it would potentially encroach on the privacy of individuals in public spaces—an issue that has been receiving increasing attention in the field of computer ethics and public discourse (Nissenbaum, 1998). Thus, in addition to the experimental laboratory study, Kahn et al. initiated two additional but complementary empirical investigations with indirect stakeholders: (a) a survey of 750 people walking through the public plaza, and (b) in-depth social-cognitive interviews with thirty individuals walking through the public plaza (Friedman et al., 2006). Both investigations focused on indirect stakeholders' judgments of privacy in public space, and in particular having their real-time images captured and displayed on large screens in nearby and distant offices. The importance of such indirect stakeholder investigations is being borne out by the results. For example, significant gender differences were found in their survey data: More women than men expressed concern about the invasion of privacy through Web cameras in public places. This finding held whether their image was to be displayed locally or in another city (Tokyo), or viewed by one person, thousands, or millions. One implication of this finding is that future technical designs and implementations of such display technologies need to be responsive to ways in which men and women might perceive potential harms differently.

Coordinated Empirical Investigations

Once Kahn et al. identified an important group of indirect stakeholders, and decided to undertake empirical investigations with this group, they then coordinated these empirical investigations with the initial (direct stakeholder) study. Specifically, a subset of identical questions was asked of both the direct stakeholders ("the watchers") and indirect stakeholders ("the watched"). Results show some interesting differences. For example, more men in the watched condition expressed concerns that people's images might be displayed locally, nationally, or internationally than men in the plasma display watcher condition. No differences were found between women in the watcher plasma display condition and women in the watched condition. Thus, the Value Sensitive Design methodology helps to bring to the forefront values that matter not only to the direct stakeholders of a technology (such as physical health, emotional well-being, and creativity), but to the indirect stakeholders (such as privacy, informed consent, trust, and physical safety). Moreover, from the standpoint of Value Sensitive Design, the above study highlights how investigations of indirect stakeholders can be woven into the core structure of the experimental design with direct stakeholders.

Multiplicity of and Potential Conflicts Among Human Values

Value Sensitive Design can help researchers uncover the multiplicity of and potential conflicts among human values implicated in technological implementations. In the above design space, for example, values of physical health, emotional well-being, and creativity appear to partially conflict with other values of privacy, civil rights, trust, and security.

Technical Investigations

Conceptual and empirical investigations can help to shape future technological investigations, particularly in terms of how nature (as a source of information) can be embedded in the design of display technologies to further human well-being. One obvious design space involves buildings. For example, if Kahn et al.'s empirical results continue to emerge in line with their initial results, then one possible design guideline is as follows: We need to design buildings with nature in mind, and within view. In other words, we cannot with psychological impunity digitize nature and display the digitized version as a substitute for the real thing (and worse, then destroy the original). At the same time, it is possible that technological representations of nature can garner some psychological benefits, especially when (as in an inside office) direct access to nature is otherwise unavailable. Other less obvious design spaces involve, for example, airplanes. In recent discussions with Boeing Corporation, for example, we were told that for economic reasons engineers might like to construct airplanes without passenger windows. After all, windows cost more to build and decrease fuel efficiency. At stake, however, is the importance of windows in the human experience of flying.

In short, this case study highlights how Value Sensitive Design can help researchers employ multiple psychological methods, across several studies, with direct and indirect stakeholders, to investigate (and ultimately support) a multiplicity of human values impacted by deploying a cutting-edge information technology.

UrbanSim: Integrated Land Use, Transportation, and Environmental Simulation

In many regions in the United States (and globally), there is increasing concern about pollution, traffic jams, resource consumption, loss of open space, loss of coherent community, lack of sustainability, and unchecked sprawl. Elected officials, planners, and citizens in urban areas grapple with these difficult issues as they develop and evaluate alternatives for such decisions as building a new rail line or freeway, establishing an urban growth boundary, or changing incentives or taxes. These decisions interact in complex ways, and, in particular, transportation and land use decisions interact strongly with each other. There are both legal and common sense reasons to try to understand the long-term consequences of these interactions and decisions. Unfortunately, the need for this understanding far outstrips the capability of the analytic tools used in current practice.

In response to this need, Waddell, Borning, and their colleagues have been developing UrbanSim, a large simulation package for predicting patterns of urban development for periods of twenty years or more, under different possible scenarios (Waddell, 2002; Noth et al., 2003; Waddell et al., 2003). Its primary purpose is to provide urban planners and other stakeholders with tools to aid in more informed decision making, with a secondary goal to support further democratization of the planning process. When provided with different scenarios—packages of possible policies and investments—UrbanSim models the resulting patterns of urban growth and redevelopment, of transportation usage, and of resource consumption and other environmental impacts.

To date, UrbanSim has been applied in the metropolitan regions around Eugene/Springfield, Oregon (Figure 16.3); Honolulu, Hawaii; Salt Lake City, Utah; and Houston, Texas, with application to the Puget Sound region in Washington State under way. UrbanSim is undergoing significant redevelopment and extension in terms of its underlying architecture, interface, and social goals. Under the direction of Borning, Friedman, and Kahn, Value Sensitive Design is playing a central role in this endeavor (Borning et al., 2005).

UrbanSim illustrates important aspects of Value Sensitive Design in addition to those described in the previous two case studies:

Distinguishing Explicitly Supported Values from Stakeholder Values

In their conceptual investigations, Borning et al. (2005) distinguished between explicitly supported values (i.e., ones that they explicitly want to embed in the simulation) and stakeholder values (i.e., ones that are important to some but not necessarily all of the stakeholders). Next, Borning et al. committed to three specific moral values to be supported explicitly. One is fairness,

Figure 16.3.   **Results from UrbanSim for Eugene/Springfield, Oregon, forecasting land use patterns over a fourteen-year period. These results arise from the simulated interactions among demographic change, economic change, real estate development, transportation, and other actors and processes in the urban environment. Map (a) shows the employment density in 1980 (number of jobs located in each 150 × 150 meter grid cell). Darker area indicates higher density. Map (b) shows the predicted change from 1980 to 1994 (where darker area indicates a greater change), and map (c) the predicted employment density in 1994. In a historical validation of the model, this result was then compared with the actual 1994 employment, with a 0.917 correlation over a 1-cell radius.**

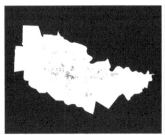 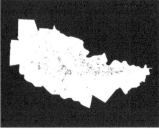 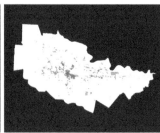

(a) 1980 Employment   (b) Change 1980–1994   (c) Resulting 1994 Employment

and more specifically freedom from bias. The simulation should not discriminate unfairly against any group of stakeholders, or privilege one mode of transportation or policy over another. A second is accountability. Insofar as possible, stakeholders should be able to confirm that their values are reflected in the simulation, evaluate and judge its validity, and develop an appropriate level of confidence in its output. The third is democracy. The simulation should support the democratic process in the context of land use, transportation, and environmental planning. In turn, as part of supporting the democratic process, Borning et al. decided that the model should not a priori favor or rule out any given set of stakeholder values, but, instead, should allow different stakeholders to articulate the values that are most important to them, and evaluate the alternatives in light of these values.

Handling Widely Divergent and Potentially Conflicting Stakeholder Values

From the standpoint of conceptual investigations, UrbanSim as a design space poses tremendous challenges. The research team cannot focus on a few key values, as occurred in the Web Browser project (e.g., the value of informed consent), or the Room with a View project (e.g., the values of privacy in public spaces, and physical and psychological well-being). Rather, disputing stakeholders bring to the table widely divergent values about environmental, political, moral, and personal issues. Examples of stakeholder values are environmental sustainability, walkable neighborhoods, space for business expansion, affordable housing, freight mobility, minimal government intervention, minimal commute time, open space preservation, property rights, and environmental justice. How does one characterize the wide-ranging and deeply held values of diverse stakeholders, both present and future? Moreover, how does one prioritize the values implicated in the decisions? And how can one move from values to measurable outputs from the simulation to allow stakeholders to compare alternative scenarios?

    As part of addressing these questions, the research group implemented a Web-based interface that groups indicators into three broad value categories pertaining to the domain of urban development (economic, environmental, and social), and more specific value categories under that. To allow stakeholders to evaluate alternative urban futures, the interface provides a large collection of *indicators*: variables that distill some attribute of interest about the results (Gallopin, 1997). (Examples of indicators are the number of acres of rural land converted to urban use each year, the degree of poverty segregation, or the mode share between autos and transit.) These categories and indicators draw on a variety of sources, including empirical research on people's environmental concepts and values (Kahn, 1999; Kahn and Kellert, 2002), community-based indicator projects (Palmer, 1998; Hart, 1999), and the policy literature. Stakeholders can then use the interface to select indicators that speak to values that are important to them from among these categories.

This interface illustrates the interplay among conceptual, technical, and empirical investigations. The indicators are chosen to speak to different stakeholder values—responding to our distinction between explicitly supported values and stakeholder values in the initial conceptual investigation. The value categories are rooted empirically in both human psychology and policy studies, not just philosophy—and then embodied in a technical artifact (the Web-based interface), which is in turn evaluated empirically.

Technical Choices Driven by Initial and Emergent Value Considerations

Most of the technical choices in the design of the UrbanSim software are in response to the need to generate indicators and other evaluation measures that respond to different strongly held stakeholder values. For example, for some stakeholders, walkable, pedestrian-friendly neighborhoods are very important. But being able to model walking as a transportation mode makes difficult demands on the underlying simulation, requiring a finer-grained spatial scale than is needed for modeling automobile transportation alone. In turn, being able to answer questions about walking as a transportation mode is important for two explicitly supported values: fairness (not to privilege one transportation mode over another), and democracy (being able to answer questions about a value that is important to a significant number of stakeholders). As a second example of technical choices being driven by value considerations, UrbanSim's software architecture is designed to support rapid evolution in response to changed or additional requirements. For instance, the software architecture decouples the individual component models as much as possible, allowing them to evolve and new ones to be added in a modular fashion. Also, the system writes the simulation results into an SQL database, making it easy to write queries that produce new indicators quickly and as needed, rather than embedding the indicator computation code in the component models themselves. For similar reasons, the UrbanSim team uses the YP agile software development methodology (Freeman-Benson and Borning, 2003), which allows the system to evolve and respond quickly to emerging stakeholder values and policy considerations.

Designing for Credibility, Openness, and Accountability

Credibility of the system is of great importance, particularly when the system is being used in a politically charged situation and is thus the subject of intense scrutiny. The research group has undertaken a variety of activities to help foster credibility, including using behaviorally transparent simulation techniques (i.e., simulating agents in the urban environment, such as households, businesses, and real estate developers, rather than using some more abstract and opaque simulation technique), and performing sensitivity analyses (Franklin et al., 2002) and a historical validation. In the historical validation, for example, the group started the model with 1980 data from Eugene/Springfield, simulated through 1994, and compared the simulation output with what actually happened. One of these comparisons is shown in Figure 16.3. In addition, our techniques for fostering openness and accountability are also intended to support credibility. These include using open-source software (releasing the source code along with the executable), writing the code in as clear and understandable a fashion as possible, using a rigorous and extensive testing methodology, and complementing the open-source software with an open process that makes the state of our development visible to anyone interested. For example, in our laboratory, a battery of tests is run whenever a new version of the software is committed to the source code repository. A traffic light (a real one) is activated by the testing regime—green means that the system has passed all tests, yellow means testing is under way, and red means that a test has failed. There is also a virtual traffic light, mirroring the physical one, visible on the Web (www.urbansim.org/fireman). Similarly, the bug reports, feature requests, and plans are all on the UrbanSim project Web site as well. Details of this open process approach may be found in Freeman-Benson and Borning (2003).

Thus, in summary, Borning et al. are using Value Sensitive Design to investigate how a technology—an integrated land use, transportation, and environmental computer simulation—affects human values on both the individual and organizational levels; and how human values can continue to drive the technical investigations, including refining the simulation, data, and interaction model. Finally, employing Value Sensitive Design in a project of this scope serves to validate its use for complex, large-scale systems.

VALUE SENSITIVE DESIGN'S CONSTELLATION OF FEATURES

Value Sensitive Design shares and adopts many interests and techniques from related approaches to values and system design—computer ethics, social informatics, CSCW, and participatory design—as discussed in "Related Approaches to Values and System Design," earlier in this chapter. However, Value Sensitive Design itself brings forward a unique constellation of eight features.

First, Value Sensitive Design seeks to be proactive: to influence the design of technology early in and throughout the design process.

Second, Value Sensitive Design enlarges the arena in which values arise to include not only the workplace (as traditionally in the field of CSCW), but also education, the home, commerce, online communities, and public life.

Third, Value Sensitive Design contributes a unique methodology that employs conceptual, empirical, and technical investigations, applied iteratively and integratively (see "The Tripartite Methodology: Conceptual, Empirical, and Technical Investigations," earlier in this chapter).

Fourth, Value Sensitive Design enlarges the scope of human values beyond those of cooperation (CSCW) and participation and democracy (Participatory Design) to include all values, especially those with moral import. By moral, we refer to issues that pertain to fairness, justice, human welfare, and virtue, encompassing within moral philosophical theory deontology (Dworkin, 1978; Gewirth, 1978; Kant, 1785/1964; Rawls, 1971); consequentialism (Smart and Williams, 1973); see Scheffler (1982) for an analysis; and virtue (Foot, 1978; MacIntyre, 1984; Campbell and Christopher, 1996). Value Sensitive Design also accounts for conventions (e.g., standardization of protocols) and personal values (e.g., color preferences within a graphical user interface).

Fifth, Value Sensitive Design distinguishes between usability and human values with ethical import. Usability refers to characteristics of a system that make it work in a functional sense, including that it is easy to use, easy to learn, consistent, and recovers easily from errors (Adler and Winograd, 1992; Norman, 1988; Nielsen, 1993). However, not all highly usable systems support ethical values. Nielsen (1993), for example, asks us to imagine a computer system that checks for fraudulent unemployment benefit applications by asking applicants numerous personal questions and then checking for inconsistencies in their responses. Nielsen's point is that even if the system receives high usability scores some people may not find the system socially acceptable, based on the moral value of privacy.

Sixth, Value Sensitive Design identifies and takes seriously two classes of stakeholders: direct and indirect. Direct stakeholders refer to parties—individuals or organizations—who interact directly with the computer system or its output. Indirect stakeholders refer to all other parties who are affected by the use of the system. Often, indirect stakeholders are ignored in the design process. For example, computerized medical records systems have often been designed with many of the direct stakeholders in mind (e.g., insurance companies, hospitals, doctors, and nurses), but with too little regard for the values, such as the value of privacy, of a rather important group of indirect stakeholders: the patients.

Seventh, Value Sensitive Design is an interactional theory: Values are viewed neither as inscribed into technology (an endogenous theory), nor as simply transmitted by social forces (an exogenous theory). Rather, the interactional position holds that although the features or properties that people design into technologies more readily support certain values and hinder others, the technology's actual use depends on the goals of the people interacting with it. A screwdriver, after all, is well suited for turning screws, and is also amenable for use as a poker, pry bar, nail set, cutting device, and tool to dig up weeds, but functions poorly as a ladle, pillow, or wheel. Similarly, an online calendar system that displays individuals' scheduled events in detail readily supports accountability within an organization, but makes privacy difficult. Moreover, through human interaction, technology itself changes over time. On occasion, such changes (as emphasized in the exogenous position) can mean the societal rejection of a technology, or that its acceptance is delayed. But more often it entails an iterative process whereby technologies are first invented and then redesigned based on user interactions, which then are reintroduced to users so that further interactions can occur and further redesigns can be implemented. Typical software updates (e.g., of word processors, browsers, and operating systems) epitomize this iterative process.

Eighth, Value Sensitive Design builds on the psychological proposition that certain values are universally held, although how such values play out in a particular culture at a particular point in time can vary considerably (Friedman, 1997b; Kahn, 1999; Turiel, 1998, 2002). For example, even while living in an igloo, Inuits have conventions that ensure some forms of privacy; yet privacy is not maintained by separated rooms, as it is in most Western cultures. Generally, the more concretely (act-based) one conceptualizes a value, the more one will be led to recognizing cultural variation; conversely, the more abstractly one conceptualizes a value, the more one will be led to recognizing universals. Value Sensitive Design seeks to work on both levels, the concrete and abstract, depending on the design problem at hand. Note that this is an empirical proposition, based on a large amount of psychological and anthropological data, not a philosophical one. We also make this claim only for certain values, not all—there are clearly some values that are culture-specific.

The three case studies presented in "Value Sensitive Design's Constellation of Features," earlier in this chapter, illustrate the different features in this constellation. For example, UrbanSim illustrates the goal of being proactive and influencing the design of the technology early in and throughout the design process (Feature 1), and also involves enlarging the arena in which values arise to include urban planning and democratic participation in public decision making (Feature 2). The cookies work is a good illustration of Value Sensitive Design's tripartite methodology (Feature 3): conceptual, technical, and empirical investigations, applied iteratively and integratively, were essential to the success of the project. Each of the three projects brings out a different set of human values (Feature 4): among others, informed consent for the cookies' work; physical and psychological well-being and privacy in public spaces for Room with a View; and fairness, accountability, and democracy for UrbanSim, as well as the whole range of different, sometimes competing, stakeholder values. The cookies project illustrates the complex interaction between usability and human values (Feature 5): Early versions of the system supported informed consent at the expense of usability, requiring additional work to develop a system that was both usable and provided reasonable support for informed consent. The Room with a View work considers and takes seriously both direct and indirect stakeholders (Feature 6): the occupants of the inside office ("the watchers"), and passersby in the plaza ("the watched"). Value Sensitive Design's position that values are neither inscribed into technology nor simply transmitted by social forces (Feature 7) is illustrated by UrbanSim: the system by itself is certainly not neutral with respect to the democratic process, but at the same time does not on its own ensure democratic decision making on land use and transportation issues. Finally, the proposition that certain values are universally held, but play out in very different ways in different cultures and different times (Feature 8), is illustrated by the Room with a View project: The work is informed by a substantial body of work on the importance of privacy in all cultures (for example, the deep connection between privacy and self-identity), but concerns about privacy in public places play out in a specific way in the United States, and might do so quite differently in another cultural context.

We could draw out additional examples that illustrate Value Sensitive Design's constellation of features, both from the three case studies presented in "Value Sensitive Design's Constellation of Features," earlier in this chapter, and in other projects; but hope that this short description demonstrates the unique contribution that Value Sensitive Design can make to the design of technology.

PRACTICAL SUGGESTIONS FOR USING VALUE SENSITIVE DESIGN

One natural question with Value Sensitive Design is, "How exactly do I do it?" In this section we offer some practical suggestions.

Start with a Value, Technology, or Context of Use

Any of these three core aspects—a value, technology, or context of use—easily motivates Value Sensitive Design. We suggest starting with the aspect that is most central to your work and interests. In the case of informed consent and cookies, for example, Friedman et al. began with a value of central interest (informed consent) and moved from that value to its implications for Web browser design. In the case of UrbanSim, Borning et al. began with a technology (urban simulation) and a context of use (the urban planning process); upon inspection of those two, values issues quickly came to the fore.

Identify Direct and Indirect Stakeholders

As part of the initial conceptual investigation, systematically identify direct and indirect stakeholders. Recall that direct stakeholders are those individuals who interact directly with the technology or with the technology's output. Indirect stakeholders are those individuals who are also impacted by the system, though they never interact directly with it. In addition, it is worthwhile to recognize the following:

- Within each of these two overarching categories of stakeholders, there may be several subgroups.
- A single individual may be a member of more than one stakeholder group or subgroup. For example, in the UrbanSim project, an individual who works as an urban planner and lives in

the area is both a direct stakeholder (i.e., through his or her direct use of the simulation to evaluate proposed transportation plans) and an indirect stakeholder (i.e., by virtue of living in the community for which the transportation plans will be implemented).

- An organizational power structure is often orthogonal to the distinction between direct and indirect stakeholders. For example, there might be low-level employees who are either direct or indirect stakeholders and who don't have control over using the system (e.g., workers on an assembly line). Participatory design has contributed a substantial body of analysis to these issues, as well as techniques for dealing with them, such as ways of equalizing power among groups with unequal power. (See the references cited in "What Is a Value?" earlier in this chapter.)

Identify Benefits and Harms for Each Stakeholder Group

Having identified the key stakeholders, systematically identify the benefits and harms for each group. In doing so, we suggest attention to the following points:

- Indirect stakeholders will be benefited or harmed to varying degrees; and in some designs it is probably possible to claim every human as an indirect stakeholder of some sort. Thus, one rule of thumb in the conceptual investigation is to give priority to indirect stakeholders who are strongly affected, or to large groups that are somewhat affected.
- Attend to issues of technical, cognitive, and physical competency. For example, children or the elderly might have limited cognitive competency. In such a case, care must be taken to ensure that their interests are represented in the design process, either by representatives from the affected groups themselves or, if this is not possible, by advocates.
- Personas (Pruitt and Grudin, 2003) are a popular technique that can be useful for identifying the benefits and harms to each stakeholder group. However, we note two caveats. First, personas have a tendency to lead to stereotypes because they require a list of "socially coherent" attributes to be associated with the "imagined individual." Second, although in the literature each persona represents a different user group, in Value Sensitive Design (as noted above) the same individual may be a member of more than one stakeholder group. Thus, in our practice, we have deviated from the typical use of personas that maps a single persona onto a single user group, to allow for a single persona to map onto multiple stakeholder groups.

Map Benefits and Harms onto Corresponding Values

With a list of benefits and harms in hand, one is in a strong position to recognize corresponding values. Sometimes the mapping is one of identity. For example, a harm that is characterized as invasion of privacy maps onto the value of privacy. At other times the mapping is less direct, if not multifaceted. For example, with the Room with a View study, it is possible that a direct stakeholder's mood is improved when working in an office with an augmented window (as compared with no window). Such a benefit potentially implicates not only the value of psychological welfare, but also creativity, productivity, and physical welfare (health), assuming there is a causal link between improved mood and these other factors.

In some cases, the corresponding values will be obvious, but not always. Table 16.1 in "Human Values (with Ethical Import) Often Implicated in System Design," later in this chapter, provides a table of human values with ethical import often implicated in system design. This table may be useful in suggesting values that should be considered in the investigation.

Table 16.1

Human Values (with Ethical Import) Often Implicated in System Design

Human Value	Definition	Sample Literature
Human Welfare	Refers to people's physical, material, and psychological well-being	Leveson (1991); Friedman, Kahn, and Hagman (2003); Neumann (1995); Turiel (1983, 1998)
Ownership and Property	Refers to a right to possess an object (or information), use it, manage it, derive income from it, and bequeath it	Becker (1977); Friedman (1997b); Herskovits (1952); Lipinski and Britz (2000)
Privacy	Refers to a claim, an entitlement, or a right of an individual to determine what information about himself or herself can be communicated to others	Agre and Rotenberg (1998); Bellotti (1998); Boyle, Edwards, and Greenberg (2000); Friedman (1997b); Fuchs (1999); Jancke, Venolia, Grudin, Cadiz, and Gupta (2001); Palen and Dourish (2003); Nissenbaum (1998); Phillips (1998); Schoeman (1984); Svensson, Hook, Laaksolahti, and Waern (2001)
Freedom from Bias	Refers to systematic unfairness perpetrated on individuals or groups, including preexisting social bias, technical bias, and emergent social bias	Friedman and Nissenbaum (1996); cf. Nass and Gong (2000); Reeves and Nass (1996)
Universal Usability	Refers to making all people successful users of information technology	Aberg and Shahmehri (2001); Shneiderman (1999, 2000); Cooper and Rejmer (2001); Jacko, Dixon, Rosa, Scott, and Pappas (1999); Stephanidis (2001)
Trust	Refers to expectations that exist between people who can experience goodwill, extend goodwill toward others, feel vulnerable, and experience betrayal	Baier (1986); Camp (2000); Dieberger, Hook, Svensson, and Lonnqvist (2001); Egger (2000); Fogg and Tseng (1999); Friedman, Kahn, and Howe (2000); Kahn and Turiel (1988); Mayer, Davis, and Schoorman (1995); Olson and Olson (2000); Nissenbaum (2001); Rocco (1998)
Autonomy	Refers to people's ability to decide, plan, and act in ways that they believe will help them to achieve their goals	Friedman and Nissenbaum (1997); Hill (1991); Isaacs, Tang, and Morris (1996); Suchman (1994); Winograd (1994)
Informed Consent	Refers to garnering people's agreement, encompassing criteria of disclosure and comprehension (for "informed") and voluntariness, competence, and agreement (for "consent")	Faden and Beauchamp (1986); Friedman, Millett, and Felten (2000); The Belmont Report (1978)
Accountability	Refers to the properties that ensures that the actions of a person, people, or institution may be traced uniquely to the person, people, or institution	Friedman and Kahn (1992); Friedman and Millet (1995); Reeves and Nass (1996)

(continued)

Table 16.1 (*continued*)

Human Value	Definition	Sample Literature
Courtesy	Refers to treating people with politeness and consideration	Bennett and Delatree (1978); Wynne and Ryan (1993)
Identity	Refers to people's understanding of who they are over time, embracing both continuity and discontinuity over time	Bers, Gonzalo-Heydrich, and DeMaso (2001); Rosenberg (1997); Schiano and White (1998); Turkle (1996)
Calmness	Refers to a peaceful and composed psychological state	Friedman and Kahn (2003); Weiser and Brown (1997)
Environmental Sustainability	Refers to sustaining ecosystems such that they meet the needs of the present without compromising future generations	United Nations (1992); World Commission on Environment and Development (1987); Hart (1999); Moldan, Billharz, and Matravers (1997); Northwest Environment Watch (2002)

Conduct a Conceptual Investigation of Key Values

Following the identification of key values in play, a conceptual investigation of each can follow. Here it is helpful to turn to the relevant literature. In particular, the philosophical ontological literature can help provide criteria for what a value is, and thereby for how to assess it empirically. (For example, "Conceptualizing the Value," earlier in this chapter, described how existing literature helped provide criteria for the value of informed consent.)

Identify Potential Value Conflicts

Values often come into conflict. Thus, once key values have been identified and carefully defined, a next step entails examining potential conflicts. For the purposes of design, value conflicts should usually not be conceived of as "either/or" situations, but as constraints on the design space. Admittedly, at times designs that support one value directly hinder support for another. In those instances, a good deal of discussion among the stakeholders may be warranted to identify the space of workable solutions. Typical value conflicts include accountability vs. privacy, trust vs. security, environmental sustainability vs. economic development, privacy vs. security, and hierarchical control vs. democratization.

Integrate Value Considerations into One's Organizational Structure

Ideally, Value Sensitive Design will work in concert with organizational objectives. Within a company, for example, designers would bring values to the forefront, and in the process generate increased revenue, employee satisfaction, customer loyalty, and other desirable outcomes for their companies. In turn, within a government agency, designers would both better support national and community values, and enhance the organization's ability to achieve its objectives. In the real world, of course, human values (especially those with ethical import) may collide with economic objectives, power, and other factors. However, even in such situations, Value Sensitive Design should be able to make positive contributions, by showing alternate designs that better support enduring human values. For example, if a standards committee were considering adopting a protocol that raised serious privacy concerns, a Value Sensitive Design analysis and design might result in an alternate protocol that better addressed the issue of privacy while still retaining other needed properties. Citizens, advocacy groups, staff members, politicians, and others could then have a more effective argument against a claim that the proposed protocol was the only reasonable choice.

Human Values (with Ethical Import) Often Implicated in System Design

We stated earlier that while all values fall within its purview, Value Sensitive Design emphasizes values with ethical import. In Table 16.1, we present a list of frequently implicated values. This table is intended as a heuristic for suggesting values that should be considered in the investigation—it is definitely not intended as a complete list of human values that might be implicated.

Two caveats. First, not all of these values are fundamentally distinct from one another. Nonetheless, each value has its own language and conceptualizations within its respective field, and thus warrants separate treatment here. Second, as noted above, this list is not comprehensive. Perhaps no list could be, at least within the confines of a paper. Peacefulness, respect, compassion, love, warmth, creativity, humor, originality, vision, friendship, cooperation, collaboration, purposefulness, devotion, loyalty, diplomacy, kindness, musicality, harmony—the list of other possible moral and non-moral values could get very long very quickly. Our particular list comprises many of the values that hinge on the deontological and consequentialist moral orientations noted above: human welfare, ownership and property, privacy, freedom from bias, universal usability, trust, autonomy, informed consent, and accountability. In addition, we have chosen several other values related to system design: courtesy, identity, calmness, and environmental sustainability.

Heuristics for Interviewing Stakeholders

As part of an empirical investigation, it is useful to interview stakeholders, to better understand their judgments about a context of use, an existing technology, or a proposed design. A semi-structured interview often offers a good balance between addressing the questions of interest and gathering new and unexpected insights. In these interviews, the following heuristics can prove useful:

In probing stakeholders' reasons for their judgments, the simple question "Why?" can go a good distance. For example, seniors evaluating a ubiquitous computing video surveillance system might respond negatively to the system. When asked "Why?" a response might be: "I don't mind my family knowing that other people are visiting me, so they don't worry that I'm alone—I just don't want them to know who is visiting." The researcher can probe again: "Why don't you want them to know?" An answer might be: "I might have a new friend I don't want them to know about. It's not their business." Here the first "why" question elicits information about a value conflict (the family's desire to know about the senior's well-being and the senior's desire to control some information); the second "why" question elicits further information about the value of privacy for the senior.

Ask about values not only directly, but indirectly, based on formal criteria specified in the conceptual investigation. For example, suppose that you want to conduct an empirical investigation of people's reasoning and values about "X" (say, trust, privacy, or informed consent), and that you decided to employ an interview methodology. One option is to ask people directly about the topic. "What is X?" "How do you reason about X?" "Can you give me an example from your own life of when you encountered a problem that involved X?" There is some merit to this direct approach.

Certainly it gives people the opportunity to define the problem in their own terms. But you may quickly discover that it comes up short. Perhaps the greatest problem is that people have concepts about many aspects of the topic on which they cannot directly reflect. Rather, you will usually be better served by employing an alternative approach. As is common in social cognitive research—see Kahn (1999, Chapter 5) for a discussion of methods—you could interview people about a hypothetical situation, or a common everyday event in their lives, or a task that you have asked them to solve, or a behavior in which they have just engaged. But, no matter what you choose, the important point is a priori to conceptualize what the topic entails, if possible demarcating its boundaries through formal criteria, and at a minimum employing issues or tasks that engage people's reasoning about the topic under investigation.

Heuristics for Technical Investigations

When engaging in value-oriented technical investigations, the following heuristics can prove useful:

Technical mechanisms will often adjudicate multiple if not conflicting values, often in the form of design trade-offs. We have found it helpful to make explicit how a design trade-off maps onto a value conflict and differentially affects different groups of stakeholders. For example, the Room with a View study suggests real-time displays in interior offices may provide physiological benefits for those in the inside offices (the direct stakeholders), yet may impinge on the privacy and security of those walking through the outdoor scene (the indirect stakeholders), especially women.

Unanticipated values and value conflicts often emerge after a system is developed and deployed. Thus, when possible, design flexibility into the underlying technical architecture so that it can be responsive to such emergent concerns. In UrbanSim, for example, Borning et al. used agile programming techniques to design an architecture that can more readily accommodate new indicators and models.

The control of information flow through underlying protocols—and the privacy concerns surrounding such control—is a strongly contested area. Ubiquitous computing, with sensors that collect and then disseminate information at large, has only intensified these concerns. We suggest that underlying protocols that release information should be able to be turned off (and in such a way that the stakeholders are confident they have been turned off).

CONCLUSION

There is a growing interest and challenge to address values in design. Our goal in this paper has been to provide enough detail about Value Sensitive Design so that other researchers and designers can critically examine, use, and extend this approach. Our hope is that this approach can contribute to a principled and comprehensive consideration of values in the design of information and computational systems.

ACKNOWLEDGMENTS

Value Sensitive Design has emerged over the past decade and benefited from discussions with many people. We would like particularly to acknowledge all the members of our respective research groups, along with Edward Felten, Jonathan Grudin, Sara Kiesler, Clifford Nass, Helen Nissenbaum, John Thomas, and Terry Winograd. This research was supported in part by NSF Awards IIS-9911185, IIS-0325035, EIA-0121326, and EIA-0090832.

NOTE

1. The Oxford English Dictionary definition of this sense of value is: "the principles or standards of a person or society, the personal or societal judgment of what is valuable and important in life." (Simpson and Weiner 1989)

REFERENCES

Aberg, J., and Shahmehri, N. An empirical study of human web assistants: implications for user support in web information systems. In *Proceedings of the Conference on Human Factors in Computing Systems (CHI 2000)*. New York: ACM Press, 2001, pp. 404–411.

Ackerman, M.S., and Cranor, L. Privacy critics: UI components to safeguard users' privacy. In *Extended Abstracts of CHI 1999*. New York: ACM Press, 1999, pp. 258–259.

Adler, P.S., and Winograd, T. (eds.) *Usability: Turning Technologies into Tools*. Oxford: Oxford University Press, 1992.

Agre, P.E., and Rotenberg, M. (eds.) *Technology and Privacy: The New Landscape*. MIT Press, Cambridge, MA, 1998.

Baier, A. Trust and antitrust. *Ethics*, 96 (1986) 231–260.

Beck, A., and Katcher, A. *Between Pets and People*. West Lafayette, IN: Purdue University Press, 1996.

Becker, L.C. *Property Rights: Philosophical Foundations*. London: Routledge & Kegan Paul, 1977.

Bellotti, V. Design for privacy in multimedia computing and communications environments. In P.E. Agre and M. Rotenberg (eds.), *Technology and Privacy: The New Landscape*. Cambridge, MA: MIT Press, 1998, pp. 63–98.

Department of Health, Education, and Welfare. *The Belmont Report: Ethical Principles and Guidelines for the Protection of Human Subjects of Research*. The National Commission for the Protection of Human Subjects of Biomedical and Behavioral Research. Washington, DC: OPRR Reports, 1978.

Bennet, W.J., and Delatree, E.J. Moral education in the schools. *The Public Interest*, 50 (1978), 81–98.

Bers, M.U.; Gonzalez-Heydrich, J.; and DeMaso, D.R. Identity construction environments: supporting a virtual therapeutic community of pediatric patients undergoing dialysis. In *Proceedings of the Conference of Human Factors in Computing Systems (CHI 2001)*. New York: ACM Press, 2001, 380–387.

Bjerknes, G., and Bratteteig, T. User participation and democracy: a discussion of Scandinavian research on system development. *Scandinavian Journal of Information Systems*, 7, 1 (1995), 73–97.

Bødker, S. *Through the Interface—A Human Activity Approach to User Interface Design*. Hillsdale, NJ: Lawrence Erlbaum Associates, 1990.

Borning, A.; Friedman, B.; Davis, J.; and Lin, P. Informing public deliberation: value sensitive design of indicators for a large-scale urban simulation. In *Proceedings of the 9th European Conference on Computer-Supported Cooperative Work* (ECSCW 2005). Dordrecht, The Netherlands: Springer, 2005, 449–468.

Boyle, M.; Edwards, C.; and Greenberg, S. The effects of filtered video on awareness and privacy. In *Proceedings of Conference on Computer Supported Cooperative Work (CSCW 2000)*. New York: ACM Press, 2000, 1–10.

Bynum, T.W. (ed.) *Metaphilosophy*, 16, 4 (1985), entire issue.

Camp, L.J. *Trust and Risk in Internet Commerce*. Cambridge, MA: MIT Press, 2000.

Campbell, R.L., and Christopher, J.C. 1996. Moral development theory: a critique of its Kantian presuppositions. *Developmental Review*, 16 (1996), 1–47.

Cooper, M., and Rejmer, P. Case study: localization of an accessibility evaluation. In *Extended Abstracts of the Conference on Human Factors in Computing Systems (CHI 2001)*. New York: ACM Press, 2001, pp. 141–142.

Dieberger, A.; Hook, K.; Svensson, M.; and Lonnqvist, P. 2001. Social navigation research agenda. In *Extended Abstracts of the Conference on Human Factors in Computing Systems (CHI 2001)*. New York: ACM Press, 2001, pp. 107–108.

Dworkin, R. *Taking Rights Seriously*. Cambridge, MA: Harvard University Press, 1978.

Egger, F. N. "Trust me, I'm an online vendor": towards a model of trust for e-commerce system design. In *Extended Abstracts of the Conference of Human Factors in Computing Systems (CHI 2000)*. New York: ACM Press, 2000, pp. 101–102.

Ehn, P. *Work-Oriented Design of Computer Artifacts.* Hillsdale, NJ: Lawrence Erlbaum Associates, 1989.

Faden, R., and Beauchamp, T. *A History and Theory of Informed Consent.* New York: Oxford University Press, 1986.

Fogg, B.J., and Tseng, H. The elements of computer credibility. In *Proceedings of CHI 1999.* New York: ACM Press, 1999, pp. 80–87.

Foot, P. *Virtues and Vices.* Berkeley and Los Angeles, CA: University of California Press, 1978.

Frankena, W. Value and valuation. In P. Edwards (ed.), *The Encyclopedia of Philosophy*, vol. 7–8. New York: Macmillan, 1972, pp. 409–410.

Franklin, J.; Waddell, P.; and Britting, J. Sensitivity analysis approach for an integrated land development and travel demand modeling system. Presented at the Association of Collegiate Schools of Planning 44th Annual Conference, November 21–24, 2002, Baltimore, MD. Preprint available from www.urbansim.org.

Freeman-Benson, B.N., and Borning, A. YP and urban simulation: applying an agile programming methodology in a politically tempestuous domain. In *Proceedings of the 2003 Agile Programming Conference*, Salt Lake City, June 2003.

Friedman, B. (ed.) *Human Values and the Design of Computer Technology.* New York: Cambridge University Press, 1997a.

Friedman, B. Social judgments and technological innovation: adolescents' understanding of property, privacy, and electronic information. *Computers in Human Behavior*, 13, 3 (1997b), 327–351.

Friedman, B.; Howe, D.C.; and Felten, E. Informed consent in the Mozilla browser: implementing value-sensitive design. In *Proceedings of HICSS-35*, IEEE Computer Society, Abstract, 2002, p. 247. (CD-ROM of full papers: OSPE101.)

Friedman, B., and Kahn, P.H., Jr. Human agency and responsible computing: implications for computer system design. *Journal of Systems Software*, 17 (1992), 7–14.

Friedman, B.; Kahn, P.H., Jr.; and Howe, D.C. Trust online. *Communications of the ACM,* 43, 12 (2000), 34–40.

Friedman, B., and Kahn, P.H., Jr. Human values, ethics, and design. In J. Jacko and A. Sears (eds.), *The Human-Computer Interaction Handbook.* Mahwah, NJ: Lawrence Erlbaum Associates, 2003, pp. 1177–1201.

Friedman, B.; Kahn, P.H., Jr.; Hagman, J. Hardware companions?: what online AIBO discussion forums reveal about the human-robotic relationship. In *Conference Proceedings of CHI 2003.* New York: ACM Press, 2003, 273–280.

Friedman, B.; Kahn, P.H., Jr.; Hagman, J., Severson, R.L., and Gill, B. The watcher and the watched: social judgments about privacy in a public place. *Human-computer Interaction Journal*, 21, 2 (2006).

Friedman, B., and Millett, L. "It's the computer's fault"—reasoning about computers as moral agents. In *Conference Companion of the Conference on Human Factors in Computing Systems (CHI '95).* New York, NY: ACM Press, 1995, pp. 226–227.

Friedman, B.; Millett, L.; and Felten, E. *Informed Consent Online: A Conceptual Model and Design Principles.* University of Washington Computer Science & Engineering Technical Report UW-CSE-00-12-2, Seattle, WA: Department of Computer Science and Engineering, University of Washington, 2000 (available at http://www.cs.washington.edu/research/tr/techreports.shtml).

Friedman, B., and Nissenbaum, H. Bias in computer systems. 1996. *ACM Transactions on Information Systems*, 14, 3 (1996), 330–347.

Friedman, B., and Nissenbaum, H. Software agents and user autonomy. In *Proceedings of the First International Conference on Autonomous Agents.* New York: ACM Press, 1997, pp. 466–469.

Fuchs, L. AREA: a cross-application notification service for groupware. In *Proceedings of ECSCW 1999.* Dordrecht, The Netherlands: Kluwer, 1999, pp. 61–80.

Galegher, J.; Kraut, R.E.; and Egido, C. (eds.) *Intellectual Teamwork: Social and Technological Foundations of Cooperative Work.* Hillsdale, NJ: Lawrence Erlbaum Associates, 1990.

Gallopin, G.C. Indicators and their use: information for decision-making. In B. Moldan, S. Billharz, and R. Matravers (eds.), *Sustainability Indicators: A Report on the Project on Indicators of Sustainable Development.* Chichester, England: Wiley, 1997, pp. 13–27.

Gewirth, A. *Reason and Morality.* Chicago, IL: University of Chicago Press, 1978.

Greenbaum, J., and Kyng, M. (eds.) *Design at Work: Cooperative Design of Computer Systems.* Hillsdale, NJ: Lawrence Erlbaum Associates, 1991.

Grudin, J. Why CSCW applications fail: problems in the design and evaluation of organizational interfaces. In *Proceedings of the Conference on Computer Supported Cooperative Work (CSCW '88).* New York: ACM Press, 1988, pp. 85–93.

Hagman, J.; Hendrickson, A.; and Whitty, A. What's in a barcode: informed consent and machine scannable driver licenses. In *CHI 2003 Extended Abstracts of the Conference on Human Factors in Computing Systems*. New York: ACM Press, 2003, pp. 912–913.

Hart, M. *Guide to Sustainable Community Indicators*, 2nd ed. North Andover, MA: Hart Environmental Data, 1999.

Herskovits, M.J. *Economic Anthropology: A Study of Comparative Economics*. New York: Alfred A. Knopf, 1952.

Hill, T. E., Jr. *Autonomy and Self-Respect*. Cambridge: Cambridge University Press, 1991.

Isaacs, E.A.; Tang, J.C.; and Morris, T. Piazza: a desktop environment supporting impromptu and planned interactions. In *Proceedings of the Conference on Computer Supported Cooperative Work (CSCW '96)*. New York: ACM Press, 1996, pp. 315–324.

Jacko, J.A.; Dixon, M.A.; Rosa, R.H., Jr.; Scott, I.U.; and Pappas, C.J. Visual profiles: a critical component of universal access. In *Proceedings of the Conference on Human Factors in Computing Systems (CHI 99)*. New York: ACM Press, 1999, pp. 330–337.

Jancke, G.; Venolia, G.D.; Grudin, J.; Cadiz, J.J.; and Gupta, A. Linking public spaces: technical and social issues. In *Proceedings of CHI 2001*, New York: ACM Press, 2001, pp. 530–537.

Johnson, E.H. Getting beyond the simple assumptions of organization impact (social informatics). *Bulletin of the American Society for Information Science*, 26, 3 (2000), 18–19.

Johnson, D.G., and Miller, K. Ethical issues for computer scientists and engineers. In A.B. Tucker, Jr. (ed.), *The Computer Science and Engineering Handbook*. Boca Raton, FL: CRC Press, 1997, pp. 16–26.

Kahn, P. H., Jr. *The Human Relationship with Nature: Development and Culture*. Cambridge, MA: MIT Press, 1999.

Kahn, P.H., Jr., and Kellert, S.R. (eds.) *Children and Nature: Psychological, Sociocultural, and Evolutionary Investigations*. Cambridge, MA: MIT Press, 2002.

Kahn, P.H., Jr., and Turiel, E. Children's conceptions of trust in the context of social expectations. *Merrill-Palmer Quarterly*, 34 (1988), 403–419.

Kant, I. *Groundwork of the Metaphysic of Morals* (trans. H.J. Paton). New York: Harper Torchbooks, 1964.

Kling, R.; Rosenbaum, H.; and Hert, C. Social informatics in information science: an introduction. *Journal of the American Society for Information Science*, 49, 12 (1998), 1047–1052.

Kling, R., and Star, S.L. Human centered systems in the perspective of organizational and social informatics. *Computers and Society*, 28, 1 (1998), 22–29.

Kyng, M., and Mathiassen, L. (eds.) *Computers and Design in Context*. Cambridge, MA: MIT Press, 1997.

Leveson, N.G. Software safety in embedded computer systems. *Communications of the ACM*, 34, 2 (1991), 34–46.

Lipinski, T.A., and Britz, J.J. Rethinking the ownership of information in the 21st century: ethical implications. *Ethics and Information Technology*, 2, 1 (2000), 49–71.

MacIntyre, A. *After Virtue*. Notre Dame, IN: University of Nortre Dame Press, 1984.

Mayer, R.C.; Davis, J.H.; and Schoorman, F.D. An integrative model of organizational trust. *The Academy of Management Review*, 20, 3 (1995), 709–734.

Millett, L.; Friedman, B.; and Felten, E. Cookies and web browser design: toward realizing informed consent online. In *Proceedings of CHI 2001*. New York: ACM Press, 2001, pp. 46–52.

Moldan, B.; Billharz, S.; and Matravers, R. (eds.) *Sustainability Indicators: A Report on the Project on Indicators of Sustainable Development*. Chichester, England: Wiley, 1997.

Moore, G.E. *Principia Ethica*. Cambridge: Cambridge University Press, 1978.

Nass, C., and Gong, L. Speech interfaces from an evolutionary perspective. *Communications of the ACM*, 43, 9 (2000), 36–43.

Neumann, P.G. *Computer Related Risks*. New York: ACM Press, 1995.

Nielsen, J. *Usability Engineering*. Boston, MA: AP Professional, 1993.

Nissenbaum, H. Protecting privacy in an information age: the problem with privacy in public. *Law and Philosophy*, 17 (1998), 559–596.

Nissenbaum, H. Can trust be secured online? A theoretical perspective. *Etica e Politca*, 2 (1999) (electronic journal).

Nissenbaum, H. Securing trust online: Wisdom or oxymoron. *Boston University Law Review*, 81, 3 (2001), 635–664.

Norman, D.A. *The Psychology of Everyday Things*. New York: Basic Books, 1988.

Northwest Environment Watch. *This Place on Earth 2002: Measuring What Matters*. Seattle, WA: Northwest Environment Watch, 2002.

Noth, M.; Borning, A.; and Waddell, P. An extensible, modular architecture for simulating urban development, transportation, and environmental impacts. *Computers, Environment and Urban Systems*, 27, 2 (2003), 181–203.

Olson, J.S., and Olson, G.M. i2i trust in e-commerce. *Communications of the ACM*, 43, 12 (2000), 41–44.

Olson, J.S., and Teasley, S. Groupware in the wild: lessons learned from a year of virtual collaboration. In *Proceedings of the Conference on Computer Supported Cooperative Work (CSCW '96)*. New York: ACM Press, 1996, pp. 419–427.

Orlikowsi, W.J., and Iacono, C.S. Research commentary: desperately seeking the "IT" in IT research—a call to theorizing the IT artifact. *Information Systems Research*, 12, 2 (2001), 121–134.

Palen, L., and Grudin, J. Discretionary adoption of group support software: lessons from calendar applications. In B.E. Munkvold (ed.), *Implementing Collaboration Technologies in Industry*. Heidelberg: Springer Verlag, 2003, 159–179.

Palen, L., and Dourish, P. Privacy and trust: unpacking "privacy" for a networked world. In *Proceedings of CHI 2003*, 2003, pp. 129–136.

Palmer, K. (ed.) *Indicators of Sustainable Community*. Seattle, WA: Sustainable Seattle, 1998.

Phillips, D.J. Cryptography, secrets, and structuring of trust. In P.E. Agre and M. Rotenberg (eds.), *Technology and Privacy: The New Landscape*. Cambridge, MA: MIT Press, 1998, pp. 243–276.

Pruitt, J., and Grudin, J. Personas: practice and theory. In *Proceedings of DUX 2003*. New York: ACM Press, 2003, 144–161.

Rawls, J. *A Theory of Justice*. Cambridge, MA: Harvard University Press, 1971.

Reeves, B., and Nass, C. *The Media Equation: How People Treat Computers, Television, and New Media Like Real People and Places*. New York, NY, and Stanford, CA: Cambridge University Press and CSLI Publications, 1996.

Riegelsberger, J., and Sasse, M.A. Face it—photos don't make a web site trustworthy. In *Extended Abstracts of CHI 2002*. New York: ACM Press, 2002, pp. 742–743.

Rocco, E. Trust breaks down in electronic contexts but can be repaired by some initial face-to-face contact. In *Proceedings of CHI 1998*. New York: ACM Press, 1998, 496–502.

Rosenberg, S. Multiplicity of selves. In R.D. Ashmore and L. Jussim (eds.), *Self and Identity: Fundamental Issues*. New York: Oxford University Press, 1997, pp. 23–45.

Sawyer, S., and Rosenbaum, H. Social informatics in the information sciences: Current activities and emerging direction. *Informing Science*, 3, 2 (2000), 89–95.

Scheffler, S. *The Rejection of Consequentialism*. Oxford: Oxford University Press, 1982.

Schiano, D.J., and White, S. The first noble truth of cyberspace: people are people (even when they MOO). In *Proceedings of the Conference of Human Factors in Computing Systems (CHI '98)*. New York: ACM Press, 1998, pp. 352–359.

Schneider, F.B. (ed.) *Trust in Cyberspace*. Washington, DC: National Academy Press, 1999.

Schoeman, F.D. (ed.) *Philosophical Dimensions of Privacy: An Anthology*. Cambridge: Cambridge University Press, 1984.

Shneiderman, B. Universal usability: pushing human-computer interaction research to empower every citizen. ISR Technical Report 99–72. College Park, MD: University of Maryland Institute for Systems Research, 1999.

Shneiderman, B. Universal usability. *Communications of the ACM*, 43, 5 (2000), 84–91.

Simpson, J.A., and Weiner, E.S.C. (eds.) "value, *n.*" *Oxford English Dictionary Online* (available at http://dictionary.oed.com/cgi/entry/00274678, accessed on May 30, 2003).

Smart, J.J.C. and Williams, B. *Utilitarianism For and Against*. Cambridge: Cambridge University Press, 1973.

Stephanidis, C. (ed.) *User Interfaces for All: Concepts, Methods, and Tools*. Mahwah, NJ: Lawrence Erlbaum Associates, 2001.

Suchman, L. Do categories have politics? The language/action perspective reconsidered. *CSCW Journal*, 2, 3 (1994), 177–190.

Svensson, M.; Hook, K.; Laaksolahti, J.; and Waern, A. Social navigation of food recipes. In *Proceedings of the Conference of Human Factors in Computing Systems (CHI 2001)*. New York: ACM Press, 2001, pp. 341–348.

Tang, J.C. Eliminating a hardware switch: weighing economics and values in a design decision. In B. Friedman (ed.), *Human Values and the Design of Computer Technology*. New York: Cambridge University Press, 1997, pp. 259–269.

Thomas, J.C. Steps toward universal access within a communications company. In B. Friedman (ed.), *Human Values and the Design of Computer Technology*. New York: Cambridge University Press, 1997, pp. 271–287.

Turiel, E. *The Development of Social Knowledge*. Cambridge: Cambridge University Press, 1983.

Turiel, E. Moral development. In N. Eisenberg (ed.), *Social, Emotional, and Personality Development*, 5th ed. New York: Wiley, 1998, pp. 863–932.

Turiel, E. *The Culture of Morality: Social Development, Context, and Conflict*. Cambridge: Cambridge University Press, 2002.

Turkle, S. *Life on the Screen: Identify in the Age of the Internet*. New York: Simon and Schuster, 1996.

Ulrich, R.S. View through a window may influence recovery from surgery. *Science*, 224 (1984), 420–421.

Ulrich, R.S. Biophilia, biophobia, and natural landscapes. In S.R. Kellert and E.O. Wilson (eds.), *The Biophilia Hypothesis*. Washington, DC: Island Press, 1993, pp. 73–137.

United Nations. Report of the United Nations Conference on Environment and Development, held in Rio de Janeiro, Brazil, 1992 (available from http://www.un.org/esa/sustdev/documents/agenda21/english/agenda21toc.htm).

Waddell, P. UrbanSim: modeling urban development for land use, transportation, and environmental planning. *Journal of the American Planning Association*, 68, 3 (2002), 297–314.

Waddell, P.; Borning, A.; Noth, M.; Freier, N.; Becke, M.; and Ulfarsson, G. Microsimulation of urban development and location choices: design and implementation of UrbanSim. *Networks and Spatial Economics*, 3, 1 (2003), 43–67.

Weiser, M., and Brown, J.S. The coming age of calm technology. In P. Denning and B. Metcalfe (eds.), *Beyond Calculation: The Next 50 Years of Computing*. New York: Springer-Verlag, 1997, pp. 75–85.

Weizenbaum, J. On the impact of the computer on society: How does one insult a machine? *Science*, 178 (1972), 609–614.

Wiener, N. The machine as threat and promise. In P. Masani (ed.), *Norbert Wiener: Collected Works and Commentaries, Vol. IV*. Cambridge, MA: MIT Press, 1985, pp. 673–678.

Winograd, T. Categories, disciplines, and social coordination. *CSCW Journal*, 2, 3 (1994), 191–197.

World Commission on Environment and Development. *Our Common Future*. Oxford: Oxford University Press, 1987.

Wynne, E.A., and Ryan, K. *Reclaiming Our Schools: A Handbook on Teaching Character, Academics, and Discipline*. New York, Macmillan, 1993.

Zheng, J.; Bos, N.; Olson, J.; and Olson, G.M. Trust without touch: jump-start trust with social chat. In *Extended Abstracts of CHI 2001*. New York: ACM Press, 2001, pp. 293–294.

CHAPTER 17

SOCIALIZING CONSISTENCY

From Technical Homogeneity to Human Epitome

CLIFFORD NASS, LEILA TAKAYAMA, AND SCOTT BRAVE

Abstract: *Consistency is a major issue in user interface design. Although graphical user inter-faces have benefited tremendously from a focus on the cognitive aspects of consistency, advances in computer technologies now allow for more socially demanding interfaces incorporating more realistic artificial intelligence agents and new modes of interaction (e.g., voice). This chapter demonstrates that as interfaces become more social,* social consistency *becomes as important as the more traditional cognitive consistency. This chapter presents experimental studies of human-computer interaction that are theoretically grounded in social psychology and the computers are social actors (CASA) paradigm. Each study is used to inform design guidelines for social consis-tency and to open new areas of research on social responses to computers in important areas such as personality, gender, ethnicity, emotion, and the use of "I."*

Keywords: *Consistency, Social Consistency, Computers Are Social Actors (CASA)*

INTRODUCTION

User interface designers are notorious for answering every question with the answer, "It depends." The dependencies include characteristics of the users (e.g., novice vs. expert, frequent vs. infrequent, heterogeneity, physical disabilities), the task (e.g., complexity, business vs. entertainment, length of time required, production vs. distribution vs. consumption), and the input and output modalities (e.g., text, pictures, voices, haptics, gestures, output only), among others. Furthermore, virtually every issue elicits debates within the design community, with designers pointing to conflicting research, judgments, anecdotes, and rules of thumb. Consumers of design can well ask the question, "Isn't there *anything* that you can *all* agree on?"

Miraculously, there is one point of consensus among designers: *Consistency is king.* Open a book on interface design and you will almost certainly land on a page that either explicitly or implicitly argues for consistency both within an application and across applications. Most producers of oper-ating systems and platforms provide formal descriptions that describe standards for everything from menu structure to sizes of icons to color schemes. Trust in standardization is so powerful that many of the tools produced to build applications for PCs, the Web, and voice user interfaces *automatically* ensure that their design guidelines are followed. Attempts to deviate from these guidelines in the name of "creativity" are derided as "showing-off."

Why is consistency such a laudable goal? While humor is based on incongruity (e.g., Morkes et al., 2000; Raskin, 1985) and magicians are admired for violating the laws of physics, there is significant evidence that the human brain is built to expect consistency and process it more readily than inconsistency (Abelson et al., 1968; Gong, 2000). In a classic study (Stroop, 1935), people were shown a word on a screen and asked to say the color of the ink in which the word was written. People took much longer identifying red ink and saying "red" when the word on the screen was "blue" as opposed to an arbitrary word, such as "ball" or "chair." The inconsistent color word seemed to *interfere* with the processing of the ink color, an effect known as the "Stroop effect" (Stroop, 1935).

In addition to making information easier to process, another benefit of consistency is transferability of learning. If computer applications A and B both use the leftmost menu item for saving and printing, a user can leverage the learning of application A and immediately apply it to application B. This is a key reason why tools associated with most operating systems or platforms enforce a set of interface guidelines: They ensure transferability of knowledge *across* applications. All standardization strategies reflect *pre*processing, the structuring of information to facilitate subsequent processing (Beniger, 1986). Even within applications, transferability is important: One of the primary reasons that interfaces moved away from modal behavior (the same command meaning different things at different times) to modeless behavior (a given command had the same meaning at all times) was to ensure consistency from one context to another.

Basic consistency is well understood in the domain of traditional graphical user interfaces (GUIs), and any number of books can help designers achieve consistency within and across their applications. In recent years, however, many interfaces have started evolving in a new direction. The ubiquitous presence of cell phones and the ever-growing desire for access to information anywhere, anytime (including while driving) has led many to consider voice interaction as an effective and flexible interface technique (Cohen et al., 2004; Kotelly, 2003; Nass and Brave, 2005). Whether getting directions, checking e-mail, or browsing the Web, interacting with a computer might start looking a lot more like talking and listening than pointing and clicking.

A related new trend is toward lifelike characters as the interface to information and services. Many companies and researchers have recognized, for example, that customers and users would often rather interact with a person than a machine: Virtual people may represent a reasonable substitute (Cassell et al., 2000; Isbister and Doyle, 2002; Ruttkay and Pelachaud, 2004). Lifelike characters have been employed in e-learning applications (Massaro, 1998), on customer service Web sites (www.finali.com), and as online news anchors (www.ananova.com). Both voice interfaces and lifelike characters (and robots, as well) fall under a category called embodied agents (Cassell et al., 2000) and bring with them a new design landscape.

Given the recognized importance of design consistency for users, how does consistency play out in this new design space? The answer is social consistency. As soon as computers start sounding or looking like people—and often even before then (Reeves and Nass, 1996)—social attributes and norms come to the forefront. In many ways, consistency in the social arena is even more critical for users than consistency in the more visual/mechanical arena of traditional interfaces (Nass et al., 2004). Social consistency is fundamental not only for ease of processing and transferability of learning, but also because it has strong affective impacts on users, deriving from the importance of social life for humans (Nass and Brave, 2005; Nass et al., 2004). To appreciate the power of the social aspects of embodied interfaces, one need only consider the raw frustration and anger that emerges when a lifelike paper-clip character—breaking a host of social norms—incessantly interrupts your work with completely useless information.

This chapter presents a number of research studies that focus on issues of social consistency in embodied interfaces. It considers consistency of personality, gender, emotion, ethnicity, and ontology (human vs. machine). Throughout, we provide theoretical grounding for the findings and describe how these results and theories could and should inform design.

PERSONALITY: IT'S NOT ONLY ABOUT "PERSONS"

Humans (and other social animals) are extremely complex creatures. Yet social life requires inter-action with any number of such complex beings on a daily basis. How do we cope with this complexity? One of the ways is by simplifying our view of others through categorizations such as personality (Nass and Moon, 2000; Nass et al., 1995). Descriptions such as extroverted vs. intro-verted, judging vs. intuiting, kind vs. unkind, and a host of other traits provide a powerful frame-work for understanding how other people will think, feel, and behave (Pervin and John, 2001).

Given that we assign personality to people and pets—and sometimes even inanimate objects (such as cars)—it should come as little surprise that once a computer starts looking or talking like a human, people will assign personality (Nass and Lee, 2001; Reeves and Nass, 1996). Interfaces that talk (even those using non-human-sounding synthetic speech) constantly provide signals of personality through vocal characteristics such as pitch, pitch range, volume, and speech rate (Nass and Lee, 2001). For example, listeners rapidly and automatically interpret softer, slower, lower-pitched speech with narrow pitch range as introverted, and louder, faster, higher-pitched speech with wider pitch range as extroverted—regardless of whether the voice comes from a human standing in front of the listener, a television, a telephone, or a computer (Nass and Brave, 2005; Nass and Lee, 2001). Words themselves (whether spoken or written onscreen) also evoke personality (Nass and Brave, 2005; Nass and Lee, 2001). For example, extroverts tend to communicate using more words overall, use more assertive language, and make more use of emotional terms than introverts (Kiesler, 1983; Nass and Lee, 2001).

Embodied agents that have a face and/or body (such as onscreen character and robots) can pro-vide additional indications of personality through gestures, facial expression, and posture (Cassell, 2002; Cassell and Stone, 1999). For example, extroverts tend to stand closer to other people and face them more directly, make larger and faster gestures, stand more upright, and make more eye contact with others than do introverts (Isbister and Nass, 2000). Particular body types/shapes are often even interpreted as indicators of personality. For example, mesomorphs (muscular bodies with erect posture, like Superman) are associated with energetic and assertive personalities, ectomorphs (tall, thin, and small-shouldered bodies, like Ichabod Crane) with fearful and introverted personalities, and endomorphs (round, soft bodies, like Santa Claus) with gregarious and fun-loving personalities (Sheldon, 1970).

Because personality is fundamentally a mechanism through which we understand and predict the behaviors of others, consistency of personality is critical (Cantor and Mischel, 1979; Nass and Lee, 2001). If a social being is unpredictable, it is very difficult at a cognitive or practical level to interact with that being. Thus, people strongly prefer to interact with others who display consistent personal-ity cues—a phenomenon known as consistency-attraction (Nass and Lee, 2001). Inconsistent person-alities not only require longer and more effortful processing (Fiske and Taylor, 1991), but also lead to dislike and distrust of the inconsistent person (Cantor and Mischel, 1979; Cantor and Mischel, 1979).

Given such negative responses to inconsistent personality cues, it would seem that the same might hold true for inconsistent personality cues in embodied computer interfaces. To find out, our lab conducted an experiment in the context of a voice interface for online auctions (Nass and Lee, 2001).

Study on Personality in Voice and Content

Eighty participants took part in the experiment. Participants were directed to an online auction site, complete with an eBay-like interface. The site included the names and pictures of nine antique or collectible auction items: a 1963 classic lamp, a 1995 limited edition Marilyn Monroe watch, a 1920s radio, a 1968 Russian circus poster, a very old church key (1910–1920s), a 1916 Oxford map, a 1920 letter opener, a 1940s US Treasury award medal, and a 1965 black rotary wall phone. The items were chosen so that they would not be of great interest to the vast majority of participants: Desire for a particular item could confuse the results.

For each item, two descriptions were created, one that would be written by an extrovert and one that would be written by an introvert. Each was based on an actual description from eBay. The different personalities were created by modifying word choice, phrasing, and the length of the descriptions. The extroverted descriptions of the auction items were filled with adjectives and adverbs and used strong and descriptive language expressed in the form of confident assertions and exclamations. There were also references to the writer and to others, such "I am sure you will like this." By contrast, the introverted descriptions were relatively short, used more tentative and matter-of-fact language, and did not reference either the writer or the reader. For example, the extroverted description of the lamp read:

> This is a reproduction of one of the most famous of the Tiffany stained glass pieces. The colors are absolutely sensational! The first class hand-made copper-foiled stained glass shade is over six and one-half inches in diameter and over five inches tall. I am sure that this gorgeous lamp will accent any environment and bring a classic touch of the past to a stylish present. It is guaranteed to be in excellent condition! I would very highly recommend it.

Conversely, the introverted description of the lamp read:

> This is a reproduction of a Tiffany stained glass piece. The colors are quite rich. The hand-made copper-foiled stained glass shade is about six and one-half inches in diameter and five inches tall.

The personality of the synthetic voice was created by manipulating various speech characteristics (Nass and Lee, 2001). The introverted voice had a lower volume, lower pitch, smaller pitch range, and spoke slowly, while the extroverted voice had higher volume, higher pitch, wide pitch range, and spoke rapidly (Nass and Brave, 2005).

When participants clicked on a button next to each of the items, they heard either an extroverted or introverted description of the item via either an introverted or extroverted synthetic voice. For all items, one-fourth of the participants heard extroverted descriptions spoken by an extroverted voice, one-fourth heard extroverted descriptions spoken by an introverted voice, one-fourth heard introverted descriptions spoken by an introverted voice, and one-fourth heard introverted descriptions spoken by an extroverted voice. Equal numbers of introverted and extroverted participants were randomly assigned to each of these four conditions.

After listening to descriptions of all nine auction items, participants filled out a Web-based questionnaire. Based on participants' responses to the questionnaire, there were clear and powerful effects for consistency. When the voice personality and content personality were consistent, people liked the voice itself more and liked the content more. People also liked the writer more and found the writer to be more credible when the interface was consistent. Consistency of personality thus proved to be critical in embodied interfaces, much as it is in day-to-day human interactions (Nass and Brave, 2005; Nass and Lee, 2001).

Designing for Personality Consistency

Whenever possible, the best way to ensure consistency is to *start* with the personality of the interface and then have all of the content *emerge* from that personality. Ideally, an entire "backstory" is created in which the designers describe the entire life story of the persona (Cooper and Saffo, 1999) of the interface, providing richness and nuance that can emerge over the course of the interaction. Even if the interface is a portal to content with a diverse set of personality markers, the interaction that provides access to the content must have a consistent personality (Moon, 1998).

In addition to consistency across personality cues, such as voice, content, and appearance, consistency of personality and context is also important. For example, many occupations have stereotypical personalities associated with them. An embodied interface for selling adventure gear should employ a different personality than an interface for online banking. The casting of the BMW 5-Series' voice interface presents an informative example (Nass and Brave, 2005). Car computers have advanced well beyond the point where they simply (and annoyingly) say, "The door is ajar." In-car computers now can tell the driver when it's time to check the oil, which freeways currently have accidents or slow traffic, how many miles per hours the car is going over the speed limit, and even whether or not there is a pedestrian up ahead.

BMW was faced with the problem of how to cast a voice that would give a BMW 5-Series driver this kind of information (Nass and Brave, 2005). They considered several roles for the voice to play. The first was to let it be the voice of the car itself, like KITT from the TV show *Knight Rider*. That idea was rejected because when there is an intimate link between the car and the voice, the qualities of the car can lead to a "halo effect" (Thorndike, 1920) that extends to the quality of the voice: Because current car voice interfaces are not very intelligent, a car voice might undermine the perception of "engineering excellence" that is so intimately tied to the BMW brand. Other ideas were to use the personality characteristics of a stereotypical German engineer (loud, dominant, and slightly unfriendly, with a slightly German accent), the voice of a stereotypical pilot (very dominant, neutral on friendliness), or a stereotypical chauffeur (very submissive, neutral on friendliness, with a slightly British accent). The engineer personality was not chosen because drivers might feel intimidated by the expectations of the dominant voice. The pilot's and chauffeur's personalities were not chosen because BMW 5-Series drivers typically want to feel in control of the machine. Finally, the designers agreed upon using the personality of a stereotypical co-pilot (male, slightly dominant, somewhat friendly), who is highly competent but fully understands that the driver is in charge; however, the co-pilot must jump in whenever the pilot is unable to perform or is making a serious error. This is exactly the image that BMW wants to convey about its cars. Similar considerations could be made when deciding upon how to cast the personality of a virtual receptionist, a complaint or service department, or a Web site for potential million-dollar investors.

GENDER: IT'S A BOY! NO, IT'S A GIRL! WHAT GENDER SHOULD THE COMPUTER BE?

Much like personality, gender serves as a fundamental means by which people categorize other social beings (Beall and Sternberg, 1993). Gender provides critical information with respect to who to mate with, who to compete with, and how to treat other people. In many ways, it seems nonsensical to think of computers as having gender, but people do often assign gender to objects (Kirkam, 1996).

A number of studies have shown that users categorize voices coming from a computer (whether recorded or synthetic) as having gender (Lee et al., 2000; Nass et al., 1997). Furthermore, users not only make this assessment, but they use the assignment of gender to guide their attitudes and behaviors (Lee et al., 2000; Morishima et al., 2002; Nass et al., 1997).

Designers of embodied interfaces must be aware of consistency issues raised by gender perception in the various aspects of the interface, ranging from the gender roles socially assigned to certain content areas and tasks to gender perceived in the authorship of texts to gender perceived in the voices and faces of animated characters. Of particular concern is the inadvertent use of gender stereotypes to influence a user's perception of the computer interface. Gender assignments are often used to deduce norms for social behavior (Costrich et al., 1975), norms for explanations of successful performance on gender-stereotyped tasks (Deaux and Emsweiler, 1974), selecting occupations (Heilman, 1979), and even for which toys children choose (Martin and Ruble, 2004).

People use stereotypes as heuristics for evaluating and predicting behavior of members of each (socially constructed) gender group, ethnic group, etc. (Fiske and Taylor, 1991). Humans have very limited processing capabilities (Newell and Simon, 1972), so to treat each individual as an entirely novel encounter would be very mentally costly without filters to categorize people into neat categories of generally observed characteristics and behaviors.

Studies on Gender Stereotypes

Our lab's first study on perceived computer gender was done in the context of a tutoring system of gender-stereotyped content areas, including love and relationships (stereotypically female), mass media (stereotypically gender neutral), and computers (stereotypically male) (Nass et al., 1997). For half of the participants, the tutor computer spoke using a recorded female voice and for the other half of participants the tutor computer spoke using a recorded male voice. Identical information was presented by both voices. Conforming to gender stereotypes, participants found that the "female" tutor computer was perceived as being a better teacher of love and relationships than the "male" computer, while the male-voiced computer was seen as a better teacher of technical subjects (Nass et al., 1997).

Although computers may not actually have any intrinsic gender, they are nonetheless treated as though they have gender by the users who interact with them. To find out whether human recorded voices were causing the social responses to these computers, a follow-up study was done in the domain of e-commerce, using synthetic voices that were clearly mechanical rather than human (Morishima et al., 2002).

Because of eBay's wide-ranging scope of products and its wide-ranging population of users, we chose to use an eBay-like interface to present stereotypically female products (e.g., an encyclopedia of sewing) and stereotypically male products (e.g., an encyclopedia of guns). Participants were asked to evaluate the item, the item description, and the synthetic voice that described the item. In line with predictions of the match-up hypothesis (Kamins, 1990) in marketing, participants were just as influenced by the gender of technology-based synthetic voices as they were by the gender of human spokespersons. Product descriptions were evaluated as more credible when the genders of the voice and product were matched. Also, voices with genders that matched the product genders were evaluated as more appropriate for the product than the gender-mismatched voices. The gender of the voices also affected perceptions of the products, and vice versa. Female products matched with female voices made the product seem more feminine and male products matched with male voices made the product seem more masculine. Conversely, female voices were perceived as less feminine when describing male products and male voices were perceived as less masculine when describing female products (Morishima et al., 2002).

A striking aspect of these studies is that all of the users in the studies vehemently denied that they thought of the computers as having a gender. An even more striking aspect is that all of the participants said that even if they did attribute gender to the computers, it wouldn't matter: after all, they said, they don't believe or follow any stereotypes! (Nass and Brave, 2005)

Designing for Gender Stereotypes

Gender stereotyping is so powerful in shaping the human experience that it plays out not only in the world of humans interacting with humans, but also in the world of humans interacting with computers. Sometimes gender matching across various aspects of computers interfaces and content may make one's interface seem more credible and likeable in many situations, but the larger societal implications of perpetuating gender stereotypes must be balanced against mindless gender-matching of all media and content (Friedman, 1999; Friedman et al., 2005). Media portrayals of gender stereotypes, such as those found in television programming, can and do create and sustain gender stereotypes (Gerbner et al., 1986). Computer media portrayals of gender stereotypes are perhaps even more problematic and societally risky. First of all, there is some suggestion that people reduce their time spent in interpersonal interactions as computer and Web use increases (Nie and Hillygus, 2002). This means that users will be less exposed to stereotype-challenging behavior (since actual people are more likely to challenge stereotypes than computer characters). Second, the social interactivity of computing might heighten the likelihood of people drawing conclusions about social life from computers, as compared to the more passive medium of television; this effect can be compounded because computer use also draws time away from television use (Nie and Hillygus, 2002). Finally, the diversity of computer software and the Web as compared to television or even real life might mean that computer-based stereotypes may play out over a wider range of activities than other social activities, further instantiating the stereotypes.

Technology provides a wonderful opportunity to overthrow gender stereotypes in the minds of users. While it might be difficult to rapidly increase the number of female employees in stereotypically male positions in various careers (or vice versa), it is very easy to give female *voices* to all of the content delivery software for top-down business directives, information technology support, or other stereotypically male positions by simply hiring voice talents of the desired gender or manipulating the parameters of the synthetic voice. Similarly, one could use a male voice reading off routine instructions for a new tutorial on timecard-stamping software to create a balancing force against gender stereotypes.

Just as people bring gender expectations *to* technology, they can draw gender expectations *from* technology (Nass and Brave, 2005). By "staffing" business software with gendered voices that counter stereotypes, people are likely to draw the conclusion that people of both genders "belong" in all jobs and in all points in the organizational hierarchy (Gerbner et al., 1986). The key point is that designers of computer interfaces must make value sensitive design decisions (Friedman, 1999) that recognize that the stakeholders in design decisions (Friedman, 1999) are not simply the owners of the company that produces the software but people in the larger society as well.

ETHNICITY: MORE THAN JUST SKIN DEEP

When two strangers meet, the question "Where are you from?" is asked very early in the conversation (Nass and Brave, 2005). There are two socially motivated reasons for asking this question. First, the answer provides an opportunity to find "common ground" (Clark, 1996, Chapter 4; Stalnaker, 1978), that is, shared knowledge and beliefs (Clark, 1996). Places are particularly fruitful bases for shared knowledge, because even if one of the people speaking has never been to the place, there is often a characteristic of the location (e.g., urban vs. rural, a famous landmark, a friend who lived there, etc.) that provides a starting point for shared understanding.

A second reason for inquiring about a person's geographic origins is that place of origin can be just as powerful as gender and personality in allowing a person to predict his or her conversational partners' attitudes and behaviors. Throughout most of human history, people's place of birth predicted their culture, language, and familial ties, because cultures appeared within regions and there was limited mobility from one region (and hence culture) to another (Anderson et al., 2002; Jackson, 1985). Thus, when someone describes himself or herself as an "Easterner," a "Texan," or a "Laplander," his or her interaction partner obtains much more than simply knowledge about natal locale. Like gender and personality, place of origin is one of the most critical traits defining a person (Hamers and Blanc, 2000; Lippi-Green, 1997). Indeed, place of origin can be a greater predictor of people's attitudes and behaviors than gender or personality, because although each person interacts with many others who do not match his or her gender or personality, the vast majority of people one encounters during one's formative years come from the same place and culture that the developing child does (Scherer and Giles, 1979).

In embodied interfaces, voice accent and word choice are some of the most powerful indicators of place of origin and culture. Because languages do not have an "official pronunciation," every speaker (human and non-human alike) has an accent (Lippi-Green, 1997; Pinker, 1994; Trudgill, 2000). "Accent-neutralization" (Cook, 2000), an active topic of discussion as telephone-based call centers move to countries with lower wages and different accents, is a misnomer: Although speakers can change their speech to reflect the most common para-linguistic cues in a particular locale, this simply involves replacing one accent with another rather than eliminating an accent (Nass and Brave, 2005, Chapter 6).

Clearly, consistency of accent over time is critical both for people and machines. If an interaction partner's voice changed, for example, from a thick Southern accent to an Australian accent over the course of a conversation, the speaker would surely be perceived as odd and untrustworthy. However, inconsistencies in place of origin and culture can crop up in another less obvious form as well, because there is another socially relevant meaning to the term "place of origin": where one's ancestors came from (Nass and Brave, 2005). This is usually referred to as "race," and is generally indicated by physical appearance (Gallagher, 1999).

Throughout most of human history, migration was very limited, so language and race were consistent: People who looked like a given race almost always belonged to the culture associated with people of that race, and vice versa (Nass and Brave, 2005). Indeed, culture and race were so inextricably linked that the term "ethnicity" has come to be used interchangeably for both (Britannica Editors, 2002). However, these two definitions of place of origin are not *intrinsically* related. Designers of embodied interfaces might initially rejoice in this fact, thinking it provides the perfect opportunity to create an interface that appeals to two user populations simultaneously. For example, create an onscreen agent whose face suggests Asian descent, but whose voice exhibits a heavy southern accent: This approach should please both groups! However, it is possible that even such reasonable "inconsistencies" would prove to be disorienting for users and lead to the same types of negative effects that we have seen for inconsistencies in personality and gender.

Consistency of Ethnicity as Exhibited in Voice and Face

To test the effects of ethnicity consistency on users, an experiment with an online e-commerce site was conducted (Nass and Brave, 2005, Chapter 6). A total of ninety-six male college students participated in the experiment. The participants were either Caucasian Americans (forty-eight participants) or first-generation Koreans (forty-eight participants). Participants were directed to an e-commerce Web site, where they listened to descriptions of four different products: a backpack, a bicycle, an inflatable couch, and a desk lamp.

Half of the Korean participants and half of the Caucasian American participants heard product descriptions read by a voice with a Korean accent that occasionally used distinctly Korean phrases (e.g., "*Anyonghaseyo*," which is Korean for "hello"). The other half of the participants heard descriptions read by a voice with an Australian accent that occasionally used phrases associated with Australians (e.g., "G'day, mate").[1] For a given participant, each description was read by the same voice and was accompanied by a full-length photograph of the same product spokesperson. The spokesperson had a different pose when describing each of the four items to give a sense of liveliness.

To hear the description of an item, participants clicked on the speaker's photograph. Half of the participants who heard the Korean-accented voice were shown a photograph of a racially Korean male; the other half were shown a photograph of a racially Caucasian Australian male to accompany the voice. Similarly, half of the participants who heard the Australian-accented voice were shown a photograph of a racially Caucasian Australian male and half were shown a photograph of a Korean male. Thus, the accent and race were mixed. Half of the participants in each condition were culturally and racially Korean; the other half were culturally and racially Caucasian Americans.

After hearing each product description, participants were asked to respond to a questionnaire that asked about the product's likability and the description's credibility. After listening to the descriptions of all four products, participants were also asked to rate the agent's overall quality. Although there was no logical linkage between the para-linguistic cues of the voice and the race of the agent, participants were clearly disturbed when the agent did not "look the way it sounded." The photographic agents that had "consistent" voices and faces were perceived to be much better than those that were inconsistent, regardless of the ethnicity of the user. Participants also found the products to be better and the product descriptions to be more credible when the two "places of origin" were consistent.

Designing Ethnicity in Interfaces

Toward the end of 2004, we made an attempt to listen to as many different voice interfaces in the United States as we could. We called airline and train reservation systems, technical help centers, in-car navigation systems, etc. While the voices and content certainly reflected different personalities and included both genders, there was a striking similarity: Every single interface sounded like it was spoken by a Caucasian from the upper Midwest, the accent that is considered to be "neutral" in the United States (MacNeil and Cran, 2004). This was remarkable, given that in the next few years, "whites" will be a minority of the country, and the upper Midwest is not one of the most populous regions of the country.

We have already dismissed the argument that Caucasians (as distinct from ethnicities that are associated with other accents) speak without an "accent"; everyone has an accent. The argument that the "white" accent is standard and hence understandable by the whole population was used in the early years of television to exclude minorities; obviously, this argument cannot hold sway. It is undoubtedly alienating for a large fraction of the population *never* to encounter someone who sounds like himself or herself when they use a voice interface.

The problem is made even more apparent in voice interfaces than in traditional media because non-Caucasian accents tend to be less understood by voice recognition systems. This provides an additional source of alienation and a feeling that these interfaces are "not for us." As with gender, it is important that interfaces capture the range of accents for both production and recognition in order to reduce stereotypes and to be more accommodating to increasingly diverse populations.

EMOTION: "COMPUTER EMOTION" IS NOT AN OXYMORON

Gender, personality, and ethnicity are examples of social characteristics known as traits: relatively permanent intrinsic characteristics. This chapter has demonstrated the critical importance of consistency when it comes to traits. Users expect embodied interfaces to look, sound, and act in a way that is consistent with the interfaces' assigned social categories. Traits serve as important baseline for understanding and predicting the behavior of others (Fiske and Taylor, 1991).

People, however, are also affected by their environment. While traits give us a broad sense of what a person will think and do, predicting a person's behavior at any given moment in time also requires attention to *state*, that is, the particular feelings, knowledge, and physical situation of the person at a particular point in time. While extroverts are generally talkative, they might be as silent as introverts in a library, or even quieter when they bump into their secret crush. The most "feminine" female will exhibit a range of masculine characteristics when protecting a child. In a group, people often submerge their identity as they blend in with and mimic the people around them (Simmel, 1985). People also vary their linguistic styles based on the communities of practice (Wenger, 1998) with which they are engaged (Eckert, 2000). While traits provide the general trajectory of an individual's life, every specific attitude, behavior, and cognition also can be influenced by momentary states.

Of all the types of states that predict how a person will behave, the most powerful is *emotion* (Brave and Nass, 2002). Rich emotions are a fundamental component of being human (Brave and Nass, 2002). Throughout any given day, affective states—whether short-lived emotions or longer-term moods—color almost everything people do and experience, from sending an e-mail to driving down the highway. Emotion is not limited to the occasional outburst of fury when being insulted, excitement when winning the lottery, or frustration when trapped in a traffic jam. It is now understood that a wide range of emotions plays a critical role in *every* goal-directed activity (Brave and Nass, 2002), from asking for directions to asking someone on a date, from hurriedly eating a sandwich at one's desk to dining at a five-star restaurant, and from watching the Super Bowl to playing solitaire. Indeed, many psychologists now argue that it is impossible for a person to have a thought or perform an action without engaging, at least unconsciously, his or her emotional systems (Picard, 1997; Picard, 1997; Zajonc, 1984). Consistency is crucial when it comes to emotion. For example, when mothers are inconsistent with their verbal and vocal emotional cues, their children are more likely to grow up with behavioral and emotional problems (Bugental et al., 1971; Gong, 2000). Within groups of such children, boys whose mothers used more inconsistent communication were found to be more aggressive in school than those with mothers who used less inconsistent communication (Bugental et al., 1971; Gong, 2000). Being able to detect a person's emotional state is extremely useful for choosing if, when, and how to approach the person in order to have a successful social interaction. Many of us have felt the frustration of being sent "mixed signals." This frustration stems from being unable to disambiguate how to interact with the person next time due to inconsistencies between his or her words and his or her paralinguistic cues, which lead to dislike of the speaker (Argyle et al., 1971; Gong, 2000). In human-human communication, such inconsistencies are often used as indications of insincerity, instability (Argyle et al., 1971; Gong, 2000), or deception (Gong, 2000; Mehrabian, 1971). If it is true that people will interact with computers in the same way that they interact with people, it is likely that such negative perceptions of voices are not desirable for voice interfaces. To find out what happens when voice interfaces present emotionally inconsistent paralinguistic and linguistic cues, a telephone-based experiment was conducted.

Emotional Consistency of Voice Interfaces

This study (Nass et al., 2001) compared emotionally consistent para-linguistic cues and content with emotionally inconsistent ones; participants all heard the exact same male synthetic voice and same content. Participants called in to a phone system that read them three news stories about clearly happy or sad events (e.g., a new cure for cancer or dead gray whales washing ashore on the San Francisco coast, respectively). Based on reports from a follow-up questionnaire, the participants found that happy stories sounded happier when read by a happy voice, sad stories sounded sadder when read by a sad voice. Consistent with the earlier results, participants liked the stories more when they were told by emotionally consistent voices than by voices that failed to match the emotion of the story, even when the voices were clearly synthetic and obviously did not reflect "true" emotion.

It appears that humans are so readily wired for picking up emotional information from speech, that people perceive emotions even in computer-generated speech (Nass and Brave, 2005). To hear emotion, one usually uses a person's paralinguistic cues of pitch range, rhythm, and amplitude or duration changes (Ball and Breese, 2000; Scherer, 1981; Scherer, 1986; Scherer, 1989). People seem to integrate those cues with the spoken content when understanding messages, even when they are coming from virtual voices.

Implementing Emotionally Consistent Voices

When computer voices are recorded from human actors, it is relatively easy for the actors to infer emotional meaning from the script so they do not have the problems that computer-generated speech does in maintaining consistency of emotional paralinguistic cues with emotional content. Given that humans can infer emotion so easily from written text, it seems as if computers would be smart enough to do the same, and could crank out emotionally consistent readings even more efficiently than human actors, but the problem of deducing emotion is a much more complex one than it seems (Picard and Cosier, 1997).

Casting Voice Emotions Within Constraints

Given the difficulty of properly casting appropriate emotional paralinguistic cues for each utterance in a computer interface, it is safest to cast a slightly happy voice (Gong and Nass, 2003) because humans have a "hedonic preference," which means that they tend to experience, express, and perceive positive emotions rather than negative ones. People who show more positive emotions are liked more (Frijda, 1988; Myers and Diener, 1995), perceived as more attractive, and perceived as appealing to work with (Berridge, 1999). Happy emotions are not always the best choice though. Humans pay more attention to and remember more about times of anger and sadness than times of happiness (Reeves and Nass, 1996). Submissive emotions such as fear and sadness are more likely to increase trust since the expression of such emotions are seen as emotional disclosure (Friedman et al., 1988), opening up to the listener, which often causes him or her to reciprocate with disclosure (Moon, 2000). Depending upon the goals of the computer interface, one type of emotional voice setting could be sufficient. Those designers who are creating both content and voice casting at the same time may generate emotional voices that match the emotion of the content provided by the computer interface (Nass and Brave, 2005).

Designing Emotions as Dimensions: Manipulating Voice Settings to Create Feelings

Another way to conceive of emotions is in terms of two dimensions: valence (positive/negative) and arousal (excited/calm). All of the basic emotions can be laid out along these dimensions (Lang, 1995). For example, happiness would be on the highly positive side of valence and slightly higher than middle level on arousal. Using these dimensions makes setting voice emotion cues a relatively simple task. For example, the more on the excited end of the arousal dimension, the higher the voice's pitch should be and the wider its pitch range; also the voice should have wider volume range and faster word speed (Nass and Brave, 2005). The more positive the valence dimension, the higher the pitch and wider the pitch range should be; also the voice should have greater intensity and more upward than downward inflections. Such guidelines provide a concrete basis upon which to tweak synthetic voice settings to make voices more emotionally consistent with the words they are speaking.

ONTOLOGY: IS IT (PRESENTED AS) A MAN OR A MACHINE?

Given the findings described in this chapter so far, the general conclusion could be that, from a social perspective, embodied interfaces are treated as humans. Users respond to computer-based voices and faces as if they exhibit very human characteristics such as personality, gender, ethnicity, and emotion. Users further expect that the computer voice will be socially consistent on all of these dimensions, much as they expect consistency from other humans. These findings appear regardless of whether the embodied interface seems almost human (e.g., employs an actual human voice) or seems distinctly non-human (e.g., employs an unambiguously synthetic voice).

Humans and machines are not equivalent, however, and it seems unlikely that users would completely overlook this fact, particularly when obvious indications of machinehood are present. When machines sound and look exactly like humans, it would be impossible for users to treat them any other way (as the user would be unaware of whether they were interacting with a human or a machine). However when machines give clear indications that they are machines, it seems unlikely that people would treat them as equivalent to humans (one need only look at popular science fiction to see that machines are often ascribed second-class citizenship, e.g., Asimov, 1991). From a social perspective, this could be seen as humans and machines occupying distinct social classes, much as humans of different ethnicity may occupy distinct social classes.

If this is true, we should expect to see a preference for consistency within these social categories: Any object that reminds one of a machine should consistently sound, look, and behave like a machine, while any object that reminds one of a person should consistently sound, look, and behave like a person. To investigate this conjecture, an experiment was conducted (Nass and Brave, 2005).

Saying "I"

Self-reference—thinking and talking in terms of "I"—is arguably the most human of human actions (Descartes, 1999). Use of self-reference (i.e., the first person) therefore presented a perfect way to test whether consistency in humanness is important to users. An experiment with a telephone-based auction was conducted. Participants were first directed to a Web site. Upon registering, they were given a scenario in which they were about to graduate and move to another city, and must furnish their new apartments. This scenario was chosen because it was potentially relevant to all of the participants, regardless of their gender and personal interests. Participants were then given a phone number to call an auction system, where they would place bids on five items, one at a time.

Half the participants (randomly assigned) used a system that had a synthetic voice. The other half of the participants (randomly assigned) used the identical system, but with a recorded voice.

Half of the recorded speech participants and half of the synthetic speech participants were presented with a system that used the word "I"; the other half of the participants heard only impersonal speech. Specifically, for people in the "I" condition, there were four uses of "I"/"my" in the introduction and two uses of "I" in each of the five descriptions. To ensure that the sentences were grammatical and natural in both conditions, a few additional changes were made to the syntax. Despite these changes, the sentences—including the amount and type of information given—were essentially the same for all participants.

Here is the introduction and example description for the interface that says "I":

> *I* will begin today's auction shortly. *I* have five items for auction today. *I* will read the descriptions for the items one by one. Please bid at the end of each item's description. *My* records indicate that you have $1000 in your account.
>
> The first item *I* have for you today is a cozy twin-size pine-frame futon. The estimated retail price is around $180. It's a great piece of furniture for any room and very convenient when your friends come over. The cover is included. It is one of the top items *I* can offer to you today.

Here are the parallel sentences for the condition that did not use "I":

> Today's auction will begin shortly. There are five items for auction today. The descriptions for the items will be read one by one. Please bid at the end of each item's description. The records indicate that there is $1000 in your account.
>
> The first item today is a cozy twin-size pine-frame futon. The estimated retail price is around $180. It's a great piece of furniture for any room and very convenient when your friends come over. The cover is included. It is one of the top items offered today.

There were equal numbers of men and women in each combination of type of voice and use of "I" or not, to ensure that gender would not affect the results. To control for idiosyncrasies in the voices, two different recorded voices and two different synthetic voices were used; all voices were chosen to be similar with respect to gender, age, personality, and accent.

Users showed a strong preference for consistency of humanness. First, when they heard a recorded voice, participants were more relaxed by the use of "I" (they didn't have to worry about what was being communicated by the use of the passive voice), while synthetic speech participants were more relaxed with the interface that did not say "I" (the synthetic voice was not human enough): It's disturbing when one's language is not consistent with one's ontology.

The "mismatch" between the language of personhood and the voice of a machine, or vice versa, affected perceptions of the interface as well. Although the interface performed identically in all conditions, with seemingly 100 percent speech recognition (bids were recorded), the recorded voice system was perceived to be more useful when using "I," while the synthetic voice system seemed more useful when avoiding claims to humanity by avoiding "I." Similarly, the synthetic speech system that said "I" was judged less trustworthy than the same system without "I," demonstrating that the attempt to claim humanity was perceived as a suspicious artifice; there was no significant difference for recorded speech.

Is there money to be made by carefully matching voice and words? Yes. People who heard the recorded voice user interface bid more when they heard "I," while people who heard the synthetic voice interface bid more when they did not hear "I."

When Not to Use "I" with Recorded Speech

Although recorded speech clearly benefits voice user interfaces—even though there are nuances that must be taken into account (see Nass and Brave, 2005)—and people expect these systems to use the term "I," designers should not assume that using "I" is always optimal. For example, when formality is desirable, the avoidance of "I" is effective (Nass and Brave, 2005).

A second domain in which the avoidance of "I" may be useful is when the system wants to deflect blame from itself. Every child's instinct is to say "the lamp broke" rather than "I broke the lamp," and in the heat of the Watergate scandal, President Richard Nixon said "Mistakes were made" rather than "I made mistakes." Similarly, when a person requests information that may not be provided, the system might benefit from behaving like a stereotypical bureaucrat by saying "The rules do not permit that information to be given" rather than "I cannot give you that information because of the rules." This strategy can also be useful when the system has to deliver bad news, for example, "That item is not in stock" rather than "I don't have that item right now."

Passive voice can also be useful when a voice input system fails to understand the user (Nass and Brave, 2005). Thus, an (actual) airline system that only uses "I" when it does not understand the user is particularly poorly designed: The exceptional use of "I" draws attention to the personal aspect of the interface at precisely the time when users are most frustrated and annoyed.

In a related way, cultural differences dictate when one should use "I" or "we." In individualistic cultures, such as the United States and Germany, people are more persuaded when the speaker, including a computer agent, uses "I." Indeed, in the United States (and likely other individualistic cultures), individuals highlighting their own identity are evaluated more favorably than are the same individuals in aggregates or groups (Sears, 1983). However, in collectivist cultures, including most of Asia, it is much more effective to refer to "we" (Maldonado and Hayes-Roth, 2004; Miller et al., 2001).

A third domain in which "I" may be problematic is when the user must provide input via touch-tone (DTMF). There is a basic conversational principle that it is polite to respond in the same modality that the user uses. People return a phone call with a phone call, not e-mail; a letter with a letter, rather than a phone call; and a spoken yes/no question with words, rather than a nod of the head. When a voice interface says "I" and then proceeds to refuse to let the person reply by voice, this might be seen as controlling and unfair: "He/she gets to speak, but I only get to push buttons?!" The avoidance of "I" may reduce the social presence (Lee, 2004) of the system and thereby make it more acceptable to restrict the user to touch-tone responses.

The absence of "I" can be a powerful rhetorical technique when the system wants the user to respond to the system's statements as certainties. For example, a voice user interface that says, "I have four messages for you" or "I see that you are free between 12 and 2 PM," or "I think that you will like these four restaurants" may seem more uncertain than a system that says, "There are four messages," "You are free between 12 and 2 PM," or "You will like these four restaurants." Conversely, voice user interfaces that want full focus on themselves and their unique capabilities likely should use the term "I," as in "I have searched through thousands of songs to find these three for you" as opposed to "Thousands of songs have been searched; here are three for you" (Nass and Brave, 2005).

Synthetic-speech interfaces, on the other hand, should *never* use "I." As the experiment showed, there was no case in which the use of "I" made the synthetic-speech interface seem better, and in many cases, the benefits of avoiding "I" were clearly significant.

CONCLUSION

When William James (James, 1890) marveled at the "blooming, buzzing confusion" of life, he was trying to understand how babies could eventually make sense of and integrate the constantly changing stimuli impinging upon their senses. Eventually, he noted, babies figure out that the physical world is not all that complicated a place. Drop anything and it falls to the ground. Even if it rolls under a table, it still exists. Even the imponderable is remarkably simple: Every snowflake may be different, but for everyone besides meteorologists, they are all the same. Though water spins down the drain in opposite directions in the northern and southern hemispheres, the physical world works in much the same way throughout the Earth. For all the seeming complexity of the universe, then, people do not have to be Newtons or Einsteins to cope with and comprehend the way the world works: managing the physical world is relatively simple and straightforward.

Although children acquire a virtually adult-like understanding of the physical world by the age of eight or so (Piaget, 1960; Piaget and Inhelder, 2000), the social world remains extraordinarily complex throughout adulthood. There are no laws of human behavior that are as reliable as any physical law. The differences between each person, unlike the differences between snowflakes, are highly consequential. In contrast to the virtual uniformity of the physical world, every new location seems to present multiple new cultures with mysterious and unpredictable attitudes, norms, and behaviors.

The world of interfaces may parallel these complexities. Although the world of GUIs, like the physical world, might seem initially complex, in a relatively short time users understand that there is not all that much going on in graphical user interfaces. The limitations of GUIs, coupled with designers' almost religious belief in the virtues of consistency across applications and domains, dramatically enhance the reliability of the users' conclusions. GUIs, like the physical world, are accessible to everyone.

As interfaces began including social representations such as voices, designers became responsible for an extraordinarily rich and complex world that they and their users can barely manage in daily life. Although the rules of GUIs can be neatly encapsulated, the rules of social life are too complex and rich to be captured—that is one reason why advice columnists are so popular! Unfortunately, while designers can justifiably plead ignorance of the complexities of the social world, users will nonetheless bring to bear the full range of social rules and expectations with which they guide their interactions with other people.

Even the seemingly simple problem of ensuring that the various aspects of an interface are socially consistent turned out to be extremely subtle and nuanced. If one then wishes to take the small step of thinking about consistency between the characteristics of the interface and the user as well, the situation becomes even more complex. For example, how does a designer select the personality of the voice when the user is extroverted and the language of the Web site is introverted? (Nass and Brave, 2005; Nass and Lee, 2001) Now include politeness (Nass, 2004; Nass et al., 1999), flattery (Fogg and Nass, 1997), specialization (Nass et al., 1996), among thousands of other social domains, and the designer begs for mercy! Will designers feel overwhelmed and simply adopt "standards," no matter how far removed they are from the realities of social life? Will they opt for a set of consistent rules, no matter how foolish (Emerson, 1990)?

We need not be pessimistic. Even the most suave person does not know all of the social rules of interaction, and other people, situational constraints, cognitive distractions, and a host of other factors lead to inconsistency that is not crippling in social interaction. Nonetheless, society does not crumble. Similarly, an interface need not be Miss Manners (Martin, 1998), Dale Carnegie (Carnegie, 1990), or Don Juan (Byron, 1988) to have success with users. While a number of academic disciplines have endeavored to precisely list every social rule for every social characteristic and culture, a complete list is likely unachievable and certainly unnecessary. In a sense, all people are experts on social interactions. Designers simply have to ask "What would a person do?" and be guided by the answer. Even if not perfect, this strategy will create interfaces that are more human, more consistent, and more humane.

NOTE

1. Because U.S. accents are not associated with particular races, it is not unusual to hear someone who is Korean in appearance speak with an American accent. Ideally, this study would have been done with Australian participants. As a compromise, we view Australian culture as closer to U.S. culture than to Korean culture and interpret the study accordingly.

REFERENCES

Abelson, R.P.; Aronson, E.; McGuire, W.J.; Newcomb, T.M.; Rosenberg, M.J.; and Tannenbaum, P.H. (eds.) *Theories of Cognitive Consistency: A Sourcebook.* Chicago: Rand McNally, 1968.
Anderson, K.; Domosh, M.; Thrift, N.; and Pile, S. (eds.) *Handbook of Cultural Geography [unabridged].* Thousand Oaks, CA: Sage Publications, 2002.
Argyle, M.; Alkema, F.; and Gilmour, R. The communication of friendly and hostile attitudes by verbal and non-verbal signals. *European Journal of Social Psychology*, 1 (1971), 385–402.
Asimov, I. *I, Robot.* New York: Bantam, 1991.
Ball, G., and Breese, J. Emotion and personality in conversational agents. In J. Cassel, J. Sullivan, S. Prevost, and E. Churchill (eds.), *Embodied Conversational Agents.* Cambridge, MA: MIT Press, 2000, pp. 189–219.
Beall, A.E., and Sternberg, R.J. *The Psychology of Gender.* New York: Guilford Press, 1993.
Beniger, J.R. *The Control Revolution.* Cambridge, MA: Harvard University Press, 1986.
Berridge, K.C. Pleasure, pain, desire, and dread: hidden core processes of emotion. In D. Kahneman, E. Diener, and N. Schwarz (eds.), *Well-Being: The Foundations of Hedonic Psychology.* New York: Russell Sage Foundation, 1999, pp. 525–557.
Brave, S., and Nass, C. Emotion in human-computer interaction. In J. Jacko and A. Sears (eds.), *Handbook of Human-Computer Interaction.* New York: Lawrence Erlbaum Associates, 2002, pp. 251–271.
Britannica Editors. *Britannica Concise Encyclopedia.* Chicago: Encyclopaedia Britannica, Inc., 2002.
Bugental, D.E.; Love, L.R.; Kaswan, J.W.; and April, C. Verbal-nonverbal conflict in parental messages to normal and disturbed children. *Journal of Abnormal Psychology*, 77 (1971), 6–10.
Byron, G.G. *Don Juan.* New York: Penguin Books, 1988.
Cantor, N., and Mischel, W. Prototypes in person perception. *Advances in Experimental Social Psychology*, 12 (1979), 3–52.
Cantor, N., and Mischel, W. Prototypicality and personality: effects on free recall and personality impressions. *Journal of Research in Personality*, 13 (1979), 187–205.
Carnegie, D. *How to Win Friends and Influence People.* New York: Pocket Books, 1990.
Cassell, J. Nudge nudge wink wink: elements of face-to-face conversation for embodied conversational agents. In J. Cassells, J. Sullivan, S. Prevost, and E. Churchill (eds.), *Embodied Conversational Agents.* Cambridge, MA: MIT Press, 2002, pp. 1–27.
Cassell, J., and Stone, M. Living hand to mouth: theories of speech and gesture in interactive systems. In *Proceedings of the AAAI Fall Symposium: Psychological Models of Communication in Collaborative Systems*, Cape Cod, MA: 1999, pp. 34–42.
Cassell, J.; Sullivan, J.; Prevost, S.; and Churchill, E. (eds.) *Embodied Conversational Agents.* Cambridge, MA: MIT Press, 2000.
Clark, H.H. *Using Language.* New York: Cambridge University Press, 1996.
Cohen, M.H.; Giangola, J.P.; and Balogh, J. *Voice User Interface Design.* Boston, MA: Addison-Wesley Publishing, 2004.

Cook, A. *American Accent Training.* Hauppauge, NY: Barron's Educational Series, 2000.

Cooper, A., and Saffo, P. *The Inmates Are Running the Asylum: Why High Tech Products Drive Us Crazy and How to Restore the Sanity.* New York: Sams, 1999.

Costrich, N.; Feinstein, J.; Kidder, L.; Maracek, J.; and Pascale, L. When stereotypes hurt: three studies of penalties in sex-role reversals. *Journal of Experimental Social Psychology*, 11 (1975), 520–530.

Deaux, K., and Emsweiler, T. Explanations of successful performance on sex-linked tasks: what is skill for the male is luck for the female. *Journal of Personality and Social Psychology*, 29 (1974), 80–85.

Descartes, R. *Meditations and Other Metaphysical Writings.* New York: Penguin, 1999.

Eckert, P. *Linguistic Variation as Social Practice.* Oxford: Blackwell, 2000.

Emerson, R.W. *Essays: First and Second Series.* New York: Vintage, 1990.

Fiske, S.T., and Taylor, S.E. *Social Cognition.* New York: McGraw-Hill, Inc, 1991.

Fogg, B.J., and Nass, C. Silicon sycophants: the effects of computers that flatter. *International Journal of Human-Computer Studies,* 46, 5 (1997), 551–561.

Friedman, B. (ed.) *Human Values and the Design of Computer Technology.* New York: Cambridge University Press/CSLI, 1999.

Friedman, H.S.; Riggio, R.E.; and Casella, D.F. Nonverbal skill, personal charisma, and initial attraction. *Personality and Social Psychology Bulletin*, 14 (1988), 203–211.

Frijda, N.H. The laws of emotion. *American Psychologist*, 43 (1988), 349–358.

Gallagher, C.A. (ed.) *Rethinking the Color Line: Readings in Race and Ethnicity.* New York: McGraw-Hill, 1999.

Gerbner, G.; Gross, L.; Morgan, M.; and Signorielli, N. Living with television: The dynamics of the cultivation process. In J. Bryant and D. Zillmann (eds.), *Perspectives on Media Effects.* Hillsdale, NJ: Lawrence Erlbaum Associates, Inc., 1986, pp. 17–40.

Gong, L. *The Psychology of Consistency in Human-Computer Interaction.* PhD dissertation, Communication, Stanford University, Stanford, CA, 2000.

Gong, L., and Nass, C. "Emotional Expressions on Computer Interfaces: Testing the Hedonic Preference Principle." Stanford University, 2003.

Hamers, J.F., and Blanc, M.H.A. *Bilinguality and Bilingualism.* New York: Cambridge University Press, 2000.

Heilman, M.E. High school students' occupational interest as a function of projected sex ratios in male-dominated occupations. *Journal of Applied Psychology*, 64 (1979), 275–279.

Isbister, K., and Doyle, P. Design and evaluation of embodied conversational agents: a proposed taxonomy. In *Proceedings of the AAMAS '02 Workshop on Embodied Conversational Agents.* Bologna, Italy, 2002.

Isbister, K., and Nass, C. Consistency of personality in interactive characters: verbal cues, non-verbal cues, and user characteristics. *International Journal of Human-Computer Interaction*, 53, 1 (2000), 251–267.

Jackson, W.A.D. *The Shaping of our World: A Human and Cultural Geography.* Hoboken, NJ: John Wiley & Sons, 1985.

James, W. *The Principles of Psychology.* New York: Holt, 1890.

Kamins, M.A. An investigation into the "match-up" hypothesis in celebrity advertising: when beauty may be only skin deep. *Journal of Advertising,* 19, 1 (1990), 4–13.

Kiesler, D.J. The 1982 interpersonal circle: a taxonomy for complementarity in human transactions. *Psychological Review,* 90 (1983), 185–214.

Kirkam, P. *The Gendered Object.* Manchester: Palgrave Macmillan, 1996.

Kotelly, B. *The Art and Business of Speech Recognition: Creating the Noble Voice.* Boston, MA: Addison-Wesley, 2003.

Lang, P.J. The emotion probe: studies of motivation and attention. *American Psychologist*, 50, 5 (1995), 372–385.

Lee, E.-J.; Nass, C.; and Brave, S. Can computer-generated speech have gender? An experimental test of gender stereotypes. In *Proceedings of the CHI 2000.* The Hague, The Netherlands: ACM Press, 2000, pp. 329–336.

Lee, K.M. Presence, explicated. *Communication Theory*, 14 (2004), 27–50.

Lippi-Green, R. *English with an Accent: Language, Ideology, and Discrimination in the United States.* London and New York: Routledge, 1997.

MacNeil, R., and Cran, W. *Do You Speak American?* New York: Nan A. Talese, 2004.

Maldonado, H., and Hayes-Roth, B. Toward cross-cultural believability in character design. In S. Payr and R. Trappl (eds.), *Agent Culture: Designing Virtual Characters for a Multi-cultural World.* Mahwah, NJ: Lawrence Erlbaum Associates, 2004, pp. 143–175.

Martin, C.L., and Ruble, D.N. Children's search for gender cues: cognitive perspectives on gender development. *Current Directions in Psychological Science*, 13, 2 (2004), 67–70.

Martin, J. *Miss Manners' Basic Training: The Right Thing to Say.* New York: Crown, 1998.

Massaro, D.W. *Perceiving Talking Faces: From Speech Perception to a Behavioral Principle.* Cambridge, MA: MIT Press, 1998.

Mehrabian, A. When are feelings communicated inconsistently? *Journal of Experimental Research in Personality,* 4, 3 (1971), 198–212.

Miller, P.; Kozu, J.; and Davis, A. Social influence, empathy, and prosocial behavior in cross-cultural perspective. In W. Wosinska, D. Barrett, R.B. Cialdini, and J. Reykowski (eds.), *The Practice of Social Influence in Multiple Cultures.* Mahwah, NJ: Lawrence Erlbaum Associates, 2001, pp. 63–77.

Moon, Y. Intimate exchanges: Using computers to elicit self-disclosure from consumers. *Journal of Consumer Research,* 26, 4 (2000), 323–339.

Moon, Y. *When the Computer Is the "Salesperson": Computer Responses to Computer "Personalities" in Interactive Marketing Situations.* Working paper #99–041. Cambridge, MA: Harvard Business School, 1998.

Morishima, Y.; Bennett, C.; Nass, C.; and Lee, K.M. *Effects of (Synthetic) Voice Gender, User Gender, and Product Gender on Credibility in E-Commerce.* Unpublished manuscript, Stanford, CA: Stanford University, 2002.

Morkes, J.; Kernal, H.K.; and Nass, C. Effects of humor in task-oriented human-computer interaction and computer-mediated communication: a direct test of SRCT theory. *Human-Computer Interaction,* 14, 4 (2000), 395–435.

Myers, D.G., and Diener, E. Who is happy? *Psychological Science,* 6 (1995), 10–19.

Nass, C. Etiquette equality: exhibitions and expectations of computer politeness. *Communications of the ACM,* 47, 4 (2004), 35–37.

Nass, C., and Brave, S.B. *Wired for Speech: How Voice Activates and Advances the Human-Computer Relationship.* Cambridge, MA: MIT Press, 2005.

Nass, C.; Foehr, U.; Brave, S.; and Somoza, M. The effects of emotion of voice in synthesized and recorded speech. In *Proceedings of the Emotional and Intelligent II: The Tangled Knot of Social Cognition.* North Falmouth, MA: AAAI Press, 2001, pp. 91–96.

Nass, C., and Lee, K.M. Does computer-synthesized speech manifest personality? Experimental tests of recognition, similarity-attraction, and consistency-attraction. *Journal of Experimental Psychology: Applied,* 7, 3 (2001), 171–181.

Nass, C., and Moon, Y. Machines and mindlessness: social responses to computers. *Journal of Social Issues,* 56, 1 (2000), 81–103.

Nass, C.; Moon, Y.; and Carney, P. Are people polite to computers? Responses to computer-based interviewing systems. *Journal of Applied Social Psychology,* 29, 5 (1999), 1093–1110.

Nass, C.; Moon, Y.; Fogg, B.J.; Reeves, B.; and Dryer, D.C. Can computer personalities be human personalities? *International Journal of Human-Computer Studies,* 43, 2 (1995), 223–239.

Nass, C.; Moon, Y.; and Green, N. Are computers gender-neutral? Gender-stereotypic responses to computers with voices. *Journal of Applied Social Psychology,* 27, 10 (1997), 864–876.

Nass, C.; Reeves, B.; and Leshner, G. Technology and roles: A tale of two TVs. *Journal of Communication,* 46, 2 (1996), 121–128.

Nass, C.; Robles, E.; and Wang, Q. "User as assessor" approach to embodied conversational agents (ECAs): the case of apparent attention in ECAs. In Z. Ruttkay and C. Pelechaud (eds.), *From Brows to Trust: Evaluating Embodied Conversational Agents.* Dordrecht, Netherlands: Kluwer, 2004, pp. 161–188.

Newell, A., and Simon, H.A. *Human Problem Solving.* Englewood Cliffs, NJ: Prentice-Hall, 1972.

Nie, N.H., and Hillygus, D.S. Where does Internet time come from?: a reconnaissance. *IT & Society,* 1, 2 (2002), 1–20.

Pervin, L.A., and John, O.P. *Personality: Theory and Research.* New York: John Wiley & Sons, 2001.

Piaget, J. *Child's Conception of the World.* London: Routledge, Kegan, and Paul, 1960.

Piaget, J., and Inhelder, B. *The Psychology of the Child.* New York: Basic Books, 2000.

Picard, R.W. *Affective Computing.* Cambridge, MA: MIT Press, 1997.

Picard, R.W. Does HAL cry digital tears? Emotions and computers. In D.G. Stork (ed.), *Hal's Legacy: 2001's Computer as Dream and Reality.* Cambridge, MA: MIT Press, 1997, pp. 279–303.

Picard, R.W., and Cosier, G. Affective intelligence—the missing link? *BT Technology Journal,* 15, 4 (1997), 150–161.

Pinker, S. *The Language Instinct.* New York: W. Morrow and Company, 1994.

Raskin, V. *Semantic Mechanisms of Humor.* Dordrecht, Holland: D. Reidel Publishing, 1985.

Reeves, B., and Nass, C. *The Media Equation: How People Treat Computers, Television, and New Media Like Real People and Places.* New York: Cambridge University Press, 1996.

Ruttkay, Z., and Pelachaud, C. (eds). *From Brows to Trust: Evaluating Embodied Conversational Agents.* Dordrecht: Kluwer, 2004.

Scherer, K.R. Speech and emotional states. In J.K. Darby (ed.), *Speech Evaluation in Psychiatry.* Grune and Stratton, 1981, pp. 189–220.

Scherer, K.R. Vocal affect expression: a review and a model for future research. *Psychological Bulletin,* 99 (1986), 143–165.

Scherer, K.R. Vocal measurement of emotion. In R. Plutchik and H. Kellerman (eds.), *Emotion: Theory, Research, and Experience.* San Diego: Academic Press, 1989, pp. 233–259.

Scherer, K.R., and Giles, H. *Social Markers in Speech.* New York: Cambridge University Press, 1979.

Sears, D.O. The person-positivity bias. *Journal of Personality and Social Psychology,* 44, 2 (1983), 233–250.

Sheldon, W. *Atlas of Men: A Guide for Somatyping the Adult Image of All Ages.* New York: Macmillan Publishing, 1970.

Simmel, G. *The Sociology of Georg Simmel.* New York: Free Press, 1985.

Stalnaker, R. Assertion. In P. Cole (ed.), *Syntax and Semantics 9: Pragmatics.* New York: Academic Press, 1978, pp. 315–332.

Stroop, J.R. Studies of interference in serial verbal reactions. *Journal of Experimental Psychology,* 18 (1935), 643–663.

Thorndike, E.L. A constant error on psychological rating. *Journal of Applied Psychology,* IV (1920), 25–29.

Trudgill, P. *Sociolinguistics: An Introduction to Language and Society.* London: Penguin Books, 2000.

Wenger, E. *Communities of Practice: Learning, Meaning, and Identity.* Cambridge: Cambridge University Press, 1998.

Zajonc, R.B. On the primacy of affect. *American Psychologist,* 39 (1984), 117–123.

PART VI

REFLECTIONS

CHAPTER 18

ON THE RELATIONSHIP BETWEEN HCI AND TECHNOLOGY ACCEPTANCE RESEARCH

FRED D. DAVIS

Abstract: *This paper examines the relationship between human-computer interaction (HCI) research and information systems research on technology acceptance. The technology acceptance model (TAM) is a motivational model of the user that traces the effects of system design characteristics (functionality and interface features), through perceived ease of use and perceived usefulness, on people's intentions to use the system. TAM was introduced in the 1980s to predict and explain user acceptance of new information systems based on usage intentions of potential users measured after a brief trial experience using a prototype of the new system. Influenced by early HCI research, TAM extends traditional user interface testing methodologies, which emphasize objective usability criteria (e.g., task performance times and error rates). Whereas HCI emphasizes how best to design the user interface to improve task performance when using a system, TAM focuses on how to increase people's willingness to use a system. Since both user acceptance and task performance are vital to a system's success, HCI and TAM offer complementary perspectives. The paper concludes by discussing the evolution and current status of TAM research.*

Keywords: *Technology Acceptance Model, Information-System Usefulness, Ease of Use, Usability, User Acceptance*

The purpose of this brief commentary is to introduce researchers to the stream of research on user acceptance of information technology and explain its relationship to HCI research. Specifically, I provide a personal reflection on the inspiration for and the development and evolution of the technology acceptance model (TAM).

INSPIRATION FOR TAM

The general problem originally motivating TAM was the high failure rate of information technology applications in workplace settings. In the late 1970s, I worked as a consultant developing and implementing hospital budget and planning systems. The growing power of computers for driving model-based and data-oriented decision support systems was evident. As an industrial engineering student, I was inspired by Little's (1970) influential *Management Science* paper, "Models and Managers: The Concept of a Decision Calculus," which laid out key concepts of decision support and specifically raised user acceptance as a key issue: "The big problem with management science models is that managers practically never use them" (p. B466).

Although the sophisticated management science, operations research, and computer science techniques I learned in class (optimization, simulation, queuing theory, data structures, algorithms, etc.) could be incorporated into decision support systems, a key limiting factor was the ability to get end users to actually accept and use the systems. In my hospital work, I discovered that systems based on surprisingly simple analytical techniques could provide considerable leverage for practical organizational decision making and, importantly, were more likely to be embraced by users than their more powerful but complex counterparts. These experiences motivated me to pursue doctoral studies in MIS at MIT's Sloan School of Management, beginning in 1980.

My main research interest concerned how to harness the rapidly expanding power of computer technology to solve real-world organizational problems by designing systems that would not only successfully exploit effective analytical techniques, but would also achieve user acceptance and implementation success. In the early 1980s, I interviewed numerous end users regarding their acceptance or rejection of various technologies including executive information systems, decision support systems, collaborative groupware, personal computing, office automation, and expert systems.

IDENTIFYING PERCEIVED USEFULNESS AND PERCEIVED EASE OF USE

One day I was returning by helicopter from New Hampshire to Massachusetts after completing a day of interviews. Watching a brilliant sunset, a simple but important insight occurred to me. Although interviewees expressed it in many different ways, the dominant reasons they cited for accepting or rejecting a new system at work strongly hinged on two issues: how *useful* and *easy to use* they found the system to be. We landed, the attendant opened the helicopter door, and my folder of interview notes spilled out. While the spinning rotor blade scattered yellow sheets all around, I was amused instead of concerned because the simple insight about usefulness and ease of use was now in my head. I recovered most of the interview notes, but never typed them up. Instead I turned my focus to the literature on MIS attitudes and implementation success to craft the idea into a dissertation topic.

Previous research on MIS implementation success factors did not align with the idea of usefulness and ease of use as key ingredients of successful systems. The current thinking in the early 1980s emphasized top management support and user involvement as the two most important factors driving implementation success (e.g., Markus, 1983; Swanson, 1974). Although numerous studies had been published on various MIS implementation attitudes (e.g., Bailey and Pearson, 1983; Ginzberg, 1981; Robey, 1979), these exhibited only mixed and inconclusive relationships with actual workplace usage of systems (for a review, see Swanson, 1982). These MIS attitude measures tapped into various feelings toward, liking of, and satisfaction with target systems, but did not specifically target perceptions of usefulness or ease of use.

DEVELOPMENT OF TAM

This situation provided the opportunity to make a specific contribution by investigating the role of perceived usefulness and ease of use as key determinants of MIS user acceptance, specifically by placing the ideas on a more solid conceptual foundation and developing valid measures for the constructs. Two key developments in the literature made such an opportunity promising. First, Ajzen and Fishbein's (1980) theory of reasoned action from social psychology drew key theoretical distinctions between beliefs, attitudes, subjective norms, and intentions as determinants of behavior, and provided explicit guidelines about how these constructs should be specifically framed and measured in order to explain a particular behavior. The theory of reasoned action was proving successful for a wide range of behaviors, and should be applicable to computer usage behavior. Second, there was a growing awareness in the business and management literature about the importance of using valid and reliable measures of constructs in order to successfully operationalize theoretical models (Churchill, 1979). Could the lack of precise theoretical definitions of attitudinal constructs, coupled with the unknown reliability and validity of measurement instruments, be to blame for the mixed and inconclusive track record of MIS attitudes as of the early 1980s?

Whether looked at from the perspective of an organization deciding to build or purchase a new software application or from the perspective of a vendor organization developing a commercial software product to meet customer needs, a key set of decision variables under the control of practitioners is the functionality and interface design characteristics of the target system. I reasoned that functionality characteristics should be chosen to maximize the perceived usefulness of a system to users, and interface characteristics should be chosen to maximize a system's perceived ease of use among users. TAM defined perceived usefulness as a potential user's expectation that using the system would improve his or her job performance, and perceived ease of use as the perception that using the system would be free of effort. TAM hypothesized that perceived usefulness and ease of use would play the role of causally linking design choices to users' intentions to use a new system. TAM further hypothesized that because usefulness was a superordinate goal for most people, it would therefore be more strongly linked to usage intentions than ease of use.

USER ACCEPTANCE TESTING: BEYOND USABILITY ENGINEERING

TAM was formulated not only to provide theoretical understanding of how system design characteristics influence user motivation through their effects on perceived usefulness, perceived ease of use, and intention to use, but also to provide the basis for a practical and effective "user acceptance testing" methodology for predicting the degree of user acceptance of a new system based on measures from users who had limited exposure to an early prototype of the system. For such user acceptance testing to be practical, I needed to establish valid and reliable measurement scales that were convenient to use in practice and were predictive of user adoption behavior in the workplace.

One particular study stimulated my thinking about the promise of early prototype testing. Gould, Conti, and Hovanyecz (1983), working at IBM, sought to understand the usability of "listening typewriters" based on speech recognition. Speech recognition technology was not yet sufficiently mature to provide a working prototype for user testing, but extensive research and development was under way, and speech recognition was expected to become commercially viable within five years. IBM needed to understand the usability impact of specific system design features such as vocabulary size, error rate, and continuous vs. isolated-word speech in order to guide research and development investments for speech recognition technology. Gould et al. (1983) simulated speech recognition by feeding users' dictation to expert typists hidden in the next room. Software was used to control the vocabulary size and error rate of concurrently transcribed text, giving users the illusion that the words appearing on the screen in front of them were being produced by speech recognition technology. Gould et al. (1983) measured the typical HCI metrics of task completion times and error rates, comparing the listening typewriter to alternative dictation technologies. Although their study included a single-item measure of satisfaction, the measure had unknown psychometric properties and unknown ability to predict actual user acceptance of speech recognition systems with particular features. My research on TAM sought to develop measures that could be used in such situations to provide a valid indication of the relative degree of user acceptance of each of the design alternatives. Just as Card, Moran, and Newell's (1980) keystroke-level model sought to allow designers to predict the objective usability of a system's user interface from the design of the keystrokes needed to perform tasks, TAM sought to predict user acceptance from measures captured based on low- to medium-fidelity mockups of a system created before writing a single line of code.

A major software vendor (henceforth, XYZ Corporation) agreed to support my dissertation research into developing and validating TAM. XYZ had withdrawn a recently introduced end-user software product from the marketplace after a dismal launch. Although the product had successfully passed the state-of-the-art usability testing process that XYZ applied to all of its end-user products, its poor reception in the marketplace caused them to realize that traditional usability testing, by itself, was not enough to assure user acceptance. In the aftermath of a seven-figure financial loss related to this failed product, XYZ needed new metrics for evaluating its products that could better gauge user acceptance. Moreover, they sought measures that could be applied early in a product's development life cycle in order to determine if a product concept was sufficiently promising to justify the full funding needed to bring it to market. XYZ had begun using videotape mockups of software product functionality as a prototyping and design tool.

EMPIRICAL VALIDATION OF TAM

XYZ Corporation wanted my research to answer two questions. First, can validated and reliable measures of perceived usefulness, perceived ease of use, and intention accurately predict workplace usage of new systems? And, second, can videotape mockups be relied upon as substitutes for working prototypes of end-user systems that have not yet been developed? In 1984, following psychometric measure development procedures, I used the definitions of perceived usefulness and ease of use to develop and pretest questionnaire items, and conducted a survey to validate the scales and perform item analyses. The survey confirmed that the perceived usefulness and ease of use constructs were not only conceptually distinct, but also empirically distinct (Davis, 1986). It also supported the idea that usefulness was a stronger determinant of usage than ease of use (Davis, 1986).

XYZ Corporation created brief video mockups for two existing business graphics software products, demonstrating their functionality and showing examples of how they can be used. These video mockups were designed to parallel the detail and realism of video mockups that XYZ was currently using to evaluate concepts for new products. I conducted an experiment on forty executive MBA students that measured their perceived usefulness, perceived ease of use, and usage intentions twice for each system, once after they had viewed the videotape mockup, and again, several weeks later, after they had had an hour-long hands-on demonstration of the software. As hypothesized, the video-based measures of usefulness accurately predicted the hands-on-based measure of usefulness, but the video-based ease of use measure did not predict its hands-on counterpart. Direct hands-on interaction with a product is generally needed to form an accurate perception of its ease of use, but non-interactive video is sufficient to form an accurate perception of its usefulness. Also supported was the hypothesis that usefulness would have a stronger influence on usage intentions than would ease of use. Because usefulness was stable between the video and hands-on conditions, and it had a stronger effect on intention, intention was also stable across the video and hands-on conditions (Davis, 1986). This experiment provided evidence that TAM could provide realistic evaluations of new software systems based on videotape mockups before a single line of program code is written. XYZ Corporation began to use TAM routinely in its new product development processes.

EVOLUTION OF TAM

My dissertation (Davis, 1986) was defended in December 1985. Two journal articles that introduced TAM to the literature were Davis (1989), which reported on the theoretical definition of perceived usefulness and ease of use and the development and validation of measurement scales, and Davis, Bagozzi, and Warshaw (1989), which developed the underlying theoretical rationale for the causal model, and showed that TAM outperformed the generic version of the theory of reasoned action from which it was largely adapted. After that, two journal articles reported that TAM compared favorably to the theory of planned behavior, which is an extension of the theory of reasoned action from social psychology (Mathieson, 1991; Taylor and Todd, 1994). Moore and Benbasat (1991) introduced an instrument to measure the various perceptions of an IT innovation based on diffusion of innovations theory, and adapted the TAM measures of perceived usefulness and ease of use to operationalize relative advantage and complexity, respectively. In the 1990s, numerous published studies replicated and extended TAM and applied it to a wide range of systems and user populations. In 2000, two major extensions to TAM were published: Venkatesh and Davis (2000) published TAM2, which included various antecedents of perceived usefulness, and Venkatesh (2000) published a paper investigating various antecedents of perceived ease of use.

Lee et al. (2003) published a critical meta-analytic review that "traces TAM's history, investigates its findings, and cautiously predict its future trajectory" (p. 752). Lee et al. (2003, p. 752) state that TAM "continues to be the most widely applied theoretical model in the IS field." Although TAM's original focus was on evaluating the effects of system design features on usage behavior through perceived usefulness, ease of use and usage intentions, most TAM research has not examined the role of system design features. This gives rise to the somewhat ironic criticism that "TAM's narrow focus reduced attention on the role of technology and design" (Lee et al., 2003, p. 766). In many conference discussions lamenting the IS field's over-reliance on reference field theories, TAM is often mentioned as an example of a true IS-specific theory, which is ironic given the extent to which TAM was derived from reference field theory such as the theory of reasoned action. TAM's appeal is driven by its parsimony and robust generality across a broad range of system and user types. Its success has also had the effect of overly constraining research attention to the constructs within TAM, to the exclusion of other potentially important constructs. Lee et al. (2003) identify several directions for future TAM research. Venkatesh et al. (2003) theoretically and empirically compared TAM to seven other intention models of user acceptance that had been reported in the literature, and developed a model that unifies the key intention determinants across the eight models as well as several moderating variables (UTAUT—unified theory of acceptance and use of technology). Davis and Venkatesh (2004) provided guidelines for embedding early (preprototype) user acceptance testing within overall software project management practices.

CONCLUSION: THE RELATIONSHIP BETWEEN HCI AND TECHNOLOGY ADOPTION RESEARCH

In the early to mid 1980s, when TAM was originally being formulated, early human factors and HCI research played an influential role. This was a time when ideas surrounding "user-centered design" were first emerging (e.g., Gould and Lewis, 1985). At the time, I regarded TAM as a contribution to the practice of user-centered design, and expected rapid convergence of user-oriented MIS research and HCI research. Some convergence has indeed taken place, but at a much slower pace than I expected. The role for HCI research within the MIS literature is now well established. There is much that HCI and MIS can learn from each other. However, I think it is unlikely and undesirable for HCI and MIS research to converge to the point of unification. Both HCI and MIS have unique strengths and specializations, as well as distinct disciplinary foundations. HCI tends to be more micro in its focus, drawing extensively upon cognitive psychology, whereas user-oriented MIS tends to be more macro, drawing from social and organizational psychology (Zhang et al., 2002).

One key challenge that MIS and HCI researchers must attend to in order to strengthen the synergy is to clarify the theoretical relationship between the construct of usability from the HCI literature and the constructs of perceived usefulness and ease of use from the MIS literature. As Seffah and Metzker (2004) point out, usability remains an ill-defined and confusing concept. Narrowly defined, objective usability appears to function as a determinant of perceived ease of use (Venkatesh, 2000). However, other criteria such as satisfaction, learnability, performance, and effectiveness are frequently subsumed under the label of usability (Seffah and Metzker, 2004). From my perspective, the most important contribution of TAM has been to highlight the relatively important role of perceived usefulness compared to perceived ease of use as a driver and predictor of user acceptance. Treating usability as a catchall concept invites failure to distinguish usefulness from ease of use as an important design criterion. HCI research in MIS has the promise of bringing together HCI insights about how to design systems that are easy to use with MIS insights about how to design systems that are useful to, accepted by, and effective for their intended users.

REFERENCES

Ajzen, I., and Fishbein, M. *Understanding Attitudes and Predicting Social Behavior.* Englewood Cliffs, NJ: Prentice-Hall, 1980.

Bailey, J.E., and Pearson, S.W. Development of a tool for measuring and analyzing computer user satisfaction. *Management Science*, 29, 5 (1983), 530–545.

Card, S.K.; Moran, T.P.; and Newell, A. The keystroke-level model for user performance time with interactive systems. *Communications of the ACM*, 23, 7 (1980), 396–410.

Churchill, G.A. A paradigm for developing better measures of marketing constructs. *Journal of Marketing Research*, 16, 1 (1979), 64–73.

Davis, F.D. *A Technology Acceptance Model for Empirically Testing New End-User Information Systems: Theory And Results.* PhD dissertation, Massachusetts Institute of Technology, 1986.

Davis, F.D. Perceived usefulness, perceived ease of use, and user acceptance of information technology. *MIS Quarterly*, 13, 3 (1989), 319–339.

Davis, F.D.; Bagozzi, R.P.; and Warshaw, P.R. User acceptance of computer technology: a comparison of two theoretical models. *Management Science*, 35, 8 (1989), 982–1002.

Davis, F.D., and Venkatesh, V. Toward preprototype user acceptance testing of new information systems: Implications for software project management. *IEEE Transactions of Engineering Management*, 51, 1 (2004), 31–46.

Ginzberg, M.J. Early diagnosis of MIS implementation failure: promising results and unanswered questions. *Management Science,* 27, 4 (1981), 459–478.

Gould, J.D.; Conti, J.; and Hovanyecz, T. Composing letters with a simulated listening typewriter. *Communications of the ACM*, 26, 4 (1983), 295–308.

Gould, J.D., and Lewis, C. Designing for usability—key principles and what designers think. *Communications of the ACM*, 28, 3 (1985), 300–311.

Lee, Y.; Kozar, K.A.; and Larsen, K.R.T. The technology acceptance model: past, present, and future. *Communications of the AIS*, 12, 50 (2003), 752–780.

Little, J.D.C. Models and managers: the concept of a decision calculus. *Management Science*, 16, 8 (1970), B466–B485.

Markus, M.L. Power, politics, and MIS implementation. *Communications of the ACM*, 26, 6 (1983), 430–444.

Mathieson, K. Predicting user intentions: comparing the technology acceptance model with the theory of planned behavior. *Information Systems Research*, 2, 3 (1991), 173–191.

Moore, G.C., and Benbasat, I. Development of an instrument to measure the perceptions of adopting an information technology innovation. *Information Systems Research*, 2, 3 (1991), 192–222.

Robey, D. User attitudes and management information system use. *Academy of Management Journal*, 22, 3 (1979), 527–538.

Seffah, A., and Metzker, E. The obstacles and myths of usability and software engineering. *Communications of the ACM*, 47, 12 (2004), 71–76.

Swanson, E.B. Management information systems: appreciation and involvement. *Management Science*, 21, 2 (1974), 178–188.

Swanson, E.B. Measuring attitudes in MIS research: a review. *Omega*, 10, 2 (1982), 157–165.

Taylor, S., and Todd, P.A. Understanding information technology usage: A test of competing models. *Information Systems Research*, 6, 4 (1994), 144–176.

Venkatesh, V. Determinants of perceived ease of use: integrating control, intrinsic motivation, and emotion into the technology acceptance model. *Information Systems Research*, 11, 4 (2000), 342–365.

Venkatesh, V., and Davis, F.D. A theoretical extension of the technology acceptance model: four longitudinal field studies. *Management Science*, 46, 2 (2000), 186–204.

Venkatesh, V.; Morris, M.G.; Davis, G.B.; and Davis, F.D. User acceptance of information technology: toward a unified view. *MIS Quarterly*, 27, 3 (2003), 425–478.

Zhang, P.; Benbasat, I.; Carey, J.; Davis, F.D.; Galletta, D.; and Strong, D. Human-computer interaction research in the MIS discipline. *Communications of the AIS*, 9, 20 (2002), 334–355.

CHAPTER 19

HUMAN FACTORS, CHI, AND MIS

Jonathan Grudin

Abstract: Human-computer interaction research has been pursued in different disciplines with different emphases. Human factors and ergonomics has primarily focused on hands-on operation by people employed to operate hardware, enter data, and carry out other essential tasks. The MIS focus has been more managerial, considering decisions about hardware and software acquisition, oversight of operational aspects, and use of computer output. A third focus, embodied by ACM SIGCHI, recruited cognitive scientists and computer scientists to study users whose hands-on technology use is more volitional. These three approaches map to the early computer professions of operator, systems analyst and manager, and programmer. Better understanding of similarities and differences across disciplines may improve the prospects for interaction. One conclusion is that cultural and methodological differences among these groups have impeded efforts to find common ground.

Keywords: Human-Computer Interaction, Human Factors, Ergonomics, Information Systems, Computer-Human Interaction (CHI), Discretionary System Use

INTRODUCTION

In this chapter, the term "human-computer interaction" (HCI) is used inclusively. HCI is often used more restrictively. For example, Zhang and Dillon (2003, pp. 398–399) wrote:

> HCI places strong emphasis on understanding how users can perform certain tasks in given work contexts and on using such understandings to inform the design of technology that is both useful and usable. . . . HCI has tended to be located in Computer Science and/or Psychology programs. . . .
>
> To date however, the HCI and MIS fields have largely evolved independently with only minimum influence on each other. Leading researchers in one field tend not to publish in the journals and conference proceedings of the other field. . . . They share some common reference disciplines such as cognitive psychology, social psychology, computer science, communication, and many others. They also share many common research methodologies. Most importantly, the two fields share common research issues and problems. . . .
>
> In a nutshell we might summarize the shared research goal as being the increased theoretical and practical understanding of how information technology can best be designed and implemented to suit user and organizational needs.

HCI is also defined in terms of the cognitive psychology and computer science orientation of research in the ACM Special Interest Group on Computer-Human Interaction (CHI) by CHI researchers themselves. By contrast, in this essay HCI is extended to include related work in MIS and in human factors and ergonomics (HF&E) that is not necessarily focused on cognitive or computer science.

In a fifty-year retrospective, Banker and Kaufmann (2004) identify human-computer interaction as one of five pillars of MIS research, originating in the mid-1960s, long before cognitive or computer scientists showed interest in HCI. This chapter explores the relationship between the forty-year MIS history and the twenty-year CHI history. Essays including Zhang et al. (2002), Zhang et al. (2004), and chapters in these volumes identify interests shared by CHI and the AIS special interest group on human-computer interaction (SIGHCI).

The sixty-year history of human factors and ergonomics research is intertwined with MIS. For example, an early *Management Science* paper on the use of color and graphical displays cited five *Human Factors* journal articles (Benbasat and Dexter, 1985). The leading human factors HCI journal, *International Journal of Human-Computer Studies (IJHCS)*, formerly *International Journal of Man-Machine Studies (IJMMS)*, is twenty-third of fifty in a survey of the journals influential in MIS research (Mylonopoulos and Theoharakis, 2001).[1] Special journal issues on HCI in MIS resulting from SIGHCI workshops appear in *IJHCS, Behaviour and Information Technology (BIT)*, and *International Journal of Human-Computer Interaction (IJHCI)*, all of which are oriented more toward HF&E than CHI. Similarly, AIS SIGHCI leaders organized sessions for HCI International 2005, a conference with a strong human factors orientation.

Interaction between MIS and CHI has been less extensive. Both publish in *Communications of the ACM*. The CHI-oriented journal *Human-Computer Interaction* ranked thirty-third in influence on MIS research. In the late 1980s, the Computer Supported Cooperative Work conference series bridged MIS and CHI. Some prominent CHI researchers participate in AIS SIGHCI meetings and contribute to these volumes. CHI began with a link to the Human Factors Society, which co-sponsored the first CHI conference with ACM. The subtitle of the CHI conference series is "Human Factors in Computing Systems." Some researchers have been active in both groups or moved from one to the other. But, as with MIS, the human factors trend has generally been toward less interaction with CHI, not more.

The hope is that by examining the mixed results of past bridging efforts, we can better identify and exploit common interests and surmount or circumvent challenges to communication and cooperation. My analysis is based on examining literature, interviewing scores of participants, and reflecting on what I lived through. Its central thesis is easily summarized. Although the approaches have much in common, two differences keep them apart. One is a difference in the activities focused upon. Human factors targets nondiscretionary use of systems and applications, whereas CHI focuses on the discretionary use of software. The early MIS focus on managerial issues had more in common with human factors. The success of the Internet and the Web have created a customer focus for MIS (and IT organizations); discretion has become a more critical concern. The second difference is cultural. CHI comprised a different generation of researchers, and adopted the distinct academic culture of US computer science. In particular, human factors and MIS regard conferences as forums for work in progress and journals as repositories of polished work. In CHI, conference proceedings are the final destination of quality work and journals are largely irrelevant.

History is interpretation. This lesson of Rashomon is brought home by conflicting accounts of principals in past events. A researcher can feel more like a participant in a Solomon Asch study than like Asch himself. In the end, though, we need not have consensus on every detail to better appreciate shared ground and confront the obstacles to working collectively.

CHI and MIS: Two Disciplines Divided by a Common Language?

My first presentation as a CHI researcher with an MIS audience, in 1990 at UCLA, ended badly. It had gone very well until my host asked a question. It seemed meaningless, so I replied cautiously. He rephrased the question. I rephrased my response. He started again, then shrugged and stopped. The next day I gave a job talk on a different topic at UC Irvine. When I next saw my UCLA host, he seemed astonished to hear that Irvine had hired me.

Later I identified the origin of my confusion and loss of face. My host and I attached different meanings to the word "users." To me, and to everyone in CHI, it meant hands-on computer users. My host understood it in an MIS sense that included people who might never use a keyboard, who decide what software is needed and read printed output or reports. His question homed in on users who were not hands-on users, but to me all use was hands-on. I couldn't understand him.

This misunderstanding was not minor, personally or conceptually. There was a fundamental distinction between the CHI and MIS views of human-computer interaction. CHI formed soon after the arrival of the PC. It was primarily about a single user sitting at a keyboard and display. Most early CHI researchers were cognitive psychologists interested in the mind of a person using a computer. MIS, with its broader perspective, employed two terms: "users" and "end users." In CHI, these were rolled into one. Someone who did not face a keyboard was not a user and was not of any interest. Few of us ever said "end user"; we found it strange when others did.

This linguistic confusion was not unique. Working in industry and discovering practices that were incomprehensibly ill suited to developing usable software, I became interested in organizational behavior. Guided by a colleague in a marketing research group, I began to explore MIS. My colleague submitted an article to an ACM transactions journal titled *Successful Implementation of Office Communication Systems*, using "implementation" in the MIS sense, to mean organizational deployment. But to me—and the editor—"implementation" was a synonym for coding or programming. The paper was accepted, but the editor forced a change of title. It became "Strategies for encouraging successful adoption of office communication systems" (Ehrlich, 1987).

Just prior to participating in a panel on task analysis at a European conference, I discovered to my dismay that this MIS-oriented group defined "task analysis" differently than I did. To them, it meant an organizational task analysis, considering tasks as components in a broad workplace setting. In CHI, it meant a cognitive task analysis, breaking a simple task into components; for example, is "move text" better thought of as select-delete-paste or select-move-place?

Two Communities, Two Terminologies (Grudin, 1993, p. 113) identifies these and other terms used differently by MIS and CHI researchers. Within CHI, but not MIS, an application was a single-user, personal productivity application; anything more was a system. The term "evaluation" differed in connotation: Because a first principle of CHI is iterative design, "evaluation" is a desirable element of the design process, whereas in MIS it often referred to an assessment carried out long after the design and thus "not where the action is" (Herb Simon, quoted in Bødker, 1990).

Given that MIS and CHI share theoretical and methodological ground, why dwell on differences? Finding and exploiting the common ground requires understanding and working around the differences. Conflicting word use, structural differences in the organization of scholarship, and related problems impede effective communication.

This essay presents a view of the history of human-computer interaction as a framework for approaching these issues. It is one perspective, one distillation. It builds on earlier histories and will be followed by others.

1900–1945: HUMAN-TOOL INTERACTION

A century ago, with the spread of photography, precise time measurement, and confidence in the methods of science, "scientific management" attracted growing attention, notably in the work of Frederick Taylor (1911). More effective bricklaying and assembly lines resulted. Concern about technologies imposed on workers with little choice was expressed in contemporary fiction and in Chaplin's *Modern Times.*

Although there were practical limitations, illustrated by the failure of the scientifically derived Dvorak typewriter keyboard, more complex technologies did focus attention on designing for use. War raised the stakes as new weaponry was rushed into mass production. Design decisions affected performance, reliability, and training time, with major consequences. World War I spurred scientific management efforts in Great Britain and the United States (Meister, 1999). World War II concentrated attention on the human element in design (Roscoe, 1997). A simple error in cockpit design caused thousands of pilot deaths (Dyson, 1979). Such realizations led to research and application efforts in human factors and ergonomics that continued after World War II ended.

Scientific management and human factors research focused on hands-on tool use by workers who had no choice but to use them. Improving efficiency and safety of expert use was the primary focus, with training time also of interest.

1945–1958: HUMAN-COMPUTER INTERACTION IN THE ERA OF VACUUM TUBES

The first computer users were engineers and their assistants, interacting directly with computer hardware. The difficulty and expense led to the prediction attributed to IBM's Thomas Watson: "There is a world market for maybe five computers." With the spread of stored program computers, interaction shifted to software. Improving human-computer interaction then meant developing concepts and tools to aid programmers. Computers were too few for their handling to be a profession, but three roles were already evident:

1. Operation. Faster detection and replacement of burned-out vacuum tubes was initially a big issue. Control first meant connecting cables, evolved to switches and buttons, and later shifted to consoles with expensive CRT displays. Physical operation included keypunching program instructions onto paper tape or cards, loading cards and tapes, pushing buttons and setting switches, and handling paper, tape, and punched-card output.
2. Management. Developing and operating the massive vacuum tube computers and early transistor-based computers were challenging.
3. Programming. Stored programs aided engineer-computer interaction. Constructs such as subroutines, programming languages, and compilers facilitated programmer-computer interaction. Although not usually characterized as human-computer interaction, this activity was perceptively described by Grace Hopper, who contributed in all of these areas through the 1950s, as making computers more user-friendly (Hopper, 1952; Sammet, 1992).

Eventually each role gave rise to a profession and spawned a distinct research effort. When commercial computers based on transistors arrived in 1958, interest in improving the ergonomics of computer operation grew. Papers on the design of consoles and displays by Brian Shackel (1959, 1962) and Sid Smith (1963) launched the human factors study of human-computer interaction. The advent of integrated circuit machines and business computing in 1965 led to human factors studies of data entry and a broad range of studies of information systems management. Research into programmer support was widespread in the 1970s; in the 1980s it shifted within CHI to a broad focus on discretionary use.

1958–1965: IMAGINATION FREED FROM CONSTRAINT

Vacuum tube computers were maintenance challenges, energy hogs, enormous, and not very capable. The first general-purpose electronic computer, ENIAC, was ten feet tall, covered a thousand square feet, consumed as much energy as a small town, and in one year fifty burned-out tubes needed to be found and replaced on an average day. With transistor-based computers, people could envision technology uses that were unimaginable before.

The years following 1958 saw a singular outpouring of visionary HCI: descriptions of a future of discretionary computer use by professionals and working prototypes of elements of such visions. Licklider (1960; Licklider and Clark, 1962) identified requirements. Sutherland (1963) illustrated iconic representations, constraints, and hierarchically defined objects. McCarthy pioneered time-sharing, an enabling technology that allowed many people to use a computer in ways that only those who could commandeer extremely expensive machines could previously (Fano and Corbato, 1966). Engelbart (1963; Engelbart and English, 1968) prototyped mice and other input devices, word processing, and distributed computing. Nelson (1965, 1973) envisioned powerful hypertext systems. Alan Kay (1969; Kay and Goldberg, 1977) helped build the first personal computers as a step toward a vision of powerful portable personal computers. An inspiration to many was the early writing of Vannevar Bush (1945) describing a powerful, if impractical, mechanical device.

This burst of innovation is described in greater detail in Myers (1988), Baecker et al. (1995), and Pew (2003). These visions of empowered professionals' "augmented intellect" were a radical departure from the reality of the time, in which most hands-on use was the mundane assigned work of computer operation and data entry. The visions inspired precisely because they differed from experience.

Some of the ideas came to fruition soon, some after twenty or forty years, some not at all. Assessing the contributions of visions and demonstrations is difficult. They inspired work that eventually made some of them practical on a wide scale, although not always precisely as had been envisioned. The relationship between early visions and later developments is further explored in Grudin (2005).

1965–1975: THE BIRTHS OF MIS AND CSTG

In 1964 and 1965 Control Data and IBM launched the first powerful commercial computers, later christened "mainframes." Business computing had arrived. Operation, management, and programming became professions.

About operation and data entry, Shackel (1997) wrote: "In the beginning, the computer was so costly that it had to be kept gainfully occupied for every second; people were almost slaves to feed it." Following his early papers on consoles and displays, Shackel founded the HUSAT (Human Sciences and Advanced Technology) research center in Loughborough in 1970. In 1972, the Human Factors Society Computer Systems Technical Group (CSTG) formed and grew to be the largest technical group, with a strong focus on hardware: packaging, arrangement of external switches, buttons, tape mounts, and other controls, keyboards, consoles, and so on.

In 1967, *Management Science* initiated a column "Information Systems in Management Science." Early definitions of management information systems cited in Zhang et al. (2004, p. 147) include "an integrated man/machine system for providing information to support the operation, management, and decision-making functions in an organization" (Davis, 1974) and "the effective design, delivery and use of information systems in organizations" (Keen, 1980). The Banker and Kaufmann (2004) survey of management science literature identifies the first HCI article as Ackoff's (1976) investigation of challenges in handling computer-generated information. Work on cognitive style and system design occupied researchers in the late 1960s and through the 1970s.

Once a computer was acquired, managers were chained to it almost as tightly as Shackel's operator and data entry slaves. A system was there to be used. Of course, a threatening or disruptive system could be ignored or resisted. Sociotechnical design, incorporating end-user involvement to facilitate adoption, became part of the management literature (e.g., Mumford, 1971).

In 1970, Xerox PARC was founded and attracted researchers from the labs of Engelbart and Sutherland. A major PARC focus was to develop languages and tools to support programmers. Well into the 1970s, most professional programmers, like most managers, were not hands-on computer users. Programs were flow-charted on paper, written on coding sheets, keypunched by other people, and run by computer operators. Programmers typically picked up printed output. Efforts to understand and support this notoriously idiosyncratic and unpredictable skill led to research into the psychology of programming; Weinberg (1971) was an influential survey.

The first widely read HCI book appeared in 1972, James Martin's *Design of Man-Computer Dialogues*. A comprehensive survey of interfaces for data entry and operation, it began with a vision of a future in which users "will become the tail that wags the whole dog . . . The computer industry will be forced to become increasingly concerned with the usage of people, rather than with the computer's intestines" (pp. 3–4).

1975–1985: HANDS-ON DISCRETIONARY USE, AND THE BIRTH OF CHI

More than a decade after the early visions of empowered computer users, discretionary use was not widespread. Scientific computing enabled some engineers and programmers to enjoy access to expensive computers, but this did not carry over to business computing with its efficient division of labor. Even at universities, computer centers prevented most student programmers from even seeing a computer.

Nevertheless, people took up programming because they enjoyed it, and programming became the first profession to embrace discretionary hands-on computer use. Text editors provided an alternative to coding sheets. Working as a professional programmer at a computer company, I made this transition at my first opportunity in 1975. Many of the over one thousand studies of programming psychology—research surveyed in Shneiderman (1980)—examined programming skill in isolation, removed from particular organizational and management contexts.

Interest in this new category of discretionary users grew through the late 1970s as students, hobbyists, and others interacted with time-shared mainframes, minicomputers, and microprocessor-based home computers. *Human Interaction with Computers* by Smith and Green (1980) perched on this cusp. It briefly addressed "the human as a systems component" (the nondiscretionary perspective); one-third was devoted to research on programming, and the remainder addressed "non-specialist people," discretionary users who were not computer specialists: "It's not enough just to establish what people can and cannot do; we need to spend just as much effort establishing what people can *and want to* do" (p. viii; emphasis in the original).

The Formation of ACM SIGCHI

In 1980, substantial numbers of cognitive psychologists had very recently formed or joined HCI research groups at Xerox PARC, IBM Watson, Bell Laboratories, Digital Equipment Corporation, the Medical Research Council Applied Psychology Unit, and University of California, San Diego. The ACM Special Interest Group for Social and Behavioral Computing (SIGSOC), formed in 1969, focused on computers as discretionary tools for doing research. By the late 1970s, behavioral and social scientists with this interest were numerous enough to hold meetings in their professional association meetings, reducing SIGSOC activity (Borman, 1996). A 1980 SIGSOC workshop included research into software design and use. In 1982 SIGSOC was rechristened SIGCHI (considered more pronounceable than the alternative acronym that would have put the human before the computer, SIGHCI).

The first CHI conference, in 1983,[2] was dominated by cognitive psychologists. Two-thirds of the papers were from people working in industry, primarily in computer, software, and telecommunications companies (the latter promoted uses of digital data via modem and developed consumer software and hardware such as Unix and the short-lived Unix PC). Human factors and ergonomics was present. CHI '83 was co-sponsored by ACM and the Human Factors Society. The program committee was chaired by Richard Pew and included Sid Smith and other prominent HFS members. Brian Shackel and HFS President Robert Williges gave half-day pre-conference tutorials. "Human Factors in Computing Systems" was (and is) the conference subtitle.

However, few human factors researchers remained active in CHI. In the influential *Psychology of Human Computer Interaction*, published earlier in 1983, Card, Moran, and Newell wrote: "Human factors specialists, ergonomists, and human engineers will find that we have synthesized ideas from modern cognitive psychology and artificial intelligence with the old methods of task analysis . . . The user is not an operator. He does not operate the computer, he communicates with it . . ." (p. viii). This was a theoretical as well as conceptual rebuke. Human factors researchers were trained when radical behaviorism dominated American psychology and were generally antipathetic to cognitive theory.

Two years later, Newell and Card (1985) noted that human factors had a role in design but "classical human factors . . . has all the earmarks of second-class status . . . (Our approach) avoids continuation of the classical human-factors role (by transforming) the psychology of the interface into a hard science" (p. 221). Card recently said, "Human factors was the discipline we were trying to improve," and "I personally changed the (CHI Conference) call in 1986 so as to emphasize computer science and reduce the emphasis on cognitive science, because I was afraid that it would just become human factors again" (personal e-mail, June 2004).

Card, Moran, and Newell modeled repetitive activities of expert users. Although highly respected and often cited, human performance models never drew a major active following in CHI, which focused mainly on discretionary use by novices, the concern of the burgeoning software market.

"Hard science, in the form of engineering, drives out soft science, in the form of human factors" (Newell and Card, 1985, p. 212). There was a palpable sense that human factors was a discipline of lower status. "Cognitive engineering" and "usability engineering" were introduced. Many who had called themselves human factors engineers left CHI or adopted the title "usability engineer." I was among those who shifted from publishing in the human factors literature to CHI and *Communications of the ACM* until new journals were established.

At IBM Watson, John Gould had been a leader in the hardware-oriented human factors tradition since the late 1960s. Gould participated in CHI, but remained active in human factors, serving as president in 1987–88. Starting in 1984, the Human Factors Group at Watson dissolved as a User Interface Institute comprised heavily of cognitive psychologists formed. The latter contributed heavily to CHI.

The principal focus of the new organization was signaled by the first paper at CHI '83. Don Norman applied engineering techniques to discretionary use, with "user satisfaction functions" based on technical parameters. Many early CHI papers addressed the psychology of programming. Studies of editing were so numerous that in 1984 Thomas Green remarked that "text editors are the white rats of HCI." Unlike HF&E research, with its focus on expert use, the emphasis in CHI was on novice use. For discretionary users and for the vendors seeking to appeal to them, early experience is crucial.

By contrast, there were few CHI studies of data entry and information retrieval by trained users, despite widespread use at that time by airlines, banks, government agencies, and other organizations. Databases did not involve hands-on discretionary use: Those who managed database design decisions and read reports delegated direct use to people hired for that purpose. I identified only three conference papers on database use in CHI's first decade, and all focused on novice or casual use.

In Europe, fewer large companies focused on mass-market software. HCI research remained with HF&E, MIS, and relatively nondiscretionary in-house development and use. German DIN standards for keyboard ergonomics focused vendors' attention on human-computer interaction starting in 1980, a year in which three influential works on ergonomics were published (Shackel, 1997). Shackel and his colleagues at Loughborough continued ergonomic studies of computer use and in 1984 initiated the first graduate HCI program. One focus was "job design," the division of labor in organizational computing. They also worked with the Institute for Consumer Electronics, primarily on product safety. An HCI group at the British Medical Research Council Applied Psychology Unit, led by Philip Barnard, introduced multi-session lab studies of discretionary use, bridging the CHI focus on novice use and the HF&E concern with skilled use. The INTERACT conference series, meeting first in London in 1984 and chaired by Shackel, drew both HF&E and CHI researchers.[3]

The Significance of Discretionary Computer Use

Anyone using a computer would like an interface that he or she can learn easily, use efficiently, and remember how to use, one that minimizes errors and that is enjoyable. For this reason, the significance of this new category, highly discretionary users, was not appreciated. Priorities among the goals were different. For nondiscretionary use, expert efficiency is critical, the initial experience and training requirements are secondary, and aesthetic considerations come last. For discretionary use, initial experience, casual experience, and aesthetics often outweigh the other factors. Differing priorities led to differences in research focus and methods.

As Hartwick and Barki (1994) note, mandatory use is not totally mandatory. One can resist, sabotage, or use selectively. But short of quitting, in many jobs, such as data entry, use is mandatory. My job requires that I read e-mail and use a wide range of systems. For me, today, instant messaging is discretionary.

Figure 19.1 positions some of the events, topics, and publications mentioned in this chapter. The top row represents work in the human factors tradition, primarily concerned with mandatory, expert use. The journal *Human Factors,* with broad coverage that began in 1959, was joined by the computer-focused *IJMMS* in 1969 and *Behaviour and Information Technology (BIT)* in 1982. *IJMMS (IJHCS* since 1994) covered information systems, decision-support systems, knowledge-based systems,

410

Figure 19.1   Timeline for Events, Publications, and Topics Discussed in the Text

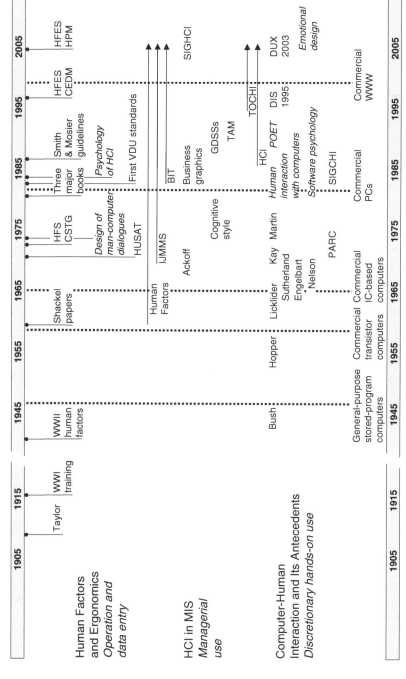

knowledge acquisition, requirements engineering, and a broad range of human factors topics. MIS HCI research appears in the middle row, with the bottom row representing CHI and its predecessors that focused on discretionary use—support for engineers and programmers, and visions of writers and prototype builders.

Books titles are italicized (*POET* represents Norman's 1988 *Psychology of Everyday Things*). Martin's 1973 book devoted to designing for computer operation and data entry is in the top row, whereas he is listed among the visionaries for the book's first chapter. Card, Moran, and Newell's 1983 book is in the top row, despite the authors' prominence in CHI and their disassociation from human factors, because their models of expert performance were intended to advance human factors, staying close to the physical interface and addressing tasks such as non-discretionary keyboard use by telephone operators. As described below, when HF&E became receptive to cognitive theory it embraced this modeling research.

1985–1995: GRAPHICAL USER INTERFACES AND HCI BEFORE THE WEB

The graphical user interface or GUI was envisioned and features were prototyped in the 1960s. Johnson et al. (1989) describe GUI development at PARC in the 1970s. But only when the 1984 Apple Macintosh survived a rocky first year did the GUI or direct manipulation interface transform HCI research. The Mac did not fare well in the large enterprises that were initially targeted, but it appealed to graphic artists and other discretionary users. As a result, the impact registered first in CHI. Even there, a prominent theoretical analysis by Hutchins, Hollan, and Norman (1986) concluded that it was uncertain how GUIs would fare. They identified benefits for new and casual users, but also noted possible advantages to interfaces based on commands and function keys for skilled users. Mouse-wary corporations, concerned with skilled use, did not embrace GUIs until Windows 3.0 succeeded in the early 1990, and even then not for tasks such as data entry.

Human Factors and Ergonomics

Government agencies, such as those responsible for the military, social security, census, aviation, and taxation, and private industries, including the financial, insurance, aviation, medical, and telecommunications sectors, continued to rely on systems with captive users. Funding at U.S. research agencies such as NSF and DARPA focused on non-discretionary uses of technology. This included massive investment in speech recognition and natural language processing, technologies avoided by users who have a choice, who are not constrained by disability, occupied hands, or the need to navigate a phone answering system.

In 1986, Smith and Mosier published the last in a series of interface design guidelines sponsored by the U.S. Air Force. Guidelines were a tool for writing contracts: An interface could be required to adhere to specific guidelines. Smith and Mosier mentioned GUIs, but their 944 guidelines did not address them. The vastly increased GUI interaction capabilities—pop-up and pull-down menus, windows, mouse button assignments, color, sound, animation—rendered a comprehensive set of design guidelines unattainable. Process-oriented approaches were needed for specifying interaction design.

A HFS Computer Systems Technical Group study of the potential impact of CHI found an unexpectedly small overlap of focus. CSTG hewed more closely to its original focus on hardware (packaging, input devices, displays) and drew psychologists working in the milieu of military and government contracting, whereas CHI focused on innovative commercial software and its development (Richard Pew, personal communication).

Management Information Systems

Use of data was a key management concern. Business graphics emerged as an important application even before the graphical user interface. Remus (1984) contrasted tabular and graphic presentations, Benbasat and Dexter (1985) added color as another factor, and many studies built on their work. The concept of cognitive fit was introduced in this context (Vessey and Galletta, 1991) and extended to other tasks. Results could be applied to online or printed reports, and studies were done online and with paper. In practice, color displays were rare in the 1980s; most managers dealt with printed reports.

Information system organization and strategy were not part of the HCI focus, but the division of labor around computing is relevant to HCI. Involvement of internal end users in the development process was actively discussed (Friedman, 1989; Bjerknes et al., 1987). Full consideration of the management of programming is beyond the scope of this study. Briefly, management hoped to increase predictability and control by routinizing programming, despite the ill-understood nature of the complex activity and the exploratory impulses that had attracted people to programming. Studies focused on in-house programming foresaw routinization; studies from the emerging, exploratory shrinkwrap software industry did not (Friedman, 1989).

Hands-on managerial use was atypical but central to group decision support systems research, which emerged from decision support systems and evolved into group support systems. Computer-supported meeting facility research was active from the mid-1980s (DeSanctis and Gallupe, 1987; Dennis et al., 1988). Key design and development was in MIS, not in computer science departments or software companies. The initial focus on decision makers and the expense of acquisition and operation set this apart from mass-market, discretionary use applications.

The Technology Acceptance Model (TAM) introduced by Davis (1989) focuses on perceived usefulness and perceived usability to improve "white collar performance" that is "often obstructed by users' unwillingness to accept and use available systems" (p. 319). "An element of uncertainty exists in the minds of decision makers with respect to the successful adoption," wrote Bagozzi, Davis, and Warshaw (1992, p. 664). This managerial view of individual behavior was influenced by early CHI usability research (see Davis's chapter in this volume).

High interest in TAM through the 1990s showed that the MIS focus, in which hands-on use was primarily non-discretionary operation, data entry, and data retrieval activity, was leavened as hands-on use spread to white-collar workers who could refuse to play. Contrast MIS with CHI: Because no one would choose to use a technology perceived to be useless, CHI rarely if ever considers utility. TAM researchers considered utility more important than usability. Usability being central to discretionary use, CHI focused on it a decade before TAM, albeit on measures of usability more than on measures of perceived usability. Perception was a secondary "user satisfaction" measure to CHI researchers, who believed that measurable reduction in time, errors, questions, and training would, over time, translate into positive perceptions. The MIS/CHI linguistic divide reappears: "Acceptance" is not in the CHI vocabulary. A discretionary user chooses or adopts, rather than accepts.

At the close of this span, the *Harvard Business Review* published "Usability: The new dimension of product design" (March, 1994). In concluding that "user-centered design is still in its infancy," it made no mention of CHI or the workshop titled "User-oriented design of interactive graphics systems"[4] that preceded it eighteen years earlier, in 1976 (p. 149).

Computer-Human Interaction

Studies of database use, speech recognition, natural language processing, and traditional task analysis and human factors remained largely absent from CHI. However, the nature of what was present changed dramatically. As discretionary computer use spread from programmers to other professions and the general public, CHI's focus on the psychology of programming dissipated. Earlier work on command naming and abbreviation gave way to research into GUI features and user interface construction tools and management systems. As text editor or word processor use shifted from discretionary to unavoidable in many settings, CHI studies of editing and word processing diminished. As PCs were networked and Internetworked, a focus on collaboration arose with the CHI-sponsored Computer Supported Cooperative Work conferences.

These shifts had profound indirect effects. CHI researchers who had worked to establish a theoretical foundation for the field found that the reference tasks on which they had labored (command naming, text editing) were no longer of interest. The space of psychological variables and technical parameters greatly expanded. Discretionary use was discovered to be a moving target, driven by Moore's Law. Published results and theory, however solid, could lose relevance. Many researchers had come from cognitive psychology, where paradigms persisted (some had arisen in engineering psychology during World War II). For some, this was unsettling, and interest in theory never fully recovered.

In 1985 *Human-Computer Interaction* was established as a top-tier HCI journal with a strong emphasis on psychological science. In 1994 *ACM Transactions on Computer-Human Interaction* appeared with more of a computer science orientation. This reflected CHI shifting away from cognitive psychology and cognitive science departments and becoming a core element of computer science curricula.

CHI as a purely scientific pursuit was difficult to sustain. As monochrome displays gave way to color with animation and sound, visual and aesthetic design became significant in appealing to discretionary users. A Visual Interaction Design interest area formed in 1992. In 1995 the first SIGCHI-sponsored Design of Interactive Systems conference series was held; visual designers were not involved, but attracting them became a priority.[5]

SINCE 1995: THE WEB, AIS SIGHCI, AND INVISIBLE COMPUTERS

Slow enterprise adoption gave HF&E and MIS time to prepare for GUIs, but the Web, connecting people with organizations and organizations with one another, had a rapid impact on MIS. The steady growth of the Internet infrastructure over the previous decade was accompanied by hands-on computer use by managers and who were now ready to make use of opportunities presented by the Web (Grudin, 2004b).

With technology in broad use, most researchers must consider aspects of technology use in one way or another. Do we need groups to study computer use in general? In 1988, Don Norman wrote that "the invisible computer of the future" would be no more noticeable than the motors that surround us today. Research, he said, would focus on objects in which software is embedded. A decade after he wrote, with the Internet bubble and Y2K crisis, computers were more noticeable than ever. Today, however, HCI research shows signs of dispersion in each of the three fields.

Human Factors and Ergonomics

As computer use has become routine in homes and businesses, human factors research and application have grown. Publication outlets expanded. *IJMMS* became *IJHCS* and shifted to monthly publication. It was joined by *IJHCI*, organizationally related to the biannual HCI International conference, which in 2003 included over a thousand paper presentations. *Behaviour and Information*

Technology, first published in 1982 and also oriented toward human factors and ergonomics, now publishes bimonthly.

Paradoxically, membership in the HFES Computer Systems Technical Group has declined in real and relative terms. Once the largest technical group, it is now significantly smaller than several others. The largest at the time of writing is Cognitive Engineering and Decision Making, which formed in 1996. The newest is Human Performance Modeling, organized by Wayne Gray and Dick Pew, which first met in 2004. This is a remarkable development. Cognitive engineering and human performance modeling originated in CHI as an effort to reform human factors from outside. Twenty years later, some of the same people have brought the effort inside.

HCI papers are published without HCI as a keyword (e.g., Peebles and Cheng, 2003). In addition to CEDG and HPM, the Communication, Internet, System Development, and Virtual Environment technical groups include HCI work. Aging, medical systems, and so on—all are infiltrated by "invisible computers."

MIS and the Formation of AIS SIGHCI

The success of the Internet and the Web changed the role of corporate IT departments and created new opportunities and challenges for MIS. Whereas IT had focused on internal operations, organizations needed Web interfaces to vendors and customers. Although the Internet boom revealed how little was understood in these areas, online services and business-to-business systems did not disappear with the bust.

The growing IT and MIS focus on discretionary customer interaction was reinforced by other changes. Embrace of the Internet led to more porous digital boundaries. Employees accessed external tools and software—search engines, consumer IM clients, blogging tools, music software, and other applications that affect organizational behavior—despite some resistance from security-conscious management. Familiarity with software use at home generated impatience with poor interfaces at work. Managers evolved from hands-off to hands-on use and are now often discretionary early adopters of technologies that benefit them. For example, managers trapped in large meetings with wireless network access can develop an interest in tablets and instant messaging.

MIS research has responded to the greater significance of discretionary use in enterprise computing. When the Association for Information Systems established the Special Interest Group in Human-Computer Interaction (SIGHCI) in 2001, Internet and Web computing was included in its broad charter; not surprisingly, most of the published SIGHCI work has been in these areas. Given that CHI has addressed discretionary use for two decades, it made sense to build an alliance with CHI, while retaining a concern with organizational and contextual factors that are often secondary in CHI.

HF&E is less central for SIGHCI. Zhang et al. (2004) define HCI by citing twelve works by CHI researchers. Five key disciplines and seven related fields are identified; ergonomics is last on the list. These two volumes include contributions from several prominent CHI researchers, but none by researchers active in HF&E.

SIGHCI aims "to promote research related to human-computer interaction within business, managerial, organizational and cultural contexts . . . [encouraging] research that looks beyond human-computer interfaces" (Zhang, 2004, p. 1). CHI's interface focus has long been seen as a limitation by those involved with enterprise system development and use. It reflects differences in priorities: Enterprises must consider domain-specific functional requirements, whereas commercial, discretionary-use software products rely on their interfaces to compete against products with similar functionality and to appeal to prospective users who have no access to training or support, or who may seek a particular style. Commercial product reviews cover usability and interface style.

Zhang (2004) lists fifteen topic areas for SIGHCI, but three are emphasized: user interface design and evaluation for e-commerce and online shopping; user studies of online behavior, "especially in the Internet era"; and the effects of Web-based interfaces on attitudes and perceptions. Eight of ten papers published in special journal issues focus on the Internet and the Web. *IJHCS* (October 2003) included papers on government home pages, use of Web-based information systems, Internet-delivered e-services, and education focused on e-commerce. It also included a paper on behavior in general computer-mediated environments. *Journal of AIS* (January–March 2004) had one paper on effects of Web site delays and one on group support systems. *BIT* (May–June 2004) comprised three experimental studies of Web usability and interface design, selected from twenty-four candidates on topics that included online consumer behavior, conceptualization of online shopping, Web site personalization, and consumer trust.

During the Internet boom, MIS rose in prominence and other academic management disciplines took notice. By the time the boom receded and MIS enrolments dropped, research in other disciplines included a greater technology focus. As with HF&E, the group specializing in technology studies had lost its monopoly.

CHI

Innovations of the previous decade that had come into routine use, such as interface design and management tools, diminished in prominence within CHI. Focus shifted to technologies that were not yet widely adopted, where discretion reigned, such as Web tools, ubiquitous computing, and instant messaging, as well as to the issues that accompanied them (e.g., privacy) and novel methods (e.g., ethnography). Only at a more abstract level is there continuity of focus within CHI: exploration of novel input devices, communication channels, information visualization techniques, and design methods.

The inclination to see interface design a wholly scientific undertaking was abandoned. Designing Interactive Systems (DIS) conferences attracted more visual designers and in 2003 Designing User Experience (DUX), with a pronounced shift toward graphic and commercial design, was co-sponsored by SIGCHI, SIGGRAPH, and the graphic arts association AIGA.

Design's first cousin, marketing, has been poorly regarded in the CHI community, but Web site design forces the issue. Site owners often want to keep users on a site, whereas users may prefer to escape quickly. CHI professionals, accustomed to siding with "end users" but designing for site owners, face an unfamiliar stakeholder conflict. Designers of individual productivity tools had no conflict with prospective customers.

The two-decade evolution of CHI is nicely illustrated by Norman's work. His CHI '83 paper used engineering metrics to predict user satisfaction based on technical parameters. *Psychology of Everyday Things* (*POET* in Figure 19.1) focused on basic usability in 1988. It was reissued as *Design of Everyday Things* in 1990, and in 2004 he published *Emotional Design: Why We Love (or Hate) Everyday Things.*

CHI may be declining in salience. Attendance at the annual CHI conference peaked in 2001 and has dropped steadily. Specialized conferences have thrived, focused on topics that include ubiquitous or pervasive computing, software agents, and design. Not completely comfortable in computer science departments, many CHI researchers have moved to information science schools and departments.

CULTURAL DIFFERENCES ACROSS FIELDS AND CONTINENTS

Differences in language often signal broader cultural differences. CHI researchers who first used computers as students in the 1970s did not see themselves as "operators." They also reacted negatively to the male generic "man-machine systems" of human factors and managerial papers of that era (still used today; e.g., Banker and Kaufmann, 2004, p. 286). *International Journal of Man-Machine Studies* did not become *International Journal of Human-Computer Studies* until 1994. These changes in terminology may seem minor, but they affected where manuscripts were submitted, how they were handled, and the levels of enthusiasm and respect for different literatures. As noted above, HFES drew psychologists focused on government contracting; CHI drew developers from R&D divisions of software companies. Attitudes toward standards illustrated the difference: HFES considered them a contribution to innovation; within CHI they have largely been seen as blocking innovation. MIS drew from governmental and non-governmental user organizations; software company participation in MIS was limited and came from marketing divisions. The cultural divide between marketing and R&D within many organizations parallels the gap between MIS and CHI.

Another distinction between CHI and the other disciplines lies in traditions of scholarship. HF&E and MIS regard journal publication as the mark of quality. Conference papers are works in progress, a means to get feedback and some recognition. CHI and much of computer science in North America regard conference publication as the final repository for most research. Leading researchers in CHI and other computer science disciplines repeatedly note the declining significance of journals. (Possible origins and ramifications of this cultural divide are discussed in Grudin [2004a].)

Table 19.1 provides suggestive data. Two leading journals are considered for each discipline: *IJMMS/IJHC* and *BIT, ISR* and *MISQ, HCI* and *TOCHI*. Numbers are rounded to the nearest 10 percent from recent figures provided by editors. The pool of conference papers is comparable across areas. CHI journals attract relatively few submissions despite higher acceptance rates than CHI conferences. By my estimate, 10 percent of CHI-sponsored conference papers progress to journal articles. In contrast, Jay Nunamaker, speaking at HICSS 2004, estimated that 80 percent of MIS track papers reach journal publication. For most CHI authors, conference selectivity is sufficient validation of quality (CHI, CSCW, and UIST median acceptance rates for the past three years were 16 percent, 20 percent, and 21 percent). ACM and IEEE guidelines discourage journal republication of conference material. In contrast, HF&E and MIS treat conference papers as works in progress, even for ICIS, a selective conference. MIS tracks at HICSS accept around 50 percent, the OCIS and TIM tracks of AOM accept 60 percent, and AIS SIGHCI events have a median of about 65 percent. HF&E figures are based on HCII and the CSTG track of the annual conference.

These differences in academic culture impede dialogue. Researchers in HF&E or MIS who submit work in progress to CHI conferences will be rejected, and efforts to polish conference papers can seem an inappropriate expenditure of energy in a journal-oriented field. After CHI reduced its acceptance rate from 34 percent to 18 percent in 1985, human factors participation largely disappeared. In interviews, some human factors researchers of that era note CHI's insistence on polished work. Others focus on methodological differences.

Computer-supported cooperative work strove to bridge CHI and MIS. In 1986, four of thirteen CSCW program committee members and many accepted papers were from schools of management. The conference included speakers from schools of management, business and policy at Arizona, Harvard, London School of Economics, Michigan, MIT, NYU, UCI, and USC. By contrast, the last three CSCW program committees had no one primarily affiliated with a school of

Table 19.1

Median Submissions and Percentage of Acceptances (rounded)

	Journals: Number Submitted	Journals: % Accepted	Conferences: % Accepted
HF&E	150	30	80
IS	200	10	60
CHI	50	30	20

management and no conference speakers from these schools. An ICIS CSCW session in 1990 was not well attended and not repeated.

Undoubtedly several factors hindered this effort. MIS researchers criticized CHI researchers for not citing relevant MIS work, whereas CHI researchers who approached the MIS literature found the terminology and style confusing or off-putting. In a Computer Supported Cooperative Work '88 panel, Rob Kling attacked the very term "cooperative work," noting that work could be competitive, coercive, or conflictual. Although valid from an organizational perspective, this confused CHI researchers who sought a "killer app" for small group support; document co-authors, for example, can usually be assumed to be cooperative.

MIS submissions to CSCW were rejected *en masse* by predominantly CHI conference reviewers.[6] Terminology and style were factors (fondness for acronyms and explicit lists of hypotheses annoyed CHI reviewers). Some MIS researchers submitted works in progress and probably anticipated the higher acceptance rates found in similar conferences in their field. CHI authors submitted polished work and successfully pushed for high rejection rates. MIS researchers report avoiding CSCW for the same reason HF&E researchers report avoiding CHI: papers of sufficient polish could be submitted to a journal and earn more credit within their disciplines. In 1992, a series of less selective annual Groupware conferences began, with heavy MIS participation. An associated newsletter, *Groupware Report*, listed relevant conferences but omitted CSCW, reflecting the exodus of MIS researchers from CSCW at that time.

Unlike HF&E and MIS conference proceedings, ACM proceedings are considered archival. Print copies could be ordered; all are now in the ACM Digital Library. Republishing conference results in journals is discouraged. With little opportunity for enforced revision, a premium on polished submissions is not surprising.[7]

Computer science in Europe and Asia is more journal-oriented, with work-in-progress conferences that are less selective and not archived.[8] This leads to similar tensions and dissatisfaction with ACM conference management. The difference in orientation is reflected in the volume of journal submissions and publications: the non-U.S. journals *International Journal of Human-Computer Studies* and *Interacting with Computers* (an eclectic journal started in 1989) publish over three times as many papers as the U.S. *Human-Computer Interaction* and *ACM Transactions on Computer-Human Interaction*.

DISCUSSION

Labeling fields by their dominant tendencies risks overemphasizing differences and obscuring commonalities. HF&E includes some studies of discretionary use. If use could be entirely mandated, major system failures documented in the MIS literature would not have occurred. Decision makers often have latitude in using a range of available systems. Similarly, CHI studies cover the design of tools, techniques, and interfaces that can support nondiscretionary use. Degree of choice could be considered a continuum rather than bimodal. For example, as peer pressure mounts on an employee to share calendar information online, at what point does acquiescence cease to be voluntary? Yesterday's discretionary application may be mandatory today. Bows remained an option when the first unreliable rifles appeared—for a short time. The first text editors appealed to the discretion of typewriter users; word processing is now generally mandatory.

The evolution of computing has a parallel in the earlier evolution of telephony. Management of telephony (like computing) in a large organization involved planning, acquisition, policy, and personnel decisions. Telephone (computer) operators were nondiscretionary, hands-on users. Ergonomic effort was devoted to reducing the time spent handling calls (computer operation). Some callers (computer users), in contrast, were initially discretionary users who had alternative channels for communication (work). Managers delegated calls (computer use) to secretaries.

In both cases, operators were phased out through automation. Direct dialing enables callers to handle phone operations; computer operators disappeared as users began installing and running programs on PCs. Other jobs involving mandatory use persisted: telephone call centers for direct marketing and customer service, computer data entry, and order processing.

Although it is not crisp, the distinction between mandatory and discretionary use is vital. This is especially true for computing. Rifles and telephones changed relatively slowly over time once their use was established. In computing, the hardware advances symbolized by Moore's Law ensure rapid ongoing evolution. Digital technology pushes into new areas, competing with existing alternatives. As performance increases and price decreases, digital technology eventually wins such competitions and use becomes nondiscretionary, but by then technology has moved on to provide a new array of discretionary options.

This perspective helps explain differences in focus of research funding. For example, U.S. agencies such as NSF and DARPA did not draw human-computer interaction program managers from the CHI community. Their funding is concentrated on topics that have little coverage in CHI, such as speech recognition, natural language, and displays controlled by brain waves. The post–World War II history of governmental focus on nondiscretionary use helps explain this.

The fate of previous interdisciplinary efforts suggests potential obstacles to SIGHCI collaboration with CHI. SIGHCI accepts 40 percent to 70 percent of conference submissions and progresses work to special journal issues. This is a great approach in a journal-oriented field, but conference-oriented CHI researchers prefer selective conferences and do not value journal publication. Sessions on HCI in MIS were organized for HCI International 2005, and special MIS HCI journal issues have appeared in *IJHCS, IJHCI,* and *Behaviour and Information Technology (BIT)*.

BIT has been edited since its pre-CHI 1982 origin by Tom Stewart, a founding member of HUSAT and a leader in ergonomics and standards development. Oriented more to human factors, *BIT* reflects the historical MIS and human factors focus on nondiscretionary use. This remains a valuable focus, given that discretionary use is often a brief phase that lasts until benefits are proved or disproved. But it creates challenges in bridging to CHI.

However, the growing MIS focus on discretionary use, design, and marketing supports collaboration with CHI, and, as noted by the founders of AIS SIGHCI, MIS topics are of growing importance to CHI. CHI developed when PCs were islands and commercial software focused on individual productivity. Designers could ignore organizational context. With those days over, CHI has much to learn about information systems, organizational behavior, marketing, management science, economics, and other disciplines familiar to MIS researchers.

Opportunities for mutual learning are abundant. CHI researchers have learned that experimental studies, still prevalent in MIS HCI, are not well suited for studying discretionary use. Participants in lab studies are extrinsically motivated and directed—a decent model for nondiscretionary users in real life, but discretionary use relies on intrinsic motivation. In routine, expert use, high volume, or high risk translate into small but prized incremental improvements that only controlled experiments can reliably reveal. But coarser methods are efficient when assessing highly variable initial use, and for exploring points in a vast design space. Some aspects of expert performance can be assessed by surveys, another MIS HCI method, but CHI researchers have concluded that behavior often does not match attitudes gleaned from surveys. Laboratory studies can reveal interface flaws, but over two decades CHI has honed more ecologically valid approaches. SIGHCI goals such as better integrating user-centered design into software development and "usability engineering metrics and methods for user interface assessment and evaluation" (Zhang, 2004, p. 1) were a CHI focus in the 1980s and 1990s that has now moved to HFES.

Building a partial bridge by eliminating one barrier—the journal/conference orientation difference—was accomplished in a forthcoming *BIT* special issue. Papers were actively solicited from CHI and MIS on user experience, a topic of central interest to each. Authors of accepted papers include no U.S. CHI researchers, but are a diverse mix of MIS, HF&E, and journal-oriented European and Canadian CHI contributors.

Understanding and bridging differences is worth the effort. A unified effort could counter the reduction in core strength in each of the three fields as the era of invisible yet omnipresent computers approaches.

ACKNOWLEDGMENTS

Scores of people contributed historical accounts. Phil Barnard and Ron Baecker inspired and encouraged my interest. Brian Shackel and Dick Pew published invaluable accounts. Ping Zhang and Dennis Galletta generously educated me on HCI in MIS. Judy Olson provided useful suggestions. Responsibility for errors of omission, commission, or interpretation is mine.

NOTES

1. The authors listed *IJMMS* and *IJHCS* separately. Combined, the journal ranked twenty-third, *HCI* ranked thirty-third, and BIT forty-seventh (Mylonopoulos, e-mail sent August 2, 2004).

2. Some consider a 1982 meeting in Gaithersburg to be the first CHI Conference. The plan to form SIGCHI was announced there. SIGCHI was approved by ACM months later.

3. For example, William Ogden, who authored two of the three CHI database papers published at INTERACT, then shifted to information retrieval publications.

4. Proceedings of UODIGS 76 were added to the ACM Digital Library CHI conference series in 2006.

5. Graphic designers participated in GUI efforts as early as PARC in the 1970s, but in a secondary role (Evenson, 2005). In 1987 computer graphics pioneers Ron Baecker and Bill Buxton co-organized the CHI conference in conjunction with the Graphics Interface conference, but this was not repeated.

6. I observed this as a member of program committees prior to the use of blind reviewing.

7. Defining quality is not simple in multidisciplinary settings. MIS and HF&E researchers focus more on theory development than do CHI researchers, and stress experimental rigor over ecological validity. Within each camp are people who accuse the other side of insufficient rigor. Nevertheless, I find general agreement that CHI papers are the more polished conference papers, at least on their own terms.

8. A causal factor is likely the lack elsewhere of nonprofit professional societies that archive conference proceedings and produce low-cost journals (Grudin, 2004b).

REFERENCES

Ackoff, R.L. Management misinformation systems. *Management Science*, 14, 4 (1967), 147–156.

Baecker, R.; Grudin, J.; Buxton, W.; and Greenberg, S. A historical and intellectual perspective. In R. Baecker; J. Grudin; W. Buxton; and S. Greenberg, *Readings in Human-Computer Interaction: Toward the Year 2000.* San Francisco: Morgan Kaufmann, 1995, pp. 35–47.

Bagozzi, R.P.; Davis, F.D.; and Warshaw, P.R. Development and test of a theory of technological learning and usage. *Human Relations,* 45, 7 (1992), 660–686.

Banker, R.D., and Kaufmann, R.J. The evolution of research on information systems: a fiftieth-year survey of the literature in management science. *Management Science*, 50, 3 (2004), 281–298.

Benbasat, I., and Dexter, A.S. An experimental evaluation of graphical and color-enhanced information presentation. *Management Science*, 31, 11 (1985), 1348–1364.

Bjerknes, G.; Ehn, P.; and Kyng, M. (eds.), *Computers and Democracy—a Scandinavian Challenge.* Aldershot, UK: Avebury, 1987.

Borman, L. SIGCHI: the early years. *SIGCHI Bulletin*, 28, 1 (1996), 1–33.

Bush, V. As we may think. *The Atlantic Monthly*, 176 (1945), 101–108.

Bødker, S. *Through the Interface: A Human Activity Approach to User Interface Design.* Mahwah, NJ: Lawrence Erlbaum Associates, 1990.

Card, S.; Moran, T.P.; and Newell, A. *The Psychology of Human-Computer Interaction.* Mahwah, NJ: Lawrence Erlbaum Associates, 1983.

Davis, F.D. Perceived usefulness, perceived ease of use, and user acceptance of information technology. *MIS Quarterly*, 13, 3 (1989), 319–339.

Davis, G.B. *Management Information Systems: Conceptual Foundations, Structure, and Development.* New York: McGraw-Hill, 1974.

Dennis, A.; George, J.; Jessup, L.; Nunamaker, J.; and Vogel, D. Information technology to support electronic meetings. *MIS Quarterly*, 12, 4 (1988), 591–624.

DeSanctis, G., and Gallupe, R.B. A foundation for the study of group decision support systems. *Management Science*, 33, 5 (1987), 589–609.

Dyson, F. *Disturbing the Universe.* New York: Harper and Row, 1979.

Ehrlich, S.F. Strategies for encouraging successful adoption of office communication systems. *ACM Transactions on Office Information Systems*, 5, 4 (1987), 340–357.

Engelbart, D. A conceptual framework for the augmentation of man's intellect. In P. Howerton and D. Weeks (eds.), *Vistas in Information Handling Volume I.* Washington, DC: Spartan Books, 1963, pp. 1–29.

Engelbart, D., and English, W. A research center for augmenting human intellect. In *National Computer Conference Proceedings 33*, Montvale, NJ: AFIPS, 1968, pp. 395–410.

Evenson, S. Design and HCI Highlights. Presentation at HCIC 2005 Conference, Winter Park, Colorado, February 6, 2005.

Fano, R., and Corbato, F. Time-sharing on computers. *Scientific American*, 214, 9 (1966), 129–140.

Friedman, A. *Computer Systems Development: History, Organization and Implementation.* New York: Wiley, 1989.

Grudin, J. Interface: An evolving concept. *Communications of the ACM*, 36, 4 (1993), 110–119.

Grudin, J. Crossing the divide. *ACM Transactions on Computer-Human Interaction*, 11, 1 (2004), 1–25.

Grudin, J. Managerial use and emerging norms: effects of activity patterns on software design and deployment. In *HICSS-37 Conference. IEEE, 2004b,* CD-ROM, 10 pages.

Grudin, J. Three faces of human-computer interaction. *IEEE Annals of the History of Computing*, 27, 4 (2005), 46–62.

Hartwick, J., and Barki, H. Explaining the role of user participation in information system use. *Management Science*, 40, 4 (1994), 440–465.

Hopper, G. The education of a computer. In *Proceedings of 1952 ACM Conference,* reprinted in *Annals of the History of Computing*, 9, 3–4 (1987), 271–281.

Hutchins, E.L.; Hollan, J.D.; and Norman, D.A. Direct manipulation interfaces. In D.A. Norman and S.W. Draper (eds.), *User Centered System Design.* Mahwah, NJ: Lawrence Erlbaum Associates, 1986, pp. 87–124.

Johnson, J.; Roberts, T.; Verplank, W.; Smith, D.C.; Irby, C.; Beard, M.; and Mackey, K. The Xerox Star: a retrospective. *IEEE Computer*, 22, 9 (1989), 11–29.

Kay, A. *The Reactive Engine.* PhD dissertation, University of Utah, 1969.

Kay, A., and Goldberg, A. Personal dynamic media. *IEEE Computer*, 10, 3 (1977), 31–42.

Keen, P.G.W. MIS research: reference disciplines and a cumulative tradition. In *First International Conference on Information Systems*. Chicago: Society for Management Information Systems, 1980, 9–18.

Licklider, J. Man-computer symbiosis. *IRE Transactions of Human Factors in Electronics HFE-1*, 1 (1960), 4–11.

Licklider, J., and Clark, W. (1962). On-line man-computer communication. In *National Computer Conference* 21. AFIPS, 1962, pp. 113–128.

March, A. Usability: the new dimension of product design. *Harvard Business Review*, 72, 5 (1994), 144–149.

Martin, J. *Design of Man-Computer Dialogues*. New York: Prentice-Hall, 1973.

Meister, D. *The History of Human Factors and Ergonomics*. Mahwah, NJ: Lawrence Erlbaum Associates, 1999.

Mumford, E. A comprehensive method for handling the human problems of computer introduction. In *IFIP Congress*, vol. 71, no. 2, North Holland, 1971, pp. 918–923.

Myers, B.A. A brief history of human computer interaction technology. *ACM Interactions,* 5, 2 (1988), 44–54.

Mylonopoulos, N.A., and Theoharakis, V. Global perceptions of IS journals. *Communications of the ACM*, 44, 9 (2001), 29–32.

Nelson, T. A file structure for the complex, the changing, and the indeterminate. In *ACM 20th National Conference*. New York: ACM, 1965, pp. 84–100.

Nelson, T. A conceptual framework for man-machine everything. In AFIPS *National Joint Computer Conference*, vol. 42. Montvale, NJ: AFIPS Press, 1973, M21–M26.

Newell, A., and Card, S.K. The prospects for psychological science in human-computer interaction. *Human-Computer Interaction*, 1, 3 (1985), 209–242.

Norman, D.A. Design principles for human-computer interfaces. In *CHI'83 Conference on Human Factors in Computing Systems*. New York: ACM, 1983, pp. 1–10.

Norman, D.A. *Psychology of Everyday Things*. New York: Basic Books, 1988.

Norman, D.A. *Emotional Design: Why We Love (or Hate) Everyday Things*. New York: Basic Books, 2004.

Peebles, D., and Cheng, P.C.H. Modeling the effect of task and graphical representation on response latency in a graph reading task. *Human Factors*, 45, 1 (2003), 28–46.

Pew, R. Evolution of human-computer interaction: from MEMEX to Bluetooth and beyond. In J.A. Jacko and A. Sears (eds.), *The Human-Computer Interaction Handbook*. Mahwah, NJ: Lawrence Erlbaum Associates, 2003, pp. 1–17.

Remus, W. An empirical evaluation of the impact of graphical and tabular presentations on decision-making. *Management Science,* 30, 5 (1984), 533–542.

Roscoe, S.N. *The Adolescence of Engineering Psychology*. Santa Monica, CA: Human Factors and Ergonomics Society, 1997.

Sammet, J. Farewell to Grace Hopper—End of an era! *Communications of the ACM,* 35, 4 (1992), 128–131.

Shackel, B. Ergonomics for a computer. *Design,* 120 (1959), 36–39.

Shackel, B. Ergonomics in the design of a large digital computer console. *Ergonomics*, 5 (1962), 229–241.

Shackel, B. Human-computer interaction: whence and whither? *Journal of ASIS*, 48, 11 (1997), 970–986.

Shneiderman, B. *Software Psychology: Human Factors in Computer and Information Systems*. Cambridge, MA: Winthrop, 1980.

Smith, H.T., and Green, T.R.G. *Human Interaction with Computers*. New York: Academic, 1980.

Smith, S.L. Man-computer information transfer. In J.H. Howard (ed.), *Electronic Information Display Systems*. Washington, DC: Spartan Books, 1963, pp. 284–299.

Smith, S.L., and Mosier, J.N. *Guidelines for Designing User Interface Software*. ESD-TR-86–278. Bedford, MA: MITRE, 1986.

Sutherland, I. Sketchpad: A man-machine graphical communication system. *Spring Joint Computer Conference 23.* Montvale, NJ: AFIPS, 1963, 329–346.

Taylor, F.W. *The Principles of Scientific Management*. New York: Harper, 1911.

Vessey, I., and Galletta, D. Cognitive fit: an empirical test of information acquisition. *Information Systems Research*, 2, 1 (1991), 63–84.

Weinberg, G. *The Psychology of Computer Programming*. New York: Van Nostrand Reinhold, 1971.

Zhang, P. AIS SIGHCI Three-Year Report. *AIS SIGHCI Newsletter,* 3, 1 (2004), 1–5.

Zhang, P.; Benbasat, I.; Carey, J.; Davis, F.; Galletta, D.; and Strong, D. Human-computer interaction research in the MIS discipline. *Communications of the AIS*, 9 (2002), 334–355.

Zhang, P., and Dillon, A. HCI and MIS: shared concerns. *International Journal of Human-Computer Studies*, 59 (2003), 397–402.

Zhang, P.; Nah, F.F.-H.; and Preece, J. (2004). HCI studies in management information systems. *Behaviour & Information Technology*, 23, 3 (2004), 147–151.

EDITORS AND CONTRIBUTORS

Francis K. Andoh-Baidoo is a doctoral candidate in information systems at Virginia Commonwealth University. He earned his MBA at the University of North Carolina, Greensboro. His research interests are in the areas of data mining, decision support and intelligent systems, and knowledge management. He has published in the proceedings of the Americas Conference on Information Systems.

Alan Borning is a professor in the department of computer science and engineering at the University of Washington. He is also co-director of the Center for Urban Simulation and Policy Analysis, adjunct professor in the Information School, and a member of the interdisciplinary PhD program in urban design and planning (all at the University of Washington), and a fellow of the Association for Computing Machinery. He received a BA degree from Reed College in mathematics in 1971, and a PhD from Stanford University in computer science in 1979. After spending a year in Edinburgh, he moved to the University of Washington in 1980. His current research interests are in human-computer interaction, particularly as applied to land use, transportation, and environmental modeling, and in integrating considerations of human values with computer system design. He has also done work in constraint-based languages and systems, other aspects of human-computer interaction, and in object-oriented programming.

Scott Brave is a postdoctoral scholar at Stanford University. He is co-author (with Clifford Nass) of *Wired for Speech: How Voice Activates and Enhances the Human-Computer Relationship* (Cambridge: MIT Press). He received his PhD in communications from Stanford University, with a specialization in human-computer interaction. As part of the CHIMe Lab, Scott studied user responses to emotion in embodied agents and non-verbal communication in virtual spaces. In 1998, Scott received his MS degree in media arts and sciences from the MIT Media Lab. As a member of Professor Hiroshi Ishii's Tangible Media Group, he focused on the application of force-feedback to human-computer interaction and interpersonal communication. Scott received his BS degree in computer systems engineering from Stanford University, where he worked with Professor John Koza and Professor Nils Nilsson exploring genetic programming, an artificial intelligence technique inspired by Darwinian evolution in nature.

Deborah R. Compeau is associate professor of management information systems in the Richard Ivey School of Business at the University of Western Ontario. Her research focuses on the individual user of information and communications technologies, viewed from a social cognitive perspective. In particular she is interested in understanding what organizations can do to facilitate individual adoption of and learning about information technologies. Her research has been published in *Information Systems Research, MIS Quarterly,* and *Information & Management,* as well as in other journals. Dr. Compeau is a member of the editorial board of MIS Quarterly.

Kevin Crowston is an associate professor in the School of Information Studies at Syracuse University, and director of the PhD program. He joined the school in 1996. He received his AB

(1984) in applied mathematics (computer science) from Harvard University and a PhD (1991) in information technologies from the Sloan School of Management, Massachusetts Institute of Technology (MIT). His current research interests focus on new ways of organizing made possible by the use of information and communications technology. He approaches this issue in several ways: empirical studies of coordination-intensive processes in human organizations; theoretical characterizations of coordination problems and alternative methods for managing them; and design and empirical evaluation of new kinds of computer systems to support people working together. A specific example of the final interest is the application of document genre to the World Wide Web.

Fred D. Davis is professor and David D. Glass chair in information systems, and serves as chair of the information systems department at the Sam M. Walton College of Business at the University of Arkansas. Dr. Davis earned his PhD at MIT's Sloan School of Management, and has served on the business school faculties at the University of Michigan, the University of Minnesota, and the University of Maryland. Dr. Davis has served as associate editor for the scholarly journals *Management Science, MIS Quarterly,* and *Information Systems Research.* He has published extensively about user acceptance of IT and IT-assisted decision making. His research has appeared in such journals as *MIS Quarterly, Information Systems Research, Journal of Management Information Systems, Management Science, Decision Sciences, Journal of Applied Psychology, Journal of Experimental Social Psychology, Organizational Behavior and Human Decision Processes,* and *IEEE Transactions.*

Gerardine DeSanctis (PhD, Texas Tech University) was the Thomas F. Keller professor of business administration at Duke University. Her research focuses on learning in distributed teams and online communities. She held visiting professor appointments on the Faculteit der Wiskunde en Informatica, Technische Universiteit Delft (the Netherlands), Erasmus University (the Netherlands), and INSEAD (in France and Singapore). She was affiliated with the editorial boards of *Information Systems Research, MIS Quarterly, Management Science, Organization Science,* and the *Journal of Organizational Behavior.* She regularly taught in Duke's Global Executive MBA program.

Gupreet Dhillon is a professor in the school of business at Virginia Commonwealth University, Richmond. He received his PhD in information systems in 1995 from the London School of Economics and Political Science. The author of five books, he has also published in journals including *Information Systems Research, Communications of the ACM, Information & Management, Computers & Security, European Journal of Information Systems, Information Systems Journal,* and the *International Journal of Information Management.* His research interests include management of information security, ethical and legal implications of information systems, and aspects of information systems planning and project management.

Andrew Dillon is dean and professor at the School of Information at the University of Texas at Austin. He has also held research and faculty positions at Indiana University and Loughborough University, and has served as a consultant on software design to many companies in the United States and Europe. He currently serves on the editorial boards of *Interacting with Computers, Journal of the American Society for Information Science, Journal of Digital Information,* and the *International Journal of Digital Libraries.* His research interests include longitudinal analysis of user response to IT, the role of aesthetics in design, and the use of hypermedia systems to enhance learning and decision making.

Batya Friedman is a professor in the Information School and an adjunct professor in the department of computer science and engineering at the University of Washington. She is also co-director of the Value Sensitive Design Research Laboratory at the University of Washington and co-director of the Mina Institute in Covelo, CA. She received both her BA (1979) and PhD (1988) from the University of California, Berkeley. Dr. Friedman's research interests include human-computer interaction; social, legal and cultural aspects of information systems; and design methodology. Her 1997 edited volume, published by Cambridge University Press, is titled *Human Values and the Design of Computer Technology*. Her work on Value Sensitive Design has engaged such technologies as Web browsers, large-screen displays, urban simulation, robotics, open source code bases, and location enhanced computing.

Dennis F. Galletta is an AIS fellow and professor of business administration at the Katz Graduate School of Business, University of Pittsburgh, and Fox School of Business, Temple University. He obtained his doctorate from the University of Minnesota. His research involves human factors, electronic commerce, and user training, especially with a focus on user attitudes, behavior, and performance. His articles have appeared in journals such as *Management Science, Information Systems Research, Journal of Management Information Systems, Journal of AIS, Decision Sciences, Communications of the ACM, Data Base, Information & Management*, and *Accounting, Management, and Information Technologies*. He serves or has served on several editorial boards, including those of *MIS Quarterly, Data Base, Information Systems and eBusiness Management*, and *Cycle Time Research*. He embarked in the fall of 1999 on an around-the-world trip with Semester at Sea, teaching IS courses aboard ship. While on land, over the years he served as the AIS VP of Member Services, ICIS Treasurer, AIS Council Member, general chair of the first AMCIS Conference, and, most recently, co–program chair of AMCIS 2003. He is co–program chair for ICIS 2005 and Editor in Chief of *ISWorld*.

Dale L. Goodhue is the head of the MIS department, and the C. Herman and Mary Virginia Terry chair of business administration, at the University of Georgia's Terry College of Business. He has published in *Management Science, MIS Quarterly, Decision Sciences, Sloan Management Review*, and other journals. His research interests include measuring the impact of information systems, the impact of task-technology fit on individual performance, the management of data and other IS infrastructures and resources, and the impact of ERP systems on organizations.

Jane Gravill is a PhD graduate in management information systems from the Richard Ivey School of Business at the University of Western Ontario. She currently holds a part-time position at the Schulich School of Business, York University. Her research addresses the self-regulated learning process, individual differences such as self-awareness and goal-orientation, end-user adoption of information systems, and user competence. Her research has been published in the ICIS proceedings and *Information & Management*. Before becoming a PhD candidate, Gravill worked for over ten years in a variety of MIS management positions.

Jonathan Grudin is a senior researcher at Microsoft Research. Before joining Microsoft in 1998, he was professor of information and computer science at University of California, Irvine. After obtaining a BA in mathematics-physics from Reed College and a PhD in cognitive psychology from the University of California, San Diego, he worked at the Medical Research Council Applied Psychology Unit, Wang Laboratories, and MCC. He has taught at Aarhus, Oslo, and Keio Universities, and currently is affiliate professor at the University of Washington Information School.

Since the early 1980s he has focused on human-computer interaction, primarily within the ACM SIGCHI organization and conferences. He was editor in chief of *ACM Transactions on Computer-Human Interaction* for six years and is currently ACM *Computing Surveys'* associate editor for Human-Computer Interaction.

Nicole Haggerty is an assistant professor at the Ivey Business School. Her research interests center on the intersection of technology and learning. She is particularly interested in research on the influence of organizational support mechanisms on post-training, post-adoption individual learning about technology and individual learning through technology in computer-mediated learning environments. Her research has been published in various conference proceedings, including those of the International Conference on Information Systems, and in the *Journal of Computer Information Systems, Journal of Informatics, Education and Research*, and *Canadian Public Policy*.

James Howison is a doctoral student at the Syracuse University School of Information Studies. His research interests include the social science of software engineering and "wireless grids" (distributed ad hoc resource sharing). For his PhD dissertation he intends to study effective practices for free and open software development. In 1998 he received his honors undergraduate degree in economic sociology and politics from the University of Sydney. In 2001 he undertook graduate study in software engineering at the University of New South Wales before transferring to the Syracuse University School of Information Studies PhD program in 2002. He was recently published in *IEEE Internet Computing* and has presented at the International Conference on Information Systems (ICIS), the annual conference of the Association for Public Policy Analysis and Management (APPAM), and the International Conference on Software Engineering (ICSE).

Jeffrey A. Jolton is a senior consultant with Genesee Survey Services in Rochester, NY, where he has worked with a variety of organizations on the design, implementation, and analyses of large-scale employee surveys. He has over ten years' experience in the design, implementation, and analysis of individual, group, and organization-level assessments. He holds a PhD in industrial and organizational psychology from Ohio University and a BA in psychology from Lawrence University. Jeff is a member of the Society for Industrial and Organizational Psychology and has presented and published in numerous conferences and publications.

Peter H. Kahn, Jr., is associate professor in the department of psychology and adjunct associate professor in the Information School at the University of Washington. He is also co-director of the Value Sensitive Design Research Laboratory at the University of Washington. He received his PhD from the University of California, Berkeley, in 1988. His publications have appeared in such journals as *Child Development, Developmental Psychology, Developmental Review, Human Development, Environmental Values*, and the *Journal of Systems Software*. His 1999 book (MIT Press) is titled *The Human Relationship with Nature: Development and Culture*. His edited volume (MIT Press, 2002) with Stephen Kellert is titled *Children and Nature: Psychological, Sociocultural, and Evolutionary Investigations*. His research lies at the intersection of human well-being, nature, and computational technologies, especially large-screen displays, robotics, and location enhanced computing. His research projects are currently funded by the National Science Foundation.

George M. Kasper is professor of information systems at Virginia Commonwealth University. He is the author or co-author of more than two dozen journal articles and several book chapters on information systems. MIT Press, Sage Publications, and others have reprinted his papers, and professional groups including the Society for Information Management have recognized his work.

Kasper has served as chairman of the Association for Computing Machinery's special interest on management information systems, and is currently the USA ACM representative to the International Federation for Information Processing (IFIP), a United Nations initiative. Recently, he was appointed AIS Representative Director to CSAB, the lead society within ABET for accrediting degree programs in CS, IS, IT, SE, and CE.

Helen M. Kelley is assistant professor of information systems in the faculty of management at the University of Lethbridge. Her research focuses on the individual user of information and enterprise resource planning technologies, viewed from social cognitive and attributional perspectives. Her current interests include investigating what management of organizations can do to enhance individual adoption of and learning about information systems technologies, and information systems effectiveness in small businesses. Her research has been published in *Information Systems Research, Journal of Global Information Management*, and *Business Quarterly*.

Paul M. Mastrangelo has been a consultant at Genesee Survey Services since 2002, where he works with large-scale organizations in the design, implementation, and analysis of employee surveys. Previously, Paul was an associate professor at the University of Baltimore, where he focused on the measurement of attitudes, personality, and biographical information. He received his PhD in industrial and organizational psychology from Ohio University in 1993, and his BA in Psychology from the University of Rhode Island in 1989, where he was inducted into the Phi Beta Kappa Honor Society.

Jeffrey May is currently a faculty member at Virginia Commonwealth University, where he concentrates on teaching programming and logical design. He holds a BS degree in mechanical engineering from Wright State University, an MS degree in environmental engineering from Virginia Polytechnic Institute and State University, and an MS degree in information systems from Virginia Commonwealth University. He currently is pursuing his PhD in Information Systems at Virginia Commonwealth University.

Clifford Nass is a professor at Stanford University. His primary appointment is in the department of communication, with appointments by courtesy in computer science; science, technology, and society; sociology; and symbolic systems. He is director of the Communication between Humans and Interactive Media (CHIMe) Lab. He has written two books, *The Media Equation: How People Treat Computers, Televisions, and New Media Like Real People and Places* (New York: Cambridge University Press) and *Wired for Speech: How Voice Activates and Enhances the Human-Computer Relationship* (Cambridge: MIT Press). He has also written over eighty papers in the areas of human-computer interaction, statistical methodology, and organization theory. Nass's primary research area is how people use social rules and heuristics to assess and respond to interfaces. His current foci are automobiles, natural language, robots, and voices.

Adrienne Olnick Kutzschan is a doctoral candidate in MIS at Queen's University in Canada. Her primary research interests are in the area of human-computer interaction and assistive technology. Before resuming her studies, she completed an MBA at Simon Fraser University and consulted in IT where she observed firsthand the challenges people face when using technology. Her research has been published in the *Journal of Management Information Systems*.

Joseph Rubleske is a doctoral student at Syracuse University's School of Information Studies. He is interested chiefly in better understanding the role that advanced information and communication technologies (ICTs) play in providing context for work teams collaborating virtually. His teaching interests include information systems analysis and design and experimental team-based projects. Mr. Rubleske received his baccalaureate in political science from Indiana University in 1993 and his master's in planning (MPl) from Indiana University in 1996. Prior to his doctoral studies, he worked as a research associate for the Center for Urban Policy and the Environment (1995–99), as a Web and applications developer for the state of Wisconsin (2000–2002) and as a senior research analyst for the state of Wisconsin (2002–2003). Mr. Rubleske's research has been published in *Public Works Management and Policy,* the *Professional Geographer,* the *Journal of Urban Technology,* and the *Journal of Environmental Education.*

Mark S. Silver is associate professor of information systems in the Fordham University Schools of Business. He received his PhD from the Wharton School of the University of Pennsylvania and has been a member of the faculties at UCLA and NYU. He is the author of a book, *Systems That Support Decision Makers: Description and Analysis* (Wiley, 1991), and co-author of "The IT Interaction Model" (*MIS Quarterly,* 1995), among other journal articles. Professor Silver's current research interests focus on the design features of interactive computer-based systems, especially browser-based systems and other Internet applications. He is particularly interested in two design features, "system restrictiveness" (how a system constrains its users) and "decisional guidance" (how a system enlightens, sways, or directs its users). The significance of these features emerged from his earlier work in the area of decision support systems.

Kathryn R. Stam is assistant professor at the SUNY Institute of Technology and associate director of the Syracuse Information Security Evaluation project. She earned her PhD in social science (anthropology and sociology) from Syracuse University's Maxwell School of Citizenship and Public Affairs. Her background and research interests are related to information technology, health and social services, and organizational culture. She has published a range of qualitative research on the topics of work organizations, community health, and teaching, and has received financial support for her research from the National Science Foundation.

Jeffrey M. Stanton received his PhD in industrial and organizational psychology from the University of Connecticut in 1997. He is an associate professor in the School of Information Studies at Syracuse University and director of the Syracuse Information Security Evaluation project. He has developed an extensive funded research program at the intersection of behavioral science and information technology, and has published more than fifty refereed articles and papers on this and related topics. Dr. Stanton's research interest in the area of information security lies in understanding the role of work motivation in guiding the security-related behaviors of employees and managers in organizations, an area of research known as behavioral information security.

Heshan Sun is a doctoral candidate in information science and technology in the School of Information Studies at Syracuse University. He received his MS in information management from Peking University and his BA in international business from Nankai University, China. His research interests include human-computer interaction, IS performance, e-commerce, information systems analysis and design, and cross-cultural IS. He has presented his work at conferences such as AMCIS, HICSS, and Pre-ICIS Annual Workshops on HCI in MIS. In addition, he has participated in several workshops and panel discussions such as the "Webshop" workshop sponsored by the University of Maryland, College Park, and the CIR workshop in Academic Management '04. His work has appeared in journals such as the *International Journal of Human-Computer Studies,* the *Journal of*

Information Studies: Theory & Application, and *China Information Review*, and in book chapters. He received the Best Paper awards at the pre-ICIS Annual Workshop on HCI Research in MIS (2004).

Leila Takayama is a PhD Student at Stanford University, advised by Professor Clifford Nass in the Department of Communication. As a member of the CHIMe Lab, she uses experiments to study the social and cognitive aspects of human interaction with computing systems. Ms. Takayama also works as a research assistant for Palo Alto Research Center (PARC) with Dr. Stuart Card. She holds BA degrees in cognitive science and psychology from the University of California, Berkeley, where she did research with the Group for User Interface Research (GUIR) of the computer science division. She is currently interested in the social history of ubiquitous computing as a vision for the future as well as how ubiquitous, "invisible" computing not only mediates human cognition and interaction but ultimately alters human embodied experiences.

Dov Te'eni is professor of information systems in the faculty of management at Tel-Aviv University, Israel. He is also the chairman of Meital—Israel's higher education e-learning center. Dr. Te'eni studies several related areas of information systems: human-computer interaction, computer support for communication, knowledge management, systems design and non-profit organizations. His research usually combines model building, laboratory experiments, and development of prototypes such as Spider and kMail. Dr. Te'eni serves as senior editor for *MIS Quarterly* and is on the editorial boards of *Journal of AIS, Information and Organizations*, and *Internet Research*. He has published in journals such as *Management Science, MISQ, Organization Science, Communications of the ACM*, and in more specialized journals of HCI such as *IJHCS, Behaviour and Information Technology, Computers in Human Behavior* and *IEEE Transactions*. Together with Jane Carey and Ping Zhang, he awaits their forthcoming book entitled *Human-Computer Interaction: Developing Effective Organizational Information Systems*.

Noam Tractinsky is a senior lecturer at the department of information systems engineering at Ben-Gurion University of the Negev. He received his PhD in information systems from the University of Texas at Austin. His HCI-related research has appeared in journals such as *Behavior & Information Technology, Human-Computer Interaction, Interacting with Computers, International Journal of Human-Computer Studies*, and *MIS Quarterly*. His recent research projects have involved the study of consumer behavior in e-commerce and the effects of time pressure and time delays on decision making and user behavior. He is currently interested in the study of the aesthetic aspects of information technology.

Iris Vessey is Professor of Information Systems at the University of Queensland and Honorary Adjunct Professor at the Queensland University of Technology. She received her MSc, MBA, and PhD in management information systems from the University of Queensland, Australia. Her current research interests focus on the evaluation of emerging information technologies from both cognitive and analytical perspectives, knowledge management systems, and the management and organization of enterprise resource planning systems (ERPs). She has served on the editorial boards of *MIS Quarterly, Information Systems Research, Management Science, Journal of Management Information Systems*, and the *Journal of Database Management*, and on the executive board of *Information Systems Frontiers*. During the first eight years of its life, she serves or has served as secretary of the Association for Information Systems (AIS), as well as of the International Conference on Information Systems (ICIS) following its merger with AIS. She is an inaugural fellow of the AIS.

Jane Webster received her PhD from New York University and currently is a professor in the School of Business at Queen's University in Canada. She investigates the impacts of technologies to support distributed work, organizational communication, employee recruitment and selection, employee monitoring, and training and learning. She also focuses on human-computer interaction issues as they relate to organizational systems. She has served as a senior editor for *MIS Quarterly*, and has published in a variety of journals, including the *Academy of Management Journal, Communication Research, Journal of Organizational Behavior, MIS Quarterly*, and *Organization Science*.

Ping Zhang is associate professor at the School of Information Studies, Syracuse University. She earned her PhD in information systems from the University of Texas at Austin. Her research appears or will appear in journals such as *Behaviour & Information Technology (BIT), Communications of ACM, Communications of AIS (CAIS), Computers in Human Behavior, Decision Support Systems, International Journal of Human-Computer Studies (IJHCS), International Journal of Electronic Commerce, Journal of American Society for Information Science and Technology*, and the *Journal of AIS (JAIS)*. With Dov Te'eni and Jane Carey, she co-wrote an HCI textbook for non–computer science students, *HCI: Developing Effective Organizational Information Systems* (John Wiley & Sons, 2007). Dr. Zhang has received several Best Paper awards at IS conferences, an excellence in teaching award from the University of Texas at Austin, and an outstanding service award from AIS SIGHCI. She is associate editor for IJHCS and CAIS, and a guest co-editor for JAIS, JMIS, IJHCS, IJHCI, and BIT. She is the founding chair (2001–2004) of the AIS SIGHCI.

SERIES EDITOR

Vladimir Zwass is the Distinguished Professor of Computer Science and Management Information Systems at Fairleigh Dickinson University. He holds a Ph.D. in Computer Science from Columbia University. Professor Zwass is the Founding Editor-in-Chief of the *Journal of Management Information Systems*, one of the three top-ranked journals in the field of Information Systems; the journal has celebrated twenty years in publication. He is also the Founding Editor-in-Chief of the *International Journal of Electronic Commerce*, ranked as the top journal in its field. Dr. Zwass is the author of six books and several book chapters, including entries in the *Encyclopaedia Britannica*, as well as of a number of papers in various journals and conference proceedings. He has received several grants, consulted for a number of major corporations, and is a frequent speaker to national and international audiences. He is a former member of the Professional Staff of the International Atomic Energy Agency in Vienna, Austria.

INDEX